Dedicated
to Khilani

Adventures in Europe and Central America:

Travel Stories and Personal Reflections
By Dennis Cleasby

A Visit to Ireland, Holland, Denmark, France, Austria, Italy, Greece, Colombia, Costa Rica, Nicaragua, Guatemala, Honduras, El Salvador, and Belize.

Published in the United States by Cathedral Art Gallery Records
P.O. Box 808, Glenwood Landing, NY, USA 11547-0808
©, 2011 DENNIS CLEASBY

Graphic Designs and Photography by Dennis Cleasby.

To learn more about the author and view an accompanying color catalog, of all travel photographs visit us online at www.denniscleasby.com.

FIRST EDITION
(ISBN-13: 978-0-9817015-3-0)
(ISBN-10: 0-9817015-3-1)

Library of Congress Number 2011905616

ISBN: 978-0-9817015-3-0

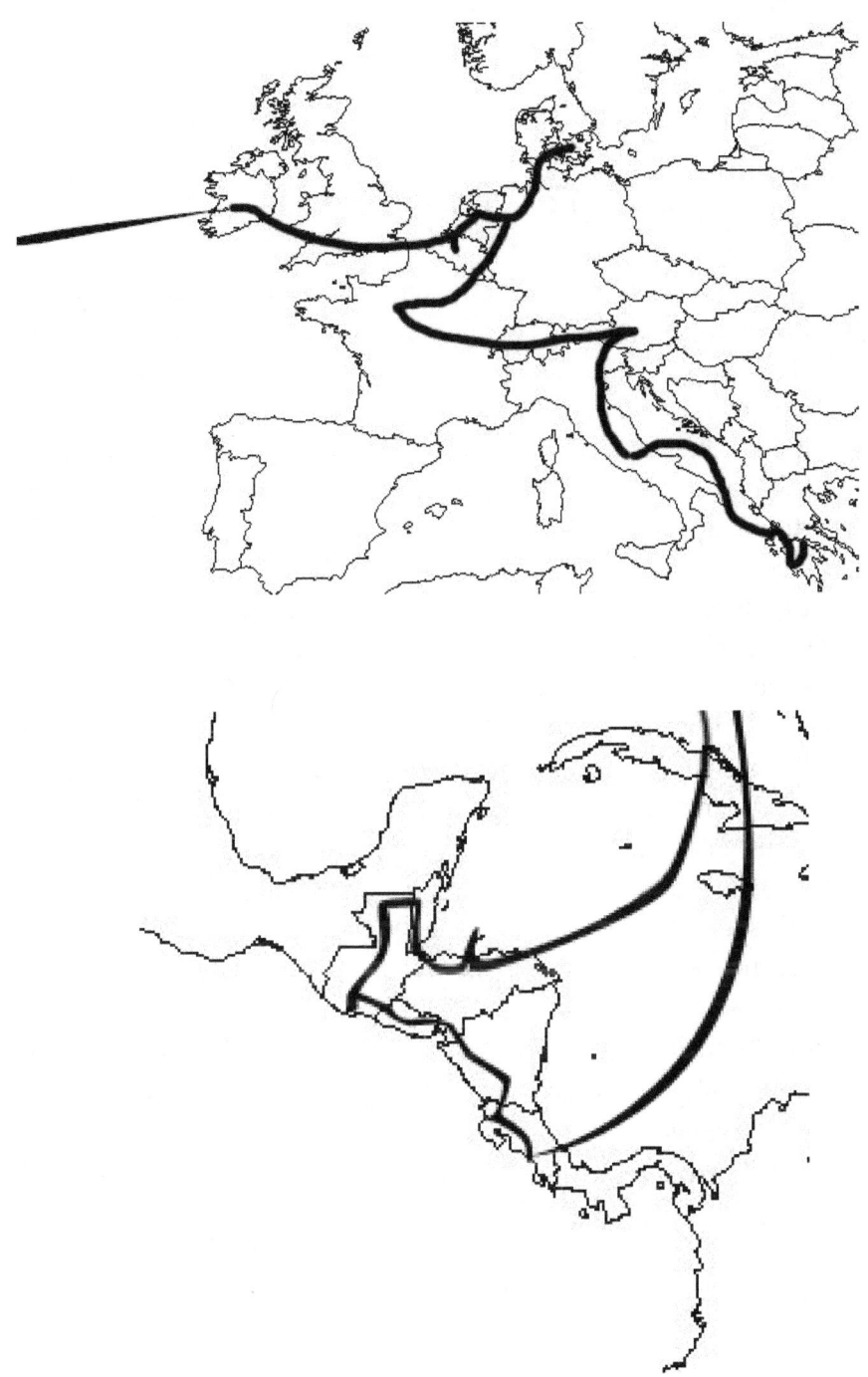

Chapters by Country

Introduction..7
Chapter 1 Ireland...11
Chapter 2 Holland..21
Chapter 3 Denmark..37
Chapter 4 Paris...57
Chapter 5 Vienna...67
Chapter 6 Rome..74
Chapter 7 Greece...85
Chapter 8 Colombia...125
Chapter 9 Costa Rica..142
Chapter 10 Nicaragua...167
Chapter 11 El Salvador..182
Chapter 12 Guatemala..194
Chapter 13 Honduras..224
Chapter 14 Guatemala..234
Chapter 15 Costa Rica...258
Chapter 16 Costa Rica/ Colombia......................................262
Chapter 17 Honduras..269
Chapter 18 Belize..313
Chapter 19 Guatemala..333
Chapter 20 Busland..380
Chapter 21 Nicaragua...385
Chapter 22 Costa Rica...402

INTRODUCTION

This book is a memoir of travels where the jigsaw puzzle of people, places, and events are chronicled, most often the traveling was successfully, and other times my words turn into advice of what to keep clear of. This book can be opened at any chapter and read. The "guide" aspect is in places we visited, but this book is also about daily situations that happened during our journeys to interesting places, fifteen countries in all. Chapter sizes depend on the number of days we stayed in each country. Within each chapter they are divided by the day.

If you are a novice this book will prepare you for the unexpected. If you are a seasoned traveler, you will enjoy the fresh, personal, perspective in revisiting where you have been. Some of the people in this book are a continuation of friendships in foreign lands. Every person in this book is real and a part of our beautiful world. The briefest of encounters can leave a life-long impression and on some occasions become life-long friendships. Maybe this book will open a door to a new world waiting for you. The book combines three years of travel.

Because publishing a book with color photography is so costly we have decided to share the full visual benefits of our journey on the World Wide Web. Ten times as many photographs can be shown on the web as opposed to a costly color book. My first book had full color reproductions and was about meeting and marrying my Colombian wife, Diana, in 2006. Please visit my site (www.denniscleasby.com) and follow the links to the photographs and artworks that I created while visiting all the countries. Each chapter has corresponding photographs on the web.

I have been traveling since I was two years old. Over the years I've stopped to live in different houses, states, and countries but the idea of being rooted in one location for long periods of time has never been an overly familiar feeling. As I have become older, I have lived in one general location (Long Island, New York for 25 years), but travel out of the country annually. I am now elsewhere at least three months a year. I love to travel. I inherited this from my parents. When I was young we were always packing up the car and heading for one place or another. At age six we drove from New York to California after living in Panama for two years. For the majority of my youth, two years was the maximum stay in one house. These moves were distressing to me as a child. I was the middle child of five with an older brother and sister, and two younger sisters. My Catholic parents wanted to live the typical suburban life in a modern home with the new car parked in the driveway. That car commuted with my father every day to downtown Los Angeles where he worked in corporate America. Seeing his life motivated me to live different, be an artist and seek new inspiration.

In my adult life I still experience the tinge of stress related to travel. Days before I leave I begin to gear up into a nervous, hyper drive. I leave my home, and realize I may encounter death around an unseen corner. In some cases this is just a ritual of safety, departure, packing, and checklists, but also a deep awareness that things are about to change, and a new adventure is about to begin; a study of life, where people and places will leave subtle, or possibly profound, impressions on me. When I travel my senses open a door of perception, I become ultra-alive, I am in my best element. I make sensory notes pushing myself to be sharply aware, to lock those notes into my memory. I photograph or paint my visual journey as well. No matter where I am, I am the universal traveler.

The best way I can describe events in the present is to relate to the past. I have always loved to explore, sometimes putting myself at risk. I remember the first time I ever told a lie. Or more precisely, the first time I told a lie and got away with it. I may have tried before, since I was only seven or eight years old, but this lie involved my thirst for adventure. A few blocks from our home in Torrance, California there was a huge reservoir for water run-off with a chain-linked fence around it. I had gone in there once before and got a good butt-whipping for getting all wet and muddy.

There was an older boy in the neighborhood and we had ventured over the fence to discover whatever was behind a forbidden, locked gate. The murky pond had us intrigued; we knew some hidden discovery was there to be explored. A fence made the expedition that much more desirable for two young unsupervised kids. I had to keep my pants dry or my mother would know what I had been up to. No sooner has we scaled down the embankment when I slipped and went swimming into the green sludge. The same was true of my compadré. The now wet cloths, of course, expanded our freedom to pursue the entire reservoir looking for creatures and whatever. I don't know if the water was heavily polluted, another reason my mother had warned me of the dangerous location, but we played like there was no tomorrow, as if no spanking were eminent.

Only after retreating to the dry street did it dawn on me I had better prepare an explanation for my mother. How could I hide a body, soaking wet with green slime? The consequences were looming and dark while the brilliant California sun dried the mud caked on my cloths. I don't remember the name of my counterpart, but I do remember what he told me next. He planted the seed of how to lie, "Make up a story". I had a few minutes to concoct a brilliant alibi. It went like this: While turning a corner, my bicycle slipped on the mud and I fell in the muddy water. I had the exact corner, the precise pool, and elaborate description of how the bike toppled as I took the terrible spill, down into a murky bath. Like most children, I added dramatic effect with woeful sorrow. Not only did my mother believe the whole story, she gave me sympathy and a warm bath. I actually felt guilty for the kindness I received, thus telling a lie wasn't so gratifying. I also feared an eventual truth rising, and my days would be numbered until she found me out. But none of this came to pass and the mark of being a liar lay deep in my conscience, but being a storyteller remained. Seeing the world, exploring beyond my home has always given me a great since of freedom.

By age sixteen, I had already lived in four countries, the United States, Panama, Pakistan, and Iran. I had seen Europe, Afghanistan, and many of the sights in my own country.

The next time I got muddy in fun I didn't have to lie. My mother in her wisdom allowed, my brother and sisters, David, Cathy, Connie and I to be children as long as we hosed off outside and took a hot shower. I remember my sisters and brother were all a part of this joyous event. It was the kind of event that would cause question years later. "Remember the time we all went sliding in the mud?" Every child needs to play unrestricted and unsupervised. Every child needs to learn how to wander and discover the world. Every adult wants to remember, traveling is a form of play to be remembered.

I am of the belief that we need to hammer swords into plough shares. When I travel I believe I am a messenger of world peace. I believe the only power of real protection is truth, an open heart, and the power of love. This is the true power of the universe, anything less than this love is replaced by a false sense of security.

I contend it is a lack of belief in the positive universe that leads to destructive wars over religion and land. In order to stave off their ultimate fears of self-realization people arm themselves, rob others, or create war. I live in a country where neurosis and anxiety is the norm and fear is rampant. Television is considered reality and reality is avoided at all costs. This avoidance is of the inner voice, which is peaceful and loving in most of us, the escape from that voice charades as "entertainment". This book is about the real world full of love and small mundane miracles.

I understand jet fuel is used every time I step into an airplane. My carbon footprint is large and looming. I am a hypocrite caught between the future where pollution is our death and the here and now in the world we may lose. We are the earth's worst enemy through pollution, but we may be the hope that saves our future as well. This world has so rapidly changed in my own lifetime; I have seen the world population increase six fold!

Returning to the past, when I was around ten, some of my unsupervised Saturday activities were to explore the vacant fields and ride my bicycle to the movie theater in Torrance, California. The movie house was a couple of miles away, up a hill, where I'd park my bicycle (without a lock), and see a double feature for less than a dollar. It was possible to be in the center of town and see as few as three people walking and one car on the street.

I have become increasingly aware of the lack of physical space that comes with being a traveler in the world. In some populated countries like El Salvador, for instance, there is no such thing as a life in solitude. The in the seventies and eighties I lived in Nebraska. My last four years in Nebraska were spent renting an old farmhouse where I painted, kept a journal, wrote music, and created photographs. I lived by my wits end with little to no money. In winter I chopped my firewood, in summer I grew my own vegetables and raised chickens for food. This time was a treasure of personal solitude. Living alone with the silence of nature has created a source of stability deep in me nothing can ever diminish. Those times created my spiritual inner voice. Over time I have come to learn my inner voice remains unchanged, and my voice is no different than the majority of people on the planet. We all have much more in common than differences. Through my travels I have come to know that sharing is in the hearts of the majority of the people in this world.

My relatively new, cross-cultural marriage to Diana is a testament to creating commonality and sharing. If I focused on the differences we would have never survived the inevitable pressures that marriage puts on a couple. The chaffing that comes from cultural clashes is just that. Over time I find the "cultural clash" has been replaced with understanding and greater love through patience. My first book on this subject (Internet Love: How I Met My Wife) describes how challenging and fun a new marriage could be. But all and all the survival of our marriage is strengthened by the intense unity that is created while traveling together. I documented the four weeks we didn't travel together but came to find we were deeply intertwined regardless of the distance. We were in daily contact and our proverbial footprints merge into a common vanishing point on the horizon.

To master traveling as a married couple is the art of teamwork. This book entails much interpersonal back and forth between Diana and me. If you take her "side", I understand. I am brutally honest about what we live through. My writing is a coping mechanism for what I encounter, the good and bad. I don't really know if my writing improves, or suffers, when I travel with my wife. I had much more time to focus on writing when I ventured out solo in Central America on my first visit. The four weeks I was alone I found it more challenging to travel because I was unable to depend on anyone but myself, and additionally I did not have Diana there to help me with speaking Spanish. I had much more time to occupy myself with writing when traveling solo versus enjoying time with my wife. I get lonely when I travel alone; conversely, I sometimes tire of the intense, constant companionship when I travel with my wife. There is no perfect answer, except to seek a balance, so in these writings that span three years, there are samples of both. Most of the book was written while traveling with Diana. Our close daily relationship was in motion even while I was traveling alone because we spoke nearly every day by telephone or computer. Our interpersonal growth is a big part of these stories.

The book, oh the book, it's not looking at the past like the introduction. I share three years of adventures with Diana, six weeks in Europe, two weeks in Colombia, four weeks in Central America (solo), and eight weeks of a return to Central America. In these pages are years of friendships, and new developing friendships, that occurred while traveling. I find myself becoming more global in perspective with each new venture into the cultures I encounter. The alternative life I sought when I was young has come full circle, to a place where the third world is often more comfortable than the first world, yet I live in both. So I've decided to share the journey with you in hopes of creating a better world and opening a few new doors to others. And also to show my wife how much I love her, by telling our story.

Om Tat Sat

Chapter One
Ireland

July 1, 2008:

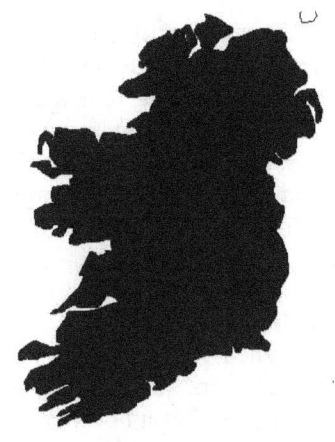

If a traveler invented a song it would be like that of a bird that has flown to the far corners of the globe to seek happiness. Not one musical note would be repeated, ever, and like the great whales of the oceans, the song would reach those in the far away depths of their souls. While I'm passing over the clouds the aircraft follows the white shores of Long Island. Under the mist only a thin white ribbon of shoreline indicates where land ends at Montauk's lighthouse. Clouds soon cover blankets of sky and the airplane is a whale surfacing for air, then returning to earth in five and a half hours to sing another song of a happy reunion with Denis and Carol, our Irish friends.

We have six weeks ahead of us. Six weeks to see Europe and visit old friends. The plan is to tour Ireland, Holland, Germany, Denmark, France, Austria, Italy, and lastly Greece. The future is a big, sunny, red ball on the horizon, and like time, it sinks, slowing to a crawl and glowing brighter because the diminishing light brings out its own importance. The conclusion of light doesn't end with the sphere swelled by the horizon. After the sunset, a longer wider ribbon drags across the sky like orange sherbet. No one remembers these colors; they are the last strands of humanity, giving birth in blood red, pulled by gravity to sleep. They fade into orange and we see the day passing in an open grave through the airplanes window. Black water below and blue heaven above, the kind of blue the Persians set to a glaze and dripped down a vase resting on its lip.

I've kissed Diana's lip. We look into each other's eyes. Very little is said when we look out of the aircrafts window and share the last thread of light. We open the night with stars and more stars. Within the hour we traversed the globe enough to begin the night and fly above the clouds like arrows from our ancestors, flung at the speed of love toward Ireland.

Since 2006 I have been married to a short, slightly weighty, pretty Colombian woman. She has straight, dark brown hair, a narrow face with deep set dark eyes, and a very light complexion. We have twenty years age difference between us. I am a balding, mustached; lip-go-teed, six foot tall, Gringo with long white curly hair. I smile a lot. Diana is more serious. She loves to fire Spanish words at me in incomprehensible speeds. The relationship has a built-in "misunderstanding" clause due to our language difference. We miss many meanings of both languages and are constantly clarifying what the other means. In a big way this keeps our relationship working positively, although that mysterious silence that comes with long vulnerable glances is the true cement of our relationship. There is deep communication that takes place between us that has nothing to do with words.

The voice of the stewardess comes over the airways and interrupts the movie about Bob Dylan. The movie stops long enough for the public address to be heard by all. Her voice carries the importance of God. In the headphones the voice delays just long enough to give the God-voice a half second echo into the future. We are in an airplane but it sounds like a cathedral with lofty ceilings and stained glass windows. I like this effect even though the movie is paused. I know how to buckle my seat belt and enjoy the echo in my headphones despite the message. A new airplane, a new journey, and I'm in church thanking the creator for all Her abundance and my good fortune to live, be married, and have wings to travel like an angel.

When we arrive, the passport is stamped and a month of visa preparation and paperwork passes with a brief ink thump. Diana is in! The border agent makes a joke that it never rains in Ireland. I tell him it's my thirteenth time and he looks at me as if he knew me. I was still smiling from his joke. He knows I am happy to be there, wishes me a safe journey and welcome to Ireland.

For some thirty-five years Denis and I have been friends since our first encounter as coworkers in a boot factor in Omaha, Nebraska in 1971. Denis is now waiting at the airport; He was sitting unseen off to the side. By the time we found an ATM and wheeled the luggage out the front door, I had circled back to see if he was inside waiting. He wasn't at the curb, which he never is. He greeted us when we found each other and we all felt home again. I'd mistakenly told him on the phone, "I'll see you Tuesday". He had come the day before only to be hours out of bed and en route to the airport at five in the morning. I told him the dates several times, but Tuesday turned into Wednesday because we left on Tuesday and arrived on Wednesday morning. Mea culpa. We laughed at the confusion of time zones during our joyous reunion. Forgiving mistakes is a healthy part of our friendship and why we have been friends since 1971.

This is Diana's second time to Ireland. She met my Irish friends the second year of our marriage. Ireland was the third country in her life to be visited. She had the luxury of being in a home of friends who made her feel very welcome, rather than being a typical tourist.

Denis is a tall, thin Irish looking man. His Irish accent is so thick it takes time to adjust, so listening is crucial to following what he, or any Irish, is saying. His peppered-gray hair is collar length. He has a broad, clean shaven chin and thick eye brows that make him appear pensive and serious. When he was young his younger brother was taken by polio. Denis in turn contracted the disease and has a slightly deformed left arm. He keeps this arm always covered with a thick Irish sweater. He has a no-nonsense, tell it like-it-is personality. His inner strength comes from being raised by a widowed mother and the tragic loss of his younger brother. His childhood was harsh. His pride is sourced coming up in the world and being self-sufficient. That we hold in common.

The day passed in cycles of sleepy stories of remembrances. The jet lag is like a bomb that never goes off but has to be carried on my back in the recesses of consciousness, heavier than anything in recent memory. There is no memory because the want for sleep in the middle of the day creates a strange drunken stupor. Three times in the day I fell asleep. I never nap, but I was like a cat looking for a soft cushion to rest on and fall into slumber. If I have coffee, which I very seldom do, the drink doesn't even wake me.

It is the strangest sensation to be half awake but very excited to be in Ireland on a new vacation. We have to remind ourselves that when we go to bed for the night it is only six o'clock at night back in New York. When back home I make sure to call Denis from New York before 6 PM so I don't wake him. And he is often times awake past midnight anyway. I'm asking myself if jet-lag is what it is like to be old and feeble.

We woke at 9:30, twelve hours of sleep and we still are not awake. It feels like we will never be. After eating cereal for breakfast, Diana and I walked down the country lane towards Galbally, the small village where Denis has lived all his life. The air is so fresh and thick with odors from farms and flowers. Our stroll is without cadence, as every effortless step is like sleepwalking.

Along the single lane is an abandoned one-room house. It's been there since my first visit to Galbally in 1971. The roof of the building has roots that stretch down to the ground and drink the water like straws pulling nourishment to the foliage that covers every inch of any reaming slate tiles. Someone lived a lifetime in that tiny one room house. Someone was born and died there a hundred years in the past. We continued on toward the small town snapping pictures, allocating memory to a camera. Nothing reminds us of home as we walk, we are alive in a beautiful picture.

The hedge along the road is a wall of knurling greenery where thorns and honeysuckle mix. Bluebell flowers grow like spikes inside the hedge, inching taller and leaving a skeletal stalk as the tops keep blooming, and waving their brilliance above the impenetrable thicket where no man nor beast pass. The tiniest and most gorgeous flowers share the stage, and spatter the walk with color. The cows look at us as if they know us and are indifferent to Diana's singing. She is singing a song she made up about me.

"You are the best husband in the world. You are my Papito".

There are swallows with orange chests jetting over the road and darting so fast they are hard to trace, follow their flight. Nothing else seems to move, not even the wind. Everything and everyone is happy. When Diana swings her arms at her side she is happy. I know this about her.

Ireland has a smell. It's a clean smell. The houses even smell like the outdoors because there is always a window cracked to circulate air no matter how cold the outside world is. The weather always has a chill. I come here for spiritual renewal and I'm never disappointed. Maybe the jet lag is New York lag. The slow rescheduling of my body's clock is nothing more than a reawakening in a place that is alive with the abundance of nature and spirit. We passed through the town square and Diana wanted me to take pictures of the men working at a tiny garden. I shook my head no, I didn't want to interrupt them working. The people here are so polite. We passed along the road where the town ends and a small river has a tiny stone bridge that crosses over to the cemetery. The black gate has been painted so many times that the shiny paint has built up a skin of enamel rounding off any edges that were buried years before. Denis's mother is buried here and I say a prayer over her grave for my friend. She died at eighty, a few months after one of my visits, five or six years back. Diana says a full rosary and won't let me talk until she has finished. We walked among the tombstones reading the names of strangers. Some of these people were born and died in my own time, living only twenty years, killed in car accidents. "Tragically taken from us". One mother and her daughter were killed on the same date and their oval pictures stand out on the black polished granite. Galbally is so small Denis knows the stories of each death. Here, life is valued. A death isn't a sensationalized event of the evening news, but a real event. He visits his mother grave enough to notice and ask about any new tombstones if he hasn't heard of a death from the local friends. He leans on his wall in front of his house and chats to get the local news. He will say a prayer even if he never knew the stranger in the graveyard.

As we circled back to Galbally on our walk there was a new crowd gathered around the square where the workers had been hoeing. I approached a couple of men and they explained that the RTE (Irish National News) was filming. Some ten years earlier Galbally had been chosen "Tidy Town" of Ireland. This is an honor bestowed on the cleanest looking towns. The news people were revisiting the event. We were asked to move away so the cameraman could get a shot. The men I had begun speaking with moved away to the curb and I asked them if they knew my friend. Indeed. Everyone knows everyone here. Denis Henebry is a friend to all.

By the time we got home up the lane we had lunch, and soon began our driving jaunt into Limerick. First we found an electronic store, bought a three-pronged adapter so I could charge the computer. Carol and Diana went off shopping as Denis read the newspaper on a bench and I watched the people as they passed by. The shopping mall could have been anywhere; the only difference was that I was the only guy wearing a plaid shirt. It made me stand out and be looked at stranger.

Carol and Denis have been married for almost thirty years. Carol is a medium sized, stocky woman with a pixy haircut, white hair, and sweet dimples. She has round rosy cheeks and laughs all the time. She keeps a light-hearted twinkle in her eyes as she often finishes sentences for you. She works as a nurse and exudes warmth towards all. She and Diana walk around, arm in arm, like two sisters from a different mother. While Denis and I have a slower, more reserved demeanor, the two women are electric with each other.

After a visit to a Chinese restaurant, we always go to; we headed home for a Bally's Irish Cream and the inability to fall asleep. It was midnight, my body wanted to watch the six o'clock news and stay alert for hours.

The following day we have decided to see the northern most point of Ireland and visit a beach where Denis and Carol have vacationed many years with their two children.

Now, we are driving north. We've stopped to visit the gravesite of W.B. Yeats, Ireland's most famous poet. Our destination is a hotel in the village of

Carrigart in the county of Donegal.

Carrigart is a small village on the inland coast. We spent two nights in the hotel that sits on the one corner in the town across from the Anglican Church. The village itself has three grocery stores, one home furnishing and souvenir shop, and a coffee shop. Other than two-dozen colorful row houses along the main road, and a park that runs behind the main street on the edge of the tidal bay, there are few other buildings. Horses can be rented to ride while the tide is out. There is a huge expanse of sandy shoreline that gives a rider plenty of open spaces at low tide.

The real attraction to Carrigart is a coastal area called the Downings. Houses spot its landscape and tiny roads lead to each small enclave where the steep hills make it impossible to build a road. We parked the car after driving onto the beach where the flat, packed sand creates a natural driving terrain. There, despite the chilly wind, beach goers splashed into the water (mostly young children) while parents sat behind colorful windscreens anchored into the sand. The beach is shaped like a crescent moon. We walked the mile, or so, up once and back again. The water was very shallow and wind surfers with bright sails speed back and forth carried by the strong wings. One father attempted to keep a kite aloft but the wind was uncooperative. He was having his son hold the kite but the wind didn't want to allow their kite to fly. On the far end of the curved beach a bright white house stood with dignity hugging the hill between large rocks and the water. In the background a huge new hotel made the house seem suffocated. Such is the contrast of Ireland, modernity is swallowing up the quaint houses where families struggled to survive the Great Potato Famine, and now vacationers take little notice of what was.

There is a coastal road called Atlantic Drive. It is maybe five or six miles and circles around from the inner bay to the far side on the Atlantic Ocean where the surf crashes against the rocks. Vacation houses are spread along most of the way until only one or two old established farms sit between the road and the coast. Those are the real houses where families, generations of families, were born and died. The newer houses have been built within the last twenty years. Many houses have house trailers parked to one side of the driveway. This is where the locals live while they rent out the main house to vacationers in the summer. They can make as much in one week renting to vacationers as an entire winter of labor.

Denis and Carol had driven the eight hours to the Downings for eighteen years. This was their favorite summer place to bring their two children. They showed us many of the houses they had rented for two weeks at a time. Stories of the children came up as we passed this place to that. Stories of old men with dogs on fishing boats where the houses no longer had the smoke coming from the chimney pipe, thus the people live on in memory only, in such an idyllic place lives pass, and the shore-rocks weather in fractions of millimeters. Nature doesn't change. It covers the well-worn path of old age where young men stepped onto boats to fish for the family meal only to disembark as old men a millisecond later. The children had all grown, the wife passed away, the constant companion became a dog that knew every routine and expected no reward for such awareness. The past is so strong it haunts you in Ireland, you can't escape the long winter because the chill never leaves the land long enough to make summer hot. A sweater in summer is common; on the shore it is a must.

The second morning we drove south. Carol knew every town. Even when I spotted six houses stranded on an offshore island she knew the name of the island. She knew the Gaelic and English names.

At lunch Diana said she wanted to know the name of a place in "Garlic". "No dear, it's Gaelic". We all had a wonderful laugh. Her shelf conscious mistakes are more relaxed when amongst friends that are as close as family. Her English is as weak as my Spanish, yet we manage despite repeated linguistic stumbling blocks. Sometimes the humor is obvious, others it is a real challenge to make clear what we intend to say. This is a theme of our marriage has that is permanent, until one of us masters the others language. Ireland is a dreamscape for my Colombian wife, yet she says this island reminds her of the farms and small houses back home. We had been to Ireland the first year of our marriage. The magic of the place and our marriage remains equally current.

We visited a cultural heritage park where a family of weavers had the last remaining member die in the 1970's. This is called the Dunlewey Lakeside Center. The original home site was preserved. All the dishes and furnishings were intact. A bed was built into a small cove in the main room. The spinning wheels had been moved to a demonstration room where we watched a short slide show and saw how the wheel created the thread for the looms. A second room had a hand-loom where Manus Ferry sat and wove his tweeds that brought buyers from all over the globe. The humble house had one electric outlet probably added a few years before the death of the owner. Each room had an open hearth and the smell of burning peat still hung on the walls. Manus died a wealthy man. He was the weaver. His brother was the shepherd. Their family ingenuity put the village on the map. Now years later, any traveler was welcome to spend cash or use credit cards in the gift shop.

Our private guide told us how the music of the Clancy Brothers put into motion a love for Ireland and Irish sweaters in the 1960's. The prices the Yanks were willing to pay for Irish tweed made the Ferry family rich beyond their dreams. Yet the farm and surrounding grounds had no sign of affluence or acquired wealth. This is a characteristic of a people who saw the English landlords the century before flaunt wealth and power. Wealth is a blessing of the heart, not a powerful flex of material comfort.

On Denis and Carol's honeymoon in 1978, while driving they wandered into Northern Ireland by mistake. One missed turn in the road sent them facing gun barrels pointed directly at their heads. Five times they were searched and had to empty the contents of their car. They couldn't turn back but had to keep driving north until they passed back into the Irish Republic only a few miles away. This tiny road was a flash point where gunrunners shipped arms to the IRA underground in Northern Ireland. Now the orange license plate of vacationers from Northern Ireland is as common as the black and white plates of the south.

The British actually conquered no one in the south and the topic of such thuggery is compared to the current occupation of the United States in Iraq. Conquering power is a waste. The occupier has the ability to use hatred as a tool of power. What has happened in Ireland has happened in Berlin, and will happen in Korea and even Palestine.

Hatred has a short affect in the long scheme of things. Those who cultivate hatred are eventually swallowed up by their own hatred. The universe has true power and true love. The listening towers in Donegal, which were used for surveillance of the citizens, are still standing on the mountaintops. The old listeners are deaf because a new language of reason is being spoken. A healthy attitude to remember the occupation of the British and to not harbor the same kind of hatred has given way to a bright future. This is a large part of Ireland's success and growth. They learned from the mistakes of the British.

Our guide told us the "Celtic Lion" (Irish economic boom) was more prevalent in the cities of the entire island. "We've plugged along at our own pace", those who are close to the earth carry a more practical view of affluence. The Irish know how superficial wealth is. They obtain a sensibility and humility that comes with hard work and awareness of the importance of family. Like our family in Colombia, no one in our circle is living in the clouds. No one is drunk with materialism, or with the comforts their labors have brought them. Their gratitude is stronger than greed.

The same man that gave us the weaving demonstration and tour of the farm took us onto the water in an enclosed boat, which had plastic windows to shield us from the elements. The rain and wind kicked up as we bobbed across the water and the guide told us the originating stories behind the names of each passing landmark. The lake had been increased in size because a dam had been built in the 1950's. Hydroelectricity was brought to the area, years after the luxury of electric lights was prevalent in the rest of the world. Ireland still has a strong foot in the past. Tradition is everywhere in the names of every nook and cranny.

We've just visited Denis' sisters, Mary Anne. Walter is her husband. Walter comes from a family of ten. They are all alive except one sister that lived in the United States. She died some twenty years past. Walter's grandfather was evicted from his own house during the time of the English occupation. The British soldiers broke all the windows of their house and set the family out in the cold. The wife and five children were forced to live in a dirt house out in the bog. Her husband caught pneumonia and died at thirty-six, leaving his widow and children to live out on the bog. The land was taken from the family by a Colonel Henry who was rewarded by the British Government with Irish land for his conquests in the Crimean Wars. Walter's father was the only one of the children that remained in Ireland. The rest went to the United States and England to make a livelihood. It was the Easter Rising of 1913 when the British were to retreat to the North. Walter told me the conditions of the oppressed Catholics, where the landowners were given as many votes as parcels of land they had. The Catholics had no vote, no representation. In all this history telling, Walter never had anger or hatred in his voice. There was a sense of deep pride in his being able to sit in his living room and own the freedom his grandfather had once lost. Their house was a mix of ongoing projects, with obvious stacks of things in piles waiting to be put away, or back where they came from.

The garden was very nice. The young, great-nephew took us on a tour of the garden picking us different berries, explaining some in fine detail. This short, brown haired child wore a smile brimming from ear to ear. He was like a child scientist feeding us everything he knew about the garden. He was very kind, alive with youthful vitality. During a dinner made from many of the garden vegetables he gave us several seeds that he placed into an envelope for us to take home and plant. (We don't have a vegetable garden.) The meal was made of only wholesome foods. They also had lamb and chicken. It was a hippie meal of whole foods, direct from their garden, in a house that struck me as being more counterculture than Denis and Carol's. I asked Denis' sister if she was a hippie. She laughed. The title has many meaning to many people.

Denis' niece is a photographer and language teacher who is starting a business with another teacher. She and I shared some photographs we each took. I showed her the photographs in my first book and she showed me some of her commercial projects. She had a camera that was huge and weighed enough to give a tourist a backache. But this is the camera she uses for weddings and professional portraits.

Just before dinner Denis' nephew gave us a tour of his log house imported from Finland. The nephew is a short, casually dressed, counter-culture lad who earns his living playing music or laying tile. The entire house had been sent as a kit to be assembled with numbered logs. It was a beautiful spacious house where the smell (of pine) alone was worth its value. Some of the upstairs rooms were a bit small for my tall figure because of the slanted gables, but it was truly a hippie home.

The young man is in his mid-twenties. He and his father lay tile for a living, but at night he works as a backup musician for a few singers. He told me how it was easy to do music in Ireland because the distances to travel are never more than five hours at most. He had an impressive collection of guitars. This is a country where the fathers share the land with their children and they are happy if the son or daughter builds a house next door.

We soon returned to Galbally back to Denis and Carols house to sleep and spend the next two days resting and relaxing. The day after our July sixth anniversary Diana and I walked into the village and ate at the one and only eatery. We were celebrating our second anniversary. We took the umbrella and had a comfortable slow walk there and back home again. At one point we sat in a tiny park and I feel asleep. The jet lag is still playing with me. On the walk, Diana told me stories about her relatives back in Colombia. Some of them I've heard before, but I don't mind. It never bores me to be with her and see how happy she is in talking about her family. They are such a big part of her life I feel bad that she isn't with them. But I also feel happy to have her in my life, and starting a new one with me.

Denis arranged for me to have a brief radio interview on the morning before we left. I was given a seven or eight minute interview concerning the new book. It was my first crack at book promotion. The man's name was Shawn Buckley. We did it on the telephone so I have no idea what the man looks like. He asked me if any of my books was embarrassing to Diana. I explained there was some sensitivity about her language weakness and how others may perceive what I wrote in humor, but the main theme was respect and sensitivity towards her. I also explained how I have lived a life of self-expression with art and music, so for me this was a common way to live and express in writing. I think the interview went well.

At one point he seemed critical that people have come to using the Internet to find love. I defended the practice and said it was nothing more than a new way to communicate and that a new global phenomenon was taking place. I could tell he was a bit critical, or more traditional about finding a mate, but I welcomed the challenge. I only wish I had said more about Diana and the life she left behind. I did compare the Colombian and Irish as people who work hard and care deeply about family. If I'm lucky I sold one book by having maybe five hundred people listening.

I often joke with Denis that he lives in a glorious place with a view of the Galty Mountains, yet he jumps in his car and drives for hours to "get away". I have spent many a day just walking up the hill (more like a small mountain) near his house and taking in the view. From up at "Darby's Bed" (a megalithic tomb) one can see for many miles. I know the entire mountain and all the paths that circle it. To get away is as simple as a ten-minute walk. The Irish are as addicted to petroleum as we Yankees.

When we visit we blend in with our guest's routines and customs. Denis and I often sit in the parlor and have a drink of Guinness before we bed. Diana and Carol sit in the living room and get to know each other like two sisters. I give a perfunctory concert of my songs were Denis sings harmony because he is one of the few people on earth who knows my music by heart. The concert is on a borrowed guitar that belongs to their daughter Laura. At times she accompanies me as well. Their son, Graham, has been away most of the times I have visited, the same this time. He does rapid-river kayaking all over the globe, working as a kayak teacher, or tour guide.

We spent a lovely and peaceful few days in the Irish countryside before we left for the European mainland. "Quiet" is the best descriptive word for our days. The hills near Denis and Carol are full of paths. Diana and I did many walks watching sunsets, talking, taking in the fresh air, and finding the open space to be at one with nature. The wisp of smoke from the fireplace wandered up and away in a traceless mirage, and so our drifting the countryside went as well. The evenings were punctuated by dinners of Irish food with potatoes, gravy, and lots of laughs. Carol and Diana cooked together; Denis and I would often be in the den watching the news or one of his favorite Irish teams. It was too short a time with pleasure and good company. Denis drove us to Shannon Airport our last morning and we arrived in Holland that afternoon. Diana's childhood friend,

Clarita will be waiting for us in the Amsterdam Airport.

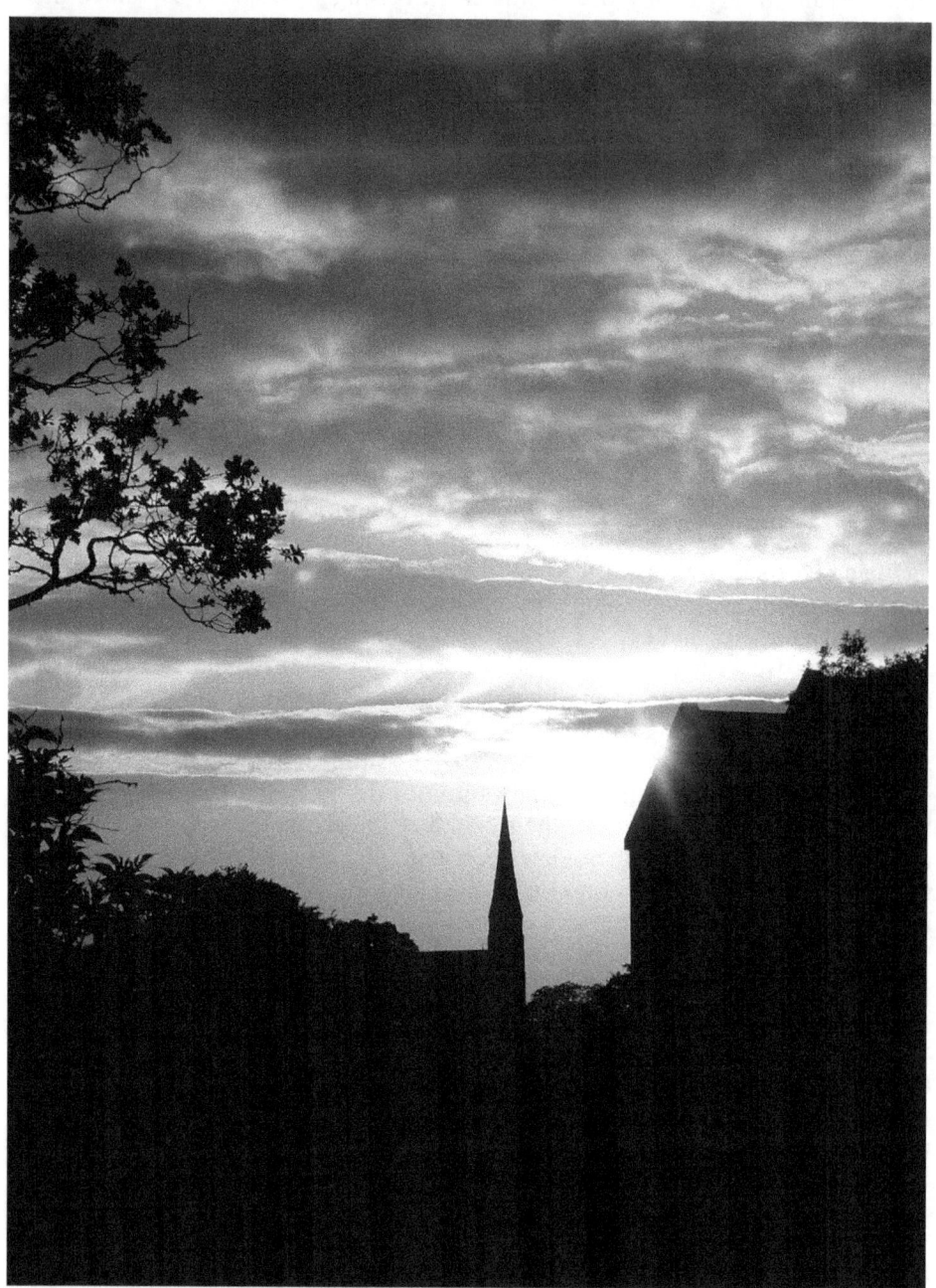

Chapter Two
Holland/Belgium

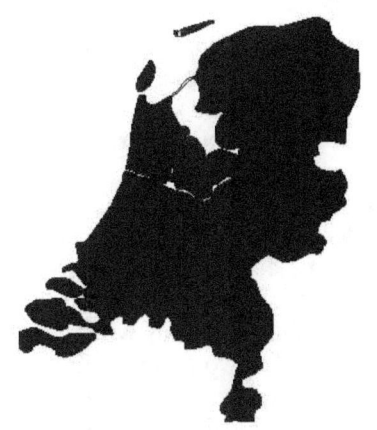

We arrived in Holland a half hour later than scheduled. As difficult as the female clerks in the New York Dutch conciliate were (a month before), the border agent in the airport was extremely effective, quick, and friendly. "Where are you going?" to which I replied, "We will be in Holland eight days and then go all over Europe." "All over? Have a good time" he said, and that was it.

The exasperating part of the trip was the second security check in the Dublin airport. After a huge line in Shannon Airport, we were forced to repeat the procedure in Dublin where our connecting flight was to the Netherlands. We were in a totally secured zone but had to exit and go through the long line and border control again.

"How long will you be in Ireland?" "We've been here a week and we are about to leave for Holland." I don't get it. I find these checks useless and annoying. Governments (especially the USA) have promoted failed policies that have created the conditions of war and invited attack on their citizens. Because of my government's ignorance and bigotry towards the Muslims of the world I have to be screened like a criminal. My view of these things is not considered mainstream, but the history of the western world's exploitation of these cultures will be taught someday. I don't at all condone the violence of the Muslim extremists, nor the violence my government has perpetrated on them as well. The result of years of mismanaged government policies are expressed in these long lines of paranoid security measures. This goes for all the western governments by the way.

Twan was waving when we exited the glazed glass doors in the Amsterdam Airport. He is a tall, medium-sized built man with no hair. He is casual and wears jean jackets and collarless shirts. Like many Europeans' he wears thin rectangular glasses and looks over the rims. Clarita was standing behind him with their baby in a buggy. She is a tiny, very thin woman with short cropped hair and a wide smile. Her body size gives her a fragile appearance, but she has strong character and is tough. The baby is Andreas, he has reddish curly hair. I had never laid eyes on Twan but I recognized him from his passport photo. He had sent a copy of his passport to us in order to get the Schengen Visa for Diana. (This is a special E.U. Visa for Colombians and other non-western countries). They handed us two bright orange tulips as a greeting. Twan speaks excellent English and the ladies were instantly streaming greetings in their native Spanish language. The airport is very large compared to the way I remember it in 2000. Now the airport looks like a modern shopping mall with expensive shops and long corridors featuring restaurants. We walked for quite a distance to get to the parking garage. We circled a couple of times to exit the airport, Twan not knowing the place at all.

We left the airport and went to straight Utrecht for some sightseeing. This was a drive that took well over an hour, past giant wind turbines and flat farmlands with well-organized irrigations systems. The highways are very modern with electric signs that indicate the traffic conditions. The city had a Turkish section where we parked the car at a meter and walked about ten minutes to the city center. We walked through the Turkish neighborhood past many shops with cloths and goods where the signage was in both Dutch and Turkish. Muslim garments for woman and fine carved wooden tables, where hookah pipes stood on top, were seen inside the shops.

In the train station we saw every kind of nationality imaginable. We cut through the station to enter the central city. The train station was like a giant shopping mall spread above with the trains below. This was a modern, busy passage with restaurants and glass displays full of colorful products. When we passed through to the other side we began to see the older city. It felt like we were passing into history where the "New" and the old blended. The buildings were old yet hundreds of young people walked around with happy grins. The old architecture is so well maintained looks new. An old building may have an exterior that is a few centuries old, but the windows, doors, and fittings are extremely modern. The brick streets were clean and little trash lay about. I kept telling Twan how clean the city is. He said to him it looked dirty. We spent five days with Twan, Andreas, and Clara.

Day Two: The second day we were heading to Delft, the famous Dutch city known for its ceramics. An electronic warning on a huge display, above the highway, said the road was closed because of a ten-truck pile-up in a tunnel. So we turned onto a new freeway and went to the town of Breda instead. This detour was a forty minute drive east. The most memorable part of this city was a Spanish war ship docked in its' center. The ship had come up a tiny canal and defeated the Dutch, some two hundred years before. The ship was a small gunboat. I thought it would be a large sea vessel, but instead a small boat no bigger than a large truck. The Dutch built shipping canals all over the country, from village to village; this gave access to the sea and invaders. The gunboat held a town hostage and parked on the water outside a red-brick fortress. The fortress was in the center of the city

The streets were curved and built in a pattern that circled away from the central fortress and canal; along one of these streets near the Spanish ship we found a meal that was amazingly delicious. We all sat on a small step a few feet away and ate food beyond every culinary expectation. The succulent chicken was cut in thin juicy strips, had a lettuce and cucumber base, and a yogurt dressing laced with dill. This was wrapped in pita bread. (We tried a similar pita chicken sandwich a couple more times on out trip but it was a big disappointment, so we gave up and concluded only this one place had the correct spices and knowledge for cooking the treat.) It was a shop, with no tables, with a counter opening onto the street.

The same day we drove to the town of Den Bosch. As soon as we parked the car and exited it, I was almost hit by a woman on a bicycle. In Europe, the bicycle lane is an important feature to learn quickly. Bicycles are everywhere. Another woman passed on a bicycle and spoke in Dutch.

"It's very beautiful here, not easy to concentrate." She commented, or something to that effect. Twan translated for me. There was no profane or indignant biker, just a friendly reminder of the local ways. The city was cleaner than Breda, but Twan said the cities are dirty.

We wandered up and down streets with little Andreas crying from time to time. If he didn't get what he wanted his eyes began spilling tears, more often than not he got his way. Diana commented on my distancing from the child, but I didn't know him and the excessive tears are not an endearing characteristic to be around. He is only two. I must sound pretty stern to access this child in this way. I think at two, at one even, the behavior we tolerate in our children can come back to haunt us, unless we, the adults, change our (yes, our!) behavior. I think children mirror in our shadows, and weaknesses. They also make beautiful little creatures that mimic all we are, the good and the bad, and unfortunately our weaknesses. I have no children so my observations are one step removed, but I work with students and their parents as a teacher.

The year before I didn't see the children in Ecuador crying and badgering their parents for things they want. Poverty imposes a type of self-control. Affluence exaggerates needs in small children and adults. I'm not saying these are bad people, I'm saying the influence of western culture is to want what isn't available, right then, and there. The infants in Ecuador are carried on the backs of their mothers, wrapped so their arms are inside the blanket, out of view. They are not crying for need and want. This is a strange observation, but I like to compare what is often a misconception of life being "better" in the western developed countries. Who really needs development when it brings on stress?

What do we do when we go to see a new city? We walk around looking at things we can't afford, and if we did buy, we would be in debt beyond control. It's not a blame game I'm playing. I see the child and the adults as victims of this Western success. We have plenty of "things" in the Western world. What we lack is balance between abundance and real need. Materialism is being promoted through commercialism. Self-control and common sense are too low on the scale of ecological living, but spiritually and psychologically these "things" can potentially distract us from what we crave the most; community, love, friendship, and family. Materialism "fills" a void when these things are unavailable.

Twan and I stood in the town square as the two women bought underwear in a shop. It started to rain and we headed for an ice cream parlor. I found twenty Euros on the floor of the shop and handed it to Twan. I was happy to have a little boost from money coming in versus out of my pocket. From some reason, Twan was paying for food all too often. On a couple of occasions I hurried and paid the tab before he could get to it. He was insisting we were his guests, but it was not a fair exchange in my view. He was doing as Clarita wanted, because in Colombia if you have house guests you pay all expenses. I heard this before in Costa Rica and Colombia. I don't know where this comes from, but it is not a comfortable situation for me. I like to share the monetary burden.

Diana and I get into these tussles about paying. She is pulling me aside telling me to pay while Twan was saying he wanted to pay. It is a kind of unfair position for me all around because in my politeness I keep both sides of the conversation private, yet I'm in the middle of all this. We had the same mini-drama in Ireland. I feel like Diana has to stop putting this responsibility on me, take it on herself. She has to learn how to accept other's generosity. To resist the kindness of others is a way of allowing guilt into a quality situation. She feels inadequate and bad about not having a way to return an immediate favor.

Back in Ireland Denis and Carol paid for our hotel room for two days. Instead of enjoying the gift I was constantly reminded that we should pay for all the meals, all the ice creams, and you name it. I know them well enough that I can return favors in different ways. Denis has commissioned three art works from me during our stay. I finished one and will send two more when I get home. They are landscape scenes in watercolors of friends and relatives houses. I've explained to Diana that if people won't let us pay we find other ways to return favors. Send a painting of their house, send them flowers, or bring a shawl from Ecuador (which is exactly what we did). But first and foremost receive a gift and keep your guilt to yourself, express gratitude, not regret for having nothing to return. I think it is in bad taste to receive a gift and say, "Oh, I need to give you something as well." This is the little side drama at play between a husband and wife that is "private", but we all do these things.

With all that said I felt very at home with Twan and Clarita. By this time we were teasing each other and enjoying a new friendship. Twan reminds me of my friend Steve, who was my best friend in high school. Steve and Twan both are a no-nonsense kinds of guys who say what they want, like it or not.

There is something serious and melancholy in Twan. His mother had died a few months past. When we parted at the train station he was chocked up and said he didn't like to say good-bye to people. That magnetic draw of friendship is what lures one to another visit. When you enter into the personal space of a stranger, friendship grows, the veil is lifted, and the shared time is so pure it instinctively causes a thirst for another drink.

The Dutch have a genuine ethic and a make conscious effort to create a just society. We never saw poverty or crime, we saw a minimum of mentally disturbed people, and the tone of society was one of optimism. An enormous part of the American psyche is culturally anchored in the Dutch. The common living rights of the Dutch in New York (New Amsterdam at the time) were a healthy influence on the Bill of Rights before the colonies were turned into British property. On my first visit to Holland back in the 1990's I was so impressed with the Dutch way of life that I wanted to live in Holland. In my opinion, they seem to be a step ahead of the United States when it comes to progressive laws and tolerance. We are "programmed" to believe the propaganda machine, the American Capitalist perspective more often than not is a social hindrance.

Day Three: We took two trains to Brussels. The first train was just inside the border, maybe fifteen minutes from Twan and Clarita's house in Holland. The second train was modern in contrast to the first, which had wooden seats and made squeaky-wheel sounds as it slowly moved along the tracks. On the second train a group of well-behaved students boarded and sat on the sleek smooth plastic benches. My teaching instincts were observing that no one was acting out.

An hour into the ride we pulled into the main Brussels station and exited onto a busy street. We crossed the wide, open street into what was an immediate tourist zone. Thin streets with shops and an overabundance of restaurants, where men spoke in three or four languages to greet and entice people inside, were packed with pedestrians. This was a pedestrian only sector of the city. A festive atmosphere with the smell of beer and the wide smile of intoxicated drinkers spilled into the walkway. Inside hundreds of examples of beers were displayed above the bartender's head. I remember one establishment had mugs with the names of regular patrons hanging from the ceiling. It seemed every bar was packed and every restaurant was empty for being so close to noon.

The streets wound around in no particular order in the old town. By the time we found the famous statue of the little boy urinating (Manneken Pis) the city streets were wide, ordinary and straight, with loud traffic, and hordes of tourists; the streets became uniform in square city blocks. We entered a chocolate shop just to find space away from the crowd, but we soon were sampling our first taste of famous Belgian sweets. The young man working behind the glass display case offered us a small taste of each chocolate we eyed. He spoke in several languages but correctly guessed ours to be English as he welcomed us with enlivening treats. Behind glass displays carefully stacked layers of chocolate varieties tempted our eyes and taste buds. Dark and light chocolates in round and square, mouth-sized, sat waiting to be tested. The smell of chocolate was a thick as the air.

It was slightly overcast as we made our way to the main plaza called Grand Place. In the square a huge bandstand was erected and live music was blaring. The tall ornate buildings with fancy scrolling facades created a cave-like effect for the music and it echoed in a messy spattering of sounds that bounced in all directions. The only place the sound was truly clear was in front, or to the side of the stage. There was a Belgian singer whose song I recognized from the sixties, but the rest of the performers were unknown to me. (In addition, they all sang in French.) It was well past noon and people filled the square, it seemed the free concert was a slight distraction because the majority of the people were more interested in the sights. The world famous square with its ornately decorated facades was difficult to take in because of the stage and live concert.

After walking several hours and seeing many Belgian waffle shops I gave in to my taste buds. I waited in line as the others walked further on, almost losing me. Diana saw me and was surprised to see me about to break my standard, strict, no-sugar diet, and consume a waffle with whipped cream and chocolate syrup. It was delicious. I couldn't go all the way to Belgium and not have chocolate and waffles. I felt gluttonous as the rest stood around and waited for me to lick the whipped cream off my face. We were getting to a point where our feet were sore and ambitions had waned.

I remember passing a hippie van smothered with animal rights slogans. No matter where we go we see a lone solider who still continues the fight for a better planet. I know these people are seen as "nuts" by most, but I admire their ways.

Nearby we found a park where a giant sculpture of an orange parking cone stood in a small plaza. Andreas ran around the sculpture in grand circles, laughing and playing. On a patch of grass, on the far side of the park, a group of Roma women sat in a circle talking. They all wore black, wore headscarf's, and looked somewhat out of place. The Roma people are like a tradition that never changes. There is permanence to their tribe. The new trend to wear a colorful flowered scarf by the younger gypsies shows some slight advance in fashion. I liked that the women were in a circle holding court like an ancient tribe in the middle of a modern city. The children on the laps of their mothers were comfortable enough to touch and sit with other women in the circle. The extended families touched lives of all sitting there; no one was isolated. There is something that is lost by the isolated lives we lead in the western world. This scene could have taken place hundreds of years ago.

The less attractive part of Brussels was apparent on the train as we left the city. No tourists walked the baron, half desolate streets where sex shops and men milling around smoking cigarettes stood in the cold with their collars pulled up. Everything seemed serious and bleak. The train was an hour, plus, ride back to the border.

We returned to Holland with the clean, well-cropped yards of the small Dutch towns. Twan told me how he had left his employer and was very blunt with the manager, telling him there was no real personal interest in him, so why pretend? He is working as a computer programmer for the security division of corporations. Because of his clearance he was able to see the income of all the company chief officers. There was some resentment due to his knowledge of such vast pay differences between employees.

As we drove through the small towns, back into farm communities, the well-organized use of land was very apparent. For centuries the Dutch have used land managers, flora isn't unchecked like Ireland.

Twan explained his mother had died a few months prior from cancer, so he was still in a mourning period. His English was near perfect with the exception of an occasional pause where he was mentally looking for the correct English word. I admired his openness and was honored by his trust.

Day Four: We awoke to gloomy skies and what looked like an eminent shower. The early rise followed a quick breakfast. I was over the jet lag, but a late to bed schedule made getting up difficult. We all grouped into the car and headed for a town that stood on the three borders of Holland, Belgium, and Germany. Diana stood on the corner of one country as I instructed her to go to Germany. Some Japanese tourists got my joke and chuckled along with us. We rode an elevator up a tall tower and looked at the forest and rolling countryside of the three countries. The shower that had greeted us when we first arrived at the parking lot was already far off to the west. The clearing skies remained for the rest of the day.

Twan drove us through small towns that looked and felt very German. Flower boxes hung from second story windows and exposed dark wooden frames contrasted with the bright white stucco facades of houses. The streets were full of vacationers and even in the countryside; people strolled on long paved walkways that snaked through the farms, over small brooks, up and down hills from one village to the next. This was a favorite pastime, to take day walks from town to town. The farmers were required to allow people to use their land and as long as they behaved, it didn't seem to be a worry. It struck me that people had a sense of sharing the land for many generations. No one was concerned that strangers were "trespassing". It all seemed so civilized. The fences separating the fields had steps built to allow the people to walk up and over into the next field. This kept cows inside and allowed pedestrians to traverse the fences.

We drove a few hours more and entered the tourist village of Volendam where shops lined the streets and families licked on ice cream cones while leisurely strolling and window-shopping. No cars were allowed in the center of the town, narrow streets had been built long before the invention of the car, and the town fathers had wisely kept the old architecture and atmosphere. We bought trinkets for the family in Colombia; small Dutch porcelain shoes, lacy embroidered scarves, and everything one could imagine being Dutch. Yes, we saw the little Dutch boy and girls kissing in a million variations on a million souvenirs. My idea is always buy a tiny thing and make it a bigger gift to give away. People love token reminders of foreign places. Our refrigerator door is full of such memories.

Somewhere on the drive home, the sun set and we drove into the small village where Twan and Clarita live. Across the street from the home a large soccer field with play area for small children. The house was in a neighborhood with duplexes that didn't cramp each other. The houses are built so privacy is tantamount. We said hello to a neighbor who was returning from his job as we unloaded the car. The proximity of the houses was not so evident because of the high windows and tall walls between. We never heard the neighbors even though their house was a few feet away. The tall fences and climbing shrubs made all sounds stay within the yard.

We slept on the third floor in a room high above the patio. Our room was one big bed with a small open space near the door where the bags made maneuvering around nearly impossible. An extra bed had been put in the room so we could sleep side by side. The window was one, large single pane that opened on a single hinge. The window didn't open all the way but just a few inches. What appeared a strenuous event to open, and push out, was an easy exercise because the gravity of its own weight balanced on the hinge. We cracked the massive windows in the night just enough to give us some air. Along the windowsill Twan had a series of tiny miniature Dutch windmills, each based on an authentic structure. Of all the art and fine objects in their house waking up to those tiny windmills a few inches away from my face gave me a real Dutch smile. I felt like a child.

The third floor had a winding stairwell that circled up into a hall. At the immediate left, a small room with a computer on a sleek thin table in a European design made the room feel empty. We had access to a computer at all hours. The bedroom was the second left with a washroom across the hall. We had a washing machine and a computer. We could have stayed there and been fairly content. Inside the washroom there was a sink to brush our teeth, so we really felt at home. It felt like a separate apartment. The spiral stairs made it even more isolated, like ascending into a private space. We were happy to feel so secure and welcome.

The next morning we all sat out in the back patio. The air had a slight chill as their tiny, black and white Terrier ran in circles, barking and playing with Andreas who rode on a small plastic tricycle.

Diana was with her best friend for life. They reminisced, sang songs, and laughed like two schoolgirls, never missing a beat, as if time had never separated them. We spent five days with them and our two wives were in heaven. They still talk for an hour or more when one calls the other on the telephone. Friends are our link to the past that makes time and aging go away. We stay young through friendship.

Day Five: We boarded a local train to Amsterdam. Twan paid for the ticket because our ATM cards were not working. It was one more grand gesture that in the hurry to get to the train he knew exactly how to buy the ticket in a vending machine, all instructions written in Dutch. Twan was sad and waved us onto the platform. Our wives were in tears of sorrowful parting.

We pulled into Central Station in Amsterdam. I know this place well, it is also very accessible. Diana stood with the heavy bags as I went upstairs to buy the 'Amsterdam card', get a map, and find where our pre-reserved, hotel was located. We made our way through the busy throngs of people, dragging our wheeled luggage across the tram tracks, to the second main street into the city. There is always that awkward moment when new in a city where one (me in this case) is standing in the middle of the tram track, looking around, only to be obstructing an oncoming public transport. This is where a loving partner is so helpful. *Watch out* was the alarming call that returned me from sightseeing mode to reality. I stand out when my mouth is wide open, holding a suitcase, and I look up. Silly me.

The hotel was a comfortable three blocks from Central Station. The sun was shining and we blended into the crowd as we strolled across street the like ice cream rolling in syrup. Amsterdam is a happy place. We soon found our hotel and registered on the well-polished front desk. A friendly, tall redheaded receptionist gave us our plastic room cards. Our room opened onto the front of the hotel's first floor, just above the street and main entrance. This might have been a problem, but with the windows shut, sound was at a minimum. Thick curtains kept out the streetlights at night, but for now it was time to find a meal, and we were getting hungry.

In the cool afternoon air our first stop was a nearby side street where we saw many shops and restaurants on our way to the hotel. The streets echo the sound of boots and shoes, old cobblestone walkways are worn from centuries of pedestrians. It was a decision between a falafel shop and gyro shop. We remembered the last gyro in Holland and wanted a savory repeat of our sidewalk meal. We never found that same quality of that first chicken gyro again the entire summer. Here is a lesson in being satisfied with an original experience rather than trying to duplicate happiness.

It was a second-rate meal, punctuated with a small piece of metal in the chicken. I didn't break a tooth, but it felt like I did. The man behind the counter shrugged his shoulders and returned to his cooking like I was a creep for showing him the steel chunk in my food.

We spent the rest of the night walking and exploring the tiny streets and channels. The light from the channels glistens and reflects itself on windows and walls of the tall, thin Dutch buildings. What are houses as wide as one small room climb heights as tall as five stories. The rows of thin houses gives one a sense of a time when every square inch of land was precious and building skyward was the only option. There is little open space in Amsterdam today. Every speck of real estate has been used for living. In years past it was used for commerce, where warehouses stood, now is living space. The channels are filled with parked house boats, some being stationary for so long those green algae has caked the sides of the vessels while deck anchors are rusted in frozen orange knots. The streets are clean, if not for sloppy tourists, there would never be a lose scrap of trash to be found. The smell of marijuana wafted around corners as people sat in half-trance, smiling or talking. Diana was not familiar with the smell at all. I explained.

Day Six: We exited the hotel and entered a deli a few doors down. Two small kittens were scurrying under a fruit stand. Diana and I paused and loved looking at the playful creatures darting at each other. Inside we bought some yogurt, bread, and sandwich materials. The man behind the counter was a cheery Middle Easterner. We set off for the Ann Frank Museum that we had passed the night before. The line was moving so slowly the night before we planned a morning visit to see if the line would be shorter. It was, but only slightly. All the way, I photographed every interesting reflection on the channels. The line was a brief thirty-minute wait; during which we stood chatting with people from all over the globe.

The museum has a maze of halls and stairwells that move throughout the thin Dutch building. Slide presentations, films, and words are projected or written on the walls, telling the story of the young Jewish girl living in isolation while being sheltered by her father's Dutch employees. At the conclusion of the tour a presentation with current topics on tolerance was shown as the audience participated in a Q and A session, presenting the voting data of the people in the room, and the overall scores from all who had participated. I liked the instant feedback and because these were very current, tough subjects that face us all concerning cultural conflicts.

On most of the topics, I fell within the norm, but on some I was in the minority. These questions involved the topics of race, religion, sexuality, and social norms. I noted reading at the time that although governments have laws against discrimination, society is sometimes ahead of what governments vote into laws. Also, we in the United States think we are the "world leaders" on civil rights, yet many European countries strike me as being much more advanced. After being sensitized to Ann Frank's tragedy my emotions were raw. Holding back tears isn't easy in such a sad place. I don't remember if I read her book or not, but I know the story and have seen numerous documentaries on her life. The cold history of that era is not that distant from our present world nor is the numerous genocides we still live with today.

Our next place of interest was the Van Gogh Museum. This large three-story museum is the best collection of Van Gogh artworks in one place. Less known works of his can be found as well as the usual well known themes of landscape and still life. The queue inside was fast moving. Once inside, the security checks and coatrooms were situated in a way that facilitated entry. I recall the security was better than the airports and seemingly more efficient.

The first floor was filled with artists that were contemporaries of Van Gogh. The wide central space of the museum had ascending stairs that lead into the various galleries of his works. This was my second visit and I saw new galleries of what must be rotating exhibitions on such topics as etchings, drawings, oils, or divisions of works by his age.

In my fledging years Van Gogh was one of my patron saints. His tragic life was enough for any young artist to identify with. In many ways he was truer to his work than many artists today. He worked without reward; well before the time when art was considered an investment, he dedicated his life to his passion. I remember being astonished at his landscapes and the inventive brush strokes that captured depth and realism, yet he was employing such wide, abstract brush strokes. To this day, I get a personal excitement looking into these works. This museum is an appropriate shrine to this Dutch Master.

We left the museum and Diana spotted a Diamond Museum. This, to her, was her Van Gogh collection. I knew it was a market to entice buyers but I went along for the ride. Behind well-secured glass counters, displays of diamonds of varied sizes and shapes stood for eyeing. Video surveillance cameras caught every hall, stairwell, display cabinet, worker and quest. The diamond cutters themselves worked inside glass viewing workstations where the guest could stand within inches of the machinery that spun and cut the rare stones. Diana was rapt and I was impatient, tugging at her shirt to keep moving. The "museum", which was a glorified department store, went up and down stairs, through a couple of building; and ended in a room with two long rows of glass counters where clerks peppered the exiting visitors with luring questions to stop and shop. I whizzed right through but Diana was another fifteen minutes drooling her way out.

This is one of our differences. I can't imagine why this is so interesting to her when she couldn't have afforded a years' worth of labor for a rock to be worn on a finger, but, she might be equally as bored with some of my interests. Any time we pass a jewelry store I keep my mouth shut and wait until she is finished with her visual bliss.

In general, we walk at a different pace. This is a struggle for me because I feel purpose and direction driven. I figured out years ago that money was something needed to complete window-shopping; therefore I learned to just walk on by. I shop with purpose intentions; my lovely female counterpart finds adventure in looking.

"It costs nothing to look", she loves to say to me. I automatically pull back and let myself linger so Diana can dream at windows. I would have exited the Diamond Museum in fifteen minutes; this was a good hour and a half venture.

Across from the Diamond Museum is a grand park. One end has the words "Amsterdam" sculpted in huge plastic letters. Tourists, like us, flock there to have their pictures taken. A man-made lake and outdoor cafes, or food stalls, with seating are to one side while the opposite side is open grass spaces. People run on the grass, play Frisbee, walk dogs, run dogs, or simply lay in the sun on blankets. At the farthest end of the park a grand concert hall (Concertgebouw) stands. It is looking well preserved, but a little out of place since the rear of the Van Gogh Museum, along the parks edge, is so modern and sleek. This park is nearly a mile long and a scenic walk. We stopped to eat the sandwich we had packed, avoiding the expensive costs of the food sold by vendors. We bought cold drinks and an ice cream cone.

Just around the corner from the giant words "Amsterdam" is the Rijks Museum. This museum is where Rembrandt's famous painting 'The Night Watch" is housed. The same scene from the painting can be seen as a life-size, three-dimensional sculpture in Rembrandt Park which is a mile, or so, from the museum. I love this mammoth painting. My favorite joy is to find Rembrandt himself hidden in the background. The work is a classic example for artist historians describing composition and how artists use visual devices to lead the viewer in and around the subject. Every seemingly aimless position of a visual device leads the eye to the center of interest without giving itself away. The light, or natural spotlight, illuminates the two main figures that stand like bold heroes as a child runs through the background into the shared light. The shadows being cast accentuates the perceived motion taking place; no one seems still from the men cleaning their guns to the main figure who has his hand extended as he speaks. The listener beside him is paused, but not standing like a stone, he is an active listener glowing in his white cloths draped in Rembrandt's light.

We had walked half the day and we were ready for an easy, relaxing afternoon so we took a channel tour in one of those long, low glass boats where the tourists sit and look like tourists with cameras around their necks. If the navigation of such a long vessel didn't make it around a corner the boat simply reversed and a second attempt brought success. The ride went from shady small channels to the grand harbor where boats from around the world were unloading cargo. This tour and the multiple trams around the city were all part of the Amsterdam Card. Major Museums were an extra charge, or a discounted fee, but the card was well worth the price paid. We had to find the correct channel tour that honored our Amsterdam Card, so we took the tram back to Central Station and walked to the dock nearby, where our card was honored. This was not as easy as it might have seemed. Only one company honored the card, there must have been ten channel tours. We asked at many tours before we realized that our boarding location was at a specific place near Central Station. We plan our days so riding a tour is late, after we are tired from walking. This is always subject to change because things inevitably change as the day progresses.

During the night in the hotel, we heard some partygoers in the halls and could smell pot coming in under the door, but for the most part things were tame. Although the street was a few feet away but the noise was bearable. The room had a second, heavy inner curtain, which blocked all the neon lights from the hotel, so sleep was not disrupted.

When we left our hotel in the morning we passed the small deli where we had bought food the day before. The two kittens were scampering around and one ran into the adjoining alley. We both let out a scream and tried to halt a delivery van that was racing toward the small kitten. Our shock intensified by the driver not making eye contact, nor seeming the least bit aware of the animal. Right in front of our eyes the wheels of the van rolled over the cat catching the hindquarters flat under its front wheel. To our amazement the cat was alive, but crawling on its front paws back under some crates of the deli. The day before I had stopped to photograph these furry toy-like creatures. Now we ran to see if we could help the one that was had vanished under the fruit displays. Diana ran inside to tell the Middle Eastern owner who came out to investigate. He seemed more interested in the size of the van and what the man looked like than the harmed animal. We never saw the cat again. When we returned to inquire in the afternoon the owner said the cat was fine. I don't believe him now, nor then. He asked again about the color and shape of the van. Because of his focus on the deliveryman I question if he wanted revenge more than help for the cat. Both cats were absent from the store at that time. He insisted that the cat was fine, but a half-ton van squashing the back legs of a cat is not going to have a miraculous healing. We expected blood and were talking about what we could have done to help the tiny cat. To this day I cringe when I rethink what we witnessed. Despite all the wonderful memories this sticks in my mind.

The day passed through miles of wandering cobblestone streets. We had the map and went to as many museums as possible to use the Amsterdam Card. There was the doll museum and the photographic exhibit of Russians early museums. These were times we were completely lost, even unable to figure out the map. The layout of Amsterdam is fairly simple. Central Station is truly central with channels and streets fanning out from there. In this patchwork of channels, streets and boulevards also span and circle out. These sectors are less systematic. Some streets end at the edge of the channels. Other streets could be as short as ten buildings, short and dead ends. But the general idea is that the city is a seaport with many channels connecting to the main harbor behind Central Station.

My first time in Amsterdam some twenty years past I pitched my tent in a campground. I stayed on an island opposite the mainland, behind Central Station.

From there, I took a five-minute ferry ride to the camp that was like another dimension full of alternative folks. Punk Rockers were still the rage, and like me, they had little money to spend on hostels or hotels. I witnessed bohemians from all over the planet who had migrated there to sample the marijuana.

I really had an eye opening experience into the new wave of variations on the "old" hippie theme. I saw Punkers with pink spiked hair make bongs out of plastic soda bottles and aluminum foil. The camp was like a scene out of Mad Max. I, while in my early twenties was considered very radical in attitude, dress and hairstyle, was a conservative amongst the tattooed, body pierced lot.

The Flower Children had babies that went even further with eccentric apparel and revolutionary beliefs. This is no different, in my opinion, than the hippies, they just look more radical. It is all a part of the counter-culture wars that rage all over the planet. This will continue and I embrace this revolution no matter how old I get. I actually feel like one of the early innovators, although the Beatniks were a variation on this theme long before my time. I enjoy Amsterdam because it feels like the United States back in the seventies; young people are exploring their new world with excitement and gusto!

My wife has no inclination toward this rebelliousness. She comes from a time and place where convention isn't to be challenged. Now, when I smell the pot there is a nostalgic connection. I simply reached a point where I no longer wanted to be fuzzy. I like full sobriety. I guess it comes with maturity; being an adult with responsibilities. I met a man who told me he stopped raging with alcohol the day he made his first mortgage payment on his first house. How long each person extends his or her irresponsibility comes with a price. The struggle that comes when stopping the drugs, or alcohol, is not an easy one. Why we want to remain immature is the real issue. How long we avoid the responsibility we have to ourselves, to remain clear about our goals, and inner spirit, is a challenge for every age. The rebelliousness comes from our parents' or our own conflicts with trusting authority and becoming authority. It all starts at home.

What I perceived to be normal when younger was far from it. The number of household moves in my childhood alone was enough to shift the ground under me. Strict parenting wasn't balanced. My parents provided all the necessities for physical comforts, but little for the inner soul and emotional stability. Physical punishment was often in the form of belt whippings. But to complicate life even further, I have come to realize my situation was not what most people experience; people are as diverse as the clouds that form overhead every day. Physical abuse leads to physical addictions. Because of the complications of the human experience we need to approach "addiction" with a spiritual approach, versus a punitive, legal solution of arrests, convictions, and jail time.

As we were nearing the end of the day in Amsterdam we walked to the Botanical Gardens. In the channel next to the garden there were swarms of police lining the edge of the water. A few policemen in scuba diving gear were dunking up and down looking for a body. Someone had seen a man jump into the water in a suicide attempt and the police rushed into action. A crowd of observers was on both sides of the banks which were quickly cordoned off with bright yellow tape.

We entered the Botanical Gardens and could see the search continue from inside a huge tropical atrium. I was high up in the skywalk when I noticed the search had been called off; no body. I learned this later when we exited to ask a few straggling spectators.

I had my camera and at every turn I was shooting pictures inside the Botanical Garden. While in the butterfly house I was able to get some quick photographs of children playing with the winged insects. This universal fascination with butterflies is always an excellent subject to photograph. The light wasn't that good and a flash was out of the question, so I did the best I could. At an outdoor café table near the entrance I was more successful taking pictures of birds that landed on our table and approached our cookies. I was surprised at how tame these fast little birds were. One flew into the cafes dining room and a waitress chased it out with a broom. This gave all the customers a bit of exciting entertainment. We sat drinking herbal teas outside, next to a palm tree in a vast orange ceramic pot. The day was overcast and getting chilly.

We had a bus that night to catch so we slowly walked back to the tram a few blocks away. We missed entering the Jewish Museum while in route, circled back looking for the front door, but it had just closed. It was five o'clock, two hours before our bus left.

We had planned our last few hours to use the Amsterdam card on public transportation before we left the city. Our last ride took us to a neighborhood north in the city. We had time so we sat on the tram and relaxed, waiting to see how far it went and where it ended.

We returned to the hotel where the desk clerk had stored our bags in a special luggage room. I fumbled through my pockets to find the baggage receipts. His insistence on me turning in the ticket assured me things were run by the book. We passed the deli in search of the small cat, but they still were unseen. Maybe it was better to not see them. The horror was bloodless, but that cat badly injured. I don't care what the deli owner said. We think he euthanized the animal and was just trying to make us feel better by saying it was all right.

At the train station there were signs for our route, it had been closed, and we needed to take a bus to the International Bus Station. After a few questions to other passengers we were on the correct bus. In the International Bus Station there were hoards of people crammed into a thin long room with windows where clerks sat. We were an hour too early to buy our tickets.

Diana sat with the bags and I went off across a boulevard to enter into a residential neighborhood. The full moon was rising above the trees and a lone woman was out walking her dog.

When I travel I try to and imagine I am living in that place. What seems so new and exciting to me must be common and "every day" to the residents. Then when I return home I try to bring some of that same newness to the strolls in my own neighborhood. I keep a tiny reservoir of "exploration surprise" tucked into my memory to see if I can turn the ordinary into the unusual. It works. Another exercise is to remember where I last saw the moon, what phase it was in, or where I saw the last full moon. These mental markers are part of traveling, part of being aware, and part of enjoying the earth more fully.

I took a long walk, making sure I wasn't so far that I would not remember my path. The houses were quiet with lights being turned on as the dusk crawled across the land in slow motion. I'm not a voyeur, but I enjoy observing how people go about their daily routines. People were sitting at their tables or watching the television, not that different from my home country. What little traffic there was would pull into a driveway and a person would walk up the driveway, tired from working all day.

I returned to the bus station and saw some of the waiting passengers were boarding a bus. Our vendor's window was still closed; we had another half hour to wait. Diana was bored and she took a walk to the nearby train station. It was my turn to watch the bags. She was gone maybe ten minutes and returned with something cold to drink. The waiting room was slowly emptying as busses were boarded and pulled out for such cities as Paris, Brussels, and other European destinations. The pay toilet was next to the waiting room and luckily a man exiting left the door ajar, so we took turns.

The station was full of Middle Eastern and African peoples. A very high fence surrounded the bus station so no one could leave or get in without passing through an un-manned security gate. We bought our ticket for Copenhagen. We sat on our bags as the bus was assigned, then changed to a different bus, and finally boarded. Twelve hours of bus hell awaited our weary bodies, which would be even wearier after the ride. We had the wisdom to keep warm jackets, eye masks, and sleeping pills handy.

The bus was full of people from all over the world. This was a class of people who can't afford airplane tickets; backpackers and immigrants getting to their new home country. These are people I have always felt more at home with since my early years of living and traveling to Pakistan. I did have a privileged situation. I sought out places where the cloths weren't pressed and the people were real and willing to talk to a young stranger. The ride was uneventful, boring even.

We were originally told our bus would be nonstop. When we got to Hamburg it was around five AM. All of us were roused from sleep and told we had to get off the bus. Then we were told we had to get our bags and stand in the cold to wait for another bus within forty minutes. An hour is what it actually took. No one explained why we changed buses after being sold a direct passage.

It was dark, gray, drizzling, and not a pleasant time. There was a McDonalds in the bus terminal, but the restroom was where most of us headed. I bought some hot chocolate and we sat on some freezing metal seats, or on the luggage. It was a miserable thing to have to go through.

We boarded our bus and were traveling for maybe a half hour when we stopped and the German police boarded the bus at a checkpoint. "Vhere are you coming from? Vhere are your papers?" their brief interrogation was with a stern tongue and heavy German accent. They had guns in holsters and fit the German stereotype of husky thugs in boots. They spoke in loud voices and announced their presence on the bus. With the EU not having borders where passports are checked, the Germans do random spot checks of busses and cars. There didn't seem interested in Diana and me. They asked some young men next to us what they had been doing in Amsterdam. One guy responded, "Smoking (pot), but I didn't bring anything with me." They passed through the bus spreading a little terror in their path, then stopped a single young, black man and escorted him off the bus. He was ordered to take his bags from under the bus and his bags were thoroughly searched. I could see heavy directives outside the bus window. Ten minutes later he came back. After he sat I turned and asked if he was ok by flashing him the thumbs up. He smiled and nodded yes. No one was free enough to speak; the silence was thick with intimidation. Repressive means are not exclusive to the past. I hate that kind of treatment of anyone. His skin color and traveling alone was what prompted the officer's actions.

After what seemed like an endless, dreary ride we got off the bus in Copenhagen. It was midmorning. I knew exactly where I was from being there so many times before.

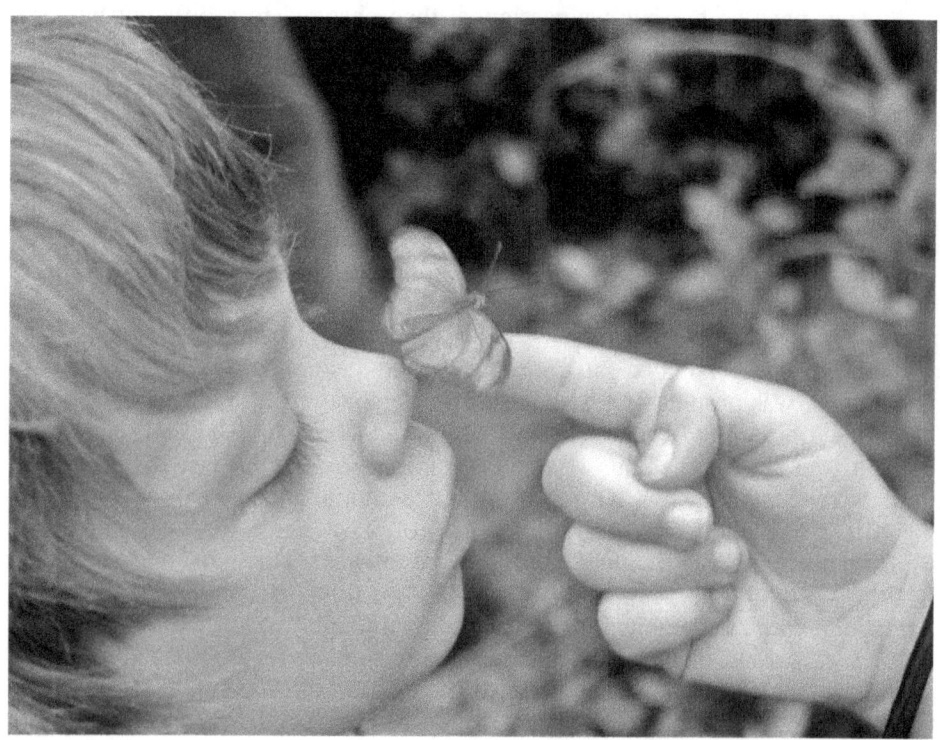

Chapter Three
Denmark

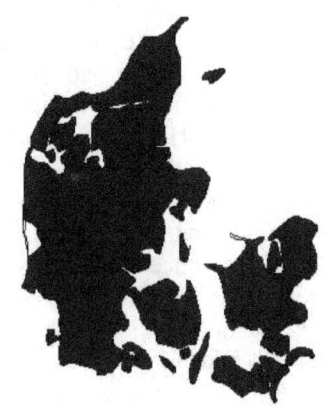

The international bus let us off behind the main train station in Copenhagen. We had our duffel bags with wheels so we easily walked to the front of the train station and crossed the street to the country's main tourist information center. Inside I took a number and waited. Diana watched a multimedia show on Denmark's tourist highlights displayed on the wall while sitting in a low chair. The sleek chair was obviously made to cause the sitter to appreciate its "Danish" design.

I bought the Copenhagen Card when my number came up. I feel really cool, when I say I've been someplace many times and know all the ways to get around. My long time Danish friend, Susser, had also given me the correct bus number to get to her house, so I knew exactly where to find the stop and where to get off. I was in familiar territory.

The street where we caught the bus was the first street in Europe to allow adult films to be sold. In Denmark, adult entertainment is shown on TV late at night. There are no giant signs saying 'sex here' or 'Adult Bookstore'. It looks like any other street with walk-in shops and display windows. Only the displays are of sex toys, blow up dolls all in boxes. The same sense of normality is placed on these shops as a street with grocery stores. In fact, grocery stores are mixed in with the sex shops; it's a neighborhood. The parks are full of topless sunbathers and no one but the Americans tourists who visit seem the least bit interested.

Sex is a healthy part of life in their country, not something people flaunt or condemn. They make fun of our American TV with its nightly violence, how it shuns all sexual content. In the USA the strange mix of detective or crime shows poison our youth. Denmark has much less violent crime than in America. I wonder if there is any connection. The "high moral standards" of the United States have created a perverse sexuality that has caused such extremism in the media. I don't understand the entire hubbub. A fifth grade teacher was fired in Texas for exposing students to a nude statue in a museum on a field trip. No wonder our children have a skewed perspective of sexuality. We still think sex is a sin in my country. It's like saying flying in airplanes is an abomination, yet we fly planes every day, and get to the delivery room on time before the babies arrive.

For almost ten years I have been coming to Denmark. My friendship's there are constant despite the scarcity of visits and distance. Computers and telephones keep me connected to Susser and Keld. I met Susser first and Keld a few years after their Las Vegas wedding. Susser is a shy, withdrawn woman with a big smile and nervous laugh. She wears glasses, has freckles, and shoulder length, curly brunette hair. She is quiet. Keld is her opposite. He is a tall, muscular man with broad shoulders and a powerful hand shake. He has a presence when he enters a room. His stature and body frame give him an air of self-confidence. His hair has become increasingly gray and thinner, yet he has a youthful smile and joking makes him seem younger than his years.

We exited the bus across the street from Susser and Keld's apartment building. The apartment building is a half block long with three floors, the top two for living spaces, and the street level has shops. On the second floor Susser was waiting as we knocked on the door. Cecilia, her daughter, was in her room with her headphones on. She came out an hour later after napping in her raised (high) bunk bed.

Cecilia is a tiny version of her mother only much thinner. She is frail and has blue eyes that look lonely. She isn't, but this is a state young adolescent girl's project due to a need for romantic love and music videos. She is consumed by pop culture and all its "necessary" technologies. The headphones, the cell phone and texting are all a part of her mix of socializing that never seems to cease. She often wears a scarf draped around her neck which accents her tomboy, short, hair style.

Space is a luxury in Denmark; every furnishing is taken into consideration as is how much space it will occupy. The tiny apartment has one of my favorite Danish features: the bath tub. The bathtub is a small, short, but deep tub. You can sit in these tubs and be fully submerged up to your chest while your feet are down below in a split-level. By scrunching into the front section one can fully submerge. They are half as short as an American bathtub.

Space is treated as a luxury in the Scandinavian countries. Heating houses for the long cold winters has caused the building of apartments to be more popular than single house dwellings. Buildings are built with small halls, and compact cupboards. Diana sees our house in New York similar to a Danish home. I have used every inch of space to store things or build shelves. I get a certain delight in seeing how inventive the Danes are about using space. Susser and Keld's master bedroom is small, so they have built their bed up on high stilts, and have a desk and bookshelves built under the bed. The living room and dining room are a single large room where furniture can be moved around to accommodate many or a few guests. The furniture is small, the decorations are small, and the house is full, yet it doesn't feel packed with decorations. Two of my paintings are positioned on the walls, which make me feel good.

We had one night to sleep in the living room before we all left the next afternoon for their summerhouse, so the sofa was rearranged into a bed for Diana and me that night. With everything being small and compact, one key thing is never minimized, a window that lets in lots of light. The entire back wall of the apartment is a series of windows. Even in the tiny kitchen, light is never a lost commodity. Every room has a disproportionate amount of window space. Light is a must in all Danish homes. The long dark winters have caused an acute awareness of lighting. It also cuts down on the consumption of electricity. The things we take for granted in the United States are seemingly based on excess versus conservation. The idea of the boundless frontier and endless resources permeates the way we live and think in the Unites States. To sit in Danish home is to realize the consciousness behind their design features. It is like constructing a puzzle of practical usage. I enjoy seeing this very much.

While we stayed overnight at their home we relived old events, looked at home videos, and laughed together over a glass, or two, of wine. I have known Susser for almost ten years and had four visits to Denmark. I originally met her through my roommate's girlfriend that is Susser's cousin. On my first visit I stayed with the same family, in their mother's and Susser's apartments.

I had met Susser's cousin (Helle, a friend of my roommate) in the states because she had stayed in my house during a visit. She returned the favor by accommodating me on my first visit to Danish. The apartment was so small I asked to move to Susser's larger apartment. I remember one of the intriguing Danish design features in that first apartment; the shower was the entire bathroom itself. The tiny room doubled as a shower with a high-mounted hose that could be removed to wash the feet. The tiles floor and walls came equipped with a tiny sink and toilet, all in the space of what would be a small closet in my country.

Susser's daughter, Cecelia, offered to take us on a tour of Copenhagen the next morning, and raised herself in the morning to do so. I have been to Denmark so many times that I know all the sights, yet I enjoyed showing Diana around the city. We saw all the tourists attractions starting with a fun ride on the Metro, first to my favorite museum, and then to the main plaza where city hall has a statue of the author Hans Christian Anderson. Across from the plaza is the main walking street (Strøget) where street performers punctuate a pleasant stroll.

The first time I met Cecelia she was shy and hid behind her mother's legs, she must have been six or seven. That quiet shy girl has blossomed into a talkative, lively teenager. She is as fluent in English as Danish, loves texting friends, and is well versed in contemporary music. She has a fascination with photography so we spun many conversations around the topic. She is very close to her adoptive father, Keld, and they hug often like any parent and child. I remember when I first met her, thinking how this shy little girl is going to turn out; she did perfectly well. Now she chatters like an energized teenager full of a thirst for the future.

There is a Danish artist named Koyer whose paintings are displayed on the blue tins of Danish cookies sold all over the world. On the cover of these cookies there are usually two women wearing long white dresses walking along a beach. This commercial use of the artist's work is good, but it gives no justice to the immense body of his work, or the true scale of these works. They are enormous and breathe taking.

The light in Denmark is particularly soft and emits a special glow from the sunset being delayed until almost 11:00 PM. Long summer nights are full of low light. Couple this with the light from a full moon reflected along the shore of the sea in Northern Denmark and one receives a hue that is pastel blue and glowing from all directions. This light is the backdrop of many of Kroyer's paintings. These realistic paintings are wall-sized and capture all who gaze into them like a mirror holds one's own face. The paintings are of families, usually his own, or small groups of women walking along a beach with a full moon low in the sky. This pristine environment gives a glimpse into Danish life and the peaceful long summer nights. The additional hours of daylight gives time an added dimension to a families bonding experience. There are several paintings of Kroyer's wife strolling along the beach. In fact, there was an entire school of realistic Danish painters that congregated in the northern town of Skagen just to capture this special light.

On one of my trips to Denmark I made the pilgrimage to Skagen to sit in the very room where these painters did a group portrait while at the town's main hotel. Around the upper panel of the room in the hotel the artists had all contributed self-portraits to mark their camaraderie and shared love for the light in this town, situated on the tip of a thin peninsula. This Skagen School of Danish painter is perhaps the best known of all of Denmark's artistic genres. Koyer was their leader and a true master of realism and light. Unfortunately, he went mad when his wife left him. But the body of works dedicated to his love for her still stands.

The Hirschsprung Museum is where these grand works are housed. Kroyer's large canvases are honored in the main gallery of the museum. This small art museum is one of my favorites in Copenhagen because of its intimate feeling and size. Diana was spell bound by the artworks. The Danish artists are an entire chapter lacking from my university studies in art history, but when I first visited the country I became an instant devotee.

While the French Impressionists were defying realism, Danish artist were perfecting it. In some ways it is a shame the Impressionist had stolen the spotlight away from these perfectionist of light and realism. The art of realism is so vast, and still on-going today, we tend to let Impressionism dominate the conversation because it lead the eventual birth of modern art, or so it was linked to their movement. We spent a good hour visiting the galleries, returning to the main gallery where Kroyer's works hang.

Next to the Hirschsprung Museum is the Kunst State Museum. We would return another day, but for now, we went back to the center of the city's main plaza next to the city hall. This vast plaza always has troupes of Andean musicians playing their flutes and drums. The sound of Peruvian flutes is always an incongruous, but pleasant mix to experience in the middle of this bustling plaza. Small groups of onlookers gather in circles around different performers from acrobats, to comics, to musicians who sell their music on the side. It is impossible to cross the plaza and not be held captive by one or more acts. We paused to listen and watch Andean natives wearing indigenous American head dresses playing Peruvian music, and then made our way toward the walking street (Strøget) on the far side.

On the walking street we stopped and watched a young couple from Argentina who slowly setup a cloth, a CD player, and tin cup for donations. We sat on a bench as the pair mounted each other in slowly and executed body contortions that were acrobatic and simply fabulous. The slow methodical pace of their set up was enough to gather a small crowd of onlookers. People sitting at a nearby outdoor café stopped their conversation and soon a roar of applause echoed between the buildings of the long shopping street. Passersby and restaurant goers were happy to reward the couple with coins in the tin can. After they finished their five-minute routine we left our bench to congratulate their performance and ask them what language they spoke. They spoke to us in Spanish, so we replied in Spanish. The slender blonde female was from Sweden, living in Argentina with her boyfriend. They were busking through Europe to visit her homeland. I admire such modern nomads.

At the end of the pedestrian street there is a large roundabout where the State Opera House stands on the left. On the far side of the opera house is one of Copenhagen's major visitor attractions, New Haven. This is a thin harbor with beautiful, colorful buildings on both sides. The sunny side of the harbor is always filled with outdoor drinkers who sit, or stand in the crisp Danish sun. The atmosphere is always very festive. People from all over Europe, mostly Sweden, come to drink the famous Danish beers. The Swedes have a reputation for coming to Denmark and raising hell, rather drunken hell. The price of beer is substantially cheaper in Denmark because of Swedish taxes on alcohol. So the short train stop over the bridge that separated the two countries allows many a drunken weekend venture for the young Swedes. I noticed this on my first trip. There was a distinct brand of loud drunk people who didn't seem to fit into Danish culture. New Haven is a picturesque place full of sporty drinkers and busty, blonde, waitresses with big rosy cheeks. Every once in a while, a drunk, Danish or from anywhere, is known to fall into the channel.

If you have ever seen a postcard of Denmark you have seen New Haven. The boats are moored to the docks and the bright orange roofs of the buildings bounce light onto the glistening waters below. The long ultra-thin, glass covered tour boats come within inches of the overhanging bridges. While in the tour boats you can touch the bottom of the bridge by reaching up if you so desire.

We walked on to the Marble Church whose dome is a small replica of Saint Peters in Rome. The building is much smaller than Saint Peters. The interior of the church is made of marble thus the name. In a visual line to the harbor, the street leads directly to the Royal Palace.

We timed our walk to get to the palace in time for the changing of the guard. These elite soldiers are a sight from the past, tin-solider-like, and decked out in blue uniforms with tall, black, furry, bearskin hats. We watched the line of soldiers walking in formation, to the front of their small guard booths, change personnel, and vanish down the cobble street with the cadence of hard boots echoing through the plaza.

Diana was standing next to one of the erect guards with a tall bearskin hat. The solider spoke in a thick Danish accent, "Three meters". Diana thought he was saying something else, she doesn't always have the correct understanding when someone speaking English to her. His accent made it impossible for her to understand. As she nuzzled up to the man, he pushed her away with his arm. She didn't understand his second; "Three meters" command and she tried to get even closer. By this time he was practically shoving her away. She turned red, he turned red, and I stood in shock embarrassed by it all. I felt bad for Diana and instantly understood she didn't have a clue what the man was saying to her. I took some pictures after she stood three meters away from the solider. Diana is the most complying person I know. She follows the rules all the way. To see her shoved away was horrible. I understood what the man was saying, yet I was helpless at expressing this to her because I stood so far way.

We left the Royal Palace without seeing anyone but the guards. The King and Queen of Denmark were not home, the sign being no flag was displayed above their residence. Along the riverbank there is a beautiful walkway. The walkway curves around an old walled fortress called Kastellet.

On the far side, and up the shore, is the statue of the Little Mermaid. The statue is on a rock mounting a few feet out from the shore. People will occasionally make the short leap into the rocks where the statue is standing. One year I was there as a man was playing around with the statue. He was goofing-off like he was going to kiss the Little Mermaid. There must have been seventy people there because all the tour buses make this one of the major tour stops. The man lost his balance and slid into the water. I was beside myself with laughter, as well as many of the onlookers. The man was drenched and very embraced by his fall. People couldn't contain themselves. Had the man just jumped and missed it would have been less funny, but he was dancing around and making a fool of himself, which added to the crowd's glee when he hit the drink.

We did the obligatory photographs of the monument to the famous fairy tale, and met three women from Colombia. We heard Spanish. Diana could tell from their accents that they were from her city. So she approached the three women from Colombia and we had a brief conversation. The women were eating candy from Colombia and shared some with us. We were delighted to have a sweet from my wife's home country.

We had to return to Susser's house in time to miss the rush hour traffic out of Copenhagen, so we headed back to the apartment building around two-thirty. We had seen a small part of the capital city, but there was so much more we didn't see. We moved all of our bags outside and loaded Keld's station wagon. He showed me his old Honda motorcycle in the garage and we spun off, briefly, into comparing motorcycle journeys. Two hours later we arrived, where a couple of days later I caught up with my writing and made the following journal entries.

We are in Sjaellands Odde, a thin sliver of land on the opposite side of the island where Copenhagen lay. In some ways this place is not that different from our home Bayville, Long Island. A five-minute walk in one direction puts us on a large bay; seven minutes in the other direction is the sea. This part of Denmark is farmland and vacation homes. Our friends Susser and Keld, and their seventeen-year-old daughter Cecile, have a summerhouse that is to be their retirement home in ten years. For now they have built a home that is a loving work in motion, a loving work in progress.

The summerhouse used to be half its current size. Five years ago, when I was last there, it was a small house and small rooms added. I slept in a room attached to the garage, separate from the main house. They kept the original house and built a second house, virtually around the first house using the original roof and a section to what became a larger, giant room. The old house was gutted to make an expansive living room. The new house is red and taller. The open spaces where the new house fit over the old house became windows. Only one half of the original roof remained. Lightly stained tan walls give an open space even more territory. What was a tiny dwelling is now a modern expansive space with four rooms and one large kitchen, and a central living and dining room.

Keld has done this mostly. He had the help of friends and relatives to do major construction. Keld and Susser took out a loan and started with a foundation. When the new roof was on, they went in and drill-hammered the old floors of concrete. Other than the cement for the floor and help from family for the roof and chimney, this is a one-man, one-woman project. Susser has been here through the whole process, and at times had to deal with no kitchen, and a toilet in the middle of the room; primitive comforts to say the least.

I painted a watercolor of the house yesterday, but today I feel like the walk on the water's edge was enough to satisfy my soul. Diana and I sat at a picnic table on the shore and talked about everything. She loves to tell me about her family back in Colombia. I feel I know them by now. The shore is filled with stones that are from two to five inches in diameter, so walking the shore is a wobbly endeavor. Not ten feet from the shore, a nice grassy path follows the shores edge, and further away another larger path is the main thoroughfare. It's big enough for a car, but seldom used for motor vehicle traffic. We walked the middle, less-traveled path looking for the perfect stone on which to make a painting.

Susser asked us to find a rock and do a painting on it. We searched while walking and settled on a flat oval shaped rock about five inches long.

We came home and Diana started at the drawing right away. Susser brought out the paints and we eventually both created the art, sometimes painting simultaneously, sometimes individually, sometimes objecting to the other's decisions, but finally finishing our requested gift to Susser. In the painting we are standing in front of three mountains and holding hands. Diana did most of the drawing and I shared in the painting and background scenery.

"This is good couple's therapy", she told Susser. And it wasn't that different than how we resolve challenges together. Each of us has the tendency to believe we know best.

Susser has a hobby/business where she paints flowers and designs on glass objects, including glasses, cups, and cognac bottles. She has been doing this as long as I remember, but with an increased yearly fervor. Every visit I see more and more painted items being created. The house has painted bottles, latrines, pots with plants on shelves, and any bare place that is in need of her painted happiness. If I recall correctly, Susser began all this by painting on a rock. Flowers and insects on rocks are her most common themes. I have several of the painted rocks in my car back in New York. Diana first asked me where they came from while driving on our honeymoon.

Susser has a large pushcart she wheels to the edge of the grassy drive and leaves it out for passing customers. The prices are labeled on each item and the money box is left open for the unsupervised sales to take place. She has some two hundred items and leaves them there while she is inside the house or out for the day. She does surprisingly well and sells enough to always keep busy. She does this only for enjoyment and as she says, "To relax". The house has her positive energy throughout. Keld's energy is in the building, her mother's (Edith) energy in the cooking, and her daughter's laughter to complete the layers of happiness that dwell in this tranquil setting.

The Danish landscape is spattered with windmills. Over many a hill and dale the giant white blades mysteriously cut through the air. It takes a few seconds to figure out what the slow moving blades are until one sees the tall column of the base. At first the long blades look like some alien spacecraft, the massive blades circle the axis in a slow silent churn. *How can that create energy when it moves so slowly*, one might ponder? From the distance the movement seems even less exaggerated. With the multitude of windmills throughout the country Denmark has become the world's leader in this renewable energy source. The Danes use half as much energy in each household as the average North American house. They have mastered the art of wind and solar energy to a level of being the world's leader in green technology. Insulation in their houses and thermal heating the floors of their houses use a fraction of the energy that powers the average American home.

Keld's house has a thermal heating system that runs through the concrete floors of his house. A criss-crossed piping system, only inches from the surface, provides a balanced radiant heat through the house. His house has so many windows that electricity is never needed for light until after the sunset. What few electric lights get used are small high intensity bulbs that require low voltage. Rainwater is captured in run-off drains, thus stored in large plastic drums, and put to use in the garden or wherever needed. Water heaters don't heat the water until needed in a sink or for a shower. Solar panels on the roof provide heated water as well. In their summer house, nothing is wasted. The garbage is separated and recycled, the biomass is composted, and whatever is left is burnable and ends up in the wood stove for heat at night.

Over the years I've seen increasing vast numbers of wind turbines on the land and off shore. Perhaps the most startling feature of Danish life is the use of bicycles. Thousands of commuters use bicycles to get around, mostly commuting to work. Every major road has a bike lane. There have been times I've seen more people on bikes than in automobiles. Susser and Keld seem to pay little heed to the energy efficiency in their lives because it is so common. It's as common as the majority of Danes being bilingual; English is their second tongue.

The sun is bright, filling the house, the windows are open and curtains are shifting with the passing breeze. Chimes are ringing from the breeze, the doors are all open, the sound in the trees outside carries the hum of rustling leaves, and

Diana is doing a drawing of me that makes me look ten years older than I really am. I laugh at the hairless head and she offers to put more hair in the drawing.

We are in a state of heavenly bliss in this place. Last night we watched the story of Frida Kahlo, so Diana is inspired. The success of the stone painting has built up her confidence as well. I'm half asleep and love the attention of being drawn. It's similar to when a barber cuts your hair or someone does your nails. It just feels good.

I described this as a heavenly place; is one of the most peaceful places I've ever been. This is my fourth visit to Denmark and my third visit to this house. Five years ago was my last visit. I went to Ireland and Denmark to do some serious soul searching and healing from feeling deeply betrayed at the end of a relationship. Susser and Keld helped me as much as my Irish friends in an entire process that took three years. So a part of this healing is completing the circle of returning in better health, being strong again, without emotional pain, being in a new relationship, and with my wife so she can meet friends she'd only heard of. She has commented on how easy it is to be around these people. Diana commented that they are hippies like me.

I still hear the constant litany of comparisons of Colombia to everyone and everything we encounter, but I think Diana is seeing the world in a different view where she is going to shed some sort of emotional skin. The first day Cecilia accompanied us we went to many places in Copenhagen. The second day it was just the two of us.

"This is very strange, are you sure this is alright to leave our hosts?" Diana kept asking me.

When it comes to the practice of unescorted travel, I might be oblivious to social and cultural norms. In Colombia, the attention of a guest is a 24 hour labor of love and leads to days of accompanied outings. The awkward angle of this "attention", as she calls it, is that the guests pay for nothing; the host has all financial obligations. In Colombia the host is expected to cover all expenses and be servant (or slave) to the welcomed guest.

Now I really don't know how much of what Diana explains, as a Colombian custom is universal, or only exclusive to her family. But I do know that Diana's surprise at not being accompanied by the host was a real concern for her. Life in South America is very insular and lived with family. The physical construction of houses with barred windows and doors is a means of setting up huge barriers between the life of a household and the outside world. Life in Denmark is almost transparent in the openness of houses and the openness of the society at large. Women sunbathe topless in public parks, sex films are shown on television late at night, and nude statues are in public areas. Attitudes are expressed in a healthy 'matter of fact' way. To put it in Diana's exact words, "You are more civilized here".

A friend of Susser and Keld stopped by and we were discussing the role government's role in everyday life. It appears that the Danish government is a better form of Democracy, more egalitarian. My friend was commenting that many rich people leave the Scandinavian countries because the taxes are such a burden that they truly don't have as much wealth. This is a country where the middle class has greater wealth and there are few poor people. The friend was saying that people don't have incentive to become richer because of their good standard of living. It is interesting to hear both sides of a story.

It is easiest to be critical of the place you were raised. I expressed the war on Iraq is a source of economic strain. It is strange to me that no one is talking spending trillions of dollars on a war and don't expect a negative impact on the world's economy. Is war good business? It certainly is immoral business.

On my first visit to Denmark I met Susser. She is the cousin of a friend of a friend, in a house I shared with four other men in New York. My reason for staying at Susser's was a bit more complicated than I had mentioned earlier. This was twelve or thirteen years ago. Back then, I came to Denmark and stayed with Susser's cousin, while Edith, Susser's mother was at the summer house. We had no romantic interests in each other, met back in New York and I was invited to come see Denmark. I wasn't a teacher yet and had very limited funds, down to the penny. Susser's cousin and I had a disagreement over the amount of money the food was costing. She asked me to pay a large sum of money, three times more than I had every spent on my own food in the United States. Even considering the cost of living here, it was a month's worth of expenses/spending in a matter of days. I felt taken advantage of and left the house so my expenses were brought under control. Susser came to my rescue and let me sleep on her sofa for the remaining week. Susser also agreed the money was a bit extreme. Now this has all blown over, I sent more money when I returned back home, and we are all friends.

On my subsequent visits to Denmark, three, I stayed with Susser and Keld. She met Keld a year or so after my first visit. They later got married in on a trip to the United States. Cecelia is the product of a previous marriage. The first time I met Cecelia, she was a tiny child hiding behind her mother's leg. Today she is the life of the party and brings a lot of energy and joy to our visit. Her biological father died a few years ago, so Keld adopted her and is now her legal guardian. In a few days she will be eighteen and talks about going to college, or acting school. Her whole life is ahead of her. She is a happy person. She and Keld are very close and spend a lot of time cuddling and playing with each other. Keld is closer to her than his own daughter from the previous marriage. The family is very united and we never see any disagreements or troubles. This isn't just because they have visitors. I have been here enough times to know these are genuine people who take life serious and who take making a family unit a cooperative effort. They see communication as being crucial to raising a child.

Cecelia has told us she was the first child her age to be allowed to leave the house and go by bus into the city to shop. I'm thinking this was at age fifteen, but she said it was at age nine. The parents don't restrict their children and the scare of child abusers isn't on the news every night. It is sad to me that I stay away from the children in my own neighborhood because I don't want to be misunderstood as a molester. Social damage will occur in a generation not allowed to play in a field, or go out unsupervised.

My fondest memories of running in fields in California and exploring nature are my links to experiencing God. It's the "fear" propaganda of American news media that I don't buy. I don't accept the sensationalism that has changed the perspective of parents nowadays. Or war either, for that matter. Americans thrive on fear; Xenophobia, fear of change, fear of being less than number one, and fear of everything except negativity. The negativity has become so prevalent that many people have forgotten what it was like before all the fear mongering began.

From my youth, I remember what it's like to ride a bike into town and see a movie, buy a piece of candy, and return home hours later without being reminded that there are bad people out there. I'm sick of a culture that focuses on potential evil. The world has millions of more good people than bad. Is there a balance in pointing out what is simple and good in life? The media have been used to create a culture of fear. Maybe this is an oversimplification, but good news is out there and not being broadcast. I remember at a young age going out unsupervised groups on Halloween. Today parents think evil is a normal part of society. The real evil is how our government promotes wars and keeps an atmosphere of distrust towards "them", where ever they are. I don't dismiss the loss of many innocent people on 9/11, but the reaction of America was far too violent. There will always be fear as long as we see "them" as not one of "us". The Danes live free of that kind of news and politic.

Today Cecilia made muffins. While consuming we sat around and talked, even in three different languages, and were all at peace. Susser cut Keld's hair, Grandmother Edith read the newspaper, I started a drawing of Diana, and the birds were singing in the background. Eventually the conversation subsided. We remained seated at the table, yet everyone drifted into the recesses of their own thoughts. Still we remained part of a tiny collective in universal harmony. This happens every day, everywhere, but the bombs going off, or the murders in the cities get the publicity. Perhaps the use of computers will make us more human if this side of life is brought out. This is the positive side to all the new social networks on the Internet. The challenge of saving the planet is a bigger problem than the negative stories that permeate the airways and media.

I have this theory that we all live in a parallel world. One is peaceful and full of love; the other is filled with evil. It is as simple as choice to decide which world we want to occupy. Heaven is a state of mind just as much as hell. I am baffled how much people in different countries choose to live in a peaceful universe while in other nations seem possessed by evil and trouble. It doesn't even have to be disputes defined by nationalities; it can be as small as a nuclear family.

I believe we create our own universe. If I sincerely need a peaceful life I will find it. The battle for earth is eventually going to settle down and I believe goodness will prevail. The leaders of governments can cause great hardship for their people because they don't believe that peace is obtainable here and now. Peace is not profitable.

Diana wanted to show her gratitude to our guests so Diana spent the afternoon preparing a bean-beer dish with chicken sausages. Diana had reserved the kitchen. The dinner was a big hit, which was as close to Colombian food as she could make it. My contribution was minimal. I helped cook the rice. Edith, Susser's mother, was usually in the kitchen making our meals.

We fit right in and whatever is suggested as a daily plan we never had cause to disagree. Diana has painted her very first still life from a bouquet of wild flowers we picked on one of our many walks. I am impresses at her skill for never having done a watercolor painting before. We are all pleased at how clear the detail is. To majority of the days we spent time reading or drawing with an additional short outing to a small town.

We had so many trinkets from Ireland, Holland, and Copenhagen that our luggage was already over-stuffed. We decided to make a small box of these things and send them ahead to New York. We packed the box with lots of extra bubble wrap. This is an extra, weightless, travel supply I always bring along to keep the purchases safe. The mailed box cost twenty-five dollars, but it was well worth the loss of this excess weight in luggage. The post office was in a small room on one side of the grocery store. The Danish government saves money by renting postal space in stores rather than create a separate building. The economic use of space is a conscience design everywhere here.

As we exited the grocery store we entered a walking street that was full of pedestrians. Mothers and fathers each pushing baby buggies and elderly and youthful lovers all strolled in the bright sunlit street. The shops had sale items on stands or in large boxes sitting out front. The street was no more than three short blocks long, but it was market day on a weekend so it was bustling with people. During the hour or so we were there, the crowd increased almost exponentially.

On a far street we wandered into an art gallery and met one of the local artists. He painted enlarged musical instruments. This was his venue. In one corner an electric guitar stood on a stand. He explained that he loved art and music, and at night he played in a band. He had left a high pressure of a job in Copenhagen and began to follow his bliss with his art and music. In European culture, artists seem more commonplace, and more importantly, able to eke out a living. This man also did picture framing, but he seemed happy to live a simple, but comfortable, life in a seemingly out of the way locale. His life style wasn't considered so radical, and his matter of fact description of how he made a living seemed oddly neutral. He didn't seem to be calling attention to himself and was more interested in being middle class than a radical free spirit. I liked the uncomplicated and unpretentious feel of both the man and his shop.

We parted ways and embarked on an adventure, soon finding ourselves at a Viking tomb. I always think things will be different than when I imagine them. The Viking tomb was a mound of dirt, nothing more than a small hill. We ducked down to enter a narrow thin tunnel that opened into an arched round room. Keld lit a lighter to get into the tunnel leading to the room, but a small light bulb illuminated the room itself. I couldn't stand up straight and the musky smell made me wonder what the big deal was. I learned this was the site where one of Denmark's most valuable art objects had been found. We saw the photograph of the flat warrior standing on his chariot. Later we saw the actual object in a museum and things took on a deeper meaning.

I banged my head leaving the tunnel and was happy to get back in the fresh air. We climbed the top of the tomb while Cecilia ran down the slope into the adjacent wheat field. Soon we were on the road again. This time we, all six, were seeking a flea market.

The only way we knew we were near the market was the number of cars parked on the side of the highway. In the distance I could see a Ferris wheel and hear the sounds of a carnival. The flea market was one of the side attractions, but we had only discussed going there.

I love such things. Diana and I eventually lost each other and the rest of our group, so we all ended up crossing paths midpoint through the rows of tents. I can't help but buy trinkets from our travels. I bought a small porcelain statue of a typical Danish fisherman. Over the years I have collected small dolls/ statues of men from many countries. This was an antique find. Diana bought some jewelry, her favorite thing to get. Keld found something, as well as Susser. Even if it is a tiny object, we always seem to want some memorabilia of where we have been. This could all lead to another box being shipped back home if we're not careful. We all eventually wandered into the carnival, but none of us were interested in the rides. We felt something universally tenuous about carnies that made the rides seem unsafe.

Our next stop was an old windmill whose tall structure was gray and weatherworn. There was an entrance fee to go see the stone wheel that ground wheat to flour, but we entered only long enough to see the one room and access. It wasn't worth the fee, but outside I got some good photographs. In Holland, we saw windmills, but it was not until Denmark that we actually walked up to one. Our brief stop was long enough to stretch our legs and set off for home.

I wanted to paint so we asked Keld to drop us off near a particular vista I had seen in the morning. I am in an awkward position when I want to paint and have people sitting around, so I asked that Diana and I be dropped off for a couple of hours. This gave us a little down time and a chance to be alone in a beautiful setting. The view included some beautiful yellow wheat fields that reminded me of Van Gogh's landscapes. The brilliant sun punctuated the setting of a comfortable picnic area making a perfect temporary studio. Prior to my sketching the scene, we unpacked our lunch and had sandwiches with cheese and turkey.

I can't really describe what happens when I start a painting, but somewhere in the first few minutes I know if the work will be successful or not. I suppose it has to do with how centered I am within my intentions. I liked this painting as soon as I began to draw it. The yellow wheat and perspective all fell right into place. The thin sliver of land over a faraway bay was just right to give the work added depth. Diana was reading as I painted and sat at the picnic table. A breeze was blowing across the land, bringing a fresh smell from the ocean.

I wore a light jacket and had a flat table on which to paint. It was a lovely setting. We were lower than the hill above and the wind was in the tall trees but not that much on us. Maybe the place has to do with my overall attitude as well, the time flew and I was able to get most of the work's foundation done so I could complete it later at the house.

My visits to Susser and Keld's summer house are always creative and a spiritual retreats. My paintings are on various walls in the house, and Susser's handy work is everywhere, not to mention Keld's building skills. The yard has an organic design, not symmetrical, or organized. A shed is at one end next to an old outhouse. Trees and bushes are growing un-pruned in a spot where one would expect a well-manicured lawn. There is no indication where the property line is and the neighbor's house isn't even visible. The layout of the house is free flowing, very open. The entire south side of the house has large floor to ceiling windows. Just outside these windows are two decks with dining tables and lounge chairs. Keld incorporated the new deck into the old one, doubling the entire size. On one side of the house there is an enclosed deck for nude sunbathing. Next to this is a garage that has been converted into Keld's workshop full of tools.

Two days before we left, we were lounging and Keld asked me to do some art on the garage wall facing the large deck. I obliged and we began to brainstorm. Instead of painting directly on the wall, which had shingled wood, we settled on a wooden plank. This would be something that could be removed and kept separate if needed. We contemplated its design and decided it would have to be a Viking theme. (For years I have called Keld Susser's Viking.) We cut out a large piece of wood maybe four feet across. It was elliptical with two Viking horns coming out of the top. We started priming the wood and then laid a black background in. In white lines I painted a Viking ship with the oars dipping into water. The sky was black with white stars and above the ship I painted the letters S and K. We took the project into the second morning where I added some final details and stars in the sky. Keld added some hooks and we hung it on the garage wall just time to catch the evening light brightly shining on my artwork. They loved it, and I know it will still be there on our next visit.

The last day was spent going to a local harbor and where Keld bought us some delicious, spiced, and crunchy fish cakes. This small harbor is a typical little port where generations of fishermen have filled their boats and feed their families, eking out a living in the cold weather of the Danish waters. The town has a few houses and businesses smattering the slight hill next to the port. We walked on the windy jetty, all the way to the end and shortened our stroll because of the cold.

Soon we piled into the car and drove a few miles more to visit a brightly colored church. The church is a sun-bleached orange-red that can be seen for miles. Outside in the courtyard there stood a gravestone for a Danish sea captain who died in a famous battle. The interior of the church was very bland with whitewashed walls, but centered in the back was a beautiful replica of a war ship; the same ship on which the captain met his demise. The ship was suspended above our heads in the center aisle. I can't remember the actual dates, but the church was well over two hundred years old and still in use. The Danish don't bulldoze structures like we do in the United States, but rather keep old buildings maintained with pride. The roof of the building had stair-step like walls that reminded me of a Dutch building. This must have been a common building style for Northern Europe at the time. It wasn't a wide structure and inside the two rows of pews made the space feel confined. The lack of windows, or rather large windows made it feel even smaller. I imagine heating the building necessitated small windows. It was a dark building inside. The red paint of the church exterior was also on the wall that surrounded the churchyard and cemetery.

Our next destination Keld's mother's house was a few miles further. The house is nestled in a grove of trees and only partially visible from down the road. The pink house and blue shutters stand out from the green of the woods. The blue flowers in blue flower boxes below each window give the whole place a fairy-tale feeling. Keld's mother has the look and feel of Mrs. Clause. I say this with respect. She has white hair, is round with bright rosy cheeks, and a smile that glistens for miles. She is truly pleasant. Superimpose the brazen behavior of drinking beer in a bottle and smoking cigarettes. She is youthful and still swigs the beers and puffs on a cig. Amazing! She may have sworn like a sailor but we would have never known because she spoke only Danish. Her character and appearance were a quirky juxtaposition of the absurd and sublime.

Her house had a few small rooms and few possessions that are small and well placed throughout. On one wall in her living room is a watercolor painting I did of her house several years ago. I emphasized the blue and pink colors and flower boxes. She lent me her apartment on one visit, so I try to reciprocate with my talent. She must have liked the art work. It was framed and prominently displayed on the wall in the middle of the room. To give an unframed artwork, and return to see it framed, is a joy beyond words. I am flattered and moved because I feel my artwork is being respected. The tiny home is somewhat like a dollhouse. In Denmark, the summer homes are small and built for sleeping, the outdoor patio is where most of the time is spent. We sat in the sun for an hour and Keld would translate what we said in English into Danish. The conversation rose and declined as we ended the visit and loaded into the car again.

Our last night was a home-cooked meal followed by some Danish cake and a short visit by the people we had met a few days before. They had stopped by to invite Keld and Susser to a party. We sat around and chatted not knowing when we would all be together again. Diana and I fell asleep relatively early with the sun still low in the summer sky. It was 10PM.

We were running late for the train. I was beginning to feel slight panic. We were so late we parked the car and left the keys inside. The car was still running but we had to catch the train. We ran for the train. The train pulled up to the station and Diana got on board. I was on the platform and fumbling through the backpack for the tickets. I was beginning to sweat. I knew I had the tickets. Where were they! I'm always very organized, but somehow I had them buried in the pack. To my horror Diana was yelling to get on the train when the doors shut. She was banging on the door. I was running alongside the train and we couldn't get the door to open. The tickets were no longer a concern. I was in sheer shock.

Diana was in sheer shock. There is nothing we could do. Diana was swiftly fading as the train picked up speed, and I was running out of breath. Then I woke up. I was lying on my back and could see blue sky out the window. The sun hadn't come up, but the upper atmosphere was crisp in that pre-dawn aura. I had been dreaming.

Thank God we were still in Denmark and our last day was still ahead of us. I got out of bed and needed to spend every second of our last few hours at the beach house doing something productive. If I was quick enough I could get out before the sunrise and capture that low angle of light that is so crucial to the paintings composition. It is the point in a sunrise when the shadows contrast with the orange glow of early light. Every blade of grass is brilliant. All is an exaggerated realism. The night is being chased away like God sending serpents into their hellish holes. Dew hangs on anything that leans sideways. Fog is rising in praise and angelic white mist is causing the tall bleached grasses to turn to gold. This spectacle of light is brief, only a few minutes. I say a Hail Mary, and then I begin to chant a Buddhist mantra out loud. I am stopping in the moment. It is the first time in days I have been completely alone. A deer I saw grazing as a sign, a miracle.

All the while I am taking pictures with the camera, walking, and realizing this is the last time I will be out of doors in total solitude for many weeks. The rest of the trip we will be in cities. Maybe in Greece I will be able to have that special experience. It's like the time I went into the mountains in Colorado when I was twenty-four. For some thirty days, I was alone seeking inner truth, writing a journal, painting and seeking.

It wasn't long before my silence was broken by a dark figure seen walking out of the woods. I wasn't alone anymore. Between the shoreline and the trees was a wide stretch of bronze grass. I was far away enough to know I was not seen. I was walking home and soon realized the dark stranger was Susser. Before she saw me I photographed her silhouette standing still. I used the telephoto lens. As I approached she sent up a wave.

"I didn't know you were here". "I woke up early and decided to take some pictures", I replied.

We walked back to the summerhouse chatting about superficial topics.

By the time we returned, Edith was already setting the table. Diana was still asleep but within minutes heads were peeking around doors, looking towards the breakfast table to see if it was time to sit down. Edith was toasting bread, taking her medication. I went in to kiss my wife good morning. She wakes in a state of happiness. She always smiles and asked me what time it is. She has done this every morning since the beginning of the trip. I always say, "I don't know". I refuse to wear my watch after the last day of school. Diana still asks me anyway. I always respond in the same manner.

Like every morning in the summerhouse we eat, make jokes, get serious, make more jokes, and finish with a few minutes of silence. This morning I join Susser and Keld in their daily vacation ritual of drinking a tiny glass of Danish liqueur. It smells like cloves, tastes like medicine, and burns the throat as it slides down. I make a funny face and provoke a chuckle from all. "It is medicine?" They laugh again.

By eight thirty, we have all the bags loaded into the car and exchange our last goodbyes and embrace. Keld drove us all on a scenic route. We drove past many inlet bays and farms, eventually into the city past the street where they live, into the heart of Copenhagen's center to the train station. We said goodbye and promised we would see each other soon. None of us know when time will bring us together again. They say Cecilia will be over to visit us in the spring.

We took our bags to the basement where we needed to store the luggage for the day because we had a 6:53PM departure time. My credit card didn't work because I didn't remember the pin. We needed money from an ATM. I walked upstairs to find all the ATM's were not working.

Jan is my other friend in Denmark. He is a very thin man in his forties. He has a pointy nose set on a narrow face with soft doe-eyes. His smile ekes out from thin lips and is one of his handsome attributes. His cloths are often baggy due to his thin bones and lack of any body fat. He is a book-worm-like man, soft spoken, and very intelligent.

I walked under the large clock in the middle of the station. At that exact moment I saw Jan walk up and we made eye contact. "I need money", I said before we even greeted each other. Then I began to laugh. "What?" "I need your money. There is no ATM working and Diana is waiting in the basement with the luggage". We know full well you don't walk up to friends and ask for money first thing. Then I said hello and gave him a hug. He likes my off-the-wall way of making fun. It had been two years and eighteen days since we last saw each other. "You look the same" he said, which promoted more laughs.

We found Diana in the luggage area. They kissed hello and gave each other a hug. Jan paid for the baggage storage and we took a train two stops to Norsport. Graciously Jan helped me. There we found an ATM and now had money to pay for the luggage and some food for the day. We walked a few blocks to the Klimt Café where we met Ursula, Jan's girl friend from a few years past.

Denmark has a murder rate that ranges between two and seven murders a year. On my third visit to Denmark I stayed with Jan in an apartment flat where the buildings are all connected and go on for an entire city block. In the middle of my first night I was awaken by startling screams. We thought the screams were coming from the apartment next door. The screams were accented by loud thumps. It was a horror to listen to. The entire event took maybe two to three minutes. We called the police, they came, and we described the beating of a woman in the apartment next door. "What was the woman saying?" Well, we weren't sure; we heard words but mostly screaming.

The next day we came home to find the police had been lead to the murder scene by one of the two perpetrators, who were both patients in an asylum. One of the men confessed to his psychotherapist. What we thought was a woman was a man from Russia. He was screaming in Russian so no one understood his pleas for help! Everyone on the block was thinking there was some domestic violence, but it was an actual murder. The two men had jarred the apartment door open with a screwdriver. The murder weapon was the screwdriver. The thumping we heard was, well guess, the stabbing. The murder was a revenge dispute. There were no newscasts about this; we found a tiny paragraph about the murder in the newspaper. I shouldn't make light of the murder of another human, but I am sure that this all happened as it did because Denmark is a Socialist nation where guns are outlawed. Whenever Jan and I get together we talk about this horrifying experience….Socialism. We also note that screwdrivers don't kill people, people kill people.

Ursula was now living in California with her mother, but commuting to Denmark doing research on Danish cultural history. Her two-month stay was being spent reading books and newspaper accounts of Danish woman who had lived in the colonial Danish Virgin (West Indies) Islands. Before these islands were purchased by the United States they were a Danish colony and active in sugar cane production through slavery. Ursula's particular interest was of accounts of the lives of women who had returned to Denmark after the island was sold and how they reminiscence about island life. We talked about some contemporary women's issues like headscarves on Muslim women, the fictitious War on Terror, and the area in California where she now lives. I gathered that Ursula was a woman who likes to spend her time on lofty academician pursuits and it wasn't long before I was trying to lighten up the conversation with silliness.

We soon parted with Jan as Ursula returned to do a few hours more of research. She and Jan were leaving for Norway by boat at 4:30, so we had a few hours to spend together. We did this by visiting the Danish National Museum of Art. There was no entrance fee, which was good because we had a few Kroner left for lunch. The museum had been completely reorganized from my previous visit five years ago. Half of the building had the Danish Skagen artists like my favorite Koyer. The other half of old building now had the modern art. The new building was filled with the Danish classical artists. The tall ceilings in the modern building were a perfect setting for row after row art works. The walls were stacked, sometimes eight paintings high, in light filled galleries where windows on the sides or close to the ceiling let in natural light. Rather than having to view the works in the usual eye level, we stood back and surveyed large walls full of works. For the monumental works this was a better way to see them. The arrangement of similar genre of works in time periods and styles was a good way to observe this large collection. We walked the building in a kind of silent reverence that museums goers do. Afterwards Jan noted how tiring it was and how sleepy the process of observing art makes him.

"I think it has to do with so much energy being focused in one place. Think of it, we are seeing years of artists lives encapsulated into a few hours", I said.

We walked to the Copenhagen library where we had to go online to put money into the bank account. We checked our individual emails. Jan had to go a few blocks further to deliver a form to the university. The library was an open, modern, bustling place. A man approached us and told us we would find a computer faster in another part of the library as we stood looking at the small line of waiting people. At the main desk we asked for a computer in English. In fact you can't go anywhere in Copenhagen where English isn't spoken.

"There's one right there", the librarian pointed. It was a standing computer station. In matter of seconds I had paid a bill in New York. It still amazes me.

We bought some sandwiches and returned to the King's Garden, a park in which Jan and I sat years before, listening to the Copenhagen Jazz Festival. The festival had already ended the week before our arrival but the park was still full of people. Sun bathers, some topless, Frisbee throwers, mothers with babies, couples, shade seekers, or people just riding their bicycles through the park. There were lots of bicycles, as usual all over Copenhagen. Even though we were in a city the feeling of being active, out of doors, and completely in sync with nature was a big part of this sunny day.

It wasn't long before Jan had to say goodbye and left to meet Ursula for the boat ride to Norway. They had a two-day getaway planned and we had spent a short but lovely visit together. Jan was still suffering from the nine hours difference of jet lag, having only arrived the day before. We squeezed in a visit in our date books months before knowing when we'd be in Denmark at the same, one and only day. This has been the nature of our friendship for some ten years now. I'm not sure of the exact number of years and don't need to. He is a friend beyond time. He came to our wedding and is now also good friends with my wife.

Diana and I lie on the grass another hour or so. We fully analyzed Ursula and his relationship with her, drew completely biased opinions about the outcome of their relationship. We did this while resting our heads on our backpacks like pillows. (We think we know so much.) We just love to speculate and be human.

A few hours later we had slowly walked into the main train station, exchanged our Kroners into Euros, sat next to two teenage girls kissing on a step, watched taxis drivers, bought a cookie, and killed time by watching the theater of life. An hour before the train left I wisely had the train passes validated in the Eurail office and got the information on how to find the correct platform. Diana sat in the station on the platform 8 (it had been changed from 7 at the last minute); I ran outside and took the keys out of the car that was still running. The guy in my dream (me) was frantically running back to the Eurail office to get the ticket validated seconds before the train pulled away, while the guy on the platform was well composed and ready to board the train with his wife, tickets in hand. We had this one down. The conductor was very polite and could tell we had never done this before by the nature of our questions, the eminence size of our luggage, and slight bead of sweat on my brow.

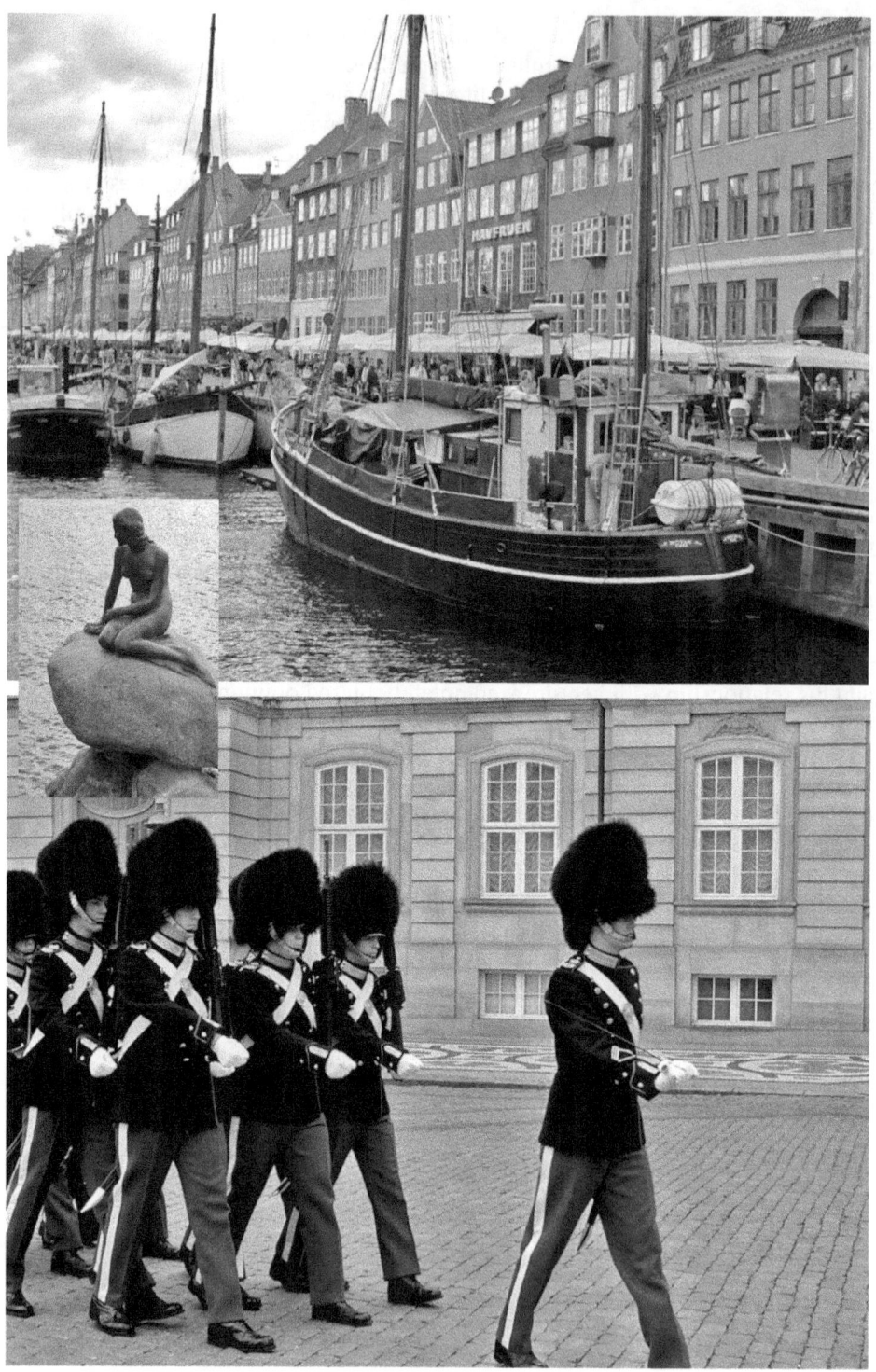

Chapter Four
Paris

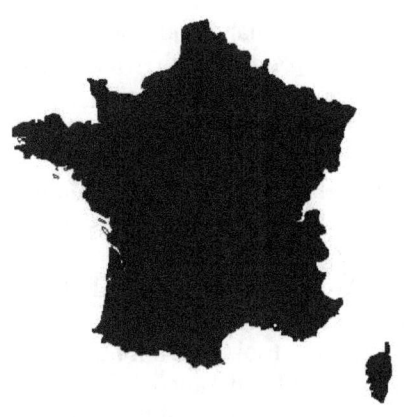

We boarded the train and discovered instant luxury. The solo compartment was designed to accommodate two people with tables that swiveled up and out of the way when needed. The most exciting feature was the private shower which contained a toilet. The sink swiveled away over the shower stall while the toilet was open. When inside the shower, the sink moved in the opposite direction over the toilet. I was hot and sweaty so I took a shower as soon as the train began to move. The train rolled alongside the highway as we passed cars, over bridges, and into the rolling green hills of Jutland; Denmark's mainland that is connected to the European continent via Germany.

The trains sleek design and rapid speed gave us visions of luxury and easy travel the rest of our journey throughout Europe. Every detail inside the train was a well thought-out design. The back of the seat folded up to become the double-layered bunk bed. The stewards were there with a snack of yogurt and cookies soon after I dried off. A few hours later a delicious meal was brought to us as we sat and looked out the window at the waning daylight along the terrain. We felt well pampered and excited to spend time in such a luxurious mode of transportation. This was our first experience in First Class!

The night passed but not as easily as expected. Sleeping in a train is not like the romantic myth. The rolling motion and noise kept me awake. I'm not accustomed to being in a tight berth where I could barely fit my six-foot frame. The window was cracked a few inches to let some of the overwhelming heat out, but the open window allowed the sound of the clickety-clack all night.

The steward woke us for a nice continental breakfast of yogurt and buttered rolls with marmalade. We were to depart in Cologne, Germany at six in the morning and had an hour before our connection would arrive. In that hour we decided to venture out of the station and see the colossal cathedral. It was a massive, very prevalent structure just outside the door of the station. Inside the station while I was looking for the information booth, Diana was buying some food at a counter. A man approached her and began to speak in Spanish. He introduced himself and explained he was a high school teacher of both Spanish and English. I don't remember his name, but we made a friend for life and only encountered him for our brief stay of one hour.

The teacher encouraged us to come across the street to see one of the most famous Gothic cathedrals in the world. Had he not spoken to us we might have stayed inside the confines of the train station, afraid of missing our train. At first I was apprehensive about the man, questioning his intentions. I could see he was interested in Diana and appeared to be awe struck. This happens when an older man has a younger wife. Men often come up to her, and flirt only to learn that the older man is her husband.

We had our luggage on wheels so we crossed the plaza, took the elevator up to the street level, and headed to the front doors of the cathedral. The Cathedral at Cologne has a famous facade that I remember from my Art History classes. The relief sculptures and arched doors are an essential symbol of the Gothic Age.

We entered into a tall dark structure where the only light to be seen was the tiny candles placed on the altar, far, far away. The massive edifice constructed in middle Ages took over six hundred years to build, concluding in 1880.

A slight stream of light came in the main chamber, but the darkness overwhelmed most of the interior. We were inside a total of ten minutes when we thought it wise to return to the train station. A small man-operated street cleaner was washing the street as we exited. The homeless men who had been camping at the door the night before began to gather their bedrolls as the spraying water missed them. The city was just waking and early preparations for the day had begun. Our instant tour guide bid us a safe journey and we soon found the correct platform and made our way to the train that arrived exactly on time; German style.

We thought the train the night before was luxurious, but this high-speed train topped the list. The seats were more comfortable than first class airline seats and could recline close to 180 degrees. We were a bit out of our element compared to the rest of the passengers who were dressed for work in fine suits with leather brief cases. The steward was a black man who spoke English and French and treated us like royalty. Hot washcloths to clean our face and hands were provided. We were given a newspaper to read, a sweet chocolate after breakfast, of a croissant roll with marmalade. This was Europe at its best. The train was in Paris in slightly over an hour. We entered a huge glass station with many faces and languages from all over the world, navigating our way up an escalator and into a cue for the tourist information booth. There we bought two tourists cards and were given directions to our hotel. The attendant was friendly and polite.

I joined a web site called the Virtual Tourist a few months before our trip. This is a person-to-person exchange of journeys and travel ideas. So I contacted a man who lives in Paris and asked him where we could stay near the Left Bank for a reasonable price. I booked three days and was happy to have that all in order before entering such a large city. Depending on one's preferences it can be done at the train station, upon arrival, or ahead of time on the Internet.

The subway was a hassle because we had our two duffel bags on wheels. While entering the turnstile Diana's bag got stuck. An African man helped her through by lifting the bag over the machine. Then we had many steps to go down. Soon another man was helping us lift the bags down the long steps. He looked like an African immigrant in street clothes. He never said a word, but silently just took the bag by one end as Diana carried the other side. Exiting the subway was equally as hard.

When we found our way to fresh air we were completely lost. The map in my hand was confusing and difficult to read. A woman from the United States passed us and told us she was visiting her daughter who lived there. She reoriented us out and put us in the right direction. We walked along side streets and into the street since sidewalk were too narrow for the bags. This is one time I truly regret being too cheap. I like to save money but to not take a taxi from the train station was foolish. The struggle through morning job commuters, up and down the steps was a crazy exercise. Diana was exhausted by the time we strolled into the small hotel on one of the side streets.

People from many countries ran this hotel. Every time we entered or left the premises there was a different desk clerk. It seemed they worked short hours and shifted people frequently. I never saw the same desk clerk twice. The bags again had to be lifted up a small flight of steps to get into the tiny elevator. There was no porter. The room was not that much bigger than the elevator. The bed was in the middle with just enough walking space to get around. Our bags were an obstacle no matter where we put them, so we placed them on top of the dresser and into a small closet. The toilet was in the same tiny room as the shower and sink. It was cramped but the large old-fashioned windows that fit long, thin, white drapes flowing with the slight breeze, made the room feel heavenly. We managed to tidy up and went out for a walk to discover Paris.

What a place! I never understood French pride and why they seemed to have such high expectation of things. But seeing their capital city explains why such high standards are maintained. There is visual delight in every public building. At the end of our street there was a park with a fountain, just two blocks from the Seine River. That day we crossed the bridge onto the Left Bank and found our way to the Notre Dame Cathedral. The staggering amount of tourists squelched my desire to go inside. Throngs of people stood in the sun waiting to see the famous landmark. We walked around the exterior and still enjoyed ourselves. Everywhere people milled about in the shade or sat at cafes enjoying themselves.

I had been to Paris once before in 1976. I lay in bed three days suffering with influenza and diarrhea. In the middle of one night I was awakened by a rock and roll band singing, "I can't get no satisfaction". The weird, surreal convergence of being very sick and listening to these singers was their thick Chinese accents. They sang in English, but between songs the dialogue was all in Chinese on a loud public address system. I had a delusional dream and to this day remember it. I was held high in the air by a beaked animal with the body of an electric fan. The bird-like creature squeezed me until my bowel movement splattered onto the fan, spreading my feces all around. This nightmare has left some kind of mark on my subconscious. I know now why surrealism had its birth in Paris. I left Paris, still sick, went back to Ireland to Denis', recouped, and went home with my proverbial tail between my legs. I had planned a three-month adventure, cut short by nightmares and fright.

This trip was nothing like my first bed-ridden experience in the city. I was twenty-two on my first trip to Paris. Thirty-two years later, I had the good fortune to return and live quite the opposite reality. Every street, every alley, every face, every smile made us fall in love with the city, and each other even more. The first day we wandered around not going that far from our hotel, staying mostly on the Left Bank exploring the tiny side streets, and eating in a Mexican restaurant where singers belted out Spanish lyrics. The doorman lured us inside with Diana's native tongue, and then enjoyed some good French wine with dinner. At one point we got up to dance and bumped into the small tables in the crowded room, no one seemed to mind. By the time we made it home we had ventured to near fatigue. The small hotel room seemed big enough for our two bodies in bed and that was all we cared about.

Day Two: The next day we took our first bus tour. I bought the tickets for the jump on and off tour for two days. Usually the plan is to sit though the tour, see what the city has to offer and spend the next day jumping off for attractions that caught our eye. Several different routes of the tour took us well into the late afternoon. We made a stop for the Eiffel Tour and waited in a short line for about forty-five minutes. The lines had the added benefit of a cooling system which sprayed a soft mist of water on the people waiting. I had never seen this before. As the fan sprayed it rotated sprinkling lines of people waiting. This made the whole experience less difficult in the late afternoon's hot sun.

We rode the elevator up the three different levels. I was scared to death. I am terrified of heights. A swell of anxiety rushed my body. My palms sweat, my eyes lose their focus, and I feel myself physically falling. Diana's hand became a comfort and like waves subsiding my emotions calmed as I convinced myself I was on a solid surface. My camera was clicking as often as I could get the courage to approach the edge. Families with children ran about like they were on a flat street. I went to the rest room and couldn't shake the fact that I was urinating very high up in the air. We had some other tourists take our picture together, kissing. The Pairs cityscape had a distinct color that was a pale white. The birds-eye view of the city had a color that gave the entire city a feeling of calm and serenity. In the far distance we could see the reverberating colors of the city in the pale, white spires of the Sacre Coure. There was so much to see we never made it to that church, but seeing it so strong on the hill made an impression. I have seen many paintings of this church. Seeing the colors and surrounding streets settled my nerves, calming my fear of heights. I found myself really enjoying the vista, losing myself in the view.

I studied the structure of the rivets and beams as we rode the elevator back down to street level thinking how genius was in its construction. A short rain shower ended as we rested on the ground under some nearby trees. I lay on my back looking at the Eiffel Tour while Diana went off to find a restroom. We ate the two sandwiches that had been saved for a late snack. A lone vendor came up to us to sell a small Eiffel Tour. We bought this for a low price and walked by the hordes of tourists being taunted by souvenir sellers. Our sale had been in a quiet place and seemed more intimate. We found our way home and walked along the river as night fell. Another rain shower saturated the streets and gave the lights a special glow. Lovers were everywhere and the city of love was on fire with light and color. Day two ended while we left the streets to lovers who strolled arm in arm towards home. The ancient past and future live in this city, but the here and now rules the day. Time spills into the Seine as people sit on the banks and hang their feet like children waiting for tomorrow's dreams and lullabies.

Day Three: In contrast to the sitting on the tour bus and having a passive day, today we walked for many miles. We saw the Louvre, the Orsay Museum, and Orangerie Museum. My favorite was the exclusive layout of Monet's Water Lilies at the Orangerie Museum. The Orangerie Museum is a nondescript building at the far end of the park (the royal gardens) that houses the Louvre on the opposite end. A square facade with no noticeable, no distinctive marks leads the viewer down steps to a series of galleries. The first galleries have collections of the Impressionist and their contemporaries. But the two spectacular galleries that house Monet's Water Lillie's are grand white oval rooms that give justice to his master pieces. The curvature of the walls added to the visibility and made the viewer step into his art. It was homage to Monet's life. The white walls gave the viewing event a spiritual overtone where people whispered or stood silent in awe in the middle of the room. For some reason the gallery was without the hordes of people we had seen at the other galleries that day. This was an intimate place.

The Louvre is a delightful circus. We gave ourselves a two-hour limit, which is unrealistic, but the sheer number of artworks could not be properly appreciated in one lifetime. The line began outside, near I. M. Pei's glass pyramid, but when inside the inner space of the entry opened and the line finished.

I.M. Pei's glass pyramid is just the correct size to fit into the plaza where the Louvre's entrance stands. The glass is constructed with thousands of triangular structures, under the glass which protects the entrance from the elements; there is a rhyme of triangular supports. If the pyramid were any larger it would seem an eye sore, but from below, inside, the purpose of this structures mystery opens and answered its purpose is to light the basement entrance. A vast spiral staircase with an elevator in the center caught my interest. Other people entered via the escalators.

We knew what we wanted to see and soon followed the crowds and signs to the Mona Lisa. We felt not to see the Mona Lisa is a sin in Dante's damnation, so we joined the pilgrimage up stairs, down long galleries, past centuries of cultural icons. I played my game of "recognize the artists and see if I could guess the correct painters name". I have seen so many reproductions of these works throughout my career that the challenge is to keep adding to my memory file. Titian, Rembrandt, Raphael, and all the masters of art were represented. The walk was slow and methodical as Diana shot photographs in the low light. By the time we reached the beloved Mona Lisa we knew it was the correct gallery because of the vast number of spectators. The problem was getting close enough to see what seemed too small, or almost event-less in size. This painting is the most famous in the world, but is smaller than one can imagine, maybe twelve inches tall. It is sheltered behind a thick glass barrier. The crowd was at least twelve people deep, so getting close takes time and patience. I loved the multinational viewers from every corner of our planet. If you just arrived on earth this would be the place to go to meet all of our beautiful human species.

I know we saw less than a fraction of the grand collection, but we also wanted to move on and fill the remaining hours with other places. The Louvre was our second museum that day. The first museum was the grand house of the Impressionists, The Orsay. Picture a grand stadium (which was a rail station) that has been converted into a museum with modern elements merged into old architecture from the 1870's. Paris's old rail station was converted into a palace for these famous painters. I know the station because Monet himself did a famous painting of the trains and steam inside the vast dome of the Orsay in the 1880's. The main station's interior yard is now an open vista where smaller galleries break off into side rooms. Statues and large granite walls divide the space but do not intrude on the large open area above the galleries. The building is almost as interesting as the art. Mixing the architectural periods was done with exceptional grace. We actually spent more time there than the Louvre.

Outside the Louvre television cameras and crowds of people were lining the street sides. We had seen barriers earlier in the day while crossing the Champs de Elysee. The morning clouds had given way to bright sunshine and crowds were standing in anticipation of the Tour De France. We weaved our way through the crowd under a television camera mounted on a crane. Soon a series of police motorcycles sped by, then the support cars mounted with many bicycles atop. These cars had commercial sponsors logos pasted all over them. I never paid attention to the Tour De France until I was in Denmark one year and my friend, Jan, was glued to the television cheering for a Danish cyclist. This piqued my interest but I am not a real fan.

I can't explain the sudden emotional jolt that struck me that day. I stood cheering for the cyclists and tears began to stream from my eyes. The moment was charged with excitement and elevated pride. All the different nations and glory of their love for sport hit me. Wow! I was witnessing history! In was overwhelmed by the surge of national pride felt by all the different peoples present. I was truly a glorious moment. I had no clue who was ahead or who I was cheering for. It was simply swept away by so much excitement was in the air. Packs of riders would speed by, and then there would be a few minutes of silence. Again the people would begin to cheer and the quick flash of the riders would sweep by in an instant. We couldn't see the long view, just the swath of colors between the heads of spectators. It was a very happy moment that celebrated all that is good about being human.

That evening we wanted to do a dining boat trip up the Seine, but the prices were too steep. Instead, we found a tour boat that was a part of our tourist card. We joined families and couples for a two-hour ride that took us too many stops. The announcements were in several languages. We sat in a row of chairs situated inside the boat. We had no choice because the seats were all taken, but by the time we had passed a few stops the seats opened up and we moved closer to the side of the long boat for a better view. The river offers a unique perspective of the city, especially at night. The city's fathers have understood how to beatify a building, and even the riverbank itself by utilizing several spotlights. The added lights give a dramatic illusion to the features of the buildings. All along the riverbank people sat and drank, strolled hand in hand, and even danced.

One park was compartmentalized into small sections of curved seating. In each of as many as seven sections, groups of people were dancing either mambo or salsa. Music blared from loud speakers and small enclaves of dancers were having a party. Some looked like beginner groups, others very advanced dancers with spectators cheering them on. One park had a rock group blasting out tunes with crowds of dancers waving their arms and singing along. Everyone and anyone were invited to join in the fun. The spirit of freedom and enjoying life was in the hearts of all. There was an air of lightheartedness. I held Diana's hand and felt in love more than the previous day. Paris had struck my heart.

I have always had this secret fantasy to come to Pairs with my true love. When I was young I kept a brochure that was from Paris. It had the silhouette of a man and woman embracing under a crescent moon and star. I had imagined the couple beneath the moon was actually Diana and me. That dream had come true. We strolled in the warm night air and enjoyed every second Paris, the city of love.

From our walk along the river after the boat ride we found the subway. We purchased a three-day subway pass and had not even used it yet. Around nine at night we made our way to the Metro and took a ride to the Arc De Triumph. I took a few photographs of the cars in a slow shutter giving the image a blur under the orange-yellow light of the L'Arc De Triumph. I had no tripod so I used a concrete pillar to prop up the camera.

The day before, high in the Eiffel Tower I saw an impressive set of buildings across the Seine. Many people gathered there to see the Eiffel Tower. This was our next stop on the subway. At midnight, the sparkling lights on the tower turn off. We arrived around 11:30 and walked past the crowds standing or walking in the dark. People selling tourist items and handbags were on the ground with open blankets. We couldn't really see where we were until we arrived at a long marble wall. Below, stairs lead to other lower levels. From this place I could set the camera and get shots of the Eiffel Tower. This grand marble walkway was part of Les Gardens Du Trocadero. Hundreds of people cheered as the lights on the tower glistened with the symbol of the EU shinning in bright yellow stars. At midnight the last light display went off. We asked strangers to take our picture and likewise we did. From our vantage point we could see street dancers playing loud boom boxes, doing spinning headstands and acrobatics. No one was out of place; all were lost in the joy of the moment. It was a party for all. The French Revolution had succeeded.

The last day we wandered the city and took public transportation, buses and subways. We visited the Picasso Museum. I think this was one of his houses that had been converted into a museum. To my dismay photography was prohibited. We had spent a considerable time finding this out-of-the-way-museum, weaving in and out of old streets. My map seemed useless with so many tiny streets to follow. After the museum, we found a small food store and sat on the curb drinking a cold beverage. It was no more than ten-thirty but the heat was beating down.

Our next destination was a bus ride to a remote side of the city. On our map I had found the house-museum of Gustave Moreau, the famous Symbolist painter. This museum was a special treat for me. The minute we entered the guards were friendly and allowed photographs. This was a well-preserved location; all the original furnishing and household items were still there. It was as if he were just around the corner in another room, sitting and pondering some new painting.

I admit I like his art more than Picasso, and I loved his house. The house is similar to my taste. Every inch of the walls had a painting, etching, sketch or an interesting wall hanging. Diana and I struggle with our different decorating styles. I like "clutter", I like busy and interesting to look at. She prefers the stark or simple look. This discussion takes place whenever we enter a home. For me this museum was full of visual delights. Small ornate jeweled boxes sat on the dressers or desks. Lamps with glass basses and fine shades sat on tables. Everything had frills and ornamented decorations. The house seemed to evoke a sense of mystery and intrigue. He had collected fine Arabian trinkets and had rich, thick gold frames on the paintings. Diana and I lost each other a few times, carefully eyeing each room for all the minute details of a man who lived like a mystic. The surprise was to find two enormous studios at the top of the house. These expansive rooms had grand windows for light. Moreau covered the walls from top to bottom with paintings. Some of the works were never completed; others were well-known, famous paintings by this Symbolists master. I was in my element clicking away with the camera.

His paintings are of angels, dragons, or saints in fantastic landscapes that allude to dreamscapes and fantasy. Knights ride horses, or unicorns, while brilliant colors splash as stars burst or halos stream overheads. Flower garlands are draped on the heads of beautiful maidens. This is a perfect world were wisdom rules over ignorance. Love is on the canvases. Victorious winged creatures crush evil dragons as the gates of heaven open. I have been a fan of his art since my early twenties. He was an inspiration to me then and now. The top floors of the house are where the real art is housed, yet to see the lower floors gave me a deeper understanding of his tastes and influences. We spent a couple of hours looking at the details of the large canvases. I enjoyed this very much, much more than the noisy crowds of the Louvre.

On our walk back to the bus stop we found an old church and walked inside to see an ancient dusty church where years of incense burning had marred the ceiling. After a short bus ride we found the Pompidou Center. The tourist card again came in handy, saving us a few dollars at each museum. Before entering the museum on the upper floors of the Pompidou Center we decided to use the free email service at the public library on the ground floor. After a short wait we were given a card with a number on it. The immense library was rows upon rows of desks with computers. We were lost immediately but a polite clerk helped us find the right computer. Of course the computer needed a pass code. Another patron helped us figure out how to begin the process. With our mission accomplished we were riding the long, enclosed glass tube up the side of the building to the top floors exhibition of modern art. I find the modern art interesting, but my real love of art comes from the Impressionist, not esoteric, contemporary canvas or installation. My specific tendencies are influenced by my mother. She instilled in me an eternal love of landscape and realism. I enjoy modern art, but it all seems so limited, too public, and too loud because of its size.

I wrote a paper once called Neo-Neo Romanticism, expressing a desire to return to intimate and romantic concepts that guided the early landscape artists. It has always baffled me why painting the earth became passé in the eyes of the modern art world. The same goes with painting the human figure. Earth and the human form will never become "out-dated", so why exclude subjects in the vernacular of modern art? This art is meant to challenge the viewer, and we were challenged. The large, spacious size of the galleries in the Pompidou Center welcomes the viewer into the grand arena of public art. I favored the large soft sculpture installations.

The rest of the day we walked around the city, aware of our hotel's location and how close it was, only a twenty-minute walk. We were nearly three miles from our hotel, in the same general area of the city. We discovered the wonderful gardens (Jardin du Forum des Holles) and crossed the street to the Gothic Cathedral of Saint Eustache. This was a quiet respite from the hustle and bustle outside in the shopping areas.

The afternoon light was at a perfect, low angle to shine through the wonderful stained glass windows. The drone of the shopping streets was total cacophony, contrasting with the quiet afternoon light streaming into the church. This set a tone for reflection and wonderment at human accomplishment as we sat in silence.

Beyond the park was a beautiful fountain where crowds of people sat with their feet in the water. We sought shelter from the heat then enjoyed watching all the people.

It was getting late enough for an early dinner so we strolled a few blocks to an outdoor restaurant. We ate some type of rolls stuffed with chicken. I wouldn't have remembered this so well, but there was an altercation between the two men calling in customers. We stood waiting at one restaurant, but no one helped us. So we walked to the next set of tables and found an empty seat. The men spoke in Arabic, but one doesn't need to understand a language to hear a verbal cross-fire. This seemed to be a never-ending scenario. It got heated because the vying parties wanted each other's customers; we watched the floor show as we finished our meal.

Being filled with starchy food, we wandered back to our hotel to sleep. The following morning about nine o'clock, we checked out of our hotel. This time we had the good sense to take a taxi and leave the struggle of luggage to the driver. Passing some of the same sights we had seen on second day on the tour bus made the city slightly familiar. We left Paris from a different train station. I think it was the western station. While waiting I was sitting on the luggage and Diana went off to find food for the train. We had an hour wait so we sat at the end of the platform awaiting the arrival of the train to Salzburg.

In Salzburg we transferred to an overnight train with a private sleeping compartment. There was no shower and the stewards weren't as friendly or accommodating as the other trains. The train was old and dirty. This became a theme as we took more trains south. The more trains we rode, the dirtier and older they became.

Paris was our favorite city. For me it was the trip to Paris I had always wanted to have. I wasn't sick in bed; I am an older wiser traveler. Diana was thrilled by the open public spaces and the obvious cultural heritage that spills onto every building, boulevard, park, and fountain. Not once did we encounter the "French Attitude" that so many Americans stereotype about these Parisians. (I often saw the "attitude" coming from belligerent AMERICAN tourists.) We found our romantic city of love. I found sheer visual joy in all the art and architecture. A return trip is high on our agenda, someday. Even a quick weekend would rekindle the magic we found. I suggest this city to anyone, forever.

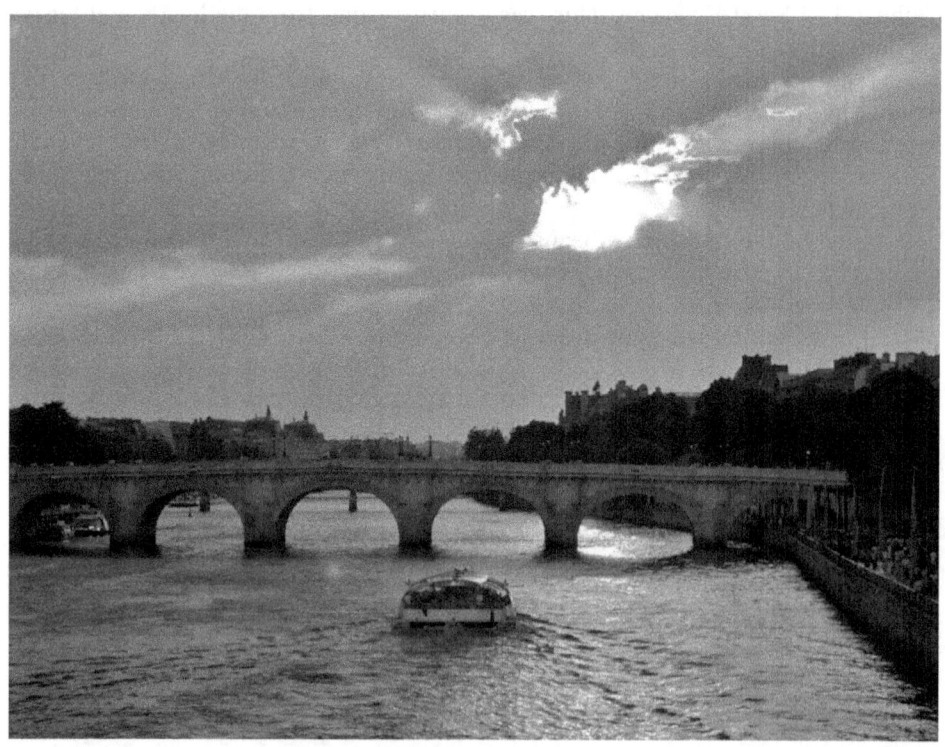

Chapter Five
Vienna

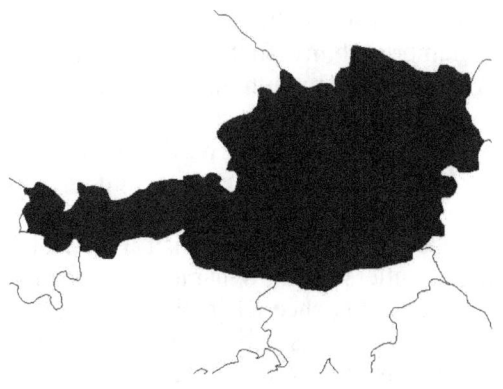

As the train left Salzburg it slowly climbed into the Alps. We sat gazing out the train window as the houses changed to an increasingly quaint, Bavarian style. Darkness began to settle in the valleys and tiny yellow lights in the houses indicated warm meals being served. Eventually, all we could see were the lights of tiny houses like fireflies in the distance. We opened the seats to the railroad berths and climbed in to sleep.

We booked our hotel on the Internet. This time we had even booked a classical concert and a few museums months before our arrival. The train station had an elevator so it was not like we had experienced in Paris. We found one Austrian young man to help us get our subway/ metro ticket and we were soon up on the street level where I recognized our whereabouts. Unlike the open glass structure of the Paris train station, Vienna has a station that was built underground in the seventies. The environment is lit by neon lighting, and poorly lit with long square corridors that feel gray. Few people fill the hall even thought it was the morning rush. The people look conservatively dressed as employees rush their way to their daily routines or jobs. It must have been seven in the morning but I was too drowsy to care.

This was my fourth time to Vienna. It is one of the easiest cities in the world to negotiate. Every night in the summer there is a free concert in the center of town. On a huge screen, performances are shown to crowds of people in a sizable outdoors theater. Cultural events play a pivotal role in this city. Vienna has an air of elegance of its own.

We liked our hotel room very much. It had a balcony, free breakfast, a big room with two single beds, and a bathtub that was from an era when the entire body was submerged in hot water. The hotel was a college dorm that had been converted into a hotel. The building was ten stories tall with long halls. We had a corner room opposite the elevator. It had a desk and plenty of space for us and our belongings. The luxurious bathtub was immediately put to use.

After a relaxing bath, we returned to the center of town finding the tourists' office to pick up our pre-purchased Vienna Card. The office was located in the central city. We then headed back to the main plaza were Saint Stephen's Cathedral stands. This is by far the most famous building in Vienna and it can be seen from most places in the city. Scaffolding covered the main spire, but Diana could see it was an impressive structure. The scaffolding had a photograph of the real spire printed on a canvas to camouflage the construction.

The first time I was in Vienna was 1965. The only memory I have from that time was seeing the statue of Strauss in a park. Years later, I returned and had the memory of my first teenage visit come back to me. I didn't recall my previous visit as a youth until I stood in front of the golden memorial statue. The trip would not have been complete unless Diana saw this.

This time on my return, I wanted to also show Diana one of my architectural favorites; a white building with a large, gold dome in the Art Nouveau style with flower patterns called the Sessions Building. I love this Viennese style building and visit it on each return. As I travel, there are times it seems pointless to know names and locations. But when returning to a place, a sort of second chance takes place, thus a need to know and identify names. The Sessions Building is one of my favorites because it is elegant and unusual. This building was built to house exhibitions for the rebel artist that broke away from the fine art institute in the early 1900's.

I recalled a street market a few blocks away, so we headed in its direction. Diana and I stroll through rows of restaurants in thin passages. Men sat smoking cigarettes, sipping coffee, looking us over because we were obviously travelers. They were speaking in a hushed tone about business, and then looking back at their coffee. Women called to us to sample their stuffed peppers, stuffed with what looked like some kind of cheese. The smells of spices wafted up as we strolled past the open bags of spices. The smell of curry and coriander made the air thick with imagination, sailing us off to far away Middle-Eastern places we may never see, but visit for an instant through homeland aromas. The people smile because they know we are traveling home with them, through pleasant fragrances. The sun is beating down as I shift my head to dodge an awning. I'm sweating, but happy to be in the bazaar.

Diana asks, "Why do you tell people I am from Colombia and learning English?"

I know this is going to be one of those moments I need to be patient. She doesn't like to standout as different. She had just been stung by a bee as we walked past the vegetables. She shook it off but not before a sting. This may be why she suddenly brings up a "sensitive" topic while she is recouping in pain.

"I don't say you are learning English, I say you are Colombian to explain that we are not both North American. One time I said you were learning English because the person did not understand you." This is a series of conversations in which we engage that I am finally accustomed to having. I am no longer feeling a surge of anger, just a trickle. I just want to get along and not have any conflict. She is satisfied with my answer and we have a truce. I feel defensive and I know it's my ego. I cross examine myself and reflect on some Buddhist readings. I've got to let go and just center myself, not feel defensive. I take a deep breath. This technique works as we cross the street and the graffiti distracts me. I begin to photograph again.

Vienna is cleaner than Paris. We rate a city by how much graffiti it has. We make judgments based on cigarettes butts strewn about and words scribbled on the walls. Of course, we admire the magnificent architecture and the art museums. Europeans are still puffing away in the cafes, outside; as we walk by we see this. We also see the graffiti in out-of-the-way neighborhoods. I shoot photographs of it sometimes. I'm looking for Banksi the political graffiti artist. I've found a couple of his works, or a few who are in the same school of social criticism known as Guerrilla Art. I love his wit and pointed criticism. I saw one today that was a woman with a mushroom cloud popping out of her eloquent hairstyle. I find myself laughing at tragic, but true, artistic statements.

Our first major museum that day was the National Art Museum known as the Kunsthistorisches. It is homage to high art. The gold stairwell leading to the second floor is enough to justify a visit. There is an institutional building, equal in size, across a grassy park that houses a gigantic collection of natural specimens. This is the natural history museum. The museum of art has some of the world's best-known art works, Rembrandt, Rubens, El Greco, and many more masters. This is the crown jewel of Austria's art collection, construction on this spacious museum begun in 1871 and completed in 1891. The collection can stand up to the Louvre, only with fewer pieces.

Vienna is, in my quality of the eyes like a small Paris. One needn't travel far outside the city center to see attractions; most attractions are in or nearby. The city tram system runs like a wheel with spokes to outreaching locations. The unique thing about the tram is that it goes in a circle around the center of the city. You can board and end up where you began about a half hour later. From that one, central tram, you can spend your first day seeing museums, parks, castles, churches, the opera, or simply shopping. It is Disneyland in a real place.

Day Two: Our second day began with another pre-purchased ticket to see the Hunderwasser Museum. This is in a neighborhood where middle class people live. The museum is actually an apartment building where the main floor is the museum and a restaurant, and the top two floors hold Freidenreich Hunderwasser work. The outside of the building defies the standard geometry of design. The inside is just as interesting. Bizarre conveys the buildings appearance. It is not a typical square building. Inside the museum, there were quotes from Hunderwasser reflecting his philosophy of life. This quote paraphrased best describes the building and its unconventional appearance. "A straight line is a sin against humanity". And so, not one straight line exists in the building, which makes for a lovely visual treat. Floors roll like waves, walls curve in and out, and stairs truly wind. In addition, there is a visual playground of color in tiny mosaics covering complete areas of the building.

His art is based on tiny rectangular bits of color that add up in swirling designs. The shapes add together to from objects such as buildings or figures.

I first heard of him in high school from a fellow student. We would gawk at his art and the imaginative, inventive way he saw the world. He died in 2000. I never even knew he was alive in my teen years, thinking he was not a contemporary, but from an earlier era. He abhorred anything straight, or with a hard edge. He spent the later years of his life sailing while calling New Zealand home. We also saw photographs of a modern village he had designed, hundreds of original artworks, and the museum building itself, an artwork. We spent a few hours in the museum then reentered reality and the straight world.

Our next stop was Gustav Klimt's artworks at the Belvedere Palace. This was a tram ride to a stop close to the train station where we arrived the day before. The museum is a converted palace. Klimt's famous painting "The Kiss" is a central attraction in this museum. This is a pleasant, spacious museum with grand gardens and benches. We spent a few hours inside and then found a shady bench to eat a picnic. We secretly took some rolls from breakfast and made a few sandwiches. A young couple from Japan lay sleeping on a nearby bench as we ate. We took a short nap on the narrow benches which were unfortunately uncomfortable since the grass was off limits.

We had bought tickets for a concert of Mozart's music that evening. We took the tram to another Castle called Schonbrunn. This was the home of the Hapsburg's and is a designated World Heritage Site; a museum where all the furnishing, gardens, buildings, carriages, and toys of the king had been preserved.

"In this room the king had his informal meetings with his subjects", was the sort of thing on the tour.

The tour was well organized and lead by experienced historians that filled our heads with all the exciting details that never return to memory. Several types of tours could be seen at various prices. We bought the "Grand Tour" verses the stable and grounds tour, staying in the main building.

Following the visit to the castle we strolled to the grounds behind the palace. Here we passed the remainder of the day until it was time for the concert.

Out of curiosity, we moved several times stopping at different gardens or fountains, ending with a picnic dinner in a special rose garden. The fountains contained within were filling the air with intoxicating fragrances of roses. Few people could be seen. We were completely alone holding hands and sharing long romantic kisses. Miles upon mile of trails where joggers ran or people stroll span the huge garden. Some of the paths stretched straight for as long as the eye could see. Others were sleepy paths with a low afternoon light that gave the entire visit a graceful sensation. The thick trees would arch into tunnels of green rows. Low fences kept people from entering the woods, in some areas magical fountains with low sculpted hills rolled surrounding the fountains, shallow ponds gave way to adventurous discoveries around each corner. Breathtaking.

The park was symmetrical, having a series of low, boxed gardens in one grand central aisle that divided the entire estate. At the far end of the central garden, directly behind the palace, was a huge sculptured fountain decorated with horses. Water shot powerful streams from the animals' mouths out the fountain.

A tall, square war mausoleum stood on top of a steep hill. The mausoleum was dedicated to the fallen solders' of the Prussian wars. It was a blonde granite structure that has little appeal.

We walked a small fraction of the grounds by the time we needed to leave for our concert. At that time the grounds were being locked. Luckily, the main gate to our concert was only a few feet away. It was held in a small recital hall that sat three hundred people at most. As usual, we had the middle priced seats, not more than two rows from the most expensive front seats.

Diana loved the gowns worn by the women performing that night. They dressed in traditional Baroque attire from 1600's and sang like angels. It was well worth the thirty dollar price and a very special evening; we dressed up in the best clothing we'd brought, enjoying ourselves the entire time. The concertgoers gave several standing ovations to the performers who repeatedly gave return bows. The Baroque Concert was good, but vacationers are an easy crowd to please. The easy train ride, and change to the tram was all it took to find our beds and pillows.

Our last day was filled touring more museums and walking until our feet ached. We knew we'd have time to rest on the train that night so we put as much strolling as possible into the schedule as possible. Our first stop was Stadtpark, where the golden mausoleum of Johann Strauss is situated. This is the gold statue that I remember from my childhood and first time to Vienna. The most beautiful tribute to the composer stands at one end of the park. In its center the composer is playing a violin; behind him a hallowed, open arch has female muses merging out of the white stone in a swimming dance that surrounds him. The gold statue of Strauss contrasted against the white background is brilliant, stone turns into music with muses circling his melodic stance.

We also went to a museum of modern art called the Leopold. Its exterior is a cold, square unimpressive building. The collective works of Gustav Klimt, Oscar Kokoschka, and Egon Schiele paintings are housed here.

We saw a painting by Schiele where a bishop is romantically embracing a nun. It made me laugh to see how he was mocking the celibacy of the priesthood. To think he did it at a time when the church was so influential is a tremendous challenge to that institution. I often find myself chuckling at the wit of art while I see people parading by wearing such sacred faces, almost a death march, as if they are saying the Stations of the Cross.

The museums are the new churches of culture yet the people are puppets of sorts. Among certain circles, submissive, liturgical behavior in religion has been replaced by silent meditation museums. They have replaced the omnipotent god, with new, beautiful tangible idols, bowing to the aesthetic masterpiece standing in His stead. I can't go to a museum and feel anything but the desire to paint. As I witness so much art I am learning from what I see, to add to my own artistic vault and creative behavior. I don't know what most people do with the information they obtain in museums. It seems so passive to look at art. To me, it's like learning how to spell, but never writing, learning to read music but never sing or play an instrument. "Making history" doesn't happen by reading or observing life, only by living it. Yet we live in a world where we are spoon feed art as if it were entertainment. This is a superficial idolatry that makes me question the art world.

The Leopold is near many other museums of antiquities, but if you are looking for early nineteenth century art this is an excellent source. The landscapes of Oscar Kokoschka are a favorite of mine. I'm unsure why his art appealed to me when I was a burgeoning artist, but even now, I identify with his works.

After the Leopold we ran into some Hari Krishna. I struck up a conversation with them. I admire their life of aestheticism so I always give them a graceful "no thanks" when they invite us to visit. The older I am the better I feel about who I am and the choices I've made along the way. My youthful visit to their California temple was punctuated by an attempt to make me stay there. I was told I was falling back into the material world if I left. Guilt doesn't motivate me into following the "one true faith". I could have been one of them, or a priest, or a sheep. Respect doesn't need to be shown through imitation.

We soon found a grocery store and bought provisions for the next leg of our journey. We were on our way to where all roads lead, Rome. In the late afternoon, our overnight train was waiting, on time at the station. It was a little grungy but its selling point was that didn't have to change trains to reach Rome.

Vienna is a compact city as far as the attractions are concerned. We never ventured that far out of the city center to get to the museums or royal palace. Approximately fifteen minutes on a tram, or bus, puts you at any location.

Had we not known of the outer sites, three days would have occupied us in the city center.

The prices of goods, and food, were high, so we ate picnic style and stayed away from costly expenditures. It is always possible to stay on a budget and keep extra money for less expensive places.

We bought some small trinkets. Diana found a blouse and I, a hanging Turkish ornaments in a second-hand store. The majority of our money was being maintained in miserly fashion. The aura of Vienna was expensive; the prices in the windows were too high for our limited funds. We did visit a few department stores but we left empty handed. We kept reasoning that adding extra baggage to our load would be a problem. We had already shipped one box home.

My second trip to Vienna was ten years ago. I had a dear friend named Sanford who married a woman from Vienna. Sanford was ninety at that time. He was a small, skinny Jewish man with no hair and a tremendous smile. I felt closer to him than my own father. He has since passed away. He was a world traveler and an inspiration to me. He was my role model. His wife was thirty years younger than he. Our friendship began by me over-hearing him talk about a future trip to Copenhagen. This was at a Unitarian Universalists Church on Long Island, New York. I was about to leave for Copenhagen and we set up an appointment. Instant chemistry joined us in a cosmic venture; we began a long friendship that ended with me at his bedside when he died at the age of ninety-seven.

Strange as it may seem his death was a spiritual moment I'll never forget. I felt honored to be there and see him off the planet.

He and I had traveled together on three continents, always meeting up whenever possible. He and his wife offered me their Vienna apartment as their guests. It was a spacious grand apartment that had seen better days. But what it did offer was a glimpse into the past and how life had been in an age gone by. The furniture was from the 1940's. The rooms had cathedral ceilings with large windows. The kitchen was eminence with two sinks on each side of the room.

Perhaps the most impressive feature was the spiral staircase that curved up to the third floor apartment. Sanford's mother-in-law had collected trinkets from all over Europe, so the house was a veritable treasure trove of goodies from the past. I was as interested in the sights inside the apartment as I was the surrounding city.

We spent every night in the main city park watching operas, or special classical music concerts, eating below the giant screen with hundreds of other spectators. The summer air was perfect; all we needed was a sweater after the sun set. Because we were with local people we had the edge on the usual tourists' stresses. That self-assurance has remained with me each visit to Vienna. On those earlier trips I was able to go by car to small villages and churches and get a real feel for the native culture. Austria is an expensive place to visit but with careful planning some of the major costs can be avoided. Find a friend!

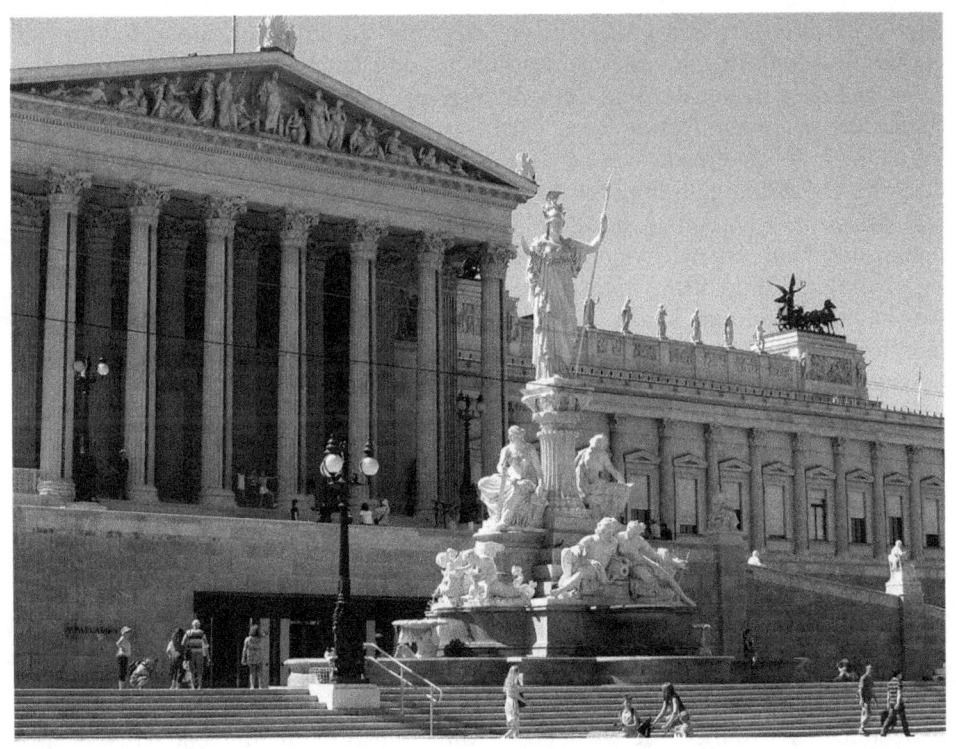

Chapter 6
Rome, Italy

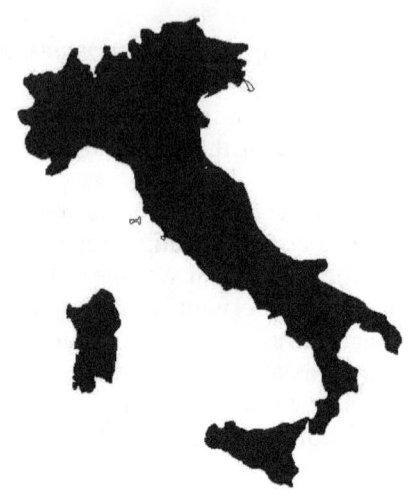

The train just pulled out of Florence. Diana was sick most of the night with acid reflux. She woke me and said it was time to get up.

In my sleep, I dreamt of being back home on Long Island. I was at work, on a lunch break, and out of the building with a co-worker. My friend and I were driving in a stolen pink 1957 Chevy convertible. The sun was bright and warm as we rode with the convertible top down, it was a carefree event. We were driving up hills, joy riding on side streets, and we were ten minutes late for the school bell. I had a new classroom but was confident my students would be ok alone. I took for granted that one of the responsible students will let the other students into the room and they would be fine until my arrival. The only problem would be my supervisor who would know I was late. Diana woke me up so getting back to my job on time, in my dream, was never concluded. I must have been subconsciously thinking about being on time for the trains, I'm certainly wasn't worried about my job while on vacation. I hope not anyway. And the dream was completely unrealistic; I can never leave my students unattended!

In the middle of the night a previous dream was with reference to my art. I was having a one-man show, but the entire show was exhibited on flat computer monitors hung on doors. I was rushing to get the monitors hung on the doors and downloading my art into the computers. It was so realistic that when I woke it dawned on me how unique the idea of having an art opening on computers would be. This could be a possible glimpse into the future. The art could be in my realistic style. The computer monitors could change images every few seconds in a slide show. Dreams are often the source of many a creative endeavor.

Traveling and writing a book may not have been the most ideal of circumstances to place myself in. To mix creative expression with leisurely intentions makes it not as fun as one might think. When we come back to the hotel I seldom have time to re-read, or digest, what I have already written. More importantly, any time for writing is out of the question. There is no down time while traveling. The daunting task of enjoying oneself and writing a book at the same time have pulled me in opposite directions. Journaling our daily events can't be put aside. The gnawing task of keeping current is an obligation and responsibility that I have to balance with pleasure or this whole vacation will become a second job.

I started a portrait of Diana I need to finish. I completed only one painting of a landscape in Denmark. It has golden fields and was the view not far from Susser's summerhouse. I feel a need to paint, write, and do sight-seeing all at once.

The next time we plan "down time" is in Greece where we booked a hotel for six days. When we get there I'll try to catch up with my unfinished paintings. The writing will not be revisited until months have passed. But if it happens, or not, I can't make myself go nuts over the responsibility of having an imaginative body of work to show. Yet traveling in itself can be a creative act. Finding one's way around a city is an expressive endeavor because there are tasks and solutions with physical results, equal to making an artwork. Many times, while engaging in creativity, I feel a great sense of release and accomplishment, just as I do from traveling. The act of expression is so healthy and powerful I believe it is as powerful as prayer or meditation. To create is to be spiritual. To travel can be spiritual if one truly engages the people and places. To be a silent observer is quasi-spiritual. I think most tourists are too passive to understand they are not interacting with the world.

We arrived at the train station in Rome and immediately sought the tourist information center. We walked to the center of the station saw an information sign, but we discovered it was for train information not tourists. A conductor misunderstood my question and sent me to the opposite side of the train station and on a long, pointless walk. Diana sat on a seat as I approached a counter in a line. I was with a woman who sounded Dutch. As she spoke to the man behind the counter I was at her side, and we exchanged eye incredulous glances. During her series of questions the male agent stopped three times, ignored her, and was interrupted by phone calls and other agents. Each time the woman had to restate her questions, again, from the beginning.

As I waited I devised a plan to ask succinct questions. I would ask one thing; get the information, and then move on to the next question.

"Where is this hotel?" He drew it on a map he had given me.

"Can I buy a pass for the buses and metro?"

He answered, "Yes, but you will have to return at noon because we have none until then. They are for three days of travel."

"Where can I buy a ticket for today to go to Saint Peters"? His answer, "You can buy them over there around the corner."

"Thank you." It worked. I was clear and direct without "agent-interruptus". Mission accomplished!

We walked away from the counter satisfied, went around the corner to find no such ticket counter for Saint Peters'. As I was walking with Diana she said she had been watching a man at the car rental counter nearby. The agent was yelling at a customer and had called the police to have the customer removed. Yes, I said the agent was indeed yelling at the customer. As the police took the man away he was saying he only wanted to rent a car.

The atmosphere in the train station was transmitting an emotional state we'd not experienced on our trip until then. As we talked about it, it seemed to be spilling into every frenzied, tense, agitated person around us. There was distinct emotional electricity to the train station. After not finding anything that looked like a ticket counter, I realized it must be one of the machines, which I wasn't prepared to deal with so we left the station for the hotel.

I had the map in hand, as I glanced over I saw Diana wasn't looking well because she had been so ill on the train the night before. A taxi was just pulling up and I motioned to him, but he pointed to the taxi at the front of the line. Another man walked up to us and asked if we wanted a taxi. I said yes, showed him the name of the hotel, and street address from the Internet confirmation sheet. He didn't seem to know the name of the street. I showed him the place on the map. It was five blocks away. He then said it would cost us twenty Euros. I instantly said no we would walk. Then he said, "OK, fifteen Euros". I was more convinced than ever the taxi driver would get me as a customer when hell froze over, thawed, and then froze over again.

In Paris a fifteen-minute ride to the train station cost us six Euros. This was less than five minutes by car and from his feigning ignorance about the address I was sure he was smarter than he let on. We walked. It took us fifteen minutes.

When we got to the hotel the receptionist barked out the room wasn't ready until 1:30. We said fine, but wanted to leave our bags. I asked to use the restroom and went to find it. When I got back we left and walked down the street to a McDonalds for some orange juice and water. On the way Diana told me that the woman at the desk told her she couldn't sit on the steps to the hotel while I was in the restroom.

"What?" She had come out and told Diana she had to move. There was no waiting room, reception, or any place, other than a desk, and small hallway for our luggage. Yet, this had been the instruction.

Diana and I remembered we needed to wear long pants so we finished our drinks, sat in the air conditioning for fifteen minutes, and went back to change our cloths, so we could adhere to the Vatican's dress code. We had forgotten to do this earlier not thinking of dress codes while traveling.

I noticed that in the short amount of time we left and returned, our bags had already been moved. A lock seemed like a good idea.

As we walked down the street Diana told me she couldn't find a way to flush the hotels toilet. I explained, with a laugh, that the toilets have a button in the wall. She was looking for a handle. I was laughing gleefully at the thought of the nasty receptionist being the next to use the facility.

Shortly we returned to the train station, found the correct place to buy the three days pass and bought four one-way tickets to the Vatican.

In Paris we made the mistake of buying a three-day metro pass only to need it to get from the train station to the hotel. The second day we planned an all-day city tour, so we didn't need the pass then either. This time we figured we'd get the three-day pass but use it the last three days of our five day stay. The bus ride to the Vatican was like riding in the back of a pickup truck, bouncing over every bump, the streets were so rough that there must be a need for special shock absorbers on the buses here.

"This is like a bus I had to ride in Medellin, Colombia", Diana noted. We laughed at the rough ride as everyone sat bouncing an inch or so off their seats in perfect unison. What seemed like a life-time, merely fifteen minutes later, we exited the bus. The columns of Saint Peter's were visible from between two buildings.

Entering the huge plaza put an expression of awe on Diana's face. This was my fifth time to Rome, but I was equally impressed each time. The grand open plaza was dotted with people coming and going. The heat was unbearable and across the plaza I could see the queue for entering the church. Of course the line was in direct sun light and it took us twenty minutes as we sweltered in the heat.

Babies were crying and parents soothed their children. The rest of us, like sheep, followed the zigzag line into the shade where the metal detectors and x-ray machines screened us and our backpacks.

I made a rhetorical comment questioning, "Why don't they just ask us for our guns?". One guy who got the joke told his girlfriend in German what I had said. She chuckled just long enough to get serious again before she was screened.

We met another woman from Norway who had lived in New York. We chatted as we passed in to the baking sun. This was purgatory before entering the pearly gates.

These kinds of public screenings are more invasions of privacy than for the sake of public safety. Humanity has lost its dignity because of the perpetuation of fear and propaganda. Forcing the public to fry in the heat, while there was ample shade, it is a real violation of everyone's being. We were all equally offended by the invasion of personal space and relative comfort, being forced into the glaring sun and asked a string of ridicules questions. It all seemed so unnecessary since the odds of any sort of incident were remote, at best. In a place that should be as open and free as possible the authorities show no faith in humanity (or God for that matter). We have let a part of reality fall into the guise of police work, with policies that only instill more madness into the system of public safety. It is all fear based and it is all hype compared to the actual number of loonies walking around with concealed weapons. A follower of Christ having to be screened to enter a place of worship is seriously wrong. I am equally certain that Christ would have the people with guns (security) get the hell out of his house, just as He chased away the moneychangers.

It was a brief wait to the next pause at the entrance where women were told to cover their shoulders and legs while men were allowed into the basilica with exposed knees in shorts. The hypocrisy was laughable. I also got a little chuckle from the Muslim women dresses in long robes who were allowed to pass through while the Europeans were screened by security. Nuns in full habit, covered like the Muslim woman, were allowed through without screening as well. The Vatican has a very business-minded set of people running it. The women that are "rejected" went to one side and forced to buy very expensive scarves to cover their shoulders, for the mere price of an airline ticket.

I remember back in 1965, when my mother and sisters had to cover their heads to enter Saint Peter's. I was told to remove my hat while priests and Jewish tourists were allowed to go into the church wearing a head covering. Would they allow the Hebrews to enter? If Jesus wore a Yarmulke would he be allowed into his own house? The extent of the dress code had me wondering if there is really an appropriate way to dress for worshiping. If security authorities could figure out a way to monitor the prayers going up to heaven they might have a set of rules for that as well. God forgive me for being so cynical, but aware.

I had promised Denis and Carol in Ireland I would light a candle for them in Saint Peter's. I couldn't complete my dear friends' wishes. Nowhere was the public allowed to light a candle. There was a small side chapel so I said a prayer there. Diana was far ahead of me in that category. She was praying the second we entered the basilica.

In a moment of silent respect I heard Diana mention how much wealth was expressed when so many poor are living in the world. A church is a business. The church is a spiritual house. There is confusion as to when and where business is not appropriate because spiritual matters are without monetary value. We will be judged for all these matters!

By no means am I saying that Saint Peter's isn't beautiful. I actually see more value in the contribution of art to the spiritual quests than the hoarding of gold and property.

Of course, saying the church helps the poor. But the calling of Saint Francis to live a life of poverty, and mirror the true Christ, hasn't been followed. Christ didn't die to start an institution. We, his followers, have grossly misconstrued His intentions.

Rome is a beautiful contradiction of past and present, organization and chaos, cleanliness and refuse. Diana says the city and people are more like those of her own country than any place in Europe.

The Romans are rowdy; from the people that run the bus tours to the shopkeepers. Today we took the "On-Off Tour". I found a package of garbage sitting on the seat in front of us. Some new customers got on board and moved the package of orange peels and plastic. The new passengers set the garbage on the cooler where the woman who sells tickets kept bottled water. She came over to get a customer some water and got angry when she saw someone had put garbage on her cooler.

Right away, I said it was mine trying to appease her by moving it away. But that didn't matter. She had to discuss this with the bus driver and let it be known that something was wrong. There is a level of expressive out bursts in the Italians that we noticed the second we got into the train station. It's a kind of emotional state that is contagious just from being here.

We did the entire tour, staying on the bus for one whole cycle, and then got off at the bus station, where we entered the tour two and a half hours earlier. The tour rode past all the famous landmarks of Rome; the Coliseum, Saint Peter's, the ruins, etc. We walked for several blocks trying to find a street market we had seen on the bus.

We found a wholesale district where the Chinese had many shops selling clothes, shoes, and purses. In one shop I began to play with a little boy. He was very short in western cloths, but with a bowel haircut and slivered eyes below. I was fanning myself with a fan I found on the bus, when the boy walked by I fanned him. He immediately took a stiff pose and thus the play-acting began. He had a shield and was pretending to be a Kung Fu expert. As Diana discussed prices and the size of shoes I was dancing around the store with the son of the shopkeeper. This went on for about five minutes as he and I pretended to battle each other, twisting and turning in spinning motions. When Diana was done I bowed to him and shook his hand. We parted as instant and eternal friends.

A few blocks later we entered a market. Diana suggested not using a camera. My reply was that living in fear is no way to enjoy life. I got some great pictures. I asked at several fish stalls if I was permitted to photograph. No one turned me down. What most intrigued me about the market were the multiplied ethnicities. The fish mongers were mostly Pakistani or Indians. The fruit vendors were other Middle Eastern peoples. The Italians were there too, all the other nationalities were yelling in Italian, selling their wares. I loved it. Every one, or most people, looked anything but Italian, yet we were hearing all these people speak Italian. As we exited I commented that "was real and very nice to see". We were the only tourists for blocks.

(It's always good practice to ask permission to photograph people. This is common courtesy all over the world. It is also common to buy goods or tip the people you photograph since you are taking their image. Buying seems to work best because they understand a real exchange has also taken place.)

We soon found a store where Diana bought a handbag. The woman selling took Diana to a far room in the store.

I began to hear what sounded like a game show in Chinese. Behind the counter, out of sight were two young Chinese men in their early twenties watching a TV game show on a computer. I asked if the show was from China, they nodded yes. Here we are thousands of miles away from China and these people are watching a show as if they are sitting in Beijing. Technology brings all cultures is closer than we think. My assumption was this was a kind of MTV show for the young Chinese, yet almost no different from a US game show. This reminded me that the world is not just inside the US borders. Asia is just a mouse click away.

Diana and I walked into a soda shop after wandering a bit. It was boiling hot outside in the heat. As we entered we heard a loud bang from a car whose radiator exploded from the heat. A blonde woman standing at a corner turned to look at the commotion. She had very expressive curves, large full breasts, long blonde hair, and the face of a man. After she left I said to the man behind the counter that she was man. He agreed.

I asked the man if he was from Iran. He said yes. "In my country we don't have transsexuals.", he said.

"Yes, and according to Ahmadinejad you don't have homosexuals in Iran either". We both began to laugh at the lunacy of such a statement. I told him I had lived there in 1965 for three months.

"This was the time of the Shah. Yes, this was a good time to see Iran". I told him that his current president and my president (Bush) are crazy. We began to laugh again.

Diana and I drank an orange soda and watched the two Chinese men outside in the heat open the hood of their car, pondering how to repair the radiator. Soon we were off walking and seeking the market we never found.

We returned to the bus station and went to get some cash from an ATM machine. As we stood there two young girls were speaking in Spanish on the pay phone. As I was getting money, Diana was listening in to their conversation. Apparently both girls had just been pick-pocketed on the bus from Saint Peter's. They were calling home to Mexico to inform their mother that all their money and passports were gone. I was a little amazed how Diana had picked up so much information just while I was punching in my security code to get the cash. They were in a state of shock so Diana in her usual, helpful manor began to console the girl that was standing next to the older sister on the phone. In a crowded bus some skillful thieves had robbed them. We have heard and saw notices all over the city to watch out for pickpockets. We pulled out some money and gave them a bit of relief until their parents could wire them money on Monday when the Embassy opens.

Five years ago, some quick thieves stole my backpack in Costa Rica. I was waiting in a bus station. One guy distracted me with small talk while the other one slid by and lifted my pack. All my money, airline tickets, passport, legal papers for my property, and two years of journal writings were stolen in two seconds. I got on the bus after running around the station and letting everyone waiting for the bus know that I had just been robbed. A stranger on the bus gave me twenty dollars. In eternal gratitude I gave more than that to the two girls. We were furious at the low-life people who would be so bad as to rip off tourists.

Diana said later that those people would find what was coming to them in the way of Karma. She is not vengeful, just aware of the laws of the universe. That is only one of the many reason why I love my wife.

We re-boarded the tour bus and went through half the tour this time. I struck up a conversation with a woman from Texas. I asked her if she was Bush fan. "Yes, I am". Diana kept silent the whole time, just listened. The woman went on about how the "Illegal Mexicans are getting a hand-out". I said I taught "illegals" in school and believed there needs to be a way to help educate people. (Diana noted later how proud she was of my response.) There is a way I speak with those whose views differ from mine which is to find middle ground, and a way to make the conversation polite, despite my thinking that these people all have a mean streak and a selfish attitude.

I asked her if she really believed we should have invaded Iraq. "If we didn't, they would be killing us at home", was her answer.

I know regardless of all facts people still insist that the enemy is out there to get us, and we have to bomb them first. I was very polite but told her I felt we had created a worse enemy by our actions. It was pointless to get into it any further and luckily for us the bus came to our stop. I said good-bye and Diana and I talked about how the prejudice toward Mexicans was obvious. This

Republican woman would have never in a million years helped the two young Mexican women with what she would have called a "hand-out". I was glad to be away from the anger and agenda of such a person. "It all about me", was written all over her face.

We walked past very expensive, exclusive shops where the women we had just left on the bus should have been shopping. Diana likes to tease me and tell me she demands to be pampered with the goods in such stores.

"Why don't you treat me well like a good husband, and buy me a purse in here?", as we walk past Gucci. A pair of sunglasses would cost me a day's wages in such a place. The closest we came to the "royalty" was when we went into a fancy restaurant where Fellini's portrait hung on the wall. We used the restrooms on the suggestion of the police in the plaza. Imagine; I wed the same restroom as Fellini! Maybe even the same toilet! That's about as close as I want to come to knowing him. It was the portrait of a dead man that told me someone was cashing in on someone else's success.

We made it back to our hotel room, and then ate a terrible dinner of tuna, cheese, and rolls. We laughed at how hungry we were so the food didn't matter. Diana knows we are spending a lot of money and never complains. I think we are about one thousand dollars over budget and we have two more weeks to go, not to mention the week in Colombia at the end of August. We only live like this because we know it is worth every penny. Fortunately, none of it is putting us in debt, credit card or otherwise.

As much as I don't like working I do like the summers off and the adventures we can live. While Diana has been sleeping, the TV is on. It is a very bazaar U.S.A. show. The people are speaking in Italian, look like Americans, and the plot is so bad, and predictable, that I don't need to know the language to understand the plot. Life is strange but beautiful. What will tomorrow bring?

Day Three: Our day started around ten. In passing, we began to speak to one of the cleaning women. We had seen her in the mornings and exchanged greetings before. This morning we asked for some additional towels. The woman, Theodora, came into the room and the conversation spun off into many directions, our professions, where we had lived, and my (partial) Italian heritage.

I told Theodora about my musical recordings and her eyes light up. It turned out she is an opera singer, just recently laid off from a prestigious Italian troupe. She asked us if we'd like to hear a little song. Right then and there, she slide the room's door shut and sprang into song. It was beautiful and so personal that we were a bit shocked. She was open with us about her loss of a job, but offered us a mini-concert. We were both very touched. Theodora held her large body arched and poised as if on stage. Her song drew up from some unseen part of her lungs and gave a deep sustaining vocal tone. We had no idea what she sang; only aware it was in Italian.

She reopened the door and motioned that her employers weren't the nicest of people, that she could be fired for such artistic expression. I thought that strange and sad at the same time. Here, an obvious talent was eking out a living cleaning a hotel, yet such creative bursts were outlawed. After that we exchanged email addresses and spoke the few remaining time our paths crossed. But every Christmas and Easter we get an email from her wishing us happiness. This is the sole personal encounter in Rome that has continued to this day.

Outside the hotel and around the corner Diana found a booth where a man from Bangladesh was selling glass (Morano) pendant jewelry. She bought seven or eight of these beautiful glass necklaces. She bought so many the man gave her an extra one free. It was fun to see how excited she got about buying all these gifts for her family and friends.

Soon we were walking to the train station when Diana found a stall where another Bangladeshi was selling sunglasses. She bought a pair. We took the Metro to a stop that was for an art museum. We never found the museum. We walked until we returned to the Fountain of Trevi. We had gone there our first night in Rome. I told Diana the legend of throwing the coin over ones shoulder and it guaranteed that we'd return some day. I didn't know it would be the second day we were in Rome. Does that count as a real return? We did return and Diana bought more jewelry. This time it was for her mother. I liked them so much I bought a tiny pendant for myself. They were made of glass with brilliant colorful flowers in a design the size of a nickel.

There is one bad thing about Rome. It is so big. On every corner there is someone lost looking at a map. In Paris and Vienna we couldn't get lost, but in Rome it happened the minute we left the subway. It was happening to everyone, everywhere, all day. It is confusing to come here because there is so much history in every building each one is special. The big attractions get lost in pursuit of finding them. I have mixed feelings about this place. We feel that Paris was the best so far. Rome is an emotional upheaval.

Day Four: We are on the train bound for Ancona. It is seven-thirty at night. I have found an electrical outlet for the computer so I am very happy to have this time to write. Ancona is the port from which we leave tomorrow at around 11. It was a scorcher today. We knew the heat would beat us before we even left the hotel, so we took our time packing and watching a TV show about Leonardo, in Italian of course. I have learned so much Spanish that I can understand a fair amount of Italian. I think I can anyway. There are many words that are similar to English as well.

The day we arrived at the hotel the woman receptionist wouldn't let Diana sit on the steps. I mentioned to the receptionist on the third day, how now we understood because a new sign was put up which read, "It is strictly forbidden to sit on the steps". (The use of English can be very harsh at times.) The night receptionist explained that there was a crazy woman that lived in the building and she would scream when people sat on the step. I'm assuming this woman has been there forever and that people sat on the steps smoking and making their presence known at any hour to the locals. I mentioned to the day receptionist that we now understood the situation.

When I was returning the key this morning she stated to me that we could wait in the reception room if we wanted to come. Somehow the conversation turned to the first day when Diana was told to move. The woman explained that she told Diana that she could move to the waiting room in the basement. I told the woman that Diana didn't understand this because she is learning English. The receptionist then commented that she was wondering why Diana gave her such a strange look. I know Diana was pretty angry at the whole event at the time. While we were walking, a few blocks away, I told Diana about the conversation with the receptionist. At first she was a bit put off by my mentioning this at all. I know the woman wasn't lying or she wouldn't have mentioned the perplexed look on Diana's face. (It was really an angry look.) I approached it in a way that explained that people of different cultures constantly misunderstand each other. Couple this misunderstanding with the passionate emphatic way Italians express themselves. It can come across as being curt.

Frequently we have marital mishaps caused by "language and grammatical faux pas". Despite our love for each other, Diana and I suffer gross miscommunications. We are at the mercy of our language barrier, often having to opt for English since she is much stronger in her second language than I. However, when people embellish stories for their own benefit it is not only difficult to verify what was stated, it makes me question my wife's credibility solely based on language comprehension which can be quite a sore spot. I should trust Diana more. Mea culpa.

I was hoping to write the entire three hours on the train tonight. Instead we met a wonderful Italian couple named Johnny and Anna Maria. They have just returned from a two-week stay in Turkey. Anna Maria is a religion teacher in a public school.

Anna Maria was an attractive middle sized woman with brown hair just below her ears. She looked like a school teacher. Johnny was a balding man with horn rimmed glasses, a round nose and round cheeks framing a wide smile.

A few casual exchanges of words erupted into a deeply engaging conversation that covered years and miles of our respective lives.

I never asked Johnny what he did but his hobby is photography. He showed me some shots and his camera. His camera was a big Nikon. I showed him my medium size Olympus. I couldn't imagine lugging around such hefty equipment. Mine is difficult enough. I actually get backaches from carrying my cameras all day.

We spent a couple of hours chatting in Spanish, English, and Italian, the four of us talking in bits and pieces of each other's languages communicating beautifully. I was speaking Spanish, Diana knows a little Italian from classes in school, Anna Maria knew a few English words, and Johnny knew a couple of English words, but we had a grand time getting to know each other. I showed them my first book on the computer with the art and photographs. Then he showed me the photographs of their visit to Turkey.

The topic shifted to all the old music. Johnny and I got a big laugh at naming names and noting the different pronunciations of the bands names in the two languages. Led Zeppelin, Cream, the Beatles all had name-sounds that I'd never heard before. Then we talked about Blues players like B.B. King and Muddy Waters. Our eyes lit up as we tossed names back and forth trying to figure out what strange pronunciations in Italian were in English. Before we knew it they had to get off at their stop. I gave them our email address and we hope to get some emails back and forth. It was a wonderful brief visit. We have kept in touch and email back and forth. We found new friends!

When we pulled into Ancona we saw beautiful beaches. Diana complained that I had scheduled the tickets so late in the day we could not enjoy the beach, as if I did this with spiteful intentions. That set off a ridiculous volley of words. The kind only married couples would ever tolerate. By the time we crossed the street from the train station to our hotel, the feud had evolved into silent anger. I couldn't insist, "I need a vacation". I was on my vacation! The hotel bed and our near exhaustion was the only solution to our impasse.

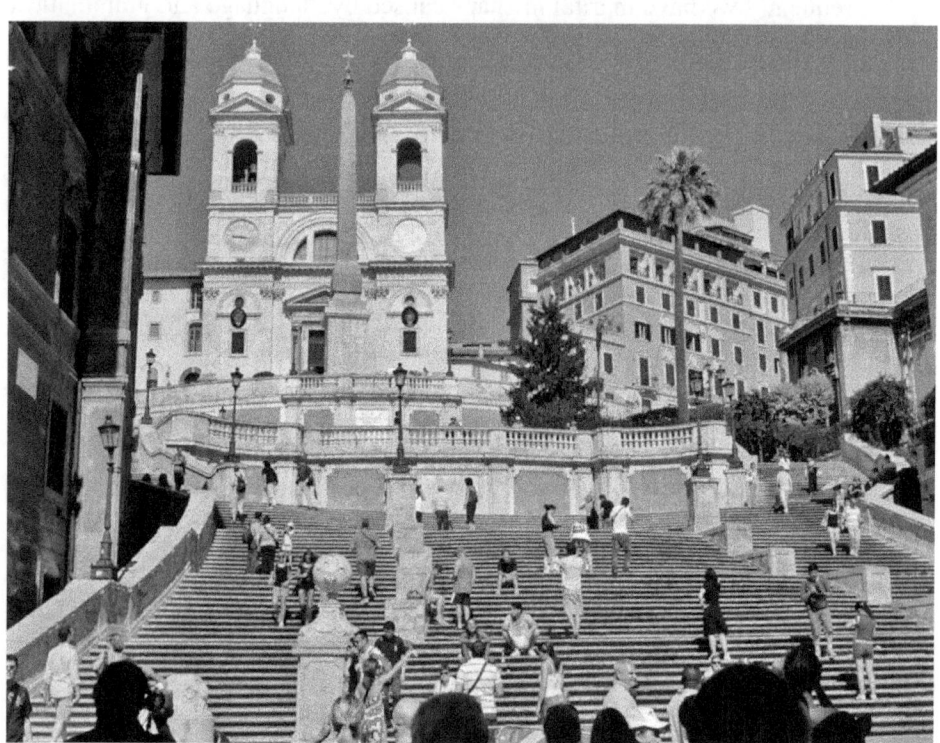

Chapter Seven
Greece

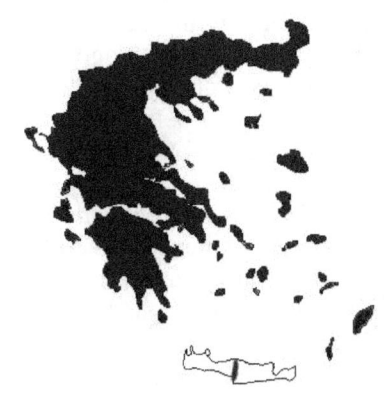

We are riding on a ferry and have just passed between the mouths of land that leads into the Greek landscape. There is a strong haze which covers the land on both sides of the boat cloaked in a gray mist. It looks hot and yet feels cooler on the boat because of the breeze. The ferry is very modern and nice. In order to avoid the expense while on the trip, we bought all our food before we left Ancona, Italy. The best deal on the boat is a huge bottle of cold water for one and half Euro. Everything else is too costly.

I don't like to procrastinate, so we left early yesterday to get our tickets for a 1:30 departure. It was 9:30 in the morning when we left the hotel in Italy. We had to make sure we returned for a noon check out. Things didn't go that way.

I made a big mistake by walking on a viaduct to the port. The hotel clerk told us to go into the port, but not how. We walked for forty-five minutes and got back to the very same road, which lead into the port. This was really a coastal road that ran alone between the port and the city. I stupidly walked, and dragged Diana along with me, to a viaduct that ran over the railroad tracks to a no-man's land of warehouses where nothing green grew. I asked one man who was walking. He said the ferry was twenty minutes away by foot. It was a hot, dry, and oddly lifeless environment. Trucks whizzed by, but seldom a passenger car was to be seen. Human feces were dried on the thin concrete walk on the viaduct and nearby the smell of a dead animal (or maybe human) was wafting up from an area with dead, brown brush.

The short morning was already becoming difficult. Diana wasn't happy walking in such a barren place. Sweat was dripping off our brows. We asked many times to find the ferry as we came across fishing boats where idle fishermen sat at plastic tables smoking and drinking. A bus ran along the same road, which would have put us in the port in a matter of five minutes, but I set us off on a wild goose chase while time was dwindling away.

A woman at the ferry counter told us we had been over charged by 150 Euro by the travel agency that I used back in the USA. Through a tiny, thin window I had to bow down and listen as she explained that we should call the agency in Greece and ask for a discount that was provided because we had the Eurail pass. I thought I was required to show the train pass, thinking we already had a discount. It was 250 Euro for the trip versus 75(about $150US difference), so I thought it was worth the effort to make the change. The agent was very nice about looking out for us.

We bought a phone card, which took fifteen minutes. An old man helped us figure out how to use it. To call, or use the phones in Europe is not easy because of the system and language. I can't read Italian and the man who sold us the phone card couldn't help, other than a few words in English. We returned three times to the seller before an old man standing nearby offered to help. The phone rang and rang. No answer. It was getting late so I went back to the woman at the thin air-conditioned window and bought the tickets at full price. They had actually been charged already to the credit card. She gave me the number of her main office in Athens and said to call them.

We returned to the hotel and I went into an Internet cafe and tried to call the company where I had booked passage. This time a man answered and gave me the usual poor customer service to which, sadly I have become quite accustomed. I gave him all the information and he repeated it back to me at a snail's pace. I finally began to get loud and aggressive after this runaround where he informed me that the ferry company offered no discounts for the rail pass. I was getting really angry as he read the "small print" and stalled me.

"Are you calling me a liar, I just told you that I was at the ferry company and they said I was entitled to a discount." He then told me I could not cancel anything by phone but needed to send an email. I got very nasty.   " W o u l d you like me to give you to one of our supervisors?"

"Yes, because you are doing nothing but wasting my time!" I yelled back. I got a supervisor who was a bit more helpful, there was no mention that there was no discount, but I needed to call back in one hour so I could speak to the actual agent who had booked passage two months earlier. She also had to go to a filing cabinet and get the actual transaction records. Yes, call back in an hour, even though the ferry leaves in an hour and a half. I said I'd call back in 45 minutes, which I did.

In the meantime, we ran into the hotel, got our bags out of the room. Diana sat in the lobby as I rapidity walked three blocks to a supermarket to buy food for the boat ride. It was now noon and we had at least checked out of the hotel room on time. I rushed back to the hotel gave Diana the food bags and went back to the Internet shop to call Greece again. The boat was leaving in forty-five minutes. The woman had not offered me her phone number the first time, but I wisely got the direct number and her name. This time she was prepared to help me, all she could. She would call the ferry office in Ancona, speak with them, cancel the original credit card order, but I had to return to the ticket office and reprocess the new tickets. At this point it is useless to point out the absurd way business is done in an age of computers, but I said nothing. I was going to save 150 Euro. I was polite to her, but the first male agent was completely incompetent.

We took the bus back to the port with our bags and got there fifteen minutes before the boat left, purchased the new tickets, and took a shuttle van to the boat. We rolled the luggage up to an escalator, showed our tickets, and stepped into a wave of air conditioning that made me think I would forget what every had just happened to us. (As detailed as this may all seem, this is an example of how crazy it can be to travel.)

Two porters in red suits greeted us and we were told to go to the reception desk where our tickets were validated. The tickets became our pass into the sleeping dorm. We walked too far to find an elevator but the air conditioning and soft background music, coupled with the smell of food, made us feel civil again. We had made it, saved a lot of money, used the system to our advantage, and we went gliding across the carpeted floors to large lockers and tiny bunk beds; six in a compartment, three high on each side.

We made a new home for the next 21 hours. My suggestion is to always book direct with ferry companies, not agencies, or otherwise overpay.

The boat's plush decor was such a contrast from the scorching heat it made us feel we were stepping into instant comfort. The passengers were Muslims in long robes, teenagers of all nationalities running around, Greeks, Italians, you name it. We saw a variety of TV parlors, bars, and restaurants. The atmosphere was definitely that of being on holiday.

Right away I met an architect named Sid who was very friendly. Upon our third encounter I finally introduced myself and he introduced me to his girlfriend. She was from France. He was from India. They both lived in Edinburgh, Scotland and were going to Greece, then eventually back to India. We talked about the way the media has exploited the war in Iraq and the perceptions they promote in most news companies. He claimed the news media exaggerate the problem in Kashmir to his home country.

I said it was never going to work when governments split up territories like in Palestine, North Ireland, Korea, and Kashmir. These solutions are the very simple; share the land. No one owns land really. An artificial line on a map doesn't work. The same goes with the line between the USA and Mexico. The United Sates is going to have to figure out that people are coming for economic reasons and they should be allowed to enter and work. Who can blame them? Ultimately the governments need to create work cards. If a person is a convicted criminal they should be deported, but really the rest of the people immigrate for good, wholesome reasons, and we should be honored they want to be a part of our "dream".

I think back every so often of the woman in Rome on the tour bus.

"If we don't go over there and get them, they will be in our land killing us." This is mine and this isn't yours. Keep out. If you think you can get a handout forget it! I doubt many Mexicans come to the USA thinking, "Oh boy free lunch". "I won't have to sweat for hours all day working at a back breaking, labor intensive job. I can just get over that border and milk the system, send money home, and be a parasite on the tax payers of the USA."

We arrived at our port, Patras, in twenty minutes and have decided to go get our luggage organized now. To catch up with the writing later is on my agenda as well.

The hotel in Ancona, Italy was directly across the street from the train station. When we arrived there we walked directly into our hotel. In Patras, Greece it had been very similar, booking hotels while looking on the Internet maps and finding close locations in terms of proximity to the ports or trains was important. We rolled down the ramp on to the port. I asked a taxi driver where the hotel was. He pointed it out to me. He spoke in English and didn't try to cheat us like the Roman taxi drivers. First we walked one block to the train station and to buy our tickets for the next day.

"It is free." "Free?" "Yes, there is no charge." We had shown him the Eurail pass, so we assumed that's the reason. Unless there is some kind of free event, we are guessing that we can just come over one block from the hotel and jump onto the train without a reservation. The man took great effort in writing out the times the train goes to Kalamata; 6 AM, noon, and 5 PM. Greek hospitality welcomed us. No one was yelling and the personal tone was vastly different from the arrival in Italy.

We then stepped to the next window, which was for information and asked where the hotel was (always get a couple of directions.) We were told to go to the square turn right, and it was on the corner. We did that but we should have been told to turn left at the square. We stepped into a liquor store where an elderly man took us outside and pointed to the hotel on the opposite side of the square. It was across the street from the train station. He said he was seventy years old and that he could still see all the street signs. Meaning, we must be blind to not see the hotel name. But he was joking and I gave him a big handshake in thanks. His wife was equally as old. She gave him his eyeglasses to read the name we had written of our email. I don't know why we did that because the likelihood of them using a computer was nil.

The liquor store looked like it was something out of the past. The shelves were all half empty and the place hadn't been remodeled since their marriage some fifty (plus) years ago. They both gave us sweet smiles from their wrinkled mouths. As if they understood love and marriage. They stood next to each other like two that had never stepped more than a few feet away from one another. They were both ancient with tanned weathered skin, short, in clean clothes that were two generations old. Seeing one without the other seemed impossible to imagine. On the wall hung a photograph of their wedding day, we explained we were newlyweds. As if this was some common bond, it was. We were in a new country.

As we walked into the hotel Diana already said three times she liked the place. "It reminds me of Cartagena". This is a port city in Colombia on the Caribbean coast. We didn't care for Rome as much as we thought we would. I'm sure we had some false expectations or this wouldn't have happened. The worst part was the heat and the size of the city. Here everything is in a short distance. We got right into our room, after a five-minute wait. Right away, we disrobed, began to wash clothing and then hang them from our fourth floor balcony. While Diana washed the clothes I rung them out and hung them to dry. The clothes weren't visible from the street. The beautiful view in front of us is a huge port with blue sky, Mediterranean-blue waters, and a breeze that will dry the cloths in no time. Several big ferries are parked right outside our window in the port.

I couldn't figure out the air conditioning right away so I asked the cleaning woman. The doors all have to be shut, or the electricity shuts off the power to the

AC. The room key also has to be placed into a special socket where the key turns on all the power for the room.

Diana is taking a nap while I write on the computer and soon we'll be on the streets for our day in Patras. I then plugged in all the electric devices to charge them up and be ready for picture taking. We were in our travel routine.

Greece is beautiful. The people have faces like road maps. They are worn and weathered and show many years of sunny skies and blue seas. Their hair is dark black, or gray from the years. Men wear bold mustaches and stubbed sea capes. Elderly women who are widows wear all black. The hot white sun makes these women stand out in strong contrasts. As they pass the shadows they look like dark spirits contrasted against the bleached walls. The architecture is a shade of white or tan. This may be because the Greeks learned centuries ago that it was pointless to fight the suns power. The sun will make anything pale. The rocks on the coast are pale, almost snow like. This makes the sea bluer than usual. The white rocks extend below the water's surface and reflect the cloudless sky. Everything feels exaggerated because of the sun and its heat. Even the youth seem tempered by the heats dominance. Their energy is less than other Northern European children. They know how to conserve their youthful outbursts as their calls mix with the heat and wind. The shadows of trees and buildings pull their voices down and cool them by measurable decibels. The heat doesn't allow for loudness, car and motorcycles are muffled by the heat. The clear blue sky is the only cooling element. But it is an illusion because the sun is always standing center stage, ready to burn anyone who walks into the street and heat. Thus is Greece, a place where green isn't green, but sun-baked green, or olive green.

After a three-hour rest, we went out into the Greek heat. It was so hot that our perspiration dried on our foreheads. The hotel is right next to the main town square facing the port. From the town square we walked straight up the center of this small city. This is a street with many restaurants and no cars are allowed, there is a broad pedestrian walkway. At the end of this walkway the street narrowed for a few blocks, and not far up an incline, a long set of stairs went directly up a hill to a large fortress. We could see the walls and headed up the steep steps. We took many breaks in our ascent because the heat was draining us of all energy. In a small park at the top of the stairs there was a young couple kissing on a swing in the shade. We walked further around the long wall, around the corner, to the entrance of the castle. It was closed. Along our way I saw a church on a side street so we headed in that direction.

The church was a small replica of San Sophia in Istanbul. The grand mosque had a tiny cousin with four cornered spires and one large dome in the center. What takes up huge city blocks in Turkey is only one city block in this small church. When we entered the shadows in our eyes fell away, we beheld a magnificent Greek Orthodox Church. The walls were filled with mosaics from the life of Christ. Vast, ornate candelabras hug from the ceilings and lead the eye to the dome where a grand mosaic of Christ with his hand in a sign of peace. The church interior is surrounded by icons in ornate frames standing on easels. These paintings of the saints framed behind glass. The paintings are not flat but where the head-halo of the saint sits a layer of silver is added to give the work dimension.

As we entered, there was a young man seated behind a desk, who offered candles for sale. We greeted him. He recounted the history of the church, how it had been occupied by the Turks then turned into a mosque. Years later, he adds, the Turks were driven from Greece and the church building returned being a Christian church. I photographed the church and Diana explored the interior as the young man spoke with another patron. We circled back to reopen the conversation. It was the church's "birthday". The church had blue and white ribbons hanging as well as other types of garlands where flowers circled the icons.

We had a lengthy conversation about the history of the church and how the Roman Catholics had split it up. He explained the Crusades were an attempt for the Roman Catholic Church to regain the rule of the Holy Lands, but it never happened. The Greek Orthodox Church filled that void not the Roman Catholic Church. The young man explained the five divisions of the Christian church that have been in place since the beginning. As we spoke an elderly, thin man came up and began to speak with the younger man. This second man was throwing in a few words that seemed understandable even if I don't speak Greek. The word "Catholic" kept coming up in a thick Greek verbal roll. The man was not speaking in a manner that was gentle. In fact, he wouldn't even make eye contact with me although I was next to him. This conversation went on for at least five minutes as we waited for the man to leave. When he did I asked what the conversation was about. "He was telling me I should be very strict and truthful in my explanation of the church to you". Diana and I both knew from the tone of this man's voice that he was speaking about us in a negative and threatening way. I don't consider myself Catholic (because the Catholic Church doesn't consider me one of their own because of my divorce), but I found it strange that a man who neither knew Diana, or me, considered us infidels and Christians.

On three occasions, on the boat the night before, I had small conversation with a Muslim man. Yet never did I experience the same kind of bitterness as in the "Christian" man. One of my points in conversation with this young man was how Jesus Christ's message is so simple, most people follow dogma more than the simple truth. I wasn't out to change anybody, but rather ask questions and learn. Every one of every faith thinks they have the key, but God has many faces and speaks in many tongues. People are complicated, God isn't.

We walked down the hill, street by street in an aimless southerly direction toward the coast. The streets were clean with sharp granite curbs; the condition of the asphalt was strong and well kept, unlike other European cities. I had seen on a map on the Internet that there was a very large church on the south side of the town. The woman at the hotel's desk also told us of the church, and the castle we tried to enter at the top of the cities hill as well. The church we sought was no disappointment. It was very large and the decorations and design was a treasure to behold. I made video and still photographs of the Greek Orthodox Church, Akti Dymaion. This church was newer than our first church visited. The size was four times larger. Again, the tiles and mosaics with Christ's stories in stylized geometric designs covered most wall surfaces. The chandeliers were immense and made of metal hanging on chains from the ceiling. Like all these churches a huge mosaic of Christ faced looking down on those below. The church was so magnetic that we spent a good hour looking at the mosaic and framed icons distributed around the building.

We sauntered back to the hotel in the slow, subsiding afternoon heat, and stopped at a grocery store to stock up on some food for the train ride tomorrow.

Day Two: The morning passed with no glitches. We woke around eight, showered and got ready. Diana had a rash or chicken pox. Big red nodes are developing on her skin. She is in a great deal of pain from scratching. I tell her to leave the patches alone; it will only make things worse. She whines about it and there is nothing I can do to lessen the pain. I process pain in such a different way that I don't reach out to anyone. This makes me feel insensitive to Diana's condition although it deeply affects me inside. The hotel seemed empty. There was no one else at the continental breakfast provided with the room. We sat in a main floor dining room.

We strolled along the road that is parallel to the railroad and harbor. There was a lighthouse at a rocky point and a small park, but the heat was causing Diana to need shade fast. The sun on her skin is causing her additional pain. We returned to the big church we had been the night before. I took pictures as Diana sat still to relieve the pain. The first thing we did after breakfast was get some medicine at the pharmacy. We bought an antihistamine and a skin cream. Diana said the cream made her sting worse. I said it must have been working if there is pain.

The Greek Orthodox Churches have no statues in contrast to Catholic churches. Instead there are icons encased in glass. The people kiss the icons and you can see lip marks on all the glass surfaces protecting the icons. The walls of these churches are covered in paintings, or mosaics, of Christ's life. I asked the young man the day before why Christ was never smiling, always serious. I told him about a painting I saw in Colombia where a resurrecting Christ was smiling.

"Yes, we have a few smiling Christ's. There is one where half of his face is serious, the other half is smiling."

This is the dual nature of man's interpretation of God, I am assuming. I suppose it would be bad for business if Christ were smiling and selling a product of salvation. We are supposed to be so caught up in saving our soul that there is no room for happiness. But what I feel is missing is just that. Happiness is realizing you have received the Holy Spirit. If you live in light you don't project darkness, sadness, sorrow, or judge others. This is one of my personal observations that keep me wondering where all these ideas come from and how they stick for centuries. Is happiness just a phenomenon of commercialism in the new centuries?

Right now we are on a small train heading south. Outside the train, as I write, the blonde, dry grass is shaded by small green olive trees. There is a scarcity of water and everything looks parched, not green.

As we pull into each town there is a conductor standing outside near the tracks. On his head is a red hat, in his hand a round sign. If there is someone waiting for the train the conductor holds up the sign indicating the train needs to stop. If no one is there, a green sign to keep going. I haven't figured out how passengers stop the train or let the conductor know they need to depart. We are the last stop so we don't have to do anything but watch the scenery and luggage. It is up above the heads of everybody else so it is easy to keep in sight. I asked a young man to help lift our luggage into the overhead rack.

The train left the station as we moved through Patras, slower than automobile the traffic. I said this must be why it will take us three hours to get to Kalamata. But soon, outside the city limits, we were clipping alone at a fast speed. In fact, it's not easy to write on the laptop. There is a lot of rock and roll going on and it isn't the music I'm listening to in my earphones. The train is short and very modern, clean, and spacious inside; most importantly air-conditioned.

As people get off at the stops they nod to other people in the small towns. They've all know each other for years. Lives pass in these small places, icons are kissed millions of times, death and birth are in a cycle of churning romance and sorrow. It is so hot outside no one wants to stand in the sun for long. The side of the street with shadows occupies where foot traffic takes place. A couple of men are waiting in a train station they sit and conserve energy. Nothing is happening except the sun and his burning reminder that light is to be feared because it is heat. Light is torture. Too much happiness is a sure sign of a lost soul. Stay in the shade, suffer from the heat, but make sure the rays of the sun don't consume you. Too much light is a tragedy; too much awareness is a sure sign of lost salvation. Never question anything, just accept answers. Even if the answer of salvation is so simple a child gets the equation, let dogma stand like a stone wall. How dare you think you have God inside you? You are not worthy. The train door is stuck closed and the people at the fifteen-minute stop can't re-enter the train. At first the conductor panics, walks away, then goes back, and gives the door a slam with both firsts. Boom, the gates of paradise open and the lost souls are floating back on board into the air conditioning; saved souls. A new male passenger entered the train. He has been working all morning. His cloths are soiled, his hands are dirty, and he is in air conditioning as the train pulls away toward salvation. No wonder hell was invented in Greece.

Diana is looking out the window at the flat farmland. The land reminds me of Southern California. Here we are in the cradle of civilization, speeding toward an unknown city suggested by my co-worker. She says there are no tourists. Our hotel is across the street from a beach. I want to write and paint a portrait of Diana that needs finishing. It was started in Denmark. That is the last time we have any real down time. I just want down time and planned this six-day stay, in the middle of nowhere, to have a place to decompress. There is a lot of stress related to travel. About a half hour before our train departed I began to feel my blood pressure rising, even if the train seat was five minutes, (really!) from our room.

In the morning we walked out a back door of the hotel, across the street, through the station and into our seats. That close, that quick. I even went back inside the station to get a ticket, which wasn't necessary because we had the rail pass. For once the pass seemed like a real bargain. All we had to do was show the pass and it was FREE! (Sort of, other than the initial payment and when there have been additional fees.) We now figure it is still cheaper, by a thousand dollars, to fly. There were eight days where we didn't use the pass because we were in cities sightseeing. Next time we will fly. The problem with flying is that the aircraft usually have to return through London. We both agree if this were to be done again we'd skip Rome and stay longer in Paris. Who knows these things until they are tried?

One of my angriest moments came when Diana was complaining that we didn't leave Rome earlier in the day to see the beach in Ancona. I bought the tickets right away, in the morning when we arrived in Rome, for the trip four days in advance, didn't know that we would want to leave earlier. I explained at the time what I was doing and became indignant when she complained upon our arrival in Ancona at eleven at night. One of my less than compassionate emotional moments comes when feeling a person is complaining about things that can't be undone. I explained to Diana everything I've done in planning the trip was to make it fun and convenient for her. So I got very nasty at her complaints. Next time she can plan a six-week vacation and see if it goes as planned. Traveling is never without hitches, and who can ever plan for stress free relationship? If I knew the days we'd be at odds I'd leave them off the calendar.

But back to a deeper explanation, it is work to travel. To see the world is not all fun and excitement. There is an exhausting effort to absorb all that is being witnessed and getting to the euphoric moments. When we were sitting in the train station in Rome I told Diana I felt like my brain and every nerve of my body was electrified. My senses were so alive I could feel everything and everyone in the motion of life. In my youth I toke recreational drugs for stimulation, and still nothing made me feel as alive as that moment in Paris. A kind of ecstatic happiness was filling me just by observing so much life and activity. Need I say I like traveling? Every possible emotion is geared to a peak.

Right now, in Greece, the train is going so fast and is so empty of people I can hardly write on the keyboard. We think we are nearing Kalamata. The train blows a horn that sounds like a big truck as we pass intersecting roads. This is Greece, Diana feels at home. She says the people and the place feel like Colombia. They are dark skinned and the climate is like the ocean towns of her country, although I think it is much greener in Colombia.

We are still on the train. The conductor, our third, has just informed me we will arrive at five o'clock. We thought it was a three-hour train ride. It is taking much longer. At one stop the conductor got off to buy a pack of cigarettes. The train pulled away without the conductor and I'm thinking to myself, "I wonder if that was supposed to happen?" Sure enough, the train stops a few minutes later, goes into reverse, and goes back to pick him up. All the passengers were laughing at the situation, but by the time the conductor got back on, no one said anything. No one wanted to laugh at him, but it was funny until he returned in sheepish, somber mood. This is life.

The train has passed through three big mountain ranges. They are filled with cacti and low bush. At one juncture the train slowed to a crawl as we passed through some dangerous turns. Some high gorges and very old looking brick bridges was another place of caution. Now we are on a flat plain. The land is greener here, but not much more than the terrain up north. There is an indication of greater rainfall in these parts. The sky has become over cast and we passed through a small rain shower. I like that we are going to a place where nature is wild. We are going to a small, unknown city, unknown to tourists anyway.

Concerning the interpersonal arena I hope to get out of doors here. I also hope to give Diana some space. She and I have been together for almost three weeks without a break, since Denmark. We have these conversations where she accuses me of making all the decisions. It's partially true, but it is also my better ability to get around the "physical world" (as I say, an experienced traveler). Who really leads and who really follows is a big question. The fact that she thinks in those terms makes me wonder how maturity (the age difference) plays into the roles we have in our relationship. I've been the major financial provider and planner for this whole trip.

It was all planned and discussed before we left. The design was to insure that we were not looking for a place to stay when we arrived into a new city. I know from experience that forced, bad, and quick decisions are expensive decisions. I don't really (and admittedly) know how to balance those types of decisions out. It seems one person has to do the planning, or there has to be joint problem solving when decisions are made in split seconds. With every specific hotel and city I asked her where she wanted to go. In one frustrated moment I told her next time she would be the one doing all the planning for hours on the computer. I enjoy putting the puzzle of travel together. It just makes me wonder why she can't enjoy the ride, or does she have to feel like she needs to be in control?

For the last two years I have been the financial provider. I own the car. I buy the gas. I pay for the house and food. I knew full well I was doing this from the beginning. I think if she were more experienced in life she wouldn't be thinking I was like a daddy. There is hardship and monotony in all daily situations, marriage is no different. What needs to be kept in perspective are the unplanned changes that will come, living through them, and the ultimate freedom on the other side of this process, hopefully a freedom for both of us, but mostly for Diana.

I'm not stupid, or blind, to know we are building something from nothing in this new marriage compounded by the traveling. That is a lot less than most people start with because we started the relationship without a long dating period. I am being resented for setting up this situation where my wife feels trapped. The lack of responsibility on her part will change with time as she becomes more accustomed to her new life, new country, new language, and new marriage. The struggle comes between being patronizing and a true partner. As the major economic provider in the relationship I have to keep in check a balance between listening to Diana, putting the relationship as a priority, and my own independence. This is not easy. Living through this is why I wrote my first book. I was venting and trying to find emotional solace! It is a big part of traveling as well. Going "on vacation" doesn't end the marital effort, and at times it intensifies it.

Day Three: Kalamata. The crystal, clear sea, and water so clear the bottom is visible as waves of light shimmer across the shallow sea floor. The motion is constant and graceful, as graceful as light can ever be at the bottom of the sea. The rhythm of moving water creates a lace-like pattern of dancing light. The water holds a memory of something that is eternal and correct. It's memorizing to watch. I want to put it in my pocket and take the feeling home. Not the water, the feeling. One of nature's little surprises. Remember me. I am your friend. I am water. I am your God; I am your endless summer where nothing is lost. For the cost of a rubber shoe heal you can drift like water on an endless shore. The morning is calling you to join the dots of heads in the water; people float like spots, dark spots wearing hats in the water. The rest of their submerged bodies are gone, heads floating on the calm water. I'm one of those heads. The first thing this morning I was out in the water like the rest of the Greeks. I am one of the youngest heads in this sea of senior citizens in the water, but I like it. This is Kalamata.

The night wasn't as pleasant. Diana has this terrible rash or what looks like the chicken pox. Her body is a lumpy-red, with red bulbous mosquito bites, or something like that.

I went out and looked at a second hotel. It was 30 Euro a day more. The hotel where we are staying is noisy. Diana suggested we look for an alternative. I went to see a very nice place, but what is nice when the street noise is the same. There was a point last night when we both were saying we could be home in New York and have a quieter time. I've always preferred the peace of nature to the noise of crowds. Who wouldn't? Here in Kalamata there are crowds at night, people coming and going, and chasing fun. There are teens in cars that drive up and down the single small strip. As they pass their car stereo systems are so load they shake the building. I'm not exaggerating. When they circle back around after a few minutes the shock is the same, but my anger level is higher because I had just regained a small, momentary piece of calm. Teenagers love to draw attention to themselves. The same thing happens in New York. The bass in the cars is so loud it hurts. So goes the night in Kalamata. Greeks are on vacation and young, middle class, people do the same wild dance of adolescence all over the globe.

I went into a bar and asked a few young Greeks where a quiet town was, somewhere along the coast. They looked hung over from the night before, were smoking cigarettes, like everyone there, and gave me a polite response. About thirty-five kilometers down the coast there is a sleepy little town. The only way there is by bus. I came back to the hotel and talked to our hotel receptionist. They gave us a "quiet" room on the fourth floor, not the second, on the side street, not the main drag, with a better air conditioner. They were very nice about it. I also explained that Diana was sick and needs the rest. We lay in the room and waited until a little after noon to move to the other floor. The bathroom is bigger, but the room is a little smaller. The price is right. (The same) May be we will rent a scooter and go see the little town. The only problem is in that town it would put us too far south to catch any buses to Athens.

I live most of my life in preconceived misconceptions. I thought this town would be quiet and a little get away. Not exactly, it is quiet in the mornings. That is when the old folks go out and float in the sea wearing hats. The side of the street facing the sea is a wall of restaurants. This is a very busy little town where all life is active along the shore road. All day long waiters and waitresses run across the busy street holding a tray full of drinks on one shoulder. I wonder how many of them get killed by the traffic. The main restaurants are across the street from the beach, while the seats and tables are under umbrellas on the beach. We ate a late lunch at such a place. The price was about thirteen Euros. The first day in a new place we always let our hunger get the best of us and don't look for the best prices, we just eat, and then start the price-comparison game afterwards. I got a succulent roasted chicken breast. Diana got spaghetti with a red tomatoes sauce. We shared bites back and forth. We sat at the same restaurant, at different tables. I was across the street seated in the main building and would dart between cars as we exchanged bites. This is about how silly it was for the waiter to negotiate traffic for each order.

The wind was strong most of the day. I wanted to fly a kite. In the morning while I was in the water it was almost completely calm. By noon the sea was rough, well as rough as a sea can get in a bay without waves. The larges waves were one foot if that. I coaxed Diana out of the room to go to the beach. I told her the salt water would be good for her skin rash. When we showed the receptionist the skin rash he immediately said, "Go into the water, the salt water will help." She listened to a total stranger more than me. But who cares, she did, she had fun even. We lay on two big beach chairs under a huge blue umbrella. The receptionist told us we didn't have to rent the umbrellas, just buy a drink from the boy. But the boy never came around, or if he did we were out in the water. We swam three separate times as the heat forced us to cool off. The water was delicious. The bay holds a layer of sand. This sand makes the water less blue than most areas. Also the shallowness of the land at that point in the bay didn't offer that aqua-deep blue that Greece is best known for.

I tried to explain to the waiter as we were leaving that I'd be back tomorrow to buy a drink. The guy only knew enough English to say, "Good bye". He didn't care. I began to feel Greek. I began to enjoy the place and put leaving out of my mind. It's better to stay put and see if we can adapt to the rhythm of a place.

The buildings are provincial, simple and square architectural forms. It seems most building took place in the seventies and eighties. There are no modern buildings per say. The majority of the buildings are four or five story living flats with shutters that pull down to decrease the suns glare inside. Even the newest hotels have a square, boxy feel. There are no postmodern elements.

The streets are paved with asphalt and feel well kept. Only in the old town and Pedestrian Street did we see cobblestone. Kalamata is on the largest Greek island that is known as Peloponnese. The second largest city of this island is Kalamata. It is best known for being the olive growing district where famous olive oils are shipped all over the world. We asked about the origins of the city's name. "Kala" means "good" while "Mata" means "eyes". This could also be related to the eyes of the olives.

In 1986 an earthquake destroyed much of the city, thus it was rebuilt in subsequent years in a uniform style that makes most of the city feel the same. The size of the cars we found to be very interesting, compact for the most part. This makes traveling through the narrow streets easy and quick. There are a substantial number of motorbikes that make up the city's population for transport.

We came back to our new room and felt a bit better. The AC was working and the room wasn't in direct sunlight so it didn't feel as hot. While we were in the water I gave Diana a stern talking to about states of mind, sickness, and how healing won't take place until she heals her attitude first. The water did help, my lecture only made her mad at me. She rattled off a series of Spanish bolts of lightning and I give an embarrassing laugh.

By the time we were grooming each other back in the room with scissors and a manicure, the anger has passed and we hold a temporary truce that lasts the rest of the day. It's my tone of love that tells her straight up, without flowers, without pretty adjectives, that she is being self-defeating. Yes, that is tough love. The tension is called "Marriage on a Vacation".

We watched the opening ceremonies of the summer Olympics. I don't know why but I started to cry. I was watching "us all" the way we should always behave. I was so happy to see the proud faces of the marchers from each country. What a wonderful way to be, to play, to play games like children. Tears were rolling down both sides of my face. I don't where it came from. I don't know why or where they went. I didn't want attention, so I let the silent moment go and felt happy to be human. We napped in the air conditioning. I woke to see Colombia and Costa Rica. I was praising my second countries.

We got dressed and went out into the afternoon heat. It was already six, but it felt like four. The sun is a mysterious timekeeper. The seasons deceive us. Then if we travel to new places we are using the wrong frame of reference from our home country. The light is different all over the globe.

I never understood the art historians explaining the light in Matisse paintings and how the light of Morocco influenced him, until I went to Morocco. What I do understand about Greece is the light gets low toward sunset and it a great time for contrast so I took the camera. We walked along the shore, the opposite direction we had been during the day when we had lunch. We found a long dock so I photographed the boats. We sauntered up the long street as the heat blew on us from across the water. The hot wind made us sweat but we didn't care.

We visited some souvenir shops and bought a few trinkets. The sun was casting an orange glow upon everything. The quaint fishing boats rocked in the wind and created a rhythmic clang of sound coming from the vessels. People began to populate the street along the shore as the day's heat diminished. The parks and paths along the shore were delightful and much less claustrophobic than the cities side streets this must be why the people are naturally drawn to the shore. Trees mixed on the sandy shore at the end of the long concrete pier. This pier is wider than the actual street. A statue honoring sailors is located at the end of the pier as well. Children were running about as their parents strolled and took in the last light of the day. We soon found our way back to the room where I painted while the Olympics were on TV.

Day Five: Kalamata. The morning started with a swim just after a light breakfast. As I floated in the balmy azure sea, the tranquility took me back to the memory of last night's dream. In my dream three friends renovated an old jalopy into a surf wagon. We rode in the old truck, it was floating, then the road gave way like a sheet of fabric, we were floating backwards, then forward. Somehow we didn't crash. We slid to a smooth landing. We were brainstorming about a new addition to the truck. It was up to me. Three horses standing on their hind legs with their front hooves holding a ships steering wheel was what I envisioned and added to the truck. The sculpture was placed in the back of the truck. Everyone seemed to like the design. I was pleased in the dream, then awoke.

A wave of contentment washed over me as the water gently rocked me. I was looking at a boat out on the water. A boat was floating free in space because there was no horizon, or rather no distinguishing color to separate the water from the sky. A thin haze saturated the horizon line. A small fishing craft was visible in the distance. It struck me that the water was so full of haze that the sky was one color. It was a wonderful sight to behold. The sea and me, holding Diana flat on the water, playing like I was going to make her go deeper than she wanted to. We were now two of those black dots in the water we had seen earlier from the hotel balcony.

We went into the water first thing in the morning and became Greek elders soaking in the salt water, which is what Diana needed to heal her skin. She was less swollen, the small red blisters are reducing in size, and she is less crabby. Yesterday she wanted to go to the doctor but I knew it would just need a few days to heal. She exaggerated the growth of the blisters moving all across her arms and legs. I think it was a reaction to insect bites but we'll never know for sure. One nice thing about the body is it heals itself, more than doctors do. (Note: This rash was much more serious than I realized at the time. One of the days we were in Rome I found a small bug in the hotel bed. I pinched the critter from the sheets and threw it out the window. Somewhere a few months later, I don't exactly remember, I was reading a newspaper and saw an article about the infestation of bed bugs in Italian hotels in Rome. I recognized the insect and was shocked to remember I'd set a villain free. The odd thing is that with all Diana's bites, all over her body, I had not one. She is sweeter to the taste than I. I have learned to be more understanding of insects. (Now if I could do the same for my wife the relationship will improve.)

We soaked in the water and frolicked together. She was finally coming out of her funk. We headed back to the shower in the room. Soon we were a few doors down at an Internet café sending emails to friends. I put more money on the credit card and looked up the spending that has been put on the credit card thus far. We are about a thousand dollars over budget, but the budget was not without a bottom, we have nothing to really worry about.

The number one bus is the only route that comes along the beach. I asked a woman to show us on a map where the city center was. In a matter of ten minutes we disembarked and walked towards a series of umbrellas-covered sellers. People were selling something but we couldn't see what. The umbrellas were only the beginning, further on there was a long building that extended for about three city blocks. It was a "real" farmers market. There was fresh produce and a fish market. It seemed to go on forever. Diana wandered way ahead of me because there was no place to get around those in the slow moving line of shoppers. There was one continuous row of sellers on both sides of the narrow isle. People crowded the narrow opening between tables and booths stocked full of vegetables and fruits. The smell of fresh fruit and food wafted into the air as it mixed with the smell of the shoppers. We were so close it was easy to smell bodies and perfumes on the passersby. The noise was that of people making bargains and asking prices. The hurried pace of daily shoppers made the air pulsate with electricity, although the walkers were tempered by the crowded path. At the end of the narrow walkway it opened into a shaded area, we found some peaches that were so good looking we had to buy five. The man selling them threw in an extra nectarine with a smile.

A few feet away a truck pulled up to the curb. From the open tailgate two men were selling nuts and grains. We bought some raisins, cashews, walnuts, and peanuts covered with honey and sesame seeds. Across the street we found some empty benches in the shade and ate to our hearts content. It was a heavenly vegetarian feast right on the sidewalk. I told Diana the Seventh Day Adventists eat that way every day. "Who are they?" I told her the little I know, but like because they are very diet conscious.

A bakery selling some strange bread was close, we walked over to the display window to see small loafs that looked more like cookies than rolls or bread. The texture looked rough and had a pale color. I bought some cold peach juice to wash down the dry nuts. The video and still camera had been put to use, but with so many interesting people walking by I continued to shoot while we ate. The Greeks are a cross section of modern, or western dressers, and old fashioned styles. A man could walk by with a donkey and cart right next to a woman wearing highs and a long skirt, the cosmopolitan and ancient mix. By ancient I don't exactly mean people walking around in robes, I mean styles that seem very dated. The most obvious being the older widows that wear all black.

Between two streets I could see the two spires of a large church in the distance on a hill. I checked the map; it was the biggest church in the city. We walked down totally vacant streets, thin enough to get one car past. This was the old part of the city. New houses stood next to wrecked, dilapidated, abandoned houses. Before we reached the church we found the city historical museum. I tugged on the door, but it was locked. We walked a few feet away and a woman popped out of the museum.

"Are you open?" It said they were on the door, until one, it was noon. "No. But come in." A middle-aged woman with well-kept hair and makeup smiled, and explained we should come back tomorrow. The museum is an old house with items from the historical past. "If we can we will return", I told her as we exited into the hot sun.

We found a narrow street to the church. Outside was a large plaza with impressive busts of the Byzantine Popes, or Patriarchs. I photographed the dozen or so pure white statues which stood about twelve feet tall. The busts rested on tall footings that had their names in Greek. The dates of their reign were in a sequence. When one died another man began immediately.

The inside of the church was beautiful. We sat for a long time in silence, on separate sides of the church. I was looking at all the paintings. There wasn't a bare wall to be found. The Greek religious art isn't realistic, but more like super-real cartoon art. The paintings are flat, colorful, with sharp edges. (Long before cubism was invented.) The colors and angular designs make them seem brilliant and bold, yet they are full of intricate detail. The works have no depth; rounded shapes are not a concern because that leads to a hint of realism. The flatness is intended to give the art a spiritual dimension, raising it to a realm separate from the natural world.

Candles in square sand boxes burned for the intentions of the parishioners or visitors. I light two for us. Massive candleholders stood on both sides of the altar. These were for the mass or special holy days. They were ornate, multi-tiered, at least seven levels high. A priest walked by us and smiled. He passed through the bright light to the outside and vanished into a white haze while the rest of the church remained mostly dark; very dark because there were no electric lights, only candles flickering.

We walked along to a small hill, to a store with colorful thin scarves floating in what little breeze there was. An old man sat outside. As we walked past I was looking to see if he was sleeping, he was so still.

"Hello", he spoke English. We went into his shop. It was a tourist shop but had a second side that sold food goods. We bought a couple of tablecloths. He told Diana he had gone to Harvard but never really was able to adapt to the American life. His English was thick with accent, but he spoke well, misplacing a few words here and there. Diana told him she was going through the same thing. We promised him we'd return the next day. I had actually spent my last money. We had a few Euros in change. I asked him where a bank machine was, he pointed toward an open town square. I didn't find the bank but we walked into a tiny ancient Byzantine church. It was very, very small. The old the bricks were hundreds of years of sun-baked relics. They were no longer red but a dark, like being sun burnt in contrast to the light, faded mortar. The exterior and interior of the church had the bricks which accented their design as they rolled over the door frame and curves of the building. We shortly passed through to the opposite door out into a small street. I had to bow my head to get through the doors. I asked another person where the bank machine was.

"What bank card do you use?" "It doesn't matter." I said. But I guess it really does. Some work for one machine and not another. The only machine was out of order anyway. We walked a few blocks and found another ATM. I took out one hundred and eighty Euros. I asked for more, but the machine rejected my request. My limit is three hundred US dollars a day.

We sat for a few minutes as I studied the map. The heat was getting to both of us. We doubled back to a fancy bar and went inside. The Olympics were on TV and there were large soft sofas. We parked our bodies for over an hour and drank our fruit juices, very slowly. We watched the Olympics and looked at Greek motorcycle magazines. It was a relief to be out of the heat in a comfortable place. We sank into the comfortable sofas. They were stuffed in such a way that it was possible to sink a few inches deep below the fabric surface. The soft fabric made the cool room that much more enjoyable as we rested our bones. The people were milling together in small groups enjoying the day and each other. Most of the patrons were young and hip looking. They wore blue jeans and thin leather jackets with colorful t-shirts. We felt at home enjoying the sofas, which we had not been able to relax sitting in since Denmark.

We headed back to the original bus stop. I wasn't ready for the hotel room after the lounging on a comfortable sofa. I asked Diana at the stop if we could just walk some more before heading to the hotel. We walked back in the direction of the bar, toward the original market we had found that morning.

I have this thing about walking circles. I look for them; or rather I make them in my travels.

For no known reason we went into a restaurant where we saw a whole chicken had been roasted and hung on a spit. The man told me twelve Euros was the price. We bought it. He said he would throw in bread and potatoes, motioning to the objects and speaking only in Greek.

We spent a half hour there. Diana bought lamb on a stick and we told the owner and his waitress our love story. There was a world map on a door so I pointed to Diana's country and then to New York. The woman, named Sylvia, was from Poland. The man offered me a cigarette and I took it. I smoke maybe once a year but don't know why. I smoked and Diana made horrible faces at me. I was going to go to hell. We were a novelty to the folks who all welcomed us and made small talk, mostly in invented sign language.

It's nice to make acquaintances even if time is brief. The man, whose name we both forgot, was very happy we came along. At first we were just strangers, but the connection made by the time we left was close to family. He shook our hands and Sylvia did as well. This is normal behavior in Greece. Everyone is very friendly. We didn't see this in Italy, but we weren't around many native Italians, only tourists and taxi drivers from other countries.

The first afternoon we arrived in Kalamata we were at a bus stop directly from the train. We began to ask for directions to the beach in English. An old man perked up and said, "Ohio". Then he pointed to himself, again saying, "Ohio". The woman, who ultimately helped us, had a better command of English, listened to him in Greek, and then explained the man had lived in Ohio as a young man. When his bus arrived he made a special effort to come over and shake my hand, a double hand with a warm grasp. He was a member of the older generation that held America in high esteem. At that moment I knew I was representing my country to a generation that had fought in World War II. As anti-American as I can get, I was proud to be there for this man. He was looking to me like I was a beacon of hope and I let the light shine for him. It's not that I have total disgust with my country; it's that I know we have not lived up to the ideals we are capable of. We can do better and I'm quite aware of how good we are. When I travel I am aware of how others view me.

We bought the roasted chicken in the restaurant and went off in the direction of the bus stop; towards the shore. A woman waiting at the same bus stop was still there. In the half hour we were gone no bus had come, we had only gained time.

There were two bus lines in this town, number one and number two. Soon we climbed onto the number one into the air conditioning. It was a welcome break. At the bus stop we found a free English newspaper that gave a list of events. Back in the room we napped, watched the Olympics, and read the paper. There was a free concert on the beach that night, across the street from the church. We had our plans set for us.

At seven, we walked back to the beach along the street, south to the church, maybe five blocks away. There was a sound-check taking place on the small stage, or what seemed to be an amateur band in practice. We found some beach chairs and ordered two fruit juices for seven Euros, ouch! ($14 US dollars) We now had the "free" beach chairs so we sat and listened to as many as three groups do their music. There was a female singer who got up, performed half a song, and retreated from the stage. I was hoping for something entertaining or at least musical, but the bands were amateurs and the music was unimpressive. The last band we saw before we left was a rap group; in fact all the bands but the young women were rappers. This last band consisted of three young men, two rappers and one on guitar. All the music was prerecorded. The lyrics and guitar were live. I heard the words, "propaganda, capitalists, and Bush". These were my kind of people speaking in Greek; excuse me, rapping in Greek. We didn't like the music despite the protest agenda. There songs were all spoken and not one melody, just single words with the second voice doing an echo for the refrain stanzas. By nine thirty we'd had enough. We expected an exotic Greek mandolin but got a typical American bump and grind.

The sidewalk was full of people of all ages and sizes walking, and enjoying their holiday. We were the only tourists amongst the Greeks. We walked nearly the entire length of the street heading to the north end of the strip, sitting on a park bench near some men with tables selling jewelry. Within minutes an old man came and sat down next to us. After a few minutes I asked him if he spoke English.

"Yes, a little bit", he responded in a thick Greek accent. He had been to the States twice as well as Italy and many countries. I asked him what his profession was. He was a historian and wrote many books on the history of Greece. I said he taught about the "cradle of western civilization and democracy".

"Yes, but what you call democracy in America isn't Democracy, the same with Russia and Germany. You have economic Democracy." I laughed and knew immediately what he meant.

"You mean we have big businesses that control our Democracy". "Yes." We were on the same wavelength and in full agreement.

His wife and teenage son came by a few minutes later, and we all shook our hands and said good night. As we sat there we watched the police come by, tell the men selling jewelry that they had to leave. The police didn't have any guns. They were very calm and polite. They also spoke to a man who was giving a tattoo to a young man. The young man paid for the tattoo and came over to our bench to dry the tattoo.

"Do you speak English?" "Yes, a little bit." "Why did the police tell these men to leave?" "They are not the police, they are the Coast Guard." That explained that they had no guns. "They don't have licenses to sell here." All the while he was drying his tattoo, which I recognized.

"Ah, the eye of Horus", I said. "You know?" "Yes, of course, the all seeing eye that gives protection.", I replied. The conversation drifted to a new topic and he explained the men selling were from Egypt, and that many people came looking for work in Greece. I explained, "Yes, we have the same with people from Mexico and El Salvador". He told me his name and I introduced Diana and myself. I still can't remember, or pronounce, his Greek name. He is twenty-two, working on the big ship that is docked in the harbor. This is the only large ship in the harbor that is very visible because it displays full lighting on the deck at night. We have seen the boat for days wondering what it was.

He had been to Aruba and Holland, and was about to set sail for Japan at the end of the month. They were transporting methane gas. He said he had visited Amsterdam and enjoyed the freedom there. He didn't smoke marijuana because the boat had strict drug testing every day. No drugs or alcohol. I told him about my friend Damian from New York who has a similar job on a vessel in the Mediterranean. Damian's job, the last year, was supplying the Iran war, despite not agreeing with the war's politics.

The man's English was better than a "little bit". We had a long conversation drifting from politics to global issues. Soon we said good night and shook hands. Diana and I walked home to the hotel to soon fall fast asleep.

Day Six: Kalamata. We spent the day in a low key, "whatever happens" mode. Not much did happen. In the morning we slept late. The door that opens to the balcony that keeps out the light was shut, so no morning sunlight came into the room. These blinds are on all the houses and hotels to keep the rooms cool from the sun in the mid-day. They are made of soft metal and pull down on a heavy track. The room was totally dark. What woke us up was the noise from the housekeeper moving her cart down the hall. If you know of the heavy steel doors that roll down over businesses in New York City, these are a smaller, sleeker version for privacy. We ate breakfast on the balcony, afterwards headed for the water across the street. First we did laundry in the sink. I prepared the sandwiches for lunch.

The water was cold at first, but we soon were giving each other piggyback rides and adventuring along the shoreline out in the water up to our shoulders. The sea is so calm in the mornings we found ourselves walking blocks while out in the water, and then returning to our end where a jetty runs into the harbor and the beach ends.

We returned to the room and decided to eat lunch instead of taking it with us to the same museum we had tried the day before when it was closing. After lunch and a short bus ride to the middle of town we found ourselves at the museum door. As we walked in, the same woman laughed, and said she was closing again. It was one o'clock. There was a group of five Spaniards, three women and two men, who also arrived at the same time, so she said she would stay open for five minutes for everyone. The bottom floor was filled by displays of old tools and equipment from a few hundred years back, before electricity. There was an olive oil press, a book press, some farming and wood working tools, as well as some very old handmade white lace. The second floor was paintings and busts of local heroes from the war, which gave them independence from the Turks. Tucked in one corner was a room with small Greek Orthodox icons housed in special glass cases.

As we were exiting the museum I thanked the woman and overheard one of the Spaniards saying that he wanted to do some translation and studies of the museum for his Master's degree. He was seeking cooperation through the local university and museum to facilitate this.

We returned to the shop we had bought the tablecloths the day before. The old man was gone and his son was keeping the store. The son was an old man also. We bought a few trinkets, but when they wanted nine Euros for a t-shirt, I told Diana to wait until we get to Athens for that. The large cities always have cheaper prices.

A few doors down we were in another shop that was also a museum, of sorts. There were taxidermy animals, birds, and butterflies (in glass cases) from all over the world. The shopkeeper was trying to make a sale so hard that we gave up and left. Every item we even glanced at he would blurt out the price. We would have preferred to simply look at the displays of animals and sea creatures. None of the salable items had price tags and we got tired of his constant attention. His frantic pushing, while quoting the price over, and over again, turned us off.

Once outside, the heat was broiling us on the sidewalk prompting us to stop in a small pastry shop and buy an ice cream and sit in the air conditioning. The whole town was strangely empty. We walked past the market that was alive with thousands of people the day before. It was as if a plague hit. Nothing was alive but a stray black cat wandering in the empty expanse. Every street was vacant and businesses were closed. The town center with large statues and flower gardens was equally as deserted. We walked all the way back to the hotel in the heat.

At one juncture, an obese woman lay behind a car in the middle of the street. She had slipped on some water in a gutter and was laying on the street while onlookers were getting her water and calling for an ambulance. One man attempted to lift her, but she let out a squeal. He then laid her back down on the hot asphalt. In the meantime, a crowd was gathering from the traffic that was backed up. Calm was in the air regardless of the emergency. The people patiently, curiously craned their necks, peering out of car windows, not saying a word.

On Sunday, everything is closed in this town. We couldn't find a grocery store or a shop to rent a movie, so we went back into the water for a swim after a short nap in the hotel. I took my watercolors with me and started a painting as we sat in the dirt in the shadow of the jetty. As I was painting I could hear two people speaking English out in the water. After painting, and the heat getting to both of us again, we went back into the water to cool off. There is no escaping the Greek heat.

The woman speaking English was talking to a little girl who was playing in the water. While in the water I walked by and said, "I haven't heard English in a long time". "Yes, where are you from?" "New York." "So am I" " L o n g Island." "So am I." "Bayville." "Well close, Hicksville, not far." The woman introduced herself; she was a teacher in Plainview, New York and in Greece for her uncle's funeral. She teaches dance. Soon her older male, cousin was in the water and he was talking with us as well. He is a brash and pushy fellow from Pennsylvania. Diana didn't care for him. I could tell by her body language. She drifted away in the water, but I was soon telling her that the man's wife was from Columbia. She asked him the city and they spoke but briefly, she was drifting away again, uninterested and put off by the man.

I got a lot of information about the area and another town named Nafplio. We may be able to visit there for a day on our way to Athens. There was something strange about the man. Diana later said he was making fun of her, displaying a kind of male competitiveness, typical of some men in the States. I was more interested in getting information in English so I stayed talking with him. He said he worked with 'computers and stuff', but when I tried to press the topic more, utilizing advanced terminology, but he seemed to go blank. I tried to ask what he did and he said, "Programming". I could tell he was lying because when I asked if he was working with systems or programs he got confused and was balking. He didn't seem like a techie. I knew, without trying, I had backed him into a corner, the conversation went dry, and so we changed the subject back to the local towns. He was a talker, but I couldn't tell if he was a crook covering up his identity or simply strange. I had this one brief encounter with an American and he seemed suspicious.

We ran into him again at sunset when I was heading toward a boat I wanted to photograph in the light. The owner of the boat was standing next to him and he asked me to take a picture of the two of them. I also explained that I wanted to paint the boat that morning, but the boat was gone after being there all week. "Yes, he took it out today." It was a medium sized fishing boat, all white, and a perfect subject for a painting. They could have been hauling dead bodies for all I know.

After taking some pictures, and returning on the jetty, I passed the two men still talking and smoking cigarettes. Diana didn't want to speak with them at all. We also passed the woman and young female child from Long Island. She was pleasant and wished us a good evening. We crossed the street into the Internet café. I searched for hotels in Nafplio while Diana wrote her mother an e-mail. We priced a half-gallon of ice cream from the little stand across the street from the hotel. I wanted to have Bailey's Irish Cream and ice cream. The woman wanted nine dollars for a small container of ice cream. We bought two cones instead; they were four Euros, about five dollars. (Yikes!!) We sat on sidewalk on the hotels furniture nursing the expensive delectable treats. We sat looking at European cars and wondering why so many brands don't get to the USA. It was amazing to see all the different cars passing by. They were all compact with tiny engines, engines that use little gas. Small equals low gas consumption, but in the States there are few small cars. We are going to buy the smallest car we can find when we get back. The new car will be for Diana's new job. I wish we could take half these cars back with us. The hotel bed and Olympics was next on the agenda. Sleep too.

Day Seven: Kalamata. It is our eighth day here but I will retract yesterday's events while we are on the bus leaving Kalamata. Before boarding the bus this morning Diana met a woman in the bus station from Bogotá, Colombia. She was with her husband who she met on line (computer), like us. The woman lives in Switzerland and has two, twin children. She and Diana exchanged their love stories as I waited outside with the luggage to load the bus. Meeting another Colombian in Greece is a big event for Diana!

Our last day in Kalamata we rented a small motorcycle. I wish we had done this sooner. We ventured to places that took us far along the coastal road south of the city. The motorcycle was barley big enough for the two of us. On a few occasions I thought we were about to take a spill. The gravel in the street when we went to start, or stop, was a problem. The wind was hot and very strong, but we found our way out of the city. The man who rented us the bike said to keep taking rights out of the city. On the non-beach side many buildings span across the land. Outside the city limits we stopped the bike at a public beach. The water was turquoise blue. The rocks under the water were white causing the sea to be clear and colorful. The water here was cleaner, more distinct than the sea in the city. The wind had picked up and we remounted taking the road further south. The wind would tilt the small motorcycle, as we seared into it like a sailboat. There were few clouds, but many seagulls filling the air. The wind seemed to dominate the ride.

We stopped again at an elbow in the road where I saw a bench on the shore. Two Greek women sat talking and glanced at us, we were foreigners. One slipped her hand over her bag. That was the only time I felt mistrust for us from anyone here. The people are very open and friendly. Diana rubbed her leg across the exhaust pipe and slightly burned a few inches of skin. It was sudden but superficial. She then went and stood in the cold water to cool the sting. I sat on the empty second bench and took pictures. The blue water was so beautiful it pulled at me like a magnet. What had we been missing all this time while in the city? This was the country life. It was another dimension to Greece we hadn't seen as of yet.

We volleyed up and down hills, through tiny villages all hugging the coast, passing a shop with seashells and handmade ceramics. There were times I thought we had reached the end of the road, but we'd pass between two, old, dilapidated, narrow buildings and off we'd be on another stretch of road. The coast was rocky. There was no sand. Cacti grew in patches amongst dry, blonde grass and low bushes. It was extremely hot even though the shore was a few feet away from the road.

We passed along hills and up a narrow road, then back towards the shore where we saw my idea of a Greek dream house. The multi-terraced, vine covered house had plants and large stone arches. The abode was at least two hundred years old, but a solar tank and collectors gave it twenty-first century flair. The house looked like it occupied a vast number of rooms tucked into the hillside where vegetation covered at least half the walls. A sleek modern sports car sat in a driveway that came winding through the terrain.

Down a steep embankment the road turned between two buildings, another left turn and we were in a small village with a restaurant, a dock and small boats moored in a tiny harbor. This time the road absolutely did end. Around the corner there was only a dead end and a tiny cove with a few sunbathers on blankets.

We dismounted the metal steed and took our backpack, a blanket and lunch. The cove was no larger than a few houses. We found an empty spot on the rocky earth and reclined to eat some nuts and raisin we'd bought at the market on Saturday. We relaxed in the shade of a bamboo grove. There were three people in the water and one woman sitting on shore. As we arrived, two people left so we had a spot to lay our blanket.

I am amazed how the Europeans share with each other. Americans have a different sense of space and ownership when being in a small area. Here I've seen people sitting at tables, go up to strangers and sit down next to them. A better sense of sharing in Europe would be considered an invasion of privacy in the USA. The same went for the small little bay. Our neighbors were a few feet away, but no one was bothered. We did not bring our bathing suits. I sat looking at the water and decided it was too attractive to leave me out. I stripped down to my bikini underwear and went into the water. It was heavenly.

I had seen sea urchins in the water and asked another man swimming in gestured sign language, where the spiny critters were. I used my hands and fingers to mimic the size and shape of the creatures. He understood me and pointed to the area where the boats were tied up. I immediately set off, out into the water swimming toward a rocky edge. The sea floor had isolated areas of green sea grass, small patches of gravel, but mostly rocks. I reached my outcrop and stood in a victorious pose so Diana could see me from the shore. Before long, I was swimming back towards Diana. I had spotted sea urchins in the cracks of the rocks and decided I wasn't going to get hurt my last day in

Kalamata. Back on shore I ate more food, indulging in the delicious peaches that grow there. There is nothing as refreshing as a juicy, fresh peach on a hot day. We lay on our blanket without a care, listened to the wind rustling through the bamboo, savoring the succulent fruit.

After a splendid hour, or more, we retraced the ride along the coast and stopped at the crafts store and bought a few trinkets. I bought a ceramic Greek sailor and Diana bought a bracelet. The shop keeper gave us a small cross as a bonus. The shop was in her home. The daughter was working outside, painting ceramics, as we pulled up. It was the only real "hippie shop" we'd seen. The woman with her two children was all making things to sell. I liked the natural feel of their environment. Nothing was artificial; all objects were made with love. As we left I said, "Peace", like we used to back in the sixties and seventies. The older woman understood my perspective instantly. We shared the same era in the early seventies, even if we lived on separate continents. The common bond of our generation had not diminished with time.

As we rode along the coast the first time I saw a fork in the road, one branch curved toward the mountains. On our return we took the road that headed up into the mountains. The small bike squealed as we drove up hill after hill, higher and higher. It was cloudy and a few raindrops began to hit our faces. We stopped a few times to take pictures as the clouds grew thick and the sky darkened. The shore lay far below and the coastal road weaved a thread along the banks. Tiny white villas dotted the mountain all the way down to the shoreline except in the higher altitudes where it was too steep. Mixed amongst the expensive vacation homes were groves of olive trees. This gave the land breathing room placing deep greens and the light-brown earth in a hop-scotch pattern of homes and farms. The motorcycle came to a mountain pass where we could see the shore in the distance. The top of the mountain was covered in clouds. Here a forest of evergreens looked out of place in the dry terrain. The cloud cover took the bleached sun look away, all looked healthy and verdant, but the sun with its harsh heat would return and replace the green with that baked-earth tone.

It was going to pour any minute. Rain was draping the sky between the highest point and the earth where we rode. We descended the mountain road and the heat returned as we crept closer and closer to the shoreline. A light rain fell but the storm was staying in the upper regions. Sun was shining along the shore as we rode beneath a low, gray bank of clouds.

A massive, single mountain range just south of the city dominates Kalamata. This mountain range is called Taygetus. A sweeping bay curves around the land but the mountain forces all roads to shirt the shore. The mountain is solid rock with scrubby pine trees growing on top, through its mid-section, and at its base. Tiny white villas dot the base of the mountain. The uniform white of all the villas are complemented by terra-cotta roofs. The rocks on the face of the mountain have a soft white tinge that reflects in the bay. It is all very tranquil and impressive. This was the same mountain that the motorcycle had climbed on the western side.

We still had a few hours of rental time. Passing through the city we hugged the shore to the north where the land became extremely flat. Farms with long stretches of young crops being irrigated bordered a newly paved road. Mist rose from the raised massive sprinklers spraying the crops. There was a racetrack for cars misplaced in what seemed the middle of nowhere. Other than those strange few buildings there was not one thing to hinder vision on the flat terrain. The shore was covered with round, fist-sized stones that would twist your ankle, in a thin stretch of land between the beach and the road. Eventually the paved road gave way to a dirt path with streaking dust clouds pulling the earth high above the motorcycle. This was the same land we had passed through the week before on the train but somehow we had no memory of the train or the flat land. This stretch was the exact opposite of the rugged, uneven, and mountainous earth that filled the southern view from the hotel and beach. We traveled to what seemed to be the edge of a new bend in the expansive bay, turned back toward the industrial belt along the city's northern port, and eventually into the city itself. Traffic was beginning to build from people leaving work, so we returned to the hotel to get the morning's departure information from the hotel owner, Nicholas. He, and his sister the other desk clerk, were crucial to our obtaining information about Kalamata.

Nicholas helped us by calling the national bus station and speaking in Greek. We could take the bus to Tripoli, change buses, and go to Nafplio on a second bus. He couldn't reach the local bus company, but he reached the bus company in Tripoli. It is a common thing here to make calls and no one answers during established businesses hours. Maybe it's their break. The buses left at ten and two from our connection in Tripoli. We'd have to leave Kalamata early to get to the bus in Tripoli by ten in the morning. The bus company wasn't answering so we got directions and drove the bike to the station. I knew the way because the station was a few blocks away from the Saturday market. By now, we knew our way around the small town. Nicholas was always friendly and we grew increasingly dependent on him for what to do and how to get there. There really wasn't that much to do, but after being over saturated with Rome the lengthy stay was a nice break from the stress of traveling.

During our stay in Kalamata it took us a few days to figure out the staff of the hotel. There were four people who sat behind the desk. A fifth person, who we saw the morning we left, was there after midnight. We were always in at night, by nine or ten, and never up early enough to see the night clerk.

A family operated the hotel, siblings and cousins. Two brothers were the actual owners; they hired their cousins, a brother and sister. We preferred exchanges with the brother and sister. Nicholas and his sister both spoke English and had a worldly feel. The two brothers were like mafia thugs. They were not at all friendly and tried to feign a working knowledge of English, but they couldn't. Every time we'd speak to them they had no idea what we were talking about, one time I even asked them to call Nicholas so I could set some daily plans into motion. The brains of the operation were the brother and sister team. I got the impression that the two brothers were spoiled and had inherited the hotel and hired their cousins to help run the place. These brothers must have had some connection to the man with the boat who hauled bodies. I know it!

We drove the motorcycle to the bus station. The station was new and clean. Inside, one man sat talking on his cell phone (not answering the phone, ha, ha) while the second man sold tickets (not answering the phone that was ringing off the wall, ha, ha). I bought the tickets for six in the morning with a ten o'clock connection in Tripoli. On the way back we saw a big modern (Wal-Mart-like) store, the same store that has a chain in Colombia. This gave Diana a little moment of Colombian joy. She perked up on the motorbike and began to excitedly yell in my ear the story of this store chain in her home country. We bought food for the trip in the bus the next day.

I dropped off Diana the hotel then returned the rented motorcycle. The gas tank was only half used. There wasn't a scratch on the bike. I paid him twenty dollars in cash. I walked back towards the hotel. Diana and I agreed we'd meet each other along the street that ran along the waterfront. When I spotted her I put my arms out and for a city block I ran with my arms outstretched. I ran in slow motion; my movement was slow and exaggerated. Cars were driving past looking at me like I was crazy. Diana was laughing at me for acting like a big fool. I can be that way with little effort. One of my secret professions is as a comedian. I enjoy making people laugh.

We'd heard English spoken, while walking, at one of the restaurants on one of our first days. On a few occasions we went in and asked for information. The couple running the small Bristol had lived in Boston and was now making a living, working very hard, running an Italian restaurant. We decided on our last night we'd give them our business after sharing so much information freely. We sat on the shore side of the street and a young waiter brought us bottled water, small rolls of French bread, and a Greek salad with cucumbers and black olives all the while darting traffic like an Olympic pro. My order was for pesto and pasta. Diana ordered shrimp and pasta. The waiter then brought us natural apricot juice which was delicious and fitting for the time of day. When we finished our meal I gave a waves and thumbs up the owners.

"Have a great trip", the man yelled back through the open door as the traffic muffled his words.

At the ungodly hour of four forty-five the phone rang and we got up. A quick shower and breakfast were all we required. The packing was done the night before. A taxi waited for us outside. At the bus stop we showed a note to the driver that Nicholas had written to make sure the bus driver knew where we needed to get off in Tripoli. I felt like a child on his first day to kindergarten class. The bus driver may have been assuming we needed some special medication as he looked at us over his glasses resembling a school teacher more than a driver. We left at six sharp. I saw a few stars in the sky, something we had not seen since Denmark and Susser's summerhouse. We were about to leave a fractional part of our lives in a town we grew to love, mostly because of the warm-hearted people.

The night slid into dawn and the houses that hugged the road soon gave way to open land with farms of olive groves. As the sun cast light on the landscape it was evident that something was wrong. Why were the trees all black with no leaves? The earth had the blanched, dead, grass mixed with scorched, black knots. It became evident that the trees had all been burned. At first I thought this was just one farm where maybe some clearing had taken place, but this went on for miles and miles. Then it came to me. Days earlier while we sat on the beach we attended a free evening concert, a woman walking a dog and holding a sign went past. The dog was trained to carry the sign, which I could not read in Greek. The woman had handed us a flier, all in Greek.

"Do you speak English?" I asked. "Yes, "What is this for?" "Did you hear about our fires last year?" she asked. "Oh, yes, I did". "This is for the victims of the fires".

As we drove along in the bus this conversation came back to me. The dawn's light and the skeletons of trees made the scenery seem haunted and bleak. It was a sad, empty, charred place. The buses air conditioning blocked any odors, but my senses filled in the void with the smell of smoke.

As we rolled over a few mountain passes, the land still wore a scorched gown. It was near Tripoli that we saw less damage from the fires and began to see green again. The earth is never really green here, only the trees that seem dark green, or greenish-brown. At the base of each burnt tree life and hope was springing forth in the form of new verdant branches. We disembarked from our bus to a solo taxi and an empty station, or lack thereof. Along the side of the road was a small kiosk to buy tickets. It was seven-thirty in the morning, which meant we had a two and a half wait for the next bus.

The taxi driver approached me and asked if I wanted him to drive us to Nafplio. I asked how much. "No", I said quickly thinking only of the cost and not the convenience. Then he got a little louder saying in English, "The taxi is fifteen Euros, and the bus is eight. You can share the ride with this other man. The bus takes two hours. I take one. The bus will be here in two and half hours. Why wait? " He had a point.

A young man standing next to him wore a sheepish grin. I'd seen the same young man in Kalamata saying good-bye to his family. In a split-second re-evaluation I said yes. I don't exactly know why I said no in the first place. Well I do, because the man didn't strike me as trustworthy right away. He was well dressed, middle aged, but I felt uneasy with his presence. He didn't give me a good vibe. We climbed into his taxi and sped away. When the man said we would be an hour, he lied. We arrived there in forty-five minutes. Rather we flew there. The unease I felt comes from an inborn instinct to avoid loud, aggressive people. The man was a taxi/race car driver and his Mercedes was a rocket to be tested for speed. He went 110 miles (not kilometers) an hour down the mountain. I was watching the speedometer. I told Diana to fasten her seat belt within a few minutes. He was a maniac. All the while Greek folk music was playing and he was driving with his left hand while he fussed with a cell phone in his right hand. Diana was pale and not saying anything. I watched the color fade from Diana's lovely, normally rose-flushed face to an ashen-gray. Her eyes widened and her lips were slightly parted in near horror, only to be replaced by frequent biting of her lower lip. She was speechless. We did get there fast. Diana was near death with fear. I was watching every curve to make sure we made them. I spoke briefly with the young man in the passenger seat. He was from the USA. He was for McCain in the up-coming election. Great. I was about to die with a young Republican. As we passed a shrine along the roadside the driver made the sign of the cross. It did not give me any reassurances.

The minute the taxi driver dropped us in the square of old town Nafplio, we were met by friendly people. The driver could not take us in the old town but he asked a man who actually walked us a block, asked another woman the directions, and she walked with us to the Pension. It was maybe three blocks from the square. Two lovely women sat inside the Pension drinking coffee, one with long dark hair, and the other with short-cropped brown hair. These were the cleaning ladies. It was 8:30 in the morning and we needed to use the restroom. Diana ordered a cup of tea, which the women refused payment. We left our bags and set off to see the magic in our new temporary home. And that there was; pure magic!

The Venetians built Nafplio and it was later dominated by the Ottoman Empire. The city is on a peninsula where a natural bay in the Argolis Gulf creates a port. The city is located in the Peloponnese province and was once an important trade port. High above the small streets we could see a colossal old fortress (called the Palamidi) that looked newly constructed it was so well preserved. The granite structure was a dirty beige color, nearly the same color as the rock on its surrounding hill. On a closer hilltop where we walked was a much smaller fortification similar in design.

The old cracked streets and morning light was inspirational and my camera was in constant motion. I clicked away at any alley, crease of light between buildings, or any surface that had character and distinction. The first building down the street was an old, small church. It had to be at least nine hundred years old. It was dark and mysterious, and smelled like years of burnt incense. We lit some candles and said a prayer together.

We strolled toward the direction I had seen two people carrying towels and wearing their bathing suits. In the center of town we found another large square and went into a shop looking at the souvenirs. The ground of the town plaza was all white marble. In the far corner stood a huge old tree where the low branches and leaves filled an area large enough for an entire restaurant to be situated. A few people sat drinking their morning coffee under this tree. We breezed through unnoticed and found ourselves inside another Greek church a block away. The inside was magnificent. The dark, unlit walls, opened up to flowing gold tiles with a grand mosaic of Christ in the apse. The gold shone in the dimly lit room, illuminated only by the small door we had entered.

Across from the church was the harbor. We sat a few minutes on a park bench where I greeted an old man sitting on the next bench. Soon a friend joined him as we finished a brief snack. As a woman strolled by I caught her attention asking where the beach was. She told us how to get there from the other side of the town, closer to our hotel. A minute later she returned and apologized that she said 1500 hundred meters, when it was only 500 meters. Who's counting? I was very impressed by the hospitality of the people already. People made countless friendly impressions within our first hour. The harbor's parking lot was almost full of cars already, in the middle stood a small-motorized train with five passenger cars. A sign said tours began at 11:30. It was only 9:30.

We followed the curved edge of the shore seeing many restaurants filled with patrons enjoying a morning meal. The wide stretch of land between the concrete edge of the harbor and the actual buildings was filled with umbrella-clad tables for customers. Hundreds of people could be seated in this long continuous array of tables. Where one restaurant stopped and another seemingly began indistinguishable except for the change in furniture. The entire length of this street was in full shadow because the sun had yet to reach above the nearby hill. We continued along the shore to a small park where a wide walking jetty split the sea. Perhaps a half-mile out in the harbor, a small island stood with a large fortress with tanned walls. In the opposite direction a path hugged the shore and narrowed as the turquoise-sea undulated in waves of blue. Off in the distance, up the path we saw the same woman who had offered us directions. She and her friend were heading toward the beach, but from this side of the small town. She had told us a short cut and they were taking the scenic route to the beach, towels in hand.

As we traveled on the path around the hill the sun was fully visible. A short distance further was a small tunnel where the path exposed a beautiful beach where people waded in the water. What side of heaven had we stumbled upon? A second hill, more like a small mountain, had the Venetian fortress casting a long shadow on the beach. This shadow was in deep blues, and as the sun was progressively filling the water with light reflecting a brilliant turquoise. Soon the beach would be in full sun. We knew after our 11:30 tour we had a beach to visit.

Retracing the path, we found the small train and took the slow, town tour past war monuments and shopping streets. In the morning heat we saw the old town and an edge of the modern city where traffic kept us at a snail's pace. The tour was merely half an hour. We walked back to our hotel and checked into our room. The water to our hotel had to be shut off for repairs, but the woman was so apologetic that it didn't seem to matter. One of the two woman workers was still sitting at a table.

I had called the day before and booked the hotel, waking up a man with a deep, gruff voice. I expected to see this man. He was still a ghost. A heavyset boy in the lobby was at the computer. When he got up I sat down. The boy came over to me and told me I had to pay five Euros for the computer. I handed it over, correctly assuming he was the owner's child. The woman who had given us the tea looked at me and made a strange face at the boy. She didn't like him. He ordered her around with a very surly tone. When the child left she told us the computer was free to the customers.

Our room was in an old house. Each step to our room was accented by the complaints of a creaky set of stairs. The door didn't seem that secure. Any real effort to force it open would have yielded all our belongings. The old room was quaint and magical. We had a kitchen, a second large room with a sofa, and a real bathtub. It was tidy, and with lots of character; old peeling paint on the kitchen cabinets, and faucets that leaked. It felt like we were in someone's apartment rather than a hotel, but we liked the place very much. The main window was double doors that lead to a small balcony on which there was a table and two chairs. It was too hot to sit in the sun during the mid-day. Directly across the street was the church we had visited earlier that morning. As the bell pealed we became more enamored with our accommodations. We had no running water, so after a hurried lunch we organized a return trip to the beach.

The walk to the beach was ten minutes. A strange abandoned hotel, with 1960 architecture stood in disrepair near the beach. It is going to be replaced by a more modern hotel, but for now it remains an eyesore. The blistering hot road to the beach wound down a steep hill where evergreen trees cast long, thick shadows; the sun intensified the smell of evergreens. We joined a small parade of pedestrians that disappeared down the embankment.

Suddenly, a bright turquoise swath of color filled our eyes. The sea was a huge jewel as the thin shore cupped the water's edge where sunbathers sat or reclined on white chairs. People crammed into an intimate shoreline, brimming with humanity, blanket to blanket, elbow to elbow. There were no vendors peddling unwanted wares, simply a collection of sun and sea worshippers. We found two empty chairs and made a home in the sun, floating in bliss, enjoying everything about Nafplio.

It reached a point where our bodies were no longer cooled by repeated visits to the water, so we left for the hotel. The dark hotel room and TV lulled us into a nap. The bell outside our balcony would knoll once every hour as the hot sun melted any ambition to leave the air-conditioned room. It wasn't until sunset that we exited and found our way to the harbor where a bright red sun sunk over the Greek mountains we had slid down that morning, at speeds not safe for humans. I could see the highway we had been transported down and wished to never repeat such death defiance again in life. The evening had begun and hundreds of people were sitting in the same restaurants. By this time all the seats were full of patrons, their many dialects filling the warm evening air.

From the harbor across the water, the very distinct Bourtzi Fortress is well lit and attracts many photographers. It is situated at the entrance of the port and undoubtedly was there to protect from invasion. Today it is a beautiful light-blonde structure that adds to the harbor's romantic air. We strolled hand in hand along the wharf looking at the expensive vessels from all over Europe. The small waves lapped on the wharf wall while boats gently swayed in sync with the tide.

In the main square we spent a few hours just sitting and enjoying watching the parade of souls that wove the tapestry of Nafplio's downtown. The massive tree that shaded the restaurant was illuminated and the seats were filled by the dinner crowd.

A man and his son were selling a toy that when pulled, sent a disk spiraling straight up in the air, the disk flashed with multicolored, tiny lights. As it lifted

114

the object spun in the air. Passersby were immediately transfixed, a bright smile unconsciously glued to their faces. Children prodded their parents or grandparents to buy them the toy, thus filling the plaza with an abundance of scampering and shrieking children. Some of the toys got stuck in the trees and boys would climb up the thick limbs to retake their prized flying disks. There must have been fifteen or twenty of these disks rising and falling with children scurrying about to retrieve them. They were all having a wonderful time. People strolled in the heat without a care as children ran and played.

The streets that splintered off the main plaza were filled with shoppers. Each shop had a specialty; candy, souvenirs, or clothes. The free open space of the plaza was contrasted with congestion on the side streets. Restaurants had people sitting on small tables outside. In some areas, a bottleneck of pedestrians would narrow and slow. The foot traffic slowed to a crawl. The old city is roughly ten blocks by seven blocks by size. Half of this area is flat, while a hill creates a stair-step of geometric houses dotting the hillside upwards. At the top of the old city is a fortress. Beyond is a gorge that cuts to the sea and the beach. The Venetians build another fortress high upon the hill above the city as well as the one on an opposite mountain. This is what made the port so valuable. It was a well-guarded town with easy access to the sea. The higher fortress had a panoramic vista, a vantage point in times of war and peace. We never went to the high fortress. It seemed out of reach and in the hot sun we had little reason to go that far.

The Fortress Palamede is highlighted by the symbol of the Venice, a lion sculptured in stone. Part of the fortress perimeter resembles a smaller version of the Great Wall of China. Its square barricades line the wall, giving ancient archers a clear shot at invading forces.

The small, old town is easily traveled by foot. We didn't have time, or feel a great need, to venture outside of the old city. It was so charming that the new city with traffic warranted us to stay within walking distance of our hotel. I did finally meet the gruff-voiced owner of our hotel when it was time to pay the bill the morning we left. I told him his son had insisted we pay for the computer. I half-jokingly made a crazy face about the son, but it was too late for jokes. The owner became defensive and said I was talking about his son! I softened the exchange by explaining I was a teacher and I understood how difficult it was to raise a child. Within a few minutes the son handed me the five Euros back. It was a learning moment for him about honesty. The woman who worked there secretly told us how the boy was spoiled and a problem to be around. Nothing can be more sensitive than parents and their children. The owner did not like us because of the situation, but he did at least make his son return the money.

The morning we left I went on a long walk at sunrise to capture the light. I walked to the top of the old town through old arches into the fortress that overlooked the city. Cacti and thick brush were overgrown. It was hot even though it was only eight AM. I was walking in time with the music in my headphones, shooting as many interesting photographic views as possible. The solitude was good for me.

On my walk back I ran into my lovely wife Diana. We explored a little more, finding a church up a set of steep steps. Inside the bright church a priest stood at the altar saying Mass. No one was in the church but him. We joined the Mass.

It was a special moment. I can understand Christ in intimate settings, but the church as an institution is something I instinctually challenge.

The priest had a gentle demeanor and appeared to be in his nineties. He spoke to us in English with a thick French accent. He had lived in Africa most of his life but was now in this tiny church for retirement. Diana asked him for a special blessing, which he gave us for our travels. We spoke for a few minutes, exchanging information on the countries we had all come from.

We returned to the hotel just long enough to retrieve our bags and take the short walk to the bus terminal. At the bus station a crowd of muscular soldiers boarded. They wore clean green uniforms and seemed eager to get on the bus. These young men had been on some military exercises and were all heading back to Athens. We waited inside the air-conditioned station as long as possible. Several buses came and left until we found the correct one to Athens. It was a mad dash to get in amongst all the soldiers, but soon all were situated in the bus and we were quietly rolling toward the birthplace of democracy.

We spent three days in Athens. A proposed rendezvous with my coworker never happened, but as soon as we found our hotel we began calling her. The bus left us off at a busy traffic circle near a subway. I learned from my mistake in Paris and we climbed into a broken down taxi. The man spoke no English but we had the name of the hotel printed out on a sheet of paper. He found our street, even drove us to the front door, up a pedestrian walkway where cars were not permitted. I paid him fifteen Euros for a fifteen-minute ride. I have no idea to know if that was a fair price or not, but I liked the old driver and his dilapidated car.

Our driver helped us lift the bags into the hotel, but it was another four flights of stairs to our room on the top floor. There was no elevator. We'd been given the name of the hotel from my coworker. It was her sister's boyfriend who had a job in the hotel while he was an intern for his medical degree. By the time we arrived he had left their employment, but he was spoken of kindly when we mentioned his name. It was my coworker who suggested Kalamata and the hotel there as well. She is Greek and knows where the locals go. I asked for a town that was not full of foreigners, which we found. But we did find all the Greek tourists who were on vacation. Athens on the other hand, was full of international tourists.

Outside on a tiny balcony, we could see the Acropolis. We were a mile away at best, and the view was lovely. The hotel's TV was the only real problem, that and being on the fourth floor, up the small winding stair well. The volume on the TV was set so low it was impossible to hear. I'm sure this was to keep the rooms noise level down. On the second floor was a kitchen and refrigerator where we kept our food.

Two bicycles were parked on the street in front of the hotel, one was turned upside-down, and was being repaired. I met the bicyclist later. He was from Switzerland and had bicycled all though Iran. He told me the desert temperature was as high as one hundred and twenty degrees, so hot his rubber tires almost melted. He tried to do most of the riding at night to avoid heat stroke. I was very impressed with such a trek. We began our conversation on the narrow staircase and ran into each other again in the kitchen where he pieced his story together for me.

After a rest, lunch, and getting directions from the hotel clerk we were on our way out the door. We were looking for a grocery store first, not the Acropolis. The city is extremely easy to get around because of the Acropolis. It stands on a plateau and is visible for miles around. The city has miles of buildings surrounding this historic site, but we only stayed in the central district. The first day we passed walking in the old town at the base of the Acropolis. This was touted as the world's longest, continuous walking-street and runs along the old town into the modern sector. This is parallel to the Acropolis. The long street entertains every desire imaginable from expensive clothes to restaurants, to cheap stores where locals buy food. Of course, the majority of the stores sell souvenirs for the tourists. We walked for hours taking in many sights and smells until we were saturated and exhausted. Bed was the best option. It was late.

The second day we started with a small train tour that takes the tourists to all the main attractions. As I stated earlier this is the best way to get an overview of what interests you and give you cause to return to see in more depth. The train tour was cheap and did the same sights as the big tour buses at a fraction of the price. My coworker suggested this to us. The Parliament (the Syntagma), the tomb of the unknown soldier, where the changing of the guard takes place, and the National Gardens are all within walking distance of each other and the old town under the Acropolis.

A most intriguing spectacle is the changing of the guard. The solders wear white shirts, white pleated skirts, white tights, colorful vests, a round red cap, and clogs instead of boots. The guns negate all the feminine attire. The stance, synchronized arms swinging, gun swinging, feet clopping and toe tapping, freezing in midair, continuing with swinging gyrations is a spectacle to behold. The purpose is to intimidate the Turks, their archenemies. The explanation I was given about the ritual was to commemorate the dead Greeks who fought the Turks. The elaborate set of moves is to impress upon the Turks that they will not forget. I think this is akin to the Nazi goose step but I'm not Greek, nor do I have a great love of the military in any country. The entire ritual reminded me of a rooster strutting around to defend his turf. This is well worth the price because it is free to the public.

We met some other new Yorkers, and had a pleasant encounter. On the next street over from the Royal Palace where a similar ritualistic military dance takes place, adjacent to the Royal Palace is the National Gardens. The metro plaza that opens onto the parliament building is an expansive, grand scene. Fountains and a sweeping view of the buildings are a pleasant place to just sit and take in the Greek shade.

The Acropolis was our main stop. On our walk to the historic site I was photographing as many interesting shadows, buildings, or angles as I could find. In one shop window I saw a large icon of Christ surrounded in a brilliant gold frame. I was interrupted while my shutter clicked; a man hissed at me that the icon was for sale, not to be photographed. I was wondering if this was for religious reasons or commercials reasons that he objected. I was also wondering what God he worshipped since he seemed more concerned about his money than my admiration for a likeness of Jesus. It was that love for ones fellow man that gave cause for me to know he was a true Christian.

The Acropolis was, is, and will always be breath taking. What began as a Greek temple to Athena attributes its partial destruction, not to time, but the munitions of war. The British used the temple as a storehouse for gunpowder. To add to this insult, the British today hoard the valued friezes that spanned the top of the building in their National Museum. The original statue to Athena has long ago vanished, but her house stands as a relic to the Greek culture that flourished some six hundred years before Christ. The structure is awe inspiring must to see. If you choose to see the temple or not, you will see this impressive white marble structure standing as a piece of heaven above the city, no matter where one stands in the city.

We entered the park grounds surrounding the base of the Acropolis. A small queue of tourists gathered around the entrance. In the park itself, the police were chasing men selling trinkets. They were playing a cat and mouse game of "catch me if you can". These Egyptian men ran here and there warning each other of the policemen's whereabouts as they quickly approached the tourists selling trinkets. The police obliged in this game with angry threats and sneak attacks that would result in one out of twenty five being arrested. (Survival versus the law!) I thought this was very interesting to see.

The queue at the base of the temple was long and luckily in the morning shade. It wound up and around scaffold pillars. The already worn steps were getting a trampling, as there seemed to be no real order to the trail of humanity. People would zigzag in a slow motion stream. All were cheery and happy to be a part of the tourist attraction. At the top entrance, security guards appeared like a silhouetted dark vision. Thick ropes surrounded the exterior of the temple to keep people off the ancient steps. There was a considerable renovation project under way which was evident by the abundance of scaffolding holding up whole sections of the temple. If you have any premonitions of quietly visiting an empty temple and having a sacred moment go somewhere else. There is nothing quiet and nothing but crowds of people.

In the hustle of footsteps and loud children scampering around, Diana and I shared a moment. We paused, looking at the far side of the temple in the blazing heat. A strong, pleasant wind was cooling the sweat from our foreheads. We had been standing on line for a drink from a water fountain I glanced over at Diana and she had tears streaming from her eyes.

"What's wrong?" as any husband would ask. "I have dreamed of this all my life, and never knew it would come true". I was very proud of her and my heart melted as I gave her a strong embrace followed by a tender kiss. At that moment all the effort and struggle of our travels paid off. Diana thanked me. Athena's grace was shining upon us and we believed in her love.

We were walking on sacred clouds. We lingered another hour. And visited the museum where headless elegant human torsos resided. We regarded the marble faces of men and women from an age that seemed to defy time and make us feel no different than those we observed.

Have we really progressed or evolved in all those years? Those frozen faces affirm our linage to the past, nothing more than a thin flash of time. How ridiculous it is to think we have changed as a species. We are no different than the Greek ancestors. There are more of us, but perhaps we are less wise. The passage of additional millennia may reveal the truth about mankind's wisdom.

Athens is full of ruins that can be walked through for a fee or seen through a chain linked fence. Some of these ruins are free. We visited a free site of low laying broken ruins, and wandered to a park with homeless men sleeping under olive trees. We found a shady spot and ate our packed lunch. As we sat eating two turtledoves danced in circles waiting to see if we had any breadcrumbs for them. Once I got the birds as close as possible I began shooting pictures. A man sat on the ground eating as a flock of pigeons arrived swarming him, eating the bread he threw out to them. We napped in the shade as the sun passed overhead into the early afternoon. A mix of homeless people and tourists shared the park. I suppose in my own country this would have felt unsafe. Maybe the heat let us drop our guard down or the fact that we were on a vacation gave us that extra excuses to enjoy ourselves.

On the pedestrian-street we found a small shop with benches and stopped for a cold drink. Three young men from France sat at the table next to us and we began a conversation about music from the sixties. These young musicians were in a band and idolized the same people as I, despite our age difference. We shared a brief conversation and I invited them to visit my web site, leaving them a card with the address.

The next morning we were up very early and took the subway to the port city of Pireas. We were huddled amongst the daily commuters with our bags hiding bathing suits and cameras. Leaving the train we crossed a pedestrian bridge as a light shower began to bath the streets. After asking around we found the ticket booth for a ferry that would take us to two islands near Pireas; Aegina and Angistri.

Aegina is a busy port where cars and people scurry about half an hour away. We had a two and a half hour wait until the next ferry to Angistri so we started with an ice cream sitting at a restaurant that skirts the harbor. The sidewalk is actually buried below umbrellas and tents to shade the patrons from the sun. But next to the doors of the various restaurants a tiny path leads down the street. A loud and active arena of people is suddenly replaced with quiet alleys where one can hear one's own footsteps within yards of the port's main street. We wandered aimlessly finding interesting photographic views and visiting a couple of Greek Orthodox churches. The churches were near empty, only old women saying their prayers, lighting candles, kissing the icons, and making the sign of the cross, drifted inside the cool shaded houses of God. The contrast of hot, bright sun, outside, made for good silhouette photographs as I caught the shadow of a woman sweeping the church's interior floor.

We wanted to see the beach so we walked to the shore away from the harbor where it was less congested. As we sat on a low wall in the shade of group of Roma were resting on blankets placed on the ground. The more we looked around the more we saw that there were many such small clans. This was not their vacation picnic; this was their home for the day. A man was sitting on the wall next to us. I offered him some cookies, sharing what we ate. A few minutes later he opened a small suitcase and pulled out an accordion and began to play and sing. The combination of his voice, the beads of sweat rolling down his face like syrup, and the heat, all filtered through the trees mixing with shadows and light. I pointed to my camera, my face begging the question. He nodded, giving permission to photograph him. Somewhere between ecstasy and sheer pain he possessed the true expression of his situation. He sang a low, sad song that lamented his life of struggle. I didn't know the language. I knew the emotion and felt the connection. I shot a series of pictures of him as he allowed me into an intimate moment of reality. When he finished I asked him his country. He was from Romania. He spoke neither Greek nor English. His humility was not an act. This was real life. The duality of life for a vacationer strikes me at times. I have the luxury of enjoying travel while the majority of the world struggles to get by. If I can be real, honest, and understanding there is no need to feel guilt. That is the real passport, to have others open up to you.

The ferry entered the Port of Aegina with a horn that frightened every bird within earshot. We had spent our two and a half hours well, now we were heading for Angistri, only a short ferry ride away. One can never say enough about the beautiful, azure seas, beckoning even on the ferry, pulling, luring, tempting a hand, a toe to caress its sweet wake. Twenty minutes later we disembarked into a small village that seemed too small to handle all the tourists. I had been to this island before, maybe eight years ago. It is a chance to get a small taste of a Greek Island as a simple day trip without the hassle of luggage and lodging.

We spent the day under the shade of a small olive tree on one of the beaches. We were enjoying watching the Greek women watch us, and whisper back and forth. Mothers with their teenage children sat a few feet away on tall stools, leaning on a tall table, smoking and drinking, while they commented to each other about anyone who passed by. We know our age difference is a topic that comes up often and this must have been the subject of their conjecture about us. The woman dressed like teenagers in tight slakes, only with an additional twenty years of wear. Their hair was puffed up high; the eyeliner was thick and black, while their eyes wore a blue shade that made them appear clownish. We whispered about them as they whispered about us, a comic situation to say the very least. As the sun moved we shifted the blanket around the tree, moving closer to the women each time. Our hushed banter was reminiscent of a 1960's melodrama.

While in the water, where we stood, the wind sent rough waves that threw cold water on our heads and torsos. If we had been totally submerged we would have avoided the chill, but the water wasn't warm enough. The bottom was rocky with sporadic patches of green sea grass. The heat was the only real reason to go into the water; the sudden chill of the sea shocked parts of my manhood.

We ate our packed lunch and splurged on a half-gallon of ice cream from a corner store. The "piggy foreigners" were actually eating the ice cream from the bucket before it melted. I'm sure the women with big hair discussed this. We'd had enough of the heat and headed toward the port and better shade. We didn't say good-bye to the women, which was topic for discussion in and of itself.

In one of our unusual rare moments Diana and I were bickering about what, I can't remember. She went off to see more of the small village while I sat, then walked to see what the vendors were selling along the walkway. We, like any couple, have times where enough is enough. I only remember that I tend to get verbally distasteful with her and live to regret it. I could be totally correct in what I am saying, my delivery is terrible, and often the source of my own guilt. I was stewing and waiting for the ferry to blow its horn. No boat, nothing. Then it struck me.

We had bought a ticket for a sleek, race-boat-like, fast boat home and the ticket showed a different port. What? How can this island have more than one port? I asked a vendor and sure enough, the other port was within view, only a long, twenty-minute walk, down the coast. Diana returned to find me in a panic and grabbing her hand to run for the boat. We rushed past the beach we'd spent the day. The women gossips were gone, thank God! They would have known we were fools, late for the ferry! We were speed-walking, sweat rolling down our faces. A car was driving by on the road and I put my thumb out in a desperate act of hope. The young couple inside spoke English and welcomed us to ride along. The tiny car was just big enough for us. It was one of very few cars we'd seen on the island all day. We had ten minutes to get to the ferry. We would not have made it had our tiny-car-saviors not come by at that exact time. In a frenzy we both forgot about whatever silly nonsense we were disagreeing about, and began a friendly conversation with the couple in the front seat. We thanked them and made a fast exit to the long jetty that ran along the harbor. The boat left five minutes after we sat in our seats. A word of caution about revisiting a place, don't assume things to be the way they were in the past. It can be a mind trap.

The fast boat back was indeed fast, bumpy, and loud. We zoomed past huge tankers and cargo boats with bright colors and rusty decks. The journey time was halved, but still a good hour to complete. The sun was getting low with good light so I went outside to a slim open passage where the water splashed and the noise was like a jet on a runway. As I bounced around I took photographs of passing vessels. It was a pointless exercise of blur and motion, no matter what the camera settings everything was a wash.

We arrived back at Pireas just in time for the sunset. The train platform was full of passengers coming, and going home from work. We squeezed our way onto a train just before it pulled away from the station. We stood in the front of one of the passenger cars all of us crammed in like sardines. Twenty minutes into the ride the train seemed no less empty of passengers, few people disembarked at the individual stations.

Suddenly, two men were having a tug at each other. People began to yell and scream. A woman was pulling at the man who had her husband in a headlock. Then other passengers began to grab at the man holding the passenger by the head. At first I thought this was a fight. Well, it was a fight, but the man I assumed to be the perpetrator was the victim. The crowd of passengers immediately assessed what was really happening. One man yelled in English, although with a thick accent, "He picked my pocket!" Suddenly what had been two men became three, a family, and many standers-by. A few fists flew but the passengers soon had two men in a strong lock-down. The two men were Slavic, acting innocent, as everyone was yelling at them. The victim began to search them and look for his wallet while passengers were restraining the men.

The train pulled into a station and stopped. The two men being held tried to escape through an open door, but they got nowhere. I stepped onto the platform from the front door and motioned to a policeman that he was needed. Soon three policemen were in the car, questioning the passengers, and no one was going anywhere. The man who'd been pick-pocketed, his wife, and children were all taken off the train along with the two Slavic men. The wallet was never found, maybe a third man had it passed off to him, but no one found the wallet while we watched the police searching through the open train door. The train pulled away leaving a small crowd arguing on the platform. The passengers all took up the conversation as we, little by little, disembarked until few, if anyone left on the train witnessed the scuffle.

We sat out in the evening air as people gathered to watch a crew of flamethrowers. Out of the corner of my eye, I watched a man steal a six-pack of beer from a shop refrigerator. The owner was oblivious to the theft. I guess I was tired of people not being caught after the train so I went up to the owner behind the cash register and informed him of the event. Within seconds, the man was nabbed and brought back to the shop. He offered to pay and the matter was settled quickly.

We had a last stroll back to the hotel. In the morning we were back on a high-speed subway built to house all the traffic for the Olympics that had taken place a few years earlier. On my previous trip to Athens it was a terrible ordeal to get to the airport. This time we walked in long polished, marble halls where escalators whisked us to the check in desks.

For the first time in all our travels we were being asked for our wedding certificate and told we could not board the plane. I got calm and assertive, convincing the supervisor we'd been on many airplanes without any problems, in and outside the United States. Diana needed a stamp that showed she was married to me, with a name change. (This was the first we heard of this, but within a few weeks of returning back home we got the stamp at the Colombian Consulate.) All was forgiven and we were allowed to board our plane.

Our direct flight to New York had been changed to a London stopover. It was exciting to circle the city and see Big Ben, and the Parliament building, as if they were dollhouses. I felt like Peter Pan. In 1965 I flew into London for the first time. Now the city is an immense modern metropolis. Mod cloths and the Beatles are old fashioned. Nothing stays the same. I dreaded the airport and the anticipated long lines for security. None of that was the same.

I offended a man from New York by making a crack about waiting impatiently in line "like a New Yorker". The man shot back at me that he'd lived there all his life and never experienced rude behavior. "I'm from New York", I said. His wife put her hand on his arm to calm him down. I tried to ease the situation with a political joke about George Bush. The man wasn't laughing and I was sure I'd made a wrong assumption about his political affiliation as well. I was in deep "doo doo" no matter how I tried to clean up, so I shut up. I didn't want to embarrass myself any further by trying to be cute like before. The line moved fast, we were soon on the same jet as the other New Yorkers, never to be seen again. (Ps If I offended you in London in 2008 while in line at the new British Air Terminal number five, I'm sorry! And thank you for buying my book. You are the exclusive recipient of an apologetic ending to our European chapters of my travel memoir!)

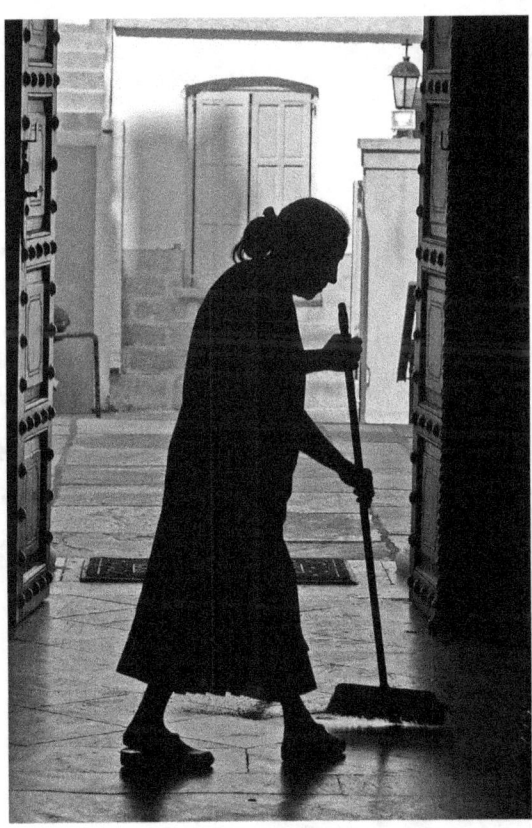

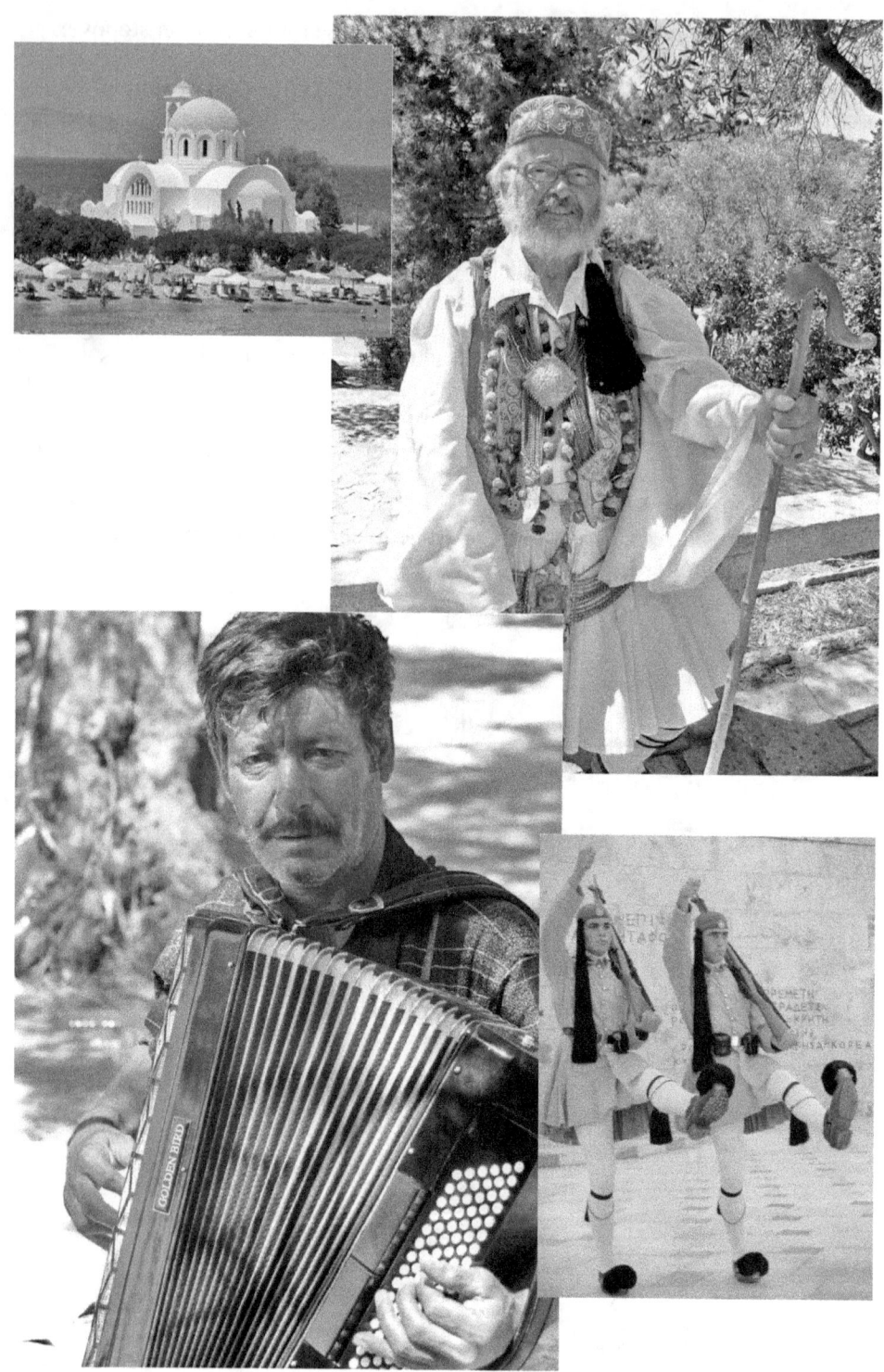

Chapter Eight
Colombia

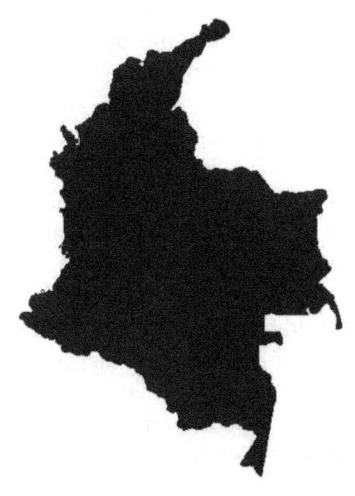

A quick return home to New York for two days, gave us time to unpack, repack and leave for Colombia. I will be in Colombia for one week, Diana for a full three plus. In the two days home we had four hours of fun, the rest was all business and catching up.

In New York a trip to the beach with our friend Victoria the first day back home was fun. We sat on a beach, that was nicer than Greece, but we had to travel half way around the world to discover such things. While on the beach, we saw two women have an argument. For the moment, I thought I was back in Italy. The police were called because one of the women was told to move her chair to the public side of the beach. She was a few feet into the private beach. The argument was about the one sunbather trespassing inches onto an invisible line. Ah, life in America. Private property on a beach is as foreign in Europe as a space ship landing in the Vatican. The cop detested what he was doing. The onlookers loathed what was happening to the evicted beach-goer. And the few using the private beach felt fully justified in their power-driven luxury. Welcome back to America.

We spent the second day in Manhattan until one o'clock AM. At five thirty in the morning we got up and drove into the city. At nine o'clock sharp I was down near Wall Street picking up my letters of incorporation for the new publishing company. Diana sat in the car and said the rosary. A cop came by (she was parked at a hydrant) and luckily said he was a Catholic too. He wasn't going to chase a woman praying in a parked car. I was gone maybe ten minutes; we had sat there forty minutes waiting until nine when the lawyer's office opened.

We drove to Madison and Twenty Third Street where Diana had an appointment with her new employer, as an assistant speech therapist. We waited in the car, and then plugged a parking meter for an hour as we went up to the building. I waited in the reception area of the business. Diana wanted me to go, but I said it was more professional to leave me outside.

"In my country the husband would go with the wife," she stated noting the contrast in cultures. She got the job, but starts in September after our summer.

Soon we were back on Long Island grabbing lunch at a fast food place and then off to the bank. We took out an auto loan for Diana's new car. I am trying to help her establish credit so the loan is in her name. We went to the local post office where we collect the mail for our house. (We have two home addresses and two post offices.) All the while we separated the real mail from the junk mail while driving. There was two months of mail to sift through. We arrived home, savored our first home-cooked meal in seven weeks, and continued to get ready for the flight the next morning. We had to leave at 3:30 AM. Bedtime was nine PM.

The check-in went without a hitch and we were just getting settled in for our wait in the airport when Diana spotted Herman, Flor's nephew by marriage. Flor is the woman who introduced us to each other. We sat and visited with him and waited for the time to board the plane. As we went through security, I met a man who lived in Costa Rica. He was a retired sanitation worker and has been living there for twenty years. His wife was back in Lemon, Costa Rica because they could never leave the house empty. Diana and I had just visited that side, the Gulf side, of Costa Rica last April. The man was a joy to meet and we exchanged stories about Costa Rica. He loved the place, as I do.

We sat with Herman and told him about our summer travels. When I first met him, and many Colombians in New York, they seemed a bit distant to me. I speak my weak Spanish with them. But I have noticed over time and many visits (He has been to our house for dinner) that the "distance" is more about people's inability, or shyness, in speaking English. My speech hops between the two languages. If I don't know a word I use English. But I now feel fully accepted by all the acquaintances we've made. In fact I am family. Herman gave me a big hug when he came over to greet us.

The six hour flight started with the drone of the flight safety measures. I listened to the Spanish version just to sharpen my language skills. I think I could do this ritual I have sat through it so many times. I love the body gestures and the pointy fingers to the exit doors. I would exaggerate every movement and make a complete fool of myself. Only once did I see a stewardess act the fool. It was so delightful. I think they have to be serious, but who can take a seat cushion that doubles as a floatation device seriously! And who can take a discussion serious about floating in water when you are a quarter of a mile up in the air! That disconnect is something that bothers me. I enjoyed the meal more than anything else on the flight. The South American carriers still have the good grace to feed passengers.

We were greeted at the airport in Medellin. Diana's father, Tuto, was there to welcome us and Aura, Diana's sister-in-law. He drove up in his car to give us a ride into town. After a twenty minute drive, we briefly stopped in Guarne, where Diana's brother lives, to leave some gifts, drop off Aura, his wife, and then continued into the descending valley of Medellin to receive lots of kisses. Guarne is a small town at the crest of the mountains that stands above Medellin. Guarne climate is notably cooler than the big city in the valley below.

Diana's aunt is here from Florida and we had a gift for her as well. The day passed after we set foot in the house at 2:30 in the afternoon, not to leave as of yet, the next morning.

Diana's uncle Fabio and aunt, Piedad, came over and we greeted them with gifts. The Spanish was making me dizzy. My ability to translate was becoming a slurred mixture of languages and lands recently visited. I was falling asleep mid-sentences, so I went to bed. I am still on a European body clock. The din of traffic, voices muffled in conversation, and house cleaning was audible before the sunrise or the time I arose.

Already, the entire household has been up cleaning, except me. I am the "privileged" artist/writer who sits, pensively at the computer. The daily ritual was off and running before I got up at 6:30; mopping, wiping cleaning solutions, dusting, scrubbing, every chore completed daily. I have no idea how dirt can ever possibly collect in this house. It's like a soul forever in a state of cleansing prayer. In the midst of breakfast and cleaning we received news of a neighbor's death. She had lived alone in the building and had secretly been battling cancer. Only Tuto, Morelia, and the woman's brother who lived in the building knew. Now, in death, the entire building knew what a guarded secret was. What was so private had become general knowledge and passed off as non-incidental gossip. How strange life is. Is there really such a thing as privacy? Is there really such a thing as private property?

Today my only chore is to buy Diana's mother a washing machine.

Day Three: I'm exhausted from working on the computer. Yesterday Sandra, who is translating my first book into Spanish, delivered the entire book. Before she arrived I began to prepare the files by using the original English files. This was a big undertaking because I was looking through massive amounts of old files to find the correct ones. I did. Then when the book was delivered I did the paste up, which took a few hours. In the night I began to do the cover in Spanish. This was a nightmare because I could not get the exact font and shadows I wanted. I'm a perfectionist. There is still one thing I couldn't figure out but it had to wait until I got some help from a friend at the job. In all it took me about five hours which wasn't that bad. Writing the first English text was a sort of 'on the job training'/ baptism by fire when it came to the computer applications. I did most of the learning when I did the original book a few months back, but remembering the details is always a challenge. I know my mood is one of emersion and tunnel vision while working. Not being disturbed by others in an intense and detailed computer arena makes me very non-commutative.

Diana is also going through some work for the new job. She requires help with the computer at times, yet last night she was an angel. She knew I was drowning in work and asked some questions in a very delicate manner. This morning we had a conversation about the best way to communicate and to answer people's requests in the shortest, most concise way possible. She always tells me I am direct and strict, but I feel my influence is a positive thing for her. I try to show her how her attitudes and moods are not centered. She has a nervous temperament when she has challenges, or tasks at hand. I can sense these moods and at times I am just plain short tempered with her. Other times I can step back and navigate the situation in a gentle way, though these times always test the relationship.

Diana doesn't give herself enough credit for the process of change and her immigration. She only thinks about the demands put on her and stresses out on the situation rather than see that this is a long process. I tell her this is a sign of immaturity, which is often taken in a negative light. Maybe I do the same thing and this is why I understand her. But at my age (57 while Diana is 37) I also feel a greater enjoyment out of these situations because I have a list of accomplishments that give me the confidence to face challenges. I have learned from art and music, they are great teachers for knowing that accomplishment is just that, a process. Art, music, and writing, all, give me a sense of completion, or expression for my moods. I can change my modes by feeling this completion. This is why I see art education as the sole means for students to have this internal dialogue that is crucial to mental and spiritual health. I frame my life from an artistic perspective, but I'm sure that a businessman can feel the same sense of internal solace through creativity.

I was using business as an example for Diana. Business is concise and factual, the product is delivered, and payment takes place. Period. It is not personal.

From an artistic perspective everything is personal because art involves the metaphysical, personal emotions, and the spiritual universe. But in business it is a plain and simple delineation. When the woman delivered the book in Spanish she wanted more money. I had no business obligation to give her more money, but on a personal level I felt I did. Regardless of this, I was not obligated to give more; therefore I stuck to our original agreement. These are the kinds of distinctions I try to explain to Diana. She is an extremely giving person. She is generous to a fault. So much that she leaves her self-loving center. It's not that she needs to "protect" herself from others. It is that she needs to focus on her own strength and not feel threatened by other's needs. I live this myself or I couldn't explain that I see it in her. I sincerely believe that when we operate in our "centers" we operate in love, in appropriate ways, and succeed. This is the challenge in life and all personal and professional relationships.

We bought Diana's mother a washing machine yesterday. After going to many shops we settled on the big department store. Diana, Toto, and I, walked to the downtown and went looking. On the way we ran into some Hare Krishna's. I had seen them the day before at the airport. We spoke briefly and I told the man who had come in from Europe, we had seen devotees in Vienna a few weeks earlier. A group of people waited to greet this man, a leader of some kind, at the airport. I feel a good kinship with these people. I can't be a member of any army, but I love that they are like priests and nuns living in the modern world. They invited us to the temple that night but we said that we didn't know if we'd attend. We went off to more stores comparing prices, maintaining our status as consumers living in the material world.

In the meantime, I bought more eyeglasses. The prices for glasses here are a fraction of what they cost in New York. The three of us romped around the city. We made jokes with Tuto and had a good time. Tourists are rare here. None are American-Gringos as they are called throughout Central and South America. The piercing stares sent in my direction are a strong reminder that I am definitely a stranger in a foreign land, no matter how much time I spend here. My presence here is a silent, yet very powerful remark about the influx of visitors, some tourists, some future immigrants who will reflect a world of the future where cultures and ethnicities will blend harmoniously. Without a word, I am telling the people to prepare for more of my kind in their future. The globe is no longer a series of isolated nations.

I often think back on my own childhood and how aware I am not only of the changes in population, but also the changes in the nationalities of these people. I saw a woman yesterday that was Chinese and Spanish descent. She was speaking Spanish with a friend. This mix of ethnicities is the future.

We came home and I took a nap. Today the washing machine will be delivered and my agenda is to look at this beautiful place and make it more my home.

Day Four: Most of the day I was here in the house, but later Diana and I ventured out around noon and decided it was time to have a break from the family and its domestic goings on. We went to a few stores, and then ended up at the Hare Krishna Center. We saw the same man whom we met the day before and he took us to meet the guru/ leader. I can't remember his spiritual name, but he was a German man in his early fifties. We had a pleasant chant and discovered we had both been in Vienna at the same time a few weeks back. We told him we had met three devotees on the street in Vienna. I also told him I had stayed in a temple in California back in the 1970's; around the same time he joined. He gave us two roses and a big hug when we were leaving. This was Diana's second time in a Krishna temple. It was striking how we were in the restaurant and went down stairs into the booming and bustling street. The drastic change in scenery and feelings of total chaos was intense. I told Diana we had passed from the spiritual world back to the material world.

I like the Krishna's despite the bad rap they get in the media. I can't join anything like they want me to. I don't even want to be a full-fledged Unitarian Universalist. The five years I devoted to the Unitarian organization were spent fighting their internal politics. I don't like politicized organizations and the same goes with being employed by organizations like schools. Right now I don't want to even think about my job because next week I will be back in that saddle.

After our visit to the Hare Krishna temple we went to the Medellin Botanical Gardens. This was a perfect place to regroup and enjoy each other's company. The park has been rebuilt since our first visit there approximately three years ago. The entrance is a grand concrete circle that has a fountain inside. It is a tall flowered-shaped structure with walls that tilt outwards. The fountain was not running. A shallow pool of water stood with lights to shine in the night. There was no entrance fee.

We have been there many times. Every time we visit Medellin we go there. This particular visit was especially nice because we were able to spend time together after days of little interaction in the house. Diana sat on the park bench by the lake while I lay on the bench with my head in her lap. Ducks would walk around our feet looking for a meal, then go back into the water, then on to the next group of people on the lakeside. The wind was blowing, the sun was out, and we sat in the cool shade of a big tree. We spent hours there, relishing our time to reconnect. We both know it will be difficult to be apart for three weeks coming up, while I return and Diana stays here with her family.

We came home and I watched TV. This time the cable TV has BBC and CNN, so I am in news heaven after weeks of being deprived of news while in Europe. I love politics and keeping up on world events.

Day Five: Friday Santa Fe de Antioquia. We needed a day to just be on vacation again. So we went to a town that we had talked of going to several times. This is the small quaint town of Santa Fe Antioquia. I love this place's charm and grace. It has narrow streets and old style houses behind walled street entrances. The streets are made of round hand sized black boulders. Instead of yellow taxis' the town has motor "rickshaws". These are three wheeled enclosed motorcycles where there is room for two passengers in the back while the driver sits in the solo front seat. These tiny taxis rumble over the rock streets with ease and make a small noise, like the buzz of a small motorcycle.

From Medellin we had taken a small bus to Santa Fe Antioquia. The small passenger bus was cramped and smelled like urine. I wasn't sure if the smell was the plastic seat covers or someone freely using the bus floor as a place to urinate. As we traveled up the mountain I could smell the brakes and was wondering if anyone else did. Yes, Diana did as well. We snaked up the mountain road and looked at the sprawling city of Medellin. It is growing higher and higher into the surrounding mountains. The bus entered a tunnel that was one of the longest I've ever been in. The ride inside the tunnel was ten to fifteen minutes long. It was filled with smog. It was new, within the last few years. Diana said it used to be a three and a half hour ride to Antioquia, but the tunnel had cut the time in half. On the far side of the tunnel we hit a small traffic stoppage. I think it was construction; it also looked like a landslide had covered one lane of the road.

We began to pass many hotels with swimming pools. The terrain changed into a tropical landscape as the warmth became more and more apparent. We passed into a new, more humid, area. When the sun began to shine and it felt like we had gone into Costa Rica. I was surprised by the sudden change in climate and vegetation. The mountains gave way to low hills and the wide River Cauca. The rainy morning and cloud-filled valley of Medellin was replaced by a paradise of heat and sunshine. The number of hotels lining the roadside painted a vacation atmosphere. This is where the people of Medellin come to soak in the sun and get some rest. Medellin is high in the mountains and change in temperature is at least ten degrees, making me feel hot while on the bus.

After a two-hour journey from Medellin's North Terminal to Santa Fe Antioquia, we arrived. In Medellin the metro stops opposite the terminal on the other side of the river and freeway, but a foot bridge traverses these obstacles. A five-minute walk put us in the heart of a bustling terminal. We bought our ticket and had a half hour wait so we bought a small snack of chicken on a corn bread. As we sat eating we watched a man approach a young woman to become friends. He was flirting with her, but she seemed politely distant at first. We enjoy watching such little dramas while we travel. We make comments, some may be totally inaccurate, but most of the time we make correct assumptions. Fun!

On our way we pulled into a small town called Parque, where the streets were barren until we drove though the town square. There, the sudden change in population was drastic. The square was filled with school children in uniforms. There was a festival of some kind. We dropped off a few passengers and went ten minutes further to Antioquia.

The small bus station was in a gated area. The ticket office was neighboring a restaurant and tiny shops. We ate a lunch of rice, salad, and spiced chicken for a few dollars each. I took some portraits of the local people dining in the restaurant. My impression of the town immediately changed in a mere two blocks. We walked up a short hill onto cobble narrow streets with a long line of white buildings that was an instant venture into the past. The noise of the crowded bus station and people disappeared. We were walking in another time where women stood in doorways eyeing the passersby, where a stranger stood out, and where children paused to look in wonder. The long street pointed us to the town square, as did all roads in Antioquia.

In the center was a large plaza with a church, park, and fountain. The park had compact booths with people selling goods. The minute shops sold natural candies, fruits, handmade items, and one or two sold souvenirs. Mostly the wares were the products that the local people used. We looked at one stall and told the young girl we would return again later. We bought a few pieces of natural coconut candy. It was delicious. Before we left in the afternoon we did return.

The girl confided that we were her only customers all day. No one was shopping that day and we spent only a few dollars. There were no other tourists with the exception of two people we stopped and spoke with. They were from Italy and stood out because of their dress and the camera around the man's neck. I stopped them and asked them where they were from. The woman was glad we were the only tourists. We told them about our bed bugs in Rome, their home town. We didn't tell them Rome was our least favorite place on the trip. They were seeing Colombia by bus, heading to the coastal cities. The small talk soon ended and they went off in the opposite direction.

We visited two hotels to see what the prices were. The first and oldest hotel in the town was in the square. The second, newer and more posh, hotel was a few blocks away. Both hotels were on a ridge that had spectacular views of the mountains. The street below had a few houses, but this was an area of the town that made me feel we were on the edge of things. The sun was beating down on us and I felt like swimming. We had no suits. We liked the prices of the older hotel and the rustic atmosphere. We discussed staying the night, but we had no clothes or provisions. Had we known we would have stayed and enjoyed the town. Soon we were sitting under a large tree in the town square drinking icy fruit drinks and looking at the "campesinos" (country folk). The Italian tourists passed us by without seeing us. We sat watching young girls attracting boyfriends, like bees to flowers. Biology is always at work, like gravity pulling people together to make babies, create new families, and continuing the life stories. It all astounds me. We are spreading over the hills and mountains in numbers that make the previous ages look like we were not here on earth. Now humanity is so prevalent that we are drastically changing the landscape and atmosphere.

A woman in the second hotel told us we could hire a motor-taxi and go to see the bridge over the River Cauca. This famous bridge was a historical landmark and a favorite tourist stop. We rode down a long steep drive after passing through neighborhoods that seemed to be the kind of places I would like to live. The long straight road curved into a flat area where the driver stopped to show us the vista. The single lane bridge was off in the distance. The sound of wood clanking as a single car passed was loud. I was nervously wondering if this would hold our weight, not to mention the trucks and cars that pass over the structure. Two steel gray, short towers stood at the ends of both sides of the bridge. It was simple and not an impressive structure. It was the bridge that linked two sides of Colombia and made Antioquia a "big" city. It was the original capitol of this State, or Province. (The Province is called Antioquia as well.)

The taxi zoomed across the bridge and we stopped on the opposite side. The driver said he would return in a half an hour, and that he was going to lunch. A boy in his late teens came up to us and offered a guided tour. The price was whatever we wanted to give him. He gave us the history of the bridge, the story of the man who was the engineer, and the dates of its construction. The man who built this bridge was Jesus Maria Villa. His story was fascinating. He was a total drunk who was fired from the project for his alcoholic antics, but eventually won the hearts of the local people to become a hero in Colombian folklore. No one would traverse the bridge until Jesus, his wife and children, and four hundred cows proved its safety by crossing over the waters of the River Cauca. The house where Jesus was born and lived was a white spec on top of the nearest mountain. He sadly died of his disease.

As we sat with the boy after the tour, two policemen rode up on a motorcycle as we sat drinking cold water, the boy continued with the history even though we had given him a few dollars and a cold beverage. He seemed to be enjoying the fact that two people had paid him and were interested and asking questions. It wasn't until the taxi returned that we pulled ourselves away and thanked him that he gave in and ended talking. He loved what he was doing. An old man had told him the story of the bridge and he was continuing, passing along what he had learned.

The three-wheel taxi ascended the long hill and we re-entered the town square after a tour of the outer roads and sights of the city. A second unpopulated square was a few blocks away from the main square. We had stopped there before, but this time the taxi passed through and up the street to the crowded center of the small town. I say crowded, but this is an exaggeration. There could have been one hundred people in all. In one corner of the square two "canteens" had music blasting and another fifty men occupied this area. The smell of alcohol and cigarettes was milling as plentiful as the men.

In the other corner of the square we entered the municipal building. It was well preserved and still in use. It was an old building with a central garden and a second balcony of offices. A local artist had done portraits of the individual officials that worked there which were hung outside each door on a common wall. As we walked past the open doors we could identify the people inside by the art. I pointed to the first man I saw, then to his portrait outside. He motioned yes. It was he. I liked this. The art on display had meaning and application to the people working in the building. We used the public restrooms. The woman's room was locked so a woman entered the men's restroom unashamedly, closed the door and did her business. It was a liberating moment. (I often see that men don't have to pay and women do. Is this because the men can stand up? I've never figured that one out.)

It was at that time we returned to the young girl in the town square and made our purchases. We did this so we wouldn't have to carry the bag around all day. We exited the square and one block away, we entered a little museum that was originally a house of a one of the founding fathers. Each room had been decorated to show the way life had been lived in years past. Some religious art was in two rooms and a show of a contemporary artist hung in a larger room lined with chairs. This was artwork of a black artist from one of the coastal cities. Large figures with striking, rainbow colors were composed in realistic arrangements. The artist was easy to understand. The art was for the people, about the people.

Our time was running out so we hastened to the bus depot only to sit waiting in the bus ten minutes past the departure time. A middle-aged couple entered and sat on the bus. They were dressed in casual clothes. The man was speaking English. He was a Gringo. "Where you from?" I asked. He ignored me.

"Excuse me, where are you from", I said a second time and louder. "Outside of Chicago." "I used to live in Omaha." He didn't want to talk to me. The novelty of being from the States made no difference. He was with his girlfriend, a Colombian, and wanted to keep to their secret relationship. Of course, my suspicions conjured up a man who was a priest, or a man who was running from the law, or cheating on a wife back home. No, he looked too straight-laced. This was Internet love incognito. There were no wedding rings being worn. Me telling him about the book would have been greeted like ice in Iceland.

The wind was blowing through the open window and we engaged in small talk between us on the way into the city. The sun was getting low in the sky and the glow of TVs in open doors was visible. People were walking home or sitting outside watching the traffic. The bus driver must have been single; he had a number of young women waving to him, as he'd honk a familiar hello. I swear some of them were waiting for him, anticipating his wave and toot on the horn.

The sky was dark and rainy by the time we got back to the terminal in Medellin. The unfriendly couple vanished before we got off the bus. They had a bank to rob. We traveled along the cement walkway to the metro and took it to the center of town. It was Friday and everyone was heading out to enjoy themselves. Bars and restaurants that sat empty all week now had occupants sitting as they had never worked a day in their lives. Music filled the air and people hocking goods were everywhere. The festive Friday night was rolling and we were going home to bed. We watched the news and soon drifted into sleep.

Day Six: The day started before sunrise. Brooms and mops were swishing the floor clean as I lay in bed wanting to get up and begin writing about Antioquia. Maybe an hour later I had a chance to write, but I needed to lay in bed first and eat later. Diana's aunt had been staying with us all week. This morning she wasn't there in the house. She had spent the night at a friend's. This meant Diana had to do the cleaning. She does anyway, but this made her begin early and make sure the daily cleaning ritual went without a hitch. Ha! There is never a hitch in this household's routine. Cleaning is as guaranteed as waking. My first priority is eating; second my art, or personal expression. This keeps me occupied while I feel like I'm waiting forever for the cleaning to stop. This is a house where nothing is out of its place. This morning the pair of socks I left lying on the bed while showering found their way to the bedside table. They knew they were out of place and had better hightail it to an appropriate setting.

I keep one dresser, or TV cabinet, cluttered on purpose. This is a big step. Last visit all my things were put away every day by Diana's mother. No matter how I tried, my things were shelved or tucked into the closet. This time I was allowed to keep a series of things out. I think this is the influence of Diana's aunt in the mix. I keep one area organized, in my way. Diana often comments that the house is in "disorder" when several items of mine are left out. I laugh every time like it's a joke, but she doesn't laugh back.

"I know exactly where my batteries and mp3 player are on top of the cabinet. This is a silly form of comfort for me. Diana's family members are letting me into their lives and I know it. (You'd think I was leaving needles around like a junkie.)

We left the house with Tuto, bought a new bathing suit for Diana, and then took a bus to her Uncle Juiro's house. He lives with his sister, Amanda. We had to meet them at 10:30 because at 1:00 we were all heading to a small town for a family gathering. Diana's Aunt Amanda is an extremely devout Catholic. She has gone as far as to ask to see our marriage certificate. It does not exist, as a Catholic document anyway. Diana said this is the first time she was not bombarded with questions about our marriage. The aunt must be letting me in as well. She, Tuto, and I had a long conversation is Spanish. Now, I know I'm ok in her book. She must pray for me a lot. We had a good visit and delivered the gifts we bought them in Greece. We gave Juiro a small statue of Pegasus, and Amanda, a small bust of the Virgin Mary with baby Jesus on her lap.

We all had soup for lunch. Amanda made me a special chicken version while the rest of the family had beef. We sat and politely conversed about our summer travels and our friends in Europe. It wasn't long before we said our goodbyes and found a taxi home.

When we got home the new washing machine was finally installed, two days after it had been delivered. The only problem was it wasn't working. The spin cycle was completely broken. We had replaced an old working machine with a new broken machine. After several attempts we concluded there would be a Monday morning call made to the store where we bought it. But, the call had to be to Bogotá, the Whirlpool headquarters. I wonder if they will come all the way from Bogotá. I know the machine won't be working for several days. I was not happy about this.

The one o'clock pickup time for the new machine turned into two thirty. I didn't mind, since I was writing and killing time in a constructive way. We left the city in a two-car caravan, phoning each other when we lost track of the other vehicle. The traffic in the city eventually thinned and we wove up and up into the mountains south of Medellin. The traffic up the mountain was slow and terrible. We had to stop many times and wait for the elastic flow of traffic to pull us up again. We didn't feel bad though because the traffic going into the city was at a complete stand still. For a good forty-five minutes we passed trucks, cars, and buses packed with passengers, all standing dead still. It was bad for us, but for them, hell on wheels. Many cars were pulled off to the side from overheated engines. Buses on the shoulder had people standing, men of course, relieving themselves. Being stuck in traffic is so common that men selling foods were running along the stopped traffic selling food. Diana told me it is that way every time she has been on the road.

At one juncture we stopped to pay a toll. The peak of the mountain had been driven past a few miles back, but we soon found the traffic was still slow and painful. I didn't feel any pain actually. I was humoring myself by taking photographs and enjoying the view. It was breath-taking, to say the least. I'd never seen such mountains except during my last visit to Colombia, only this time the mountains were bigger and the vistas took longer to take in. This country is a green paradise.

We drove along a crest of road that had houses lining both sides with steep drop-offs behind the houses. It was unreal to think these houses were hanging on the edge of the world and traffic was pounding through their hearts. The vibration of the big trucks was enough to shake fruit from trees. Children ran along the narrow walkways as if they were mountain goats. Underweight horses and donkeys carried heavy loads of fruit and timber while small shacks with stilts hung over cliffs resembling an illustration from a Doctor Seuss book.

The ride took two hours more after we reached the summit. The summit was a very high pass sandwiched between ridges. Down the mountain some twenty minutes we passed through the village of Santa Barbara. This little town hugged the top of a mountain but spread across the peak with many streets and houses. The houses terraced each other in a kind of collective leaning where one building depended on the neighboring structure to stand. Along the roadside were small shops with dissembled motorcycles strewn across their floors as the mechanics sat looking over their projects like fine surgeons. Poverty is so commonplace that it creates equality amongst the people. No one stands out. The houses have no aesthetic appeal because survival leaves little room for fine taste and frivolous art affects. A piece of trash is left unnoticed because the belly needs food. The priority of those in poverty is not to see material things as anything but a means to feed their hunger.

Far below our vantage point we could see two distinct mountain peaks that stuck out of the valley floor like two displaced minarets. Farallones del Citara is the name of these outcroppings. I didn't know at the time, but the town we were driving to visit is at the base of one of these colossal rock up-crops. La Pintada is a small elbow in the road where the River Cauca carries its brown water toward Antioquia at the base of Faralloes del Citara. There are a few hotels with large grounds and swimming pools. We are in a gated compound with guards and tall walls. It is somewhat like the house in Costa Rica, but the houses are all individually designed, not a uniform construction. We spent the night eating, watching the photos of our trip to Europe, and eating more. I was full before dinner began at 9:30. I feel asleep with the family talking at the tables in the center of the room. I was so tired it didn't take long. I fell asleep with voices and woke to the silence of night, hours later. I seemed to expect hearing voices then dozed off again.

Day Seven: Sunday. Tuto was up with a flashlight as to not disturb anyone, but since I am a light sleeper, I awoke from my frail slumber. I was in a large room that doubles as a kitchen. There are two beds, really three; the third is tucked under another on the floor. The whole tribe has just eaten and the morning cleaning is taking place. There are twelve of us in all; four children and eight adults; including one aunt, one uncle, one brother, his wife, Diana's two parents, Diana and me. The radio is playing Colombian folk music with simple guitars and accordions. Life is about being together as a family here. I sit here writing at the kitchen table as they toss Spanish conversations back and forth.

As the family shifts their daily behaviors the children have put on their bathing suits and gone into a small pool that is here in the house's patio. It is more like an oversized Jacuzzi. Tuto is listening to the mp3 player I gave him. This toy amazes him. The women are supervising the children. Morelia is outside as Francisco (Diana's brother) cleans his car and listens to the closing ceremonies of the Olympics on the radio.

Before breakfast, eight of us went into the small town and took a long scenic walk. I took the camera and caught as many typical glimpses of life I could. The main corner of the town along the highway had several men milling around. It is Sunday and no one is working. The businesses were just opening. We found a small playground where the children played on the swings. Diana and I played on a teeter-totter. Her short legs dangled far above the ground as my weight pumped her skyward, bouncing her on her butt.

We followed the road that lead to the bridge we crossed when entering the town, traversing the River Cauca again. As we crossed the bridge and I saw one green tree, so full of white Egrets that I assumed them to be white flowers. From a distance the multitudes of white spots merged into tiny objects seemingly hanging, but in a magical moment the flowers took on wings and rearranged to other branches. We looked at more of the town and entered a church. Mass was over, but we entered a side door to say short prayers.

The building had an unusual statue of Jesus smiling above the altar, no crucifixion. On the wall painted behind the statue were clouds and rays of light. It was a pleasant image of Christ, without blood. To one side of the church was a stark contrast; a Jesus at his flogging. Skin and blood were exposed as He leaned on the floor next to the whipping pole. The robe was made of real cloth. Huge gaping wounds on His back depicted torture and suffering. I was commenting to myself that few men have learned why Christ died, because torture and killing continues still today. My perception is that the message gets lost in the delivery. People should not kill people. Yet the church killed many people while spreading a message of love and forgiveness. Turn the other cheek. Go figure?

We all returned home and ate breakfast. Then the eight of us began to walk the neighborhood to see which houses are for sale. This is an ideal place to own a home because it is a guarded compound. I am thinking ahead for retirement, the plans is to live in a country where the cost of living is low, and start an alternative business in art or photography, plus keep writing books.

At this point, I have no idea about the progress of my first books sales since I have been away all summer. I need to begin the promotional aspect of this after I return. My need for a break from writing, and creating my new book on a computer happened because of this vacation. Although I have been writing all summer I need to spend the next year completing and polishing these gleanings. I put all my creative projects through a three-tier process. When I write the first draft it is straight writing, no corrections, no spell check. This is followed by going through the writing for proper articulation. The last phase is to make the writing polished. I have my work set out for me.

We found some houses we were interested in. Diana's mother will call later in a lawyer capacity, handling all the negotiations. This is a good feather in our cap. I'm leaving all the negotiations up to her. The distance from Medellin is the only problem, but the abundance of nature, seclusion, and the surrounding mountains is worth it. We have begun a process that may take years, or may not happen here at all.

Shortly afterwards we all entered the swimming pool complex and spent three hours lounging around and swimming. Diana's parents and aunt stayed back at the house while the rest of us played in the pool. The "pool" is actually three pools. These are the nicest features to the housing compound. The roads are in need of repair, but the pools are top notch. There is a main pool, and two smaller pools, one of which is for children. The largest pool is long enough to do laps for exercise.

After returning to one of the houses that are for sale to get a phone number, we all piled into the two cars and headed south toward Medellin. The tiny town was crawling with people by this time of day.

The apparent poverty was seen on the faces and clothes of the people. On the same street where the entrance to the housing compound is, we stopped and returned the key to an elderly woman sitting in a vegetable shop. The store was not much larger than the old chair she sat in. Next door to her was a mechanical shop of some kind. The men inside were filthy with black soot. Other stores were there for many years and had not been cleaned for a long time. In contrast, the stores and restaurants on the main street could have been anywhere in any country. This is Colombia. The contrasts between people being rich and poor are more distinct than most countries. The small towns have beautiful quaint and antique qualities, but the level of income is so low that fresh paint and modern elements are only on the newer buildings.

The drive home was as spectacular as the drive in. Fabio passed trucks, cars, and buses on hairpin turns. This triggered a few skipped heartbeats, as I'd warn of an approaching bus. Eventually I calmed down, enjoyed the ride and gave up being co-pilot. The climb up the highway improved the view of the distant peaks, and I felt that this was one of the most amazing places to behold. In the distance, huge minarets could be seen. Men on horses or mules rode on the highway. Children lay on the highway inches from death, while dogs darted out of houses onto the same thoroughfare. Life goes on with what seems like imminent danger to me, is merely a passing car to those who live here.

Think where we would be without the automobile. The spread of these mountaintop towns and all civilization is dependent on the very thing that will gag us all to death. Not a pleasant thought indeed, but someone better come up with a solution fast.

This time there was no traffic jam. The ride took a total of two hours, an hour and a half shorter than the day before. As we approached the summit I asked Fabio if the pine trees were native or planted. They were naturally occurring flora. My association with mountains always comes with pine trees, but here the pines only grow in the highest altitudes within groves. They mix with other trees that are tropical on the edges of these groves. No sooner had we passed the summit and the police checkpoint, it began to rain. As we headed downhill toward Medellin the sky was dark and clouds rolled across the highway in blankets that decreased visibility. Few houses and people were to be seen, as this part of the high mountain pass was unusually unpopulated.

The rain picked up and we gingerly navigated each curve and avoided any accidents. We came down the mountain to the single lane construction site. This place was the culprit for why so much traffic had backed up on Saturday. Now only five or six cars waited as men with small red signs in Spanish, spelling stop on one side and go on the other, sat directing traffic. The workers sat on opposite sides of the caved-in highway under makeshift tents of black plastic to keep out of the rain. The signs were on long poles so whoever held them wouldn't get wet from the rain. The workers sat inside away from the wetness. I am amazed at the ingenuity of human beings. In the USA, this would have been a big electrical production including a flagman. When there is plenty of inexpensive "manpower" the simplest of solutions takes place.

On the slick street we saw one down-turned motorcycle and a police investigation taking place. No one was hurt; the motorcycle rider was out of the rain in the safety of a truck's cab. The flashing lights could be seen from quite a distance along the steep declining road. We soon entered the main highway that runs the length of the valley Medellin is situated. Cars and motorcycles stopped for the occasional speed bump on this major artery. This caused me to think safety precautions were obstructing traffic and could be a problem rather than a solution to the speeding vehicles.

Sometimes I reflect on what seems like a strange event to me, from a

North American perspective, my narrow point of view. I don't know if my books would be as interesting to a Colombian as to an "American". Things that I find utterly amazing, or absurd, are so commonplace in these foreign lands that my observations are equally as absurd because they accentuate what is mundane, or unimportant, to those living here. I have to realize I live in a kind of isolated microcosm in the USA. On the one hand yes, I fully believe that all people are the same. It is the Americans that are so removed from world in their luxury that life is strangely boring and complacent. Much more physical creativity and ingenuity takes place in the third world than in the technological countries. That sounds very stupid, doesn't it? But it may be true for people here.

Survival creates a whole new range of problems versus pushing a button to get results. I can't count the number of widgets, and string and glue inventions I've seen here. I admire the people who struggle and find solutions that are practical and commercially worthless.   A couple of examples of this are inventions that I've seen as follows. On occasion I've seen people on upper floors of buildings send a bag, mostly plastic, on a string to a person standing and waiting on the street below. The bag is either for returning something, like keys to lock the front door as they leave, or delivering something. A delivery person will call on the building intercom, the person upstairs sends down the bag on a string, and no one is running up and down stairs all day. Another invention I saw was worm by a taxi driver. On the left arm he wore a jacket sleeve, not the whole jacket, but only the arm and shoulder portion. This was to protect the arm that hangs out the window from sunburn. I find these things utterly amazing and practical.

We arrived back at the gate to Diana's parent's apartment building safely. We gave everyone there a big hug. I love these family outings. I don't know the next time we will see each other. On all my trips here I've managed to be a participant on such jaunts. If we buy a house it is my hope that everyone can use it for our continued family unity. I am honored to be a part of this family and amazed at the lack of internal strife. I'm sure people talk about each other, but I've never seen any nastiness. I know I get nasty with Diana (and don't like it in myself) but she seldom verbally strikes back. It is in the American psyche to get belligerent with others. These people don't make an effort to be nice, they just plain are. I think it's because the family is close in generations. They all do group activities and there is no separation of age groups. The child rearing is more communal. Positions of authority and divisions of labor are not set in stone. The matriarchy is not so obvious.

Diana has said time and time again that I make the decisions in our relationship. She comes from a matriarchy and I from a patriarchy. I think I'm so modern, liberated, and cool, but I carry years of preprogrammed consciousness that is so deeply ingrained that I don't even know. The role I play is deeply ingrained socialization that causes me to take a hard look at my marriage and how I interact with Diana. I see my parents in my own behavior. I hear my parents interacting and consider that I've chosen a mate that can help me play roles similar to those my parents played with each other.

Early September. I have been home, alone, in New York for five days. This is the first chance I've had to write. I got up at 5:30, ate and began to work on a watercolor I promised to Denis in Ireland. His cousin has a new house he requested that do a painting of the place. Also his cousin has asked me to do a landscape of the Galty Mountains, specifically the view from their house. His wife hikes these mountains so his cousin wants to surprise her with another painting.

Someone asked me if I miss Diana who is still back in Colombia. Of course I do, but I also like the time alone. It reminds me of the times I was so lonely and hoping to find a partner. I keep busy so much that it is like she and I are together only in separate rooms. I want to use this time to appreciate her through her absence. I also need to look at my negative behavior and figure a better way to handle myself when our communication is challenging. I've sent myself to my room. I need to see both Diana and myself in a refreshed light. Distance makes the heart fonder. Considering we were together for seven weeks with maybe three or four hours being apart was a testament to our relationship's durability.

I think she needed this break from me. She is back with mom and dad. I am back by myself and we both get a glimpse of the past and future this way. She knows all my tarnished characteristics, abrupt emotions and all. I know her constant need for interaction and her insecurities. There is something in me; I often do the opposite of what is at play between us. When she pulls, I pull in the opposite direction. When she is being weak I get my feathers ruffled and tell her to toughen up. Sometimes I'm able to put my emotions aside and be there for her, feel compassion, and just listen. I know that's what I should be doing all the time, but this is my challenge. Even though I vent my anger, when it's happening I feel release and satisfied at expressing versus keeping it bottled up. Then later I feel like she deserves to be treated better.

I realized we spent on the European trip what I used to live on (thirteen years ago) in one year. This is close to what Diana made last year at her two jobs combined in Columbia. We both agree this was a "real" honeymoon. When she was in tears at the Acropolis, telling me she was in a place she had always dreamed of seeing, I knew I hit a home run with her. She was so sweet to me, thanking me. This made her happy. The gratitude she expressed confirms why she knows what is important in life. As frustrated as I get she teaches me to be childlike again, to love openly, to give, to be grateful, and to observe life as an exercise of wonderment.

We have been talking via videophone on the computer. We paid a technician to set up the video connection back in Colombia. At first, we could only send instant messages, now we can see each other, but the voice is delayed a few seconds. We were both very happy to see each other. Yesterday was the first day in almost three years I haven't talked to her. She is spending the night with an aunt and there is no computer. Think about it. Love creates tolerance and coping skills. We are still getting to know each other. We both took a leap in our lives like never before and we've both landed together in greater love than expected. Pretty good, huh?

The first day she told me she was sad because we were not together. She is at home like she was two years ago. She has to deal with her parents and their dynamics. Theirs is not a dysfunctional relationship; it's just had years to settle like sludge at the base of a lake. It's deep and thick at the bottom, but clear and thin at the top, to tolerate and cope with each other's strengths and weaknesses. I see how Diana is a combination of both of them. In some ways she is more like her father, yet she has personality facets like her mother.

This morning, life was in full circle. I went out in the kayak at seven. A few minutes into my paddling an Osprey dove into the water, maybe twenty feet in the distance, and carried a fish away. The fish almost got free. I was a surprised at the sudden splash in the water, so close to me. The same goes when we were newly married.

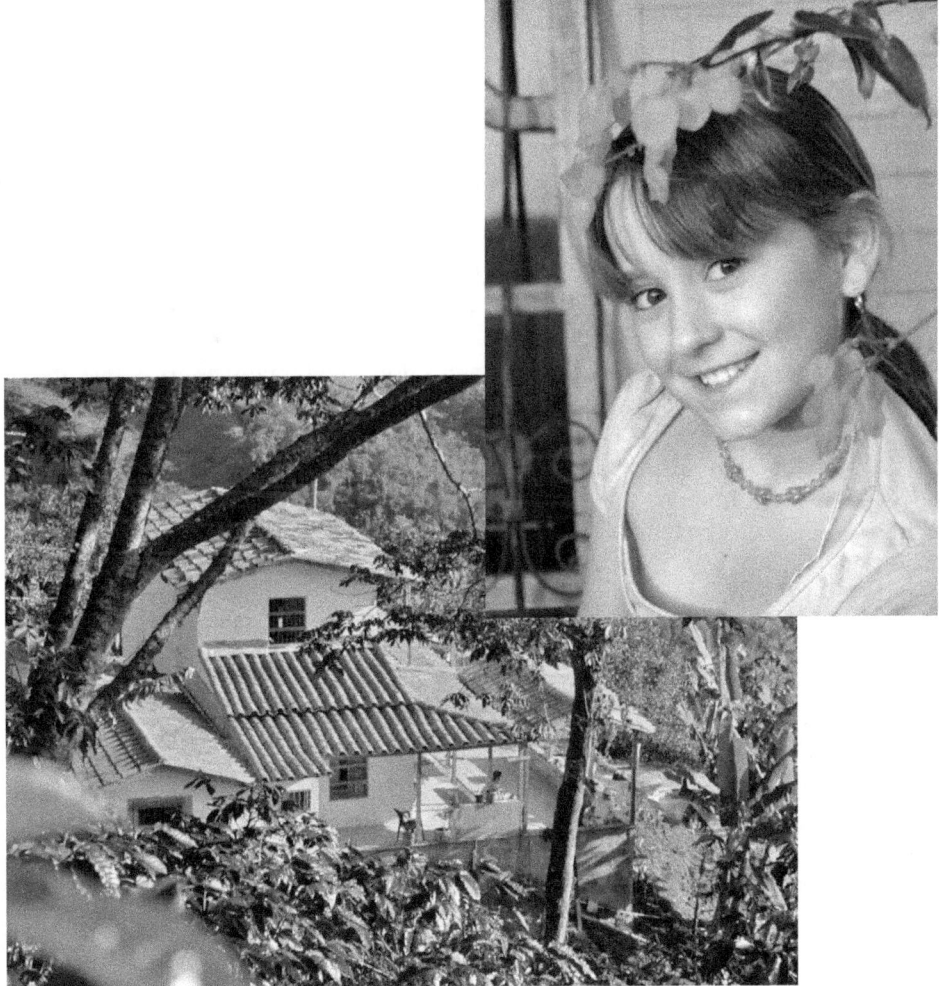

Chapter Nine
Costa Rica

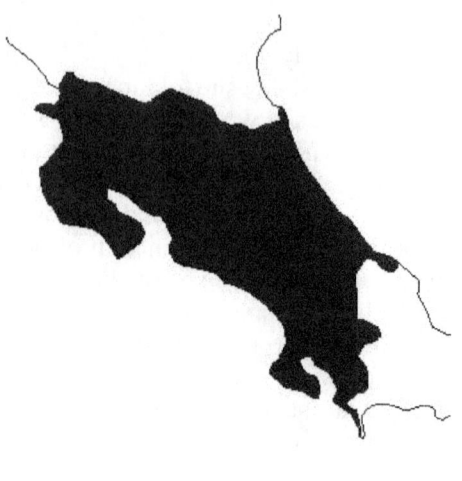

I went home from Costa Rica last February and finished the last few weeks of the school year teaching a few weeks ago in June. After an hour and ten minute ride, I'm back at the airport, Newark International, and about to leave for Costa Rica again. The woman I give a ride to work every morning has offered to give me a ride to this airport. I drove, and her husband slept in the back seat. I never use this airport, but the ticket was only $360. I bought it nine months ago. (One of the pleasures of being a teacher is knowing exact dates of my vacations.)

So much has been going on this summer already that I will have to switch gears completely and refocus on my travels and myself. Diana was supposed to be with me today, but she is home stuck in her job. She gave them a two-week notice and they threatened to sue her for breach of contract. This set a whole series of actions in motion--calling the State Board of Examiners for Speech and Language, calling the State Labor Board, calling the Legal Aid Society, calling a lawyer, then avoiding the need and cost of a lawyer by agreeing to work for five more weeks. That is five weeks she will be alone in New York while I'm in Central America. She hates being alone and I don't feel totally comfortable about leaving. It's either guilt, or responsibility, which, I don't know.

I spent an entire week focused on helping her resolve her problems with her job. On Tuesday of the second week, my summer vacation began, the skies opened, the sun came out, and my vacation really commenced. Diana had settled with a "mutual agreement" whereby she would stay until they had her replacement. She was fulfilling a part of her licensing program, working an additional six weeks, because she had completed the nine-month practicum already. The company had never had someone quit. Most people stay on after the practicum. Most of the Clinical Fellows are from South America, here on a work visa, and without green cards, unlike Diana. The company has most of the women in a type of modern servitude, a catch-22, where they repeat the nine month program, and repeat, the nine months over until they leave the country because they don't get fully licensed. They have two years to complete this, or rather two nine-month stints. Few pass the test so there is a cycle of new foreign employees that are paid below US standards for such a profession.

The people at the State level are aware and not too pleased with how this is going down with workers and the revolving door of immigrants on temporary work visas. The corporate rats threatened to sue Diana and force her to sign a paper. She wisely refused any signature and said she had to speak with her lawyer. She is not used to the way things are done in the USA. This doesn't help, but she is learning that threats and putting on legal airs is all part of the culture. I kept trying to reassure her, sometimes to the point of my own mania and hysterics. Before this was all coming to a head I, unfortunately, threatened to divorce her if she didn't stop obsessing on the job. I was seriously angry at the way she was treated by these people and the amount of hours that she was spending working; at least sixty to seventy hours a week. No time was going into our relationship. She was their "best in the division", but she was getting crazed over efforts that verged on being seriously taken advantage of. She is a perfectionist that is superb at what she does; evidence being that no client parents ever had any complaints, and she mastered driving all over Long Island. I could go on and on about her positive attributes. That's why I married her, but she thinks she is less than what she is. She needs a good shot of self-confidence. My leaving for five weeks is a shot of self-doubt and loneliness for her.

Funny how a few paragraphs could never describe the whole emotional upheaval that our lives took for a couple of weeks. We were so sure that the whole thing was going to happen that I bought her plane ticket, only to spend another nine hundred dollars, and eventually cancel her ticket all together. But soon she will be with me in Costa Rica. I savor down time and solo time, but Diana is quite the opposite. Her deep, reflective mood of the last few days was accented by outburst of sudden tears. This is the second longest period of time in her life she will be alone. The first was ONE WEEK last April. I married a woman who had lived at home with her parent's for 35 years.

We have been married for three years now. Despite all the cultural, language, and age differences we have a solid relationship. I am very pleased, but I know she thinks she married a crazy man. (Sometimes) My emotions and out bursts are something she has needed to adjust to. I have on occasion been completely in the wrong. Unlike the day she had swine flu and was going to go to work! My only outlet was my anger under those inappropriate circumstances. I dislike this part of my personality, but I also know myself well enough to keep a healthy perspective on my reasoning, justifications, and self-absolution. She would have gone to work, exposed children, and nearly killed herself had I not become outraged. (My delivery was still inexcusable.)

Mind you, I live with a woman who speaks broken English and I have to constantly interpret what she is saying to understand her. She has words for such things as 'root beer float' that I am the only person on earth who knows what she means. And, every time she tries to express this need for a delicious thirst quencher, she says it differently, and incorrectly. Usually after two or three attempts I understand her meaning. The list is pretty long, but in a sad way she is becoming less incorrect and more Americanized.

I believe the effort that goes into all "differences" is the cement of our love. But image, if you will, the lunacy that I feel when listening to a series of words strung together, incorrectly, and all the while paying attention to the emotional content and the true meaning. It is stressful. My tendency as a teacher or maybe anyone instinctively, is to correct; give the proper phrase or word. This often has to be set aside and we just continue the conversation. I notice my patience can be a great factor in how I relate back. (Duh!) Because I'm short fused, during a disagreement, I will retaliate with multiple corrections of her syntax. This all gives me reason to respect and admire what my wife goes through on the opposite side. Now I notice her correcting herself, putting the words in the correct order, or trying to use the correct verb tense. But honestly, the rain in Spain stays mostly in my brain.

It's the first morning and I'm back to the place I never want to leave, Costa Rica. I come home and my tribe is here, my friend Jose and his family. I walked into their house as if I were across the street for a few minutes although it has been six months. The hugs and hello are a bit deeper each time. We don't "separate" because we have continuation of a shared journey. I bring trinkets for his children. The first time we all left to go to the beach I locked myself out. My key was in full view on the table, but I locked the door. He has a duplicate key allowing me to get back in the house. Jose always helps me.

I have the routine of getting here to Jaco down like clockwork. Jose mails me the bus ticket in advance. This time I took a taxi to Alajuela, delivered some guitar strings to Francis, a friend who works in the store of Oscar. I bought my condo from Oscar. I visited with Oscar and explained the whole story of Diana's absence in my broken Spanish. Francis and I went to lunch and had a good chat about the politics and corruption of Central America. Corporations and drug cartels take money under the table. Monies grease all the wheels. Francis told me how the mining companies are here to begin operations despite strict environmental laws and regulations. He claims the President has skirted the laws to allow this, as well as take kickbacks. President Oscar Rafael de Jesús Arias Sánchez has won the Noble Peace Prize and is currently negotiating with the two sides in Honduras, but it appears, to Francis, that someone is getting a nice bonus in a Swiss bank. I have seen what mining does in the Appalachian Mountains and don't wish that on anyone, especially this beautiful country. I had plans to visit Honduras, but my money won't go to a country that uses its military to roust a President in the middle of the night in his pajamas and whisk him out of the country. This is why Costa Rica is stable. There is NO corrupt military because there is NO military.

I was soon in the market of Alajuela shopping for avocados and mangos. The bustle and familiarity of the city next to the airport is a favorite way to acclimate to my new surroundings. I remind myself I am a citizen of the world and a quasi-Costa Rican. I bought my fruit from a man wearing a dirty shirt in one stall in a market with hundreds of tiny booths. The stalls sell anything from food to clothing. The tiny aisle is small enough to reach across and touch the shelves of the opposite shop. The air is full of cooking smells from the occasional restaurant. The restaurants have single counters with short stools that are bolted to the floor. Inside each counter is a kitchen with three of four people packed within elbowroom of the counter. Huge vats of boiling food are being cooked on propane stoves as the customers dine. The people instinctively know how good, and healthy, everything bought in the market is. The smell of fresh food, meat, dried flowers and herbs, or sweets is wafting from each stall. In contrast to the fragrances of cuisine a sudden burst of plastic from tennis shoes can hit the nostrils. A blind man could find his way exclusively from the odors. Sellers call out slogans to attract buyers and remind me I'm back in my home away from home.

I returned to the electronics shop where my friends work, said my last good byes, and then caught a taxi to the highway where everyone waits for the bus. The taxi driver was not so friendly and seemed a bit guarded as he fussed with his meter, which he never seemed to turn on until a tourist got in. As he dropped me off and the fare came up on the machine, I knew the jig was up. His meter was twice what it had just cost me to come from the airport. There was less distance traveled. I gave him what I paid the other taxi driver and he held his hand out for more money. I protested and walked away. He sat there long enough to know he was dealing with a quasi-Costa Rican and knew there was no bullshit to be tolerated.

I stood, sat, walked around for half an hour until the approximate time for my bus only to see a bus with 'Jaco' written on it go racing by. I was waving and jumping at the driver who seemed to not care. I was doomed. I had missed my bus because of this stupid, lazy driver who wouldn't stop to pick me up. As soon as I got to the bus stop I asked some other travelers if they were going to Jaco. None, but after the bus speed by one of the men confirmed to me that was indeed the bus for Jaco. The next bus would be in one hour and a half, he told me in Spanish. I was there with my two bags and a backpack.

My exposed, emotional guts were strewn all over the highway. I was bleeding like an injured man in need of medical help. The worst possible thing in the universe had just happened to me. One by one the other passenger boarded their respective buses and I was alone about to be robbed at gunpoint in a country with NO military and no protection for a stranded traveler. I began to reflect on all the preaching and lecturing I had been giving Diana about life, and her mind as her worst enemy. Of course I justified all this, as my stress was less severe and not as neurotic as my wife's. If she were there I might have even blamed her for missing the bus.

Twenty minutes later the real bus pulled up as if it were expecting me. The road construction out of San Jose had delayed the traffic. This was one small detail the sneaky taxi driver had disclosed to me as he tried to also convince me to drive me to Jaco. It would only be one hundred dollars versus three dollars and fifty cents, that's all! Ah the unsuspecting travelers who listens to the unscrupulous helper.

While I was throwing the luggage in the belly of the beast I was stitching up my proverbial wounds and laughing at all the self-imposed calamity. Then it came back to me that Jose had mentioned my seat was reserved from the airport. The driver knew to stop for me because of the computerized reservations. I apologized to the other bus driver who had fled the scene of the murderous crime and felt like a complete fool. I did see the same bus driver in a few hours because he was on his return route from Jaco, and had stopped to get some money from my driver. He didn't see me. I was crouching low in the front row seat number three from guilt.

I put on my headphones, soon found the twelve hours of travel and heat sent me into slumber land. A good portion of the bus ride was lost to dreams, of what, I don't recall. The driver's daughter sat on the lap of another female passenger. She would look at me with long questioning glances, not the kind of quick embarrassed look kids in the USA give to adults. She was willing to feel safe with a stranger. I was too sleepy to engage in conversation. I had mopped up all my emotions with gratitude because of the knowledge of consistency of Costa Rican buses--late, but always there when need be. The tropical heat was causing beads of sweat to form around my neck. I had slept through the tourist's favorite crocodile bridge, past the small towns, and not that far from my destination. People exited the bus one by one and as usual when we arrived at the main terminal in Jaco I was one of the last passengers. I hailed a taxi, loaded my luggage in the trunk and pulled into the complex where the head security guard, Eric, motioned me through like a king in his carriage. I was home.

The house was clean. I had leant it to a farmer friend, also named Jose, and his wife Cassandra for three or four days. They had turned off all the electricity, which also turns off the refrigerator. I soon figured it all out and had the fans blowing cool air through the main rooms. I have to leave the refrigerator on year-round or else it ruins the unit. My carbon footprint runs a long thin vein all the way to Costa Rica from Long Island.

Fifteen minutes later I was at Jose's door getting hugs and trying to wash away that feeling of loneliness that plagues me when I travel. It's a kind of low-level gnawing that I have to keep in check. I think its original source was in my childhood when I was uprooted, either traveling, or moving to a new country or town. I become unsettled whenever I begin to pack my luggage. It increases as I near the travel date. On my way to the airport my blood pressure is high and I imagine death by all kinds of means, falling from an aircraft, getting hit by a car crossing the street, or at gunpoint from a robber. All attempts at tricking my ultimate demise, the moment I will never have one ounce of control over--my death. Sometimes I wake in the middle of the night and wonder what death is like. I guess I'm trying to find what brought me here and what will take me away, in hopes that I have some say in my state of being in the great beyond. I might say a small prayer. Diana prays in her sleep and it has influenced me. If I have an aversion to formalized religion I might just mediate on my feelings, knowing God knows I'm plugged in. Even as a child I believed that I could propel myself into heaven at the second of death if I thought about it hard enough. That frightening emotion is the same one I savor when I trek to new places and seek new sensations. We love what we hate.

I was back at my house putting on my swimsuit and into the water of the Pacific Ocean within the hour of my arrival. Jose and the kids were in one car; Laura (Jose's girlfriend) was in the second car with her daughter, niece, Gabriel, and his friend. I know Gabriel for a year or so. His parents were Hare Krishna's and he rebelled. I have bumped into him in assorted shops where he has worked. It's a small town; it's a small country. It is a big ocean and I love to be so small in it. I stop to thank the unknown creator and give her a moment of respect. Then I let the waves carry me at the speed of surf as my body projects ahead of the current. Bodysurfing is one sport I can do well, as Jose and Gabriel ride the waves on their surfboards. My enthusiasm wanes as I tire but within the first few minutes I had already caught three waves. Jose was still pedaling with his board to get into position. It was cloudy and hot outside the water. Inside the water I was in a state of bliss.

A short time later I sat on the beach with everyone else as we watched Jose and Gabriel surfing. These waves are not to be joked with. An occasional nine footer would rip up to the beach and we'd be looking for the black dot of our companion's heads. "Oh there he is". In the tribe we look after one another. Protection from death is a constant unspoken reminder.

About a month ago I went dancing with Diana to what is called, "English Dancing". You know, those lines of formal bows, exchanging rotations, and circling motions that you see in the movies. We spent an evening at a local church trying our best to not look foolish and stupid. But we had a delightful night of revisiting our childhoods and feeling totally insecure, totally inept, and falling all over our feet. I have a sneaky love for chaos and finding humor in watching things dysfunction. That night I was beside myself in laughter. All the while I was keeping an eye on the authority figure, a large oversized, matronly woman in a long dress from the 1930's. She had her hair pulled back in a bun on top, wore horn rimmed glasses, and once verged on screaming at the room full of adult-children of non-dancers. I assume most of us are damaged from the previous generation of parents. The female "Caller" did an excellent job of keeping her composure and a stern sense of instructional demeanor as people fumbled into fumbling gyrations of footwork, fun and funny mishaps. Diana and I got to be children with several of our acquaintances from a wider circle of friends, Victoria's friends really.

That night I had dreams of dancing and dancing. The day's activities had merged into my subconscious mind. At one point in all this dancing I was suddenly approaching skeletal figures of death. Not one death figure but two! When I was released from my partner to spine around, I was face to face with death. To my surprise, twice, both figures lifted their forefingers and motioned, no. Neither one of them would dance with me. I took this as a wonderful sign that I'm not about to check out soon. I have two more near misses before I join the worms and decompose. I did lie in bed for a couple of hours thinking about the dream before I was released back into sleep. In my time off from teaching I can afford such awakened time reflecting.

So, on my first morning back here I am catching up and writing my journal. Children are already in the swimming pool and I've had two visits from Khilani and Eligh. Laura's tiny, young niece tagged along. Her name is also Diana. Her mother has drug issues and the little girl is spending time away in a safer environment with relatives. She is either seven or eight years old.

As I'm writing, a big yellow butterfly just went dancing in and out of my door. Jose is going to take me grocery shopping when he comes around. The kids told me the adults are still sleeping. I know what "sleeping-in" on a Sunday morning means to couples.

While cleaning my house I was thinking about Diana, my wife. I rode my bike to the Internet shop and had a brief conversation with her last night. She was in good spirits. Flora, the neighbor from El Salvador is spending the night with her. Sara her daughter is there too. We are all in good hands. We are all looked after. Each day is a gift because we have each other and we have friends who care about us. The only distance between us is what we create through loneliness. **Day Two:** I was startled awake by the sound of a weed-whacker. I got up ate breakfast and felt my mood, a bit blue. I tried to call Diana last night but she was out. I am a being that loves to be in contact with others. The change to being alone is a dilemma. It wasn't long before I was back to Jose's home.

Yesterday my single task was to get groceries. It wasn't until the late afternoon that Jose and a Laura took me in their car. First we went to the beach and I got my second encounter with the sea. The water was a deep green and as warm as a bath but there was a strong rip tide and the surf was extremely rough. I don't remember it being that strong here ever. Khilani was knocked over and had two waves toss his tiny body one after the other. No one seemed to mind or panic like a typical North American. Jose watched as his son bobbed in the water, but knew his son was like a fish in water. The Lifeguard came over and explained that the children needed to swim closer to him down the beach. The Lifeguard knew Jose and they talked for a while. All the kids went south, I went in the water and the current carried me north in seconds. After a third wave I gave up and went back to sit with Laura's sister and boyfriend.

Day Three: The third day was a great bit of fun for me. I went down to the local Internet café and got permission to hook up my laptop to their system. I was delighted that my "Magic-Jack" worked. I made my first free phone call to a friend Damian in Florida. We spoke for a while and updated each other on what was going on, all the problems Diana had with her job, my flight, and the gossip around the condominiums.

My spirit was lifted even higher when I called home and Diana answered the phone. She immediately said how much she missed me. I had been upset the morning before for not getting to talk with her on Sunday night when I called. Now we were talking like I was in the next room.

Diana seemed in a good mood. I check her responses for cracks in her emotional wall. There's a kind of instant meter that kicks in as I sense her mood. The concern is always about her state of being. She is stressed out from the job and the renter upstairs causes her a great deal of anguish. The last time she was alone the tenant upstairs in the house threw away a few of my things. Diana confronted him about his yard cleanup. This isn't the only issue we have had. Property has been taken, or "borrowed", without being returned. There have been a few requests to pay back or return items. I admire the way she challenged this guy. I suspect there is some hidden bigotry against her because of her accent, but there is no way to prove this.

I have rented the basement apartment for nine years, never having a bad word with anyone. But things changed when the new tenants moved in. My near deaf, ninety-five year old landlady was replaced by pounding, footsteps of a running and jumping five-year old child. The sudden poundings have caused me to startle hundreds of times. I have contacted the landlady's son who lives two houses away. He has written letters and tried his best to intervene. Unfortunately the last encounter was a yelling and screaming couple from upstairs, protesting my hitting the ceiling with a broomstick to stop the noise because it is "improper behavior". There were four children visiting the house and the noise was unbearable.

During the yelling, as I sat inside refusing to exit my door, and I heard Diana being called a witch, there was such a flurry of words being heaped upon me that the words didn't register with me until Diana asked me what the word "witch" means. I was being called a coward and some other lowly form of existence for not coming out to be verbally assaulted. I called the landlord who lives two doors down. He said he would come and try to calm things down. I went outside just long enough to be hit with a further verbal barrage of complaints like never being thanked for replacing the firewood. I remember I did thank him thinking, that I am thanking this guy for putting back what he took without permission in the first place. These are the kind of encounters my foreign bride loves about my country. The day I used my broomstick, there were three or four visiting children, running like lunatics throughout the upper apartment. If a picture of bombs falling on Dresden comes to mind, you are correct. The circling overhead from room to room, held like an aerial pattern for twenty minutes or more. Then I went for the broomstick. I am so, SO sorry.

I listen to Diana's voice for assurances that her life there is going well despite my absence. I'd ask her how she was a few days earlier "I feel, ok", with a long exhale, was not really being what I wanted to hear. I suppose it will be much better when I get the phone hooked up in the house and we can feel like the closeness is within technology's reach.

Today is one of those brilliant, sunny days where the light is defiantly tropical and the heat is a few degrees cooler than hell. There is a smooth calm breeze that runs through the house thanks to my elaborate ventilation system of fans in each window. The mountains that hug the coast a mile away are full of gray clouds, but here there is full sun. Three children are here at my new table, painting in watercolors. I got the table from Eric the security guard. Maybe someone left it when they moved out. It was perfect for an art worktable. Khilani, Eligh, and Gloria, are playing with the paint at the new table. I have the stereo blasting New Age music and I've been at this computer for an hour or so. Life is lovely. This is the way the tribe is supposed to be.

Thursday, July 23: Rain, rain, and so much rain the water came on the front porch of the condo. After the rain, I had just gone into the pool to cool off from my morning household repairs when Jose pulled in the complex. His two sons came into the water, and Jose went in his house to clean before Laura returns.

Khilani had a big cut on the bottom of his foot, so after swimming we all went to my house and put on a bandage. (Eligh had a tiny scratch, but he deserved a bandage and some attention as well. He made a bigger fuss than Khilani.) Just around the time we were putting on the first aid dressings the rains came down in an unbelievable torrent. This is the rainy season; and they call it "winter". I suppose because it is so cloudy, less sun.

I think about these kids and wonder how they will turn out. I have known both of them since infancy. I know both of their mothers and each personality involved. Both children are spending time at their separate mothers. Little Eligh spends six months in the USA in Utah and the other six month Costa Rica. Eligh is the younger brother and takes a lot of ordering around. He is a skinny little fellow with light brown hair, a big head. His emotional body posture is often him holding the head down with his shoulders curling inward toward his chests. He is very shy every time he is reintroduced to me, yet within a couple of days we are best friends and his timidity is gone.

Khilani is a few feet taller, looks identical to Eligh; only he is missing his two front teeth. They both have bowl haircuts, and look like a couple of bookends together. There is no guessing they are brothers. Jose leaves them to play and is not hovering around to see if they are all right. They play in the pool unsupervised and pretty much have the run of the entire complex as their playground. Eligh is very submissive. Khilani is a little too independent and can be sassy with excessive laughs when Jose gives him a directive. Being a schoolteacher gives me some insight into the prospect of their futures, but I may be completely wrong in saying that Khilani will give Jose a hand full of challenges in a few years. He is a little wild at times. I noticed as soon as Laura (Jose's girlfriend) and her daughter leave, a lot of whining and taunting begins. Laura runs the tribe and knows exactly when to put a child into the corrective discipline mood. I instinctively get into my fathering mode around these kids. All and all I enjoy everyone's company and the way the children come in and out of my house at will. If the door is open, they are welcome. In fact, in a few minutes they will be here for lunch.

I lock a few cabinets for safekeeping. My tools are locked behind a door I built below one of the kitchen counters. My clothes are locked away in airtight bags in a tall white cabinet. These two areas are safe, but the rest of the house is open for occasional guests that's have used the house. NO renters, just family and friends. My one attempt at renting ended with a tenant living there for two weeks without paying the rent. He was evicted.

When I first bought the house I raised the roof on my back patio room. I raised it about four feet so air would be able to flow through the entire house. What was a small opening in the rear of the house became an expanded roof with open ventilation all around. The air was like a tomb when I bought the house. The air conditioner blew its exhaust into the small patio room and it was at least 120 degrees in there. That was my first project here. I expanded the patio room up, made additional storage space on the primary roof, and built a small meditation platform where I could see the meadow behind the house. A vacant lot has since replaced the Brahma bulls and beautiful white egrets that ate the insects around the bulls. Now exposed earth and weeds grow in abundance. The economic downturn has secretly given me back my quiet view minus the animals.

Friday, July 24: I am up at 5:45. The light was coming over the mountain straight into the house so I took some photographs. It's a rare clear morning for the rainy season. The air is crisp and the early light makes the greenery extra green. The light comes over the local mountain directly into my living room. The combination of light and music makes it a very special situation.

I called Diana yesterday and was immediately struck by a barrage of computer problems. I could tell right off she was in panic mood. Why? Because in ONE month she has to do a report in a program she doesn't know. First off she couldn't save what she had already begun. I knew it was the same problem she had many times before. The title had some incorrect notations or keyboard commands. She kept reading me the message on the screen over and over, and wouldn't let me get word in to help her fix the problem. Then I got angry and told her to be quite long enough so I can give the instruction. Sounds simple enough? Well not so. The phone line had a strange cutting out, blipping out sound every few seconds like a stuttered voice, the Internet café was loud because the attendant was blaring his music, and Diana's panic was all getting to me.

I told her in an email (later) that the only stress I had encountered all day was she on the phone. That was within seconds of beginning the call. It's like being hit over the head or attacked. A computer isn't usually the problem so much as the person in front of the computer. It can only do one thing at a time and it can only do what it is told. In addition Diana spoke with her Supervisor and the company has not filed her practicum, (State papers) yet. The supervisor had "no idea" she needed to do this. Nonsense! Diana agreed to stay if they would file BEFORE she left their employment. They haven't kept their end of the agreement, therefore I think she should just leave and come down here to Costa Rica. I told her this, and told her she needs to contact the female supervisor that said they would file the practicum with the State. This is all part of her licensure as a Speech Therapist.

Diana is not a proactive person. She reacts and gets exploited. This is a frustration to me because she is years younger and hasn't taken control of her destiny in the present. She has the long-term future goals, but the immediate issues are something she avoids or just doesn't yet know how to foresee how problems multiply if she stays neutral. On top of this she is telling me she misses me and she has been crying at night because of loneliness. I get a visceral reaction because I know her and I know she can do better. This is what happens when one marries a person twenty years younger and from a different country.

When we first got married I would get very defensive whenever the "culturally different" card was brought up. Spiritually we all have the same challenges no matter what cultural background. It may be a bit arrogant on my part as a white male from the leading nation in the world but it is more complicated than that. I have been a global citizen since my birth and living in

Panama when I was two years old. Diana is a female with all kinds of Latino imprinting on what the role of a woman "should" be. Even the way she approaches machinery (computers) is so passive that it affects her success, or lack thereof.

In an email the other day Diana said this time away would be good for us. And she added this would also be a good time to find if I am the "right woman for you". She has often said I would be better suited for a hippie woman like my friend Victoria. A big part of my attraction to Diana is her foreign character and a bigger part is to engage in HER needs. It gives me great pleasure to solve, help, to be of service, and express dedication to my wife, as well as an involved partner. I am a man in constant motion. To incorporate that daily internal and external motion into my marriage is something I have succeeded at. A 'take charge' attitude is a successful and healthy approach. The emotional component is what I have a tendency to miss. I don't know if it is because of genuine maturity, or just wanting to quickly smooth things over, that causes me to distain emotional upheaval. I also don't believe "Miss Right" is somewhere out there in the ether. Miss Right has to be nurtured in a committed relationship that evolves over time.

This could also be a myth that woman are raised with. I was as well. My father once told me, after I asked, the right woman would "appear" in my life. That I would know I was in love and am struck like lightning. He described it as if some kind of guardian angel would swoop down and pull me from my daily purgatory. I don't think my father had a clue that marriage is a struggle and constructive effort. His philandering early in his marriage proved his lack of self-discipline and lack of moral conviction. Granted, these things only come with maturity and experience, or deep-rooted religious fear in childhood. This is my cultural baggage, or rather my spiritual baggage.

A relationship is an entity unto itself. Preconditions such as compatibility and values are important, but more important are what we do to construct the relationship. Each person begins anew and "old baggage" is a positive, or negative, influence depending on how we proceed; we learn, or we regress by repeating behaviors.

Diana and I have a balance that she may not understand yet. Her nervousness is balanced by my methodic unemotional approach to most situations. Yet when I am the one in an angry mood she calms me and uses the correct words that I know are good for the situation, and me. The way she approaches her life is keeping her from appreciating what she has. I insisted she leave her place of employment. This was a gigantic step for a woman who comes from a country where employment can be life-long. She has stepped into an unknown future. I know I bring in enough income for two families, so I'd rather she advance in education than be stuck in a job where she was a slave to time and her own overzealous sense of obligation.

Her mother, Morelia, has been a hindrance to Diana's liberation. The criticism for leaving the employment has been harsh and at times downright mean-spirited. Of course her mother has the interests of her daughter at heart, but her mother lives in a country where poverty and religious obligation are the standard by which life proceeds. You just don't leave a good paying job because you don't like it. You stay as a sign of character. Suffering is good for the soul!

I saw how Diana was conflicted by her mother's input, so I wrote Morelia an email in hopes of curbing the criticism. Morelia didn't answer me, but she later asked Diana if I was angry with her. I didn't tell Diana about the email because there is no way I can never come between a mother and her daughter. I have a good relationship with the entire family, so I knew it was risky to write and politely say "back off". I think I did what was best for my marriage. Morelia is a good woman who is wise and willing to listen. I believe all this will pass.

Saturday, July 25: What a day yesterday, Friday! Wow! On Friday morning Jose, Laura, and several people all set off for a surfing adventure to a beach called Boca Barranca. The beach is a rivers mouth about one hour north of Jaco, near Puntarenas. The plan was set in motion, Thursday the night before, to leave at seven in the morning, pick up two Argentine brothers, and find the large waves that had been in Jaco the night before.

This is how it all began. On Thursday in the late afternoon I went to the beach in hopes of using my boogie board. When I rode up to the beach on my bicycle I couldn't believe my eyes. The waves were from eight to a gigantic fifteen feet high. A gringo in a car was just pulling out and said, "I wouldn't if I was you, big guy." I didn't. It was too rough and way beyond my league for a boogie board. I instantly went back and put the boogie board away and got out my two cameras. While I was leaving the house I saw Jose and Laura as they drove away, told them about the surf, and returned to the beach. Jose and Laura were sitting in the car looking at the waves by the time I cycled there.

I sat and observed the ocean taking photographs of the surfers. Soon, a couple named Greg and Dahlia came walking up. I had known them briefly five years earlier and run into them the day I went to the grocery store. We reacquainted ourselves. I had a better memory of events and another common friend that had since moved away from Jaco. Greg is America and Dahlia is Costa Rican, they have two children, a boy and a girl. Dahlia admitted that she was drinking more then and her memory was incomplete. Greg is a cook, but not working at the moment. Now they both have sworn off drinking. We all sat and visited as I shot pictures of the towering waves and tiny surfers. The beach was full of spectators with few people in the water.

Later Thursday in the night I went to Jose's for a few minutes and the plan for the next morning was set into action. Seven o'clock turned into seven forty-five. Jose was miffed because Gustavo (the Argentine) had called him and reminded him he was late. This set a verbal exchange off between Jose and Laura. It is a reoccurring conflict about time and when things need to happen promptly. I got into it by telling that I am in constant conflict with students who come to class late. I dock the students' points off their grade. I gave up creating a scene at the classroom door. I stand there with my book and take the points off. They know the routine and I don't give them the opportunity to act out. So Jose was the late student. I also said, "Your word is what is important. If you said seven, it should be seven." Jose didn't like that.

We picked up Gustavo and his brother. They look like twins. He wasn't offended when I asked him in Spanish if he was the younger brother.

Three years ago Jose introduced me to Gustavo. I bought some tortellini from Gustavo, who had a small home/cottage industry at the time. It was delicious, all organic. He now has opened a restaurant, and taken up residency in the back of the business with his pregnant wife. I was at their wedding on the beach a year, or so, ago. It was a beautiful celebration where all the people, tourists and locals, stood behind a table adorned with tall palm branches and flowers. They both wore white clothing and had flowers in their hands. It was beautiful and special as the longhaired minister performed the vows concluding with a long kiss and applause from the spectators.

Gustavo and his brother drank Mate in the back seat passing it back and forth. This unusual drink is exclusive to Argentina. It has a long metal straw that goes into a small gourd. The whole contraption looks like a big pipe, only one drinks the cool contents taking one sip, then refilling the bowl, and passing it to the next recipient. The bowl is full of herbs that don't get drunk because the straw is below in a lower chamber where the liquid gathers. The ritual of passing around the drink is not unlike the marijuana joint being passed from person to person. The drink tastes like strong green herbs or iced tea. A thermos filled with the cold Mate is used to refill the bowl. The small fist sized gourd is decorated with some carved designs that make it look very mystical.

I have the odd task of disclosure when discretion is required. Jose and the friends are all in recovery from drugs and alcohol. So the company I keep is very safe and healthy for an ex-pot-smoking hippie. (I'm still a hippie at heart.) I have attended some twelve-step meetings like Children of Alcoholics and Narcotic Anonymous, but I find I'm too rebellious to make a religion of such endeavors. I participate when the need arises, but I'm anti-institutional just enough to be true to myself first. I fully embrace the spiritual aspects of improving myself. The recovery program requires a great deal of conformity. Being on time is common in the recovery program, a common courtesy, and shows you respect others time and how you are perceived. This leads us back to Jose and his insistence that he need not be punctual and people should cut him some slack.

After we loaded the boards on top of the car and were driving down the highway, Laura handed me a twelve-step book and asked me to read the daily meditation out loud. In paraphrase it was about wearing masks and falseness of the ego. How when we stop using drugs we continue to wear the mask of self-delusion until we mature. I could feel the seat under Jose getting hotter, but no one said a word. In the custom of 'twelve-stepping' it is impolite to point the finger of accusation. It wasn't long before the all eight of us were speeding down the highway and laughing together as the radio was blaring American Pop tunes. We were all on the road to finding our best way through sobriety.

Like a band of gypsies were all piled into the small five-seater passing motorcycles and buses. Jose, Gustavo, Gustavo's older brother, Gloria, Laura's ten year old daughter, Khilani, six years old, Eligh, four years old, Laura, and I, and the police on the side of the road. The police have the same shaded hiding places every day along the highway. Everyone knows these locations and additionally a friendly passing driver will blink their car lights to let one know the police are ahead. Before each station, the children were instructed to duck down in the back seat. It was a game to them but would have lodged Laura a hefty fine for over-occupancy in her vehicle.

A few minutes into the ride we pulled up behind a gray van which had Gabriel and two more fellow surfers. Our tribe consisted of a young teenager, and Janet, a law school graduate student from Michigan, whom I later met at the beach. Unbeknownst to me, we were all heading to the same place, Boca Barranca. The tribe was assembled like a moving herd seeking the surfers' illusive dream of swells and surfing. It was a fun day already. We yelled greetings back and forth as the old highway gave way to the new modern freeway that has recently been completed. From the front seat Laura and I spoke about the look of the highway stating there was no difference between those in the USA and the new one here. I remember the drive to Puntarenas years earlier being very rough, full of holes, and even unpaved for short portions. Now it was a different place and time.

My first time to Puntarenas was maybe nine years back for the yearly Carnival. The town lay at the end of a long peninsula. On the furthest point west a ferry runs to the opposite side of the water where unpaved roads and small beach towns like Montezuma and Mal Pais are populated by surfers and adventurous tourists. It is secluded and sparse. I have been to that isolated part of Costa Rica once, years earlier. Puntarenas is a strange thin strip of road that has one very large building that is an International Hotel at the entrance of the peninsula. On one side of the road is a mangrove estuary with assorted birds, the other a beach with shanty houses of impoverished people sitting on porches or standing in shaded doorways.

There is nothing attractive to seeing idle poor people. Their depression oozes over the two-lane road and slows the on looking drivers in cars as the emotion of their poverty covers each passenger like slow moving syrup. At the farthest end of the town the city is no more than five or six blocks deep while the majority of its buildings hug the single road in and out. Having a small solitary street is its first handicap. Nobody stays in Puntarenas. It is a place to pass through on your way to beautiful beaches. The dingy unpainted houses and lack of typical green vegetation is a sign of need for economic growth. The only time of year this place comes alive is before Lent for Carnival. And alive it does become.

A parade of marching school bands, civic organizations, and partially nude, prancing woman revs up the blood as the street is packed with lively spectators. As the women wearing nipple-pasties giggle their breasts, the men whistle and hoot like wild animals. A Religious organization, or marching band, could be following the flatbed trucks carrying the feathered females. I have never seen anything like it. The strange dichotomy of religion and sexuality are expressed freely in the same parade. The sidewalks are nearly impassable.

As I walked through the crowd I was with Monty, a man I met on my first trip to Costa Rica. Not feeling my usual self-confidence, I didn't feel safe and soon noticed we were being followed by a group of young thugs, all wearing black. As we paused they paused and looked away at the parade. I pointed them out to Monty. A few minutes later I noticed them come close, stop and turn away immediately. Their sudden abrupt absence was very noticeable. "What did you say?" I asked Monty. "Nothing." He smiled. He then lifted his shirt and exposed the butt-end of a revolver stuffed below his belt. "Oh!" was all I said. I never spoke to him about it then or after.

Guns are not something I relate to since my sister was shot and killed by her cop-boyfriend. My sister's death was deemed an accidental death by the police investigation. There were no witnesses and the forensic evidence did not add up. Years after my parents died I pushed to have the case reopened. I was told 'accidental death' cases are not considered a homicide, therefore the police are not obliged to investigate them as a cold case. This convenient glitch in the law resulted in a policeman not held accountable for murder. The fox in the hen house did the investigation, and ultimately covered-up the other guilty fox. This was a large contributor to my own rebelliousness, early marijuana use, and a complete distrust for authority. My sister was twenty-seven. I was twenty. My mother's drinking accelerated, my father had an affair, and our family was devastated enough to never be in the same room as 'one' after the funeral.

What could have happened that year at the carnival luckily didn't, and what shouldn't have happened, didn't anyway. I have returned to the small town a few times since, but my memory is forever imprinted with a wild night in a place that gave me very odd and perplexing residual emotions.

From the river's mouth at Boca Barranca I could see in the distant blue haze of the solo, tall hotel that didn't seem to fit in. The landscape that exemplifies paradise had a big square box sitting on the horizon. We pulled into a gravel road that ran opposite the highway up to the river. Turning toward the coast we drove a few feet more, stopped the car at what looked like a rickety hotel built on tall stilts. Under the building were several parked cars locked behind a high chain-link fence. Two attendants watched over the cars. One was sweeping the floor; the other leaned back on two legs of his chair in the sweltering heat and shade. Music was coming from an unseen source.

We unloaded the surfboards and cameras from the car and split into two groups. I stayed with the kids while the adults went surfing. I stayed in the shade of the building next to the river while the children played in the river. I laid out all my paints and began my first painting this season. After half finishing, or getting to a point I needed to stretch my legs, I asked the kids to go with me out toward the shore. I wanted to photograph the surfing. The humidity was thick as we walked along the stony bank of the river. As we neared the shore Laura was returning with her board. She took the kids back and I continued across the river to the opposite side and a better view of the surf. The river was cold, and up to my waist where it merged with the seashore. I was wearing plastic clogs, which made the rocky bottom easy to navigate. As the ocean tide mixed with the river the temperature difference was inconceivable. The ocean was as warm as a bath.

The surf broke in extended waves that gave an unusually long ride to the dark figures standing on their boards. A ride could last as long as one minute, or more, because of the angle of the shore and adjoining river. This was not a typical brief, five second long, surfing experience. I waded out into the water and stood up to my waist in the surf photographing with my telephoto lens. The video camera got even closer shots. I then returned at the same time that everyone was retreating to the beach hotel. We ate snakes and drank some juices, as we reloaded the boards on top of the car. Gabriel used a makeshift shower under the hotel to wash the seawater off his body. One of the men watching the cars told him he had to pay for the shower. This brief exchange was met by surprise. Gabriel had no money; it was back at the van a block away at another hotel.

When we began to pull away the man approached the car and asked for money for parking. Jose protested and a small argument ensued. The man said it was a private road and we had to pay him. Jose paid for the parking and Gabriel's shower. By that time Gabriel was returning with money but everyone told him to put the money away because Jose had just paid for everything. As we pulled away Jose, shouted a disrespectful thank you and a string of Spanish I could not understand. I asked what he had said. "Thank you for the big log around my neck." We chuckled and went on our way.

I thought we were returning to Jaco but we took a dirt road toward the ocean a few miles after the turn off toward Jaco. A bus was making a run so I half expected a small town. We passed a lone pedestrian as we flagged two men on a motorcycle down. Jose asked directions to a beach. Everyone pointed west and we continued on. At one point we were passing a grove of mango trees, so the men piled out of both vehicles and climbed a tree for fresh fruit. Two men on top of the tree flung mangos to the waiting catchers on the ground. We proceeded on the dusty road for another ten minutes slicing mangos and passing the tender yellow delicacy around.

When we reached the beach the road became muddy and narrow, no town, no houses, nothing. I shouldn't say "nothing". We parked the car and walked up a steep hill to see the most spectacular view of cliffs and crashing waves. Off in the distance a couple of houses were built, but a large space of land lay between the houses and the cliffs. The ridge ran approximately a half mile long with the drop to the ocean of nearly one hundred feet. At the far end was a high point that jetted out into the ocean and a small curved beach with an unusually steep slope. It was low tide and the surf was knocking away at the volcanic rock. Behind the beach were an estuary and smaller cliffs north along the shore. What was distinct to this place was the rolling green hills and low vegetation. It reminded me of the 'Cliff of Moher' in Ireland. So we all dubbed it "Tiny Moher".

Eligh disappeared as the tribe walked along the precipice. Uncharacteristically, Jose panicked and ran back to see where he was. Our fears were he had fallen off the edge. In the far distance I could see Jose raise his open palm as his body relaxed. He found little Eligh. He was with Janet from Michigan who had been lagging behind the rest of us.

The men, except me, all went surfing on waves that were close to ten feet tall. From our higher vantage point on the cliff we could see their tiny heads dip below the surf as they made their way beyond the breakers. I sat on a higher peak and took out my paints again. I choose a view looking north the same direction as the four surfers. The rest of the group continued walking north to the rocky end, near the surfers. I was left alone to be creative. Over an hour passed, the tide rose and the surf began to throw mist straight up the volcanic wall. The waves were making great thunderous sounds like gods banging at heaven's door. No one was to be seen except the surfers; the cliffs were void of any people. The emptiness was blissful. I sat for over an hour painting and basking in the solitude. This was a place to return with Diana.

To the north and south the shore curved for miles. South was a stretch of blue mountains where clouds were building and a rainstorm was showering Jaco, or the jungle outside of Jaco. We would encounter rain on our route home. Soon the non-surfing group reassembled where I was painting. It is always show and tell when an artwork is created. The children were becoming impatient and Laura elected to leave while the rest could follow in Janet's van. We slowly maneuvered the car back down the steep cragged road. I gave directions as Laura gingerly maneuvered the car avoiding rocks on its bottom. When she came to the dirt road we all piled in and began to find our way back to the main highway retracing our route. As we neared Jaco and its rainfall, I asked Laura to take me to the farmers market. It was just before closing time, leaving me precious few minute to complete necessary shopping.

As we pulled up, the first vendors were taking down their tents. I ran from place to place purchasing pineapple, oranges, lettuce, onions, and a chicken cut into parts. It took all of ten minutes. The farmers market is one of the shopping delights of Jaco. Every Friday, vendors set up shop at the south end of town on a dead-end street. It is a mix of Tico (an endearing term for Costa Ricans) farmers and Mennonites women in long clean, pastel colored dresses operating a green grocery. The Mennonites' specialty is baked goods. There was one stall with souvenirs, but the rest were wholesome fruits and vegetables, a cheese stall, fish, and a poultry vendor were also there. The market used to be a few blocks from my home, but because of the traffic closing down a major artery, it was moved. Since a major grocery store was built at the far end other road that may have been the real reason. Big business is big business and tends to move things out of the competitive range. The new location is farther from my home, that's my real complaint.

I made three trips to the car loading each group of parcels and dashing to get my shopping done before closing time.

Laura wanted to go to one more beach to surf, so we went to the northern most beaches in Jaco. The waves and tide from the full moon were pulling the tide up under the car tires in the parking lot. I have been to this beach many times but never observed water on the costal drive along the shore. We all went into the water fumbling along the wet rocks floor, complaining all the way. It wasn't sandy, but a terrible task to maneuver without pain on the soles of our feet. I was with Gloria, Khilani, and Eligh playing in the surf trying to cool off. It was my first time actually swimming in the water all day, even though everyone else had gone in before.

A big dog with a chain collar took a liking to Khilani and Eligh and began to play with them, too roughly. One time the dog ran at such a clip that he struck Eligh in the back of the head as he dropped below the surf. The enthusiastic large dog was young and full of pep, but untrained. The dog even nipped Khilani on the eye lid making a tiny cut, that's when I intervened and did the 'Dog Whisperers' training on dominance. The dog became less aggressive, but the damage had already been done. I sat on a log watching the children and an occasional strong wave would nearly knock me on my back. I'd balance the camera out of water's reach. When Laura returned she showed a cut on the back of her scalp that was about an inch long. The strong surf had thrown a rock out of the water clobbering her as she fought to stay on the surfboard. It was time to go home. All of us were struggling with some kind of hassle and just wanted to go home, so we did.

After eating I called Diana and tell her about the surfing adventure and creative day. It is lovely to be here, even if I miss my wife very much, and think of her constantly. She'll arrive in a month.

Sunday, July 26: I stayed in most of the day. Around four I rode to the beach to look at the water. I met an American for the second time, one night at the Internet café. Rick was introduced to me by a Canadian woman (Liz) that I've known here for years. Rick seems a step above most of the Gringos living down here. He's not alcoholic and doesn't do drugs, the predominate characteristic of the majority of American men here. He does visit the prostitutes. Out of loneliness, he said, because his wife died. It seems to me this is an addiction of sorts. There are many, many elderly American men here who come for the (legal) prostitutes. They walk around like packs of wild dogs at night with a beer in their hands. This kind of group mentality allows for bad behavior. Yet I think the legalization of this trade is better than what we have in the majority of the USA.

The cat and mouse game of catching johns and prostitutes is a waste of money and effort. The "morality police" are a derivative of the old days when religion set the cultural standards and waged war on "sin". Even when I was single it was not my choice to engage in sex with prostitutes. When I was young I had a few one-night stands with friends of friends. The older I got the less attractive, or exciting, I found this to be. Sex is big business both here, and the States. The problem is it seems to attract the lowest type of societal members, druggies and alcoholics, two classes of people whom lack self-control and self-esteem. In addition, prostitution shows no respect to woman. Religious institutions are not successful (enough) to build self-esteem in society. Prisons as opposed to treatment facilities and hospitals are seen as the current solution to addiction, so the vicious cycle continues itself out in the world. My hearts sinks when I meet a good man here and then find he is living that kind of life. Maybe it is a type of longing for a fraternal friendship that has never been in my life,

159

simply, wholesome with camaraderie and normality. Jose remains my best friend here for all the above mentioned reasons.

I rode my bike into town after I sat on the beach for an hour. I saw a woman from where I have always bought my ceramic gifts. My sister, Clare, broke her last gift and asked me to replace the small flat ceramic pot. As soon as the woman saw me, she recognized me and asked if I wanted more. Last time I bought four at once and used them for Christmas gifts.

There is a group of these woman and men who walk the beach, or congregate at a certain intersection in Jaco, to sell their wares. When they walk the beach they display three ceramic jugs in each hand to show the tourists. Their fingers stretch to grasp the holes in the neck of each ceramic. They walk with heavy loads of ceramics in their backpacks all day, up and down the beach. They come from Nicaragua and have darker skin than most Tico's.

As I was making my purchase, one of the male vendors from the beach a few days earlier, saw me making a purchase. He smiled and was happy I was now buying the exact flat, low design I described to him that I was wanting. The sale wasn't his, but he was happy for the woman and me. He has a scrawny beard, sun glasses, and a straw hat made of thick palm leaves. There are many such beachcombers who sell sunglasses, jewelry, cold beer or soda. I have become acquainted with a few of these people over the years.

Yesterday I saw two young men carrying a very heavy cooler full of cold drinks along the beach. Each one had his body slumped to one side from the immense weight of the cooler. They slipped in the sand and had to stop every few feet to catch their breath. The wheels on the cooler were useless in the sand. I'm sure that was the original intent, not thinking wheels don't roll on sand. This is not that different from many of the banks who were loaded down with their bad investments, selling product, and fumbling in their own lack of forethought. Life is full of lessons and metaphors. Bad planning is on the beach and Walls Street too.

Monday, July 27: One of the strange phenomena of life in Jaco is the social strata and how they affect each other in mysteriously antiquated ways. Life here is like living in the pre-technological era of a small town in the USA. Information is still received via word of mouth, a more importantly people interact more. Even though hundreds of people descend upon this town every day, they all come together causing chance encounters to be meaningful. What is a brief encounter on one level can become a critical link in one's destiny. One need not be a voyeur to witness these events; they happen because people are in proximity. The tribe is part of a larger whole, one thread in the beautiful tapestry that is Jaco. The stranger next to me on the beach is aware that I am not a tourist, but a local, with whom to associate. The lack of technological distractions creates intimacy and interdependence. People look you in the eye because you have a deeper meaning to them.

Life in Long Island, New York is not much more than brief encounters that will never have any influence on one's destiny. A kind of indifference radiates from everyone who wears a mask of pretense. Status separates people. The cars the wealthy choose as status symbols turn into a type of uniform, no one stands out. A brief hello in a supermarket line will never go beyond that moment because of the sheer number of people that live in my county. I can go years and never see the same person twice. Here, not so.

The one place I did have a small community, my gym, has closed and scattered my friends to many other clubs, although I recall one series of events where I saw a woman at my gym in a local fast food place, and a big hardware warehouse. I went up to her in the store and told her where she had been that day. She laughed and said how strange coincidences can be. That was the first and last day I ever saw her. In Jaco, life is much different, more personable, and rooted in practical reality. This is the kind of world Diana comes from and has had such a hard time adapting to life in the States. It is my hope that we return to her native country to live someday. But by living in New York she takes the risk of losing a piece of her soul like I did when I gave myself to the seduction of money and comfort of the east coast. Life is expedient there, but life is much deeper than being a part of a sea of humanity focused on survival. Small details are considered uneventful, when indeed miracles are taking place every moment of every day. To me, my life in Nebraska, twenty years ago, had the same level of intimacy as Jaco.

Yesterday morning I sat and had a twenty-minute conversation with Liz, the Canadian woman. She introduced me to Rick who the day before gave me the information about the bus to Nicaragua and how to get from the Panamanian Highway to Granada. He called the ride "the chicken bus" because livestock travel along with the passengers. That was just the ride I wanted. Rick gave me the name of a town where I would have to stay, because the International bus doesn't pass through Granada. Sunday, I saw him sitting with a group of Americans while I was riding my bicycle to the Internet cafe. I asked him where I could buy the tickets for the bus to Nicaragua.

As I sat with Liz, another man passed on a bicycle. He, Liz, and I, exchanged greetings. Later that day I was at the beach with Jose and family. The same man, who I later found out was named Scott, stood watching the sunset and drinking a cold beer from the cooler strapped to his bicycle. Scott pointed out that we had said hello that morning while I was sitting with Liz. Scott and I talked about Colombia, where to visit, and if life there was safe. He wants to travel there and see it after years of living in Mexico and Costa Rica. He prefers the cultural richness of Mexico to the lack of such in Costa Rica, but the trade-off is the convenience of life here on the beach. When I meet people I always want to ask them how they got their money, how they live on enough to just get by, how they keep traveling, and what set of circumstances lead them to where they are. Scott mentioned that he was recently single and that the reason he stuck around so long (sixteen years on and off) was because he had a Costa Rican girlfriend. There is also an air of secrecy to most of the American men here. I don't know if it is because of the prostitution, drug trade, or my false speculations, but Americans here don't come forth with personal information as readily.

When we all piled out of the car to be on the beach, Gabriel was there. We had also picked up another young woman who had me watching her purse. I sat and read and the others went into the water. Gabriel had his surfboard back at home he explained to me during our greeting. I read my book about the life story of Albert Einstein as everyone went about his or her leisurely activity, the children to the water, Laura and Jose to the surf, the teenage girl first to her cell phone, then the water. The beautiful women and their shapely bodies distracted me while I was trying to read. Few people are fat here. The air, ocean, food, recreation, and walking keeps most Ticas in shape, while the blubber hangs on the gut of the Americans, me included. Here, I lose weight by walking, swimming, and bicycling. The food is different. Whole foods return my body's metabolism to its correct state. My car is sitting in the driveway in New York.

Rinsing off the sand and taking a brief dip in the condominium's pool with Gloria and Eligh was lit by the sunset on the horizon, thus ended my day. Khilani was at his mother's. My few chores around the house, painting a ceiling and sealing the porch roof for leaks, had long been accomplished. It was time now to watch a movie Jose had lent me, 'Goya's Ghosts', about the life of the Spanish artist.

Tuesday, July 26: I turned the computer on and called Diana right away. We spoke a few minutes and I hung up to sign the papers for the installation.

A few minutes later, I was on the phone with Diana again. It dawned on me that for five years I had never used a telephone in this house. To have any communication with the outside world, I had to ride my bicycle for a mile and use the Internet and phone in a café. Now for the first time I was walking, sitting, in my house and talking to the USA. At no cost, I might add. It gave me the realization how isolated from technology the house had been. My sanctuary was changing. Spending five dollars to call home was now a thing of the past. The plan to bring the small computer, buy the telephone jack, and keep myself plugged into the techno-grid was now a reality in Costa Rica.

Soon I was reading emails and looking up bank statements to see how the money was. I went to the beach and did some body surfing, before telling Diana I would correct her English on some documents for her job upon my return. I am plugged in. But I also see how the new technology will cause me to spend less time by myself, and more time communicating with others. There is always a trade-off to seclusion, vacation, and how much do I really need to be on the treadmill of busy-work with technology. Besides I can keep a journal on a laptop, years earlier I needed to convert my words from a handwritten book to the computer. Not anymore.

I called my cousin Frank, to see when he would be coming because I plan to leave and travel on Thursday. The only occurrence other than receiving the Internet was injuring my butt. While setting up the hammock I failed to notice the nylon rope was frayed. I reclined in the hammock then a few seconds later I landed, squarely on my butt. I thought I broke my tailbone. The pain was intense, but a swim at the beach loosened up my muscles and I was fine. By 9:30 I was asleep. At 5:30AM I heard Jose's car start up. He was off to work for a few days, repairing boats in Puntarenas. He was laid off a few months before, now he was taking any odd jobs to get by.

Wednesday, July 29: I have been busy all day with house repairs, phone calls, and packing for my departure tomorrow. I started the day by calling New York State Board of Examiners. This is where Diana is having her practicum filed, but the company has been dragging its feet. I called so many times an interest developed her case. The good people there are looking out for Diana. She agreed to continue working for five more weeks if the company filed the practicum while she was still employed. Her employer hasn't kept their end of the bargain, so I feel she should just get on an airplane and leave as soon as possible. We will see what happens. Before, when she tendered her resignation, they threatened to sue her for breach of contract. As I explained before, it was a big ordeal to convince her that this was a lawyer's bluff and corporate America at its worst. Diana came up with the compromise to stay until they hire her replacement. Yet the reason she is leaving is exactly the way things have gone all along. Dysfunctional is a kind word. So now the State has called the company asking for the form. Diana has a meeting tomorrow with her supervisor, who I am sure did not expect the State to play her game back with her. Karma is a beautiful thing if you live your life on the correct path. I have been Diana's guardian angel. The company usually hires foreign workers who don't have American husbands, few if any of the workers even have green cards.

After breakfast I called Diana and told her about my conversation with the State. Diana's is having car trouble, so I called the landlord two houses away (in New York) and asked him to look into the car situation. I then started a project that lasted all day but ended in semi-success because of unexpected rain.

I called a few friends today, including a former colleague now retired, a couple who live on a farm in Iowa that I have known for thirty plus years, and my friend in Ireland, all with my new Internet phone jack! Between phone calls I was packing, which I really began a few days ago by placing anything I need on the bed next to the backpack-on-wheels.

When I go through customs at the border I will have to open everything and repack again. I hear it is a lengthy process where passports are taken and the wait time can be up to an hour.

The day has been lonely despite my many telephone conversations. I miss Diana. She needs my help right now, so I don't want to be out of phone reach. Despite all that's going on, I must travel. It is a spiritual quest I am driven to take; a pilgrimage. I venture into the unknown to know myself better. It's like seeing an old invisible friend who only comes out when I am in the universe of unknown places. My nerves are on edge before any sojourn, but that is part of the challenge, I have to step out of my comfort zone. Travel fills me up more than anyone can; it makes me happy to be alive. I feel in conflict about what are Diana's needs and what I am about to do by traveling. Am I being selfish? Is there anything more I can really do for her situation? On a spiritual level it can be our over-dependence and over-involvement with others that makes us stale and not grow. To be overly comfortable with one's life is a danger and can cause paralysis of the soul. Letting go of people and situations can promote growth. To travel, encounter strangers, and leave a silent, unspoken message of love and peace is an art that comes with experience. Human beings are really electric; we touch each other in many unseen ways. A quick glance by a stranger can be deeper than realized. We walk around thinking much less of ourselves than should be; we are spirits that touch each other in our sleep. We bring heaven to earth every day. We get closer to living what was meant to be. I see life as having a purpose, a deep purpose. The conclusion (death) is better than we think.

Tonight Diana asked me not to publish the second book. I thought it was going to be because of some embarrassment in the first book. No, she doesn't want to spend the money and to have me suffer from lack of sales. I explained an artist does his work because of a drive to be creative. The previous conversation she was crying because she missed me. The irony is that I end up being the one who is nurturing and consoling, but with an obstinate nature. "Stop the crying. Everything will be all right". There is a kind of role that I take on to counter her emotions. Inside I feel she is being unreasonable, but I don't live her life, I don't understand her emotions and the manner in which she copes. By understand I mean I don't have the exact same sentiment. I try to have empathy, yet her yin is my yang. It is the opposites, and commonalities, that keep us embraced in this relationship. It is not a mistake that we need and/or reject the emotional component of what is confusing and difficult, yet beautiful and successful despite the hardships. I am sure my distancing baffles her, yet she follows. This is the one relationship I longed for most of my life. I don't think I would have been mature or patient enough before; I was not ready yet. We have reached a kind of plateau where the constant of knowing we are there for each other is laying the foundation for deep awareness in ourselves, individually, and each other. I trust her more than I have ever trusted anyone before. Our fidelity is true, and a strength that is very liberating.

Thursday, July 30: I was up at 5:30. I gave Diana a call before I left for Nicaragua. She told me about our neighbor, Flora, who has a tooth abscess that turned into a big infection. The neighbor is from El Salvador and has a daughter that is becoming Americanized. The daughter refused to let the mother use her new camera, a birthday gift from the mother. The mother called Diana late last night and wanted to borrow our camera, so I was giving Diana instructions on how to charge the battery. The mother is ashamed of how the daughter made a big scene. From Diana's perspective this is just another indication of the bad values that the children learn in the USA. I don't know the whole story, but I feel sorry for everyone. I fall into simple explanations of what makes kids behave badly, but this is an interesting twist. I told Diana that the daughter needs to be disciplined and the camera should be taken away for a while.

I have my rituals for leaving the house, putting away things, cleaning, and emptying the refrigerator. So I took all the perishable foods and put them in a plastic bag, and then walked over to Jose's to give him the food. He was just getting ready for work, and leaving his house, and we had a short visit after he returned from a moment of meditation at the beach. He was telling me how the night before his co-workers stopped off at a bar and got drunk. He sees the mindset that alcohol induces and the way people carry on while under the influence.

In his recovery program he is keenly aware of the trap such behaviors can have. I admire his strength and dedication, but mostly enjoy the fact that we openly discuss life beyond addition and delve into spiritual concepts. He is crucial to my survival in this town because there is so much of the underworld and its chemicals. He is my link to sanity when the sleazy side of life surfaces here. At my teaching job in New York I have a professional environment that is structured to uplift people, but here in Jaco the by-product of society's ills, like drugs and poverty, is very prevalent and obvious. What can give life great purpose is to learn how to battle these endless distractions that retard the soul.

Now I travel. I laugh at myself so often when I travel. Every preconceived notion of what a place will look like is always very different than reality. I left my house at 8:30 for the 9 AM bus Puntarenas. I took a taxi to the farthest end of town to make sure I got a seat. The travel agent told me if I bought my ticket on the bus to Nicaragua from the middle of town, there would be no seats. This proved to be false since there were empty seats as the bus passed my condominium complex. The time allowed me to have a nice visit with a woman who sat there with her child at the bus stop.

The woman's son was sick with a cough. The clinic she wanted to visit was only taking people suffering from the flu (swine flu, I don't know), so she had to go to a second clinic. She worked as a domestic, running food to vendors for a woman who cooks from her home. She said there was not much work to be found in Jaco, yet she had two sons to feed. Her other son is older, twelve years, and he was at home. I asked if the father was involved. No, she had two sons from two different men, no husband to help with the expenses. She had come from Nicaragua four years earlier. I told her I was about to go there.

As we sat there the boy jumped up to squash a caterpillar with his foot. He missed and brushed the insect, rolling it a few inches. Before he could repeat his attempted death sentence on the bug I stopped him. I picked up the caterpillar and showed the boy that it would become a butterfly, holding the long insect in my palm. It lay motionless. I then returned it to a green leaf as it crawled away. For some reason the boy began to cry and hug his mother. He realized my protest to protect the caterpillar was a criticism of his behavior. I reassured him that it was all right and alive, pointing out the way it was climbing up a twig. He soon stopped crying and listened as his mother and I conversed more in their native dialect. I thought they were waiting for a bus like me, but soon they crossed the street and headed in the opposite direction. The bus was exactly on time. It pulled up at precisely 9:00 AM. I threw my pack into the lower storage space and boarded the bus. I was about to visit a new country.

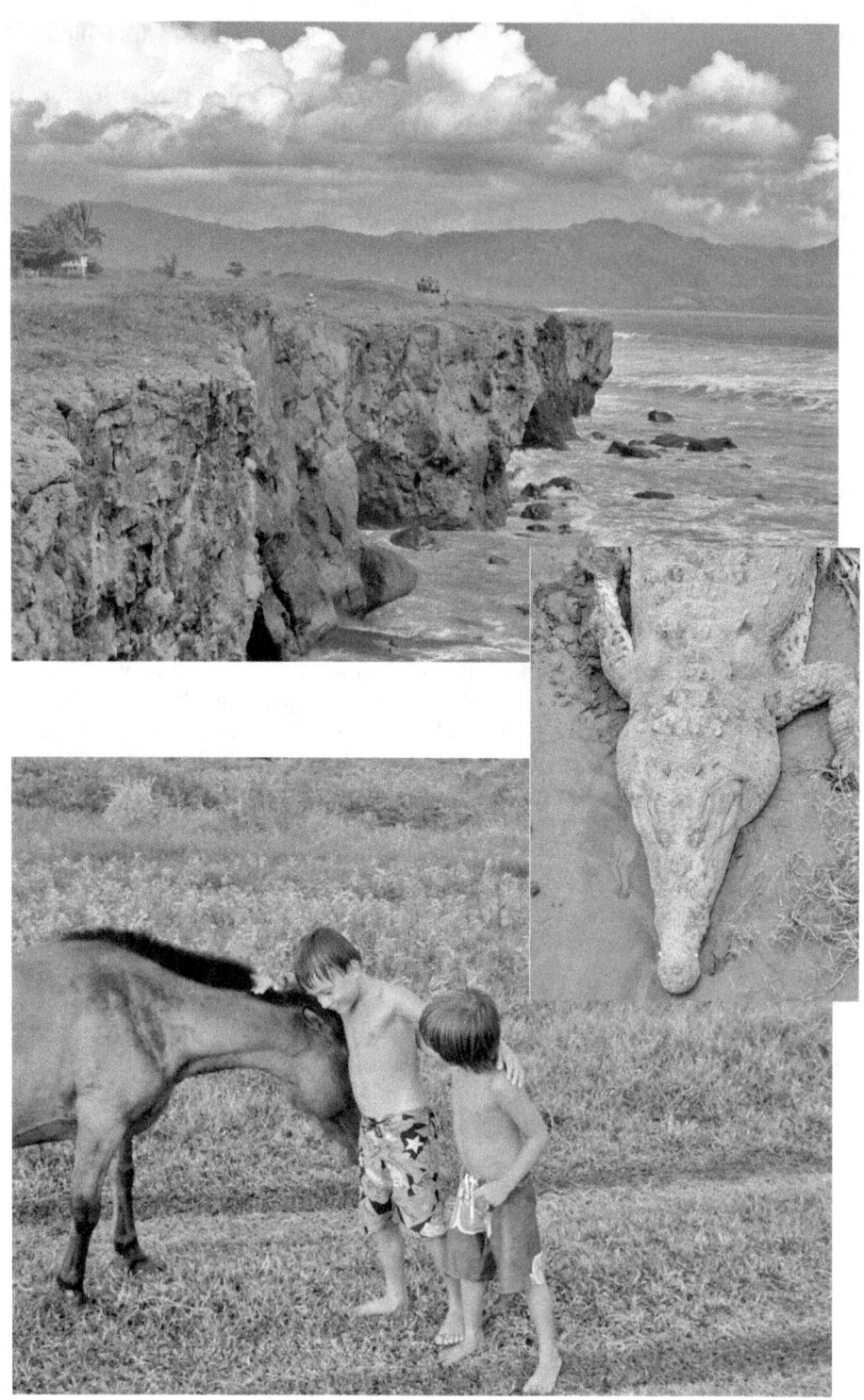

Chapter Ten
Nicaragua

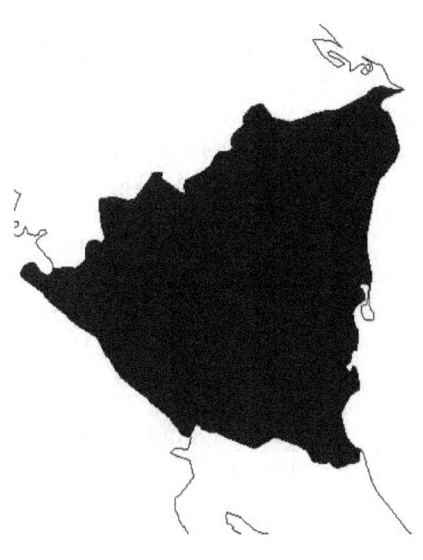

The driver knew some of the people and gave familiar handshakes as they boarded. The route we passed was the same direction I had traveled with Jose and the tribe a few days before. We passed the usual police checkpoints and cars blinked their lights to signify what was coming ahead. By the time we reached the outskirts of Herridura, the next town to the north, only one person was standing and she eventually found a seat. Before we reached my stop I walked up and asked the bus driver to let me off where I could catch a taxi to Barranca.

A woman exited the bus at the same time and she reluctantly agreed to share the taxi ride with me. I asked her if she worked in Barranca and she said she was catching a bus to Santa Ana, another town. I expected a town at the bus stop, but it was only a restaurant on a busy highway with two rusty bus shelters with people seated on its benches. I asked the restaurant worker where the town was, thinking I could walk around and see it. It was down a small valley and out of view. Very well. It was 10:30 and my bus arrived at 2:30. So I had been sitting there reading and watching the different people come and go in the restaurant. A rain shower passed and a few customers came in to eat, but other than the man selling pineapple with a loud call as each bus pulls up to the stop, the time has passed with ease.

Now I had about one remaining hour in this loud intersection with all kinds of traffic. A near collision between a van and a car caught my attention, but so far all are safe and sound, including me. Although I always notice my nerves while traveling, my heightened awareness of sounds is working well. I feel safe, but a little unsure of myself whenever I venture into the unknown.

The bus arrived and I climbed onboard. I made the same mistake I made many years ago when boarding an air-conditioned bus in Europe. I forgot to bring a sweater and long pants. It has been a bone-chilling, freezing ride, so much so, I even asked a stranger to borrow her sweater to put around my legs.

The drive north is beautiful with a different type of terrain than the central coastal area of Costa Rica. The land is more developed and there are fewer forests. I saw strange red fruit hanging in trees, round orange-like fruit growing out of the bark of trees, not hanging on branches like most fruit, and green ground coverings that looked like tiny ferns spreading along the highway. The land is flat. It opens up in expansive vistas where at points the land stretches for miles.

The predominant livelihood of the people in this area appears to be cattle and sheep farms. Odd-looking brown birds with long necks and the bodies of ducks are perched on fence posts. The land has mostly been cleared for the cattle farms. Some of the farms showed signs of prosperity, but the majority of the houses looked like poverty was as common as the heat. Paint was seldom seen on the worn, wooden surfaces.

The border was a mix of mud, filth, and strewn trash. People milled around sitting on boxes and logs playing cards. The bus passed a single, wooden plank raised above the road and entered the border area. We then exited the bus, and were met by a dozen boisterous men asking if we wanted to exchange our currency. The passengers went single file into an open room, stood in a line, and got their passports stamped. The ceiling had a big gaping hole and behind a glass partition a blinking computer server sat on a wooden shelf. A woman was sweeping the floor and piles of dirt lay in the middle of the mostly empty room. Back on the bus a man who worked for the bus company came and collected our passports and took our money. He promised to return with change in dollars, and the passports.

Next, the bus then moved on through a small border crossing into Nicaragua. Inside the border a maze of parked trucks but not a man, woman, or child was to be seen. There were dozens of trucks but not a human in sight. That all changed rapidly when we pulled into a central island where hundreds of people stood milling around, some were travelers, but the majority of the people were there to make a living. People sold food or offered taxi rides.

A young man mumbled in Spanish as he instructed me to remove my luggage from under the bus, go stand at what was to be the beginning of a line. This particular border agent, who looked to be around twenty and sloppily dressed, told me to wait there. A few minutes later, he and an older man said something to me in Spanish that I didn't understand. The agent told another fellow to move away as he pulled a dirty desk out of the way. I assumed they were going to search my luggage, but didn't. They motioned to me to show the papers I got when crossing the border on the Costa Rican side. I had unknowingly cleared my top pocket and stuffed the papers in my backpack. Not to worry, no one was in a hurry. They took the paper and told me to go stand by the bus where another man replaced my luggage back under the bus. The entire entourage of passengers then stood around for about fifteen minutes until a woman dressed in a uniform stood calling out our names, handing our passports back. We then re-boarded the bus.

While I was waiting, I met a tall, blonde man from England who had been on the bus. He soon left taking a taxi to a town on the Pacific coast. A woman named Anna came up to me and asked if I would be willing to share a taxi when we arrived in Granada. She had light brown hair, a small body frame, and looked very pale and fragile. She is working as a massage therapist in Costa Rica and on a three-day trip into Granada to renew her visa there. I agreed to help and we talked while waiting.

In the distance I could see a perfectly, symmetrical cone-shaped volcano with a whiff of smoke coming out of its peak. In this busy mix of people the lure of nature was like an anchor in the chaos. Nothing looked clean or constructed as if some higher plan had been originally executed. It was simple without pretense; only functionality.

I had been told by Rick back in Jaco, what to expect when crossing the border, so I knew why, explaining to the British man that our passports would be returned. He noted this was very unusual to not keep one's passport in hand.

The last rays of sunlight were shining on the volcano as we passed huge white windmills in the foreground. In the middle of nowhere, it what seemed unchanging, a backward country, yet tall white, modern windmills spun in groups that seemed odd and out of place. It began to rain and the road took on a rough and bumpy feel. We entered a dark landscape with no lights, and no people to be seen. Night fell.

Friday, July 31: Granada. During first day in Granada and I have one fact to offer up: it was founded in 1854. The buildings are ancient Spanish structures with fresh paint and a sense of history from days gone by. The town has a Spanish feel.

When I exited the bus last night Anna and I got a taxi. The taxi driver and his wife described another hotel that neither of us wanted but for some reason, maybe a commission, and the driver offered us an alternative. We stopped at Anna's hotel first, I intended to go on to the hotel Rick had suggested, but I stayed here at 'Amigos' at a rate of eighteen dollars a night. The people seemed friendly enough and the hotel was close to the center of town. My room had a big double bed, a TV, and a fan. That's about all, but it serves its purpose. The hotel had a long row of rooms on the right side, while the dining room was situated in the middle separated by two open air patios with chairs, tables, and plants growing up the wall. It is not well finished; the building is worn and old. The toilets barely flush, and the shower has lukewarm water, but good pressure. I don't think I'd bring Diana here, but for the money I am spending it is perfect for my budget. I derive pleasure from living cheaply, way below my means.

The first thing I did was to call Diana. The computer phone wasn't working, so I had to put the line directly into the hotels outlet. We spoke and for some reason ended up arguing about the neighbors upstairs. She didn't like when I pounded the ceiling with the broom to get the children to stop jumping. She thought that a polite, face to face, conversation would have been more appropriate. That had taken place months before, but to no avail. That time I didn't go anywhere but straight to the broom closet. Several negative encounters over the neighbor using our things without permission, or even returning them, resulted in an uneasy situation. They often walked into our section of the yard unannounced or unapologetically. Then it struck me, I'm on vacation and I'm on the phone arguing about an event that happened a month ago. There was something wrong with the whole conversation, so I got pissed. I went to my room seeing Anna on my way and trying to describe to a total stranger how difficult marriage can be. I know when I am detailing my personal feelings to a stranger that my feelings have no real relevance to that person. This is only an indication of me being unable to cope with myself.

I watched TV for an hour then turned off the TV to fall fast asleep. I woke in the middle of the night from a dream where I wanted to encourage a group of friends to promote socialism with a new computer campaign. This was a type of computerized propaganda blitz that I wanted to put into motion. I had no idea where this dream came from, but I awoke with the emotional intent of a man driven by strong idealism, wanting to change the whole world, and feeling fully capable of doing so, at that moment. By the time I awoke at 7:30 my sleepy ecstasy was replaced by groggy apathy and hunger. I ate the complimentary rice, bean, and scrambled egg breakfast that comes with the room. Not long after that, I placed an unsuccessful call to Diana and was out the door with my back pack and two cameras concealed inside.

What a place! The street was filled with cars, colorful bikes, horse drawn carts, venders of everything imaginable to eat, with flies buzzing endlessly overhead, and shops with men calling out what was for sale. I went straight to the city center which is a park ringed by grand, well-kept buildings. The smell of spicy food cooking and sweets would hit my nostrils as I passed selected sellers.

The first building I entered was big yellow church. This is the cathedral that dominated the entire city. The interior was plan with brown tile floors, more pale yellow paint on the walls and almost every door opening to the outside street. The pews took up the middle section of the building while vast empty areas made the sides of the interior seem like an empty street. People prayed in reverence. I said hello to God and took some photographs, exiting on one side of the building into a long wide street that lead to the shores of Lake Nicaragua. The shoreline made for some interesting views of what looked like an ocean.

I returned to the central park and sat on a bench with two old men who were in their late seventies. They asked me where I was from and if I had children. One fellow had a large bandage on his right ear. The bandage didn't look very sanitary because dried blood and yellow stains, hopefully some medical dressing, hung on his ear like a piece of cabbage. The bandage jolted my memory of art school and Vincent Van Gogh. I asked him if he knew of the Dutch artist Vincent Van Gogh. He didn't. The one event that gave poor Van Gogh such renowned notoriety was a meaningless question. I am sure Nicaragua has a rich cultural heritage yet in this case the man had never heard of a typical art education icon, Van Gogh. I took a little pleasure from the European cultural void I was delving into.

I found an ATM machine, and then circled back to the street the hotel is on, just to make sure my bearings were correct. Following as before, to the central park in a slightly different path. I do this kind of "walk-about" to get myself acquainted with my surrounding first, before venturing toward further destinations. My second pass through the park, to the far side of the church, sent me walking down the long wide street that lead to the lake where the port and a friendly guard offered to allow me into a gate and up the stairs to photographs from a high vantage point. The wind was picking up and it was much cooler there than the thick air in the people–packed streets near the hotel. Following along the lake there was an ice cream vendor, but the man protested that my bill was too large for him to make change. So I entered what looked like a burnt out building and bought two bottles of water.

It was a sort of restaurant but God knows what kind of abuse had created such an empty, sparse space with only a few plastic tables and chairs on the outer patio. Behind an archway a woman offered me a drink of beer as she sat alone at another plastic table. She wore a cheap necklace, earrings, and had a purse sitting on the table. She looked to be in her early forties. I said no, she insisted that I do it for her. I looked a little deeper and could see she was alcoholic, lonely, and her head was bobbing from years of consumption. I repeated the polite refusal and she looked back at her drink as if an answer to some long perplexing question was going to emerge.

When I sat at another table drinking my water, the woman I had bought the water from joined me. Her husband, or lover, came and sat there first. We talked for a few minutes then they both got up and I moved back across the street to buy my ice cream. On a low sea wall, as the hot wind melted the ice cream, I ate fast. A woman and her son sat a few feet away, so I asked permission to photograph them. The woman said yes, but instantly turned allowing only the boy to be the subject. The people are very shy and unpretentious here. It is their character to be humble and not draw attention to themselves. I find these camera-shy moments very refreshing to encounter, but not so easy to photograph.

Within a few minutes, it began to rain and I went back to the shelter of the strange restaurant. By this time, no one was there and the ghosts of the people had vanished. This side of town was empty and I slowly walked my way back up the wide street towards the central park.

I passed a house that had a plank with 'artist' written on it, around the corner a young man painted a hug head of a bull. The bull was made of Styrofoam. Inside a large open door two women were painting cacti made of Styrofoam. A short man dressed in all white stood there and I asked permission to come in. Hanging on the wall above the studio was a grand painting of the artist and his studio. His name was Pedro. I could see a younger version of him standing in the painting and pointed out that I recognized him in the work. He then pointed out the two sisters who were much younger in the painting; these were the same women painting the cacti. I asked him if he liked Velasquez, because the painting reminded me of the artist. He said many artists influenced him. Some of his Spanish was too fast for me, but I caught most of the conversation. He then took me deeper into his studio and showed me a church restoration he was doing of Saint Sebastian. I photographed him next to the statue. Pedro asked me to come to his house where he had a small gallery, but I told him I would return the next day. I wanted to go buy my bus ticket to El Salvador. A man had given me directions on how to follow one street all the way. I had a reason to return and have a longer visit.

This residential street was much different than the rest of town. Richly colored painted houses with expensive gates and courtyards stood next to shanty houses. Inside each house owned by the dwellers, the front door stood open. As I would pass from door to door, I would glance in and look at people sitting in a half circle of chairs around a television. Inside the repeated dark rooms, door after door, was a series of returning eyes looking back at me. Some people said hello while others only returned their gaze to the out of sight televisions. These front rooms were vast, and the doors, with beams of light from beyond always lead to an inner courtyard where vegetation hung in baskets. All these secret worlds enticed me. Maybe forty minutes later I found my bus office. Actually I found a different bus office, but the results were the same; I bought my ticket for Monday morning at 9:30.

I was getting hungry and returned to a sidewalk restaurant that I had passed on my way. The female proprietor had moved back from New York after living there for twenty-two years. Two of her sons, one in his early teens, the other around eighteen, scurried about the restaurant helping her. I bought a chicken, rice, and spaghetti dish for two dollars. The woman looked like she had been working hard. She wore a long soiled apron, had short, pulled back, black hair, freckles, big brown eyes, and a broad smile, when she would stop long enough to pause. We struck up a conversation about the young people in the USA, their lack of proper values, and how difficult it is to raise children in the USA. She was arrested for striking her daughter in an attempt to discipline her. I explained the youth in America know exactly what their rights are, but many have no knowledge of how to respect each other, or others property. The woman, whose name was Ruth, I later found out, had such a bad experience with her daughter that she moved back to Nicaragua. Her daughter had stolen money and was hanging out with nineteen-year olds, when she was only twelve. In an effort to raise her two sons correctly, Ruth came back to Nicaragua leaving her daughter with the x-husband. She told me the story of how a judge in court didn't care about any of the circumstances of the girl's behavior, only that her mother had slapped her. It was a sad song, yet she still had hope for her two sons. The older boy briefly told me how good his grades were in his first year of college. He still holds an American passport.

I said my goodbyes only to return a few minutes later because of torrential rain. This was like the downpours in Costa Rica. Walking is pointless in such a shower. The only alternative is to seek shelter from the storm. As I stood in the door, Ruth offered me a seat in her living room opposite the restaurant's living area. Inside the living room was a nun and a mechanic, soon followed by a young woman who was an architectural student at the University. The nun was having her car repaired, the mechanic was there to get out of the rain like the rest of us, but he soon departed. As the mechanic left and I began to speak in English with the nun. She introduced herself as Sister Sara. The conversation drifted to my uncle in the Philippine Islands who is still doing missionary work. She said she wanted to visit the Philippines so I gave her my uncle's address, as well as my e-mail address. The rain continued but the car was ready, so Sister Sara went out to receive it. She was going to return to Managua where she lived.

I was in Ruth's living room for approximately forty-five minutes as the rain poured on the streets. On a table in a gold frame was the license for the restaurant. That is how I found the name of the woman who had served me lunch and invited me into her living room. I talked with the young architecture student, but she soon left as the rain diminished. I said my goodbyes for a second time to Ruth and her sons, as the rain faded into a slight drizzle. I needed a taxi, found one, and returned to the center of the city. I exited the taxi in front of a used clothing store, which I entered in order to look for a raincoat, finding a very nice jacket with a hood for ten dollars and reluctantly added this piece of necessity to the other contents of my luggage, but wore it the few remaining blocks in the rain to my hotel. It was worth a hundred dollars, a recognizable brand of jacket. Who says there are no bargains in Nicaragua?

I was wet and tired, so a nap followed. When emerging from my room Anna and another American gent were talking at the central table in the hotel lobby. I called Diana and she was at a neighbor's house nursing her friend's for a tooth abscess that had developed into full-blown infection. I called Diana on her cell phone. Soon I was walking down the wet pavement toward the grocery store to stock up on some salad supplies, water, and yogurt.

Later, Anna asked me to escort her to the same grocery store. As I walked with her she explained why she chose not to walk alone, men were indeed giving her catcalls and the look-over. She shopped and we took a long circular walk through the closing market, to the central park, and back to the hotel. Anna has to leave Costa Rica every ninety days to keep a legal residency in Costa Rica. She is Swedish, living in Costa Rica, and working as a message therapist for a beauty spa.

In our many brief conversations over the past two days, we have been exchanging and piecing our separate lives into mutual stories. As I was telling her about Diana, her leaving her job, and the whole story of how I met Diana, Anna was asking several poignant questions, finally disclosing her current dilemma with a live-in boyfriend in Costa Rica, who happens to be from Nicaragua. "The project" which I classify my relationship with Diana at times, is what makes us strong and true despite the cultural difficulties. Anna was explaining many of the same challenges that come from loving someone from a different country. To paraphrase her: "Sometimes the smallest little things in language go unnoticed because of the differences in language". "Yes, but those differences a can become what cements the bond", was my response. (Also paraphrased) It is not easy to keep love and nurture commitments under any circumstances. The theme of conversations brought us to understand the common concerns we had. Life has a mysterious role in what brings strangers together through common needs. A stranger in a border crossing can end up becoming a healthy sounding board. We returned home to the hotel where I sat writing, took a break to shower, then called Diana for a third time today. I then returned to the computer to cultivate my disciplined writing. I've invited Anna to go to a small town tomorrow where I've read there are many artisans.

Saturday, August 1: Today was a busy day for my photography. I went out after breakfast to call Diana. It must have been around 9:00 AM. I started in the market a few blocks away from the hotel, the same market that I had seen while escorting Anna to the grocery store. As soon as I left the main street I looked for the first entrance into the market. I feel so silly at times because my landmarks for my travels are U.S. shopping malls. For starters there is not one shopping mall in all of Granada. The market was a very dark maze of slim paths that had vendor stalls. That is a very simple description for what was a complicated array of split-levels, sprawling alleyways, and varied heights of ceiling coverings ranging from corrugated steel to cardboard boxes. On parts of the path, sun light and open sky, would soon give way to dark smoky corridors where vendors called out the items they were selling. In some places the floor would be blood soaked from meat drippings, and other places with mud from the rain that fell the previous day. All kinds of creative fly swatters with large fabric ends were waved over the food to keep the flies away, but the shear multitude of flies was impossible to discourage.

The people were the real treasure to behold; thousands of faces with lines, dark skin, smooth skin, baby skin, skin wrinkled from old age, or on newborn babies, all populate this place. No one was unpleasant, no one seemed to mind my asking for photographs, and often I was being asked to take their picture. It was a sea of humanity, and a sea of poverty, yet how strange to look beyond all this and feel true happiness coming from the people. Every face was an open flower. It was truly amazing. What on the surface would invoke sadness due to a harsh reality, is not the case if people know nothing different. The meek have inherited the earth on this part of the planet. Yes, yes I am romanticizing about a life that would be tough on a daily basis, but the spirit of these people is one of happiness as a result of survival, not happiness that came from attaining material goods, educational goals, or economic status. In Nicaragua, there is a big difference. There is no middle class here.

After the market I found the church bell tower, climbing up a narrow steel stairwell, and passing large circular windows on my way up. The last narrow set of steps forced me to duck and contort my body because I was wearing my backpack with cameras. The damp smell of mold and concrete was drifting from below and suddenly the air thinned and a fresh breeze came over my forehead. At the top, the draft was ten degrees cooler than the earth below. The simple concrete bricks made me feel I was in a construction site more so than a tourist attraction. Scattered bricks and broken boards were strewn on the floor. A good view of the city was to be seen with the four tallest structures in Granada being other Catholic churches. A low set of verdant mountains lay west, while the city and terra cotta roofs spread for a few miles between. East were the gray waters of Lake Nicaragua, the source of the cooling winds. It was a pleasant five minutes to stand and gaze at the bustling plaza below.

After I descended, I asked the attendant, who was accepting donations to enter the tower, where the museum was.

"Did you see the blue church in that directions (pointing), go one block, take a right for two block and you are there." He spoke in Spanish. Within minutes, I was walking into a spacious courtyard with very tall palm trees. Galleries of a few ancient ceramic artifacts, and a life-sized diorama of how the indigenous people's houses were built, all stood in a separate room. In the back of the museum were large stone carvings of Pre-Columbian figures. A sign designated this section as the Institute of Nicaraguan Culture. The figures were weathered and it was difficult to figure out what they represented. Each figure had a written explanation describing what was being portrayed. For instance, one figure had a leopard's body and the body of a man morphed together. This was a leopard God.

This section of the museum had no walls, only a corrugated steel roof. Further on, there were photographs of the city from one hundred years ago. I recognized the front façade of the market building I had visited that morning. The stark contrast time had waged on the building was drastic. It seemed no repairs had been attempted in one hundred years. Now, vegetation had grown, died and was left to stand on the building's weathervane. Next another gallery had nine religious icons, mostly of Saint Anthony, followed by a final gallery of art by a local female, modern artist.

Soon I was walking towards Pedro's studio. On my way I stopped an American who was carrying a small blonde boy with blue eyes on his shoulder. Dilbert was his name and he had the air of a Southern gentleman. He was married to a Nicaraguan and had moved from Costa Rica within the last few months. He preferred Nicaragua to Costa Rica. Why?

"Lines! You don't have to wait for hours in a line to get things done here. I got my driver license in two hours here".

He sold his property overlooking the ocean and made enough to come here with his family. He was going to start a new deep-sea fishing operation for sports fishermen. I told him I was from New York. He knew the Fulton Fish Market in New York City.

"I used to ship a truckload of fresh fish there to sell in the market."

He made his money in fishing off the coast of North Carolina. He tried to return to the States after Costa Rica, but lasted three months.

"I can't take it there anymore."

His sister-in-law is Valerie, the woman whose hotel I was going to stay in before Anna introduced me to 'Amigos'.

"Are you the guy that came in this morning and didn't stay at the hotel?"

"No, I have been here for two days." We concluded with a goodbye, as I went to find Pedro.

Again Pedro was in his studio, this time at an easel instructing a young man on perspective. Within a short time Pedro took me to his house up the street to show me his gallery, which was located inside his house. The houses gallery was in a dark, long thin room. A few chairs lined the walls, but it was unclear if it was a sitting room or a true gallery. The only light entering the room came from the open front door. He had paintings of famous Nicaraguan poets and musicians, self-portraits as a young artist, and various sculptures in wood. These were his favorite works; the prized works that he would never sell. I know his sentiment, there is some artwork treasured so deeply that they belong in the home. In this house were many extended family members. One son stored his DJ and karaoke equipment in the entry room. Babies and young children ran around the house, and Pedro's older sister came out to be introduced. We entered the two main rooms of the house but went no further. We then sat together on his front step talking. Dilbert walked by across the triple-wide street not seeing us. I did some short video clips of Pedro's artwork and asked if I could paint his portrait. Tomorrow. Most of the conversation was understandable to me but a few times I got stuck misunderstanding his Spanish, so I would ask him to clarify what the words meant.

I returned to the hotel where Anna sat watching TV. She decided to stay in and not go to the market in Masaya as we discussed the night before. It was so hot, and I was hungry, so I made a tuna salad and shared it with her. We once again compared notes on the challenges that comes with a cross-cultural relationship. Her boyfriend's name is Early. They live together in a small town in Costa Rica. He has a good job and is a responsible, hardworking man. He is twenty-four, and she is twenty-six. Later that night I sat with her for a couple of hours. I intended to do my writing, but we ended up speaking about what she is contending with in her relationship with Early. I told her about my friend Jose and his past marriage to a Gringa from Utah. The biggest challenge is economics and how little money she will be living on, if she stays in Costa Rica. She wants to settle down, but she is not ready. My advice to her was to give things a couple of years. Too many people rush into things only to find they are not ready. We talked at length about relationships, marriage, commitment, and where all this could take her. By the time I went to bed I was too sleepy to even try to put my day into the computer. I could hear Anna in the next room get up, shower and leave at six the next morning. We had already said good-by the night before.

In the afternoon I walked a few blocks and found the bus to Masaya. I arrived in a dirt courtyard and within seconds, boarded the bus. An old, orange school bus with stickers of Christ on the interior drove off for a joyful adventure. We wove our way through Granada's side streets making stops and eventually finding the highway. No one paid until midway through the ride. One time we stopped and I caught the glimpse of a young man passing his bicycle to another on the roof of the bus. Each bus had a storage rack on top where an attendant sat and loaded bikes and boxes for passengers. The bumpy ride took forty minutes.

Masaya was a better experience than the morning's market. The bus pulled into a dirt plaza with muddy pools in holes and trash strewn everywhere. The street leading into the bus plaza was lined with shanty, one-room houses where poverty was rampant and an air of destitution was part of the demeanor of the children and older inhabitants. Some of the shanties doubled as barber shops. Buses pulled in and out with a chaotic frenzy with attendants yelling the name of their destination while hanging out of the door. The dirt plaza was maybe half the size of a soccer field. I asked a man where I could find the artisans and ceramics. "Four blocks down and to the right". This time I saw tourists buying things. What had been a market for food in the morning, this time was a vast market for any and everything. Large sections were devoted to specific goods. Shoes, clothes, meats, legumes, vegetables, all had an area where a theme of product type was its specialty.

This market was ten times the size of Granada's. I walked for over an hour, and never touched the four directions. I assume the market wrapped around the central bus plaza, but I was only in one quarter where most items geared toward the tourists. I didn't buy anything except water, although I was tempted. I'd return on my way home in a few weeks, but then I wanted to travel as lightly as possible. The crafts were slightly crude, but here and there some woodcarvings, and ceramics, caught my eye. I was holding out making purchases until I got to Guatemala where the Indian fabrics interested me the most. My time was mostly occupied with photography.

Once again, I was having fun with the people and being asked to take pictures. Husbands would goad their wives to get in a picture; coworkers would push each other to get into the photographs. I held my camera tight to my chest because Pedro told me this market could be dangerous. So far my lucky angel has stood by me. I was talking with a woman from England who had just come from El Salvador. She warned that El Salvador looked and felt dangerous, a detail I would not tell Diana when I called her in a few minutes. I went to bed planning a way to get through the border and safely to a taxi. Visual projection is an attribute needed on a safe sojourn. The hotel is full of backpackers today. I think every bed in the house was slept in because the woman who operates the hotel gave up her room to accommodate some guests.

Monday, August 3: Right now I am in the lap of luxury on a bus that is fully air-conditioned and with blue-suited attendants. I have a nine or ten-hour ride to get to San Miguel, El Salvador, so I have lots of time to write and catch up on yesterday's activities.

My morning was spent writing on the computer and calling Diana. I sat in the hotels dining room and wrote the previous day's encounters. Around noon I went out on the street and was struck by heavy sunlight and grueling heat. On a map I saw where I could walk directly to the beach leading away from the town's central plaza. The first thing I heard was the sound of music swimming up the street. Somewhere trumpets and some other horned instruments were repeating a short song. As I walked toward the lake I found the source of music. A four-piece band was standing in the shade on the far side of the road while a man stood in the sun, pulling a two-wheeled cart from house to house. At the door or gate of the houses, mothers and their children stood praying to a shrine of the Virgin Mary that was mounted on the cart. The band would play the short song, and then move on up the slightly inclined street to the next household's worshipers waiting in their portal. A locked coffer stood at the feet of the Virgin where an offering was placed. I assumed this was a church sanctioned function because of the locked box. I shot photographs after making a small donation. The man pulling the cart was red from sunburn. He would remain in the street, in direct sunlight facing the worshipers, as the musicians stood on the opposite shade under the eaves of houses.

The street was bare and hot, only a few young men stood in small groups on elevated stoops, and an occasional car, or horse-drawn cart would pass. Time passed the same way, as it would have one hundred years before. The heat drove everyone out of its reach to the dark, cool shelter of home. The closer I came to the shore, the poorer people and conditions of the houses. I noticed that many of the people here say, "hi", instead of "hola". This must be an American influence the locals feel safe in saying. I stopped into a small store with safety bars and a woman behind the counter to buy some water. A man with no shoes or shirt walked down the middle of the street looking dazed and drunk. I thought to myself, the absence of women on the street is a sign that this is not a place to linger long. One scruffy-looking man approached me to shake my hand. I declined his invitation; he in turn began to curse at me. I shrugged my shoulders and made sure he was continuing on his way before I turned and walked toward the water. The wind and air were becoming fresher, and the heat was decreasing, like my previous walk to the lake, it became much cooler with a stiff breeze to dry the sweat off my brow.

Not far from where I had walked the day before I found a bridge with a fortress-like building, a gate. A female attendant stood stopping those who entered; I gave five Cordova (one dollar) to enter the park. The walkway along the beach wound a curved path along the shore. A low stonewall ran along the walk where people enjoyed the shade by leaning on the wall, or sitting on multicolored concrete benches that were in need of paint. In the distance I could see many bathers in the water. I walked for several minutes, then sat on a bench in the shade near a family of picnickers. The adults sat on the ground while the children ran back and forth to the water. They were all enjoying each other's company. No one noticed me.

Men selling ice cream rang bells and called out, women walked by with large wooden planks balanced on their heads while holding a two-legged stand in one hand. Old women selling single cigarettes and candy had trays strapped across their laps approaching various groups of people. On the shore a crowd of youngsters was burying a girl in sand, laughing and having fun. A couple with a young boy sat on the bench next to me. The boy stripped naked and ran off to frolic in the water. No one was diving under the water, only jumping with the small passing waves, created mostly by the wind, coming for miles across the empty, gray lake. No one was wearing bathing suits, boys and men wore shorts, and the girls wore shorts and tank tops. The grown women went into the water in street clothes. This must have been a cultural norm for modesty.

I began a watercolor painting of a large tree, the shadows it cast, and the small dots of heads playing in the water. I was in the shade but by the time I had finished the sun had etched a small red burn on my sleeveless arms. People would pass, stop and look at the art being created. Three people sat on the opposite bench watching me paint. Another group stopped and told me in Spanish it was a beautiful painting. Later as I exited the park, they stopped me again and asked if I would take a picture with one of the girls and my painting. It was a very pleasant way to pass the afternoon. Making art always makes me feel good about myself, and others.

I stopped to buy a tortilla from a woman. It was a corn tortilla layered with a flat thin pancake-like white cheese; this was smothered in an onion sauce with a dash of cream cheese that spread like milk. I didn't know what I was getting, but it was a delicious treat and just enough to satisfy my slight hunger.

As I exited the park gate the attendant had left and I found myself striking up a conversation with two Dutch men who were in their early twenties. Their next country to visit was Costa Rica, heading south from a trip that began in Mexico. I suggested they visit Jaco. We talked about the drug scene in Holland. Neither of them had never even smoked pot. The drug use in Holland has never spread despite all the fears of such liberal laws tolerating soft drugs. It is a rite of teenage passage to defy authority in most Western countries, while in Holland these two young men hadn't even smoked a cigarette.

While we walked, a man stopped us and asked us if we like this young girl standing there. The man was laughing and seemed to be joking, but we couldn't tell if he was her pimp or just playing a joke on the girl. Another woman was next to the girl selling fruit. One of the Dutchmen said it was disrespectful to do this with the girl's mother standing next to her. The other woman said she wasn't her mother, but was laughing at the whole scene. The teenage girl said nothing, but seemed to be embarrassed. I still wasn't sure if this was serious or a bad joke, but we passed and continued on our way. I liked these two Dutch guys even more. We walked together as far as Pedro's house where we said our good-byes.

Two children sat playing a game inside the room of the open door. One of them went off to find Pedro. He emerged from a back room, still buttoning up his white shirt. We exchanged greetings and I showed him my watercolor landscape. We soon sat on a group of chairs as I began to sketch his portrait. The portrait took forty minutes or more, I didn't want to tire him from sitting so long, so it was a quick, a good-enough likeness. I always think I can do better.

I was honored to be his guest. I gave him a copy of my book in Spanish and was soon walking into a church across the street to see what this new building was like. It had been closed the other two days I walked by.

The sun was getting lower on the horizon and seemingly came straight down the long wide street. Thousands of tiny white flies were being blown up from the lake on the wind. The flies were swarming people sitting at the occasional outdoor restaurant. Other tourists walked into the swarm then tried to get away, but it was impossible. The late afternoon sun was at a perfect angle to create a spectacle of the dancing, white, sparkling bugs. The central Plaza was full of people lazing in the shade to escape the heat. I found a seat and asked to sit with a man reading a book, he agreed. My friend with the Van Gogh bandage on his ear soon came up and sat between the two of us. We shook hands again, and continued the conversation where we had left off two days before, repeating some of the same information. He remembered I was from New York and had no children. He made a joke that my male organ wasn't working. "No, my machinery is fine", I said in Spanish. We all had a good chuckle. It is very rare for a Latino man to not have children so he considered me an oddity.

The man reading on the bench soon became part of the conversation. He was also a school teacher. He taught in a primary school. He struck such similarity to my friend, Mark in Colombia that I asked to take his picture. So once again I had another photograph of my bandaged friend with a companion. In this town most people know one another, even the beggars came up to my bandaged buddy and greeted him. We sat for a good half hour and passed questions back and forth. Sometimes my Spanish was atrocious, other times they knew exactly what I was saying. If I didn't understand their words I would stop and ask for further explanation. Once again we parted as friends.

I needed some change for the taxi in the morning, so I found a man on a street corner who gave me change for a US twenty dollar bill. These money changers are found all over the city but are in greater abundance on the street where three or four banks are. I suspect this gathering of banks is because of security concerns. The moneychangers' mill around street corners holding thick wads of bills in their hands, speaking to passersby in a polite unassuming voice, this is sharply contrasting to most vendors who spend the day yelling at the top of their lungs on the border crossing. As I finished my transaction an old man who was American exited a taxi with a young girl. He approached the moneychanger and was soon handing the girl some money, a sad statement on the lives of both people, but a greater shame on the side of wisdom and power.

After preparing a big avocado salad, I called Diana. Soon I was back in my room organizing my few things so they would fit in my backpack. Also, the best time to use the computer is before the majority of the people return. I took my salad to my room and watched the news. The highlight of my day is calling Diana, so I waited until I was organized and had free time to talk. I assured her that the following day in El Salvador I would call as soon as possible, but if I couldn't find an Internet connection I would try to call from the new hotel.

In the morning I went out for one last hour, walking to the central plaza, inside the church to say hello, and back to the plaza. As I was coming out of the church I came upon Pedro in a chance encounter. We said hello and good-by one more time. He is the one Nicaraguan I saw on all my four days in the city. Our paths had crossed consistently and I hope they will someday cross again.

I had paid my bill the day before in a funny encounter with the young female hotel clerk. I left the hotel in the morning and was around the street corner when I swore I heard someone calling out, "Dennis. Dennis." I looked around, up in the air, back down the street, and once again, "Dennis. Dennis." No one knew me there. Was I hearing the angels of death summoning me? A second later the young woman came running up to me out of breath. Between pants she asked me, in Spanish, to pay my bill. Did I still have the room and reservation for that night? "Yes."

They wanted to include my money in that week's balance, so we returned to the hotel where I paid the seventy-two dollars for four nights, plus two dollars for a lock.

I was asleep by 8:30 and awoke at 7:00 AM. I took a taxi to the bus station by 9:15, but the bus arrived at eleven. An American named Luke came in and we struck up a conversation with a Dutch woman who had lived in Costa Rica for sixteen years. The bus was very fancy. I felt like I would use this company again.

They served us lunch of sandwiches and sodas. We made a brief stop in Managua still making our way north toward Honduras. Nicaragua looks very rich in vegetation while expansive stretches of land lay unpopulated, not even with farms. The land seems mostly flat but we have passed through several mountains on a highway that is well paved. Low stone walls of volcanic rock are built in some areas while barbed wire fences separate other strips of land. The forests are not as "tropical" and the land seems more arid than Costa Rica. The mountains look more inviting because of the open patches of green grass, but there are not many cattle ranches. This is wild, uncultivated land with few inhabitants.

The black and red symbol of the Sandinista revolution is painted in a variety of places. I saw neighborhoods in Managua where the black and red flag of the FLNS were proudly waving. The FLNS is the party that took power after the revolution. These were very poor, but in a sense, better constructed shantytowns than I've seen in any other countries. If there can be such a thing as a government sanctioned shantytown this was it, the houses were occupied by the poor, but the way these houses were constructed had a feeling of order. These houses were built to help the poor. They were not the typical mismatch of found, discarded construction materials. This was the result of the Sandinista revolution that had taken place, helping those in need. This fascinated me because at least an attempt to help organize these neighborhoods was taking place as opposed to having them in outlawed and dangerous ghettos.

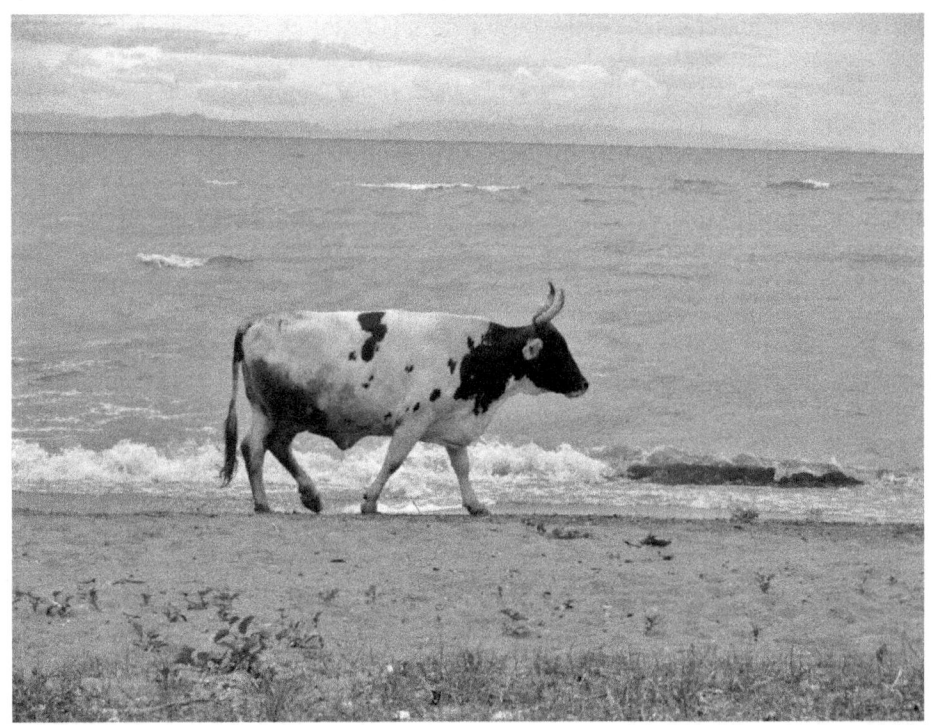

Chapter Eleven
El Salvador

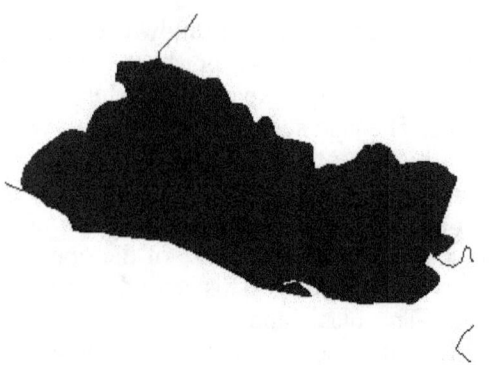

Tuesday, August 4: El Salvador. I am seated at my computer, four young children flanking me like sentries, watching my every move and keystroke, lest any flicker of the monitor escape from them. I am on the Island of Meanguera. It is situated off the coast of Southern El Salvador. The children are all skinny, barefooted, and a few of them have runny noses. I am such an oddity that they follow me and look at me like I am from Mars. My white skin, white hair, and height are something, I am sure, they have never seen before. But this is the end of my day. Many miles, a boat ride, and how these children came to be with me took an entire day.

My day started early, rising at 5:45 to get up and go to the hotel lobby to call Diana before she went to work, she wasn't home, not to worry though. I called her cell phone. She pulled off the road while driving and took my call.

The day before the bus ride was very nice. I'd brought a warm jacket. The other American on the bus, Luke, was shivering. He had spent two years in the Peace Corps working in Piragua as a health volunteer. I liked Luke the minute we met. He talked about his experiences nonstop. His stories were so interesting, and he was so motivated, that I didn't tire of his energy.

The Americans, and many people from other countries, hide from the law in Piragua. I was told it was uncommon for anyone to divulge any personal information since the majority of them were criminals, or living in some kind of underworld. There are two languages for communication in this country, Spanish and the indigenous dialects. He was curious about any current events in the States because he had only a few periodicals to read while living as a volunteer. He also wanted to know about the new movies. We were the only two laughing at an English language comedy on the bus. My stop came before the end of the movie and we quickly said our salutations as I exited the bus to a lonely, vacant highway stop. One streetlight buzzed as taxi driver woke to get my business.

Last night I arrived in San Miguel around 9:30PM. My first impression of the city was that this was a stark place. There was a solo street light shining at the gas station that was the bus stop. A taxi was waiting for a possible customer. I had read, and heard, so many bad things about El Salvador that I thought it wise to just get in a cab and go straight to a hotel I found in the Lonely Planet book. The driver didn't know the hotel; the Kings Palace. I told him the name several times and he said he knew where it was, he didn't. He called his brother on the cell phone and after a long roundabout drive, which I am sure was to increase the fare, we found the hotel across the street from the main bus terminal, just as I said. He didn't have change for a twenty and could only give me sixteen dollars, making additional dollars. He then pulled a big wad of singles out of his pocket when he was putting away the twenty I gave him. This pissed me off, but I said nothing. The guard at the hotel gate agreed with me, it was a ploy. This was my second impression of a new country. The guard escorted me into the hotel carrying my bag. Behind me he was pulling a big steel garage door down, the castle door and drawbridge were being closed for the night at the *King's Palace*.

As the taxi driver had been speeding down empty side streets I had visions of a robbery, actually more like paranoid fantasies. I guess the vibe was what made me suspicious. The guy was driving all over in a place that I know isn't that big. But I could tell this was a page out of hell if a person is walking alone at night. The only person I saw was a lone homeless man lying under a stairway. A black cat scurrying across a dark street was my third impression. Once night falls, the whole area is devoid of people. I mean this is one empty place and seemingly for good reason. The cats don't even venture outside because the rats own the streets after dark.

As I stood at the front desk sweat streaming from my brow and torso, I was asked for my passport. The desk clerk would accept my Visa card but there was a five percent surcharge. The room came to a little over twenty-nine dollars a night. My card was declined twice so I went into my cash reserve. Nothing was going as planned, so nothing surprised me.

The hotel was a three-story building with a swimming pool in the middle on the ground floor. If a car's driver wanted, they could have driven straight into the swimming pool. The street, lobby, and pool-side all merged into a continuous driveway. I had no way of knowing how many guest were in attendance, by the time I was being escorted to the top floor, the pool's two occupants were gone and the lights of the entire compound were all being shut off.

Although it was just past midnight back in New York I wanted to call Diana to put her mind at ease. I'm not sure what would be worse, waking her or having her lie restlessly awaiting a confirmation of my arrival. I opted to call. Our neighbor (the woman with the abscessed tooth) is from this town; San Miguel. She had told Diana how dangerous it is at night.

I showered and was about to watch the news on cable TV. I, despite all of the countries and luxuries I have been afforded throughout my travels do not consider myself wealthy or privileged. I have been in many an inn, hostel, or hotel that never "turndown" the blankets. Such was the case here. As I pulled back the blankets, not to reveal a complimentary chocolate, but a wolf spider was rousted from his slumber. It assumed a defiant stance, as if to challenge my claim to its bed. There was a brief skirmish. We both rested well that night. Only one of us woke the next morning.

I was awakened once in the middle of the night by a man sneezing in the courtyard. His explosive outburst echoed and jolted me awake. My assumption is that it was the night guard. I drifted peacefully back into a sound sleep, arising well rested, without the use of the alarm.

The idea of putting this hotel across from the bus station was a stroke of genius. Not only was it five minutes from the bus, but only another five until the bus pulled out of the station. The well-built bus jockey put my bag under the bus and I stepped into a very cool, air-conditioned ride. The bus jockey helped an assortment of travelers from woman with baskets to boxes, all the while running along the side, calling out the name of the city we were going; La Union. This guy was in great shape and worked hard for his money. The bus driver and he had a rhythm that kept things in constant motion, not a second was lost as passengers boarded the bus and the accelerator was punched. If the bottom of the bus was opened, the driver gave an extra millisecond pause, but the jockey never skipped a beat. When the team works well together (like in Costa Rica) the jockeys graduate to a drivers position, after years of being an apprentice.

The climate of El Salvador was drier than that of Costa Rica. The densely populated land was not revered in the same manner either. Trash strewn about was visible everywhere, including discarded bicycle tires carelessly tossed skyward, dangling from branches like dead leaves, refusing to fall to the earth.

Poverty is a careless friend to mother earth and the green movement. People who live at the bottom are not concerned with anything but survival. It isn't a careless thought, or deliberate negligence, as much as an uneducated value that comes with living in an immediate, struggling reality. Citizens stripped of self-worth though a life of poverty cannot find within their wounded psyches, strength to care for their environment.

When I departed the bus in La Union I asked where the beach was. I pulled my backpack on wheels down cobble-stone streets where trash and pools of rancid water leaked downhill toward the bay with gravity. People looked at me as if I were an alien, which in a manner of thinking I am. After asking a few more times I was certain I was at the only docking station; Playa Pequina. The least likely man finally confirmed the name of this landing, he looking homeless and starving. My Gringo (in Spanish) accent caused me to be more misunderstood than not, but overall he understood my question.

This is a place centered in the middle of the third world. Trash is everywhere and people mill around in the heat so uninspired that a heavy sadness is even in the eyes of the horses. It is bleak, yet in contradicting terms, the life being lived is full of a type of passive contentment; nothing is absent in a void of desire. Many faces passed by looked at me sitting in the shade of the building and said nothing, but once in a while an old man would come up to me, act silly to get a laugh. His tone was friendly and polite. The people I assumed were strange, homeless people with a destitute look actually had a function at the port. One guy who I just assumed was some dirty, barefoot homeless youngster proved to be a hard working helper who ran and got plastic bags for departing passengers. The passengers who needed to waterproof their purchases would pay him to get the plastic bags that kept their things dry. Another man sat next to me and began to follow me as I moved around the port, telling me his story of crossing the US border on foot, living in Washington DC, and eventually enjoying his first and only airplane ride as a deportee back to El Salvador, compliments of the US government. He told me he had not worked for three months and had not eaten for a few days. I slipped him a few dollars, and he thanked me. I found it hard to believe he hadn't eaten with so many food vendors around; it may well have been true.

People walked through the caged, open-air waiting room selling anything imaginable. One woman who was selling clothes had half the body of a mannequin hanging from her belt while she carried a pile of clothing that obscured her face from view. Women balancing plastic buckets loaded down with fruit, food, or sundries walked around politely describing what it was they were selling. A man with a variety of plastic blow-up toys passed, followed by two women with leather belts encircling their bodies with what appeared to be a hundred extra pounds.

Men draped large canvases over a skeletal frame on two boats in the nearby shallow water. This was to keep the sun off passengers. It was a bus-on-water being prepared as a trickle of passengers climbed on board with the assistance of the town's other inhabitants. What may have appeared as a chaotic mix of unrelated proceedings evolved into a well-choreographed departure, being replaced by another empty water-bus seeking passengers.

The next boat that pulled into the small harbor looked promising. A man wading up to his knees pointed to me standing on the shore, I began to wave, and he waved back. My ride had arrived. Herbert wore a large white shirt and white New York Yankees cap. He came onto shore and told me his grandmother, who came along for the ride, was going to do some shopping. When she returned she was upset that someone had pulled a flim-flam and short-changed her, costing her twenty dollars. Our nine o'clock meeting time ended up being a twelve o'clock departure. Salvadorian time is not New York time, no one is in a hurry, and I am their guest.

Herbert is a soft-spoken man in his mid-twenties. He swaggers when he walks and hunches his shoulders with attitude. Under that ball cap was a round-cheeked face with thin eyes that look deep, yet quickly into mine. He has that typical macho-bravado that says, "I am tough", yet underneath it all he is a gentleman. His body has no fat but is muscular. He stands five feet ten inches tall.

We recognized each other when we first came face to face. He was never my student but he attended the school where I teach. He had been there maybe five years before. His sister and a cousin were my students the previous year. It was a suggestion by Nancy (My student), and a few other students from this island, that I visit their island home. This is how things happen for me. A silly, half-challenging suggestion has turned into a real adventure. The political problems in Honduras this year have set my compass to this country instead of my first plans. I originally wanted to visit Roatan Island, Honduras, but that's just not possible right now.

Nancy's uncle's boat was my transport. A forty-five minute boat ride over bouncing waves, pelicans darting away from the sights boat's direction, and fishermen warning of their nets in the water were a few of the observations I can recall. Nine of us were speeding toward the island. The women covered their heads with towels to keep the sun away. I sat in the middle and guessed which island we were heading for, because there were some five islands in view. It was when we passed around a second island that we went straight toward the last remaining island. I knew all options had been narrowed down.

All the passengers unloaded the boat by helping each other carry the plastic bags onto the shore. This was accomplished while wadding up to our thighs in water. I could see a tiny village from the water, but not much more was revealed when we initially walked up the small street. The village is called Barrio Angle. They told me that the islands population is approximately two thousand people. I was waiting with Herbert for his grandmother, Blanca. One of the young boys with us was Herbert's nephew, Roberto. He has a cheery smile and big wide eyes. He would become my first candidate for a portrait. He was the last one to board the boat. He had vanished for a while, but managed to reappear just in time to leave from La Union.

The island had about five boats tied and floating in the small harbor. Another twenty boats lay on their over-turned bellies in storage. The sun beat down on the blistering concrete. The only few people milling around were the town drunks who eyed us as we paraded up the hill with my luggage and the household shopping contents. Horses tied to rocks, pigs grazing in empty lots, a real water well, cracked and dilapidated houses, and smiling white teeth shining from dark doorways all morphed together as I regarded this place. Dogs barking, roosters crowing, and the voices of the inhabitants all built into a song of life and the pace of a world where no cars are passing by. After sunset, a long line of women balancing plastic water jugs on their heads saunter down to the water well then retrace their way back to their houses on the hillside. This daily procession has gone on for generations. The woman wait for the sun to set, then the cooling night air draws them down the hills to the well. They return with their heads balancing huge water jugs. They gossip and looked at me knowing I was a stranger, someone who had come to their far island.

Herbert has given me his room in honor of me being a guest. The bed has no mattress; it has woven strands of plastic wicker. He has one dresser cabinet and few cloths. He wore his best cloths to greet me. The room has a TV, fan, and stereo. I spent the next half hour in the hammock on Blanca's (his grandmother) porch enjoying the shade. Her blind husband sat silently next to me, in a matter of minutes I had fallen asleep. When I awoke I returned to my room, put my things on the bed, and began to take out my paints. Roberto sat patiently in the hot room as I sketched him and began a watercolor. Herbert showed me the single Internet house (a room attached to a house) where three computers are linked to the outside world. Diana was happy to hear from me, but the reception is very low. We talked long enough for me to assure her I was safe and there were no kidnappers with guns to my head asking for donations.

One of her granddaughters helped Blanca start a wood fire in a shack, next to the house. That is their kitchen. They fried fish and presented me with a plate of rice and tortillas. I was filled with new friendship and real flavors. The three houses in this compound are the family of Blanca's. Nancy's (my student) mother owns the house Herbert is living in. Herbert's brother, girlfriend, and newborn baby daughter live in a second large room of the same house. The new born is Herbert's brother's child. Just up the hill, on the other side of a short wall, a third house is where a second daughter makes a home. There are maybe seventeen people here, most of who look alike and pass between the houses as if they were all one big house. There are many animals--a parrot, two dogs, three chickens that are tied at their feet, and one chicken that has been allowed it to remain untied due to good behavior. There is an outhouse where rainwater collected in a big orange barrel is used to flush via a large plastic jug. Next to the outhouse is a shower, but I chose to douse myself with water I pulled up from the well just after Roberto and I went for a swim in the ocean.

Roberto first entered the water near the boats, but I protested and got him to go to the other side of the harbor because the water was dirty with watermelon rinds floating on the surface. We crossed a concrete bridge that ran along the shore and past the police house, to a concrete slope that is used as a boat ramp. I slipped on my butt and zipped into the water on the green algae. This got a good laugh out of the two hefty policemen swimming in the water on the edge of the ramp. We were all soon enjoying ourselves in the rolling surf.

Wednesday, August 5: The heat is almost oppressive. I have been like a sloth in this heat. I walk slowly, talk less, and feel no need to hurry for anything. I have defiantly set my body to the rhythm of this small island, Meanguera. After I wrote on the computer for almost three hours last night I thought it wise to be more sociable. I entered Blanca's house and she offered me one of the hammocks. Every house has two or three hammocks strung across a central front room. This room is a kind of dining room, and living room where people lounge to escape the heat during the day. At night they still use them. Behind this front room is a partition made of tall cabinets. Inside there are four beds, some in the corner, some along the wall, and there are bunk beds. There are no true walls in the house; the beds are all in one room with no sense of privacy or personal space. A dresser drawer is in one corner, but the drawers are open and nothing is folded or organized. The whole house is without order, or order as I know it.

The ceiling is separated by open spaces between the roof and exterior, brick wall. Insects and lizards can come and go at will. A foot below the ceiling, a double row of bricks with square holes acts as a ventilation system. This runs along the entire four sides of the house. Wind, when there is any, can pass through and cool the house. The one window in the house is closed shut. All doors and windows have a double purpose. The outer bars can lock, and then there is another covering plate that can be opened to let air flow through. Herbert showed me how the door needs to be secured by first closing the plate, locking it in place, then closing the barred-door with a double dead bolt. There are few windows, mostly doors, but they are seldom opened wide, only left ajar. This causes the houses to be dark. The houses are burglar proof, but they are only locked when people are away, which is very seldom. My room is always unlocked, the children come and go, and no one's gotten into my things. I am safer here than anywhere. There is no crime because everyone in the whole village would know about it if it happened.

I couldn't fall asleep, so I watched the only English channel to be found, whose subtitles were in Spanish. The movie was Apollo 13 starring Tom Hanks. When the lights were out, the village sounds were filling my room. Dogs barking, roosters calling, radios blaring music, TV's yelling, and best of all the sound of my fan whose din was loud enough to drown out the other noises. Herbert and most of the village was getting up at 4:30 to catch the boat to Nicaragua. I heard him rise and I lay awake long enough to see him pass through my room. At five, I heard a horn blow that indicated the boat was leaving but I don't remember much more than that. I thought just Herbert was going, but it seems everyone but the blind grandfather and one uncle, Alfredo, went to see a big soccer match. The local island team was in a soccer match that transformed the place into a ghost town. Alfredo's family, a couple of children, and the grandfather who smells like vodka, are the only people remaining with me here.

I awoke around seven and had the luxury of lying in bed and listening to music through my earphones. I then began to paint and finished the portrait of Robert even though he is in Nicaragua. Two small children were soon in my room looking at the curious white man making art. My next task was to call Diana, and then spend half an hour on the phone with my bank asking them to clear up the hold on my credit card. The phone's reception was very low, but it all went well. I am free to use my plastic again.

Alfredo, my student's uncle is my designated host today because everyone else is gone. He and I walked for over an hour over the top of the ridge through the last few houses at the edge of the village and beyond any paved road to see a beach on the far side of the island. He proudly showed me the soccer field while in route. He is a soft-spoken short man who lives in the house behind Blanca's. He is fifty-one, diminutive, a slight muscular build, and dark skinned with light gray hair. I can follow most of what he is saying, but still there are times I can only agree and wish my Spanish were better. When we returned, his wife had a plate of rice, yucca, and chicken waiting for me. I ate like a king. Thanked them and retired to my room for a short siesta. I listened to my music and drifted into a half sleep.

Alfredo and I agreed while walking, he would take me on a boat ride. I offered to pay, at first he declined, and then agreed to take my ten-dollar offer. (The night before Herbert suggested I make a small donation.) At noon, the agreed time, he sent his young friend. In a silent gesture and turn of his finger, he indicated it was time to go. The three of us walked up hill, turned left along a path that eventually became steep broken stairs to the water's edge. Close to the water was the public laundry area. Young girls were washing clothes in sinks that were built for everyone's use. A row of these sinks, with flat ridged openings for scrubbing and rolling the clothes, stood a few feet from the steep wall on the water. A water tank on an upper embankment served as the source to wash the clothes. The soapy water ran into the small harbor just next to a white hotel built into the side of the hill. We boarded the small craft, the same boat that brought me here.

Alfredo, his young nameless friend, and I perched in the front of the boat.

We were soon bouncing across the water, turning the visible corner of the island, and circling to the side of the island which we had walked to see from far above earlier that morning. One cove had a small hotel owned by Spaniards. We stayed long enough for me to photograph it, but then rounded another isthmus of rich, verdant land. On the opposite side was a beach with many bathers. I climbed out of the boat and the young friend helped me move my bag ashore. As we passed the swimmers, one of them recognized me from the day before and said hello. (Last night two brothers had passed me in the street and stopped to speak to me.) This time I chatted with them, their mother, and several cousins. They were here on vacation from Jamaica, Queens on Long Island. One thing lead to another and I showed the boys how to body surf. Soon, a troop of seven of us was lined up catching the small waves. These weren't really waves, but enough of a swell to give the children and me a push into the shore. This went on for twenty minutes, when I encouraged Alfredo's friend to join us in the water while Alberto sat in the boat out on the water. We motioned for Alfredo to pick us up; we three then went further into the far bay, and circled toward our homeport. Another island is off to the east, so we went to the other side of this land's mass where pelicans darted from trees as we hugged the rocky shore, close enough to see schools of tiny fish jumping to escape larger predators. It was a very scenic place. I clicked furiously away with my camera and then we headed back. By then the port of Angel was in view.

A man sat on the rocky step cleaning three barracudas as we pulled up. I disembarked with my bag and shot more pictures. I was amazed when Alfredo's young friend lifted the entire engine onto his back and carried it into a nearby shed. This young man was maybe eighteen and the engine was larger than he was. We exited past a new group of girls washing clothes, then up the long steps. Alfredo said he was going to wait for a friend and sat on a low wall. I came back here to Blanca's house to write. I am being very piggish and using a small electric fan to cool myself. Maybe an hour passed when Alfredo brought me a big bowl of fresh watermelon. Two small boys, the same as this morning, and the blind grandfather who goes in the house from time to time to get more drink, have accompanied me. The grandfather drinks in private, but I can smell the results of his behavior. The day has become overcast. Roosters and pigs are walking about, and life goes on as if I were just a shadow in this oppressive heat. Tomorrow I will leave and head toward my new destination; Guatemala.

Thursday, August 6. I am in San Salvador, on a bus, about to leave for Guatemala. I just called Diana to tell her I am safe and what my plans are for the day. I have been awake since 4:30 and now beginning to feel it. Nothing has been wrong but I feel unsettled. It is nothing more than fatigue. Getting to sleep last night was a struggle, even with the sleeping pill. The drone of a soft rain lulled me to sleep for a short while, but the heat and dogs fighting yanked me awake. The fan was blowing to keep me cool, yet my neck was sweating.

My alarm went off as set, so I was up and brushing my teeth when Alfredo came to the door. I didn't expect him, but was happy to have someone send me off. I had packed all but my clothes the night before, it was just a matter of dressing, turning off the fan, and locking the door as Herbert had asked me. It was dark out and the only sign of life was the echo of roosters calling to one another. I recall wondering why this animal had been a part of human history, maybe they are natural alarm clocks, but from my point of view they just make noise. Thomas the apostle knew three rooster calls; to him the rooster meant betrayal.

As we walked down the small road toward the water, Alfredo carried my backpack on his shoulder. He began to tell me not to trust anyone, not to talk to strangers, not to let anyone touch my bags, and to be safe. I understood completely. When the young man that was with us on the boat yesterday walked up Alfredo told me not to trust him and gave an angry stare.

"Isn't this your son?" I asked. "No, he is a scoundrel who won't work".

I was confused. I thought the young friend was his son at first, or a part of the family. Things seemed fine between them the day before, friend or not, but now there was a rift taking place. The young man gave a nervous laugh with a half-smile and walked away. Alfredo continued to warn me against this young man. The boat was scheduled to leave at 5:00, but we didn't board and depart until 5:45. One of the two brothers I was teaching to body surf the day before was there at the harbor. He was hunting for crabs to use as fishing bait. I gave him my card and told him to e-mail me when he returned to New York. He borrowed Alfredo's flashlight and returned if after catching two tiny crabs. He went on a different boat since they were going to visit family on the mainland. I was impressed he was up and so alert so early. I shook hands good bye with Alfredo and was soon onboard.

The sky was turning bright red as we pulled away, a few minutes later the sun burst over the horizon into our eyes. The sky was a creamy orange sherbet with a red sun that caused a sensation of melting colors blending together. There were twenty people on the boat, a mix of teenage girls, young children, mothers, and several men. We all climbed over a very large plastic bin full of fish covered with chucks of ice. The bin was in the back of the boat. The mother of two girls that had been speaking English at Herbert's house a few nights past was there with one of the girls. They live in Florida. Other than the young man, I was warned to avoid, I didn't recognize anyone else. One time I caught the eye of the young scalawag, but he kept to himself and sat in silence like everyone else on the boat. I thought it so strange that no one was speaking in a place that had no privacy and where the very same people had been standing around together a few nights earlier. I wondered who was praying, who was lost in thought, and who was just plain bored with life. Some women wrapped themselves in sheets, another sat bowing with her head in her lap, and the man calling directions, standing at the bow of the boat, gazed into the empty horizon.

When that same man began to collect the money as we neared land, the boat was suddenly filled with the sounds of conversation. The man steering the boat in the rear was talking away with a woman when someone told him to watch out for a fishing boat. He didn't hear but soon a handful of people were directing him to take heed. A communal sigh, followed by a group laugh, broke the remaining silence. Now conversation was passing freely between passengers. When we pulled into the inlet to disembark at La Union, the barefooted man who had approached me when I was there before, was there, knee deep in water. He took my bag and carried it to the dock. I wasn't off the boat yet, but my bag sat safely as people came and went not noticing. I slipped him a few quarters with a thank you. I now knew he was the designated porter, or maybe self-appointed porter. The other very dirty boy who was walking about helping people get plastic bags was now pulling a boat out and laying the anchor. Groups of men sat together and talked, it was still early and few sellers were hocking their wares. The port was still asleep in a place where human activity never seems to cease; it only slows in the middle of the day from the heat.

The woman from Florida and her niece offered to show me the bus terminal and I accepted. It was a few blocks out of their way; we talked as I pulled my luggage. The woman and her two daughters were returning to the States the following week. I thanked them as we parted. I didn't notice what happened to the young man who was so bad the uncle had to warn me. He vanished into the port and became part of the blur of personalities I encountered. I was very impressed with the friendly, open people of the island. I could see why my students boasted proudly about their life on this island.

I was the first person on the bus. It was dark and cold, so I slipped into the long pants I had tucked away in my bag. The jockey put my main luggage under the bus. I positioned myself above the storage compartment to keep a safe eye on my bag. Soon, a slow trickle of passengers was arriving, the first being an old man with a white cowboy hat. I bought a chicken sandwich and pineapple juice from one of the vendors that boarded the bus. Soon we were off and I was watching the world go by. The parade of people walking and carelessly tossed trash never seems to tire my visual lust.

As the bus pulled out of the station I began to reflect on my visit. Yes it is unusual to visit foreign lands, even more unique to visit people in their homes. I was honored to be a quest in a place that has seen few Gringos. I was flattered to be a fly on the wall and see the real lives that these people live. My thoughts were about little Roberto and his future. Such a sweet young boy deserves a guardian angel, someone to watch over his life. Alfredo and his boat will cast off from that island thousands of times in the future. He will fish and transport people, and the days will pass as he grows older, maybe completely unaware that a boat ride and walk with me will return in my memory as a wonderful timeless event. Blanca will cook, clean, call the little ones to dinner as they grow old. She may not be appreciated for all her hard work. She won't expect appreciation, she won't ask for reward, she does this out of an understanding that life and the family around her are all a gift. When I return home I will think of these people and how the deepest meaning in life is often lost by the material comforts that bury the real spirit of humanity. Maybe we are lucky the entire world is not living like the spoiled Americans I live around in New York. Maybe these people give humanity its soul through struggle and survival.

Mid-way through the journey I asked the jockey for change of a ten-dollar bill. He handed me two fives, I gave one back and asked for singles. He said nothing and walked to the front of the bus. He didn't return for many minutes so I went with my trash, handed to him, asking for my change in the same moment. He took my trash and threw it out the bus window. Little Roberto had done the same thing a few days before when I couldn't find a trash container in the house. This is why trash is on the sides of the road and in the courtyards of the houses in an endless display; no one thinks to use receptacles. It baffles me. It angers me as well. When I saw Roberto spitting on the floor of the house I said nothing, but wondered why. Spitting, by anyone and anywhere, is a common incident. The same goes with trash. The bus jockey told me he would bring me the change; I had to ask a second time after several passengers had paid him and he was passing me by. I don't think he was showing disrespect. He was simply avoiding me in the hope the "rich Gringo" wouldn't mind losing a few extra dollars. I gave him a dollar for helping me find a taxi when we pulled into the bus depot at San Salvador. This is why I wanted the change in the first place.

The ride was somewhat different, the landscape changed with big green cone-shaped volcanoes popping up here and there. These perfectly shaped volcanoes added to an interesting landscape. It wasn't a flat terrain. It was hills and valleys with few empty lots, some farms, but mainly houses and people lining the sides of the road. This is the most densely populated country in Central America. It feels that way, and this is one of the reasons why it feels unsafe. The poverty is rampant. As we passed through small towns an invasion of hockers jumped on the bus. I mean *invasion*! A surge of people selling food would make a line through the bus, calling out in loud voices what they had. It wasn't a pleasant experience because they would get right in my face and yell, or just drops something like a piece of candy in my lap and walk on to return later. As if that weren't enough, they would ask again if I wanted to buy.

One small town had a very strange way of selling things. A woman boarded the bus, and had a singsong way of calling out the items. The end of each word was drawn out and the last note was sustained. This wasn't one person's way for selling; the crews that entered from that place all utilized this unique lyrical delivery. Some people selling entered in one town and didn't leave until the next, maybe ten minutes later. My favorite was when a woman came onboard and had two, foot long skewers of cooked meat. One false move by the driver and someone would have lost an eye, but who knows, maybe eye is a delicacy here.

My jockey helped me find a cab, as he had promised. I asked for the cost of the fare before I got into the cab. It was to be five dollars. I know this was MY price, but I wasn't in a mood to haggle. I was safe inside the cab and we left the terminal area only to enter a thick sea of people and traffic. The tinted windows on the cab added to my security. I made small talk with the driver to feel him out. He was fine, a hardworking man with two children and a wife who cuts hair. It was a fifteen-minute ride, up a steep narrow ramp where security guards checked us in. I paid the driver and entered the terminal. My bus would leave in an hour and a half, and they accepted my Visa credit card which put me in a better mood already.

I assumed I was going to have a three-hour wait. Never believe anything you read or hear about time schedules when traveling. What could be hours, or minutes, is unpredictable. Next to the terminal was a restaurant where I ordered chicken, rice, and pineapple juice. A TV show with Spanish overdubs was playing as the few customers ate and watched. It was a TV show on the Guinness World Book of Records. People do such foolish things and even worse people sit in a mindless stupor in foreign restaurants and watch to kill the time. (Me) I asked the woman operating the restaurant if there was a phone where I could call the United States. She directed me to the hotel downstairs. I made a quick call to Diana. I was safe, she was at her office, and we spoke around two minutes. I will call her later when I get to Guatemala City and settled in my hotel. The bus terminal is safely tucked below the hotel. I sat and talked with a woman and her daughter, and within fifteen minutes the bus pulled up. I didn't want to see any more of El Salvador, the capital, maybe another time.

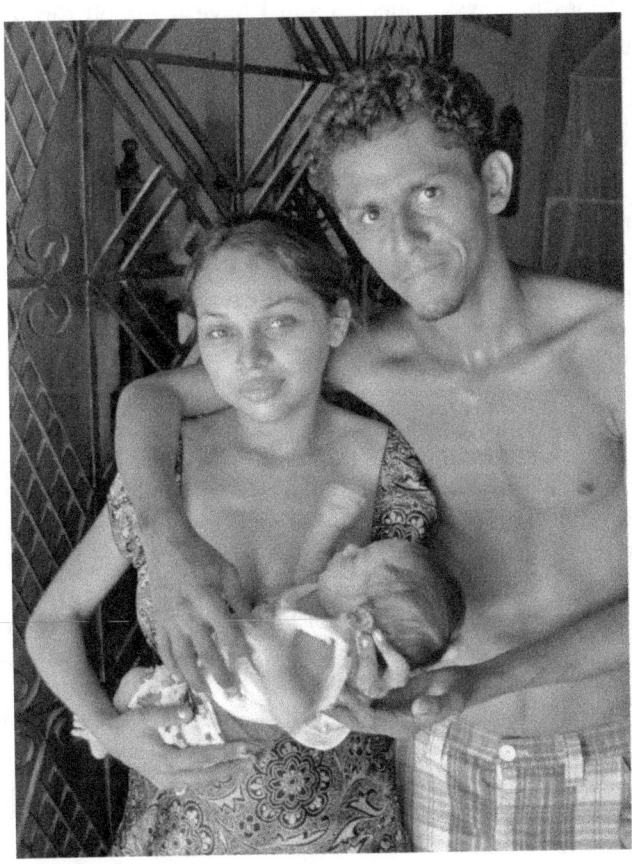

Chapter Twelve
Guatemala

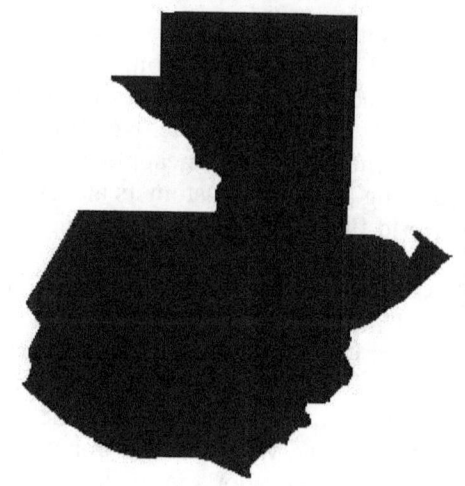

While traveling north-west to Guatemala, I encountered an American family, headed by Robert an insurance salesman from Florida. It is always a pleasant surprise to meet people and exchange stories. Robert went into detail about his involvement in his local Catholic church, how he had raised money for the Knights of Columbus. But what struck me was his open pride in his faith, how happy he was to be a Catholic and stating his devotion to his faith unlike most Catholics' I have met.

Currently we are now parked at the border between El Salvador and Guatemala. My passport was collected and I have the good fortune of sitting in an air-conditioned bus instead of standing in a line. Bus is the best way to get around Central America, this is the same company I came to El Salvador with; 'King Quality'. It is a stark contrast to the way I lived the last few days on the island in El Salvador.

I have to keep myself in check when it comes to judging the way people live, but I have a low tolerance for the way people disrespect mother earth no matter what their economic circumstances. The earth that feeds them needs to be respected; instead I see abuse and neglect. Spitting in a house seems to be a real unhealthy or unsanitary way to live. I temper my judgments with knowledge that education is what has given me a better life, but this has isolated me in a way. I can't help but feel angry at trash being thrown from a moving bus or car. The consequences of any act are very evident to me, or anyone who thinks about thinking. There is something lacking if people stay living in ignorance by default. I don't understand how this hopeless condition is so prevalent. Are all of lives conditions a simple array of choice, as I have been taught to believe, versus a set of inescapable conditions? Is poverty such a trap that is so inescapable that nothing can alter a desire for improvement? I feel emotionally lost for valid reasons, yet I know I am coming from a place of privilege. I didn't go to my student's home island to change anyone. I was a mere observer. But I do hope in some small way I can be of help by them observing me and how I behave.

Little Roberto struck me as a child who had a future because of his strong personality. I asked Herbert where Roberto's father was the second day I was there. I was a bit shocked to hear his father was dead. Blanca was raising the two boys; the mother lived up the hill. Herbert didn't know how his uncle died. This also baffled me, but I didn't push the subject. The blind grandfather was alone the day everyone went to Nicaragua for the soccer match. By the end of the day he was slurring his words from alcohol, talking to himself on and off, and sometimes speaking to others, mostly the children. The children seemed amused and knew he was babbling. His blindness was caused by being struck in the forehead by a rock while drunk. His eye was gone on his right side, and his other eye did not function. The day he was around his wife, Blanca, he didn't drink, or seem drunk, most of the time he sat in the hammock or in a chair and said nothing. I wondered if he had lived with anger because of his accident; yet he didn't seem to be angry, or have a mean bone in his body.

Herbert told me he was deported from the United States after being arrested. He "lost his papers", as he put it. I didn't feel it was right to question him on his arrest, so I just listened. A peculiar thing has happened to me as I have aged. My sense of judgment into black and white answers is not as acute. I am not as opinionated about "oppression due to imperialistic authority" as the cause, or source, of the worlds' injustices. To think the rich and powerful are the cause of poverty was my mantra when I was young. With the Age of Imperialism behind us "blame" is not as clear. A better description would be that we currently live in an age of corporate imperialism. Does generating wealth for a few create the conditions for poverty? Does taking people's natural resource leave them in poverty? On a simplistic level I would say yes, but poverty is more complicated than blaming a Capitalistic rapist. I think a responsible capitalistic system should share the wealth. This is not what happens and that is a clear blame and shame.

Oppressed people are a product of not being well educated, or at least this is my current mantra. But I often think it is a matter of wanting, or desiring, to be educated that brings about the real change. Motivation is the key component.

I also wonder why religion doesn't spark a sense of desire for improvement. Certainly a practice of loving others (and hope for this) should inspire people to change. Is it all as simple as where we are born, who gives us birth that gives us destiny? Is it as simple as praying for those less fortunate? I think not, praying can be a very passive answer. Sometimes when I am teaching in my classroom I wonder if some of my students will crack their sociological shell and get to a better place, a better life. Not just a physical place, but also a spiritual place where they realize their potential and purpose. I find myself being smug at times because of their rejection of my values. Can I proselytize and speak down to my students, or I can open myself to them and show them my heart. I think this is more effective to show my personal compassion. I hope my visit accomplished something in this village. I hope I have broken down some stereotypes and built a new view of my country and my profession. I have no way of really knowing. There is no payout, or no feedback.

Inside the border of Guatemala the road has become so rough that I can't write on the keyboard. The bus driver is on a timetable he has to meet. I find it strange that borders separate these people. As a tourist I will never know the distinct qualities that created these borders because I am on the outside looking in. The people look the same. I hope to see indigenous peoples here. The diver is a maniac! I have to stop for now.

Friday, August 7: As the bus arrived in Guatemala City I began to ask the American, Robert, questions about the money and if there was a metro system. The couple with a small baby next to me overheard me and helped with information. The dollar, contrary to me understanding, is not accepted here. So the first thing I had to do was find an ATM. The bus stopped at the hotel, luckily, Robert encouraged me to get out there, and handed me a sandwich. I said my good-byes the Robert and his family and the other couple. Inside the hotel a porter offered to help me go to another connected hotel and find a cash machine. The porter explained that the King of Spain had stayed in the hotel. A series of locked doors (he had a pass-card) and we walked into another world of gold and gilded furniture, soon to return to the other side where my bags were. The porter stored my bag, returned it, and introducing me to one of the taxi drivers waiting outside; I was all set, looking for cheap accommodations.

I was soon conversing in Spanish about my travels and my life back home. The first hotel, which was in Zone 1 on the opposite side of the city, was booked full. The man behind the desk told me to try the Hotel Seville on the next block. I paid the desk clerk two dollars to call Diana and tell her I was safe. I would make a longer call in the morning.

I awoke freezing cold in the night. The temperature was around sixty and quite the contrast from the night before on the island. I had traveled by boat, by local bus, and by International Bus the length of El Salvador into the heart of Guatemala for fifteen hours. I was soon asleep, waking with shivers, and putting on long pants and a sweatshirt in order to sleep and to raise my body temperature.

In the morning I went to the lobby and the new receptionist, Albert, offered me the computer line behind the counter, which was connected to a lifeless computer. I called Diana. This was a brief call because she was about to begin with one client. She decided to decline the company's offer of a "leave of absence", which made me very happy. I was preparing myself to be calm after she had mentioned it the day before and was considering their offer. I have to put myself in check often because I know I get nowhere when I am pushy and angry, but I was privately wondering why after so much trouble she would even take one second to think this over. A big part of me coping in the relationship to knowing when to bite my tongue and shut up, this is not as easy as it may seem. My mind works in a much different manner than Diana's. What I may assume is my own self-assuredness when it comes to decision-making is nothing akin to Diana's style. I make decisions and spend little time rethinking myself. This is problematic when I have rushed only to regret myself later, but for the most part I live with my chosen path. The challenge comes when I need to let love and kindness guide me through, and be kind, when I am vehemently opposed to what she was proposing as a possible alternative. This could be a culture, gender, or age difference. I don't which, I just know I better be good and patient with her.

When we spoke tonight on the phone I could instantly feel my blood pressure going up and my tone of voice getting an edge when Diana listed all the things she has done and given up to come to the United States. "So what's your point", I asked. "Well I ask that you not have any fights with the man upstairs."

Once again, I was angry that this history was a topic, the history of her sacrifices and the man upstairs. I said something about the distant miles, the vacation being in progress and I was far removed from spending less than one millisecond all day thinking about the man upstairs, closing with the angry phrase, "This is bull...." And it is, but we changed gears and moved on to better and more realistic subjects like what I did all day. What I love about Diana is that she can be overly obsessive and in a heartbeat be able to let it go and move on. I think she is better than me in many ways. This is what keeps the attraction in balance.

I must say I woke up in a good mood because I slept something like ten hours. Within an hour I was in the lobby calling Diana and speaking with Albert whom I had just met. I called him Alfredo by mistake, and he said no, Albert, like Einstein. The one real book I am currently reading became our new topic of discussion. I showed him the book.

I had my day pack ready in the room and walked down to the street, past the armed security guard into a day I knew was going to be all mine. And that it was! Alfredo's strong warnings, the bus jockey's money game, and people repeatedly warning me to be safe in El Salvador, may have put an unwanted edge on my visit, but this day went completely right in Guatemala.

The street was dirty, full of people, cars zooming by, everything is covered in soot, and the sky was overcast, but within minutes I had a wonderful exchange with an Indian couple selling fried plantain on a street corner. I don't have a clue what the money here really is. I held out a fist full of change and asked the man to take what I owed him. He gave me a mini-lesson on the coins and took five what-cha-ma-call-its. We all had a good laugh because I explained it was my first day there, and they understood I was clueless and trusting. I couldn't find a place to sit and eat, hoping to find a small plot of curb, so I stood at the back street of the market watching a tiny girl rolling clay on a low wooden table. Her mother passed in and out of the door carrying ceramic pots. I was thinking how the children follow by example and inherit a wonderful work ethic regardless of the overt hardships. A child in my country would be demanding attention; this child was in a healthy environment because she wasn't the center of attention.

The stairs leading to the back of the market is where I entered. There were beautiful ceramics and crafts that dazzled my eyes. After the disappointment of Masaya's crafts I could instantly see this country has a cultural depth that is nowhere near what I had experienced thus far in all of Central America; forms are realistic, not crude, fabrics are intricate and colorful, detail is carefully followed, and artistic expression is well cultivated. I was in a better mood than ever. I began to freely spend money for the first time on this entire trip, which I must admit I am the product of a consumer-based culture. I bought an electric adapter for my three-prong computer plug first, and then I gave in to my real shopping gene and bought a beautiful black embroidered vest with floral patterns for around twelve dollars. I still don't know what the money here is worth in dollars exactly. I got a feel for the bargaining style by first entering a shop and a woman cutting her original price in half by the time I left. This wasn't a devious plot on my part, by the time I saw something that I knew I had to have, I knew

197

how to lower the price and feel out what was no longer a negotiable bottom price. In 1965 I learned from an Armenian man named George in Teheran, Iran. I was fourteen. He said if they tell a price, cut it in half and begin going up from there. George worked for the same company as my father. He taught me a valuable life lesson. The sellers don't respect anyone who does not negotiate.

I was at a shop that sold herbs and potions asking for the rinse that Diana requested me to buy for her hair. A young woman and her mother came up and asked to help, speaking in English. The woman had just returned from working at Disney World in Orlando, Florida. She had a face that was shinny from make-up and a smile from cheek to cheek. They helped me buy the potion made of a plant. Back home our neighbor from El Salvador gave me the Spanish name of this liquid that helps with hair loss. Diana made a special effort to get the name right, so I needed to find what she requested. I was unable to have time to look for while traveling the day before in El Salvador. I thanked the two women and bought two small baby food jars of the thick dark blue potion.

I hadn't eaten breakfast so I went into a section of the market that had restaurants in portioned-off sectors. I sat at a long table with an elderly, stoned-faced woman and ordered rice, chicken, and salad. I made small talk; the woman was unmoved. I was eating, she was eating, and the ice finally broke when another woman from a distant stall sat next to me and started to ask me the usual, where are you from, where are you going, how long have you been here. Our energy slipped into the elderly woman who suddenly came alive and began to play with us. I asked permission to photograph her, knowing a few minutes earlier that she considered me off limits, now we were friendly. She gave a beaming smile, delivered a row of teeth, and even returned some of the happy energy. After the second woman left, I began to ask what countries this woman had visited and how long she had worked in this place. For thirty-seven years she had returned to work in this restaurant where she rented the space by the month. Her daughter and grandchildren worked there as well. The only country she had ever visited was Mexico. What started out as a silent meal turned into an enjoyable encounter and certainly not my last that day.

Across the street and on a side street I found a plastics shop; every imaginable thing made of plastic was there. I bought a plastic pump-bottle for Diana's hair tonic. An elderly man helped me and the familiar parade of questions began, "where are you from, etc." He told me he was pure Italian after I asked him if he was a Gringo. I explained I was also part Italian, part German, and part Irish. This prompted a joking rebuttal that I was some kind of a mix, a complicated breed. A woman and her husband began to boom with laughter, the likes that made me note to myself that these are happy people in this country; they know how to laugh and joke around. The man's daughter smiled and packaged up my purchase, and I continued the small talk for a minute or more, then I was out the door to further adventure.

I decided in the morning if I did one or two things that day it would be enough. I didn't want to care about making a list of sights to see. I had asked where the grand park was located. I had seen it on the map, so I found my way to the cathedral across from the park and went inside. This was a beautiful white interior church with a slight flavor for the Rococo style. Glass displays of various saints lined both sides of the church. The central alter was spacious with four marble columns that supported a false, roofless structure leading my eye up into a white apse. People knelt and prayed. On the right side was a chapel; a priest was giving his gospel in a dramatic booming voice that erupted in a crescendo that began in a near whisper. Before his sermon, while the readings were being spoken he had been sitting in his chair, his head halfcocked, in a pained expression that caused me to wonder if this man was obsessed with the suffering of Christ. I was feeling cynical so I left. Savonarola and his fiery, 1400 sermons came to my mind. Lucky for me, I live in this century. The dramatics put me off.

Across the plaza was an impressive green building. I was told I could enter for tour in fifteen minutes, so I found an ATM, which didn't work at first, but with persistence I managed to get two withdrawals, enough cash to get me though Guatemala. I returned and was politely told I had to wait another fifteen minutes; I had just missed the tour again. The building was the National Palace of Culture. This fine grand building could have been anywhere in the world. It is a jewel of architecture and yes, spacious as well as clean. The guide told me I could have an English explanation of the tour, but I wanted to listen in Spanish so I would learn. The green color of the building was the process of two chemicals mixed, one causing oxidation with the other. (I can't remember the compounds names in Spanish).

A massive mural depicting the history of Guatemala, the Mayan religion, and the Spaniards arrival was painted on the wall behind the stairwell. Another similar mural was painted on the descending stairs we exited after the tour. In the center of the building an impressive reception room was adorned with the flags of each of the Guatemalan territories. This is where the Guatemalan ruling class welcomes many Kings and Presidents. In an open door I could see an Indian woman (Mayan) in traditional dress sitting at her computer. I can't explain why, but I get deep joy from seeing these people. I had the same feelings in Ecuador. The woman wore a long black skirt with thin colorful accent lines. Her blouse was pure white in contrast to the skirt, with puffy shoulders, long sleeves, and colorfully embroidered flowers around the neck and chest.

The tour proceeded on to concert halls and wide-open patios that were covered by modern stretched white canvases. The building was four stories high with repeating columns that ran in symmetrically arched patterns with long halls where closed doors lead to offices. On the ground floor plants surrounded short elaborate fountains as light from the white canvases ceiling filtered into the open plaza. The scale of the wide impressive halls and stairwells built of dark crafted wood was a visual delight. People in suits, women in traditional dress, some carrying brief cases, and one politician with a driver who wore an earpiece passed through the main entrance. It was indeed a wonderful place to visit.

I sat in the Central Park. It was more like a grand plaza with no trees. As I sat and drank some cold water, I asked some people sitting next to me about the "Transmetro". The taxi driver had pointed it out to me the night before. I could take this double-length bus to the far side of the city and return for one coin. I got my bearings on my map and headed in the direction of the bus system. There is a similar mass transit system in Bogotá, Columbia. This is an elongated bus that bends like an accordion in the middle as it turns. The magic is that the bus has its own streets or exclusive lanes, thus not being affected by the cities massive traffic jams, a few which I witnessed while on the Transmetro. At the southern end of the Transmetro a large station built on high concrete stilts has a capacity to move thousands of passengers at rush hour. A distribution market for vegetables was visible from the high platform.

I sat speaking to an old woman who was seventy-seven. She was going home to feed her mother, who was ninety-two. She asked me where I was going. I said nowhere, just riding the Transmetro to know the city. A mother and her daughter overheard us speaking and the little girls began to speak with me as I said good-bye to the elder. They wanted to speak some English. This lead to a short conversation and them subsequently leading me up to a policeman, asking him to allow me to return to the other side of the departing platform without going through the line down the stairs. This friendly young man in a green uniform escorted me and we had a short pleasant conversation. "What are you up to", he asked in an approach that I could tell he had been taught to ask. But it was way too casual to be real.

The Transmetro is a very modern episode in this city. Just inches away from what could be considered life that has been the same for a hundred years, is a bus system from the future. At each stop policeman or porters wearing fluorescent yellow vests open each door and escort the passengers onto the bus. Order and politeness are the standards being set. The Transmetro stops at designated raised platforms, just like a subway car. A turn style where a coin is dropped into a slot is carefully guarded and each person entering the glass station is observed by at least five attendees. The bus has three doors that open like a subway car, no one crowds the doors, everyone is expected to go in single file and follow the helpful lead of the attendees.

An observation I noted while on the Transmetro, and walking later, is how the streets are lined with chain-linked fences so no one can jaywalk. The sidewalks are very wide. Built onto the chain-linked fence are shops, or stalls full of goods. As one walks down the side walk both sides are for shopping; on one side is the building with stores, on the other side are these small shops, most of which are constructed of a plastic roof and partitioned by makeshift walls or the actual good themselves. I saw very inventive ways of displaying good. For instance rows of hanging DVD's dangling in a single strand, but side by side, creating a wall of sorts. Clothes, shoes, you name it; this is the common peoples shopping district. It is no shopping mall. The DVD stalls had a certain flare because most of the men working in them had body spikes and pointy-gelled hair like in a Japanese cartoon book. They seemed more interested in watching the loud movies being played than trying to sell anything. The sheer number of these stalls was overwhelming. Not one of them had legal product. In some places the booths were two or three rows deep with these tiny shops. How all the people survive is a miracle to me. Is it humanly possible for all these people to sell enough to survive? There were more DVDs than people living in this city.

I stepped into a church that had long green shinny sashes hanging from each repeating columns. The fabrics arched down the center of the church. The afternoon light was perfect for photography. Outside the church more shops, but no DVDs, religious items. I found a hardware store and bought a wire brush for my house in Costa Rica (always plan ahead) and made my way back to the market to buy more lotion for Diana. My plastic receptacle had enough room for one more baby jar of dark-blue potion. I bought a sandwich and headed back to the hotel to eat, shower, and call Diana. It was five o'clock, stores were closing, and long traffic jams were forming along Ninth Avenue, where my hotel is. I took a walk to the top of the hotel stairs and spent half an hour photographing the volcano off to the west. It was indeed a great day with so many nice people to encounter. Tomorrow a four-hour bus ride and a new city, but I will be passing through here again in my way back to Costa Rica.

Saturday, August 8: I am in Chichicasanando, I came home from the Internet place just in time to avoid a good drenching shower. Most of the day was spent traveling. As I rode the bus I read that I can catch a shuttle directly to Antigua, my next destination. So I will cut my plans by a day and do as much shopping as I can in the morning, before I leave at 2 o'clock.

My main reason for wanting to travel by shuttle bus is fear of another bus driver like the one I had today. One can imagine the excitement of a Disney ride, roller coaster, and spaceship all bundled into an unfortunate nerve racking joyless ride. Being thrown from side to side on curves at the speed of light is best left to a fearless guy, which I sometimes see myself as, but not in this instance. This bus ride was unreal and dangerous, although the local people all took it as an everyday occurrence. It probably was. Whenever there was a car, truck, or bus in front of us the driver had to be pass, and where he passed did not matter; a blind curve, a steep incline, or flat land in the middle of a busy town. Maybe the driver was trying to break a record. One time I remember seeing a long, straight stretch of highway that curled up a hill, the view was at least a mile long. This was the drivers chance to press the accelerator to the floor, lean on the horn to get pedestrians off the road, and not slow down for a truck that entered the highway, but yes, pass with the gusto of a heard of screaming elephants.

The views were wonderful as we left Guatemala City and gradually made our way to the country where farms on small, well-kept patches of land were tucked into every inch of land. The towns were very dusty and a thin layer of silt was on everything. One of the towns we passed though was supposed to be where I changed to another bus. I was told to stay put; I didn't need to change buses. The prospect of changing buses was a bit scary and didn't appeal to me in the least. I was confused by the new instructions but went along with things. A kidnapping was out of the question in such a crowded bus!

At one stop the back door flung open and a man climbed into the bus asking me if I was going to a town they kept repeating and yelling. I was in the second to last seat and was poked several times until I finally got the point across

I was going to "Chichi", as it is called for short. While the bus was pulling into one small town the jockey opened the back door of the speeding bus and disappeared. I couldn't figure out if he jumped off or what happened. I assumed he was gone, but a few minutes later the door opened and he reappeared. I put one and one together and figured out that he had climbed the ladder attached to the back of the bus. He climbed up on the roof. I had seen him before, and in fact handed him my luggage, when I first arrived at the designated bus for Chichicasanando. Most of the trip he disappeared.

This was the town that two days earlier Robert had told me was a must, as far as markets to see. In the morning Albert, the receptionist, had helped call the bus company. After checking out, he went down to the street with me and hailed a cab. I thanked Albert and said I would return in a few days. The cab driver was a young man named Byron. He is twenty-six and has a wife and baby boy, just over a year old. Somehow the topic of marriage and divorce came up so we both found we had been divorced and remarried. He asked me if I liked to go watch nude woman dancers. I taught him the meaning of the word karma by explaining whatever good I did in life came back to me, just as is true of the negative. He got my point. We had such a good time talking that he over shot the turn, and in fact got completely lost. He stopped and asked another taxi driver where to go. This took five minutes.

We returned to the correct area and fond the bus stop. At first the jockey grabbed my bag, and before I knew it, the bag was on top of this brightly colored school bus. Byron protested and told the jockey to bring the bag back down. Half puzzled the jockey complained and Byron negotiated a special price for me to have the bag on the seat next to me. He then told me not to give the man any more money under any circumstances and to watch for robbers. I was the first on the bus but within minutes others were loading up and venders were passing through hocking food. I bought a piece of fried chicken and tried to pay less than the offered price. Instinctively I knew I was given a higher price from this man. The next woman that came along selling the exact same thing was selling it for five quetzals less to the other passengers. This is something I didn't encounter (knowingly) in El Salvador or Nicaragua. I was on my own now and soon about to get a good fright. The first time the diver slammed on the breaks, because of a near accident, I knew it was going to be a rough ride. I'll give him credit for not killing anyone, or me, along the way.

I can see from the lay of the farmland that the people have a feel for natural design. The houses were similar to modern dwellings in Costa Rica, or the opposite extreme, shacks with barefoot children playing in the dirt. Woman walked along the side of the highway balancing any, or everything, on their heads, just as they did in the city. I started to see this in El Salvador, not in Costa Rica or Nicaragua.

With only a few exceptions the highway was new and very well built. In places where construction was still in progress the bus would switch over to an opposite lane on the other side of the highway, never slowing. He never did any moves with caution or grace, only a quick jerk of the wheel and we bounced over a dirt divide onto newly paved concrete. This switching back and forth was a prevalent factor in the zigzag route this maniac took. Oh, I'm back to that driver again!

The native women here dress in the most beautiful, dignified manner. The blouses are full of embroidered flowers in large colorful patterns. Or the blouse can be a multicolored weave with rows of brilliant analogous colors. A wool shirt made of solid colors is joined together in sections, in other words the fabric is not one large piece of cloth but a collection of pieces held together by thin multi-colored strips of cloth. The ankle long shirt is wrapped around their waist and overlaps so no flesh could ever possibly be exposed. At the waist the fabric bunches up, but a wide belt that usually is as colorful as the blouse, with wild patterns and nearly blinding colors, holds all this together. The skirt, belt, and blouse are very, what we would call, "color coordinated". I guess the objective is to put odd colors and patterns together, or maybe it has only to do with what they own and wear. The shoes are black pumps with slight wide heals. The young girls and mother dress alike, but the men wear western cloths: how boring compared to the woman!

When I got into Chichi the jockey motioned me off the bus while the majority of the people sat motionless. I climbed out the back handing the backpacks to him on the ground below. Two young men in matching vests, wearing official tour guide vests with red hats and badges instantly greeted me. Oscar introduced himself. I told him the name of the hotel I wanted, he said it was full and he knew of a closer place. Their dress promoted trust so I allowed Oscar to carry my bag on his shoulder to the hotel he recommended. He in all probability was lying to me, but sure any adventure after that bus ride would be safe. Did I have to mention the bus driver again? I never actually saw what he, the bus driver, looked like. I could only see the back of his head and a sliver of eyes in the mirror. I didn't want him to be looking at anything but the road, certainly not me in the rear of the bus and my whiteness whiter than usual.

The hotel is a dump. I pay something like twelve dollars a night. Before I even saw the office Oscar brought me straight to the third floor and showed me a room with a private shower and toilet. It was fine for one night. I wouldn't bring Diana here, but for me it's fine. "Where's the TV?" "Oh, the boy will bring it. Do you want this room with the balcony or the room in back with a view of the mountains?" I chose the balcony overlooking the town.

Back in the office, I was introduced to Sebastian who lived in New York for twenty-six years. He and Oscar both spoke good English. The office looked unsecured with keys hanging on nails. It was really very secure because Sebastian sits on the balcony of the second floor and sees whoever comes down the street. A bell hooked up to a motion detector sounds every time anyone enters the building. I began to fumble in Spanish and Sebastian blurted out, "Speak English". I could tell he had that New Yorkers bluntness that he brought back with him.

My room has two beds, a shower with an electric fitting on the shower-head, and water that drips when fully turned on. There is no water pressure. The same goes for the faucet on the sink, which wiggles because it isn't bolted down. The room has a wooden door with a cheap lock. The outer door to the balcony is solid metal. The balcony is wide enough to fit a single chair.

I showered and was out the door in minutes to see the market. As I walked on the main street a wedding procession was in front of me. A woman wearing a white veil, and her soon to be husband, were followed by maybe twenty people all dressed in their fine Indian garments. I could see the white tower of the church and the steep, jagged steps where people were entering the church. The view was of a long narrow street that dipped into a shallow valley and back up to another hill. Stalls were already set up and vendors were calling to me. I asked the price of one large bed cover, one hundred dollars. I was a bit shocked, but knew I could put that figure in half. I followed the wedding party into the church.

The church's floor had long pine needles strewn up the center isle with white rose petals occasionally sprinkled on top. The pews were ancient, the wooden cabinets that held the statues of the saints, and Christ, we over a hundred years old. Any paintings had long since faded and been worn away where people had reached up and touched them. Everything had a dark layer of soot from the years of candles being burned. In the middle isle were slightly raised platforms made of slate, these were about two feet square. I tripped over one while enter the pew. These platforms on the floor were for candles, which some had groups burning, while others were empty.

The Catholic Church has embraced some of the ancient Mayan rituals, including placing candles and pine needles on the floors or perhaps the Mayan faith have embraced Christianity, because the feel of the church was one of something ancient. Outside a pile of smoldering incense burned at the bottom step of the church, and this kind of offering was at various locations inside the church. There were candles all along the sides and center. Fine white embroidered, lace curtains hung in an upside-down V-shape from the middle ceiling of the center aisle. This design touch I liked a lot. It gave a feeling of aesthetics that was nowhere else because of the age and dinginess of the church. The main alter had a grand monstrance where a row of five candles progressed up, stair-stepping a series of elevations that were also adorned with white flowers. It was beautiful and a grace filled place. I stayed for the service. There are many times I feel more attracted to the Catholic Church while traveling than I do in my country. The spirituality seems more genuine in these remote places, or I am too jaded with cynicism in my own country.

At the end of mass people filed out as the bride and groom gathered with their families near the front alter. I went out hoping to get some pictures of the new couple. The wait was long so I ordered a papusa and paid. I had noticed a strand of fireworks laying on the third step. This was going to be loud. My food was still being cooked when the fireworks rattled all those within a mile of earshot. I took pictures as the couple passed down the steps, all the while my ears still ringing. Many people were served before me as I waited for my food. I chatted with one family who came and went before I received my plate. I just let things happen the way they are supposed to be without making any fuss. It looked like the dozen, or so, cooked papusa were good enough, but I waited until I was handed my plate as the husband-cook instructed his wife to give me a plate. My interpretation of this long wait was that these people take care of their own first, I was the alien traveler, and these would be repeat customers. I have no idea really why I wasn't served in order.

I was still hungry so I bought some fresh corn on the cob. The corn was white with charcoaled burns from the fire. There was nowhere to sit so I wandered around the increasingly emptying market to where the last food vendors were closing shop for the night. On a far street I looked at some bed covers. The beginning price was 800, just like the woman's price I spoke to before the wedding. I walked away several times, was called back with multiple offers until we settled on 350. I was doing better than expected. When I first approached the booth, the man frantically pulled down the bed cover, knocking his small boy on the head. The child began to cry, the sale was more important. I was more concerned about the child at that point, but the mother interrupted with a series of quotes as the husband also rang out prices. I wasn't sure which cover I wanted at first, so I changed to another item, leaving the first interest and ended on a second choice. This is a tactic George the Armenian taught me. Start looking, show some interest, change your interest, and buy after acting disinterested. I can't say that was my exact intentional plan, it did work though. I bought a brown quilted bed cover for Diana. It is a colorful treasure.

I was hounded down the street until I entered the Internet shop at the far end. Woman trying to make a last sale followed me. I kept holding my price at 100. The woman tried to trick me by switching the large red weaving with a smaller version, but I saw this and didn't hand her the money. Instead pointed to the fabric I wanted. I felt battered by this entire attempted switch. It's impossible to just look without being badgered and verbally harassed by the hockers.

What I have in mind I will buy tomorrow, but I be darned if I feel like it's something I don't really want. I have a space in my house in Costa Rica where I want to hang a tapestry. It's got to be the right size and shape, but by even looking I can't find what I have in mind because the sellers are at me like mad dogs. After that and talking to Diana on a bad line I was pretty spent. The connection is broken up so much at times I have to ask Diana to repeat herself. I did solve one problem; the volume is no working because I replaced the batteries on the phone. I didn't see that it took batteries until yesterday. This has been my main complaint about the phone jack I bought. The sound stutters and breaks up depending on where I am using it and the time of day, the busy times of day cause a static that is terrible, mostly at night. Sebastian gave me my key and I was soon eating cashews and typing as the rain began to fall. Tomorrow I prepare for the shopping battle and plan on looking at many choices before I arrive at my decision. I will defend the capitalists' mentality and be self-serving! I shall defeat the hockers on their own ground.

Monday, August 10, 2009: I have arrived in Antigua, Guatemala. The grass is always greener on the other side of the street. My hotel here in Antique was a little loud last night and the room is small, so I went to look at a more expensive hotel across the street thinking there would be some improvement. Not so. The other hotel has no TV in the room and the Internet is not wireless. Here in my current hotel I have managed to get the wireless Internet and can even be in my room to privately talk to Diana. So I'll stay put but asked them for another room where there is less noise. None of the rooms have windows that open to real air, only an inner courtyard. The air in my room gets stuffy because there is poor ventilation. At one point last night I opened my door a crack to get some air moving with a from a small fan screwed into the wall. For the most part it is a good second-rate hotel, a step above my hotel in Chichicasanando.

Yesterday was the second day on the entire journey I went without writing down my experiences. This can only mean one thing; my day was full, full, full. I was out the door at 6 A.M. in Chichicasanando. I ate a fist full of cashews for breakfast, and a swig of remaining orange juice. I wanted to catch the morning light for good pictures. It was a day to remember. I spent around two hundred dollars, the total of which my travels may have cost me thus far. I stated right away with buying exotic belts for gifts. The market wasn't even in full swing yet, but I was. I wandered to the edge of the town where a large arch stood; looking like it was the main gate in years past.

The vista of a long sweeping valley filled with the smoke of kitchens stretches out from the hill on the opposite side of town. This gave the scene a dark, unfriendly overcast look. Where the hotel was, the mountains impeded any additional growth of the city. I was photographing the valley when an entire family of native Indians in traditional dress came closer to me. I continued photographing; the people were too far away to be of consequence in the picture. As they neared me, one man said, "What's the matter?" He motioned his arm in a kind of half protest, half question. "What's the matter?" He repeated a few times. He didn't want their picture taken. I walked over to show them I was not photographing them by displaying the images on the camera, but his negativity continued. He had an attitude. "See you later." He said in an angry macho voice. "No you won't, I replied", in an equally macho voice. That was the only time this trip I have encountered this anti-tourist sentiment. No matter what charm I tried to ease this man's anger, he hated me. Somebody did him wrong and he still wanted revenge. I continued up to the top of the arch on some winding stairs to get a better view of the smoky valley. From that vantage point I could see this town was larger than I thought. Beyond the old walled city was a valley filled with rooftops and smoky chimneys.

I was soon back in the streets were the market was becoming increasingly active. What may be a quiet street in the middle of the week becomes a thick, almost impassable, pedestrian walkway lined with vendors on both sides. There is no real size of the market and no designated selling spot. The first person to arrive and set up is the manner a location is decided. In Ecuador the vendors all had to pay a tax and displayed a receipt, which was checked by the police. Here there was no such system; this gave things an extra layer of competition and disorganization.

At the foot of the church steps the incense was burning in a large fire that gave a nice order to the market, but where I had eating food under a plastic tent at a table, now was gone and the church steps were filled from top to bottom with flower vendors wearing the beautiful traditional Indian cloths. The Indians and light filtering through the smoke of the incense was a good subject to photograph. Now and then I take out the video camera; if I'm not in any ones face they don't seem to mind being filmed.

I continued to shop and went inside the only store I was in all day. It was a shop for woman's cloths. I found the exact flower design Diana wanted; small embroidered flowers along the neck. I bargained the price in half, as was the mode of all my negotiations, sometimes even going far below the half way mark of the first price quote. It was nine o'clock and I had told Oscar I would consider an 8:30 tour. I returned to the hotel with a big bundle of shirts, blankets, weavings, and was very happy with myself. I asked Sebastian to call Oscar, he handed me the phone. Oscar was still home and he could meet me in fifteen minutes on the steps of the church. I asked the price again, we negotiated the tour for twenty dollars for two hours. I took a shower and was there in twenty minutes. He was waiting with a big smile.

Spending time with Oscar made being Chichicasanando more enjoyable. The second I got off the bus he showed he was a good companion. At the church steps I told him I still wanted some more fabrics. He led me to his family's business. I bought five large fabrics; blankets and wall hangings. We arrived at what was about $125US dollars for four tapestries. The negotiations went on for several minutes. I didn't have that much cash, so we left and found a cash machine. I gave him the money. He didn't return to pay the woman, we continued back to the hotel in a three wheel "Tuk Tuk". This is a motorcycle with an enclosed passenger compartment on the back; we called them rickshaws in Pakistan when I was a teenager. I ran in the room and left the package, coming right back to the Tuk Tuk. We rode through tiny side street toward the base of the mountains that were visible from behind my hotel. We paid the driver about a dollar and disembarked to enter a mask museum and shrine. The shrine was to Mayan and Christian deities. It had that old smoky look where soot and years of candle burning leaves nothing looking shinny or new.

We walked past an inner courtyard where a group of Italian tourist was getting a lecture on the museums contents, continuing further up the hill where a small, sheet metal shack housed a Mayan shrine. This was a series of dark charcoaled rocks (deities I assume) with one small stone cross on one side. It was a spiritual place, but not what I expected. The black burned rocks were ancient but typical rock shapes. This is a Hindu practice as well, to have stone deities.

At the top of the mountain a larger more elaborate shrine stood on a flat platform. An old Mayan god made of stone stood surrounded by several rock formations, all black from years of ceremonies. The Mayan deity stood about one meter tall. Smoke pits with smoldering coals burned in front of the main alter. A shaman stood with two woman, reciting prayers from a small handful of folded papers barely forming a book. He was praying over the fire pit and making offerings, dropping various items into the fire, first handing them to the woman, then passing them into the fire.

Behind the shaman was another smaller alter/shrine with a charcoal-black stone cross. (I read the Mayans easily adopted the Christian cross because it was already a symbol in their religion. This symbolized the four directions; north, south, east, and west) Liquids, fruit, and sundries were thrown in the flames, some causing the fire to blaze higher. At one point, a firecracker went off. The woman stood with their hands folded repeating the words spoken by the shaman. To the right, an elderly shaman swung a makeshift incense burner back and forth. The incense burner was a medium size coffee can with holes punched by a can opener which made v-shaped punctures. Smoke and fragrance filled the air as the old man chanted incantations. I picked a small group of flowers and made an offering, saying a silent prayer.

Compared to Christian, Hindu, or Buddhist rituals the purpose was the same, Incantations, prayers, offerings, and a designated medium, or priest, to communicate with the God in a service. The "dirty" appearances of the altars were strange to me. In Western and Asian rituals the altars are clean with marble and gold, this was smoke caked on to stone deities never to be touched or cleaned. The spiritual ceremony is more important than the opulent environment. I remember traveling to Bali. I was so excited to see the Hindu temples only to arrive at empty open-air campuses. Where's the temple, where's the deity? I expected a shrine, flowers, and the whole "show". It was a real revelation a few days into the visit that I was "inside" the temple all along. The food and flower offerings at every doorstep, the reverence to all peoples, the well-dressed traditional peoples WERE the temple I sought. I felt a little shallow, or too Western, when this dawned on me. So I try to look beyond my expectations and am always pleasantly surprised when I can withhold judgment long enough.

We returned to the mask museum at the base of the footpath, reentered for a brief look. Oscar asked me if I didn't mind walking back to the town. It was very close to the village. Oscar asked me a favor, to write a letter of recommendation so he could come to the USA for a year, work, and bring enough money back to build a home for he, his wife, and year old child. I said I would consider this but also discussed the importance of him remaining legal and out of trouble. I don't know if this will come to pass, but the enthusiasm and strong desire to make a better life for his family was apparent.

We were soon inside another mask shop where a show of traditional dance was taking place in a special courtyard. The costumes and music were authentic. The costumes were embroidered with gold and shiny sequences that sparkled. Long feathered hats and wooden, painted masks hid the faces of the three dancers. The dance was a celebration of the defeat of the Spaniards. I did some filming and gave a small donation at the conclusion of the dance as they passed the mask. We were back on the main street (Fifth Avenue) and I went to a small street restaurant as Oscar said good-bye. I had already paid him when we started. We had one more appointment. This was when I left at 2 o'clock. I would pay him the balance of my shuttle ride to Antique when he helped me board the correct van. I sat at a street stall and ate a bowl of rice with red beans, and tortillas. I returned to the hotel to shower, pack, and gather together my newly acquired goods. I had a cheap plastic zipper bag already to load; I brought this from the States knowing I'd need another lightweight bag for the bus. Sebastian called me a Tuk Tuk from his seat on the balcony and I was heading for the Hotel Saint Thomas to rendezvous with Oscar.

I exited the Tuk Tuk in a street filled with tourists and Indian woman trying to make a last minute sale to the departing tourists. A man came up from behind me, and said in a low threatening voice, "Give me your bag!" It was Oscar pretending to be a robber. We laughed and he helped me load my bags into a waiting van. As I sat in the van a woman stood below lifting up garments to sell, beggars stuffed their open palm into the window, and young children selling stuffed animals dropped the toys through the open window to the waiting tourists-passengers. I gave some loose change and bought one last toy for Eligh back in Costa Rica. I had shopper's fatigue; in a flurry of purchases I exhausted my resources and allocated expendable capitol into the local economy. (The night before I was listening to Allen Greenspan on TV, thinking this guy doesn't know shit, but he can use the English language better than a dictionary.)

I was talking to a man named Armando the entire trip to Antigua. He is from Mexico on vacation, like me traveling alone. We hit it off so well we both decided to find a hotel and dine together last night. It is the first "restaurant" I have eaten in this whole trip. The street and markets have been my major source of food. Its 11:30 in the morning and after a short trip to take some photograph, I have been writing for three hours. I need to stop and go see the world outside waiting for discovery.

Day One: My day has been spent walking through Antigua. I covered a greater distance than my walking in Guatemala City because the city lends itself to foot traffic; it is flat, built on a grid, and everything is close. The city is very nice. There are charming cobblestone streets and long rows of old houses with brightly colored wall-faces. The buildings are all one story high for the most part. There are tourist police everywhere that makes the traveler feel very safe. So many Europeans and North Americans are here that it was not long before I found myself talking to the many tourists. One man was in a group that was missing an eighteen-year-old girl, but he seemed she had simply wandered off and nothing dangerous had happened. I can't recall all of the brief encounters I had today, but all were very pleasant. The contrast between Guatemala City and here is very stark. This is vacationland; time in the city reflected the struggles of ordinary life. There are less people, less traffic, and in general, a quality of life that appears to be very good. I would live here and feel very comfortable.

I began the morning by taking a short walk to the market, returning to eat, and washing almost my entire wardrobe. The young man working here said I could use the hand method because I was not permitted to use the washing machine. I hung my clothes on two lines above in the tiny washroom. It had an exposed sky so my clothes were dry when I got back that night. On my morning walk I saw where the main central market and bus station are located. Around noon I was finally ready and begin a full day of photographing. People seem to be the most important subject matter here. I must have shot seven hundred pictures, putting the camera in my bag for safety, but pulling it out so often that I finally gave up and carried it around my neck.

The market was a maze of tiny walkways that seemed to go on forever. I only passed through one sector; in the center was the "food court" where the smell of delicious spices and cooked food drifted into the massive labyrinth of tiny stalls. Is it humanly possible that every booth that sells products sells something every day? I can't see how. This market was even denser than the one in Guatemala City; it was larger and had more people per square foot. I crossed a dirty street and found another market that was specifically for tourists. It was like something I'd expect to find in Southern California, with a series of courtyards organized around fountains with beautiful flowers. The shops weren't as dense and the aisles were wider, but it was full of tourists' goods. I saw a shirt I liked and started to bargain, but I left when I saw the shirt had a dirt marks. I also got a feel for how much the shirt would sell for. Ten minutes later I had two shirts, one for me, one for Diana. The prices are higher and bargaining is a little more difficult than Chichicasanando. I knew I was wise to go there first and had pretty much satisfied my buying urges.

I walked the long length of the city and found the main square. A young Guatemalan Indian girl came up and tried to sell me something. I wasn't interested but she kept persisting. She was very pushy and even told me I was "ugly" and "rude". I kept thanking her and laughing as she insulted me. I told her she should be happy and not so upset if someone didn't want to buy. This went on for a good twenty minutes as I sat there and rested. Sometimes she would break the beginnings of a smile, catch herself, and return to the scowling face. Another Indian woman selling jewelry came and sat at my other side. She listened to the young girls insults and would look at me and crunch her brow in amazement. The older woman asked me if Jesus lived in my heart, I replied yes. Under the circumstances I was doing well; maybe not sainthood, but a lot of emotional endurance was at play. When the two women began to speak in Spanish I began to speak in Spanish. This astonished the young girl who had been cursing me in her native tongue all this time. I got a little thrill out of her now knowing I was fully aware of what she was up to. The young girl finally left and the older woman said she was a devil. She also tried to sell me something, but I declined. She wasn't pushy and indeed we enjoyed the truce that had been reached. We were just sitting and talking. I often tell people that my wife is from Colombia (something Diana often hates). I do this just to make small talk and explain why I know Spanish. It is an endearment to Spanish speakers.

Visiting the old city palace I found it was closed and under renovation. I entered briefly to take a photograph because a worker invited me in, and said I could shoot some pictures if I wanted to do so. Next I enter the ruins of a grand Cathedral, then visit a cluster of ruins, The Convent of the Pillar of Zaragoza, Santa Clara Church, and The Recollection Church and Convent. Wandering through these adjoining archaeological ruins was a peaceful time. The wind was softly blowing and small groups walked along following a tour guide. Traveling alone is a luxury is some ways because tour guides don't stop me; many guides are here in the city wearing a vest and badge like Oscar's. This city has been hit by so many earthquakes that the Church gave up on rebuilding, thus the skeletal ruins of many old buildings have abandoned domes and only the remains of thick walls.

Three volcanoes surround this city, the most permanent being Volcan Agua. This cone shaped mountain is visible from every street and stands like a green giant looming above the city. The typical cone shaped volcano a child would draw is here in reality. It sweeps up and the end of long narrowing streets and is covered by foliage with the exception of a few miles of rocky earth at the top. Clouds build and then evaporate all day, at the top of the volcano cumulus clouds look like a childlike rendition of cotton candy clouds.

Above the city skyline, I could see in the far south-eastern corner, at the base of a small hill, a dome of a grand cathedral. I made my way towards that corner of the city. The hills stand up and streets lean up to their base where restricted expansion ends the buildings. This was called the Church of San Francisco. Most of the walls were stark white, with the shrines of a bloodied Christ in a variety of displayed places. I asked a custodian for permission to photograph. He didn't answer but asked where I was from, "The United States". "Ok, you can take only two pictures." I wonder if I were from Canada, I would have been allowed more photographs. He disappeared behind a column, leaving only his fingers visible from where I stood; curling around a column. Perhaps he was listening to see if I took more than two photographs, I didn't. He was soon sweeping the floor, as was a woman at the back of the church. I left the building and saw a group of woman crying at the door. Someone had died and they were comforting each other. More tourists passed them and I thought it important to remember day-to-day life is a struggle, not a vacation.

I was beginning to tire and the sun would soon be setting behind the mountain, so I headed in the direction of my hotel. On my way I passed an old Franciscan monk and we struck up a conversation. He was slowing making his way up the street as I passed and said hello. He seemed interested in speaking English, although he would throw in a Spanish word occasionally from lack of vocabulary. He was Italian born and had been sent to the States to learn English. His superiors in Rome told him he was going to be sent to China so English would be necessary. He was also instructed to learn to speak a Chinese dialect. This was in California in 1944. Because Mao Zedong was beginning his revolution, the priest was ordered to remain in California. He became a teacher there. I told him he might have possibly taught my uncle who attended seminary in Santa Barbara. The priest spent eighteen years in Santa Barbara, and then was stationed in Panama in the late 1950's. When I was young we often visited the Mission at Santa Barbara to see my uncle.

I asked how he had come to Guatemala. He had fallen down while waiting in a hospital, sitting on an emergency cot. Both he and the cot plummeting to the floor. He showed me the four holes in his head. He had only been in Guatemala for four months; recuperating and perhaps not returning to Panama. At the corner of the long street we said our good-byes, and I went to find the papusas I had the night before, sold at the side of a big yellow church near my hotel.

I met a one-eyed man named Fernando just as the sun was setting. I was sitting on the step of a church eating an ear of corn I had bought. This well-spoken man (in English) was a world traveler. We met because his dog came up sniffing my ear of corn. "She loves to eat corn", he said. I asked him why the husky had one eye white and one eye dark. "I guess they breed them that way so they can see in the snow". After a few minutes I got up the nerve to ask him how he had lost his eye. He explained that an accident had blinded him many years before. Fernando was a real character. He had traveled by bus to Montreal and flew to India to study under the same guru as Mahatma Gandhi. "I washed dishes with Gandhi's son in the ashram", he told me. We sat and visited for over an hour exchanging stories and laughing at things only people our similar ages would know. The names of songs, the names of movies, musical groups, it all clicked and we had some good chuckles. He said I was only one of the few people he encountered who understood his references to popular culture. He is two years younger than me.

We talked about diet, politics, and religion. He said he was vegetarian until he got the dog. He had to start eating meat again to help the dog survive. He wore sandals and an Australians adventures hat, where one side of the hat is bent up. His clothes were bright blue and yellow shorts with a lightweight green jacket. He shared his favorite mantra with me and I chanted two of mine with him. His mother had passed away and lived to be ninety-two. She was never sick a day in her life and passed away without every taking any medications. He was making an income from a rental property in Guatemala City, and began to grow corn on his farm where he currently lives. Most of his life he worked in his father's hardware store until his father's death. When his younger brother took over the business the money began to disappear. We agreed to meet again tomorrow around the same time, sunset.

Tuesday, August 11: I called Diana tonight when I returned to the hotel. She was unfocused and full of worries. The people selling the apartment we bought in Colombia called her and told her they needed more money for a special floor tile we ordered. Diana started in, "I have no money to pay for this, you know I will not be working after this summer, etc.". I have repeatedly told her I would help her with money. She sounds so desperate over a small problem that it pushes my buttons. When I offered a solution, to deposit the money and have her mother withdraw the funds with a bankcard we sent her. Diana just kept going on about not having any money to pay for this. She loves to make problems bigger than they are, and she doesn't try to think her way into solutions, she loves to worry. It's not like, "Hi, how are you?" It like being punched in the face with a bunch of negativity. Is life that traumatic? The wall Diana puts herself inside is so ridiculous. If she really wants this fancy tile in the new apartment then we will get it, but trying to free Diana from her worries is the real issue. I get angry when I have to deal with such an inexperienced attitude about problem solving. I asked her to not say one more time that she didn't have money. She hasn't even left her job (having an income) and she already is projecting problems on her life. This is screwed up.

I woke at 8:00, had breakfast, and after writing for several hours, I decided to stretch my legs by walking to a nearby market. Much to my chagrin, most of the stalls were unopened. I had read somewhere that Mondays and Thursdays were market days. Now I knew that the information was accurate.

Later I walked to the yellow church two blocks away. I painted while sitting on the edge of the curb. The light was perfect because the noonday sun was strong. I had found a strip of cool shade on the curb. I painted a view of the street with the yellow arched passage and the volcano in the background.

As I sat painting a fellow artist came up and introduced himself. He sells his work on the street and showed me a few pieces. He was with a woman who was his student. She showed me her painting of the same archway. Both of them struck me as very talented. By looking into their paintings I took some ideas on how to handle my own work. It was a brief but constructive encounter. I returned back to the hotel and continue to finish painting, I still need to add some more details, but the majority of the work is completed. It was already three thirty.

Soon, I left with my blank paper in the backpack in search of new subject matter, but ended up walking to the far side of town where I had been the day before. This time, I went closer to where the mountain meets the city. I visited a church, bought a muffin, and sat in a small plaza with a fountain and green grass. Two homeless men slept on the grass. It seems to me that was the first time I saw such people here in this city. As I was walking I noted that this was a better side of town. The hotels looked more expensive and the homes with high walls and green gardens felt like a more affluent environment. As I walked back towards the city center I passed exclusive art galleries and high-end restaurants. I entered a few galleries to take a look and say hello. It was getting a bit late. I stopped to buy a small snack of avocado on a tostada from a woman selling food on a curb. I sat with a family and ate a strange sandwich with spaghetti inside. The choice was noodles with bread or on a crispy tortilla. The family next to me liked that I was sitting on the curb and eating with them. I did too. We made small talk.

As I came into the small park next to the yellow church I could see Fernando with his husky. We exchanged greetings and I asked how long he had been waiting. Only fifteen minutes. I asked him if I could paint a portrait of him. He agreed. As we were walking and trying to decide on where to paint, I thought it an excellent chance to do his portrait instead of another street scene. We sat on a park bench and he told me about one of his female employees leaving that day. "She told me if I was bored with her she would leave." "Maybe she is in love with you." I said. "Maybe". I then told him of my frustration with my cousin and him not coming to Costa Rica. People love to live their lives in chaos and seem to forget they can control things by doing a simple exercise---planning ahead.

Fernando pointed out the brilliant cloud formations. He talks a lot about the mother Goddess and how she is always exposing life's beauty. His philosophy is a mix of many Eastern religions. I stopped painting and walked to the street corner to see the whole sky, and take a parting shot of the sunset with my camera. In our conversation I told Fernando how tough my students could be. "You want to get along with your students better? Take celery stalk and rub it on a photograph of the entire class, rub it round and round. Then take the stalk and burry it upside down in the earth. That will solve the problem". He told me he uses white magic. I told him Diana had a similar belief system. She has told me to take a picture of a person, put honey on it, and place it in the freezer. "Whatever works", I said, thinking anything is possible if you believe it. Fernando is a perfect personal encounter. He is full of little bits of information I wouldn't hear anywhere else.

As the light was fading two women came up and said hello to Fernando. I continued to paint as they spoke. It was getting so dark I couldn't see, so I returned to the hotel, he stayed chatting with his friends. Fernando is going to take me to his farm in the morning.

I was feeling very productive and happy. That was short lived until I spoke with Diana. Our relationship has always been based on me helping her and getting her to a better place in life. There is no such thing as a conflict-free relationship so I take it all in stride and make myself cool down by writing and expelling energy.

Wednesday, August 12: I had a very peaceful day, wonderful day with Fernando. I woke to the alarm at 8:40 and had just enough time to eat breakfast, load my painting gear, and be out the door for our nine o'clock meeting. I was standing where I had been painting him the night before when he pulled to the corner in his white car, honked, and motioned me over. I climbed into the back seat; his new employee was sitting in the front seat. She is a seventeen-year-old Indian girl, with a wide smile and good energy. She wore blue jeans and had shoulder length hair. Fernando introduced us and we turned right, down the cobble streets of Antigua. I made a brief stop at the pharmacy because the woman had promised me a free month of birth control pills if I came back the next day. The pharmacy clerk would be in later. We buy the same birth control pills that are for sale in the USA, for a fraction of the price. (One of the perks of traveling so much is the price comparison. The quality is exactly the same in many cases.)

We made a stop at the rear of the city market, where the local bus depot is a mere dirt lot. Buses pulled in and men leaning out of the door yelled the name of their next destination. The new employee went into the market to buy some bones for the dog (Percy is the dog) to chew. We next gassed up the car. Fernando had asked me to remind him we needed gas when we left town, which I did. A ten-minute ride brought us to the tall metal gate that was the front of his house. He was tooting the horn, which I didn't understand at first, half way down the street. This was the signal for the cook to open the gate. We pulled the car into a carport where a second newer car sat; it was his "good car".

His house couldn't be reproduced in any movie set; it was too original. The first room we entered was the library. On one side of the room stood three book shelves, a piano was on a second wall, and half way into the middle of the room were speakers, and three stereo systems; nothing was connected or plugged in. Two chairs were in the room, but they were plastic, and situated in a way that looked like no one had ever sat in them. "How long have you lived here?" "Oh, about a year."

He put the dog on the piano keys and explained that Percy was playing a piece by Schaumburg (twelve scale and un-melodic). Fernando had discussed the dog's piano talent with me the night before; I now knew the whole story. We entered a kitchen were two old electric stoves sat mounted on low brick support walls, under the stoves fire was burning. "I have recycled these stoves and fuel them with wood instead of electricity". The cook, who he introduced me to, also had another open fire in a pit. She was cooking some rice in a pot. The kitchen ceiling was covered by makeshift corrugated steel where two panels had been moved aside to allow the smoke to escape. I could see that these were moved back into place if a rain shower were to occur.

He showed me a dark room to the side of the kitchen where another older kitchen was. The newer kitchen was built more in the open. A young man was laying brown tiles with white grout spilling up between each tile. How long until it dries I asked, "Maybe two days." A big tall cabinet stood in one corner, but the rest of the old dark room was a collection of disorganized cooking utensils and a sink with a dripping faucet.

We continued the tour to his bedroom and a thin hall with books, and boxes of books, stacked to the ceiling. Together we sat on an old sofa that had a deerskin and cushions from a number of different sofas. I showed him some of my art and photographs of Diana on my laptop. He would interrupt with short stories, or grab a book from the shelf on a parallel topic as we conversed. He then opened up a series of cabinets with rows of small bottles. This was his laboratory for aromatherapy. Small labels with names, or esoteric notes, were placed on each bottle; as chaotic as the rest of the house seemed these cabinets were well organized and very functional. It came up that I had prostrate problems and he was instantly looking in some resource book tucked away on shelves in his bedroom. His bed was the centerpiece of the house. It was up on a high platform, with clean white sheets and neatly made up. Over the four bed posts, at the corners, hung a white mosquito net, over the mosquito net was a blue sheet that blocked light coming in from a skylight above. Everything else in the house seemed to be unorganized and in a topsy-turvy state, but the bed was that of a king. (The housekeepers did the room every morning.)

He had the helper run out and pick me some herbs and handed me a green concoction of mashed herb and oils. "Put this on the prostrate and see if it helps." He left the room and I applied the mix to by skin next to my prostrate inside my underwear. He was soon back and we were onto the topic of astrology. "What is your sign, when were you born, when was Diana born, what year?" He handed me a pile of Mayan astrology books and I dove into reading as his new employee messaged his hands with oils. He lay face down in his bed. I was on the sofa in the small hall reading away, wondering what exactly he was up to, but it was all just part of the daily responsibilities of his female employee; cooking, cleaning, planting, running errands, whatever his whim or need. (No it wasn't sexual, if that wasn't clear.)

He showed me his solar kitchen, up a ladder, on top of the old dark kitchen. One was a commercial solar oven, the others some boxes with glass doors to trap heat. The food inside looked strange to me. He handed me a black banana, which had been cooked in the solar oven. "Is this a plantain?" "No, it a banana." I began to peel and eat the black banana when he protested. "Eat it from the sides so the gases can escape from the center out. Like the monkeys do!" I did so. We walked down the shaky steps out to an orchard of lemon trees. The entire yard and path leading to the orchard were lined with black plastic bags with small plants, flowers, herbs, green shoots of starter plants, and some dead plants.

Beyond the orchard was a goat chained to a rope. The goat wagged its tail as we approached, and liked to be stroked. On a cleared plot of land was his corn crop. The corn was a few days old. Black plastic bags were strung on tall poles to scare birds away. This was the most organized sector of the vast walled compound, yet it appeared that half the corn was dead or gone. Wild weeds covered most of the remaining yard. In a walled off section he showed me where the goat, who's name I have forgotten, had done such a good job of clearing that he now had the animal eating the rest of the weeds in the remaining yard.

The two of us sat at a table in the first kitchen, with the open ventilation, and had a delicious meal of chicken, squash, carrots, and a vegetable that tasted like a potato and squash at the same time. As we ate we passed the bones and vegetable skins to Percy who stood patiently on the floor, eating our scrapes. When we finished Percy stood on his two back paws and licked our plates. Fernando gave a chuckle to this. A minute later the cook was screaming that the dog had eaten the reaming half of the roasted chicken that was covered on the same table. This was another laughing event. "Percy is full today", I said. I mentioned the show called the "Dog Whisperer" to Fernando. I explained that to discipline a dog is not as difficult as he may think.

After lunch, we went into the library where I completed the portrait of Fernando I had started the night before on the park bench. He was thrilled with his new gift. As I painted, he read out loud from the Upanishads and various poets that he favored. He showed me some of his mother's photographic portraits from when she was a young woman. Our topic of conversation drifted from subject to subject.

Fernando is a mad man and genius. I have a deep respect for this wildly eccentric man. We hit it off instantly and it is no doubt that we will always remain friends no matter how seldom our path may cross. He is an assortment of spiritual beliefs combined with New Age practices. We have much in common, yet I feel slightly more grounded. I am sure not many people would care to carry on a conversation with this one-eyed, scruffy, unshaven beatnik wearing shorts and an Australian adventurer's hat. I savor such chance encounters.

I told him about my dream the night before where his dog rolled over on his back and instead of me rubbing his belly; the dog's skeleton and organs were exposed with the fur being rolled aside. Where the joint met the upper shoulder there was no muscle, only flat bone against bone. Fernando took this as a sign and intensely listened to my dream. He then began to cry and ran to his herbal cabinet and brought back a remedy for his dog's joints. "I didn't know she was in pain". He sat on the piano stool, held the dog on his back like a baby, and had the new employee rub the dog's upper leg joints. The dog knew he was being treated and loved the attention. I have no idea what the dream meant.

I interpreted it to mean the dog would have joint, or arthritis, pain in the future. But the fact that I even had this dream must mean something on a spiritual level. In the dream the dog was communicating a message to me. The message I didn't really know. Strange, yes, but who really knows. What is ancient and primitive in all of us may seem completely absurd in our modern world. Dreams are not something to be taken lightly. I often find myself remembering segments of my dreams from the night before as I pass through my day. As dramatic as Fernando may seem to some, I found him to be quit real and crazy, both. Sanity is a relative thing when traveling. I don't go traveling to find what is "ordinary". I treasure character and individuality, and seek common ground with strangers who may be a little strange, or wiser than the rest of us.

I have only half described his house. His inventiveness was undomesticated and yet very revitalizing. Creativity was spilling from every inch of his messy house. Things were held together with wire, scotch tapes, and plastic string. He made wind chimes out of aluminum pipes. His entire universe was filed with purposeful design that spiraled forth from intellect. He was a fun friend in what may have otherwise been an eventless day, walking from place to place.

We loaded all five of us into his car and left for the bus station, afterwards we stopped at a framing shop. I helped him pick out a matt and frame for the painting I gave him. You may not understand what this means to an artist. I have given many paintings away in my life, but to have one framed and hung on the recipients wall is a true honor, and sign of true appreciation. We returned to the pharmacy, the woman forgot the pills again, so I will be back tomorrow. Fernando then asked me if I wanted to see the city from above, on one mountain. He drove the wrong way up a few one-way streets, explaining the nuisance of having to go so far out of the way if he had gone the "legal" route. We found a grand view of the city and volcano. We lay on our backs and shared more stories about life and all the intricate episodes we have lived through. It was getting late as the white clouds above the volcano pushed upward, as if an eruption were taking place. He took me back to the park where we had met and agreed we'd see each other same time, same station, my last evening; tomorrow.

Thursday, August 13: In the early morning I went out seeking light. It was 7 AM, and I poked my head out the front door of the hotel to see if the sun was shining or overcast. There was direct light, a good sign. I took one camera, the biggest lens, and went off to find some strong contrasting shadows. I found them. I realized how addictive digital photography makes the process versus using film. To get that instant high and have an endless supply is a junkies dream; see how technology is so destructive! Well, maybe it isn't that evil. The sun was overcast a few times but she cooperated and I shot over two hundred photographs in two hours.

My path took me to the central plaza and away again toward the volcano. It is so easy to photograph with the volcano in the background because the mountain dominates the entire city. I did, (maybe stupidly), so many photographs of the volcano behind subjects in the foreground that I tired of the scene. I went to a section of the city with few, if any, parked cars, so I was able to get the aesthetic, "old time" feeling. I felt very safe because at almost every street corner there were police standing, or groups stationed in trucks. I knew I had passed out of the tourist zone when I could no longer see any police, but I still felt safe.

I found the major street, the central market is on, and went into the market. It is Thursday and market day, and indeed it was. I passed through the familiar maze but ended in the rear of the market near the bus terminal (a large patch of dirt with buses racing about). This was the best part of my morning, although I only took a few photographs. The bustle of the market was in full swing and it was only 8:30 AM. One sector had a roof with tall, chained link fences for containment. The sheer number of shoppers and Indian woman on the ground was staggering and a visual potpourri. The women were squatted on their knees or sitting flat on cushions. They all wore the traditional dress and varied in age and size, from very young to ancient with wrinkled faces.

I can't say there was an atmosphere of overt joy, it was a working environment, and the daily routine was on their faces like a road map. There were so many people and the rows were so small, due to over-population, that the crowd was almost impassable and claustrophobic. Men carried loads twice the size of themselves, slipped through the tiny paths past the vast number of salable obstacles at their feet. Baskets of fruit and vegetables in small mounds opened just enough to allow foot traffic. The colors, the colors, the colors, were brilliant. I shot some still pictures by holding the camera at my side and just pointing to get whatever was in the picture. This is a hit and miss process that seldom produces a good photograph. I just wanted to capture what was typical. Being photographed is really considered a nuisance to the Indians. I did ask permission to shoot vegetables and flowers, leaving the woman out of the picture.

I was looking for cashews, but was told only in the central market, obviously not a daily staple for the people. I bought a coconut sweet, one brown, and the other white with large thin strips of coconut mixed with tons of sugar. A third sweet was like butter brittle with a mix of various nuts, the only recognizable looking was a pumpkin seed. I haven't seen any pumpkins come to think of it. I exited the chain linked compound where a policeman stood with a long riffle, which is usually the custom for banks, jewelry stores, and the fancy hotels. The market was spilling out to the edge of the parking lot where trucks and cars created a kind of courtyard. The automobiles were parked so close that they seemed to be an intentional barrier. I walked to find the major street passing by men working on platforms throwing cement (stucco) onto wet walls. In the far distance I could see an opening where traffic was moving and I knew that was the street that would lead me to my hotel. The hotel clerk, a young man in his early twenties, greeted me with a hand shake and knuckle touch.

One distinct scene I will never forget was when leaving the market that day. For the majority of my trip in Guatemala I have seen little hunger. I saw this in Guatemala City but not Antigua. Chichicasanando was real life, but Antigua had been without the usual "street-life" characteristics. The city is kept sterile for the tourists. But in the market I saw hunger that was equal to the worst I've ever seen. The far backside of the market had a walled compound where the day's trash was piled as high as a building. The homeless, young, old, children, babies, teenagers in their bare feet were sifting through piles of trash for food, eating as they found something. A few older men turned to stop and look at me. They snarled at me like angry dogs. One pointed to my camera around my neck in a daring gesture to NOT photograph. He was angry about his state of being and wanted nothing to do with it being on display. I felt sad and guilty for having witnessed this. My safety was at risk so I passed by as quickly as possible trying not to notice, trying not to cry.

I had a day of short jaunts out, but spent time in the hotel just chilling, watching the news, resting up. I went out around four in the afternoon to find a museum of Colonial Art, but it was closed for renovation. I stopped in the pharmacy that had promised me a free month of birth control pills, if I returned. This took two days instead of one, but I had all the time I needed and returned twice to receive the promotional package (a $22.00 savings). I buy in bulk to save money, so got almost a year's supply for Diana.

I wanted a small snack so I made my way to the church where I had met the Franciscan priest. Across the street in a long plaza I noted woman-selling food in the evenings. I bought a cheese papusa and sat on the edge of a fountain eating. The vendors put salad and hot sauce on top; the salad is cabbage with chili sauce. I asked for a little sauce, a little was still too much. It was HOT! I was still hungry so I bought a second crispy tortilla with avocado. I see these foods as I'm walking; remember where they are located and return for "dinner" later in the day. Lunch is the big meal. What takes me weeks, and months, to work off the excess weight, takes a couple of weeks of bicycling, walking, and manual labor when on vacation. My eating habits in the States are just that. My body feels more in sync when I walk all day.

I made my way back to the church plaza to meet Fernando as we had planned. As soon as I walked up the sidewalk I could hear him tooting his horn. Percy, the dog, was stationed at his usual perch on the window of the drivers' side; half on Fernando's lap, the other half leaning out the window sniffing the wind. Perfect timing, we had both arrived at the very same moment. The designated "time" was to be "around sunset". (I don't wear a watch all summer.)

Fernando asked me where I wanted to go. "I don't know; take me somewhere I haven't seen outside the city". "How about a macadamia farm?" "Great!", I answered. We exited the city on the same road that lead to his house, so I had him show me the turn off for his house. If I return next summer I wanted to get my directions clear. We began to come into another small village, but eventually came to the countryside. I could see low hills with farms, which had sectioned off the divisions of ownership. The air was cool and we were enjoying the drive.

We pulled up behind a funeral procession that was nearing a large traffic triangle. "We can get ahead if we go around, that way." So Fernando instantly pressed the gas and we zoomed past a line of waiting cars, turning left in front of oncoming traffic, a large bus, in particular. He laughed wildly as the bus driver cursed him out. "What did he say", I asked. "He called me a mother fu…." Our attempt to get ahead of the walking funeral procession didn't work; a policeman, who was standing in the middle of the street, stopped us. There was still a small gap open before the people came to the intersection, so Fernando asked the policeman if he could turn right onto a street that veered away from the crossing. The policeman granted his request. "See, I don't have to stop for anything", he said being full of himself.

His driving is a venture into the absurd because he passes on curves, anything that is moving slower than he. Remember this is all done with only one eye! I asked how he judged depth while driving; half hoping this may introduce some caution. "Well, I use two points and compare the foreground", he responded. "But at night this doesn't work." I noted the increasing darkness as we pulled off the road onto a dirt road. In his search to find the road, he slowed the car to a crawl for quite a distance. This brought about another angry gesture from a car behind us, the universal greeting with the middle finger flashed out the window.

We pulled into a patch of forest and a sign indicated the macadamia farm. There were some parking spaces, but Fernando continued on to the collection of building where a big dog greeted us and began to play with Percy. The whole compound was mysterious and very tropical. The sky was gloomy and overcast from low clouds that looked like rain was possible. The combination of no sunshine and trees gave the environment a dreamy feeling. We passed a garden and fountain surrounded by exotic tropical flowers. Unseen birds sang in the trees with high shrills, calling to each other. Butterflies were dancing from flower to flower paying no attention to how close we passed. "The owner is a Gringo friend of mine. He has become a tycoon from the money he has made." The surrounding forest was with macadamia trees where thousands of green bulbs hung, ready to be harvested.

We passed up a small path with fresh wood shavings; the air was delicious. In a hut with no electric lighting I could see a man standing behind a glass counter. We entered. It was so dark I didn't notice two other men, one standing, and one seated next to the door, until my eyes adjusted. Behind the counter a large sign said, "If we have nature as our religion, the church will be the trees". It wasn't written in correct English, but the idea came across. On large, white transparent sheets of Plexiglas in red letters, several testimonials to the cures of macadamia oil were displayed. Other testimonials hung on a nearby wall in frames. The man behind the counter offered us both a small palm-full of tasty macadamia nuts. A white chocolate followed this, then a dark chocolate with a nut buried inside.

Fernando encouraged me to buy something from a variety of healthy selections. I bought Diana some macadamia oil and a baggie full of bee pollen. Fernando was pushing me to buy larger quantities, but I explained I was trying to keep what remaining cash I had so I could take taxis' in Guatemala City. He offered to loan me some money, but that wasn't my point. I don't like being forced into anything just to please someone. I told him I could buy these things, like honey for instance, in my own country.

We walked back into the garden; the men were just closing shop for the day. A butterfly with transparent wings was suckling a flower and we paused to observe it. "This is a sign from the Goddess." (Fernando makes constant reference to the "Goddess" in his conversation.) He speaks in English, which is another reason we found our friendship so compatible. We have the common background of having an interest in Eastern Religions, and Philosophy. He lived in India to seek knowledge in his early twenties. His house had lots of pictures of Hindu deities amongst the collection of art affects. This is something I enjoy myself and have in my classroom back home.

In our conversations I mentioned to Fernando that I was dyslexic. "I have an oil that can cure that! I have invented oil that can cure cancer." I had used Fernando's natural remedy on my prostrate the day before and honestly felt no different. But now I was sure that we were crossing a barrier between fantasy and reality. It is my feeling that modern medicine is off track. I know modern medicine is a far cry from witchcraft, but I also believe that spirituality plays an important role in our healing. The tragic myth we in Western "Civilization" miss is the body has the capacity to heal itself, and more importantly to stave off illness if we are eating correctly, exercising, and aware of our spiritual being. Doctors are no better than witch doctors if we don't recognize the God/ Goddess within each of us. Health is not in the pill first, it is in the belief that wellness is achievable. "Belief" is the spiritual dimension we take for granted. We give way too much authority to the doctors when the source of healing comes within first. We are putting the cart before the horse. I know Fernando was little far out, but I believe his spirit is purer than most Western doctors.

We drove back to the triangle in the road and went in a different direction away from the city. This was a high road that skirted the city and gave us some nice views from above. Fernando noted that this road was not used by tourists or the usual bus routes, therefore it was a new highway, but little used. We passed into another small town and Fernando showed me where he had lived with his ninety-two years old mother when she passed away. He showed me the gate of a community, not the actual house. His rent was over two thousand dollars a month in the old house. I found this very costly, but it seems his family was well off. His father had owned a hardware store across the street from the Calvary. That location was supported by the military. He told me he was not close to his father and his father had sold the business to his other brother. "Sold, not passed it along?" Fernando went into his explanation of his father as being a difficult personality to grow up with. We had one more thing in common.

I finally got up the nerve and asked Fernando how he lost his eye. This is very noticeable because the eye drupes open and has a red base instead of an eyeball. "I was shot in the face. It was the Goddess who saved my life because I flinched at the right moment and the bullet went through my eye and exited beside it. Otherwise the bullet would have gone directly into my forehead and killed me."

"Who shot you and why?"

"I was driving along the main street in Guatemala City. I passed a car and made a man angry."

"Why would that make someone angry?"

"Well at the next light I got out and broke his mirror for honking at me. When I tried to break his window he took out a gun and shot me."

My only question was, "Was that before, or after you lived in India".

"After."

He then went on to tell me that the man was very rich and he never pressed charges. He had a private investigator locate the man, but because of his wealth, and prestige, Fernando didn't bother with any further reprisals. He told this in a way that admitted he got what he deserved, and he had no anger toward the man with the gun. But I was a bit shocked at the whole story; "I didn't want him to feel any more regret, if indeed there was any". He told me in such a matter of fact, seemingly emotionless manner that this life-changing event had come and gone in an instant.

Fernando then changed the subject telling me about a wheat-like crop called amorist. I had only heard of it in health food stores and wasn't sure exactly what it was. "Oh you have to try some." He instantly pulled into an open-air market, left the dog in the car, and was gone. He returned with a small package wrapped in plastic. "This was the main staple of the Mayans", as he was explaining he unwrapped the brown square, handing me a piece, motioning me to take a bite. It had the flavor of brown sugar and a soft texture that pulled apart like taffy. In appearance it had thousands of tiny round white balls. "The Mayan kings asked for as much amorist as corn from their subjects." He was chewing on a piece and gave the dog a piece as well. "Go buy a couple of packages for your trip tomorrow." I did, but again was a little put off by the instruction to buy something. They did come in handy.

Because it was dusk cars were using their lights, a slight rain shower was beginning as we pulled into traffic and Fernando made a U-turn without really looking. He simply blew his car horn nonstop and circled around almost coming face to face with the oncoming traffic. A man in the car we almost hit yelled something, but this didn't affect Fernando in the least. I think his partial blindness has given him overconfidence while driving. It certainly hasn't given him any extra precautionary abilities. Before I knew it, and could recognize where we were, it was time to leave. He pulled up to the plaza where we had met three nights before. We said our last good bye. I have his address and will send him a DVD of my travels. He has no electricity, but I encouraged him to use the DVD player of two women friends. "They must have one." "Oh, I bet they do!"

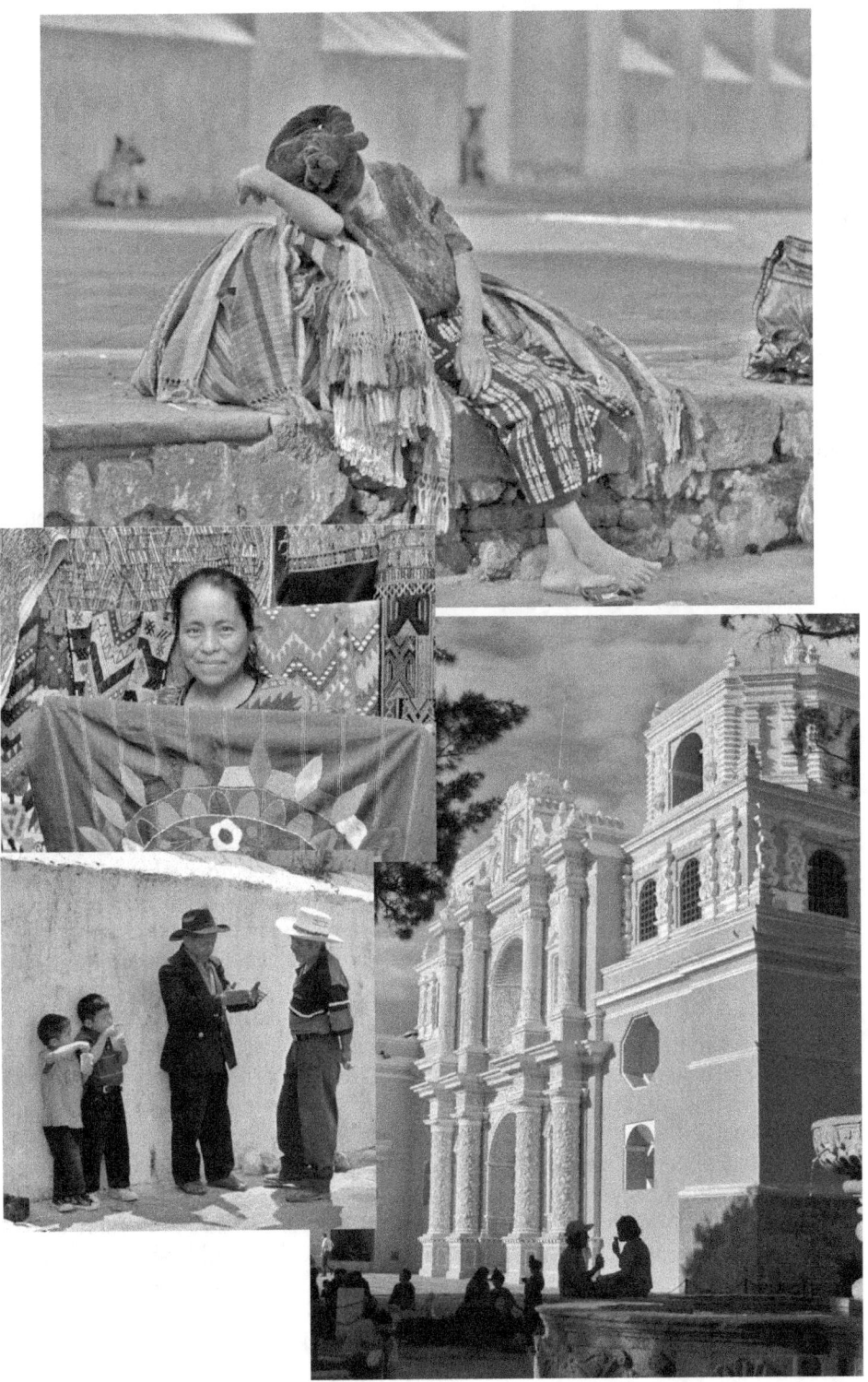

223

Chapter Thirteen
Copan Honduras

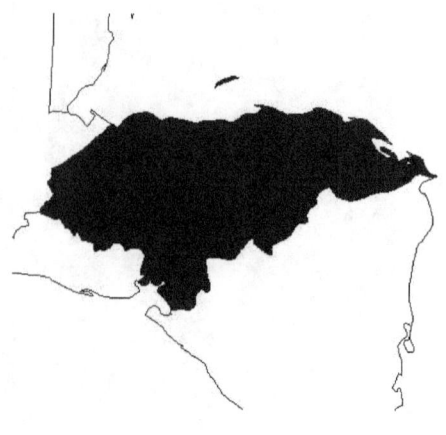

Friday, August 14: Having slept and completed my pre-travel ritual by 3:00 AM, I was up and ready for the shuttle to Copan, just inside the border of Honduras. I was awake at 2:30, drifting in and out of sleep. My mind won't allow sleep when there is a task at hand. I spoke with Diana the night before and was happy we are back on the usual terms, I got my "stuff" out and she didn't mention the past two days of verbal scuffling. We spoke about the remaining week, of missing each other. I sent her an email the night before trying to clear up what I think could be better communication, or a healthier way of being aware of each other. The relationship is a work in progress. At a little after 4:00 AM the empty shuttle arrived, I was the first passenger. We went to two more stops, picking up two women from Spain, and a couple from New York City. The man had a house in Hermosa Beach, Costa Rica ten minutes away from my house. He and his wife had traveled up from Panama, stopped in Costa Rica, and were going to fly home from Guatemala City.

The drive was strenuous because the road was rough. I was writing on the computer most of the way but first lay length-wise on a long passenger seat. I didn't really sleep but closed my eyes and listen to my mp3 player. Before we crossed the border to Honduras we slowed down considerably for the cows that were walking in the highway. I knew we had reached the border when a long line of semi-trucks was parked beside the road. The drivers were nowhere to be seen, but later materialized at the border where small groups stood around talking. The shuttle driver hurried us through the immigration process on the Guatemalan side; this was one brick building with three doors. "Go to door number four", an agent told me in English, only to baffle me more. I had to pay an extra three dollars, or something, because I was staying two nights. The female agents were very pleasant. I assumed there would be another stop in Honduras, no we sped down a winding highway with speed bumps with a sign saying 'hazardous incline'. Speed bumps were built in a series of three or four, one after the other. They were not small, but rather high, giving us an extra bounce as the driver rolled over them.

When we pulled into Copan I instantly noticed this wasn't Guatemala. Men walking around in cowboy hats, and women dressed in shoulder-less tank tops, was something I hadn't seen for a while. The streets had garbage and the poverty was very noticeable. The driver had stored away a dozen roses in the back of the shuttle. Earlier, when we stopped for a restroom break, he had taken them out and sprinkled water on them to freshen them up. He pulled up to one store, called out to a young woman, and handed her the roses. "Is that your girlfriend?" I asked. "No, it is her sister." All of us in the van were happy for him; I gave him a little "congratulation". Less than two blocks later the van pulled up to the office of his company and we all plied out.

Suddenly everyone was gone but the driver. Men were surrounding me, yelling in my face. Men were grabbing my bags and telling me, "Ten dollars, and ten dollars". It was worse than I can express. I almost had one bag carried away, not because of thievery, because the man wanted me to follow him to a hotel. I yelled "Silence!" in Spanish, which calmed the small mob down for a moment. I guess the driver thought I would go with one of the men on the street. He was completely detached from the loud event and stood there as if this were common. He had unloaded my bags then stood back as an observer. He puzzled me. I was fighting off a pack and he was looking at his shoes. I then asked the driver for help, motioning him into the office of the company. We entered and I confirmed my Sunday departure, and then asked the man behind a desk for a hotel. He shrugged his shoulders and pointed to a display propped on his desk advertising a hotel. His lukewarm endorsement only added to my frustrations, but it was my only choice. I told him, and the driver, that the men on the street were like a pack of dogs. This got a little chuckle.

The driver and I piled my three bags back into the van (one is a large bundle of fabrics I acquired from shopping in Chichi). The driver pulled up to the corner, maybe three buildings away, turned left, drove to the middle of the next block and stopped. It was that close, that simple, and worlds away from being torn to shreds in a street competition. The driver and I were laughing, but I felt like I had been released into a lion's den at the company office. I know how genuine their plight must be. Their faces showed suffering far beyond what I'd ever known, but with people grabbing at me it was hard to find time to feel any compassion. I signed up, paid with my credit card and was in my room within minutes. My room had two double beds so I used one as a platform for my luggage. My first task was to get to an ATM machine. I had no Honduran money.

I suffered instant culture shock. I have been going from country to country and noticed slight differences, but here in Honduras it is poles apart from Guatemala. Besides the obvious change in the smallness of this town: the tiny narrow cobble streets, the short length of blocks, the hills, and broken down feeling of things. It feels more third world here. But the major change came in the way people relate to me. Few understand my Spanish, they don't make much eye contact, and no one seems to return a smile. The hotel clerk, the shopkeepers, the people overall seem suppressed. (There is a current political problem with their President having been flown out of the country at gunpoint in his pajamas, but there is something else in the air here that is thick.)

In the central plaza there was a gathering of young dancers in traditional dress; the girls in long white skirts and blouses while the boys were in baggy shirts and loose pants. Few people seemed to pay any attention. I found an ATM, but it kept rejecting any amount of money I asked for. I went into the bank and asked for help. Again, it was like I was from the moon. A bank clerk was leaning on a desk flirting with a female employee. I sat at the desk almost under their noses and felt like I was interrupting something intimate, sexual even. Was this a bank or a brothel? They both attended to me, but had to take my issue to another assistant manager, who in turn escorted me back outside to the ATM. He finally concluded that the machine was out of money, and directed me to another bank across the plaza, or rather two blocks away where there was nothing like a bank, but houses. I circled back to the plaza and found the bank. How? I saw two guards with shotguns standing near a door; a sure sign from the 'Goddess' that money was near, as Fernando would say.

With money in hand I was off to find food in a market. I had walked right by this market before, not noticed it because the door was so plain. There were a few women selling cooked food from baskets, sitting on the sidewalk, but the arched doorway was up a step and practically indistinguishable from any other door on the street. Inside this archway, packed with humanity, were vegetables in low straw baskets. The door was so small and filled with bodies that it was nearly impossible to tell what it was. I bought two avocados, but refused to pay when the woman quoted a price around six dollars. Inside I found a woman who was honest. I paid around a dollar for two. I also bought salad fixings and headed back to the hotel, of course showing the crook my avocados on my way out. (She didn't like me either.) I did a double-take return to the market when I realized I had no eating utensils.

The market was tiny, it was nothing more than a courtyard sized opening. But it was packed to the hilt with people, stalls, and dirty water running between the cobblestone and gutters. It was quite filthy. Garbage was everywhere. The stalls were so small and low that I had to crouch down to enter. Dogs were milling about, and people sat picking their noses in boredom. (I'm sorry to be so crude, but it's true.) I asked the hotel clerk if there was a refrigerator I could use for my milk and he looked at me like I were from Mars. Now I've been to the moon and Mars, and I still feel like there are a few more planets to cover. "No, not for the guests", he returned. I had to wrap my milk in a towel and hope it will keep until the morning in this heat.

On the drive here I noticed a dramatic change in the terrain. The cool tropical location of the day before was replaced by an arid landscape with occasional cactus. The most noticeable shift was the heat. In the middle of the day, while I ventured out to the bank, I saw men on the sidewalk sitting in any possible strip of shade. The sun felt like I was back in Costa Rica. The heat rising off the streets caused me to thirst for liquid. My body was tired and heating up. I had no time to lose though. I went to the corner and entered a restaurant thinking it was a tour company. I got directions to the Copan ruins and hailed a three wheel "tuk tuk". I was on my way to the Copan ruins almost an hour after arriving here.

The entrance to the archeological park is about two miles away. We entered countryside a block from the city plaza, passing over a narrow bridge that arched up into a small hill. Beyond the bridge the road suddenly widened and the claustrophobic feeling of the town was instantly gone. Grand open green fields with cows were along the route. Shade trees with coolness in the air replaced the smothering heat as we drove further on. Just before the park's entrance uniformed school children smiled and waved for donation, pointing to the large plastic jugs. They stood in the center aisle where a speed bump slowed the traffic. This was also a military-police checkpoint. We barely slowed and passed other vehicles that were complying with donations. A bit further along the road we turned right into the parks parking lot. It was clean, well-spaced, and inviting.

As I approached the building a man welcomed me, he started to give me information. Not until the end of a two-minute explanation on some historical facts did he politely tell me the tour he was offering was optional for thirty-five dollars. I said I was going to explore on my own. I went to a tiny round glass hole with air conditioning billowing out, stuck my face as close to the opening as possible. No one was inside selling entrance tickets. I asked a park attendant where to pay. By then another woman standing outside the door snapped to. She ran inside the door apologizing she was not there. She took my dollars, gave me change in dollars. I asked for their local currency, but it wasn't possible.

I had spent almost all my Honduran money already. I had no knowledge of the amounts of money I was spending, as often is the case while traveling. I thought I had taken sixty dollars out of the ATM. The groceries and vegetables seemed outlandishly high in price. How could I spend so much on so little? Well later I found I had only taken out thirty dollars because I went online and looked at my bank balance; a pleasant surprise in another wise disappointing day. Until I entered the Mayan ruins!

I walked into a shady path with wide spaces, following the general direction of things where a man in a cowboy hat stopped me, explaining I could also enter a small archeological village with the same pass for two days. He then began to explain the layout of the park pointing to a map that was displayed between two steel poles. It wasn't until a lengthy fact filled narrative that he politely offered me a horseback ride that would be leaving at three o'clock. Again, I was taken aback by the polite approach after being nearly assaulted by the screaming men in the street when I first arrived. I entered into a chain link enclosure where a man asked to see my ticket. He smiled, welcomed me.

Hidden in the branches of tall trees multi-colored macaws called to each other; their plumage slightly showing red, yellow, and blue feathers through the leaves. Tree branches shaded the path. After a short walk I entered a large flat green field where a stone pyramid rose from the earth. The green field had once been a vast stone plaza, but now was a well-kept, mowed lawn. (I read this on another plank. I am not that intelligent!) In the scorching heat I made my way to the pyramid and began to shoot photographs. As the midday heat shone down on me, I tried to see myself around the year seven hundred A.D., the time of this civilization. (Actually, I am very intelligent. Facts like this come to mind without any reference. I know everything about every Mayan nuance of information. Scholars have called upon me to pontificate my wisdom to the masses. Not once have I opened a book, or studied this Mayan civilization. What planet comes after

Mars? The moon?)

I walked in a trance of amazement. I was astounded and bewildered because such beauty also included human sacrifice. I said this to one of the hired tour guides. He said, "Just like today". I laughed and said, "Yes, we call it war". That put things into a better perspective for me. We have reached the moon. Yet we continue to slaughter each other in the name of our Gods, politics and progress. Things seemed so much like seven hundred A.D. to me right then, the only part missing was the people going about their daily lives, the pyramid builders, and the king walking around wearing feathers and thick gold bracelets.

I passed the next three hours missing no part of the enormous complex. Just like all the Greek statues in hundreds of museums around the world, some guy has a thing about knocking off the noses of statues. This same guy (Yes guy, I seriously don't see women destroying art.) had defaced and vandalized any statue with a nose all around the world. I was wondering why this is so? Is it out of hatred for a "barbaric civilization"? Is it always an adolescent male venting against authority? Is it because the nose projects out of the face? Somewhere along the great timeline of history the noses of statues became 'THE' article to obliterate. This is not weathering; this is a distinct human behavior against art that baffles me to no end. So is war, which is still is a thriving business today.

To the south of the grand plaza (I am using the map given me at the entrance.) was a slightly higher pyramid with two structures. The first pyramid was a tall as a two-story house. Beyond were two taller pyramids with stairways leading up; a canvas canopy to protect it from the weather covered one, the most elaborate stairway. This was the main alter, with carvings centrally spaced up the steep incline. I circled behind the second pyramid to the backside where a path permitted spectators to pass up to the top. There low wires strung across areas too fragile for foot traffic and guards were stationed within view of the entire complex. I snuck behind one of these wires, picked up a mammoth rock, and broke the nose off one of the tall statues. Not really! I scratched my name into a wall. That's a lie too!

From the top I could see another taller pyramid that stood to the south. As I went west I came upon a deep plaza with stone steps surrounding all but an opening at the southern end. This plaza was a stadium. Each individual step was designed to be just about the height of the stretched leg of a man. The stones were perfectly built and amazingly well preserved except where the forest was spilling onto the site. Tree roots crawled down the rocks like giant pythons. The dynasty had lasted nearly four hundred years, but time replaced the unscathed surfaces with erosion and the occasional tree that found a source of water below the stones. I had been up for so many hours I had to lay down under the shade of one of the trees. I put my hat over my eyes allowing myself to take a short, well needed, nap. When I awoke, I ate my amorist, followed by a tangerine, and some water. I lay there for a good forty-five minutes listening to the calls of exotic birds with beautiful vocal melodies. High in the clouds I counted the black dots each of which was a circling buzzard. A soft breeze rustled the leaves accented by the subtle conversation of two guards on the far side of the plaza. This was the serenity I had been seeking.

After re-centering myself, I reluctantly left, walking a mile, or more, to the entrance. I paid to see the museum. This was a gigantic, stadium-sized, building with an open-air ceiling, there a Mayan pyramid stood in the center. The roof opened to the sky letting the elements fall on the reproduction of a Mayan pyramid. This pyramid was actually an exact replica of one of the altars inside a grand pyramid on the grounds. The figures on its face were in bright, reddish-orange colors. It was painted with green faces of birds and humans that projected out in relief. The immense size of the museum housed some of the actual tops (really the size of houses) of the pyramids, which had been reassembled stone by stone. Few people were visible inside the museum, but their voices drifted into the air and merged with that of the swallows darting to nests hidden within the steel structure. A long ramp covering two sides of the length of the cavernous room led the museum viewers to a second floor where more hieroglyphics and statues of gods were spaced throughout. Female guards lazily hung their arms over the edge of the railing while sitting on large white concrete benches.

My fatigue was getting the best of me. After briefly looking at the gift shop I climbing into a "tuk tuk" with two other schoolgirls then zoomed toward the town's central plaza. The price was still ten (whatever's) even though there were two other passengers. I walked around a while, entered the church to say hello. The church was unimpressive and crud. I went back to my hotel for a homemade salad dinner, the news, and a delightful hot shower. I was ready to record my day, which has been so long that I had been writing as soon as I woke from my nap and into the entire evening, only to break long enough to give Diana a short call from an Internet shop across the street. My night's sleep was horrible. I woke many times in the night; a strong rain shower lulled me back into slumber land.

Saturday, August 14: I was awake at six writing. At seven I went out to see how the morning light was. Perfect. A slight overcast on the far hills was a good contrast for the well-light streets and bright colors. The plaza was remarkably full of people for such an early hour. I asked a man who had been kissing his girlfriend on the corner, after she left in a "tuk tuk", why all the people were sitting around. "They are waiting for the market or the municipality to open." I shot photographs to my heart's content, not wanting to invade any ones privacy, and using my telephoto lens. I returned to the hotel to write, eat, shower, and get my art supplies ready. The hotel desk clerk broke his predicable silence and downward gaze with a warm question. He is studying English and needed examples of the word "should". I heard him and another worker trying to pronounce the word (incorrectly) while sweeping the floor of the gardened hallway. "Should, with a D", I said. He soon returned to my door with an assignment from his instructor asking my help. "My Spanish is good at listening, but my writing isn't". I gave him several examples of the word "should" in English sentences. He was pleased and SMILING!

(Hours later....) Now I am back after a fact filled day of sightseeing at the Copan ruins with a guide. I wanted to paint, so I lugged the bag around all day only to find I had forgot my brushes. Oh well, I just had to lie on my back and watch the buzzards in clouds for an hour after lunch. What torture there is in life?

The man I had joked with the day before about war became my tour guide. While he was giving a tour our paths crossed, he openly shared information with me. He did the same for anyone within earshot, engaging them while still with me. When I returned to the ticket office in the morning I was approached by several men, I turned them down and was lucky to find Fidel in a small shop. I sought him out because he seemed open and wise. He is older than the rest of the crew. He has worked there for twenty-six years. The twenty-five dollars I spent was well beyond its value. I knew I was missing out on exactly what I was looking at the day before. I also have a habit of getting an overview of an area and then going back into greater detail if I have the next day to return.

We began at the outset with him feeding me information; so much I wish I could just pull it all up in my mind even now. I considered taking notes it was so interesting. We first stood beside a Cieba tree. This was the tree that the Mayan made their cotton fabrics from. On the tree hundreds of thorn spikes jutted out, making it impossible to climb. How the Mayan did he never told. A tree beside the Cieba had small caterpillars bunched together. Originally I wasn't sure if it was the insects or moss on the tree. I brushed the back of my pointing finger gently across the black spiny surface of the insect. "Ouch!" I didn't expect to be stung by a soft looking bunch of critters! My finger instantly swelled up and tiny white blisters appeared. I was lucky to vaguely touch; this could have ruined my entire day the pain was so bad. For half the day the finger hurt from imbedded hairs too small for the eye to see. That taught me not to judge a worm by its soft, fussy cover. (This sting was painful for weeks after my return.)

In the park Fidel stopped at an overview map of the entire archeological compound. He began to explain the class structure of the Mayans. The kings were at the apex, with the artisans and priests being the middle class. Framers were the low class and slaves/ workers were at the bottom of the strata. Only the king and upper class lived within the actual city walls where we stood. The farmers were in the nearby valley as well as the slaves. "Just like the class structure today. The rich live in the cities and the middle class live outside." he said a few times. I understood his point of life not changing that much through the centuries.

The city was built in line with the four geographic directions. He also added the Cieba tree extends its roots in the four global directions. Fidel set a compass on some of the directional crosses authenticating their correctness. I questioned if the pyramids were built of only stone. No, there were originally hills there and the pyramids and temples were built on top of them.

We passed along to enter the largest plaza and crossed the field to a large sculpture. As Fidel held a long thin pole with a feather on the end he pointed to specific discussion topics. Such names as "Thirteenth Rabbit and Smoke Jaguar" were carved in the hieroglyphics. The history was chiseled into rows of kings and dynasties the entire length of the stone surface. The king's linage was through blood. They wore no gold but rather their most valued items made of shells and jade. There was no gold in the hills, so the Spaniards overlooked this location.

Only the king wore a jaguar skin. Around his waist and ankles he wore shells that jingled as he walked. Both the priest and king wore the red and yellow feathers of the macaw for ceremonial offerings.

The Mayans only sacrificed those of their own tribe on one occasion, after a football match (or type of game they played). When the losing teams' captain lost a match he was beheaded and offered to one of their gods. Silly me, here I was thinking they slaughtered their own people all the time. No, in fact they only sacrificed the people of the opposing tribes. If they were fortunate enough to be of the highest class they were spared sacrifice by death and taken as slaves to contribute to their city. An artesian was spared death because his talents were valuable. This is not the case in my country where the National Endowments for the Arts has been targeted by the ancient Mayan ax. Artists are at the bottom of the pool, unless they achieve fame, and by that time they have sold out anyway.

The most interesting misconception I had was there use of war as a constant ritual. It was only allowed three days a year. Yep, on the solar equinoxes they went out to capture human sacrifices. The rest of the year they only sacrificed macaws. I saw the altar to prove it. I also saw the round altar where they had a cup, the size of a small skull, which they placed the head of the humans sacrificed, and a lovely carved trestle, for the blood to flow down in a circle, wrapped around the huge round stone. The blood of the sacrificed was collected and burned so the offering would rise up to the heavens, thus, of course, pleasing the hell out of their god. Fidel told me today certain Indian tribes still carry out such pagan rituals. They use chickens, not people.

During the cities rein all the structures, including the large plaza were coved with adobe, this was all painted white. So the entire city was white washed, including the ground of the plaza, the stepping-stone bleachers surrounding the plaza, and the pyramids themselves. The only exception to the use of white was the immense statues of the kings with the historic hieroglyphs. These were painted in bright red. Some of the red still partially covered a few of the statues. The vast plaza served as both a stadium and a market.

At one side of the plaza, closer to the tallest altar, there was a court for playing a type of football. Only the ball was a very heavy rubber and it didn't bounce. The players wore shin guards, stomach pads, and helmets. The game had no time limit. Two opposing teams had as long as it took to hit the stone head of a macaw placed high up an inclined slope. A wide strip of open space was running between this "valley" of two slanting inclines. Three stone macaw heads were equally spaced at the top of the slanted rock incline; there were a total of six macaw heads in total. Think of the cemented banks of a river in the middle of a modern city, for instance, the Los Angeles River. This embankment ran the length of a very short city block. And again, in case you forget, the captain of the losing team was beheaded; a good reason to not be a team captain or athletic back in the day. Maybe the captain was inspired to play very, very good, considering his life depended on it!

One of the most priceless aspects of taking a guided tour was the information on the hieroglyphics. As obvious as the pictographs were while being shown by my guide, the reverse was occurring while I walked through alone. I couldn't see one tenth of the images before they were described to me. By the end of the tour I was recognizing the faces of animals and people emerging from the abstract stone surface. A strange visual parallel between Asian sculptures and the Mayan was the oriental looking beards that the kings wore. These pointy beards looked like something Genghis Khan would have worn. These people are the genetic descendants of the Asians and this is often easily seen on the faces of peoples here.

One statue of a king was two sided. On the eastern side he was depicted in his youth, the opposite, western side he was depicted as an old bearded man. Fidel pointed out the numerous references to Mayan folklore; a crocodile with faces emerging from its mouth, monkeys dancing, leopards dancing, and endless serpents winding throughout the sculpture.

At one point my mind wandered from being saturated with information. Fidel stopped and asked me to listen closer. He didn't miss a beat if a listener wasn't tuned into his lecture. I was receiving it all like a sponge. I kept thinking about my students and how I could incorporate these images into my lesson plans. A young boy, whose parents weren't near, reached over a wire barrier and touched the stone, Fidel reprimanded the boy explaining that the acid in his hands was damaging to the stone. He was stern and equally as stern to an adult who had climbed up a pyramid to take a photograph. This man took pride in his job and valued the site as sacred. I admired this. For twenty-six years he made a living helping others understand the Mayans.

He told me he had bought a little farm and grew corn and vegetables. He had seven children and was raising them as Catholics. He worked a few days at the historical site and the rest of the week he was farming. But importantly, he had educated himself by attending the lectures of visiting professors.

I knew he was getting hungry and was looking at his watch. We sat in the shade and he shared a drink of cold soda with me that another security guard had carried in. There was no drinking water available during the two hours of the tour. I had a little bottle but it was soon depleted within the first half hour. It was scorching hot. As often as possible I stood or sat in the shade as he offered endless information. He joked how many people had semi-complained that there was too much information to retain. This was his passion. He had attended numerous seminars from noted archeologists. He had details, dates, and names at the ready for all visitors.

We said our good-byes and I went to eat my lunch of avocado, crackers, amorist, and a tangerine. I returned to the shade tree where I was the day before. After lunch my disappointment of not being able to paint evaporated into the clouds overhead. I lie on my back and saw the faces of birds and Mayan Kings in the clouds. Five vultures flew in circles and I imagined myself to be one of them. Ants crawling through the grass, which seemed to be impassable, were already carrying the crumbs from my crackers away. Tiny ants crawled over me, and flies with golden bodies were at my hairy legs, but time drifted by like a slice of paradise; heaven is here if you seek it.

I left the chained link compound and walked through the parks nature trail. Signs with information on Mayan civilization were posted along the trail. Mounds of earth were marked as the locations of previous home sites. The jungle had swallowed up everything that men struggled to make, years melting them into seconds as thick vegetation was the victor.

That morning before I went to the ruins, the plaza was filled with a long, long line of people standing to enter the municipal building. Fidel told me this was to distribute money to the poor. They were receiving a monthly payment. He joked that it was the government's way of keeping the peace. I think it goes more along the lines of a barrel of a gun. The checkpoint outside the city, on the way to the ruins, is not a concern for the tourists, but I didn't feel the soldiers were as friendly toward the locals who stiffened up when we drove through. One shopkeeper told me the trouble was in San Pablo and the capital, not in Copan. "This place is too small to muster political momentum".

But there is an undercurrent here that (according to Fidel) the people are not happy. They lost their President Zelaya. Another shopkeeper told me new elections would be in two months, as if that would negate the events of a few months ago. I'm not here stirring up any trouble, poking, I'm an observer reporting what I see and hear. I am also being very careful what I say. Maybe I'm reading this all wrong and see things through my own, Liberal, rose-colored glasses. The poverty and deep provincialism of the local people is nothing like I have encountered in other countries. I leave tomorrow and begin a three-day hop back to Costa Rica. My two days here was enough to make sure I use a bus that drives directly to Nicaragua. I am glad to be a United States citizen and treasure the freedom that is extended to me through travel.

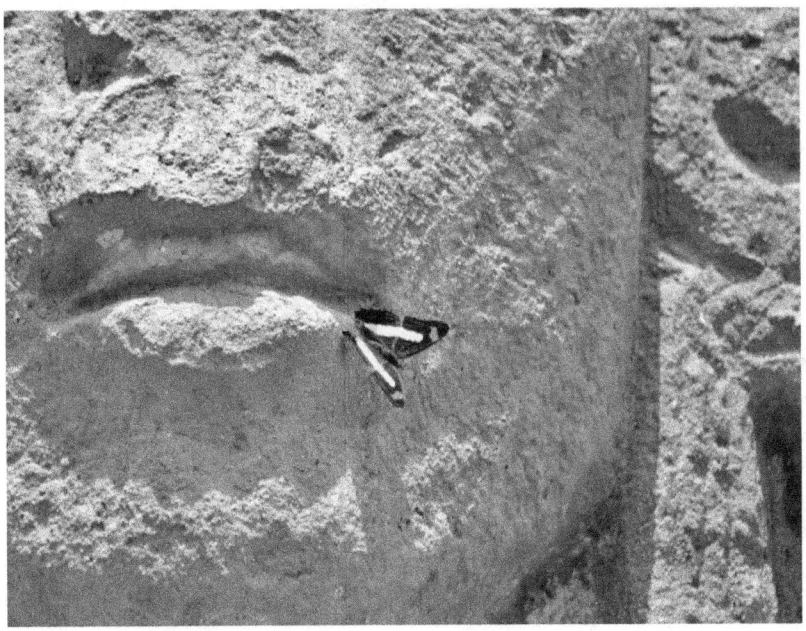

Chapter Fourteen
Guatemala City to Nicaragua

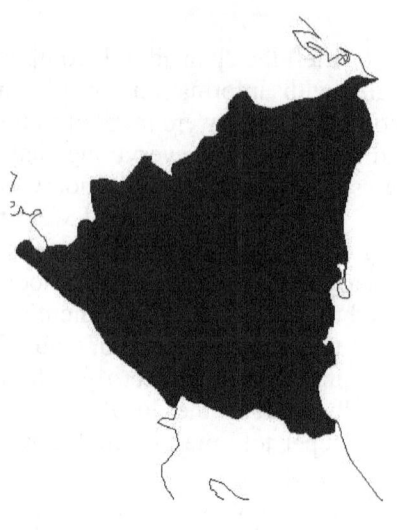

Monday, August 17: I am back at the Hotel Seville in Guatemala City. It is two o'clock in the morning. I am suffering from the usual pre-travel restlessness. Despite taking a sleeping pill I am awake and emotionally ready to leave at four. I slept five hours, more or less. It is surreal here and the bus journey itself is enough to wake me early. I have a thing about missing departures. Maybe a conflict with Diana on the phone has me keyed, but the one strange, surreal fact is a man somewhere within a few blocks is talking into a microphone. I have no idea what is being said because the Spanish is so distorted that muffled words are not being heard clearly, but rather a robotic voice. The short bursts of information are very interfering with my ability to fall asleep. A first, I thought it was a bingo game and the numbers were being called, or even some kind of church where other people, without microphones, give testimonials. The end result is that it is strange and oddly evil. Is he selling something? Is he gathering up political prisoners? Are stray dogs being euthanized?

Diana told me not to write on my computer on the bus because my retinas would detach. I tried to explain that it was like being on an airplane. "My brother (A doctor) once told me never to read or write while driving in a car because it would destroy my retinas."

"Well, I have been writing for weeks now and nothing has happened," to which she answered "Yes, well this is bad for your eyes. And someday don't blame me when your eyes go bad from writing this way." I told her that this to me sounds like more *FEAR BASED* than genuine factual information, but I will continue to write because I enjoy doing so. Somehow (and I haven't the foggiest clue how), the conversation went into me causing her to leave her job. I asked you to leave your job because you were miserable and constantly complaining. *NOW YOU ARE COMPLAINING THAT YOU DON'T HAVE A JOB*. Technically, she is still working until next Friday. First you were unhappy with the job, now you're unhappy for quitting. Your goal is to pass the Praxis test and get a better job." (The Praxis is a licensure test for Speech and language Pathologists.)

She told me she has no gifts for me when she arrives next week in Costa Rica. I said the best gift she could give me is to be happy and stop complaining about not working, not having any money; I will take care of this. Any conversation that gives the slightest whiff of complaint, when she has repeatedly drummed her fear of having no income, makes me feel like she is never going to be satisfied. After all the help I put into her leaving the company, calling the state, contacting lawyers, now she is upset about leaving her employment. I don't have the patience anymore, the honeymoon is over and I become like a pit-bull the instant that kind of self-pity, "poor me, what am I going to do", stuff starts. I can go days without anger at anyone, but the millisecond I sense her acting badly, I become vicious. Maybe it is also that I feel disrespected and what I am offering her is completely invalidated by her attitude. The only thing I asked was she stops complaining, go back to school, and pass the Praxis test. I will cover most of these expenses. With all the interpersonal understanding of her emotional baggage, I still go ballistic when I encounter such negative behavior. This is also the twenty year age difference between us at work. I try to keep it all in perspective; someday she will grow out of this, someday I hope I will mellow more.

When I left the hotel at 3:15 I asked the desk clerk who was using a microphone in the street. He looked blank, shrugged his shoulders, so I looked out the front door and saw a man standing in the back of a white truck. He was standing on a truck full of newspapers giving instruction to other smaller trucks as they pulled up, loaded, and drove away. The mystery was solved, but it didn't make me any happier that this monotone voice droned me awake. These are the kinds of things while traveling that makes it both difficult and educational. How strange could such a thing be for the middle of the night?

At three thirty I pulled up to the bus station after a nice visit with an elderly taxi driver. I told him about the street newspaper microphone, that I thought it was a church, or late night bingo game. We had a good laugh, but he agreed it was a nuisance to the hotel patrons.

Yesterday was one of two days I didn't log entries because of the travel involved. It all worked out perfectly. I left Copan, Honduras and returned to Guatemala City. At almost noon I went to the hotel lobby. Two North Americans women were waiting for the same shuttle. At exactly noon the driver pulled up and I found a safe place for my big bag of Indian fabrics in the back of the van. I climbed into the back seat across from the blonde woman (I never got either ones name.). The other woman was a red head seated in front of me. Two European men and three Honduran women were the other passengers.

The hotel in Copan turned out to be very pleasant. It had two out of doors hallways with rooms along a ceramic tile floor up the middle. Tropical plants with beautiful tall red flowers almost touched the ceiling of the clear Plexiglas as they reached into the passageways space. Between the room and the path were all green gardens, so the open sky was above the plants and a covered walkway protected people from rain. I had the farthest, corner room. I suppose they gave me more privacy for staying two nights. The ceramic tiles squeaked any time someone walked down the path, which was a nice way to know I wasn't alone, but in the mornings the clerks had to get brooms from a closet next to my open window. I am a light sleeper; no one can sneak up on me. The room had a fan, but was so hot that I left the screen door open all the time. I once saw another hotel client in a room midway down the hall, but for the most part I was in a very secluded environment. I came and went all day, all three days, always kept my key, and in many instances walked in and out without ever seeing a soul. This could be an opportunity for robbers. My impression was that nothing had been stolen, nor would be, just because the town was so small. I felt safer there than many places, despite the lack of street police and the gulag checkpoints along the highway.

Before entering the van at noon to return back to Guatemala City, I had promised myself to get up early and paint. By 7A.M. I was out walking the streets looking for subject matter. I found what I wanted and had in mind, but took a walk around the block to see if I was certain. The old, white and yellow church in the plaza seemed like the correct choice. I found a nice shady, low wall, and laid out my instruments. A man sat watching over my shoulder on my right side, then a drunk sat on my left. At first he was quiet, but then began to beg for food or money. The other man and I both were asking him to leave. He continued, and then stood up staring me in the face. The other man sprang into action by jumping into the drunk's space, arms akimbo, and opened his chest muscles like a rooster. He gave him a lecture about not bothering the tourists so they'll want to return. I was a thankful guest as the drunk staggered off. We had both threatened to call the police, but I never saw a policeman in the whole town, only at roadblocks where the military were stopping and searching cars.

As I sat painting in the shade many people came and went. For a brief period of time, three young children sat in front of me talking, then whispering. One picked up a big yellow pencil talked to me about it, and gripped it harder in her hand. The whispering built to frenzy as they plotted to steal the grand, yellow prize. But I was watching out of the corner of my eye and explained I needed the pencil for other art works. It was a peaceful lesson on leaving other's property alone. They soon went off in the direction from whence they came. I had a variety of brushes, paint boxes, single water color tubes, and my plastic bowls for water and mixing. As crowded as it was at times, with spectators, I could keep all my things in full view. The poverty here is terrible. The need to snatch something to sell would have been a meal for some of these kids.

By the time I had painted in the yellow lines on the façade of the church I realized this was going to take much longer. I had two hours and promised Diana I would call her. I collect my supplies and thanked the man who helped me with the drunk. I was back to the hotel, not more than a half block away, and out the door with the laptop and phone. We spoke briefly, and I assured her I would call when I was safe in Guatemala City. The next hour I showered and made sure my bags were all loaded. At five minutes till twelve I turned off the TV, and never saw anyone who worked at the hotel again, only the two women waiting for the shuttle. I left the key behind the counter as we left unnoticed.

The drive was a thrilling, unsafe, tormenting, roller coaster ride up and down, sideways, and especially hard on the tail bone which is still sore from falling in the broken hammock three weeks earlier. The woman knew each other's names, but had only met the day before when coming into Honduras on a

236

shuttle from Antigua. The conversation started out quite lively; where you have been, what countries, where are you going. One woman, the red head, was a nurse. The blonde was unemployed and doing some volunteer work in the villages, she was divorced for thirty years, the nurse was married and had a son, and they both had children. We talked about the Mayan ruins. They had visited a bird sanctuary in Copan as well.

In my usual, yet polite, way I wanted to get a feel for their stands on Obama's health care plan. The nurse was for it; the blonde (who had worked for a company that sold marketing for health providers) was against it. I'm not making this up. The two opposing views sat, one in front and one next to me. The nurse and I went into a lengthy agreement on the need to help those who were without any coverage, how most people would keep their doctors (unless they changed jobs and policies), and how this was so needed. The other Blonde stayed out of the conversation, more or less remaining silent. Maybe they had spoken before because the nurse was full of ammunition.

After a pause I engaged the blonde woman asking point blank why she didn't want health care reform. "Well I have friends from Canada and Columbia, and they have told me about the long lines and waiting periods." "Yes, I've seen the lines in Costa Rica; it can take all day to get helped. But we are the only country in the western world that doesn't have health coverage for the poor." She responded, "I do volunteer work in some clinics (back in the USA) and all those people get help." "But the insurance companies are dropping people, they in turn have huge medical bills, and a large percentage of them have to file bankruptcy and lose their homes." I was trying to get a feel of where she is coming from. Her answer, "I don't know any of those people." (As if this was a myth made up on the news.)

"They want to push through these changes and they haven't even read the bill." "Well the bill is in process, it's not even finished yet". "They have added on all kinds of pork barrels spending." I agreed with her that the bill should be read and that the politics of added "pork" was a horrible part of making bills and caused problems. We had at least met some common ground, but it was clear to me she was getting her information from her political party rather than being analytical. I went on to say that the spirit of what Obama was trying to do was to help a problem that will bankrupt itself if we don't do something now. That my own insurance wouldn't be affected or taken away, but I sure felt the poor needed to be helped. I may have softened her stance a little, but I have no way of knowing. I did see that the two women were not going to engage with each other through me. This is what I see has been happening in my country for over twenty years. The divide has grown and no one seems to be able to listen if someone has a differing view.

There are times I won't engage people who I see as vastly different from myself. In the hotel there was a North American man standing drinking a soda in Antigua. He was going on about China owning the US economy and the debt was going to bankrupt the country. I said we should be helping the poor. I said we should bring Socialism to our country. (I really didn't like this guy, so I was hitting him with both barrels.) "Yah, Socialism like in Cuba?" "There is a vast difference between Communism and Socialism, the people in Denmark and Norway seem to being doing just fine with Socialism." This guy then began talking down to the female hotel clerk. I was finished with him and walked away. But he continued with her, "You don't understand how the system works." "Yes I do" she retorted. I heard enough from this stiff. But when I asked if he voted, "No I don't vote." That was enough and I excused myself only to run into him in the lobby an hour later still going on, only this time he was bending the ear of a couple from Oregon. "My friend and I have opposite views," was all I said to them and passed on through the lobby. If I never knew a word of what he was saying I would have been put off anyway. His loud, aggressive demeanor was obnoxious.

I'll only say the political machinery is now set up to have no compromise. There are issues so deep that the opposing parties are only continuing to leave the needs of the people behind. In that void corporations have had a field day with the environment, special interests, and love the division; for them it makes greater profits. Somewhere between hating government and needed government we have to make it work for all the people, if not we will have another revolution. That would be a mistake.

The shuttle driver dropped off two European guys in a spot that was pretty desolate; they were going to wait for a bus to another part of the country. Wooden shacks with barefoot children selling candy and nuts invaded the open door of the van as they disembarked. A woman passenger from Honduras (whose laugh was exactly like my friend back home, Latifa) bought caramel candy and shared it with everyone in the small van. She asked me in Spanish the typical travelers' questions. She was going to Antigua. There were a mother and daughter sitting between us; they were from Honduras as well. Little did I know these two silent women would become crucial to my plans.

We were on a two-way highway for at least three hours. The land was parched and dead corn was everywhere. I could see this was not corn planted by machine, but hand planted on steep inclines where no machine could possibly go. Cactus were growing in abundance; some farms had cactus fences where the close planting restricted any passage. These were the type of cactus where many arms reached into the dry air, reaching, even crying for rain. This was a desert. The land was filled with low trees and farms where the earth had been scratched to poke holes for corn seed planting. The blonde woman said this is the worst drought in forty years, and the soon-to-follow economic devastation would be hardest on the indigenous peoples who hadn't seen any rain all season.

We wound our way down one mountain range to another. Almost four hours into the trip we came to the outskirts of Guatemala City. Trucks, with colorful lathes tied across their hoods, struggled up the highway. By now we were traveling with three lanes on each side of this super highway. The trucks with their colorful decorations were a "bus" for indigenous people coming from small towns. The trucks had so many people loaded in the back, and passenger seated inside, that the trucks would putt-putt along, just barely making it to the crest of each hill. Our driver passed on the right, left, between, or where ever he could. His goal was to make it a six-hour return to Antigua. His cell phone rang as we passed another car within inches. He would tailgate anything that moved, including large trucks packed tightly with Brahman cows. Manure was everywhere. The cattle's horns almost pocked each other's eyes out.

A motorcycle helmet went rolling down the hill from an accident where the driver had skid off the road. He was all right; the bike lay on its side propped up against a concrete drainage ditch.

We were getting near my drop off point. I was to be dropped in zone 11, and needed to get to zone 10, and then zone 1, where my hotel was. A mother and daughter were also to be left in the city. We hadn't spoken up to that point. But we, all three, were suddenly left on the side of the highway, only to become instant friends with a common task, or more accurately a big problem. The shuttle driver assured us he would drop us with a competent taxi driver, someone who knew the city and could help the women find a good hotel. Picture this; three people on the side of the road, buses passing, pedestrians running across the street, stores with doors wide open and shop keepers leaning out talking to each other, stray dogs barking, and people passing along the sidewalk. The best part, a store selling appliances was directly in front of us, but outside the store's front door were two speakers as tall as me, blaring music at deafening levels. There were two taxis. The shuttle driver handed us off to an old man with a hand painted, royal blue car where the doors didn't completely close and the trunk didn't latch shut.

At this point the three of us suddenly realized there was strength in numbers and our common goal was to get the hell out of there. We couldn't have asked for a worse shaky, environment, couldn't hear each other, or the taxi driver who seemed to understand nothing we were asking. We loaded our belongings into the royal blue dilapidated taxi. The trunk wouldn't close, my big bag was half protruding out the back, he didn't know of a hotel for the two women, and he hadn't heard of the Weston House where I needed to go buy my bus ticket for the morning ride back to Nicaragua. We struggled for a good five minutes standing next to the blasting speakers, yelling in the old man's ear, trying to see if he knew where to take us. As fate had it, the woman decided to get the bags out of the blue taxi and we all moved down the street to where a man stood next to a white taxi.

He couldn't hear us because of the loud music and seemed completely uninterested in wanting to be hired. He stood with one arm stretched across a street sign, crossed one leg, and didn't move; we leaned into his ear yelling our needs.

In our conversation, if you can call yelling a conversation, I told the women I knew of a good hotel that was cheap, but I had to buy my bus ticket first. Suddenly, and instantly things gelled together; the driver, the women, and I all agreed to pile into his tiny white taxi and go to the bus station. I assured the woman they would like the hotel where I had stayed before. We set a price, and the tone of hellish chaos on the street transformed into heavenly, comradely kinship. We had all sized each other up and were about to embark on an hour ride though some of the best sights of the city. The driver knew where the Weston House was, so we had a good start.

The Weston House was the exclusive Hotel where the King of Spain had stayed. I briefly walked through a few days before to use an ATM. We pulled up into the curved drive and a doorman in a brown suit looked down on us like we were riff-raff. I had my two bags stacked on my lap, obscuring all but my head. The doorman said the bus station was at a hotel around the block. We circled around and sure enough this was indeed the same place I had said my good-byes to Robert from Florida. The doorman who helped me wasn't there, but another man soon approached the taxi. We were in the wrong place to buy a bus ticket. He went inside and found us the address, wrote it down, and handed it to the driver. We had to go to another side of the city (zone 8), so I could buy my ticket.

All the "zone" stuff is about the lay of the city. The best way to establish a taxi fare is to tell the driver the zone you are going to. It also has to do with the socioeconomic structure of the classes. If you are rich you live in one zone, poor, another part of town.

I explained to the driver my Spanish was so, so. He said the same was true of him because he spoke an indigenous tongue that few knew, or understood. He was from a town close by, but worked in the city. He started to sing and we all began to laugh and joke with him. He said he had thirty children, which caused my mouth to drop and challenge his truth. Yes, I've been divorced and have thirty children. I think he meant with grandchildren, because he was giving details I could not fully follow.

We got lost in a small neighborhood and asked a truck loaded with police where the bus station was, they soon put us in the correct location where I went bought my ticket. My departure wasn't 6 AM, but 4 AM. This is why you go to buy a ticket in advance, don't believe brochures.

The two women were traveling from Honduras in order for the daughter to go to an eye clinic the next day. The police we got directions from were so nice to us the women commented on their politeness. I asked them if my feelings were correct about the military police in Honduras. "Yes, these men were very bad and bullies", not only because of the political trouble but all the time. According to my guide Fidel, and a German shop owner who is married to a Honduran (where I bought a flag-pin) the town voted for President Zelaya. There was a strong military presence to make sure this little isolated part of the country was in compliance with the new political reality that Zelaya had been ousted. The vibration of tyranny was real. That is why I knew this two-night jaunt would be just enough to test the political temperature, and leave. (I didn't tell Diana I was going to Honduras because the US news channels were showing all the riots there.)

I knew the street where my hotel was. We made our way there in a short time, still conversing and joking, even singing a Catholic song together, which I sort of knew from going to church with Diana. The bellhop knew me and helped me carry my huge bag of fabrics into the lobby. The woman registered first and I asked if the price was ok. Sure! They wanted a place with a restaurant and this was their dream location. They were happy, I was happy; we all had a city tour as the driver named the important buildings, and we sang together. This is why I like to travel; strangers become friends and lifesavers for each other. I can't say I was in any eminent danger; I just don't let myself get into vulnerable situations, or linger long when I sense peril. This all was actually delightful, and we all rejoiced in it. I paid for the taxi and gave a nice tip. The driver seemed double pleased. His fare was less than the first night I arrived when I took the taxi from the hotel. We had driven three times as far. I am so pleased to encounter honesty and the real price. This meek taxi driver shall inherit the earth or at least sleeps with a clear conscience.

I signed in and the porter helped me take my heavy bag to the second floor. After I settled in I called Diana, then she instantly pushed my wrong button. Being so far away is a good thing when I'm angry, yet she feels, and knows, when I ratchet up my fervor through the phone line. It was more of the same disagreement upon which we have become excellent at disagreeing.

Before dawn, I was on the bus and leaving a city I had grown fond of. At the border of El Salvador the agents made me open my locked suitcase, but left the knotted plastic bag alone after seeing it would be twenty minutes to unravel. They asked what the boxed birth control pills were for. I said they were for my wife, so we have no babies. The agent looked like he was going to keep one, and then he returned it after I explained they were for my wife. A plump boy who looked like the son of the border agents was feeling my bag of fabrics, but he put the bag back into the bottom of the bus. If I wasn't keeping a close eye on my things who knows what would have happened. There are simple rules to follow: always be polite, tell the truth, and never do anything stupid at borders. There is no better axiom for travel. Now I am back in San Salvador sweating in the terminal. We had a delay of forty minutes to change a bus due to mechanical troubles.

(Hours later) I have been on this bus all day, passed through three countries, and kept myself content with writing, food, a biography on Einstein, and my mp3 player. There are movies playing in the bus but they don't interest me.

I have a plan in motion. If I get to Managua before the last 8:30 shuttle to Granada I will go there, otherwise I'll find a hotel near the shuttles. A woman on the bus told me where to catch the shuttles in front of the university.

I passed the border into El Salvador, the most populated country in Central America, with the most trash littering the sides of the highway. It seemed to have little farmland and miles of houses along the side of the causeway. As we passed San Miguel I saw the same gas station where I had been dropped off two weeks earlier. The street corner was packed with people standing, waiting for buses and soaking up the heat.

When we passed into Honduras the houses had a Spanish influence with low, terra cotta ceramic roofs. I saw some "track housing" where small colorful, two story homes all stood in rows. The fronts of the houses had a curved turret where the half circle extended up to the roof. This was out of proportion making the rest of the house seem too small. The economic difference between the two countries was immediately apparent. The Honduran side had a feel of antiquity and better living conditions; this was very different from up north in Copan. There were many cone shaped mountains and a fairy-tale-like quality to the small rolling mountains. The military, black boots were present along the highway at periodic checkpoints.

At the Nicaraguan border I was asked to open my bag again, only this time the agent asked me what was in the large roped bag. I said Indian fabrics and ceramics. "Where are you going?"
"Costa Rica". He waved me to put my bags back in the bus, and that was it. This country has the most potential for ecological health. It is expansive; the largest in Central America, very green with few people. There is little, if any trash along the side of the highway, even where houses are standing.

This country could be the most eco-rich country if they prepared for the future with wisdom. I see how important these countries will become for food production as the United States becomes over populated and needs new imports. There are grand flat plains and mountains. The rich soil could become the breadbasket of this hemisphere. If the politics of Costa Rica (with no military) and the richness of the verdant land were combined, this would become a very wealthy part of the globe.

I think of Diana often throughout the day. I have this fear of losing my temper at her behavior. It is such a bother for me to have to contend with her "worried psyche". It is very different from how I have approached life. I have to be very patient with her and make sure this coming week, after her arrival, is a real honeymoon. I have bought many gifts, but told her the best gift she can give me is to not worry. I want us to be relaxed with each other. I hope all the usual pressures of her job won't be there. I hope. She needs to decompress, and focus on her well-being. I wish we had more than a week, but we also have a few days when we return to New York before I go back to work. I need to practice what I preach, and stop worrying as well.

Tuesday, August 18: I have had such a burst of energy, and a race to absorb as much as possible my last day before I return to Jaco, that I am on a natural high. My mental door is open today. I connect with people and feel free. The spirit of all my intentions is good and I feel good: *"On the Road to Shambala"*!

This was the case last night when I arrived in Managua, Nicaragua. The bus ride was good; two British young women on the bus were good company when we briefly spoke. The minute I got off the bus, inside the terminal gate a man came out of the shadows and asked me if I wanted a taxi. He was beside the bus when I took out my two bags. I turned him down because he was asking twice the price. I had been warned by a woman on the bus that told me the price of a cab should be around ten Cordoba's. Unfortunately I was mobbed by a group of tax drivers who all wanted my business as I exited the other side of the terminal at the street. They stood outside the tall, chained link fence and gate of the bus company like a pack of wild dogs, biting at me for a job. The local rule for tourists is often to double the price, not just here but anywhere. I also got the name of the bus terminal I needed to get to. So at the gate, I took the bait from the most assertive cabbie, and was in his cab just to get away from the other hounds.

I gave him the name of the microbus terminal and started off. He engaged me in some small talk and then "befriended me", took me in his confidence, and told me it was extremely dangerous to go to this bus station at night. I knew the buses ran to Granada until 8:30. It was 7:30. At first I said just take me to the bus terminal. He persisted and told me again how there were many thieves in this place at night. I was too tired to think. I asked him if he knew of a hotel near the bus terminal. I took the bait like a big fish and he was letting the line out. He made a few turns and basically went a few blocks from the bus station. I have a keen sense of direction, and I know when and where I am. I am like a butterfly to the magnetic poles; it is really about distance and timing too.

He knew of a hotel that was cheap and safe. From the way he described things I was lucky to be alive right then and there. His name was Alberto. He had saved my life and shook my hand to prove it while introducing himself. We pulled up to a hotel and he helped me unload my bags. It was twenty-seven dollars a night, had Internet (I could call Diana), air conditioning, and was safe. Yes, it wasn't that bad.

The short drive to this place gave it away, that he was going to get a commission. He did. I went to my room, got my phone and computer, and was back to the lobby just in time to see the desk clerk hand him a twenty-dollar bill. I don't think he got that much from bringing me; he must have brought in a few other big fish that day. I removed the fishhook from my mouth and asked the desk clerk to use the computer line. I was offered the cable behind the desk and sat down, picking up the occasional phone calls for the hotel, handing the phone over to the receptionist. On my way back to my room the first taxi driver I refused in the bus terminal walked into the hotel. He shook my hand hello. I don't mind the fact that these people need to make a living; I just hate deception of any kind.

My room was at the far end of the hall. The hotel had people from many countries. A group of five travelers sat in a small patio, laughing, and drinking beer. It was actually a nice place. I just wanted to get to Granada and have less to contend with in the morning. The room had a hot shower, TV, and a window air conditioner that turned itself on and off all night. I had a hard time sleeping, watched US TV for the first time in weeks (David Letterman), and fell asleep to the sporadic buzz of the air conditioner. I was awake at six, had two pieces of toast, thinking I would ditch the taxi driver, Alberto, who had "arranged" an eight o'clock pick up. But he was sitting in the lobby at six thirty. We reloaded the bags and I got to see firsthand the dangers that I had escaped the night before, in broad daylight. It was dangerous, but I could have handled myself.

It was a wild place. The second we pulled in Alberto stopped in front of two microbuses, one had the curtains drawn, so I motioned for the men of the second microbus, that I could see inside, to approach the cab. Before I could get out of the car my bags were taken out and going in two separate directions. I ran up to a skinny young man about twenty years old, grabbed my bag back, and retreated to the microbus where my other bag had already been placed in the front of the windshield. I cursed the young man angrily, and was instantly in the microbus. All my things were safely together. The young man was laughing in a kind of embarrassed, sheepish tone, and then made a gesture to the other men of my microbus. I came to find out that this was the bus jockey for the other microbus company. I wasn't the object of thievery as much as the object of competition between the two bus companies. Someone running off with your bag is a pretty stupid way to greet them and try to drum up business no matter what the compilation is.

This wasn't the end of the dueling. The bus jockeys yelled the name "Granada", tapped people on the shoulders, and got very aggressive in trying to drum up business. They seemingly cajoled many people into their separate microbuses. The two buses would even gun their engines, do false starts, and created this dance of aggression with the vehicles themselves. The first bus pulled away and the bus jockey gave a kind of challenging hand gesture to the other bus. The curtains were drawn so it was hard to tell how many passengers were inside. My bus was almost empty as we pulled out. The bus jockey disappeared out the door. We made a U-turn through a traffic light and ended up across the street from the bus terminal at a stop. There the young man who grabbed one of my bags, and the second jockey who whisked my bags onto his bus, were continuing a yelling match. Both were trying to get passengers onto their respective buses. These competitors weren't the only guys doing this. Big buses were stopping, microbuses were stopping, people were getting on and off, and all the while the jockeys of every transport were aggressively trying to attract customers to their individual buses. It was mayhem!

The two buses did some kind of cat and mouse game, back and forth, the entire way to Granada. When I thought we had lost them they would pass while passengers were loading or disembarking. I witnessed a curious event. I am not sure what it meant, but at one stop a man in an orange shirt with a clipboard, some kind of traffic or bus monitor, stood up and eyed the microbus driver. The driver secretly handed the jockey some money. He in turn secretly slipped it into the waiting traffic monitor. Then an even more curious thing happened. The driver of the microbus made a hand gesture to the bus monitor, some kind of sign to screw the other bus behind us. I have no idea what happened, I don't recall seeing the other bus after that, but we were tooling down the highway at a terrific speed, screeching to halts to release passengers, and then barreling at break-neck speed to the next sudden stop.

I saw a few events while on the bus that caused me to believe the driver and jockey were not so upstanding, as I originally felt befriended when my bags were safely plopped into the microbus. One woman asked to be dropped off at a hospital on the highway. They wouldn't stop for her, but continued onto the next intersection. She pleaded, and protested, and she got angry. When she exited the bus she announced that the next morning she would be taking the other microbus in a snarled tone anyone could understand.

When we were almost in Granada the microbus jockey came up to me and told me I needed to pay more because of my bags. I took my finger and gestured no, and said no three times. He conceded and sat on the dashboard next to the driver. Under his breath he was saying something about the stupid Gringo. I turned to an older man across the aisle and made eye contact, and motioned the universal gesture, finger rubbing, for money. He agreed with me and said I didn't need to pay. Then I said in a very loud voice (In Spanish), "I can understand Spanish fully, but I can't speak it." He and I then began a friendly chat that ended when he exited the bus a few minutes later. I made sure to give the jockey the evil eye and keep him uncomfortable with a long deep stare. I don't like deception and I was getting tired of being treated like a Gringo just because I am a Gringo. This must be because I am the product of the sixties and a desire for equality.

When we pulled into Granada I knew where I was. I wanted to stay on the microbus another block, but I was more or less told to get out there. I could have insisted, but I took the path of least resistance, walked the extra block to enter a familiar place: the Amigo's bed and breakfast. I got a warm welcome from the people who work here, and said hello to the man who's booming voice had awakened me a couple of weeks prior. He is a Cuban named Oscar. I was showered and out the door within an hour. I paid a taxi to take me to the bus station to get a reservation for my pre-paid ticket I bought weeks before in Jaco. It was ten o'clock when I walked two more blocks to wait for the bus to Masaya. I was going shopping again!

I found the correct bus stop to return to the center of town. Three men were milling around, I asked if this was the bus stop. They replied yes. One of the men motioned in his stomach that he was hungry and put his hand out asking for money. "No friend," was my response. I wasn't comfortable there so I moved down the street to the next corner, stopping first in a dark store to buy a cold drink, sitting on the high curb in the shade. A man came staggering up, in a warbling voice asked for some money, first greeting me with a handshake. At that exact moment two other men were walking by. I turned and walked with them. The drunk was still dazed wondering where his prospect had gone. I knew this street from my first time in Granada, towards a further corner was a park with a low stonewall and a church. I sat on the wall in the shade and took photographs. There was no one on the street. Two men lay sleeping in the park. I had moved two blocks away from where the original three men sat. I knew I was safe until I was ready to board the bus.

This time the bus ride to Masaya was very different, before I had traveled there on a Sunday, market day. This time it was a slow ride with few passengers. At the edge of town the bus jockey jumped out and ran up to a time clock, punched it, and returned to the old yellow bus. I later asked him what this was for, piecing together his company had to match a twenty minute schedule from the center of town to that stop. He placed the blue time card behind a huge round magnet that secured the paper to the metal surface above the windshield. Above the driver was another magnet with all the legal documents for the bus. Pretty cleaver, the wind was no problem.

In Masaya the bus passed barbershops where clumps of black hair lay in piles on the dirt floor. The hair was also collecting, in great mounds, outside in the gutter where all was swept. Dogs on short chains guarded shacks. Sometimes the shanties would have a small courtyard, half the size of a car. An occasional dark face would be staring out from the interior, watching the passing traffic which was slow and backed up, as the buses entered the immense dirt field used as the bus terminal. I got out and headed into the heart of the market for the shoe sector.

In the morning Oscar, the Cuban with the booming voice, had asked me to lend him a cable for his camera. He had photographed the owner's daughter's birthday party. She worked part time as one of the receptionists. I lent him the cable. In conversation I said I was going to Masaya. "Can you do me a favor and buy three pairs of sandals like this one". He showed me a low flat brown sandal with punched designs on the exposed surface. "Sure", I replied. He gave me instruction to buy three for 180 Cordoba, no more.

I went to the first booth and found exactly what I was looking for, instantly. I tried to negotiate the instructed price. The girl came down slightly, but refused the price I was offering. She said 200. She called to a sister and asked if 180 was ok. "No, two hundred" was the answer. So I went caddy-corner to the next shop and found three more pair, size 38. The woman there spent a minute trying to help me find the right sandal; there was an entire wall with this particular style, hanging. The price went back and forth until the man sitting at the desk approved the price. I heard a voice directly above me, looking up there was a man sitting on a tiny platform suspended from the ceiling, completely unnoticed until then. Behind him in the ceiling I could see hundreds of shoes piled in disorganization. This was the stock clerk, perched on a security observation deck, and storage facility in a space barely large enough to fit the plump man. He had shoe polish smeared on his face, hands, and clothes. He and I had a good laugh when I asked why he was sitting up in the heavens like God. I asked for a photo and the man behind the desk preened and gave me a handsome smile. I paid for the shoes. He then directed me to the restaurant sector. I was hungry.

A female worker calling out, "Soup, soup", directed me onto a concrete table covered with a red tablecloth. Sun streamed in from thin openings above where the roof separated the tin roof from other structures. The kitchen was behind a concrete wall where big vats of food sat warming. There was no electricity, no gas, and just open wooden stoves. Blocks of ice were chipped away when my drink of cold mango juice was brought to me. One large chunk of ice sat on a counter; this was the whole days' supply. I had rice, chicken, salad, and beans. Several large women worked there, one grandmother sat talking to a man dressed in a blue shirt. I asked him his profession, "Dentist". We dined together conversing back and forth. He had gone to school four years beyond college to enter his profession. His shop was behind the market on a main street I never got to. The grandmother had worked in this eatery for twelve years. She was the matron and her daughters all worked there. They paid a weekly fee to rent the space in the market. At the next table I asked a young man if the woman he was sitting with was his sister, "No, my mother". She liked that I said she looked so young. I thanked them and was off to find more goods. The dentist left prior to me, telling the familiar owner he would be back tomorrow for lunch.

I waited to buy goods in Masaya until my return because I didn't want to lug extra weight until the last minute. I had bought a heavy bags worth of bed coverings in Guatemala, now I was ready to add to my cargo, and that I did; I bought three wall hangings, dickering prices, and another shirt for Diana.

I passed a group of small schoolgirls, asked permission from their teacher and a nun in a white habit, to take a group picture. The children were wonderful and happy to pose. I later passed a shop where the same group was all getting measured for clothes. "Are you buying new uniforms?" "No, we are buying them shirts". "Do the girls live at the school?" I asked. "Yes, it is a boarding school." I took more pictures and asked if they had computers in their school, " N o . None". A minute later, while I sat buying a shirt in the same stall, the entire group returned with a small scrap of paper and several email addresses writing on it. "I will send you the pictures." They were all pleased as punch. (I sent off the photographs a few weeks after my return to New York, receiving a short thanks back.)

I continued wandering the dark corridors of the market. Earlier, I had seen a young man with long dark curly hair and his red-headed buddy in the market. I noticed him because he had a big black bruise and a broken nose. I passed them a second time and struck up a conversation as they priced a t-shirt. "Where are you from?" "Israel." We resumed friendly conversation and they asked me to continue through the market with them. We spent a few minutes talking and stopped at a machete salesman. They were interested in buying one, and curious about the airport security issues that ensue.

I asked the fellow with the broken nose if he didn't mind me asking a political question. He obliged. "What do you think about the wall?" "Well, it is, as you say, a necessary evil. I know the rest of the world sees this as unpopular, but in the last three years there hasn't been one suicide bomber." H e continued, "I know this is bad for the Palestinian people because it is taking their land and causing great hardship, but we need this for security." I r e s p o n d e d, "Every wall that has ever been built in the modern era by governments has always, eventually been taken down." "Yes, this is true, and we hope someday this will be taken down, but for now this is needed."

I thought he gave me an honest answer and the short exchange gave me a different perspective of an issue which I have most often had more empathy for the Palestinian's. I wanted to ask him further about the recent incursion into the Gaza strip, but they were engrossed in their bargaining. "Shalom" and we parted; I was near the bus terminal by this time, and ready to leave the market.

The return ride was equally as mellow. I sat next to a man whose name I couldn't pronounce, nor now remember. He was going to Granada from Masaya to look for work. He asked me for a job, but I explained I was a traveler. His sister was in school to be an engineer, but when asked why he didn't continue school he explained his economics were bad. He had a girlfriend eight months pregnant and his need for a job was urgent. His sister only attended the university all day Saturdays, working a full week in a super market. His spirit seemed down and I wished him all the luck in finding a job that day. He left a few blocks before the small terminal. We waved to each other, I passing my arm out the bus window.

I knew this place from before and wanted to see the main street down a thin dirty alley with drunks and garbage. This must be the roughest place in an otherwise pretty tame city. The open doors of the small houses were dotted with the faces of their destitute inhabitants, who lived without privacy, no personal sanctuary, dignity or a sense of true humanity. This was desolation row.

At the end of the street two old fat women sat with big fluffy aprons over their chests. I asked one where I could buy a watchband, taking out my broken example. She waved me down the street and said on the left side. In a matter of minutes I found a man with a small open box displaying an assembly of products from hardware to watchbands. I held out my watch. He could help me. "This is the best band. The other one is not good." We settled on a price and he was taking the band apart with some tools when I sat down and relaxed in the shade. A shoe repairman was sitting next to me at his sewing machine. I asked him how he moved such a heavy piece of machinery, or did he leave it there every night. He moved the heavy object with a two-wheel cart.

"Do you pay a person to do this?"   "No, he moved it himself all the way from his home." Soon I was trying on the new watchband, it cost me less than a dollar. It needed to be made smaller and he obliged taking out an extra link. I shot both men's photographs thanking them in return. The repairman behind the machine said I should pay him for the picture. "No, you should pay me!" This got a good laugh. He was joking with me in his easy tone, and lack of aggression, or even anger. That was the difference from the people who are serious.

I had a bag of merchandise that I wanted to take to my room, so I continued up the busy street, until I arrived back at the hotel. When I climbed the stairs to my room the clothes I had washed and hung on the railing were laying on the balcony. I picked up my clothes and went to put the key in the door. The door sprung wide open with a slight pressure while putting the key in the keyhole. My heart sank and an instant panic attack ensued. My passport and money were on the bed, the cameras were all there, and my bags hadn't been touched. Things were exactly as I had left them. Strange! If the door was opened had actually any one come in? I turned my attention back to the door, checking the lock, returning outside and pushing on the locked door; it swung wide open again. The deadbolt lock not only didn't function, the gap between the door and the lock was so wide they never engaged. The door latch was so far from the wall half that any slight push on the door opened it. A rush of relief passed through my body like a cold shower.

So I then took a shower, spoke briefly to Oscar to see if he was finished with the camera cable, handed him the shoes, and was back on the street with only my camera and large lens. I went back to the market, waving at the shoe repairman and watchband seller. He joked with me that he was extremely tired from sitting all day. I returned to the corner where the two women had directed me to the watchband merchant and started a long conversation with both of them. They were selling lottery tickets. One woman encouraged me to buy, the other said, "This is a rich man, he doesn't need our lottery tickets, and only poor people buy these tickets." I told them about Diana, my life as a teacher, my student's nationality, and countries I liked.

"And what about Nicaragua?" "They are the best people I have encountered while traveling". I could have been making this up, but it was coming from my heart. There is something extra special in the people of Granada. I don't recall anyone being negative with me. I would approach strangers and they gave goodwill in return. I entered the market and two girls asked me if a third teenager could go to the United States with me. I asked for a picture and was invited to take several. I walked through the market that was about to close. A female street cleaner was sweeping up the organic trash from the days market. As I passed one group of maybe ten people sat playing a bingo-like game. One person quickly called out the cards she was selecting from a deck while the listeners hurriedly placed coins, corn, and bottle tops onto a sheet with a cross section of illustrations. The cards were similar to tarot cards with various real and mythological characters illustrated on them. The "bingo board" with a completed row would result in a winner. The prize, I didn't have a clue what it was (maybe money), nor enough knowledge of Spanish to ask what it was. They all made jokes and I took photos of the cards and hands of the dealer.

A moment later I passed by a pool hall and was invited in by a bunch of young men. I asked for a picture, getting off as many as I could without being too obtrusive. The encounter was less than two minutes long. I was carrying a camera worth more than five years of salary to these young men. One guy shook my hand and I thanked them before leaving. I have a belief that the combination of karma and knowing safety comes in numbers can keep one safe, and never linger long enough to become a target of some unscrupulous whispered plan to mug the Gringo. People are always cordial and I am too. Internal fear is the biggest handicap to travel knowing when a brief encounter is should end is a judgment that falls on the side of safety. This is not just based on lucky chances. It is based on believing that there are more good people in this world than evil ones.

I came up to a woman with a cart yelling at the top of her lungs the name of what she was selling. I said I could hear her "singing" for blocks. "Yes, I am like an opera singer", she boasted with a healthy laugh. The thick milk-like drink was poured into plastic bags with straws and sprinkled with cinnamon; all the while she was chanting the name of the drink to attract buyers. She wasn't put off by my not wanting to buy any. I asked if it were like yogurt. No, but I was still unable to know what it was. Whatever it was milk based. She had a wooden cart with round wooden wheels where old tires had been sliced to fit the rim thus save the wood from the cobble streets of Granada.

I went on the Central Plaza took photographs of the deep setting sun reflected on the domes of the yellow cathedral. The light was getting perfect. My last day in a new place was going to end soon and I walked about with an enthusiasm that verged on exhilaration and ecstasy. I walked thought the park looking for my old friend with the bandaged ear. Instead I heard a voice of someone calling me. It was the schoolteacher who looked like my friend in Bogotá. I asked where his family was. He spends time alone in the park reading most evenings. I asked about the old man and he pointed to the opposite side of the park. I soon found my Van Gogh look-alike, standing as he spoke with two others. We exchanged a short greeting and I was off taking more pictures.

In the park I overheard a man speaking English with a souvenirs vendor.

"I don't trust you!" I stopped, was curious about the English and what might be taking place. They actually knew each other and the Gringo who was wearing dark glasses and a baseball cap said to me, noticing my curiosity, "Oh, I'm just pulling his leg. I've known him for years".

I never got to the bottom of their exchange because he and I were soon sitting next to each other having a lengthy conversation on politics, our relationships with foreign women (Diana in my case), and my life and his. Larry introduced himself with a handshake.

I read somewhere once that we never truly know ourselves, and who we are, unless we have the ability to be alone, that in being alone we cultivate the deep understanding of self. I feel an equally important aspect to living is finding one's self in others. Larry and I had this exchange of spirit. Maybe it comes from craving to just sit and rant off a conversation in English, and hear the all-important political views of those I encounter, but it was very enjoyable to meet a kindred spirit. He is a retired high school teacher, living in Nicaragua for five-week stints, and an ardent supporter of Obama. I told him about my discussion with the (why help the poor?) Gringo in Antigua. We agreed on health care, and the politics of Washington.

"They ought to outlaw lobbyist!" he proclaimed. "Not only that, there needs to be a bill passed that will end the pork barrels, make a bill so it can only cover the single topic at hand and include the line item veto" I added with enthusiasm. What a drastic change from the man who asked me why we should help the poor. Like me there is a substantial difference of ages between our respective mates. Larry is eighty-two; his girlfriend is thirty-six. We had a heart to heart talk about the cultural differences that come with loving a woman from another country. It was a lively exchange of ideas where we had agreement on almost everything. I gave him my email address and phone number. He lives an hour away from me, in Connecticut.

It began to rain and I made a quick, paced strut to the street grill that sells papusas. I bought my two papusas and headed back to my room for the nightly news, sitting in front of my fan cooling off the food and myself. It was hot; the further south in Central America one goes the heat increases. I was back in the lobby to call Diana when Oscar came up to me asking for help, again, with the camera and cable. "I can't get the cable to move the pictures from the camera to the computer." Oscar has a thick Cuban accent; sometimes his accent, or incorrectly used words, causes me to ask him to repeat what he says. So we have a mix of my bad Spanish, his bad English, and our mutual will, to get things done. He has been in the hotel for over two weeks and got involved with the daily running of the hotel. He will clean breakfast plates off tables, or go to the market for the cook. He's a handyman at heart, actually a retired plumber on disability. In my comings and goings our paths have crossed many times and our level of comradely has grown. I told him about the door-lock and he was on it, instructing the owner she needed to fix it. (He would have, but he was leaving the same day as me, in the morning.)

The first thing I noticed about Oscar was his deep smoker's voice reverberating throughout the entire hotel from the room above. I was now in the room he had occupied, down the steps, and to the far lobby, where he had his morning cigarette. His coughing, booming coughs, woke me the first morning. His cigarette smoke drifted all the way back to the upstairs because the hotel is half buildings and half garden, despite the open-air lobby the smoke wafts its way throughout, then out of the complex to neighboring buildings.

The most frequent topic Oscar and I discussed, many times, was my phone and the input jack. "Yes, I can call anywhere in the world, as long as the other party has a computer and the input jack. Or I can call anywhere in the USA for free, from anywhere in the world with this jack". (I'm not into product endorsements!) Oscar was fascinated and wanted to buy one, so I told him where, the price, and the eventual subscription fee that came after one year. Oscar isn't a computer guy so I eventually had my computer and physically showed him the way it works. He lives in that time frame where computers are a strange, obstructive device, designed solely to bring frustration to the user. (Diana is just coming out of that state of being. Many times I have had phone calls from her asking me what to do when on the computer. But the ultimate mastery of the computer has more to do with the emotional state of mind of the user than the computer. Tell this to anyone who is beginning and they haven't a clue. I call it the "Zen of Computers" because the goal can only be achieved with meditation-like patience.) Oscar has a brother in Costa Rica and he wants to save money with this device by calling him on the computer.

I knew by the way he wouldn't listen and kept turning on the camera the wrong way that his computer knowledge is limited. He is a big loud, strong man who's assertiveness can be put-offish to people. But this energy is terrific if dealing with the physical world. He had a half smile, a big build, and red hair that made him seem unfriendly at first but he is a friend to anyone, if they can get beyond his thick skin and loud voice. I grew fond of him and felt like I would hope to see him again sometime. This has happened to me many times, this is also how I have cultivated global friendships. An aspect to this that isn't as convenient when traveling alone. It is easier to approach people as a solo traveler. I also am needier as a single voyager, which pulls me toward others. Oscar, the receptionist, and I all stood at the computer choosing what pictures to add. As they both looked on I gave a small lesson on how to locate the camera on the computer, creating files in the computer.

While at the dining room later on a wild, shirtless Spaniard with a thick strand of beads struck up a conversation with me. He was visiting the entire Western Hemisphere, soon to go to San Francisco, and then New York. I was torn between just talking or writing, so I created an exit by telling about my first book, then second book, pointing to the vacant computer on the table. Oscar came by and gave me a large glass of cold water, but I avoided distractions. The next day I needed to be up at six for a seven o'clock departure.

Thursday, August 20: After yet another sleepless night, I resolved to rise and shine, despite the sun's absence. It was three-thirty. I had a tense night and always fear sleeping through a wake up time. This is a completely unfounded fear that has never happened for at least twenty years. I wake well before the alarm clock and can't go back to sleep. I tossed until four-thirty and got up to shower, and turned on the TV news. No one was in the room next to me on the balcony so I opened the door and let the fan pull cool air into the space. I was carrying my bags down at 5:30 when Oscar was up having his morning cigarette.

"Do you want me to ask them to make you breakfast?" "Sure, I thought the kitchen didn't open until seven." "No, today they are making breakfast early for some other people. I will tell them for you too." So an unexpected breakfast came with the help of my friend. I sat at the big round table in the lobby where a fan mounted on the ceiling, circled and cooled the room. My room was vacant, my three bags were in a row on the floor in front of me, and I had an hour before I needed to leave.

The people who were leaving early were a family from China who now lived in Vancouver, Canada. I had met the mother the previous evening because she couldn't get her wireless computer to work. I apologized it was because I had to unplug the antenna/modem in order to use my phone. This started another series of questions about the phone, leading into "where are you from". She and her husband had relocated to Canada at the time of the hand-over of Hong Kong to Communist China. I told her about my visit to Hong Kong and Schenzen. I asked her about her family. She, her husband, and two teenage sons were traveling in Central America. In the morning our paths crossed again and she asked me about the bus company, route, and time schedule. They were leaving on a local bus near the rear of the market, heading to the border, renting a car, and going to visit Costa Rica.

I took a cab to the bus station where six people sat on the stairs waiting for the door to open. At six thirty it did. A sleepy clerk who had confirmed my reservation the day before was rubbing his eyes allowing the passengers to pass into the rows of chairs inside and in the shade. The sun was already hot on the skin. A tall hefty Gringo with dyed hair was sitting on stoop. "Where are you going I asked?" He sized me up and in a near whisper said, "Jaco". "I am too. Are you getting off at Barranca?" to which he replied, "yes, a buddy is picking me up." "Do you think I could ask him if he can take me along?" He seemed to be so timid I wasn't sure if it was out of mistrust, or just that he was a quiet man. The latter proved to be the case when he said, "I'll ask him when we get there. I don't know how much room will be in the car." He was a man of few words, so I turned my attention to the street and the car wash next door where a brand new police truck was getting buckets of water thrown, scrubbed by hand, and looking perfect by the time the three policemen pulled into the street. Mothers and fathers walked their uniformed, well-dressed children to school, horse drawn carts with drivers clicked their cheeks to encourage the animal, and life in the city was waking for a day of labor. More passengers filtered in and at three minutes after the hour the bus pulled in.

The two borders crossings were a strange cross-section of a nuisance and necessity. On the Nicaraguan side we had to exit, stand around, and re-board the bus. This took around twenty minutes. It gave me time to use a restroom where the pipes were not working but a large barrel with water was put next to the sink for washing hands. A plastic milk carton with a handle was cut open and served as a pitcher. The soap dispenser was working fine.

As I stood there I struck up a conversation with a tall, thin German lad. I began by asking if he was Swedish, "No, but I lived there for a year".

We spoke with great fervor for the short time we had. We bypassed the quaint formalities and went directly into politics. He had spent time in Cuba and was intrigued by their system of wonderful education and hospitals, but contrasted by abject poverty.

I was interested if he knew about the current "health care debate" in the USA. He said it seemed ludicrous to avoid this issue when the health of the people was a basic need of any civilized country. Bush came up, and he told me how damaging this man had been for the prestige of the country. We had a brief chat about the German political system and how the recent coalition governments made the party differences pretty much indistinguishable.

`"At least they are working together, unlike your country." We saw things pretty much eye to eye. I continued and asked what he thought about Internet freedom being challenged.   "It is impossible to control the Internet, nor should it be." I added my concern about the abuse of young children through pornography.   "Well oddly enough it is the people who are for the free and open Internet who are helping track down these people."

Our bus was leaving so we went from sweating in the humidity to shivering a on freezing bus.

"From the oven into the freezer", I said to a few people as we reseated ourselves.

The border was a strange mixture of trash, chained link fences, and nature. It was a no-man's-land where the trash came from, I had no idea. On the Costa Rican side we disembarked and were directed to a long line in the sweltering heat. I saw the Chinese woman from Vancouver, yet again and tapped her on the shoulder. She was alone on line in front of me alone. Her husband and two sons soon cut in, with one son complaining about the heat in perfect English, while his mother's accent was very prevalent. He struck me, as being spoiled while his parents must have worked off their finger's to get into Canada. She in fact told me her sons didn't like trips because of all the trash.   "Well, there is trash in China, as well". For an awkward moment I felt I had crossed cultural line of criticism.   "I mean it is a very clean city because there are constantly people sweeping the streets, but there are sections that are just as dirty as New York City, I said trying to deflect my opening and be diplomatic. She then asked me many questions about travel in Costa Rica. They had a rental car waiting. I suggested they not drive at night, that the highways were full of people walking in the road. We then went into a mini-tour describing what I knew about the country. I suggested Jaco, of course.

The line began to move sporadically after five and six minutes in rapid bursts, and then endless pauses. By the time we entered the building the Chinese woman was cut off from her husband and sons. The policeman wouldn't allow the husband to pass. He was frantically waving his arms yelling, "We are family. We are family". The policeman would have none of it. This kind of excitement was only met with a firm but polite extended arm telling him to stop and go back where he was. It made me laugh to myself. The policeman saw I was with the woman, but perhaps he was thinking the man was saying I was in his family too. I just know the woman relented and returned to be with her family.

That was the last I saw of them as I entered an air-conditioned room. I had been there before on my way into Nicaragua, only this time I was in a line on the other side of the room. Two doors were wide open and the line moved as a plain clothed man asked for the health questionnaire, I had filled out while on the bus. He was stopping almost all the people, when he came to me; he looked at my form and waved me on. I had passed inspection! I filed it out correctly. The most important line is 'where will you be staying in Costa Rica'. If you put hotel, they want a name, and an address. It was so humid an air conditioner mounted in the ceiling was dripping water on the floor. The chilled air exiting the machine was creating a fog. I am serious. It was so hot the cold air was creating a microclimate. The man behind the glass partition stamped my passport twice, stopping to look at all my entries into Costa Rica and giving me another stamp after his pause. He shrugged his shoulders in apology. Outside, moneychangers with fist-sized bulks of bills waved them to attract business.

While on the customs line, the strangest incident occurred. We were instructed to remove our bags from the bus and bring them to a waist high platform, built out of long narrow boards with spaces between. The inspection table was about the length of a bus. We stood, and stood, and stood in the heat, dripping with sweat, looking forward to the deep freeze of the bus even if it would form icicles on our noses. A British woman in front of me told me she had seen the customs agent sitting in his small room through an open door. He sat there for twenty minutes while we roasted, then came out to inspect. The inspection was a hand wave from right to left, motioning those he passed to take their bags back to the bus. He asked the British woman what was in the box.

She said, "Ceramics" and he waved her on. I had my huge bag wrapped in ropes, many, many ropes. "Is this yours?" he asked the British woman.   "No, it's mine," I answered.   "Ok" and he waved me through.

An American from the bus depot, going to Jaco, was behind me in line. The inspector stopped and left the line, thus leaving him and all those behind him wondering where he went. I don't know. By the time the American got to the bus to load his bag I was joking with him that I could have had dynamite, and they wouldn't have known. No one's bags were opened, only brief questions, and then waved on. Back in the bus we drove into the country, passed what looked like a strange mixture of poverty and modernization; new shiny trucks sat parked in front of shacks with no paint.

Eventually after the border houses were built in thick groups and began to look more like neighborhoods. The structures thinned giving way to verdant, filled with trees and thick undergrowth. I was back in Costa Rica!

Maybe ten minutes after the border crossing the bus stopped. I looked out the window at a police checkpoint. This was a small building with a man sitting inside writing; another man stood outside and ordered the bus jockey to open the belly of the bus. He did, and inspected the first compartment where there were no bags. The bus jockey then entered the bus and called out the tag number of a bag, describing it was a black suitcase with a lock. He was barely audible from the noise of the bus and music. Some people began to scramble for their receipts and eventually a woman left the bus. She came back a minute later. I couldn't see the process from my seat because the second compartment door had been opened, blocking my view. The jockey returned and yelled out a second number. No one responded with several attempts, so he came to the center of the bus. In Spanish he was giving a description of a bag. My receipt was buried in my backpack somewhere, but I could tell it sounded like my bag from Chichicasanando. Does it have "ropas?" I asked, making a hand motion to indicate ropes? (I misspoke. This mean clothes.)At the same moment I realized there is no such word as "ropa" for rope, but for cloths. No matter, it was my bag, so I exited the bus. The younger of the two policemen had already removed half of the ropes. But I had secured two more nylon ropes. He was still unraveling the first set of ropes around the bag. He began to question me what was in the bag. "Blankets, ceramics, a wooden masks, and fabrics", I said in Spanish. He asked again and what they were for. I repeated the same as before and adding in Spanish, "Gifts for my family, for birthdays, Christmas."   "What else", he asked.   "Nothing, things for my house." He asked me twice if I was in business or selling these things. "No, for my house, for my family." The older man was standing behind my shoulder; I didn't really pay any attention to him. He was directing the other policeman to ask some of the questions, but I was not focused on him at all. Suddenly, the older man abruptly ended the questioning, and directed the young policeman to order my bag back into the bus. The ropes hadn't been removed any further, and the actual bag was never completely open, just unzipped enough to see the top blanket. I had nothing to hide and their system of questioning with a second person off to the side proved to be an effect method. I was telling the truth, thanked the policeman and returned into the bus.

As I was returning to my seat a young woman from Boston joked with me, "Oh, it's your fault!"   She and I had spoken briefly while in the customs line. She was complaining that Costa Rica was the only country that had us take our bags out of the bus and stand around waiting. "Well, there is a lot of smuggling in this country", I said somewhat defending the process and shifting the conversation to where she was from. "I live in California, but I'm from Boston."

"How about you?"   "I am from Nebraska, but live in New York." This continued into further details about who each of us was and where we lived. So by the time I came back on board the joke was half about me defending what had taken place ten minutes prior at the border. Outside the older policeman sat inside his booth again, writing down a note about the two inspections, which produced nothing. We were speeding down the highway again.

I showed a young man next to me my art after he told me he enjoyed to draw. I was typing on my laptop most of the way, breaking off to converse with him now and then. He was going back to work in Costa Rica from Nicaragua. I had met his young niece that morning while sitting on the steps of the bus company in the hot sun. She ran up and hugged him. I asked her if he was her father, "No my uncle". She had a small conversation with me while her mother and uncle talked. She was in her uniform and about to go to school. I told her I was a teacher and it was very important she study for good grades. I enjoyed speaking with her and noted to myself an American mother wouldn't allow her daughter to speak to a stranger or ask where I come from. The uncle, next to me, had all the right work permits for living in both countries. It is very common for Nicaraguans to work in Costa Rica and send money home. The relationship is much like that of Mexicans working in the USA and sending money home. The standard of living is so much higher right across the border that many "Nicas" illegally enter Costa Rica for work. And just like my country there are people who (stupidly) look down on those less fortunate.

I was getting really tired of pecking my computer on the bumpy bus ride. It was a slow, tedious method to keep things working correct, almost erasing my entire work a few times. I was just at the end of my patience when the bus pulled up to my stop. The big American motioned me it was our stop when I looked at him a few seats back. My computer was stuffed into my backpack; I shook the hand of the man next to me, moved my hand over the rear of my seat and shook the hand of the German in the seat behind me, gave a nod to the British woman, and passed out of the cold into the heat. The same man selling drinks I had seen weeks before was yelling-out his wears to the open windows of the local busses as they stopped. I was thinking to myself how I had traveled all that time, seen so many people and this man was doing the same thing day after day. I also realized he wouldn't have known me, or ever possibly remembered me, yet I did him. I saw myself in him. When I return to my job life will be routine and I will become invisible to the world again. At least to the world "out there", as I say.

A woman and two children asked us to share a taxi to Jaco, but we declined and explained we had a ride, we were not sure if there was room in the car or not. I asked the silent American how long he had been living in Jaco. "Seven years." He seemed to explain his silence by telling me he was diabetic and had a splitting headache. I was a bit surprised he had disclosed personal information. The ride he had arranged was not there at the bus stop. On is cell phone he made a few calls and established a replacement pickup. We were to look for a gray car.

Twenty minutes later a gray, low-rider with black lightning bolts painted on the sides, and roaring pipes, pulled up. Two young men sat slumped with their head barely visible. My American buddy had become friendlier by now. I think he was glad to have company while standing on the side of the highway. Taxis' and cars alike propositioned us. "You need a taxi?" One car looked like the two men inside would have slit our throats and taken our money. (I'd like to exaggerate for the thrill of the novel, but it may have been true.) A sudden bond of trust was building as we stood waiting.

The car these young men drove was a race car and they needed to prove it. They also needed to prove their early manhood and drove back to Jaco at speeds that split our lips. The quiet American told me he was the manager of the local, popular prostitution bar. We discussed a few minutes more, but his being seated in the front and the sound of loud pipes was too much. It began to rain, but this only slowed the driving slightly. I sat in the back seat with one of the young men and we smiled as the music drowned out any possible conversation. My long journey ended with Eric, the security guard at the condos, looking shocked and dismayed at the car as I emerged from the back seat. I was home, too exhausted to explain myself arriving in a strange car with three unlikely, and dissimilar, passengers. I lugged my gear inside the gate, put things in the house, and soaked my well-traveled bones in the swimming pool. I was home at last!

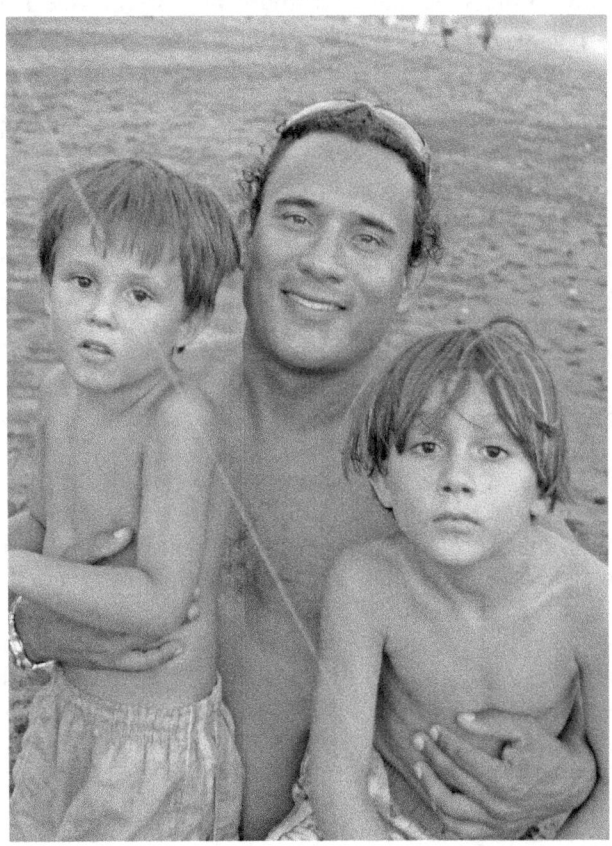

Chapter Fifteen
Costa Rica

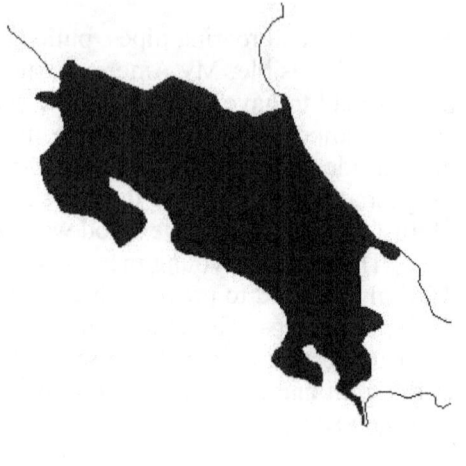

Saturday, August 22: My first night back home in Jaco I was in a kind of stupor. I sluggishly unpacked my bags, except the one with all the Guatemalan Indian goods. I want to do this with Diana. I had no memory of what I actually bought and want to share the surprised with Diana. I watched TV and my "Gee, I'm back home now what?" funk set in. I was bored just as I knew I would be. There is a type of readjustment that must take place, but I didn't help things by doing little else but watch television. I should have been writing; instead I lay in bed for hours unable to sleep, mentally skating through where I had been and what I would do tomorrow.

On my way to the supermarket while riding my bicycle I passed Johnny, the young man I hired a few years back to help me repair some walls. Johnny was at the side of the road mixing concrete at a house adjacent to a small river. Johnny is a thin, boney man in his late teens. He has black hair and deep set eyes that seem to beg for attention. He has a girlfriend and a daughter. They live with the extended family in a dirt floor shack not far from where I live in Jaco. We exchanged greetings. I stopped to shake his hand hello. I asked him if he could work for me next week. The thought of getting someone to help me do some painting had crossed my mind the day before, so here was my solution. He was leaving Sunday to do some work in another city. I had one day before Diana's arrival, so we arranged to have him come Friday morning at seven. Despite his good work I was weary of hiring him since he had a habit of showing up when he chose instead of the agreed time. His late arrivals were a topic of concerns and Diana and I often discussed the role of being a teacher with patience versus a cop with a curfew.

I keep a bicycle in Jaco. It is yellow, has fat tires an added basket to carry groceries and such. I have painted it yellow and plastered stickers of the Hindu deity, Ganesha, on the cross-bar. I christened it 'The Yellow Submarine'. While out running a different errand on my bicycle I saw Johnny again, this time asking if his girlfriend wanted to clean the house. He had seen me in April, asked if I needed him, and also offered her as a possible house keeper. So I killed two birds with one stone. I was going to clean the house myself for Diana's home coming, but I moved my house painting plans up from next week. I would hire his girlfriend, and complete a project that would have cut into my time with Diana.

Johnny had a daughter a few months old when we first met. He had not shown up for work one day and I fired him. I depended on him and his irresponsibility was a bad sign. Jaco is small town and I had seen him from time to time. He seemed to be loopy a few times I ran into him, and I was wondering if he was smoking pot or drunk. I just knew he had lost me as a customer, so his subsequent request for day jobs was dismissed during our brief encounters. This time he was working and appeared sober so an opportunity for both of us arose like a gift from above.

We live our lives in harmony with "God" or the universe, but no one is "pulling the strings". The deity, or Goddess as Fernando would say, is living within us all, not the heavenly father with a long white beard! So what we make of our lives in our choice.

Of course, I questioned myself about the appropriate tax ramifications. If I ever run for President or Congress this may come back to haunt me, hiring a person for a day job needs to follow strict labor laws. I will need to file this, claim him as an employee, and make sure I make the correct tax equations. I say keep the government out of my life! This is the very thing that makes me say, "Big government is bad. Why should Washington be like big brother? We don't need taxes, they only go to help a bunch of illegal immigrants that come to our country and milk the system. In fact, these illegal dark-skinned-different-from-me-south-of-the-border "people" (We should build a wall to keep them out.), are only here to break the law, run drugs, and create gangs." (I actually heard this conversation once in the steam room of my gym.) Thank the Goddess I'm in Costa Rica and I can hire Johnny legally! (Actually US tax laws don't apply in Costa Rica and I made this all up to sound like a Republican. Did you believe it?)

Johnny and Fabiana, showed up at seven twenty. I was up at six thirty preparing the house for being painted. We all dove into separate projects. I know Johnny's work mode, so I gave him the task of painting the roof with a roller. I painted the bars of a "cage" above my patio I had built five years ago. Time and the elements had worn the addition to the houses designed to deter burglaries. By two thirty Fabiana was done working, paid, and out the door. Johnny continued until he complained of a headache at four o'clock. I was still painting the front porch to have an extra homecoming shine for Diana.

I was in the ocean cleaning all the paint thinner off my body at five, playing in the surf with Jose, Khilani, Eligh, and Laura. We all watched the sunset together.

Some new neighbors next door are from New Jersey. We took an instant liking to each other. I offered them my ladder to fix the rain from seeping down the face of their house. I showed them my repair job, and explained my methodology. There are no gutters, so an extra shelf of aluminum retains the water.

Saturday, August 29: I am once again in the airport at the end of another summer and a wonderful journey. Diana arrived a week ago and I haven't been writing once. We spent days going to small towns and to the National Park, Manuel Antoine. I need to learn to balance marriage and my creative time better. I find myself enveloped in my relationship focusing time and energy on her, on us, putting my writing aside. I have plenty of time to write or paint when I travel alone. When I am with Diana, she comes first and "I" become "we".

We were in a kind of funk the last two days. I felt like I was in a box and wasn't very pleasant to be around. This only worsened her attitude and we were not good to each other. On top of this we waited all day yesterday for Jose. We made plans to go to the beach and they never came to fruition. This happens more often than not. He doesn't come by to tell us that things have changed, he just leaves the condo compound, and we are left to figure out things for ourselves.

My relationship with Diana is going through a growth that is not always pleasant. We have a lot to work on. My patience is too short and her expectations are too great. I know we have a good relationship, it is just not easy to keep the communication on a level it should be. Much of this is due to the language difference, but I also think she is so independent that she fails to realize that a simple thing like walking down the street, or crossing the street, is something that works better if coordinated together. I get frustrated when we go for a walk and she always ends up a half block behind me. She says it's because she has short legs, but I have seen her with other people and she makes an effort to keep up.

She started to complain about not having a job the first day and I went nuts. She quit her job, came down here to be on vacation with me, and began to regret her decision right away. It is easy to find troubles to make one worry and not to be at peace.

The last encounter I had with tourists was the day I arrived back in Jaco. I met a young German couple swimming at sunset. They had just arrived that day. I warned them how the surf was rough but usually not dangerous. As we all sat talking there were small sand crabs biting us. We said good-bye and we hoped to see each other the next day at the shore.

Two days later and I was at the beach with Diana, Jose, and Laura. The tourists passed by and I called them over. They sat with us for a brief visit. They had missed their bus that morning and decided to stay another day in a different, cheaper, hostel. This time I had a pencil and gave them my email address. They'd like to visit New York someday, so maybe they will write me. That was the last time I had a chance encounter with anyone like a trekker. I did see Mike the quiet American man in the taxi whom I met on the bus from Granada, but just long enough to say hello while I passed him on my bicycle.

We had a great summer. I fantasize about having a job where I do nothing but travel, but honestly that would become stale just like teaching can. I have the better of two worlds. I can keep my politics and my profession together, and have little to compromise at this point in my life. The compromises come in my personal life. As much as I think I have grown within our marriage I know I have much more to learn. I feel so grateful to have the gift of traveling and seeing the world. As much as I see differences in cultures I can't help but begin to see those characteristics as the surface features of each soul. While digging deeper into the top soil of humanity I find us all so similar that a great question comes to mind. Why do people insist that the differences are more important than the similarities? It seems half the world is aware we live on planet Earth, the other half still living in their homes, neighborhoods, state, or country. I believe we will make this place heaven on earth, eventually.

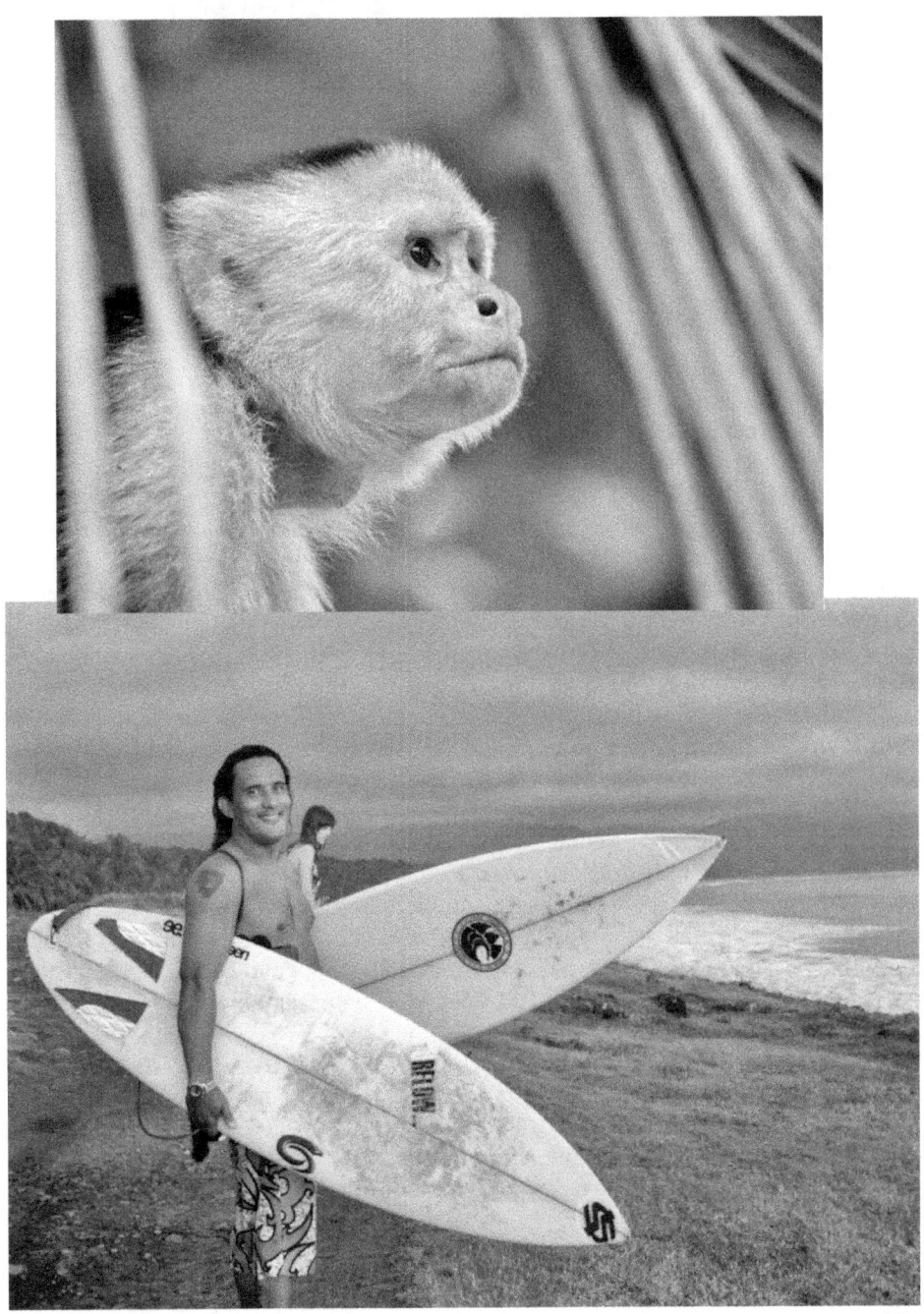

Chapter Sixteen
Costa Rica/Colombia

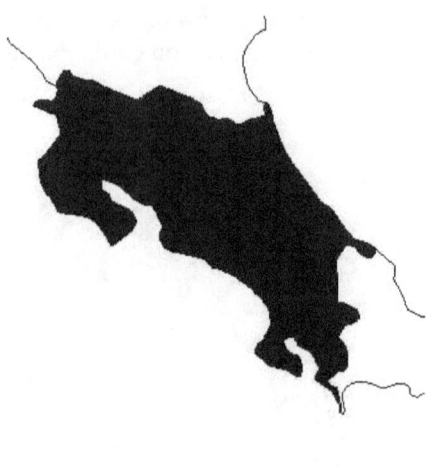

February 20, 2010: Again, we are sitting in an airport about to leave Costa Rica for New York. Six months have passed since my last visit with Jose, Laura, Gloria, Khilani, and Eligh. There has been a six day lapse in my writing of this book. I did nothing and felt wonderful about it. The deadline for this book is "whenever". When I do the final draft my work pitch will increase and I will be sucked into the project like a leaf in a whirlpool, but for now I have a relaxed approach.

For more than twelve years I have been going to Costa Rica, at first for week long vacations. Each time I went I magically rendezvoused with Jose. Our paths crossed in unplanned ways until we made it a point to enjoy each other's company. He moved into the same condominium complex without even knowing I had a place their as well. But even before that I would see him and Khilani on the beach, and run into them in the supermarket, almost daily. Jose and Khilani's mother (Nina) split up, but long before that I was like an uncle. I watched Khilani grow up from a baby in his mother's arms to a toddler sharing his father's surfboard. When Jose moved next to me I became the lifeguard in the swimming pool, or the one to pick him up when he scraped his knee on the skateboard. A light knock on the door, morning, noon, or night was little Khilani wanting to paint, play, watch television, or get some food.

When Eligh was born the two of them became inseparable. Eligh looked like a smaller duplicate of Khilani. If it weren't for the missing tooth in Khilani's smile it would be hard to tell them apart, other than the apparent size difference. They both had bowel haircuts, bleached blond hair, and golden skin from the mix of their North America mothers and Jose's dark Costa Rican complexion. Eventually it came to be that Khilani would call me 'grandpa'. He never knew his real grandfather. My gray hair and fathering instinct put me in this category in his little eyes.

The biggest change to this visit was the death of my little friend, Khilani. The loss occurred over a month ago, a few days after Christmas. I immediately went through the initial stages of shock and disbelief. I couldn't reach Jose but I did reach Nina, Khilani's mother. It was heart wrenching and I couldn't keep from crying; so much so, that long periods of silence on the phone had to be explained. He was tragically run over by a small truck while on his bicycle. Nina was on a bicycle a few yards ahead of him, turned to see him being crushed. I don't know much more than that. To see your only child killed within your sight must be an unfathomable loss. I tried to comfort her, yet within myself I was tormented by this news. I missed the memorial. A group of over four hundred people gathered on the beach in Jaco where they spread his aches and said prayers. Understandably it was very sorrowful.

I had known Khilani since he was an infant of only three months. For the past five years we lived in the same complex of condos. He was in my house much in the same way my own child would be, eating, watching TV, and drawing Transformer cartoons. I had Christmas gifts ready to bring for him when I received an email from Laura with the bad news. I always brought him Spiderman toys. So a big part of my time in Costa Rica was watching him grow and having fun with him. Jose, Laura, and Khilani had moved out of the condominiums a few months earlier to a less expensive place on the other side of town. Jose has been unemployed for almost a half year, so he was forced to tighten his economic belt and find a rental house within his budget.

After Diana and my arrival back in Costa Rica, Jose and I talked when were at the beach our first night. As usual we had a spontaneous, unplanned meeting just before sunset. He was there to surf for the first time in over a month. He had been working on a sports fishing boat in the south, by Panama. I was there to use my boogie board. We hugged like two brothers. It was a long, long hug that was punctuated with a kiss on the cheek. We had a conversation about Khilani and his tragic passing. I had spoken to Jose a few times since his sons' death, but this time we were face to face. His strength amazed me. He was not grieving, but rather accepting that it was Khilani's time to leave us. Jose was keenly aware of his, mine, and all of our mortality. I attribute this to Jose's deep spiritual insights rather than a cultural attribute to his country. Jose's references to nature often lead me to believe his connectivity to the ocean is not a typically Costa Rican way of thinking. Where his son went, we all go. None of us has a choice, so we need to love all we can the short time we are here. I didn't know how I could have held back tears when I saw Jose, but the conversation was sober and uplifting. Jose has become increasingly important to me because we talk about things that make life real. There is no nonsense between us. I thought it more important to let him talk than to fill the air with my words. Hearing him express his son's death as a purposeful event and as a lesson in love was inspiring.

"He is back where he came from, one with the universe. He is still with us in love." I don't know how I would handle a son dying, but Jose's words and actions certainly taught me a lesson about dealing with great loss.

Jose is a spiritual man who weights the consequences of daily life and how living a good life is our essential purpose. I admire him greatly and our bond has grown much deeper over the years. Part of that bond was his son Khilani and the time we all spent together. As Khilani grew I used to think he would grow up and remember his childhood with me. I looked forward to knowing him know me. Maybe this is my ego but to lose him so early in his life felt that part of my own history dissolved and become empty. We don't love with the intentions of getting any of it back, but we do expect a kind of reciprocity or equal treatment from the universe. We feel cheated of the imagined future when a child dies. Khilani's love was perfect and unconditional. He was giving, honest, and warm towards all people. I also saw recklessness and a wild side that often caused me to wonder how much trouble he might become to Jose when he was older.

He visited me in a dream one night although he didn't show his face to me. I was teaching a child how to draw, like I often did with him. I was giving some minor instruction and really just playing at art as I would with any child. In the morning I knew it was Khilani coming one last time to say good-bye. Jose told me of his dream the night he died. Khilani was with him saying he didn't want to go. Jose told him, rather instructed him, that he must go back and be good. Khilani was obedient. Like a fog lifting, he left us and we all realized how his presence was love we would dearly miss.

His laughter in the condominium complex always gave the environment life, now the silence without his voice is sadly empty. The condominiums didn't have his cheerful calls coming from the swimming pool beckoning us to join him. No one was knocking at my door wanting to come in and play or watch TV. Jose had moved his family a few months ago while I was back in the States. I knew he wasn't living there anyway, so I used that to buffer the loss. I missed Khilani and his little brother Eli coming over to ask for a drink, or to share playtime. I feel sad for Eli not having a big brother also growing up, growing past the age of his older brother, always having a faint memory of someone older who was there for him, to help, guide, and protect him. We all die; not discussing and accepting death is what causes so much pain. If we accept our own mortality, death isn't so drastic, but more importantly we understand a need for tenderness while here. We join those who died before us and become one with where we came from. Love is the passageway through which we travel. Love is eternal.

In my view, most Americans have a tendency to live in a fantasy future instead of being in life, in the here and now, absorbing and enjoying every moment. Too often we say/think/ teach "I can't wait until…", believing life is a destination rather than a journey. We are perpetually planning to obtain more rather than be content with what we have. We are conditioned from childhood to be planners of our futures and missing the essentials of the present. Our daily lives are saturated with materialism, entertainment, and commercialism to such a point that death comes and few are prepared. Those that die and those close to them are left hollow because we avoid the topic of death and focus on all possible distractions from our ultimate conclusion of life. I sometimes think wouldn't it be magnificent if death was a glorious and wonderful event. To be joined with the creative force of the universe and understand every galactic nuance is to be one with God. Life as we know it may be nothing more than the mere separation from God. Death just might be the ultimate cosmic joke on human beings. To sore forever in the bliss of the universe is a far cry from the hell we invented here on earth.

A second lesson to this trip is our encounter with young Johnny. Three years back Johnny was working for us and Diana and I spent much energy deciding how best to deal with his inconsistent work schedule. We have since hired him a couple of times but the message hit home when Diana had a small talk with Johnny. He said we had taught him a great lesson about responsibility. One day he had the nerve to show up at noon and we sent him home. Diana and I had lengthy discussions about the best way to handle him. The question was to be a teacher or to be an enabler of bad habits.

Well, fast-forward three years and Johnny told Diana that he appreciated the lesson on punctuality he had learned from us. His girlfriend is pregnant with their second child, due next month, and he has to work every day to take care of his family. Diana had conversations with him three years ago about living a better life and it seems some of our intentions for him have come to pass. We went to their house with a business proposal for Fabiana, but instead closed the deal with Johnny's mother.

Their house is literally a shack. There is running water and electricity, but the floors are dirt and the walls are crumbling. There were three shacks where the entire extended family live. His grandparents, his mother, and some cousins all live in a kind of dirt courtyard shaded by trees. Chickens and roosters run around as dogs bark or lie in the shade. I think they are from Nicaragua, which in Costa Rica is considered second class or lower class. These are the workers who cross the border to find work.

The third bit of news is about a tree that I used to lie under on the beach. The tree was well over two hundred years old. It was at the edge of the beach next to a low concrete wall. The runoff from the nearby hill kept the tree alive. It was my favorite place in Jaco. The long branches almost touched the ground and many a family had spent happy hours under that special tree. A developer, who had bought the land for speculation, and to build a resort, bulldozed the tree. I was very upset by the death of this tree.

This tree was my friend and cut down in the name of greed by my own countrymen in a foreign land. I despise this kind of behavior in a country that prides itself with a love of nature. Many an afternoon that tree shaded me after a swim. It was a trusted landmark where generations of families picnicked and took refuse from the sun. I'd spent many a memorable day with friends there. As the sun moved we'd relocate the blanket and food as that tree gave us shade like grace from above.

On our third day in Jaco we went back to this beach to boogie board. We crossed the small river and I saw a man who had also crossed the river. As we rounded the corner to the small cove the man was, by then, returning. I told how the tree has been destroyed. He happened to work for a real estate company that was trying to sell the property. The developer had gone bankrupt and the land was up for sale again. This was truly a criminal act to destroy this tree. The bastards who killed the tree didn't every profit from their murderous actions. It was a senseless act. They came in, altered the landscape, and before they could go any further with their business venture, they went bankrupt. Nature had the final say on their greedy behavior, yet the tree was lost like so many other trees that are raped by businessmen who have no conscience. I was happy to hear the story of the fallen businessmen, but wondered if they even thought about the significance of trees (or nature) and how beauty is lost under such negligent circumstances. I'll never get over the way of the world full of greed.

Jaco gets bigger all the time. There are many big building projects that have been halted because of the economic crisis. I am well aware that development means jobs and a growing standard of living. But I have a secret pleasure in seeing these things fail. What would it take to convince people that a simple life versus a "life of luxury" is a better plan for the entire planet? At some point the attempt to sustain high standards of living will strangle the plant to death if we don't stop killing our mother earth. Jaco has become a small town of tall, empty, haunted buildings that are shells. Half of the high buildings in town are vacated construction sites, yet some new projects continue to begin. There aren't enough tourists to fill the buildings that stand now, so how it is that new construction will solve the problems? It is all a bigger disaster waiting to happen.

In December, we went to Colombia again. This was my first Christmas there. The ten days we spent there flew by. I saw the lights of Christmas in Medellin. This is a huge barrage of lights hung over streets, the river, and along the entire length of the road that follows the river. Plazas and parks are turned into dazzling displays of colored lights. One night we rode in a party bus called a "Chiva". The Chiva had open sides and rows of wooden seats. As people boarded, and the music and merriment began in the center of town a few blocks from Diana's parent's house. Strangers sang with strangers. A beverage was passed around while we visited many of the sights around Medellin. Entire parks and village squares were light up. Inside the Chiva music was blasting as revelers continued the festive mood. We stayed out until three that morning. It was very unusual to see and hear.

The reputation Colombia has because of illegal drugs is so sad, while the people and their spirit are so brilliant. Diana had always told me she missed Christmas in her country. I now know why.

The overall theme of the displays was water, so various light displays turned into tears, waterfalls, rivers, and raindrops. Each park or square had a nativity displayed. These ten-foot tall scenes were made of chicken wire with colored plastic weaving between the wire grids. Other animals, trees, flowers were also displayed with lights, just as the nativity scenes. From a distance, the displays looked like giant inflated toys. Along the river some of the lighted figures were as high as two story buildings. Strands of blinking lights stretched across the river as the water reflected all the moving colors. It was visually exciting and pulled each viewer into a fantasyland of candy colored lights where thousands of spectators wandered, singing, playing maracas, or strolling arm in arm with their loved ones. In all my days I have never seen such an extensive festival and so many happy people.

After Christmas, we visited the finca (farm) of Diana's Uncle Fabio. He had bought an old house and refurbished it. I contracted the flu, so my input into the daily chores was minimal. They seemed to clean morning, noon, and night.

I did a painting and either stayed in a favorite seat, or read a book. The farm is way up in the mountains with a tiny view of the lights of Medellin at night. Diana's other Uncle Turo asked me to take photographs of the renovations so I made him a packet of pictures.

The weather was hot and sultry during the day contrasted to very chilly nights. The land yielded all kinds of fruits and vegetables, so we enjoyed natural foods. Because the farmhouse is so far from any food stores we loaded up on supplies and had to carry them down a steep row of slippery, wet, mud steps. They need to build a road to the house. We parked at a neighbor's house that is a cousin to Diana's mother. The cousin's house was higher on the mountain and maybe a hundred years old. It had an open, long thin veranda with green support posts and green doors leading into rooms. The home felt very Spanish in style with hanging baskets of plants and long wooden benches to sit on.

During the last three days we went to a second finca near Diana's brother's house in Guarne. He owns a farm with his other brother-in-law. This was a small yellow farm perched atop a local mountain. This house was even colder than the first. There were maybe fifteen of us altogether. We celebrated New Year Eve there. The small house has entire families in one room. Diana and I slept on the floor on an air mattress while her parents slept on a bed. There was not one inch of space to walk to the bathroom in the middle of the night, so I almost squashed my wife and fell on my in-laws. The view was breath taking with green hills and the small town far below in the valley.

I am not a drinker, but I was asked to taste a local mix of what smelled like gasoline, alcohol, and kerosene. I took one sip. That was all. I hated it. I really don't need a drink to make me stupid. The music was blasting and a wild disc jockey was doing some crazy, joking, announcing on the radio.

At midnight the whole place exploded with song, fireworks, and dance. To keep with tradition we ate twelve grapes, lit candles, and many people wore yellow underwear for good luck. I was not one of them.

Then in one of the craziest moments of my adult memory, everyone began to grab their suitcases, backpacks, or whatever, and ran outside, circling the house yelling, "I'll see you next year". You can't imagine how this struck me as so weird and wild. I began to laugh hysterically and thought the whole house had gone completely mad. This is a Colombian custom that I faintly heard described before, but none of that came to me until well into the festivities that followed.

The party wasn't just adults. It was every age in the family, from the very young to the very old. The last event before sleep was the burning of the old year in effigy. A hay-stuffed figure was laid outside and set ablaze. The New Year had arrived. We had a blast. I left the next day from the top of the mountain, getting a ride to the airport from Diana's brother. Diana stayed another week to be with her family. I had to return to my job.

While back in Costa Rica last August, we met a couple. I saw them in the church and stopped them in the grocery store. They were Daisy and Larry. We invited them to lunch but plans fell through. That April, I was in the bank and bumped into Larry again. We had him and Daisy come over for lunch in the middle of the week. Jaco is the type of small town where people's paths cross all the time. Larry is from California, grew up in Colombia, and married Daisy in

California. She was born in Colombia.

They bought a piece of land and built a hotel and two houses. The houses sold, but the hotel is barely floating economically. They had to rent out a front house of the hotel and are living in one of the hotel rooms. Without coming across as too critical I think they are doing what most Americans do when they come to Costa Rica. They build with an attitude of unlimited success, over extended their finances, and have to pull back to survive. I have seen this time and time again. Business is slow in Jaco. The Americans who move there don't realize that the successful businesses were established twenty or thirty years ago. The majority of the businesses have come and gone. There is a kind of exuberant mentality that people have here because the cost of living is lower than the United States. Unfortunately, the level of economic activity in the States is unobtainable in a third world country. Smaller is better. Small steps are a more cautionary approach to grand schemes.

We have become close friends with Larry and Daisy. We call them on the computer-phone and hope to see them next summer. A repeat visit to Central America with some additional countries is our next planned sojourn. Only this time I will have my lovely wife with me. Oh, yes we are getting along fine, money is tight, and Diana is working as a substitute teacher. She will go back to college next fall. She wants to become a classroom teacher, and will continue to study for the Praxis test. I don't how or why, other than pure intent, but we are getting along better than ever. This coming summer will add some chapters, no doubt. Then I have the boring task of trying to sell my book. It's more fun to live the adventures than sell them.

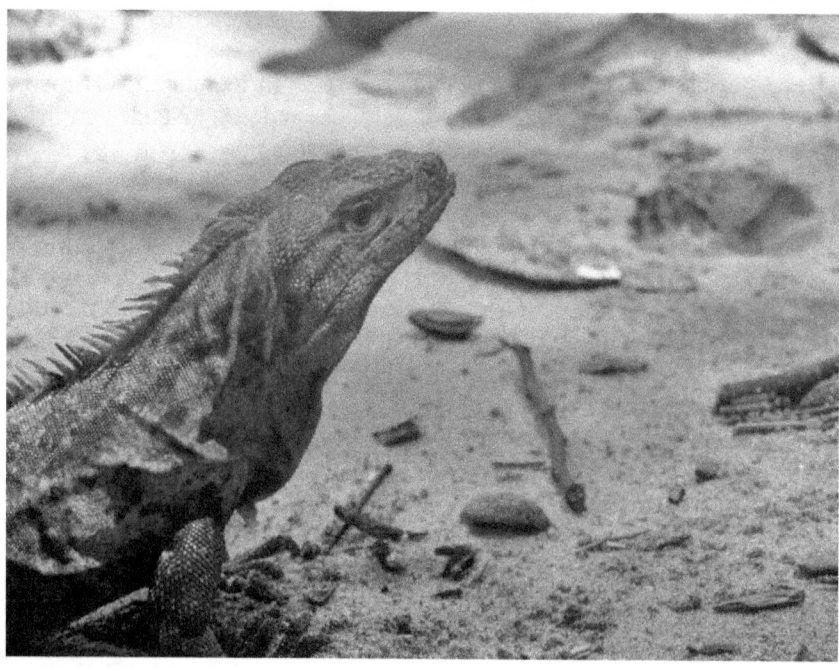

Chapter 17
Honduras

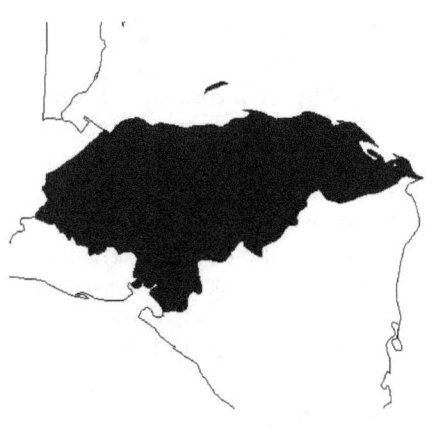

July 4, 2010: Life is a preconceived notion that forces us to be creative, to change, and adept. The creative process is a survival mechanism. The ritual of creating develops a spiritual self; an inner conversation where we "play-act" the world's creation and our own creation. Our purpose to live becomes the ritual. This creative ritual takes on many personal manifestations. For me, they are Music, Art, Writing, and Photography. I began as a writer and artist in my childhood and turned to music and photography in my teens. I have cultivated all these art forms my entire life, at some periods focusing on particular disciplines, but ultimately mixing and overlapping these expressions. I began to document or save my art and music when photography taught me the possibility of preserving my expression. I was fifteen when my real-life journey began. Looking back, I was happiest when sharing and creating with others, which led to my ultimate profession as a teacher later in life at age forty-five. Being a teacher gave me economic stability and the ability to travel the globe. I have always distinguished the vast difference between fortune and fame. By design, I have been more fortunate than famous and prefer the back streets to the boulevards. On a trip to Bali, Indonesia, I was very excited to see the Hindu temples because I had a preconceived notion what they would look like. This was based on living in Pakistan when I was a teenager. The empty Hindu temples were deteriorated and abandoned by the Hindus who had fled to India during the partition of the two countries. I was fascinated by this mysterious void and later studied that religion. When I arrived in Bali I expected grand temples and golden deities like those vacated in Muslim Pakistan. In Bali however, the temples were vast open-aired plazas. Much to my chagrin, the deities were carved in stone arches or doorways. I expected drastically different scenery of Vatican-like luxury with gold and heavenly depictions of Brahma, Shiva, and Vishnu. None of that was there and my heart sank. On the third or fourth day I had a stellar realization. I had been fooled by my imagination and preconceived notions of how life was supposed to be. The temple was indeed present only not in a physical structure. The art, music, and religion were so predominant in the environment that I had completely missed out, due to my own mental stumbling blocks. The incenses in the air, the morning offerings in each household doorway, the garlands in the women's hair, their dress, the men's cloths, their attitudes of respect, the happy smiles of playful children all came crashing down on me as if I had lived in the dark and seen light for the very first time. The temple was in the people, their food, their dress, their rituals of daily worship, the entire world, and living inside me as well. How foolish I had been to miss the true temple.

So when I travel, or prepare to travel, I switch gears and loosen my own expectations and prepare to free myself. I do this by keeping totally occupied, or more exactly, preoccupied. The night before we left for Honduras seemed like an endless, sleepless night, which never ended. The waiting for months turned into a lengthy, nonstop wheel in motion. I never stopped moving that last day in New York. Up until the hour we left, I nervously barked at Diana while working on a project for the Brooklyn Museum. Diana came into the room and told me Flora was on her way, intending me to stop that very second because mind you, I had been nervously waiting all day while finishing up a paragraph.

The bags had been placed in the car hours earlier and at 11:00 p.m., Diana and I were standing in the dark street where Flora's car was already parked and locked. I could see two women's silhouettes coming up the hill, so I mimicked a spooky voice and made a howling sound. They froze and began to squeal. I didn't know it then, but they explained to Diana that they had been watching a scary vampire movie so a good deal of laughter came from my prank. We all climbed into the car, and I drove to the airport within forty-five minutes. We were four hours early and the line was already beyond belief. It was midnight by the time we'd said good-bye and joined the "full to capacity" line, up and down, back and forth, move a few feet, stop, move a few feet more, stop, pick up everything, get comfortable enough to scratch one's butt while no one is looking, but someone always is, then move to the front of the line anticipating something bad will happen, although it never does. The process always makes me edgy.

We had our boarding passes, were stopped going through x-ray machine because Diana had a suspicious bag full of chocolate powder. We told the black female attendant how great our new diet drink was and how many people are using those shakes to lose weight and she let us go ahead. What a perfect place to do a product analysis.

As I sat there listening to music and watching the CNN news caster spout bad news, a friend from my job walked by. "Norma!" I shouted, which caused people in the immediate vicinity to pause and see what was happening. What was the chance of one of those cosmic connections in which a female custodian from my work place was walking to a far gate? We visited a few minutes and she told me she was going to El Salvador with her granddaughter and mother. I later went over and got a photograph of them all, meeting the granddaughter who promised she would be my student when she entered the high school. I love those unplanned meetings. This was a perfect moment for writing a book, as if everything is connected and part of a bigger plan.

In another unplanned moment I also saw one of my ex-students who I am totally convinced stole a small digital camera off my desk the second week of school last year. He saw me at the airport and never acknowledged my presence, another reason to deepen my suspicions that he really did. We could never prove he stole the camera, but his absence from my class the next day fermented my awareness of his lack of eye contact the rest of the year, and even into this year in the hallways. I'll never know, but I would stop him once in a while and talk about the camera, just enough to be on the right side of the law, and out and out accusing him of theft. I would say things like, "What kind of camera are you using these days?" He is so cold he never gives himself away. I decided I would give the photographs to Norma as a gift and curse this student under my breath everything I see him, while always wearing a polite smile.

We boarded the plane at 3 A.M.. Diana slept a few minutes but I never so much as blinked. I had been awake for almost twenty-two hours. Except when I had a brief nap that day around noon. The day we left for Honduras I was up at five o'clock in the morning, even though we were not due at the airport for some seventeen hours. I was up futzing with the MP3 player trying to add some last minutes songs. I went for an unusually forty-five minute walk in the morning and wanted to begin that ultra-awareness of a new environment that comes with traveling. It worked. By the time I was walking down the embankment of the driveway I didn't recognize my own house. I was in a different land already. The light was changing in ways that heightened my awareness. The birds were exceptionally happy. Diana asked me why I didn't wake her for the walk, and then added, "It's OK if you need to get away from me once and a while." This irked me because she never would have wanted to walk and made a quip remark about a perfectly honest attempt at my spiritual fine-tuning. Some things deserve total privacy.

I took half a sleeping pill as soon as we were boarding the plane, woke up long enough to eat airplane food, and fall back asleep until a few minutes before touching down in San Pedro Sula, Honduras. The airport was like Omaha in the 1950's. Luggage carts were pushed into place by men and our bags were twenty minutes apart despite them both holding hands when we gave them to the nice security man at the x-ray machine back in New York. They were whining and complaining by the time the second one burst through the plastic curtain that was so transparent we could see exactly how slow the process was. We were the ones complaining to each other by then. The sleeping pill made me feel like I swallowed a pillow case full of feathers, and Diana was leaning against me looking like someone who had escaped the loony bin with some sleep deprived illness. It was all fitting together like the sad condition of the airport.

There were three baggage claims, two x-ray machines, and an air of relaxation that made me wonder why we had given a second thought to not bringing the dietary shake because we were afraid of some drastic tariff being imposed on us for bringing in "commercial goods". I had to walk back and hand the customs sheet to the guard manning the x-ray machine. He looked shocked that I was going out of my way to hand him a form that many passengers had painstakingly filled in with lies and misinformation. We had eight weeks of dietary shakes, cleansing powders, and hands full of snacks to complete our weight loss plan while traveling. We were sure they would fine us for bringing in a vast commercial enterprise of dietary supplements. The whole place was as sleepy as we were; no one paid us more than a quick glance. We got a hundred dollars' worth of limperas (Honduran money) and were at the door getting a taxi in no time.

There is something about the people of this country that seems repressed. It's like Ireland without the happy music that wishes a silent revenge toward the English. The taxi driver was dull from no exposure to a world of possibilities. Nothing could have shaken his life. I am sure if we return in fifty years he will have the same expressionless, polite laugh. My theory about his country is that the military-controlled government has secretly suppressed everyone from living a life in the open. I felt it last summer when I visited. There is a dullness here that I don't feel in other Central American countries. It may be the poverty. It may be the heat. It may be in the water for all I know. A few near misses from other cars didn't raise an eyebrow on the driver, yet Diana gave one of her Colombian gasps. This didn't seem to faze him either. He was polite and drove us around the streets a few times until we found the hotel's front door.

The dark interior of the hotel added to the dull lack of expectation. We got one of the better broken down rooms on the second floor with walls the color of rusty poop. The window is blocked off by the air conditioner, which has a row of curtains half blocking the vents. The shower has nothing but a sawed off head where the cold water has not the slightest hint of heat. Who needs heat? This is the tropics. The shower curtain was just short enough to soak the floor with water, but who's complaining. This is an adventure one could never find in the well-groomed world of North America. The sidewalks invite a cautious eye for each and every step. Nothing is in a state of perfection; this must have an effect on the people as well. Excellence is an idea that only works for the politicians that must be pocketing every penny allocated toward sidewalk maintenance. Diana pointed out that in Colombia people would fall and sue the government for injuries if such conditions existed in her country. My comment was, "There you go being an idealist. What are you some kind of socialists?" For all the anticipation of this trip, for months now, I am feeling very grumpy.

I'm getting ahead of myself. The first thing we did was take a shower then went naked into the street and inspected the sidewalks. It was quite fitting because we noticed we were in the midst of the red light district by the number of ladies with cleavage leaning up against walls like they were having intercourse with men in their eyes. Diana poked fun at the places I bring her, but she knows well enough that I will protect her, but never shield her from the real world. It is what it is, here.

Our first stop when venturing into the dreaded heat was the cathedral across from the central park. The church is dilapidated and in need of a new coat of paint, but our intentions and prayers was not for the building, but for the people who live less fortunate lives than our own. As much as I make fun and get sarcastic I know there is serious work to be done for the poor in Honduras. The sad syrup that plagues this country is like a sleeping giant that is about to wake with laughter. It is hope that keeps poverty from killing all who enters her womb. We entered a different type of poverty in the shopping mall around noon. This is the poverty of modern shopping malls where everyone pretends to be wealthy. It is the social sickness of pretense.

As if we had nothing better to do we went to the local Taca Airline office to get our air miles registered. This spun us in an emotional downward spiral as we waited half an hour only to be told Diana could not be credited because her passport was back at the hotel. I was given a new air miles card and we walked a block to the newest, central shopping mall, lunching on a local plate of papusas and tea. The fried pancake-like dough was filled with chicken and the tea was full of white sugar. Why not start at the bottom and work our way up? This was exactly the way the rest of the day went, after we ruined our imaginations with a douse of shopping mall lust and buying nothing. We walked around the mall and wondered why on earth we had flown four hours to get away from New York. It was here right in front of us. After a few minutes we rebelled, left the mall, and found ourselves in a ceramics store of all places. It was a high-end company with walls of hanging tile displays. This was more trendy than New York, but when exiting the store Diana asked the gun totting security guard where we could find a crafts market. That is when our day really began. The first half of the day was spent in reverse until we dipped our feet into the true travel mode.

The security guard gave us the name of a market and after a short taxi ride we were looking at true wooden carvings of Honduran handicrafts. We found one ceramic piece and bargained an unplanned purchase. It was beautifully painted with Spanish floral designs. We didn't see anything else like it the rest of our hour in the market. The market was alive with smiling people. We had found the heart and soul of this city. The atmosphere was not one of fearful anticipation, but one of friendly invitation. Shopkeepers invited us in to see the woodcarvings, the flowered blouses, and the multitudes of handmade objects. Most of it was too crude for my tastes, but we were at last in the world of creativity and hopeful ambition.

One whole side of the market had women patting tortillas and slapping them onto huge flat skillets. Three such aisles of woman working at these tortillas were like a visit to another land in the past. White mounds of batter lay in heaps the size of pillows as the women kneaded the dough. Some of these small kitchen stalls had two women at them, one cooking while another flattened the tortilla, but most of the women worked alone. We bought a strange cookie that looked like piecrust and tasted like leather. A young woman uncharacteristically walked up to me and asked me for a small piece of cookie. I obliged and took this as an act of acceptance as a group of ladies laughed at such an overt gesture being taken in friendship. We had begun our journey and the spirit of what makes us all enjoy people shown from Diana and me. After months of preparation I was beginning to feel like a traveler again. The transition is not quick or easy.

Now the future was opening up to us by way of serendipitous messages. We stopped and sat at a lemonade stand. An old woman proprietor sat silently reading a newspaper as we cooled ourselves in the shade. Then a young man came up and bought himself the cold drink. We struck up a conversation and he led us to the park where a concert was to take place. Without our knowledge, this was the central park across the street from the cathedral. We had gone full circle from our morning to a delightful day of unplanned wanderings.

We did venture out of the hotel later in the afternoon, after a short nap and drying our sweaty clothes. This is when we actually noticed the prostitutes who were not really as visible the first time we headed toward the central park in the morning. Prostitutes don't keep bankers hours and why you were foolish enough to believe this before I'll never know. Our second outing was to find a three-pronged electric adapter for the computer and to find a plastic bowl and spoons so we could eat. All was complete when I convinced Diana to walk back to the central park to see if the five o'clock concert had begun. It was five thirty and the band was still doing the sound check, hitting on individual drums a dozen times to see if it was annoying enough to drive impatient, waiting people away. It worked. We left, but first I made a joke in Spanish to a young man next to me that the music concert was boring. He got the joke despite my weak language skill.

Back at the hotel Diana asked the desk clerk if it was dangerous at night in the hood. She asked it in a way that prompted an honest, cajoling answer. "A little bit." We went out the front door. This set in motion an entire series of paranoiac speeches from Diana about the dangers of this god-forsaken place with prostitutes (alright, we actually only saw four milling around hotel doorways). Diana was beginning to froth at the mouth like a vampire about to be shriveled by sunlight. As the sky increased in darkness, she repeated her danger mantra until I gave in and ended the party by going back to the hotel. You'd think there were gunshots and blood on every street corner the way she was acting. Every attempt to sooth her nightmare about to happen, was only met with dismissal of my American-over-confident ego. Did I tell you about my first visit to Colombia where I was unequivocally told I would unequivocally be robbed if I dared take my camera out in public to be used? Diana made it all up to me later by agreeing to marry me. (I didn't say that.)

On the way back to the hotel we saw guns, lots of guns, but not in the hands of robbers. As we passed every store we pretended all the security guards were really holding a toy gun. In fact, all the men in every store, in every bank, and a few with hidden guns, were all just playing an incredible spoof on us. All the guns are toys. All the men in this country are pretending to be safe. We went inside the hotel to feel safer.

We have a reservation for a bus to La Ceiba at ten thirty in the morning. I made the entire reservation myself on the phone, in Spanish, and remembered all the digits to my Visa card (in Spanish!). Tomorrow I hope to buy a real gun and see if I can scare some life into the Honduran people, except those at the crafts market and the women tortilla makers. I think all these people secretly keep firearms under their children's beds.

Day Two: Heldman just gave us a ride to the bus terminal. He is a plump, jovial taxi driver who laughed and laughed. The joking started when we passed a cemetery and I told him the cemetery was my future home. He said we all must die - it is necessary. Then a speeding car almost ran into us and Heldman said we might be going home to the cemetery now instead of later. He had a great laugh and made jokes the entire fifteen-minute drive from the hotel to the bus depot.

When we arrived he helped us with the bags. He asked us to call him when we return and promptly wrote his phone number on the airline tag still fastened to the handle of the luggage. As I stood in line, ten minutes later Heldman returned inside the bus depot to give us the correct phone number. He had mistakenly written down the wrong information and wanted to make sure he got the fare. It was only five or six dollars but perhaps a good bonus for such a short distance.

On the ride in the taxi with Heldman the World Cup soccer game was on and he was cheering for Germany, who was ahead 4-0. Heldman spoke English in the worst possible way. Whenever he spoke we had to ask him to repeat the phrase a couple of times. This added to the fun because he was so bad at his words. Diana ran with the conversations in Spanish comparing her country to the USA. Heldman listened intensely.

Last night in the hotel I was writing while straddling my legs across Diana as she slept. It was around ten-thirty in Honduran time, but because of the time difference it was two hours later in our body clocks. I fell asleep with the earphones in my ears while listening to the Moody Blues. Every once in a while I would wake and hear a favorite song, then drift back under water. I thought it strange that besides being in a sleeping state my mind, I would pop up and bounce awake like a bubble being burst. I would enjoy a few seconds of music, go right back to sleep again, but my favorite songs would bring me back to awareness. It was a delicious sleep as we lay in the air conditioning. I pulled the blanket and sheets off the second bed in the room and we cuddled in a cocoon-like embrace.

I woke somewhere around five, put the music back on and lay there thoroughly enjoying nothing. I couldn't distinguish the light coming through the window as dawn or just the hotels neon light. It was the latter, until the real sun was evident by the glow through the dirty plastic, covering the window. The window had been sealed with an unhealthy amount of duct tape that was peeling away from old age and heat. Dust from the street was coating the tiny openings. It was a part of the room we chose to ignore. The same goes for the area between the bed and wall. I made sure the pillows were tucked between the wall and the edge of the bed to keep out spiders. I am almost sure they were living under the bed. This was the best hotel possible to avoid a false sense of luxury and break into true traveling. But look, it's like I say. You can stay at a dive and travel for two months versus spending all your money in two days at a costly hotel. Pretense is wide-open to interpretation of what real luxury is.

By the time I was up and drinking my special health elixir Diana was beginning to smile from under the covers. She asked me for a kiss, like she always does, by silently stretching her arms towards me and puckering her cheeks. I knew she was in a good mood, because she wasn't complaining about her allergies and headache, like many a day back in New York. I was out of bottled water so I went down stairs and bought two cold waters. In the room I made my special breakfast shake, followed by another for Diana. By then she was up and moving around the room. At seven we were out the door with a slight protest from Diana about possible danger and no stores being open. "The light, the light, it's all about the early morning light, silly," was all I could say to explain my lust for photography.

The streets were indeed barren but the light was good. We found a double boulevard with a sidewalk up the middle and a statue of an Indian holding a bow and arrow. A group of men stood and watched us as they were waiting for work at the nearby super market. A few blocks later we crossed the railroad track that I had seen the day before. This was a neighborhood I wanted to photograph as the city was waking up. Along the railroad tracks shacks had been built covering most of the immediate area next to the tracks. Men were rolling giant spools of cable to the street side of the track to display their goods to sell. This was the electrical supplies district. Huge piles of wire and plastic tubing were being moved to make room inside the wooden shacks where the sides were packed with tools and electric accessories for sale. We said good morning to each shop keeper as we walked along the railroad tracks making sure we didn't trip in the lumber ties where open gaps were calling to our ankles. One man refused my asking for a photograph, but a few stalls down the way I was granted permission by three men to shoot away. We walked to the end of the street where a police booth stood empty. We crossed the street to join a gathering of people who had exited a bus, walking toward their perspective daily jobs or errands. I was wearing a Hawaiian shirt with yellow flowers and blended in like a Chameleon.

One side street looked like an invitation into a thick market so we took a right turn, walked several blocks until the market became too congested with stalls. I knew I was pressing Diana's sense of safety already so I assured her we would go back. En-route were make-shift stalls jimmy-rigged together with every imaginable flat surface to display cloths, shampoos, shoes, tools, you name it. Each stall had its own specialty. I noted one booth where a woman was carefully hanging bras on a thin wire by the hooks on the backs of the bras. Creativity was abounding for the more inventive the display, the more possible sales that day.

Another corner stall had tiny chicks chirping. I thought we had come upon a bird market. Indeed small chicks in low plastic crates were colored in various bright, iridescent colors. A crate full of purple chicks, another of bright red, another of blue, or bright yellow all moved in waves as the woman selling the birds reached into the crowd of tiny birds to pick one out and place it in a box for a customer. I asked the man buying the chicks how long until they were big enough to eat. "Two months," he said. The strange colors and innocence made the cute birds very unappetizing to us.

The market streets continued on for half a mile. We walked a fraction of the distance. In the middle of each street was just enough room for an occasional taxi to squeeze by. This made little, if any, room for pedestrians. The taxis would be driving over the trash that was swept into the middle of each street. The morning cleaning was in full swing as people cleared the trash from under the stalls and sidewalks moving it to the center of the street. These piles of garbage varied in degree of size and stench. Some had the added benefit of purification, spoiled fruit and vegetables while tiny rivers of dark gray water rolled between the tires of taxis. Gravity was at work! This water would eventually follow the law that all water subscribes to, and end up in the sea.

In the middle of one intersection was a sewer hole where the cover had been missing long enough for a considerable amount of garbage to accumulate down inside. I am positive the local people hadn't a clue why the Gringo found this open hole so fascinating and stood there looking down in amazement. This is why Americans get a bad name. We visit foreign countries and look at the most mundane holes in the middle of streets and even speak to our partners about whatever the hell is so interesting about a garbage pit. In the local people's eyes we suffer from a lack of excitement and humor. There is something seriously wrong with people who need such entertainment. Tourists, indeed, are very strange to the locals.

The smell from the open sewer was so good we decided to move onto the next piece of excitement, a McDonald's. I bought water as Diana used the universal restrooms that services desperate travelers all over the world. The air conditioning was a welcome break and we spent at least forty-five minutes eating some Weight Watchers snacks we smuggled past the armed guard at the door. I have a perverted sense of ownership of McDonald's when I visit foreign countries. No one would ever dare to ask us to leave because we didn't buy anything but water. We didn't bring our own supply of water so we were forced to buy theirs. I imagine to myself that the local employees think we are secret spies from the United States, there to judge the cleanliness and speed of service. They know McDonald's originated in my country and I was personally responsible for bringing this delicious enterprise to the native peoples much like the Spanish missionaries to the indigenous peoples of Central America centuries before. They brought small pox and European viral infections while today we bring cholesterol and quick service. I am so proud.

After the break from the heat we crossed the street to the cathedral where I was quick to pull out the video and still cameras. Someone had installed speakers throughout the church and soft, new age music was playing. I really liked this touch. It was a modern subliminal concept at play in a church, but it worked well. I was moved to say a prayer and thank God that the missionaries had brought Christianity to this land, thus McDonald's as well.

Diana has asked that I specifically write about an incident where her life was nearly snuffed out. The taxi drivers here own the streets. There is a sense of entitlement to the power of hurling down the street in a metal box, at speeds capable of breaking bones into thousands of fragments. This was easy to read in the eyes of one taxi driver as he stared expressionless at Diana as she dodged one such lunatic. To use the horn or brake would have caused too much expenditure of energy from the heat. I can see the drivers now gathered after work, sitting around showing that priceless, blank expression to each other, and then bursting into laughter as they describe the various shades of white my wife turned as death brushed close enough to feel the wind of eternity. Not only is this look, or blank-look, present in the drivers, but the passenger in the front seat was also wearing the same kind of expression as well. It's not even a "what a stupid idiot look", it is an expression that can only come from a people who live in a world devoid of happiness, or to whom there is no value to human life. They may secretly enjoy such a death for all I know.

Diana came to the conclusion about the people the same as I did a year before when I visited the Copan ruins. These are not a happy people here. They smile only if smiled to first. The desk clerk at the hotel looked like he had gone through extensive training on how to flash a smile. The only problem was he ended the broad, sweeping smile just a little too soon to give it any sincerity. As soon as his teeth were exposed he clammed up like a teenager wearing braces. My favorite moment was when I asked him to help me make a reservation for the bus today. No sooner had I asked the question when he snapped out, "No". I repeated the question, thinking my Spanish had somehow insulted him. "No" meant he would have to charge me by the minute for any help on the phone. I agreed, much to his surprise. But when he kept calling the same number for information, listening to the "wait music", and hanging up I began to calculate the cost of sending a man to the moon in Honduran terms. Finally a break in his face came when he walked over to the computer and looked up the phone number himself. He had been calling information, and not the actual bus company. Five minutes had already gone by and I was wondering if he was going to charge me for the "wait-music" time as well. I have no idea if he did or not. I just allocate it to that Vacation-Money-Expenditure list. I don't quibble over the small stuff, which is why we stay in hotels that have to charge for phone minutes and have duct tape around the air conditioners. We live like royalty, relatively speaking.

Right now as I catch up on the writing we are hurling in a giant metal box toward the coast. A teenage girl with a cell phone is driving the European passenger bonkers. The cell phone has an annoying jingle that goes off every fifteen seconds. Each time the phone rings the young jumps out of an attempt at snoozing. I think she is texting. (Something I refuse to learn to do.) The European finally looked at me with a cold, "I could kill her," look. This look, she no doubt learned from the taxi drivers here, only she isn't as good at it. She let a fraction of a disgusted expression into her eyes that gave her foreignness away. The woman at the window directly behind her has been speaking for at least an hour on her cell phone. The chatter between the two is like bricks being thrown through windows.

The bus has hit flat land and the coastal mountains remind us of Costa Rica. The mountains are green and protrude upward like a quick conversation which is all we have had as Diana sleeps and opens her mouth just enough to say nothing and not snore. We are getting close to La Ceiba where we plan to spend one night before we take the boat to Roatan and the expected paradise.

Day Three: We have arrived on Roatan, but I will need to backtrack in the process of explaining how we got here. Today my motto is "always be willing to change and adapt". There is nothing worse for a marriage than sticking to a vacation plan, unless one intends to divorce. We found our first "paradise hotel" on Roatan but within the hour, booked five days at another hotel with air conditioning, a refrigerator, a microwave, high ceilings, large plate glass door, and a porch with a hammock. From what I have described, guess what was lacking in our first, and current, physicality? It was lacking all the above, plus it has a ceiling fan and a room the size of a closet with one double bed and one single bed built into the walls. The area not occupied by the beds is an isle just narrow enough to get to the bathroom. Nevertheless, there is hot water here, unlike our neighbor's cabin. (He told us so.)

When we first arrived Diana said nothing. The slightly glazed (oddly similar to a San Pedro Sula taxi driver) look as she lay in bed swatting mosquitoes was enough for me to understand. She was sea sick from the fast ferry and had not spoken for a while when I took the decision completely on my own to save the vacation and marriage. She has said some five times, "I will say nothing," meaning a change was needed to a new hotel. She has felt guilty because when we went to look at a hotel close by, (the first and only one we looked at) I explained to the desk clerk the first hotel was too "rustic" for my wife. I played up the hero/husband role a bit too much and she didn't appreciate my ability to play at a little drama.

The day before in La Ceiba we found an excellent hotel called "Casa De Espania" (House of Spain). That experience rapidly spoiled us and left us unprepared for the first "rustic" hotel in Roatan. Back in La Ceiba, the teen-age girl on the bus with the texting compulsion joined us in the taxi as we began to look for a hotel. She was very helpful and gave us a few ideas on the much-anticipated trip to Roatan the following morning. She stayed in the taxi, which was taking her to the boat for she was leaving that day, while we stayed in La Ceiba for one night. The girl explained she lives in Roatan and had been visiting friends in San Pedro Sula for a month. The taxi driver told us the hotel listed in our Lonely Planet guide was closed, but he knew of an excellent place, and that is was. The owners of Casa De Espania were a husband and wife team with three grown daughters. The daughters' photographs were displayed behind the front desk. Upon our arrival we were shown two choices of rooms, and we picked the front room with a TV and balcony over-looking the street. The man was a large mouthed, handsome, dark eyed Jew. His wife was a beautiful dark, slender, woman with long black hair pulled back into one long braid.

The hotel was no more than a year old with antique furnishings, and a dining area tucked under the stairs on the first floor. The entire roof was an open terrace with a spectacular view of a mountain peak called Punta Sal. This mountain is within the boundaries of the National Park Jeannette Kawas. Its distinct peak is very visible from the hotel roof because it looks so out of place. The usually rounded, smooth green mountains are contrasted with the Punta Sal that looks like it belongs in the Alps, more so than Honduras. It is the highest point in this part of Honduras and the second highest in all of the country.

Diana loved the feel of the town. The streets were lined with tidy sales shacks (stores) all painted a special, uniform, turquoise blue. The sidewalks had the typical ankle-breaking holes, but there was organization and an attempt to keep things clean. The turquoise shacks were lined along the outside of the sidewalks on the street, leaving just enough room for a single car to pass, but inside was a cave-like walkway where fat women sat in front of electric fans in the shade. Standing by the ATM machines at a bank was a security guard holding a long rifle. He was seated at a white, plastic lawn chair. He told us to use the machine on the left (there were two) because the machine on the right often swallowed the cards, not returning them. I always listen to men with guns.

Three blocks down we came to the beach where a woman was screaming at her unfaithful lover, while pointing her finger in his face. Some kind of scuffle was heating up between them as we walked close to the shore and asked an ice cream vendor if he sold water. The vendor pointed to a soda house where men sat watching the World Cup Soccer match. We crossed the street to enter. One man leaned at me like he knew me for years and stammered some drunken Spanish greeting even Diana didn't understand. The woman behind the counter was oddly out of place. She was beautiful, wore a long dress that touched her ankles, and had hair pulled back into a single black ponytail. She struck me, as being so beautiful that this may be the reason so many lonely hearts sat silently in the shade, most seemingly unaware of the soccer match. As we were exiting to return to the beach with our water a younger patron put some money in a jukebox. It began to blast a Bob Marley song several decibels above the already loud soccer game. We could hear the music all the way while walking. No one protested that it was too loud to hear the match.

By the time we returned to the beach the woman and man who had been arguing were tussling over a bicycle that the man had been leaning on. The woman extended her finger toward his face like a knife. The small drama got the attention of the police parked under a shade tree and several others sitting on the trunks of dead trees in the shade of the same tree the police were parked under. Somehow, mysteriously, the woman began to calm down, sat down, and asked the man to join her. They both let go of the bicycle and even gave a small kiss to each other. What we all thought was going to involve a police action became disappointingly peaceful. The gathered crowd was soon disinterested. We turned our gaze toward a shaky pier in the west where the sun made the figures standing on the pier look like silhouetted skeletons. There were three trees that looked like a good place to sit so we headed toward the pier.

Within a few steps towards our destination the same ice cream vendor approached us on the raised walkway, motioning us over, and began speaking out of the side of his mouth, secretly. He spoke to Diana in a hush. "Those men lying under the tree are druggies and they will rob you. This is why the police are here." I hadn't really noted these men, but to be on the safe side for my wife we changed directions, returned past the now snuggling couple, to the far side of the beach. We were now on the same street as our hotel, stopping at a children's playground to take some pictures and sit in the shade while we drank our water. A woman in a hammock allowed me a few pictures as Diana sat, and then took the camera from me to shoot some of her own. A few raindrops began to fall and we started back to the hotel just in time to get out of a shower that lasted a couple of hours. We lay in bed, watched TV, and later showered to wash away the sweat that had drenched our shirts.

As the rain was ending and we'd had our fill of TV news, we ventured out for dinner and another look at the town of La Ceiba. By now the shops were closing and a variety of closing exercises were in motion, from sweeping the trash into neat piles on the street corners, to plastic tarps being rolled up. We walked on the side of the street where there were enough canopies from the overhanging buildings to not need the umbrella for the last few, light drops that came from above. We went into one souvenir shop to take a look. A few blocks away we entered a church where four well-dressed women informed us that mass would begin in a half hour. That gave us time to grab a quick bite to eat or so we thought. We'd passed a Chinese Restaurant so we doubled back to order some food. After waiting nearly five minutes at the counter, the casher told us we had to have a seat to place our order. This didn't make sense because some nine people sat along a row of chairs waiting for take-out. They didn't sit at tables but we did. We waited another five minutes when I said we should leave and find a place that would serve us that very day. Not once did we see a waitress. Two other men sat patiently looking toward the kitchen door but no waitress ever appeared. We left.

We found of all things a Pizza Hut. Diana went to the salad bar and in her fully honest voice asked the man if I could share her salad. He told her if she did, she could not return for seconds. By now we were sharing the salad as we watched every employee there, nine in all, watching us as if we had robbed a bank. Again, like MacDonald's, I own these corporate enterprises because I am an American. I said to Diana, "I'd like to see them stop you from going and getting seconds." But we both agreed the salad was so bad it wasn't worth being shot by the guard at the door. Forty-five minutes later our 'Chicken Shish Kebab' arrived which we ate and paid for. On my way out of the restaurant I handed the security guard with the gun the two complimentary sweets the waiter had given us. He knew it was for not shooting us for sharing the salad bar.

The church service was well into the gospel by the time we arrived. The priest was telling a story about a man who was always too busy to share his salad with others. Not really. It was about a man too busy to pray, so Christ said he was too busy to remember to let him into heaven. Diana interpreted for me in a whisper, but I hate when she whispers to me in church because she is really speaking in a loud, hushed tone. The church was modern and had good energy. The people were well involved and this felt like a real community. Towards the end of mass a woman who had been shaking our hand during the greetings began to wail in a sorrowful tone in the back of the church. She had received word of a death in her family and the word spread through the church like wild fire in a rash of whispers. The entire church felt her sadness. My annoyance at Diana for whispering in my ear seemed pretty stupid by then.

We walked home on streets vacated by all but the lone, armed security guards. In one street a man and woman played Mexican music from a music system, which was extremely loud, while above them a single, burning light bulb hung. They sat at a table with CD's for sale. The music could be heard for blocks before we saw them. Who would be out at that time other than people scurrying home, and who would buy this at that time of night? We had no idea. This was their passion, the music of Mexico. We returned to our room to make a few phone calls on the computer. We spoke to Diana's cousin in Florida, and our friend Victoria in New York. Diana tried to call her mother but no one was home. We soon hit the sack.

In the morning we were up at five-thirty and walked toward the beach at six. We had to wake the owner to let us out. He was polite and gracious. The beach had a few people; one man sat and ate as the pigeons flocked around for scraps of his food. We returned to the street that ran parallel to the coast. I was fully engaging the camera capturing the precious morning light. On our walk we passed a bar full of men yelling and drinking like there was no tomorrow. Indeed they all seemed like lifelong devotees to the bottle in an establishment that must not have ever closed. What a wonderful environment with such upstanding citizens! I commented to Diana that if we were alone in an ally with anyone of these characters, they would have a knife at my throat for the camera. We knew the safety of being on the street in the morning light where the sun was casting delightful shadows. An intoxicated man invited us into the bar but we declined. Beyond the small bridge and the "community" of drinkers we found a street that ran along a river or canal. The light was perfect for reflections where red Fire Trees and Water Lilies gave color a new meaning. It was a beautiful place to be.

It wasn't long before we were crossing back over another bridge towards a part of town we knew from the night before. We walked up a street with numerous turquoise blue stalls where shopkeepers were opening for the day. One man refused my asking for a photograph while the others standing near him jousted him with ridicule. I understand this may be the only sense of power over others that some have - to refuse being photographed. We passed along to another street where the variety of shop owners were cleaning, gathering supplies to sell, or unloading trucks with vegetables, fruit, shoes, or whatever. We saw a unique taxi driver pass by selling crabs. He had one hand on the steering wheel, and the other with a hand-full of crabs hanging, tied into a group with string. He wasn't calling out, or honking, just simply hanging the crabs from the driver's side to attract customers.

As we passed a group of woman there was a loud conversation-taking place. One of the women was practically jumping and bouncing as she animated a story. The others sat in rapt attention next to her on a small wall or stood leaning into her story line. As we passed I tried to catch what was going on but they spoke too fast for me to follow. "What was that about," I asked Diana. She said, "They were eating at a restaurant and found two mosquitoes in the food". I was intrigued by the loudness of this woman's tale and couldn't resist being nosey. I wasn't disappointed in the least. Diana continued telling me all the details she had picked up in the brief passing.

We returned to the central park and crossed in front of the church where the same priest was speaking to the congregation from the night before. A row of waiting poor and crippled people sat along one wall in front of the church. They were the same army of needy folks that we'd seen the night before. I took several shots of the church from different vantage points on different streets. The building had two tall towers and a large dome all in an Old Spanish style. The structure dominated the skyline from all over La Ceiba.

As we neared the hotel we stopped and bought two meals to be eaten later in the day after we arrived in Roatan. Diana sat and spoke with a man and two women who were cooking. A few more blocks closer to the hotel we stopped and sampled some flat, large, chip-like bread coated with garlic on one side. The big black woman selling the dried bread seemed to be astonished at our boasting of the good flavor. I asked her permission to take photographs, and then asked her niece, who was wearing huge blue curlers. I snapped a few quick photographs. Diana and I work well as a team in these situations. She flatters the client as I fire away with the camera. These casual settings make for good photography.

Back in the hotel we packed up and exactly at eight o'clock our taxi driver from the day before returned to give us a pre-planned ride to the ferry. He almost secured a pick up for when we come back from Roatan, but my instinct told me the price was inflated. A side conversation with the man taking the luggage affirmed the price was fifty limperas more than usual. We bought our two tickets for one hundred and ten dollars, which included a round trip. This was one-third the price we would have spent to fly directly into Roatan. We know how to save money - use buses.

On the ferry I happened to strike up a conversation with a retired American bus driver who lives in Guatemala. He seemed lonely and glommed onto a brief introductory "hello" that lasted almost the entire boat journey. Diana was literally turning white from seasickness and was trying to sleep off the nausea. The man started by saying how screwed up the world was. I should have known then it was going to be a crazy ride, but I, in my ignorant lust to encounter others, feed into the fire of back and forth conversation. He hated Obama, he thought that health care was being "forced down our throats", and that the oil spills in the Gulf of Mexico was the end of civilization. That I half agreed with. He said Obama was a Socialist. I said I was a Socialist and that the country needed more men like Obama. It wasn't a confrontational encounter in the least. He seemed to be seeking answers more than being stuck in an ideology. He listened to me in a way that I felt given a few months, and no Fox News, he would have come around. The man needed attention.

I hate being unkind, but aside from feeling politically, and completely unable to connect with this man's words, I felt him to be somewhat stupid. This is a word teachers should have stricken from their vocabulary, so I use it in shame. He was considerably less than a dull tool in a shed. There was actually one thing we did agree on – 'Pork Barreling'. This practice by the Congress should be outlawed and no bill should ever contain a single item that is not relevant to the specific law being written. (Ah we agreed.) A bridge to nowhere in Alaska, an extra billion in Medicare for Nebraska, or a library to some dead senator should never be permitted into legislation that is for "all" the people. (Do I watch Fox news?)

I don't mind a good difference of opinions, but what convinced me this man was stupid was his description of his traveling to Roatan. He left Guatemala

City (he lives in a small town near that capitol) and rode in a bus to San Pedro Sula, Honduras, for twelve hours. He was in San Pedro Sula's bus terminal three hours when he boarded a different bus for La Ceiba. He spent the night in La Ceiba (thank god we didn't run into him there) and was on the ferry for Roatan at nine thirty like us. Now, how long was he planning to stay in the beautiful tropical island of Roatan? Two Hours. Seriously, I was in shock. And what are you going to do there for two hours? "I hear they have good casinos," was his response.

By this time Diana was whiter than the sea caps splashing from the waves of the bouncing boat. She looked at me with a taxi driver-cold-far-away-heartless-detached expression and said, "Make this parrot shut up." This was hushed during one of the few pauses where the man was not engaging me and looking at the TV playing an American canned-laughter comedy. She placed the words just as the canned-laughter smothered anything in possible earshot. I said my Colombian wife wasn't feeling well, hoping to quiet his endless conversation. The word Colombian spurred another twenty minutes of stories of how he had been married to a Colombian woman. He even graced Diana with a few Spanish sentences to verify her already exploding curiosity. I couldn't get him to let go. He was at my ankle like a dog that hates bus drivers or postmen. I turned toward two young men wearing cornrows and Bo Derrick beads in their hair. They mumbled how stupid the man was in Spanish and continued speaking in English. The young men and I began with a point of strong agreement.

The young men were locals so I began to drum up information about this or that. I asked to share a taxi to the West End Beach, and they agreed. A few minutes later the eldest said he was in a time squeeze, needed to get a taxi right away and couldn't wait while we got our bags. We shook hands as the boat docked and I mumbled something about "white bread" under my breath that got a good chuckle from them both. We parted on another agreeing note.

The luggage retrieval system was one of the most unique I've ever seen. It was a good thirty minutes when I was able to get our bags. A giant, black man stood next to me patiently waiting. He was there long before I arrived but he didn't seem to notice my receiving my luggage first as the attendant handed me the bags. Everyone's bags were rolled in on big carts where the luggage was stacked, maybe six high. A triangular shaped counter with the luggage inside, and the shouting people screaming and waving their hands was the "system". The attendants were being heckled by the passengers to grab their bags for them. It was like a dogfight without gapping bloody parts. The attendants were trained by the Honduran taxi drivers to never let expression be shown. Even a "thank you" didn't prompt eye contact as they suffered though their labors. It was a tourist mob scene.

I had Diana stand next to a group of Honduran soldiers thinking that would ease the seasickness. They looked at her, looked at me, and whispered something about a possible drug-kidnapping incident, but Diana kissed me and their suspicions retreated. She was so pale I was beginning to think I had married a Colombian albino. Just as I got the two bags I became engaged in a dialogue with my American nightmare.

American: "Do you know how much they want for a taxi to the casino?"

Me: "No", was all I could say.

American: "Eighty dollars."

Me: "They must have seen you coming, our taxi will be twenty".

American: "They say the drive is one hour there and one hour back, that gives me no time to gamble because the ferry goes back in two hours at one o'clock".

Me: "Why don't you stay the night, or two nights?"

American: "Because I've already paid for my hotel room back in La Ceiba and the ferry"

Me: "Well stay anyway. How much was the room?"

American: "Nine Dollars." How much are you paying for your hotel?

Me: "Thirty dollars."

American: "I heard there wasn't a place for less than one hundred and forty"

This was all going back and forth as we exited the boat depot and a bevy of taxi drivers began approaching us yelling into our faces. At that point, God intervened in the form of an Archangel disguised as a taxi driver who whisked us away before we could know what was happening to the stupid American. We quickly negotiated a fifteen-dollar fare and were off toward the town called West End. I did get a glimpse of the man as I turned back. He was on his knees begging for mercy as a pirate was lancing his vocal chords for speaking out of turn. This stuff can't be made up. God puts people in our path for emotional nourishment and creative subject matter. There is no possible other explanation. In the one hour he has to gamble here he may lose everything. The only footnote needed to add is this. While on the boat, he explained to me that he had a SLIGHT gambling problem.

Now let's do a quick math equation. I don't gamble, but I know to sit at a poker table must be at least twenty dollars to open a bet, maybe less. Let's recap: To pay for a twelve hour bus ride, stay in a hotel for nine dollars, spend over one hundred dollars for a ferry ride to Roatan, only to plan a two hour stay is the best possible, most cost-effective way to stop a gambling habit. The man is a genius.

The taxi ride was a little depressing. We both noted that we'd had a different impression of the place from the Travel Channel. I expected a high standard of living, or men in suits, but the same kind of poverty on the mainland was all along the road leading to West End Beach. The taxi driver wisely didn't have change for the twenty-dollar bill I handed him. I told him to keep it anyway and thanked him for his pirate friend with the sword back at the boat dock. These people all know each other here. It is a small place.

Our cabin was just as bad as the taxi driver tried to warn us. I instinctively don't believe taxi drivers. They get commissions from hotels and always tell me my destination is a bad deal. He tried to warn us about the mosquitoes, we (I) didn't listen. He tried to tell us that the cabins were very small; we (I) didn't listen. He tried to tell us that the cabins were as bare as a baby's butt; we (I) didn't listen. I suppose Saint Joseph went through the same bullshit when he got Bethlehem. He had a reservation and wasn't going to slip from the plan no matter that the reservation was a stable. He'd booked the place months before on the telephone and was told he would be charged on his credit card for the first night. I had no choice, just like Saint Joseph. One night is one night. So we've experienced the worst of a place in order to gain something better. Again this is all the work of God in our lives. So we arrived on a donkey and Diana was recouping from the seasickness of rocking on a donkey's back.

The port town of West End is so small it is like something out of the Wild West. We have seen some of the same people that were with us on the bus to La Ceiba. The woman from the bus, next to the teenage "texter", is here as well. Her name is Ashley. She told us how to sneak into the fancy resort at West Bay (the next town over) and do some excellent snorkeling. We walked the length of West End in about ten minutes just as the Lonely Planet book had described. We have stopped in a few tourists' shops to get ideas; most of the goods are from Guatemala. I'm telling Diana to wait until we hit the mother lode in Chichicastenango, Guatemala. That is where prices will be the best.

Here, there are the most creative speed bumps I have ever seen. Old ropes from ships are laid across the dirt road and the cars have to slowly maneuver over them. These are the ropes that hold huge vessels at a pier, so they are large enough to stop a car. The streets are nothing more than sand pits where pools of water sit and splash as cars drive by. The one street in West End runs along the shore, where shops, restaurants, and hotels filter back into the land. The water-side is the beach with some establishments on stilts over the water's edge, or long piers that run to buildings built on stilts far out on a pier. West End is a small hippie town where most of the buildings are hidden back inside the trees. Such was the case of our first hotel with the tincy-whincy cabins.

The first night in our tiny cabin was not the least bit disappointing if you like mosquito bites the size of quarters (on Diana's butt, not mine. I can't see my own butt.). The night included a power outage and sweltering heat where pools of sweat form in the area between the chest and shoulder blades. When the power went out and the ceiling fan stopped I was typing while my feet were draped over Diana's legs. The sudden darkness unleashed a flurry of small moths, or gnats that attacked my computer screen. At first there were three, or four, which caused an interesting pattern on the computer screen, but within a minute there were well over fifty bugs running around the computer screen like there was an orgy being missed. I could no longer keep the computer on my lap. This tiny army of infiltrating bugs was getting in through the window screens. I turned off the computer, risking my life from an impending massive invasion. By doing this I managed to free myself from the responsibility of writing for that day.

It was somewhere in the middle of the night that the electricity returned only to blind me from the light bulb directly above our sleepy heads. This woke Diana who sleepily stumbled to the bathroom to pee. I was too sleepy to move and asked my wife to shut off the lights. She shut off the fan instead and that got my attention. "No, No, not that one!" I said, as I drifted back into slumber-land with the sounds of tropical insects and a cooling fan. I woke freezing a few hours later, thinking to myself I was such a spoiled human being as I pulled the covers off Diana (so she later reported to me in the morning). This is something I manage to do in every place we have ever slept. I get the lecture as if it is something I lay awake intentionally planning. The exact moment she falls asleep I steal her covers and laugh to myself.

In the morning we made the transition to the new hotel down the street in three minutes; it took two trips to the new hotel so we didn't have to pull the luggage on the sandy street. We have spent the last two hours setting up home, playing house. Our bags are unpacked, we have showered, the AC is on, the music is playing on our portable speakers, and life is pretty damn good. The only crisis has been the water running on our floor from the refrigerator. One of us unknowingly unplugged the refrigerator. I'm not laying blame, but there are two people here and I know I never touched the plug. However, we did use this opportunity to defrost and clean the small freezer.

Day Five: There are two roads in West End, one into town and one along the shore. From our hotel named "Coconuts", in the very center of town where all roads meet, there are three directions to travel. We went on three walks yesterday in each of these directions, my favorite being the road out of town that winds up a hill past some jungle and houses nestled off the road. The forest looked very inviting, but there were no trails. The major task of the day was to unpack and organize the room, but other than our walks, giving the passports to be locked in the hotel safe, and a call to Colombia we stayed put. We are doing a cleansing fast so it is better to stay in the hotel and do our drinks every three hours. It is all-liquid for one day and a vitamin drink every morning for breakfast. This is a weight loss and health program. Any smells of food or advertisements on TV are pure torture.

A crab next to the walkway to our room dashes into his hole every time we pass. The grounds aren't the garden with flowers like the other mosquito infested hotel, but we have a big room with two double beds, a big shower, and have the luggage under the table where I write on the computer. We have this kind of feeling "now what" because there is not much to do here. It is also the life style where there are many druggies and drunks who congregated at the noisy bar across the street from our first hotel. The local bar has Wi-Fi (Internet) so we sat at a side of the bar, outside and used their signal. The first day we were here a young boy gave us the password when we asked. We later spoke with his entire family while buying a smoothie in a restaurant. The family is from Boulder, Colorado and I knew the street where they live. (I lived in Boulder back in the 1970's.) They crossed paths with us many times as we sat on the front porch of the cabin in the first hotel. They seemed to like to hotel but they had a large cabin. You know how we felt.

Today the plan is to snorkel. The sun is out and it is our fourth year wedding anniversary. What a lucky man I am. Diana is in the frame of mind that I love most about her. She hasn't fretted over one thing for a couple of days. She is smiling a lot and is happy. This is what a vacation is supposed to do. I know back in New York life isn't so easy for her.

We headed out of the hotel at eight thirty in the morning. We had walked to a dive shop two nights before to inquire about times and prices. At nine we were to leave, but the plan changed because the scheduled deep sea divers did not show, so it was only Diana and I. Instead of a boat we went in a truck to the next town over, West Bay. I was planning to do the same thing only by water taxi the next day so we paid ten dollars each to go snorkeling in a place we could have taken a taxi to get to. Our guide, Dan, was a forty-year-old Australian. He is mixture of Asian and Caucasian. I was in a bit of a funk from the lack of a boat ride and knew we could have done this on our own. Dan and the other person, a young Honduran chap drove us to West Bay. We parked the car, and walked a narrow path to the beach situated between fancy, expensive resorts. The beach was picture perfect with white sand, crystal clear turquoise waters, and a good mile of more fancy resorts. We put our packs down near the path under a palm tree in the shade, lubed up with sun block, and entered a blue heaven.

The white sand extended into the shallow water about the length of a football field, where sea grasses then dominated the underwater shore. Past the sea grass was the real adventure. We had floated quite a ways when the change into coral and breath taking scenery began. The fish and variety of coral sudden appeared. The first coral looked like anchored fans waving in the rolling waters. They were connected by one thick root at the base. This coral began to appear at the end of the sea grass. Then large, round coral, some looking like human brain bulged and erupted into clumps of corals the size of large trucks. We saw a school of squid that looked like they were swimming backwards, their fins were in the front of their bodies. Dan pointed out a stingray and we swam to a deep section where starfish lay far below on the white sandy bottom. I tried to swim down but the pressure on my sinuses was too much. Dan told me to hold my nose and push, but I couldn't master this decompression method and gave up on diving below the surface.

When we entered the water Diana was a champ and seemed to be doing fine. She can't swim so we brought along her life jacket from New York. We brought our own snorkel gear as well. About fifteen minutes into the dive I looked over to Diana who was swimming so hard that I thought it strange. She wasn't kicking her legs, but thrashing her arms to move through the water. Her mask was completely fogged up and she was not having much fun in her first snorkeling experience. I tried to explain a few basics, but she interrupted and told me she had swallowed water. She was dog paddling and gagging on water. I was more interested in the views so I more or less, ignored her, thinking she would manage by herself. Forty minutes into the swim she was heading back to shore so I followed. She had swallowed a considerable amount of water.

I was a bit miffed and swore I wouldn't get upset at Diana's state of hopelessness. Lucky for her we were with other people. She said I looked angry. I was but didn't want to show how perturbed I can be to my wife around others. I know this is without good reason, I know it is her first time in this environment, but I still find it hard to believe she didn't ask for help, or more importantly, figure out that something was wrong and she could find a solution. I should have given her a lesson the minute we entered the water. Between three grown men and Diana we all failed her. I then failed her again by getting upset with her inabilities. I feel like she is helpless in the natural world. I would be asking for help and trying to figure out how to correct any problems. She was miserable and said nothing.

All my anger finally came to a peak at dinner, after a completely lovely day of napping, making love, and making art. Diana painted a picture of herself snorkeling and I did a watercolor of a flower. At dinner I posed the question and by then I was angry all over again.

"If something isn't working for you, don't you consider that you are doing something wrong?"

I was very careful to use the right words. I bit my tongue. But God was I feeling like an angry fool who was as compassion-less as the devil. I get in these states of mind where I want to explode at her for being so inexperienced. When she pointed out a rash that was on her skin I just said I didn't care.

"Do you know how many complaints you give me a day about your problems?"

I went into a lecture about having a positive state of mind and how much her issues in life were self-absorbed and draining on my energy. There is a word in Buddhism that described the flame of anger and how, with proper training, one can overcome falling into the trap of anger. I have not mastered that discipline. I am only at the level of thinking about squelching the flames when it is too late.

Of course this was our four-year anniversary celebration and I couldn't help but feel worse for falling into negativity myself. We sat at an outdoor restaurant a few feet from the water's edge inside a type of wooden booth with bright red cushions and red fabric draped over the two sides, opening onto the ocean. The sun was low behind a vast gray bank of clouds. Diana began her speech about not being the right woman for me, which only makes me angrier because I think she should be seeing herself as self-actualized in control, and not a victim of a miscalculated relationship. Later I stopped while we were walking home and said there is no perfect relationship, the real issue is how we take responsibility for our own actions and work at being better for each other.

These things seem to bottle up in me, and every four or five days the cork releases. Maybe I'm very intolerant of illness or the level of "complaining" that my own mother exercised when I was child. My mother was always sickly and had a million things that caused her to drink. Part of any relationship is based on the need to verbalize what is bothering us, but this has to be tempered by an awareness that just so much of our needs can be taken on by our partner. I talked about all this at dinner. Diana was sad, but eventually pulled us out of that hole by changing the subject before I got too intense.

This is why I love her. She doesn't challenge me for a fight. She gets angry, I push her buttons, and she shows me she is a better person than me by not fighting back. We held hands on the way to dinner and in the dark on the walk back home. We stopped in a few souvenir shops on the way. The prices here are astoundingly high. The man in the grocery store, who holds our passports in the hotel safe, told us where the prices would be better. He directed us to the main town called Coxel Hole. A refrigerator magnet from Honduras was five dollars. I'd have to love the storeowner to buy under such conditions. Tomorrow we will rent a motorcycle and see more of Roatan. It is growing on us here.

We are beginning to recognize the same people and they are nodding back to us. A man (Jim is his name) at the tourist booth was helping us set up the motorcycle for the day when his landlady walked up and needed twenty dollars for the electric bill. While we were doing our business Jim asked me if I'd be kind enough to advance him the twenty dollars for the motorcycle rental, which I obliged. I guess he needed me to come along at that moment. Jim has been in that tourist booth every time we have passed the one street that runs along the water. I don't think he is going too far to not be able to track down.

West End is where the people "without money" come. The contrast between West End and West Bay is like a ghetto. That is an extreme comparison of course. Here in West End the tone is rustic and unpolished. There are half a dozen pricey hotels and restaurants, most situated on the water's edge or built at the end of long docks. But the majority of places here are showing a need of paint and renovation. West Bay in contrast is like Miami with costly hotels. Here in West End the road is in bad shape. The paved street ends at the entrance to West End and a sandy, bumpy, road with large, deep holes begins. The "holes" are maybe seven feet across which gives the road a roller coaster feel. West End is in need of some street repair. How one repairs a sandy road with more sand I do not know. Blacktop wouldn't be appropriate. In West Bay the roads are all paved with gold.

There are more tiny chapels here than people. I have seen at least six and there are more nestled behind the buildings that hug the shore road. Some of the buildings are very tidy with carefully painted doors and corner panels. They have fences that are painted the same color as the house. Directly next door there might be a shack that hasn't been painted for years. Local people have managed to squeeze in small businesses between the shops where investors (outsiders) have built air-conditioned touristy shops. So walking down the street is a patchwork of new next to old buildings. You can tell where the local people live, and work, versus the newly built properties from investors. It gives a feeling of financial invasion and poverty living side by side.

Here the architectural mix is the same as the combining of different peoples from races. It is a planetary crossroads of cultural styles and genetic pools. The architecture is both modern and old school. The locals are African in origin, or a mix of Honduran/Hispanic peoples. English is the major language but it isn't the kings English, or the United States English, or Jamaican English, but more closely related to the Jamaican style of language. As we walk around we hear a few distinct English words but the rest is difficult to understand. There are Rasta's with long dreadlocks. I assume the one on the scooter, who is a permanent fixture up and down the road, is the local connection for 'weed'. We get a whiff here and there as we pass bars.

This morning the day laborer here in the hotel had a little puff that drifted into the air back in his cabin. I like the sweet smell for nostalgic reasons but hate the thought of putting any poisons in my body. Diana has no relevant connection. There are many foreigners here who run businesses. There is another level of people who, like Costa Ricans, live here for the cheap drugs and alcohol. Street people are well accepted as part of the local fabric.

The day was quite lovely. We didn't rent a planned motorcycle because the motorcycle wouldn't start; a scooter was all they had. Jimmy, the tour salesman, was there sweeping the road in front of his stall around seven forty-five. He told me James, the cycle shop owner, would be along, but he would give him a call on his cell phone. Around eight thirty he walked around the corner and I gave him all my info and paid. When the bike wouldn't start we switched to the scooter. I think it was a better ride anyway. The seats are wide and my legs are easily passed to the street with open design. We don't have to mount it like a bicycle.

We left on our journey with two packs, a bag with snorkels and fins, and food for the day. Our first stop was the town of Coxel Hole. We were struck by the poverty and number of black folks homes in a state of disrepair. On our way through the town we turned up a street and heard a man yelling in English, "One way". There were no signs, but it was a one-way street. The man spoke in Spanish and Diana asked him where the shops were. He obliged but his directions still did us no good. We went up a hill that was a dead end and the police station. This was the first time I almost spilled off the vehicle. At the top of the hill I turned and applied the front brake too strong. We skidded and I braced us with my foot just enough to keep us from falling. We found our way back to the main highway (more like a single road) expecting to find some souvenir shops. Nothing. Coxel Hole was pretty broken down. Naked children ran into the streets and people milled around like nothing could move them short of an earthquake. We were there maybe five minutes and left.

Our next stop was a boat dock where we had a perfect shoot of the huge cruise ship that was about to dock. I asked by motion for permission, to take some pictures from the dock. The American owner shouted back, "Sure". He was a gringo all right. He was there with his wife and son. He stapled a sign on the dock, 'Free gift with a $20 purchase'. We took our pictures and entered the small gift shop in his home's basement.

"Where are you from", I asked as we passed him now sitting with his son and wife.

"Ohio, then Florida, now here for two years. And we love it".

He returned the question and I answered "Nebraska, and New York."

Diana said, "I am from Colombia" (Note there was a time she would get upset with me for telling people she was from Colombia. I think being in Central America has a different effect on her versus telling people in the USA.). We bought our single souvenir here, a magnet of tropical fish saying Roatan. Financial disclosure would show that I loved the man due to the price; five dollars.

We ate a few walnuts and had a drink of water on the dock as I took a few more pictures, then rode off. When we were speaking the man had explained that the cruise ships brought tours to him. He had two boats that took them around the shore for a tour. As we were tooling down the road I couldn't help thinking to myself, "How does a guy come to Roatan and get connected to the cash flow of a cruise line company?" People have lived here all their lives and never had such an opportunity. Shops line the road with people scrapping out a living on pennies and this guy is "plugged-in," has a beautiful house, a private boat dock, a deep sea fishing tour boat tied to the dock, and sells tours on his two other boats. It baffles me how these things happen.

We rode through a slight detour called French Harbor that was pretty run down. Houses lined the shore and in between we could see the beach but this was no luxury resort. People have houses on the beach, but some were so poor a broken pain of glass would be left that way forever. We saw a very modern police car parked at a station. Diana noted that the car was fully operational with a computer mounted on the dashboard. Strange that such poverty existed and such wealth was displayed by law enforcement. We passed over a bridge where two men sat selling green plantain near a canal with boats tied to docks lined both sides of the water. The water was dirty, the houses were in need of paint, and an overall run-down feeling saturated a neighborhood where living from the sea was a daily struggle.

A few miles down the road a grand complex with all the modern stores stood out like a shiny new penny. The mall was empty of cars in the parking lot. There was even a 'Wendy's' with a drive through. From that point on we noticed more nature, a few resorts with fancy entrances, and fewer and fewer people walking on the sides of the road. We entered the half of the island that was true to the way things used to be before modernization.

The highway rose to the higher ground and on both sides the sea was visible. Far below on the shore resorts with white sand beaches could be seen. Turquoise bays with white sand mixed amongst sea grass below the surface made islands of dark colors within the water. It was windy and pockets of heat would slap us in the face and make our bodies ache, then around another turn or down a hill the heat would give way to a chill blown in from a shady rain forest. Fire Trees with red-hot flowers made them seem beyond any possible real color. Brahma bulls and baby cows walked like the heat was so common they never knew any difference for generations. The slow pace of life had become a genetic trait. Palm trees mixed in with the rain forests. Once in a while a single palm tree would reach far above all the rest of the forest and bend with the wind, by now the wind was strong enough to tip the scooter from an occasional quick gust.

The American man back at the dock had given me the names of a couple of resorts that would welcome our business, so we turned into Turquoise Bay when I recognized the signage. The hill was so steep it was dangerous and for a second time the front brake grabbed a hold and almost set us onto the steep, I mean very steep, decline. We knew we'd have to make the trip back with both of us on the scooter, a dangerous thought.

When we arrived at the resort a man welcomed us and asked if we would like to use the beach. He told us he would bring us drinks if we liked. He also said there was a restaurant on the premises. I said we had sandwiches but we'd like a drink. We walked past the swimming pool, where a diving lesson was taking place, down some wooden steps to the white sand and a row of white plastic lounge chairs that had big shade huts made of palm leaves. A young, heavy black woman that offered a message or hair braiding greeted us. Another woman sat under a round hut in the shade where beads and tourist trinkets were for sale. We were the only four people on the entire beach. We ate our tuna, avocado, and mayonnaise sandwich. Soon the waiter was there with a list of drinks on a menu for offer. We bought two Pina Coladas at five dollars each. Bugs were biting us so we entered the water for a few minutes to cool off. We exited the water and then used the last of a bug repellent we had brought along. This was a poor calculation on my part.

I did a painting as Diana studied her English grammar exercises. It was very hot. By this time the diving class had entered the water at the farthest end of the beach. We snorkeled again. I gave Diana a needed lesson on how to flap her legs and not use her arms so much. I then explained the best way to use the mask so she would not swallow any water if she knew how to operate everything. She seemed fine and knew how to do the snorkeling. I swam ahead and looked at the bottom, which had a grand field of sea grass. There was one tiny blue fish and one strange fish buried in the grass. Nothing else. No coral, nothing but a good mile of sea grasses.

After swimming maybe a half-mile out, it was time to give up, the bottom was no longer visible. This was not the Roatan I expected. Diana sat inside the water close to shore for fear of the bugs. As I was first entering the water she screamed from the vast number of red welts that had covered my entire back. I felt them biting as I squished them with blood flowing out of the tiny creatures that bore into the skin drinking my blood. Vampires of Roatan. Sounds like a good title for a trendy novel where one could get rich and buy one of these empty, bug infested, resorts!

By the time we tried to sit back on our white benches it was too late. The tiny bloodsuckers were out-numbering us, swarming us we headed out. Our white paradise was fine until the last of the bug spray ran out and nothing could hold the bugs back. The painting was done, the gear was packed up, and Diana sat in the water until I gave the signal that the bloodsuckers had given us the all clear and we left. I asked the woman under the shade what the bugs were and how she took such punishment. She replied, "They are sand flies, and I just rub my arms all day".

I'm thinking what about the rest of you? What about the other woman that lay sleeping in the heat? Was she dead from loss of blood? Should we call an ambulance? Later in the shower at the hotel my back looked like a fatal case of chicken pox. Diana was covered as well, only worse.

Because of the steep incline Diana walked back up to the top of the hill. It was a good half-mile. I was proud of her for being such a good sport. She had left well before me. I passed her and had time to stop, take a short walk for some photographs, at which time she caught up with me. At the highway we turned left and headed deeper into the island's westerly tip, coming to a view were the island was thin and the sea was close on both sides. At a bus stop we sat in the shade and drank a fruit drink we had brought along. We took a ten-minute break as vans of local people, or delivery trucks, waved at us as they passed. That was as far as we could go. "Do you want to head back now?" wasn't off the tip of my tongue before Diana said, "Yes".

By the time we retraced our return the wind was very strong, and the sun had burned my arms and legs so badly that Diana laughed at my color. She loves to say I look like white cheese. Now I looked like red cheese. Our scooter ride then involved one slight mishap. I was pulling off the road to shoot a photograph and spilled the scooter on the gravel. I jumped off as the scooter tipped but Diana rolled off and hit her tailbone. She is still in a lot of pain. We didn't crash so much as the whole thing slowly tilted on its side. Luckily she was wearing the life jacket and had a slight scratch on her upper arm, but she hit a rock with her butt. I felt bad, like I should have been more careful but it all happened in a split second. I instinctively saved myself by jumping off and left her to roll off onto her bottom. I ran, she rolled. The scooter wasn't even scratched because it was laid down, more so than dropped. We picked ourselves up and got back on after I took the picture.

After the spill I felt immensely guilty and offered to stop at a Wendy's fast food. Diana refused and pointed out a natural juice bar that was in the shopping center we had passed before. I would have offered her gold and jewelry at that point but she only wanted a fruit drink. NOT American fast food. The drink was delicious. I, of course, told the man and woman working there about our spill, telling them how Diana had jumped off and caused an accident. She pushed me! They knew I was exaggerating the whole story and had a good laugh. I was very proud of Diana for understanding and going along with the joke.

When we came back to the hotel and parked the scooter, I asked if she'd like to snorkel in our beach at West End. (Half Moon Bay is the name of the bay.) Diana agreed. To my surprise and delight I swam out and saw beautiful coral reefs right here in Half Moon Bay. They were amazing. Diana stayed in the shallow water but I convinced her that the reefs were more accessible from the sides of the small bay. The snorkeling was better than the first day with the two hired divers. That day we had driven an hour and half to find that which was better in our own backyard. Isn't life silly that way? Diana wasn't as excited as I was. She stayed close to the shore. I thought she was missing the best parts by not venturing out further.

We ate a home cooked meal of tortillas, beans, cheese, and avocados (added after the micro wave). It was perfect. We watched the US news on the television and ate to our hearts content. How perfect a day it was! After the dinner we took another ride toward the beach the divers had taken us the day before - West Bay. As we stopped to take photographs on the crest of a hill a man asked us to help him open his scooter seat compartment. He had a thick Irish accent.

I said, "I won't help the Irish", which got a good chuckle from him. We couldn't help so we asked a local man at the same hilltop view to help. He obliged. I introduced Diana and myself to Michael O'Connor. (What an unusual Irish name.) He was on vacation and a high school teacher like me. He was alone at the moment but with a group of seven other teachers trekking throughout Central America, beginning in Costa Rica. I asked him if he knew my Irish friends the Henebry's. He didn't but he was from Tipperary, knew the Galtey Mountains, and all my favorite places near to these mountains. The wind was so strong it was feeling dangerous up at our high location overlooking the sea. We said our "so-longs" and rode to West Bay just long enough to turn around. The wind was ferocious.

Before it got too dark we were home to call Colombia on the computer. Diana talked to her mother while I stood on the beach and met a polite young, thin, black man named Pinkie. He works on the glass bottom boat and told me a story about getting the diving bends, which caused him to give up diving for a living. He has been out diving again but thinks it's wiser to work on a boat or on dry land. We stood on the shore chatting and watching the sunset for a long time.

As I stroll home Jimmy, in the tourist booth, was chatting with Ashley the teacher from California. We met her on the bus. A circle closed when I saw the two of them chatting. It was one of those unexplainable cosmic moments when two totally, unrelated people, I had met, were now speaking together. I passed them both, not saying hello or interrupting them. Life is a beautiful thing, this is one beautiful place and we are into it now. We are settled in and will hate leaving in three days.

Day Six: One of our most important cultural lessons yesterday was something that we found very interesting as teachers. At an intersection we could see down directly into a school. The school was nothing more than students sitting out of doors, a bunch of chairs and a broken black board that was a being written on by a standing student. The group sat in the shade of a tree and could see us above on the street. Diana said I should photograph them to show my students how lucky they are. I don't think my teenage student's minds are capable of comparing luck to poverty. They think of only what is right in front of them and not abstract concepts. The new students who come to the USA have that reality to compare to, but those who grow up in my country can never grasp their true good fortune. It is the parents, or lack of parenting, that foster attitudes into the children. Some parents don't appreciate their environment while others do. This is all handed down to their children. When you were young and sitting at the dinner table did your mother give you, "Eat your food because there are children starving in China"? I grew up feeling quilt, but I didn't have a clue about China.

I told Diana a story about one of my students from a few years ago. One day we saw him on the street as we drove through the town where I work. This young man was an excellent student of mine, polite, soft spoken, and worked hard at his class work. On one occasion we sat together at my desk and had a private conference. He was a senior and I asked him what plans he had for college. He hummed and hawed around for a while then asked me to keep a secret.

"I'm not living at any address, so it is hard for me to do the college applications."

"Why, what's going on?"

"Well my dad was arrested and I have been living on the streets for a while."

This was a case where the student was the parent, had all the right motivations, but was a victim of many circumstances beyond his control. I can guess he never made it to college because when we saw him he looked homeless. I hadn't seen him for over a year at that time.

Now how about something a little more mundane from today; one of the tiny nuisances of the tropics is the vast number of ants. Our hotel room had ants so small they are difficult to see, but on top of the white microwave oven they're easy to see. They run at clips of speed that makes them look like little jets zooming across the white surface. These little guys are everywhere. One day I wanted a snack so I lay on the bed eating some garlic bread-like chips we'd bought from the woman on the street back in La Ceiba. As I watched TV and ate the chips I felt ants running all over my arms. Much to my horror, I could see them in the plastic bag. Things went from bad to worse when I realized I was eating ants. The ants had infiltrated our food. The next day I had to painstakingly empty the almonds we brought from the states. Each remaining almond in the bag was inspected; I had already eaten some of them as well. To clean the remaining almonds in the bag was of minimal problem. How many I had eaten I do not know. The almonds are now in a double sealed plastic zip-lock bag. We have sealed all foods and secured the parameter!

There is one irritating custom here in Roatan, rather all of Honduras. The moment you think there is peace and quiet a taxi driver will toot his horn. Even here in Roatan on a morning stroll a taxi driver will purposely sneak up and toot the horn. The toot gives a jolt to one's body, giving the digestive system a thrust equal to coffee. This event happens so much it is irritating. I have not seen one taxi without the accompanying "toot, toot". This kind of salesmanship is not that different from the man selling sun glasses to us while we were in the water snorkeling. From the beach, some thirty plus feet away in deep water, while we were wearing our snorkels and masks, the man waved at me. He motioned to the sunglasses; I motioned to my diving mask and shrugged my shoulder with a question. He got my point and laughed. The taxi drivers don't laugh, they taunt, they toot-taunt.

As I stated before, it is our four-year anniversary and we were walking hand in hand along the road. Two or three venture capitalists in the form of taxi tooters snuck up and blasted the "toot, toot" question. "Do you want a ride?" The only time this didn't happen to us was while we were on the scooter. The very second we dismounted the scooter on a vacant, abandoned road a taxi would give a first toot, and then appear from around a corner, or a tree, or from under a rock.

In both cities, La Ceiba and San Pedro Sula, the taxi drivers were wilder with the horns than the island of Roatan. They would see us from a good distance and begin the "toot, toot" in rapid succession, machine gun style. I hate this and feel like the ministry of culture needs to give courtesy classes to the same taxi drivers who give those blank, far-off, glassy-eyed looks as they attempt to kill us. In addition, some of the drivers here have very little respect for people on motor scooters. More than once we noticed that an unwanted game of chicken was being played with us. The larger the truck the bigger the toy, the bigger the toy the greater the aggression, and a projected power ready to squash small bugs on scooters. Just an observation I'd prefer to forget about. Oops, there is a taxi driver "toot, tooting" me outside the hotel window. Time to go.

In the morning our day began with a scooter ride to Flower Bay, the part of the island that lay south of the West End and West Bay, on the other side of the island from our hotel. After a steep climb up and over the mountain we came to a coastal road that runs the length of the water until Coxel Hole. Along the shore there were homes built on stilts over the water, vacant lots, broken foundations where houses once stood, and lots and lots of trash. The trash was so bad the water would be several yards deep with chunks of floating plastic, wooden logs, and Styrofoam in thousands of different sizes and shapes. The extra dimension to the floating garbage was the thick level of poverty. Nowhere was there a break from the low income and sadness of life without money. Few houses had a fresh coat of paint, most had no paint, were worn, termite eaten, and bleached by the sun. There was a new landing dock for large vessels, which stood out like a sore thumb. This was built from new investment money. We went slowly and hugged the side of the road as other cars and motorcycles passed us. There was no need to hurry.

We came into Coxel Hole from the lower side, the side near the shore I was trying to get to the day before, while going the wrong way on a one-way street. We passed the short length of the downtown, passed the super market, the very small municipal park, and came to the end before we knew it and found no parking place. I knew by now the road circled back to the shore, so we asked a taxi driver how to return. "Left, and then a quick left", so we did. This time, when back on the shore road, we asked a well-decorated police chief where to park. He told us, but I found an empty spot in a gift shop parking lot. We went right into the gift shop, looked but didn't buy. Our first brief walk took us to the municipal park where we ate a snack of granola bars we brought from the States. I took a few pictures of men's sculptured busts on tall podiums and asked a man sitting there who they were. One was of a local hero. The other was the man from England who gave Roatan to Honduras. This was one hundred and twenty years ago.

We crossed the street and bought a drink of tamarindo, a tropical fruit we also get in Colombia. As we sat on some red plastic chairs we began to speak to a man sitting at another table. He was the money runner for the local super market. He made the deposits for the big store we planned to shop at. It's funny how a first impression of a person as some kind of street person is erased within a few minutes of conversation. This is a fear reflex or some kind of self-preservation by projecting negativity. The man sat next to us for a long while as we all shifted from one piece of conversation to another. He wore a t-shirt and looked poor, but he was a regular guy with a steady job and great personality.

We passed up and down the street to the end of the row of shops, crossing to the opposite side, and stopping at the Catholic Church that was pretty bleak. We shopped for some groceries and left after an hour and a half. This time we went back to the road along the shore at Flower Bay. Where the road turned toward the mountain we went straight, found a cantina, parked the scooter, and found some seats on the water under a shady palm roof, part of the bar. A television was on behind the bar counter. Not a soul was in sight. I took out the paints and started a view of the shore and two houses. Diana was embroidering. We were perfectly content to be there in the shade and alone.

We sat for a good forty-five minutes when a woman from across the street came over and served us two Seven-up drinks. She had to leave and left her son to watch the store, although it seemed unnecessary since we had been there for so long already. All of a sudden three other men appeared - a well-dressed man, a very sickly, elderly man, and a thin man who brought out some coral in hopes of selling it to us. Diana told him we couldn't take it on the airplane. I took some photographs of the old man and gave him some money. He sat next to me as I painted, and about five minutes later said, "That money can't buy me anything" so I gave him more money. "This can buy me something," was all he said. "I'm a sickly old man who doesn't have anything," was the depth of his conversation to me a few minutes later. Then he wandered off down the street.

A new stranger came in and joined the men at the bar watching TV. I continued to paint. Diana entered into conversation with the men, but I was focused on my painting. We spent over two hours sitting a few feet from the water and slowly milking the drinks. Eventually, I was bored painting so I took a walk to the street and went a few houses in each direction shooting pictures of dilapidated houses, and caught one of a beautiful young boy in front of a bright yellow house. One of the houses had a strange, scrolled message drawn on a white piece of canvas. It was posted at the entrance. The words were in English, about Moses and the flood. An illiterate person wrote it but the idea was to find redemption and keep those with bad spirits away.

Inside the shack was a woman singing in chants over and over again. As I passed back a second time the woman was chanting something about the white man. She had seen me walking along the dirt road. I looked at what I thought was a figure inside the dark building, which was actually only half a house. One side of the structure had a roof but all the walls were caved in. Inside a strange chanting figure was moving in the shadows. My assumption was a person with schizophrenia was living in squalor. Seeing me, a white man, set off some fears. I was an intruder. I know we were in a place where tourists never came.

On the porch of a yellow house where the women came to get us the drinks, a young boy sat washing clothes in a plastic tub. He had come home from school, come into the cantina to say hello to his older brother minding the store, and went to the yellow house. After changing into street clothes from his school uniform he sat on the top step and washed the cloths. This was a good household and the boy was doing his chores with no one home telling him what to do. I went back to the bar. Meanwhile, the three men at the bar changed the station from a movie to soccer, and back and forth. We left and thanked them.

On the scooter Diana began to tell me about the conversations she was having while I painted. The first, very old man, whom I had photographed and given the money, was critical of her.

"Why are you with this white man? You are a disgrace to your race. You are a Latina, who has no business being with a man who is old enough to be your father." (He guessed her age to be eighteen.) "You are giving him sex for money."

After the old man left she had a similar conversation with the other older men at the bar. I asked her how she responded to these kinds of accusations.

"I said nothing and smiled. This wasn't true and I could not change their minds", she said to me.

I was pretty hurt by all this. I felt in some way I should have defended her. Maybe not hearing all this was better for me. I got a sick feeling in my stomach that she had to encounter such prejudice. "Racism isn't just in white people", I said as we rode the scooter returning back to Coxel Hole. "I felt the old man hating me just because I'm a "rich white guy," I told Diana. (Rich by his standard of living.) We didn't talk about it much more, because I know I wouldn't have been nasty had I heard the conversations. However, it disturbed me deeply that people would see us as sex-for-pay people. This all defied my ego. I knew I would never change these people's perceptions of us. We are tourists to them, that's all.

We circled back through Coxel Hole. We waved to the Hispanic man that told us we were going up a one-way street the day before. He recognized us and returned the wave. Riding back to the highway that leads to the West End is a very pleasant drive with houses on stilts, saw mills, and luxury resorts that dot the shore as one gets closer to our town. The first day our taxi driver showed us a resort where daily dolphin shows were free. Across the street was a Botanical Garden. We returned home and took a nap, cooling off in the AC. The dolphin show started at four so we left in time to take in the Botanical Garden first or so we thought. Our clock in the room was wrong and we arrived at the Botanical Garden with only a half hour till closing, which didn't give us enough time. We crossed the street only to find our dolphin show was at ten thirty the next day. The taxi driver and the Botanical Garden employee had told us the dolphin show was at four o'clock. The guard at the gate of the resort assured us that it was two years in the past. Word had not traveled very far or fast, not even across the street to the Botanical Garden.

The beginnings of the trail were well kept with some walkways and grass huts for group lessons. Each plant was well marked, orchids were in bloom, and plants we pay a few dollars for at a nursery back home were growing wild. A few of the giant specimens of plants were unbelievable in size. The pathways were lined with benches and meandered through the lower sector of what was a dry riverbed. As we ascended the trial became dirt. On what looked like a simple map with a single path became many paths, all more or less leading up and up to what the signs said, 'mountain path'.

We were the only people in the entire park as noted when we paid and saw no cars in the lot. Some of the most interesting vegetation was thick, dark groves of palm trees. These were not the kind you see people climbing up, but branches of leave that sprouted from the ground and fanned out. It was hot and muggy, yet the higher we climbed along the path, cool breezes would brush our faces. Occasionally, ropes had been strung along the path to help hikers pull themselves up the steep trail. At the top two wooden platforms with benches sat overlooking the coast and the diving resort far below. The resort was mammoth with an island and air conditioned huts lining the shore where mangroves skirted the shore. This was where the dolphin show was to be held. At the summit the palm trees had strange seed packets where the entire strand of seeds was half the size of my body. On the end of each seed (the size of a golf ball) there protruded a double hook, something one would not want to brush against.

We knew it was near closing time by then and headed back down, thinking we were retracing our footsteps but not so because of the number of trails. The area was covered with paths that all lead us downward. At the bottom we thanked the two young attendants and went back to the hotel for a dinner of bean burritos made in the microwave. I wanted to show Diana the far bay with snorkels so we went straight to the beach, walking as far along the shore as possible to reach the coral easier. The heat and sweat from our hike made the water look inviting.

The entire day was perfect up to that point. Diana got cold feet to swim and I got angry. I was a total ass, but I still am baffled by her fears. I swam, circling back to the shore as I was trying to get her to go farther out; it was actually shallower toward the reef than where she was swimming. I could stand on the sandy bottom at some points. Diana had retreated to the shore. "I saw it," was her response. She hadn't seen anything and I was pissed so I went back to get her. This was a mistake because by then I was too angry, wondering what on earth would cause a grown woman to be so childish. Fear is a powerful motivation, anger is worse. I asked her to come into the water again, she entered, and I steered her towards the rocks along the shore. She would have none of it. I was so hot the water surrounding me was boiling. After some unrepeatable words I was out by myself swimming alone trying to enjoy the reef.

The snorkeling was so much better than the first day I wanted Diana to see how different the reef was. When we paid the two guides to go with us in West Bay we swam the length of a football field just to see the reef. Here the reef was a quarter of the distance, hugging the sides of the bay. By that time I was as upset with myself as with Diana. But I swam out to see the reef. The sea grass was sprawling in the central area of the small bay; this is all Diana had seen. Out where I was the fish were thick and extremely vast in numbers. The colors of tropical fish were in hundreds of beautiful designs. The coral was round, skinny, flat, purple, red, yellow, or brain-like. It was multi-complexioned and a sight so beautiful I was astounded. I stayed out there a good hour. When I tired I would simply tread in the shallow water.

That night and into the next day I shut down from anger. I didn't want to write. I shouldn't have spoken. My wife is a much better person than I. In addition to all my anger, Diana was in a lot of pain from the boil-like swells where her mosquito bites were getting infected. She rubbed then so much; or rather they swelled so much that she was suffering greatly. Just like two summers before in Greece I have no tolerance for whining and whimpering. Unfortunately, I don't have much patience with her needs in those times. She claims the rash was worse than the one she got from the bed bugs in Rome. She had more on her body, for sure. I just tend to lay inappropriate blame when this kind of thing happens, all the wrong approach on my part. When Diana asked if there were mosquitoes in Belize I snapped back, "No, they don't allow them to cross the border, they are illegal there".

The next day was half a wash. I was pretty much without any company because Diana refused to leave the hotel room and air conditioning because the night before I got a very disturbing email from Jose's ex-girlfriend back in Costa Rica. Jose had been saying they would meet us in Nicaragua and she was refusing to speak to him. I was feeling like I was sick, mentally sick with anger, and hopelessly out of control over a silly snorkeling event my wife wouldn't do. Diana finally lightened up before I did. I apologized profusely and went out to snorkel alone again. I was feeling guilty and proposed we see the dolphin show.

We rode the scooter to the ten o'clock show and sat in a shaded area. I kept looking over at Diana's growing, red welts and realized this wasn't just a matter of positive thinking and mind over matter. A family of Honduran tourists was sitting between us as we watched the show. The crowd cheered, the two trainers did an excellent job and all were very happy with the performance. The heat was getting to Diana as the last dolphin trick was performed. I was thinking I'd better come up with a few tricks of my own to save our suffering relationship. We paid to enter a small museum dedicated to the island and the early peoples. The displays were of ancient artifacts and houses of the first black settlers. Photographs and items were displayed in dioramas.

Back on the scooter I proposed another attempt at snorkeling, but she would have none of this. I knew I was still in the doghouse. I returned the scooter to James who was sleeping in the shade. I didn't want to disturb him so I just let him sleep in peace. I sat with Jimmy, the tour-booth salesman, and told him about my dilemma with my wife. He was there for me and gave me some well needed, up-lifting advice. "Buy her something sweet, and tell her you love her".

It was around one o'clock that I went to the store and told the female clerk that Diana was suffering from bug bites. This was the same woman that showed us the hotel room. Jimmy had also told me to buy Diana a lotion called Cactus Juice. "No, no," protested the woman. "Put vinegar on the bites". Five minutes later the sting of raw vinegar was being applied to my wife's arms, back, and legs. An hour later after I returned from snorkeling the swelling was incredibly better. Diana's face showed signs of my attempts at reconciliation were paying off. The home remedy astonished me.

I wasn't going to spend my last day in the hotel room so I went out in the afternoon to shoot pictures. I wanted to capture as much as possible with my camera. I was out of the doghouse and thought it wise to just take some time to myself and try to stop beating my angry horse. I spoke with strangers, took photographs, and ended at the restaurant where we'd bought the guanabana ice cream the first day we arrived. The same man was not there. Only this time a white female and black female were sitting at the counter. They were close friends. The dark woman was wearing an apron, so I assumed she worked there as well. I found that she was the sister of Rudy, the owner. She lived in Massachusetts, as well as the tall white woman who was a dance instructor. We all were Democrats who like Obama, but I soon found an alternate point of view to the ex-president of Honduras (Zalia) who had been ousted in the middle of the night the previous year.

These two women didn't like Zalia and likened him to Chavez of Venezuela. I didn't agree with the non-democratic manner of the coup, but we all respected the differences. Soon the white woman's husband came to the restaurant. He introduced himself as David. He had been out buying cigars before they leave by airplane the following afternoon. I wished I'd had more time with these pleasant people. I ordered a guanabana ice cream, ate it as we all talked, and ordered a second one for Diana just before I walked back to the hotel in the sweltering heat. The ice cream was melting fast so I hurried home. I gave Diana another peace offering and she was in better spirits all around. Jimmy was right.

I went back to see James and had a short visit him with another kindred spirit. He and I were almost the same age. He had the scooter rental business for five years. I showed him the two paintings I had done. He recognized both locations. We exchanged stories about our lives and how it seemed the younger people were missing out on the 'peace and love' we'd experienced in our lives. James was well traveled. He'd been to the USA working, lived in the Cayman Islands, and had been as far away as Japan working on a ship. I asked him if he had grandchildren. Yes indeed, five in all. I told him about the travel book and he shared his idea of putting his memories into a book as well.

"This would be very important to your grandchildren", I told him. He agreed.

"If I could tell all the things I've lived through, man oh man", he said with a chuckle.

Of all my "new people" encounters on this island he was my favorite. If there was a problem with the scooter he was fine to help. He switched machines when the first one had brake problems. The last day he offered us the scooter free the entire day. We only went a few hours, but the offer was there. He was deep and I could feel his truth as he talked. He spoke of the world and how a better world was there for his grandchildren. We shook hands in a double handshake, and said "God bless". His eyes beamed with sincerity and honesty.

Diana and I ate an early lunch, watched American TV, and I went out one last time to snorkel. I wanted to absorb as much of the precious underwater view as possible. I'd bought a disposable underwater camera and finished the twenty-seven shoots by the time I returned to the shore on the opposite side of the bay. It was beginning to get dark and I walked along the road in my bare feet, meeting a woman from Manhattan. We discussed the differences between Costa Rica and Honduras. She favored Costa Rica, had been robbed in Honduras, and thought that Costa Rica was much more civilized. She stopped at Sundowners, the local bar, and I went along stepping on pebbles and bouncing my way home. She had a broken toe and didn't walk very well. I looked like a child fumbling my steps trying to miss the sharp rocks.

The sun was just about to set. The one, and only, night there was a beautiful sunset would be an opportunity for making pictures. I rushed back outside with the camera and took over a dozen photographs of the evolving light. In the far distance, near the horizon, clouds drifted up like mushrooms casted long shadows on the silver water; the light overshot the clouds and created a golden sunset. It was my last night in a little hole in the wall that had grown large inside my heart. The short acquaintances were solid. I have no idea if we will return, but I felt satisfied that I'd at least met a few of the local people, the people who were born and raised on the island. When I travel the connections I make with people are what make my journey special.

The rest of the night we were packing and getting our things organized for traveling in the morning. Jimmy had arranged our taxi at five-thirty, and that is exactly when it arrived. The driver was a Latino-Honduran from the mainland. He and his wife had a small restaurant. He drove to bring in some extra cash. We didn't drive to the port on the lush, green route; the driver took us along Flower Bay where the poor people were already awake, bathing in the sea. If the taxi driver who gave us the ride the first day had gone this route we would have had a negative impression of the poverty on the island. Maybe they tell all the divers to go along the outer route where the forest is green and the water is clearer. It is a few minutes longer to go that way, but the resorts are a better view than the struggle on the faces of the poor people. I can't say I preferred the sheltered side of the island, I just hope people like James can survive and keep smiling against all odds and the harsh reality.

We have decided to not return to San Pedro Sula. We canceled our hotel reservations and will go directly to Puerto Cortes on the shore. Maybe it is like La Ceiba, a little tamer than the large city. One man in the bus station said it was a nice town. We will not have to hassle with a taxi back into the bustle of San Pedro Sula or catch a bus in the same terminal. A direct route will make things easier. We'll have a day to see a new, different place and leave Monday morning for Belize. Why go back to where we've already been and where taxi drivers kill tourists.

Day Eight: Heldman Alas is the Hondurans bus company we bought the round trip tickets from San Pedro Sula to La Ceiba. After a painless ferry ride that took an hour and a half we were hurried into a cab at the dock. We lucked out, getting our bags relatively quick by going to the opposite side of the luggage stand. The majority of people were yelling for their bags and I stood quietly as a man came up and asked me to point out the bags. Within seven minutes of exiting the boat we were sharing a taxi with two other Hondurans passengers. They were dropped at the main highway and we were driven to the bus terminal. The fare was fifty limperas more than the taxi driver we turned down the week before. (That's about two dollars and fifty cents.) I'm constantly counting pennies. It is a secret pleasure knowing it is really only pennies in Central America. The bus ride gave me time to catch up with the writing. I even got in a nap before we returned to the main terminal in San Pedro Sula. The boat ride had been so smooth Diana was in good spirits as well.

In the terminal we exited the bus and were not allowed to leave with our luggage until Diana dug through her purse to produce the baggage claim ticket. The first day we entered the bus we were quite put off by being told our backpacks were too large to be carried into the bus. This is one of the few times I put my foot down and showed disrespect for the female security guards. It wasn't personally aimed at them, but I was insistent that the backpack with the cameras and computer would not be separated from me. The two women guards were not used to someone telling them no. They stood there and told us to step aside as other passengers passed. They offered no compromise so I took out many clothes in the backpack, put them on, or carried the computer in my hands so the bag would fit inside the metal frame (just like those at airports) that showed the allowed size. The women let us pass. I said this was very stupid in an obnoxious manor. The guards were expressionless. We were not about to be intimidated by the guns or metal detector the guards carried. They did check to see if we had firearms.

The security was excellent in fact. It was as thorough as at an airport. We'd heard about some bus hijackings by guerrillas so we weren't opposed to being screened, but to be told a backpack was too large was very strange. A few less items taken out were all we needed to do. When returning in the bus terminal in La Ceiba, the screening was just as intense. We even had our picture taken as we boarded the bus. The bus companies made all the foreigners feel safe, and the free cookies and drinks were also a big hit.

When arriving in San Pedro Sula we left the bus and exited the gate. Life changed back to reality and instant travel mode. We had to carry the two bags up three flights of steps to a vast shopping mall that was the central bus terminal as well. Rows of shoe stores and a wide-open central promenade stretched a city block long. Each length of elevation in the central promenade was utilitarian for luggage on wheels, and steps and ramps were side by side. We began to see windows for bus companies and asked for a bus to Puerto Cortes. We were directed outside.

As we neared the door I asked a man where the bus for Puerto Cortes was, he pointed and directed us to a row of vans. We were whisked away again as a man grabbed our luggage. This was fast. We were wondering if there was a problem and if this was the typical, frenzied drama of the pace in this terminal. When the first man grabbed my luggage, I told him to help my wife instead. He pulled the bags up to a minivan. I was looking for a bus. Before we could blink the doors were closing and we were pulling out of the station. The stranger I had asked at the door for the correct bus was kind enough to be standing at the sidewalk to ensure we were safe and sound. I gave him the thumbs up and he waved back. That little extra care lifted my spirit from a very chaotic state to a split second of human bliss. The bliss ended because we were barreling down the road at speeds very uncomfortable for human standards. The music in the van was blaring so loud we both got headaches from the pounding beat of Reggae tone songs.

The ride was supposedly an hour and a half to the port city but was twice that long regardless of the breath-taking speeds on the side streets of San Pedro Sula. The van didn't go to the port directly; it made many stops in San Pedro Sula first. All the while the driver honked the horn to attract riders and the jockey at the door jumped off and yelled to get customers. I'd experienced this once before in Nicaragua. Diana sat in a seat behind me with her large bag straddling the seat next to the window. I sat next to the window and the bag was in the isle. We had to pay for the use of the seat, double the usual fee, but we were happy because the entire fare was as much as the taxis ride to the bus station in La Ceiba. It was a wild ride neither of us was very happy to experience.

About ten minutes into the venture I was thinking this is not Roatan, this is hell, and if I think this is shitty Diana must be thinking it is one hundred times worse. I turned to look at her and our eyes locked in one of those speechless agreements only a married couple knows what it means. The oddest part of the driver's wild behavior was the rate of speed on the highway was slower than on the busy, jam-packed streets of San Pedro Sula. The highway was where he seemed to become human again.

In the minivan I asked a woman in front of me about the hotels in Puerto Cortes. I'd read about one called the International, but the woman knew of a cheaper, "better" place that was very safe. When we arrived she was kind to us and walked the two blocks, and entered the hotel to make sure the price was going to be honest. The clerk stood behind a barred-in counter and the price was forty dollars for two days. We went the extra mile and got the air-conditioned room for five dollars more. The clerk is a Honduran woman who lived in Seattle and has a US citizenship. The people were very nice. The security guard even walked us to the bank.

On our walk he used his phone and set up an appointment with the water taxi company that will take us to Belize on Monday. Diana spoke to a man named Roberto on the phone who said he would be at our hotel in an hour to sell us a reservation on the boat. One rule of thumb for traveling is there is no rule of thumb. When reading, or getting information from books, or on the Internet, this information may not be accurate. We had the phone number for the fast taxi and called from the USA a few months before. We were told there were absolutely no reservations and we had to be there at seven o'clock for a nine o'clock departure. Either these people had a tremendous change of heart about business tactics or we had been feed a line of bull by all our sources. It makes no sense to me how these things happen and how things change from day to day, but they do. I think this is done as soon as word gets out that information has been put to ink. Someone is planning and someone is changing information so someone can be baffled and amused, stranding travelers! It is a secret plot.

We walked after getting money at an ATM leaving the security guard who returned to the hotel. The town is very tame. The busy sector of this town is maybe seven blocks, by two blocks long. We asked the security guard where to get shrimp with rice and he directed us to a Chinese restaurant a few blocks away, right next to the Burger King, across the street from the Pizza Hut. The mountain of rice was so large we took half of it for lunch tomorrow. After dinner and a quick walk through the central park we meet Roberto (the water taxi agent) back at the hotel and paid for the boat to Belize. He even included a taxi pick up, and a stop at the immigration office, at no extra charge. The total was fifty-five dollars for everything. I think they release misinformation to give travelers unexpected happiness and it worked. The lack of confusion here is getting to me.

Roberto was a well-spoken, handsome man with straight black hair. He is in his early forties. He is the owner of the water taxi company. He speaks Spanish and English. The first thing he asked Diana was she Colombian? "Yes." "I love Colombian woman." The second question was, "Are you married?" "This is my husband". I missed all this. I was contemplating the correct time the travel book had said the boat left and the actual (twelve o'clock) time Roberto said the boat would leave, some three hours difference. After setting up the travel arrangements we were back on the street for an evening stroll. We bought a second souvenir, a ceramic piece. The style is from a particular town here in Honduras where the white glaze is accented by black, curly designs. The souvenir shop was so full we had to climb around and try not to knock anything over. I was allowed to climb into the attic where the shelves were twice as cluttered. A quick walk home and the hotel room was a prized respite. The remaining time we spent watching TV and called it a day.

Day Nine: Puerto Cortes. If you ever want to see what a ghost town is like come to Puerto Cortes on the last day of the World Cup Finals. Spain and Holland were up against each other. We walked around town and saw as few as a dozen people. The morning walk wasn't as stark when we went to church at eight o'clock and saw typical life in this small town. A man named Ralph was there at the church door. He had introduced himself and told us the night before what time church was on Sunday morning. This time we didn't get a chance to talk to him, but nod hello across the pews. After mass, there was a fundraiser selling rice, salad, and chicken for about two dollars and fifty cents, so we bought two meals for dinner and carried them home. The walk was about a mile to the hotel. We were drenching wet from the heat, Diana showered, I just stunk, took off my shirt, and we spent many hours watching old movies on the television.

The best movie was "*The Day the Earth Stood Still*." I remember being mesmerized by this movie when I was a child, yet I didn't recall one scene or the story line at all. It was a Sci-fi classic about a robot and alien being. It was the third movie we had seen. We'd had enough and needed to leave our hotel room. The room felt more like a jail cell the longer we stayed and watched old movies. The windowless room added to this feeling.

The room has a bed, a light bulb, a small dresser, and most important, a TV. It is a very "funky" place, as Diana has now adopted this word into her

English vocabulary. I find this language very cute and a bit strange. Her English is so "text book/proper" that this use of slang ("funky") is one of my obvious, bad influences. We burst out of there with our laser guns poised ready for aliens, tourists, or locals.

In Puerto Cortes our re-entry into earth's civilization was to find none. We walked toward the tall, white wall that ran several blocks along the dock, only to find no place to enter. The entire town is blocked off from the port behind this wall. I was hoping to find some way to get some photographs of ships. We passed a seaman's club where the sound of the TV blared. On a corner I popped my head into a bar where all eyes were glued to the World Cup Game. "What is the score?" I asked." "Zero to zero." The bartender yelled hello in English and said, "Come on in my friends". It was not the kind of place a woman would set a foot in so I declined and we kept walking. Everywhere, everyone was watching the game. I was beginning to wonder if the movie we'd seen was reality. No one was on the streets and if they were they stood motionless, outside windows peering in at a TV in a trance.

It was outside a Wendy's that Diana noted the restaurant had free Wi-Fi. We decided to watch the game like all the people but first go back to the hotel and get the computer. A half hour later we were walking back, when on our way we heard that Spain had won. Actually we were talking to a security guard in a store when I heard the long "Goal" shouted. I pointed it out to the guard that had a radio blaring. Spain had won their first World Cup. We had talked about this a few hours before. We both wanted Spain to win. Why? Because they had never won before, Holland had won twice. We missed it in TV, but could hear the town exploding from inside hundreds of houses, bars, and unseen locations.

As I turned on the computer inside the Wendy's I got a call from my friend Jose in San Diego. He was there with his son, Eligh. The TV was so loud from the celebrations, we used typing to communicate. The plan is to see him in about three or four weeks. It's hard to imagine that we have been gone from home a week already. The time here in Puerto Cortes has been strange, but a nice rest from what we knew would be the hectic, grunge of San Pedro Sula. Puerto Cortes is void of activity, but off the main streets it actually looks like a decent town to live in. At the Wendy's we spent two hours in the air conditioning catching up on our Internet. I paid online for Diana's upcoming college course, and checked to see how our finances are. Diana wrote her mother an email and explained that the phone was out of the question until we get to Belize. We left as the management wondered how two people could loiter for so long after buying two ice creams. We have exactly five dollars (In limperas) left and if we calculate right we will have enough to buy lunch for the boat tomorrow.

As we walked back to the hotel a young woman approached us and asked in a thick British accent where to catch the ferry tomorrow. We told her the information and she said she would meet us at nine in the morning when we leave with Roberto's taxi. Her name was Harriet. We are all heading to Placencia, Belize. There are so few tourists here it is correct to assume that the travelers are all heading to Belize via water taxi.

I wasn't ready to go back and watch more TV so I asked Diana to go in the direction we'd not yet been in the town. This is when our day really began and we entered the "travel zone," that exploration zone. We walked to the far side of town, so far the road passed over a small bridge and a lagoon with mangroves. White birds flew over a small canal on the opposite side of the road. The idyllic scenery was spoiled by the realization that trash was floating on the edges of the murky water. Some of the houses we passed were dilapidated wrecks with no paint since they were built. Shadows of people inside the dark windows looked out at us. I took photographs of one place after another. Some houses were like small, well-kept gated palaces, a vacated lot with wild ferns and trash could be right next door. Poverty in paradise is what we mostly encountered.

As we strolled and turned the corner toward the hotel I saw two children out in front of a house. A woman sat inside a small cantina on the same property. The cantina sold sodas and candy. The woman in the shop smiled and she could see that some of the children were greeting us. I asked the children if they were brother and sister. "No, cousins". This chance encounter lasted maybe ten minutes as the first two children ran into the house and called two more cousins out. I asked permission from the woman sitting inside the open window of the shop to photograph the children. She obliged.

By the time we began with two children the photographs expanded to six, and then seven people being photographed. Diana offered to send the pictures via the Internet. The teenage sister of the first little girl gave us her email address. I gave her my web address. As I took pictures I tipped the camera and showed the excited children their own images. They were excited to see themselves and there was an electric atmosphere at play. We feed the fun and spoke for a short time, asking ages, where they went to school, their grades, etc.

It began to rain. We scurried off toward the hotel. A showered pursued us so we took shelter under the corner awning of a closed, vacant store. We joined a band of men and women getting out of the rain. As soon as the decreasing rain slowed to a light sprinkle we set off the last three blocks to our hotel room, a shower in the bathroom, and more TV. The church dinner of rice and chicken was taken out and we dined on the bed. Tomorrow we go to a new country, our first time in Belize.

The first thing in the morning, before our nine o'clock pick up, we were out the door at eight and running errands to buy food for the day. We entered a market we'd not seen the two days before (it would have been closed on World Cup Sunday anyway). The entrances to the market were obscured by new construction. Once inside we could see this from the inside, from the outside all we saw was a building under construction. The market will be much larger once the new expansion is finished. This was a real market, the kind we love to go in and explore. We found the center where the usual restaurants always seem to be. An old man waved us over when we began to pass. He must have seen the questions on our faces. The real question was, "Is it safe to eat here". We bought four baleadas. This is a local tortilla with beans and scrambled eggs. This is something we'd managed to get a few times from vendors on the street until I finally asked Diana what the name of the food was. Our lunch was bought for the boat. It was eight-fifteen in the morning.

The faces in this market were timeless. One old man had a cowboy hat with strands of garlic draped around his neck. His skin was weathered to an extent that he had thousands of wrinkles spaced across his face. His right eye was gone and in the vacant spot his skin wrinkled as if there never was an eye. All his clothes were beige, as if he was intentionally colored-coordinated. Another old black woman had a beautiful flowered dress with puffy selves, an apron, and her hair braided back like Heidi. She wore a circle of colored beads around her neck and smiled from ear to ear. It was Old Heidi as a hippie. The people here seem pretty mellow. The only drama is there is no drama. Life goes on as usual and we were happy to be in the middle of things.

On another street there were wooden stalls with blue tarps to keep the rain off the merchandise. This must have been where the markets expansion placed the un-housed vendors. The street was closed off to traffic. Diana bought some pumice stones to rub off her calluses on her feet. The woman asked for one limpera for two, but ended up giving her four. She must have liked Diana and changed her mind about the tourist price when Diana spoke Spanish. We stopped on a corner to buy an avocado and met the only sour man in the whole town. He was bitter and snarled the price of the avocado. We only had a one hundred limper note. He groveled that he didn't have change. He wanted ten limperas for the avocado I handed him the avocado back and started to walk away when he suddenly realized he was about the lose a sale. Out came the correct change. We priced avocados a few blocks away. They were only eight limperas. Why is it that the grumpiest people are always the cheapest as well?

Diana bought more embroidery thread and the last of our remaining money was handed over to a homeless man who was so skinny he had not one spec of fat on his body. I'd seen him three or four times before as we walked the same route away from our hotel. He didn't say anything. He looked at me as I approached, knew I was handing him something, and instantly hid the money, as if it was a secret exchange he didn't want anyone else to see for fear of being robbed. He sat on a cardboard bed behind the bus stop. This was his home forever.

A small black truck that was there to pick us up was there exactly at nine o'clock. The driver was a heavy-set jovial man. One other couple, and the British girl (Harriett), we had met on the street the day before, were there as well. These three people were all British. One other quite Honduran jumped into the back of the truck with the bags and the rest of us. Thomas and Lucy were the British couple, whom we soon introduced ourselves to. They had really good energy and we liked them right away. Thomas "is educated" was Diana's assessment of him. The tires on the back of the truck were sagging from the heavy load, but all was fine.

We drove a quick mile and were told to go into a building to get our immigration stamp. The office had three people sitting at two desks, within five minutes our passports were stamped; and we were back into the truck for a longer ride out of town, across a bridge, to a dock under the same bridge. From our vantage point we could see the opposite side of the giant cranes and walled shipyard we tried to get into the day before. This was across a wide harbor with pelicans diving into the water. There floated a few small boats. The fast "water taxi" would leave at noon and it was only nine-thirty. Diana and I handed in our luggage and went off to find something to take photographs of, and we did. Within the same block near the bridge was a fish market. I took out the camera and began to fire away, mostly at fish. The first stall permitted me to photograph the fish. A young girl was swinging a rag to shoe the flies away from herself and not the fish. I then noticed a sheet of gummy flypaper with thousands of flies stuck on the surface making a buzzing sound so loud it was a chorus of agony. I began to photograph the dying flies when the girl's mother protested and moved the stuck flies away. I respected her request and felt she was justified in not wanting the word to get out about the murder of thousands of innocent flies. So, just pretend you never read this, just like the photographs of flies I never got to take. Deeper into the fish market the people seemed very friendly and very willing to pose for my pictures. Fish, people, crabs, and cutting boards were my subjects.

We entered into the darker regions of the fish market and found the usual restaurants, but just outside was a landing dock, a fish butcher's stall for cleaning fish, and a group of young men sitting along a wall. I looked at them and yelled a cheer for Spain winning the World Cup. This was a great icebreaker. They returned the enthusiasm and allowed me to take their picture. I saw an old man cupping water out of a dugout boat and walked over a plank to take a picture of him. I took a photograph of his back as he swiped the water from the shallow boat. He wasn't looking my way. I then said hello, and he glared up at me. "Can I take your picture?" I said in Spanish. He was disembarking and was cranky. I helped him up onto the concrete pier and he said he didn't want his picture taken. "It's not my custom", was his response in Spanish. We then began to chat. He asked me where I was from and I showed him Diana standing back on the other side of the pier. He turned out to be very pleasant and we talked for a few minutes. It's like most people, you give them a little time and they warm up to you. I passed back over the wooden plank to the main pier and he joined me. The young men that cheered for Spain sat and watched us as we continued to talk, ending with a warm handshake and saying good-bye to all.

Back to the boat nothing was happening, more local passengers, not tourists, stood waiting. We sat on an old, orange, Styrofoam lifeboat and watched the pelicans dive after fish. One man was sitting across from us taking our picture so I took his picture and smiled. He and another younger man were sailors from Poland. They showed us the boat that was docked across the harbor where a shipment of soybeans was being unloaded. Their English was very weak but we managed to get in a good conversation. They worked on a route between New Orleans and the Caribbean Islands, as well as Honduras. Behind where the man had been sitting, after we said good-bye, I walked around the shore on a concrete path and found Thomas, Lucy, Harriet, and another young man all sitting at a table. I greeted them and said I would go get Diana to join us.

We spoke a good hour, laughing and talking about travel plans, comparing where to go, and what not to let happen. The other man's name was Jacob. He is an Israeli/Egyptian/American born citizen, who is working as a peace corps volunteer in Belize. He was heading back on a different boat. Once again we had a nice visit with Thomas and I was impressed with his ambition and open mindedness. He owns two computer-based services, one a video-panoramic business that caters to investment property brokers, the other a new business that does online video interviews for college applicants. He had a good brain and a stimulating thirst for life. Diana had some good conversation with the others as Thomas and I hit it off. The time passed quickly and we decided it was time to go back to the waiting boat.

The same immigration agents we'd seen in the office that morning were at the boat by then. The captain and a helper lugged giant, plastic vats of gasoline onto the edge of the boat. The captain stuck a big plastic tube into the mouth of each vat and put his mouth over the remaining opening of the containers and began to suck. This created suction and the gas ran into the boats gas tank. About twenty people stood around and watched. The mix was of local onlookers, travelers, and just curious people there to see the foreign tourists. The female immigration agent then called each passenger's name from a roster and asked to see the stamped passports. I looked over at Thomas and we were both thinking how redundant this process was. We rolled our eyes and politely stood as our names were called and we embarked. The boat had maybe twenty-five passengers in all.

A portly agent we hadn't seen before came on board and began to help hand out life jackets, making sure everyone was wearing one. Lucy joked how this didn't seem like the most "reassuring" procedure. These were the old fashioned, orange life jackets that wouldn't really keep an adult afloat. I began to see images of a tourist disaster out at sea where we hit some ungodly object and the entire boat would sink. I thought to myself, "I will quickly take the jump-drive out of my backpack, where all my writing is backed up, and put it into a water tight container I have. That way I'll not lose my writings into the sea." I had the whole thing all ready in my mind. I then wondered why I wasn't thinking of saving my water-shy wife first. What a selfish artist I am! She would agree with this completely.

Diana drugged herself with two Dramamine; we ate the baleadas, drank some water, and sat ready to leave. As we pulled away from the dock I yelled, "Adios Honduras!" A few people waved and cheered. The majority wondered what the hell the crazy Gringo was doing, and what was so flipping fun about riding a boat. I just got that World Cup fever thing for a split second and the rush of seeing a crowd sprang my vocal chords into action. Anyway the pelicans liked it. Diana sat in the exact middle of the back of the boat between a boy and his mother. I was off to one side wearing the headphones and listening to my iPod. Every once in a while I would look at Diana unable to see her eyes behind the thick dark glasses she wore. Then she would crack a smile and I'd return a smile.

That's how I knew she wasn't turning green and white from seasickness. This time the drugs worked! This could all lead to a career of heavy drug use for my wife. Who knows, I might even smoke a joint if drugs work that well. The bounce of the boat and wind left no room for such fantasies. We were busy keeping our balance facing into the strong wind.

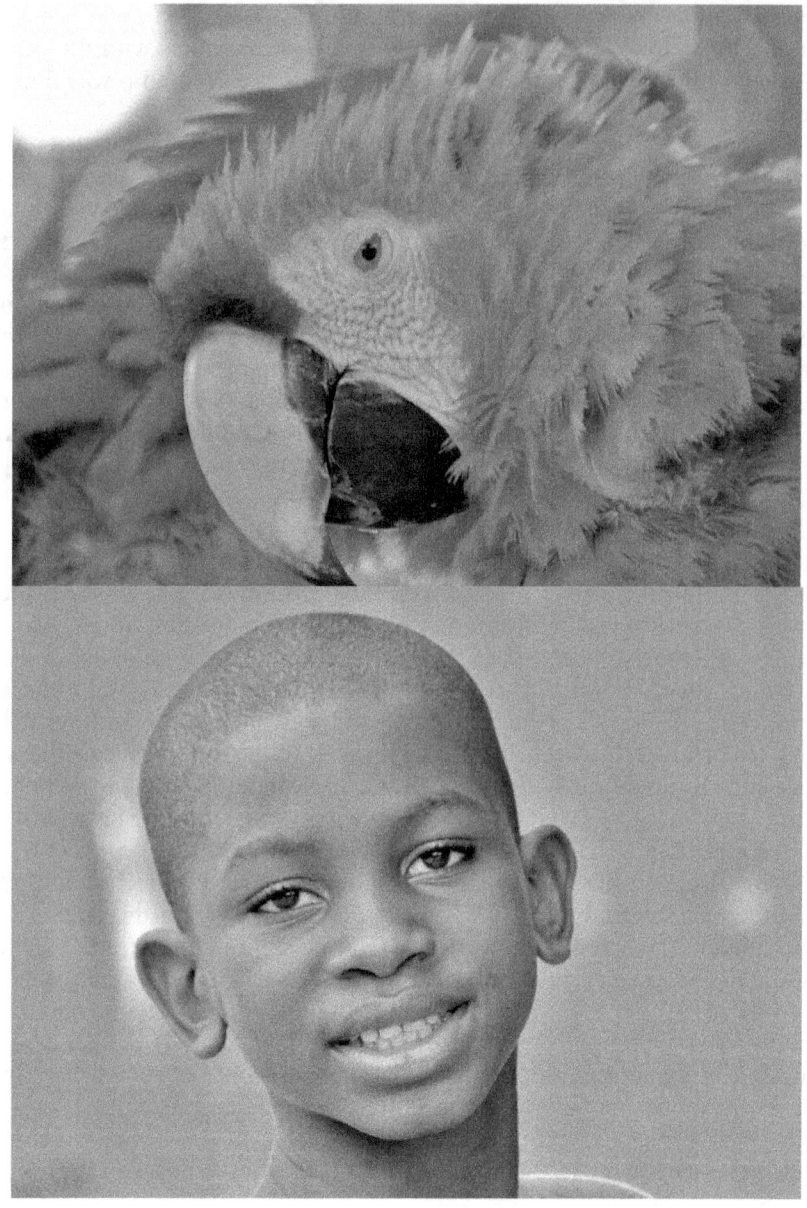

Chapter Eighteen
Belize

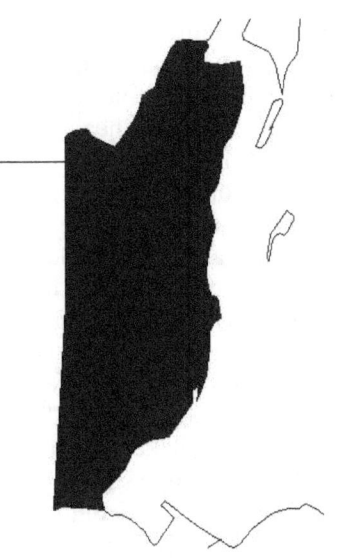

Day One: We arrived around three-thirty in the afternoon to a very sleepy place in Belize. My first impression is one of silence, or quiet. All we can hear is the wind; there are no other sounds. No people sounds, no car sounds, no airplanes, nothing but the wind. With this silence comes a void I can't describe yet. Even in Puerto Cortes there was street noise, traffic and a bustle of morning activity. On the water taxi the time flew by in a pleasant rhythm of slight turns and rolling waves that took us to a port called Mango Cove, Belize. Here the water taxi passed into a channel of mangroves past a big resort on an island. I thought we were in Placencia, but this was our first of two stops. The boat slapped into a mud embankment that was as high as the bow of the boat. The crew began to throw the entire luggage through an open portal in the front of the boat and put the luggage onto the wet, muddy soil. A dark, portly immigration agent came on board and began to call the passengers up one at a time. I saw him but didn't know my name was being called. Thomas, or someone, called to me and I went to the agent. My name was called at least three times. I must have been stoned from the fantasy joint and this guy knew it. "How long are you in Belize," he asked. For some reason I was too stoned, or totally unprepared, for this question. "Uh, five or six days, I guess." Wrong answer. I got back to my seat and Diana, who was directly behind me, compared stamps and signed dates. She could stay an entire month, I was only allowed ten days. He could see we were together with the same name, same country, same blue passports, but I was being punished for being too stupid to not have the answer on the tip of my tongue. I felt like one of my grumpy students back home, and felt like "the man" was unjustly messing me up. Not to worry we'll leave in less than nine days just to get back at him.

Everything on the boat was being exited, including the people and packages. We all climbed through the open portal in the front of the boat onto the mud and sand, standing there with no one saying a word. That sudden silence I was describing at the beginning of this chapter was already at play. Well there was one exception. A tugboat parked next to us had a crew of three or four horny men who chirped out catcalls as the boat pulled into the mud. I wasn't sure whom the calling was for and to what benefit this would be in attracting the women on board as prospective wives or lovers. It struck me as being in extremely poor taste, so I winked back at the men and shook my ass, yelling my phone number, name, and future address in Belize. This is how it's done isn't it? I didn't meet Diana this way, but who knows, it could very well have happened this way. Men all over the world find women this way. Don't they?

Soon another heavy-set customs agent arrived and asked us all to open the "top zipper" of our bags. So I opened the "top zipper" of the bag, which contained only our clothes on a separate, smaller part of the larger bag. The customs man only looked and felt in the "top zipper" part of the bags. The explosives and contraband in "bottom zipper" part of the bag were completely ignored. The way he put his little fingers into each bag was as humorous as his silly instructions. It was as if he didn't want to really be looking anyway and had to make it look as if he were searching for nothing. Then he came to a local woman who had been on the boat next to Diana. He grabbed a big bottle of orange soda and barked; "You know you're not allowed to bring this with you. Next time I'll take it from you." I was baffled and thinking, "Wow, great, a country that outlaws fattening sugar drinks!" The verbal spanking was a joke, but what the hell for; I could not figure it out? Diana said they weren't allowed to bring in food. I caught one slight detail of the bottle that made my thinking change. As the agent lifted the bottle out of the plastic bag of food, I saw the bottle was opened previously. Nothing had been drunk. Aw ha! She was bringing in heavy water to moderate a nuclear reactor, or does some nuclear fission research without a permit. No wonder the customs man was so pissed. Belize is a hot bed for homemade nuclear toys! Not to worry, Diana and I had no such contraband and we were allowed back on to the boat. The luggage was all put back on the boat. All the local people had left in taxis and strangely, only foreign tourists were remaining. The woman with the heavy water was in a taxi waiting. Diana and I sat at the back of the boat.

A taxi driver came on board to get a drink of water from the cooler at the back of the boat, directly in front of us. This was the same taxi driver that had the woman with the nuclear, heavy water, and bottle. The passenger was waiting in his taxi. The driver was right in front of us, talking to one of the crew. "What's he doing? Is he watching me?" He was saying this, giggling like there was a childish prank being played. The "he" was the customs agent. Before a word was said, and with the slightest of hand movement, a white sheet of paper appeared out of the taxi driver's pocket and was passed to the boatman. In one orchestrated gesture the crew member pulled out some money and the two men made an exchange. I jumped up and began to scream, "He's selling nuclear secrets!" The customs man ignored me, the entire boat was deaf to my plea, and we pulled away. My calls were being drowned out by the sound of the motor.

As soon as the taxi driver finished the drink of water he had (allegedly) come on board to get, as we were exiting, I asked Diana, "Did you see that?" "What?" I knew it was impossible to explain since the crew member was too close and the sound of the boats engines was drowning out my voice. "Never mind", was all I could come up with. (You never read this and whatever those two men were passing was somehow related to the men on the tugboat asking for my phone number. It's so evident; I am still in a state of shock to this day.)

Ten minutes later we pulled up to the sleepy dock of Placencia, but first made a brief passenger drop at a lonely, vacant dock. The captain then said, "We are there." This was the first and only words we heard him say the entire trip. We disembarked and stood outside the boat. The captain handed a first bad to Diana. It wasn't hers. Then he began to hand all the bags to Diana. She suddenly took on a manly air and was in the seaman's labor union. Diana took it all in and helped like a champ. We wheeled our luggage off the dock and stepped into total ignorance. You know that dumb, blank feeling of how do I get where I'm going, and I don't have clue what to do next. Thomas and Lucy came from behind and kick started my thinking.

I went into an ATM and got some money. I'd already exchanged twenty-five US dollars for fifty Belize dollars at the dock back in Honduras with one of the crew members. No, not the one selling nuclear secrets, a different guy. The ATM only gave large bills and our next move was to take a taxi. I know taxi drivers never have change, so I walked into a grocery store to be proactive about the taxi driver that didn't even exist yet. As I went into the store the girl behind the counter saw me looking for the smallest, tiniest, cheapest thing on the shelves, so I could get change. "You don't have to buy anything, I'll give you change", came out of her lips without me even telling her I wanted change for a taxi driver that didn't exist yet. My God what was going on! First the heavy water, then a boat full of foreigners, now this. "In New York they wouldn't think of giving me change," was all I said. She liked me.

As I left the store two black men sat low, slouching on some chairs, leaning back on the wall. "Need a taxi?" one of them said. "Yes I do". Now I was getting really spooked. Everybody here is a mind reader, or there is some really good stuff being smoked on a daily basis. No sooner had I said yes than a man came from around the building and began to take the bags from Diana. I knew this game all right. Take the bags and begin driving before we have established the true currency exchange about to take place. "How much?" "Five dollars." "Three dollars" I snapped back. "Five dollars". "Three". "Five dollars" "Three" "Five dollars" "Three". "Five dollars" "Three". "OK, three", he finally said. He knew I was tough like a New Yorker and meant business because I had already got the change for the five-dollar bill inside the store he never saw me enter, or get the change from. The sudden collapse of our instant bonding ritual saddened me. He gave in way too easy. He liked me as well. He knew I knew even three was twice what a local would pay for the fare.

He drove us down the road toward Lydia's Guest House, past Harriet, Thomas, and Lucy who we had already said our good-byes to before the use of the ATM. I stuck my hand out the window and waved to them. The drive was maybe three minutes, one Belize dollars per minute of travel, just as I had read in all the travel books. The driver was really very nice and had such a mellow tone of voice that I asked him to stay and have supper with us, perhaps marry our first daughter whenever she was born but he declined.

We walked up a thin concrete walk to the front of a house with a high porch on the second floor. I walked up the steps and said hello through an open screen door. Two women were inside, and one was lying on a sofa. "Excuse me," she said, as if that was a bad thing to be doing while watching TV on a hot afternoon. "Not to worry," was my response. Lydia liked me too. Diana left the luggage and I asked her to help me decide which room we wanted. There was a full apartment below Lydia, there was a room in the house next door that had a shared, public bathroom and a balcony with a view of the beach, and there was a house in the back, but the Internet reception wasn't that good there. We chose the prize behind door number one; Lydia's basement apartment for thirty-five dollars a day, the most expensive place with good Internet reception.

Lydia gave us the full tour of our apartment, and we like it a lot. We can use the air conditioner but that is ten dollars a day more. We are going to rough it and use fans. We have a kitchen, shower, refrigerator, and toilet; it even comes with a bed to sleep in. The first thing we did was go to buy groceries. The second thing we did was buy Diana some bloody sand fly lotion. (Bloody because they suck blood.) The third thing we did was buying some tiny ice cream and walked along the single (carless) walk-path that runs the length of the beach town. We are at the far end of the village, away from the dock. We came home and Diana did some laundry while I set up camp. Soon we were off to the beach and walking hand in hand. Lydia came down and gave us the code to the Wi-Fi Internet, but we still can't get the computer phone to work. The call to Colombia will have to wait.

At one point in the evening a very nice man stopped by to ask us if we wanted to purchase, "Some nice buds". "No thank you", I said. Diana thought the devil had come to sell the keys to hell. I assured her it was a harmless gesture and the custom of island people to grow their hair like Bob Marley and offer mind-altering substances to white tourists. His dark, bushy silhouette standing at the screen door with no light to see his face may have been a little shocking to her, but I knew the people here have an uncanny way of reading minds and finding what you want even when you don't want it.

Day Two: Placencia. Every night for the last week my lovely wife has been applying vinegar to her bug wounds. The ritual begins at bedtime every night. We fall asleep and all throughout the night I smell vinegar. I am dreaming of salads, tossed, cabbage, Caesar salad, anything that calls for a vinegar taste. She has no idea the smell doesn't leave her body or the bed. She is too encouraged by the medical properties of her newfound home remedy against sand fly bites. Yesterday, we bought a natural medicine made of marijuana. It was twenty-eight Belize dollars (fourteen US). The tiny plastic container is more expensive than the 'weed' they are asking me to buy as we walk around. I spent a great deal of time this morning looking through my bags thinking I had lost fifty Belize dollars. I checked all my pants, and all the passport wallets. I swore I had one hundred Belize dollars when we arrived and used the ATM the day before. Where had I spent, or dropped, my money? I asked Diana how much she paid for the liquid marijuana medicine. Then I realized where the money had gone. It was more expensive than the groceries we stocked up on. I know this is the beginning of a real marijuana habit for Diana. Just like a true addict she has crossed that barrier, that threshold of spending more on the habit than on food! I am appalled. A good Catholic girl is not only using marijuana, she smells bad as well! I prefer the vinegar odor to a drug addicted Catholic Colombian. This starts with the gateway drugs, like marijuana, and then leads to heroin addiction via vinegar.

I was up writing for three hours last night. This morning at first light, before the sun broke over the clouds, I was out photographing. The only sound here is the quiet wind. The house colors are all soft pastels and strangely contrasting. One house is dark purple, with a bright yellow railing and pink ballast. The one characteristic of the change between Honduras and Belize is the way houses are painted. They are all painted. In Honduras there might not be any paint, due to poverty. But here the painted houses are a true cultural statement. There is a tidy pride to the town - the long concrete path with the names of the homeowners is stenciled into the actual concrete. This is a good example of how personal these people are. No one passes on the beach or the sidewalk without saying hello. A lone woman jogger on the beach this morning even made eye contact and said good morning. No one wears shoes; no one wears anything but shorts and t-shirts. The children are all pleasant and tonight on our walk home I noted that this was the kind of place where children run around after dark and play. I like them for being so open and unafraid of the "boogey man". My God, a place where children can be children!

The pace of life is astoundingly slow. In addition the people never raise their voices. The children even are soft spoken. Lydia was speaking to a man from her balcony today as I sat painting, sitting below. I tried for the life of me to listen in but gave up. I was closer than the man below on the sand and all I could hear were whispers. It is a quiet place and the people are quieter than the wind. Lydia is so mellow and soft-spoken I have to strain to wrap my ears around the curvy English she speaks. They all have this kind of English that has no edges to it. The multi-syllable words are cut short into two syllables. There is also a kind of downward-twist at the end of every phrase. It's not the Jamaican "MON" stuff; it's more mellow and softer.

As I was painting a view of the house across the walk from her, she said, "That's a bad place, bad luck for us". I thought she was saying that my painting was bad luck, some kind of taboo code I was breaking. She was talking about the building across from her, more precisely the thatched roof on the house. "We asked them not to put it there, it's a fire hazard". I wasn't quite sure what she meant. I hadn't fully adapted to the Belizean telepathy yet. "The house has the same electric pole as we do, that could bring a fire to our house", she went on. Then it all added up. The thatched roof was extremely flammable, and electrical storm might set the roof on fire through the wires, thus sending the fire through the wires to her house." I guess we have a different type of wiring in the USA. This didn't seem to make sense about fire traveling through electrical wires, but I was beginning to believe her. The only burnt out buildings we had seen, three in all, were all coincidently thatched roofed bars or dwellings. "Who is the owner, an America?" I presumed. I was right. "He also built so high (the thatched roof) that he blocked our view of the ocean". I was ashamed of the "know-it-all," "have-it-all" attitude my countrymen spread around the globe. "He built it to rent to tourists, but he had to rent it to locals. No one rented it but them," she continued. "We asked him to put on the steel roof." I almost tore up my painting of the house then and there, but I'm too egotistical to destroy my artistic work. I felt bad for Lydia.

After my morning walk-about and a stroll to the grocery store to buy bread we made lunch. I went into the communal kitchen next door in the same house, and borrowed the blender. I made us a drink of peach, pineapple, and vanilla soy milk with crushed ice that set the world ablaze. The flipping thatched roof across from us was burning - the drink was so good. We were in heaven.

I spent almost two embarrassing, hours with tech support in a live conversation trying to get the phone to work. It exhausted me, and I failed only to find out from Lydia that these services, like Skype and Magic Jack, are not allowed to operate in Belize. It was a real waste of computer time. (Something I have done more times than I want to admit.) Around one o'clock in the afternoon I lay down, pulled the eye mask over my eyes, and fell fast asleep for two hours. I could not move. The heat had overwhelmed me, even with two fans running. The wake up was like being pulled from death. I'm not sure I even am awake right now. It feels like a dream here. I woke up by the time we went into the water in the late afternoon.

The water was warmer than the air outside. The beach was strewn with dead seagrass, sticks, and plastic of all assorted sizes and shapes. The wind was carrying the waves into the shore like a storm. It wasn't easy to maneuver through the muck that started at our ankles and stayed thick until we were waist deep. Beyond the dark sludge we could see fresher water. I saw fresher water, meaning less dirty, but still dirty. Remember the movies, *'The Creature from the Black Lagoon'* or *'Swamp Thing'*? That is what Diana and I looked like when we went through that dead swarm of sea stuff. We bounced in the water up and down, getting slapped in the head a few times by large waves. A group of children were playing on the beach and walked past our shoes and towel. A small girl picked up Diana's tiny shoes and looked at them like the sudden find was a discovery to keep. We waved politely and the others in the group looked at their younger sister and let her know those tourists waving to get your attention out in the water would consider this action thievery. She didn't notice us before. Just about then I felt a sting in my right foot that felt like I had lacerated my entire leg. I expected a piece of green glass; instead a crab no bigger than a penny was locked into the side of my foot. I wasn't sure what it was until the legs began to squirm as I pulled it away. I didn't advertise to Diana anything about pain or a small creature. It was a miracle she was even in the water after the snorkeling event in Half Moon Bay when I pretended to turn into "Swamp Thing" and hassle her into a crying frenzy for not wanting to see the coral. Now, let's change the subject.

We had to shower all the crud off our bodies when we got home. I went out to paint my picture on the front porch, borrowing a table from the unused apartment next door. Diana made a spaghetti dinner to die for. After dinner I repeated the fruit drink I'd made in the morning. We were filled, happy, and satiated. Life is pretty good here.

After dinner we went on a walk pretending we needed some bananas (we had a few), but the fresh fruit stand was closed and all the Chinese grocery stores didn't have any. It seems Chinese own every grocery store we've entered here. They play Chinese TV, or songs, on the speakers. A tiny subculture is well entrenched here. There is even a Chinese restaurant, really two. Blacks, or Hispanics, own the gift shops. The shops vary from top end, ice cold, air-conditioned stores with tiled floors to shacks where poor black folks have one light bulb burning. There seems to be an artist colony of sorts where painters, or wood sculptors, eke out a living. I like this about Placencia. Again, quiet, peaceful, dignified, and quiet.

Day Three: Lydia's Guesthouse is very clean, low budget, and real. There are two main houses. We are staying directly below Lydia's house and share part of the building with the communal kitchen. We can smell the bacon and eggs the other American couple from Seattle cooks for breakfast. They are tattoo artists and both have tattoos all over their bodies. I think his name is Jeff. He showed me his collection of tattoos; he gets one for each place he has visited in the world. A Hawaiian tattoo might be right next to another country. His ankle has a tattoo that wraps around; at the bottom nearest the foot there is a series of shark teeth. He said this is supposed to keep sharks from attacking while swimming. It makes sense; if I saw a bunch of teeth on a tattooed leg I sure wouldn't be biting it! There are three other young gents that are staying in the dorm rooms here. They are a mismatched trio of two Brits and one Yank from San Francisco. Their "volunteer job" in Guatemala was cut due to a bankruptcy, so they are touring around for a while, "deciding what to do next". They gave me some advice on how to get into Guatemala, the town, the buses, etc.

This morning we walked in the direction we'd not seen yet, away from town. After a conversation with the Tattoo couple, I asked Diana to consider one last attempt at snorkeling. Jeff told me the snorkeling was breathtaking and well worth the money on a day tour. We followed the sidewalk north until there was nothing but a sandy path. The walk was a good (but too short) venture to see what else is around here. We walked until we had to merge with the shore, and continued until there was too much growth to walk along the sandy, narrow coast. I began with a subtle request, more like begging Diana to please consider one last attempt at snorkeling. She was very reluctant, and then twenty minutes later gave me a stern lecture and a list of requirements. I was to stay with her, which I said was no problem. We were to be at a local island, not far, and if she was tired she wanted to get off the boat onto the land. I agreed, but in the back of my mind I'm thinking I don't have a clue as to the possibility of there being a way to get to land from the snorkeling boat. As we walked we passed a few people, an old man carrying a machete as long as he was tall, and a young boy. The people here always greet us, even the Honduran or Mexican laborers say "hi" or good morning in English. It's a little strange to hear common English coming from these workers. The coastal walk became a dead end so we circled back when we came to the highway and a flat, strange moonscape that is about to be a development of some kind. There was a boat, but nothing else, no buildings, nothing but flatness. I was happy to get the okay for a snorkeling trip. I may end up being a liar of some kind but most negotiations are painfully inaccurate by the end of the transaction. I've suddenly become a businessman with the skill of moving great financial mountains, more like the skill of having bloody knees.

We returned for a brief drink, of which I am better at making than business deals. I have the blender going every few hours now. We walked to a Diving School and got a forty dollar "discount", after some real negotiations, and will be going out tomorrow at eight-thirty in the morning. The man's name is Shen. He is from Belize, lived in New York and settled in San Diego for twenty-three years. He had a car detailing business that tanked when gas prices skyrocketed a few years back, so he came home and started a Diving School. He was very reassuring to Diana after she told him about her first experience in Roatan with the divers who left her alone drinking seawater she didn't pay for. Shen is a soft-spoken, well-mannered black man who I am sure will take good care of Diana, better than I could.

We needed cash for snorkeling so we went to the bank and got out three hundred Belize dollars. I only had fifty. We then asked around for the fruit stand we had seen the day before. In all the grocery stores the vegetables and fruit look pathetic. But the single fruit and vegetable stand was where it is at. The elevated shop is open aired with three rows of a variety of fresh goodies. The woman is Mayan and from Guatemala. Diana spun off into a Spanish conversation I wasn't following, but for a word here and there. Spanish words like "Robbers" or "dangerous" were sprouting like spring vegetables in a bean sprout factory. I knew she was being pumped by the conversation and got in on the tail end of things. The town we need to cross the border into – Guatemala was the current topic. The woman suggested we hire a guide, but I knew we were going in by bus and we'd not need a guide until we get to the Tikal, Mayan ruins. Diana was buying into the danger a little too much for my liking, but the woman at the fruit stand was saying how safe her life was here in Belize. I could see the motion picture playing in Diana's mind. It wasn't a James Bond thriller, more like a kidnapping and murder movie.

We bought a pineapple, mangoes, bananas, a star fruit (I have no idea what it is), and two oranges. Our next stop was to pay Shen and walk home in the heat. I mean boiling heat. The wind had died down and the land had a dome of air that was sitting under a magnifying glass. I was wet with perspiration and ready to put that fruit through the blender with ice, serving my lovely wife first. A nap was soon to follow. Meanwhile a visit from Lydia put Diana's rampant fears to rest. The "hire a guide to go through the border stuff" was silenced. Lydia gave us the instruction on how we can get to Flores in one day from here, if we leave at six in the morning. The second bus at seven is slower and makes many stops. Lydia's suggestions calmed the murder movie I was trying to put out of Diana's mind. Funny how I am always accused of being the control freak, yet I have absolutely no influence on the "fear factor" in her. I have no influence where I want influence, yet the ongoing accusation always makes me laugh when it comes up.

There is a cycle to our relationship. (I suppose any relationship.) Diana sulks a few days after I've verbally attacked her (like over not snorkeling in Half Moon Bay, dare I mention that again) then she begins to come out of the protective shell and fight back. She is wise by not arguing at those critical moments, but she gets back at me in a slow, torturous way. I'm a little reluctant to tell this secret. She loves to pick the pimples on my face even though I don't have any. She is my private dermatologist. "This is for the verbal abuse you gave me" is often her justification for these painful encounters. The feel is masochistic because I like the attention but hate the pimple-popping pain. I like to be touched but this is truly painful. She claims that people pay top dollar to have such skin treatments. I don't believe her.

Dinner was a second day of spaghetti, which was left over from the night before. After dinner, we walked along the beach and then the sidewalk path that runs the length of the village. We stopped in gift stores, browsed, but bought nothing in deferred gratification for the Guatemala street market. We met an interesting missionary named Shara from Canada. She was passing us on the walkway when I jokingly said she didn't use her blinker while passing. She laughed and we got off on a tangent about Health Care. She said she was from Canada and I said, "Where you have health care?" We entered into a twenty-minute conversation about all the taboo subjects, religion, politics, abortion, health care, and were on the same page pretty much. She is there for a summer camp for teenagers. We have walked by this camp and seen the teenagers many times in different activities. The first day the teenagers were in a herd on the beach having relay races. I thought it was a school outing but at night when we walked by, the teenagers were sitting out, or walking around, in an unfenced area. Their bunkhouse has lights and there is always some kind of fun vibe coming from the camp. The open "unsupervised" atmosphere would be a legal field day for lawyers in the USA. Shara works as a youth counselor back in Canada.

After the path ends, and the dock where we arrived in town begins, there is a gas station, an ATM, and shop that has parrots in a large cage. Just past the birds in the large cage there is an ice cream shop. The owner is from Seattle, Washington, like so many of the transplants here. Every night when we have walked by this shop two young kids have come up and handed us tiny samples of ice cream. "Free," they say as they smile and hand it out to all who passes by. The first night we declined to buy thinking of the sugar and calories, but tonight the fishing line was in deep water and we, the fish, bit. The ice cream was homemade from soy, and was it gooooood. I got orange vanilla, and Diana a raspberry vanilla. The owner and operator said he wasn't getting rich, but was making a lot of people happy. That sounds so Seattle to me. He was a nice man. We liked him.

At night this town comes alive. If one were ever to visit Placencia in the day and never walk the main and only street at night you would not know the place. At night everyone is out walking, and the soccer field is full of kids. At night the wind is softer than the voices we pass along on our stroll. Everyone greets everyone and the restaurants are full of people. It is a drastic transformation of the population from the heat-induced, sleepy-eyed people, into awake and bustling with activity people. I understand how the heat drives everyone under a shady tree, but also how the night brings life where none seemed present. I like it here.

Lydia's place is very pleasant. The raw feel of the house gives what Diana calls a "honeymoon cottage" feel. The walls are painted a light violet with a white trim on the edges and dark-red corner molding to accent the ceilings and boards that run up and down the walls. The white paint looks like frosting on a cake, good enough to eat. There is a half wall that separates the kitchen from the bedroom. The floor has big gray tiles with a row of white running down the middle. The kitchen is a simple, corner cabinet with a sink and bright green propane stove. The walls are all exposed and if you look hard enough you can see daylight coming through cracks. The corner posts and support beams are rounded-off logs, the paint that coats everything makes it all lovely and rustic. This is my kind of place; Diana says it is our new honeymoon. She also said she hated our real honeymoon, camping in Maine and New Hampshire. Life is a series of learning experiences some, we will not repeat. When she says these things I become the tolerant one with the shoe on the other foot. But I will add, "Didn't I bring you here? Isn't this enough to make up the difference". She had never slept in a tent in her life up to that point. I should add we went to Washington DC and stayed in a hotel for threes first. She seems to only remember the tent!

Every night a cat comes to our door and meows. I tell him we have no food but he comes back anyway. The cat has dread locks and smiles with big white teeth. Diana warns me, reminding me of the cat I once fed in Costa Rica that would come into the house. Here we have a screen door, with white checkerboard wood behind the double screen, one to keep mosquitoes away, and the other to keep robbers away. An axe would give instant access.

From where we sit on the porch in the shade of Lydia's porch above, we can see how thick the sidewalk is. I would guess the sidewalk that runs the length of the village is twelve inches thick. Where the sand has been washed away a layer of conch shells has been laid as a foundation. Many of the concrete buildings in town have this same shell foundation. It must work because all the building foundations are fortified with these massive conch shells. This is a testament to the once-upon-a-time abundance of nature here.

Iguanas live in small openings under the sidewalk. Whenever we walk to the beach we can see the footprints of birds, lizards, and humans indenting the sandy surface. Humming birds battle for territory in mid-air dogfights that make jets look like snails in slow motion. Big black sea birds suspend themselves on wind currents like kites, staying afloat for hours. At night the sand is so white that it looks like snow under the streetlights that line the walkway. Placencia couldn't get more pleasant, what with free ice cream samples, free smiles, warm greetings, and a soft-spoken people who look you right in the eye and keep smiling.

Day Four: Snorkeling. Somewhere close to two in the morning it began to rain, a heavy rain, the lightning, and then it really began to shower lightning. One hit across the path so hard we saw sparks and jumped out of bed. I thought the American's house with the thatched roof was going to be up in flames, and ours to follow. All we could do was lie in bed and wait for the fire trucks. The storm passed and the lightning decreases as I counted the lightning bolts flash, counting, one thousand one, and one thousand two, until they were too far to care anymore. The storm was now five miles away and becoming a new dream as we rolled over and slept again.

The rest of the night I could hear Diana praying for Jesus. (She often prays in her sleep. This is true.) In the morning she told me she had a nightmare with a witch. I assume there was lightning as well. We were up by six-thirty and a new storm passed through. Diana said she wasn't going snorkeling if there is lightning on the water in a boat. "Give it some time, this will pass, and I don't hear any lightning anyway." I want to say more but remember I'm a loving husband with compassion and the heart of Buddha (sometimes, less than more).

I like to prepare so I get organized early. It's little things like getting all the snorkeling gear and packs ready on the bed, only to come back a few minutes later to see everything moved and rearranged on the floor. I attribute this kind of disconnect with Diana to me as a child who had one brother who was much older and Diana living with a mother who controlled every spec of her daughter's bedroom. There is no other possible explanation, other than she is trying to purposely, and methodically drives me insane. This goes on at home as well. I put a flower vase in the window, rightly placed in the light only to find it moved within minutes. She claims I am the "boss." Not true, I didn't grow up in New Jersey, and I never met the E Street Band. I did say hello to Clarence Thomas in the airport once. He confirmed I was not the "boss" because he didn't recognize me. Anything I put down gets moved.

The snorkeling adventure was scheduled to begin at eight-thirty. At eight-fifteen the rain had come, stopped, and precisely at eight twenty-five began to rain again, more than ever, except for the lightning bolts like the middle of the night. We were ready and down at the Diving School where a pleasant young man named Lyman were greeting four other customers besides Diana and me. Shen was off getting the boats organized. Soon a new couple arrived. They were going deep sea diving and a second boat was needed to fit us all in. While passing Shen the night before he stopped to tell us that the other people coming had all paid for a full day and would we mind if we went out a few hours longer. Diana asked if she could sit on the beach instead of snorkel, and he said, "Yes, of course." She was very happy with his response. I was glad to get a full day tour for the price of a half-day.

The rain didn't stop for another hour, so we had a chance to talk with all the other Americas waiting. There was an American, from North Carolina, named Dewey, his two teenage children, and a woman we first thought was Dewey's wife. Later she told us they were not married, not boyfriend/girlfriend, and was each celibate. For the majority of the day we thought they were married, but there were some signs otherwise. Lastly, a couple from Malibu, California named the

Andersons. His name was Richard, like my dad. I remembered. Richard announced that he was an actor from television and movies. This kind of bravado always makes me suspicious. His wife was a schoolteacher like Dewey and me. We all became a mini-culture and began to talk about where we were from and what we did. A third diving instructor showed up with a young girl named Ashley. With the last people and an appearance that the sky to the north was clearing up, we all headed to the dock on the other side of town. Two boats were fetched and we boarded from the dock. This was the side of town we thought were poor folks shacks; instead there was a channel where luxury homes (not all) had private boat docks and big yachts parked. We had completely misjudged and not even cared to cross the road to "that neighborhood." It looked rough from the side where the soccer field lay. How unusual that we might judge things that looked uninteresting from a distance. I am often surprised by my own stupidity.

There was a large dock with freshly laid gravel and the smell of hot tar. A warehouse and small booth were in the same location where the local "Hokey Pokey" water taxi had its landing. This taxi runs between Mango Creeks (where we went through immigration and were exposed to radioactive substances) and Placencia. We boarded with our gear. The boat passed houses looking somewhat like they belonged in Florida. On one side were the "land houses;" and the other were houses that had to be accessed by boat. We were almost shocked to see this having been here three days and not realizing the wealth and real estate property values, not to mention the potential for investment and commercial speculation with my meager salary.

We pulled around the peninsula of Placencia to a resort where a second diving tank was picked up. When the boat pulled away from that dock Shen took on an official voice and announced that he would be our captain. I hope so because no one else was driving. He was there to welcome us to Placencia Diving School. We had already been with him almost two hours that day, but we knew the expedition was on its way at that moment. He announced that the ride to Laughing Bird Caye was about a half hour. I liked him and the way he was assertive and official.

True, the ride was a half hour (Belize time) and we arrived at a tiny island with a house, picnic shelter, and restrooms. The vegetation was palm trees and underbrush with footpaths well marked by using giant conch shells turned so their pink bellies showed the way. There was one other snorkeling tour with five or six people, and two "rangers" that lived on the island. The islands was tiny, so much so that the buildings dominated the look and feel, but not so much that one could walk to either end and feel secluded and totally at peace without traffic and aspects of modern civilization that usually come on tiny islands. The length of the island could be walked in a matter of five, maybe three minutes. A major bus line ran the length of the island for the American tourists who were too lazy and not comfortable with nature, making frequent stops at the bathroom, house, and picnic shelter. The ride took maybe one minute because the island was so small and the driver went about forty-five miles an hour. All kidding aside it was paradise with white sand, diving pelicans that could have cared less about the petty tourists, and turquoise-blue water that was exquisite. We had arrived.

I've already explained the delicate negotiations that took place with my lovely wife to go on this venture. I asked Diana if she liked the place. "Yes, but you promised me that you'd stay with me in the water." She was setting herself up for a shark attack. I know my wife. We unloaded our gear (we brought our own equipment, food, and the water color paints) and I instantly found a picnic table to begin a sketch of the lovely setting. I picked a view with palm trees in the foreground and the furthest point of the island where a grove of palm trees grew. Between was a pool of turquoise water. I had no time to waste if I was going to snorkel and paint. I laid the basic design in and noticed that the others were waiting for Diana and me, so we quickly got our gear and entered the water with the troupe. Shen was the leader and Lyman was the special agent assigned to Diana's special needs. We put on the fins; Shen gave a brief introductory ecological explanation ending with "Take only pictures, leave only foot prints," neither of which I was about to do in the water.

We entered the water like cats on the prowl, maybe fifteen feet away from the shore, in water shallow enough to stand in. Diana began to panic. "Poppie, I can't do this". She was shaking like a leaf holding my hand so tight the circulation was gone. It was at that moment that I realized what an insensitive bastard I had been back in Roatan. Feeling my wife so afraid, so vulnerable, so weak, so helpless, made my self esteem sink to a level it deserved to be. I began to scream "Shark, shark" in hopes of diverting any guilt away from myself. (NOT!) I took her and held her and said I'd be right there every fin-flip of the way. She was really scared and due to my behavior toward her back in Roatan I knew I'd better do it right this time. Besides there were six other people to make sure I behaved myself. I exorcised my father's teaching style from my mind, cast the demon of Diana's older brother (who repeatedly dunked his non-swimming sister and who instilled a lifelong love of aquatic sports), and became the compassionate Buddha I always wanted to be. The handholding went on all the way. I could feel her tense and trembling. I had no idea of her fright until that day and time. I knew she didn't swim, used a life jacket, and did the dog paddle, but what I take for granted in water is from years of swimming, with lessons at about age nine.

Eventually, towards the end, a single finger replaced the handholding. We swam deeper and further; all the while Shen making sure Diana was safe and comfortable. This was the attention I should have given her the first day back in Roatan. The coral bottom started as a rocky, white, rough surface as we entered the water. Eventually big clumps of Coral were spaced between soft, white, sandy bottoms. The bottom was a gradual slope maybe fifteen feet toward a shallow incline where we could stand. Diana was able to understand how to blow the air through the snorkel to clear the water out. I had shown her this before, but Shen was able to get the point across. It was a good forty-five minutes into the dive when the fingers, and hand, were let go and Diana was swimming without help. This was a big move. I was very proud of her. It is hard to relate to what I assume is common, but this was a big deal and she did it for me. She would have preferred to stay home.

The snorkeling was beyond beautiful. Schools of fish were gathered around and under the coral, hiding from predators, but seemed to have no fear of us as we floated overhead. Shen dove down and picked up a sea cucumber that looked like a huge, black turd. When he raised it to the surface water squirted out and he exposed the reddish under belly. "These fish are very important to the Ecosystem; they clean the coral and bottom". We would stop now and then where Shen would give a brief explanation to what we had seen below. "The parrot fish are what creates the sandy bottom of the sea because they chew the coral and poop out the sand". *That's a lot of sandy poop*, I was thinking. How can that be true? If I ate sand it wouldn't become concrete.

We saw varied types of coral that grew toward the surface like dancing, purple peacock feathers. Huge conch shells moved along the sea bottom almost camouflaged; only being noticeable because of their movement, I dove down and picked one up just to have a look. They have growths of green algae and seem like a floating hotel for other creatures. Shen pointed out a barracuda and hogfish amongst many unspoken points to various fish swimming while we were below the surface. The coral wasn't as dense as Half Moon Bay in Roatan; some places were open zones of white sand where white swimming fish were almost invisible on the sandy bottom. I felt the coral was closer and easier to get to in Roatan, and we didn't have to pay forty dollars each to get there. But the island was a treat and a true getaway well worth it.

We knew we were paying a fraction of the cost the others had paid for the "full day," so we stayed to ourselves and painted as the others ate the provided lunch. We had tuna fish sandwiches. How appropriate. I felt rushed when painting, not knowing how much time we really had, but I finished most of the painting, and took time for a ten-minute walkabout to photograph the island. When the second invitation to go back snorkeling was offered Diana declined. I had enough of the painting to be satisfied and was ready to see the coral reef again. This was a shorter dive that I cut even shorter by returning sooner than the others. When I left Diana invited Ashley to sit with her in the shallow water near the boats. When I returned they were sitting at the picnic table and Diana had begun a watercolor of the palm trees and sea. I love it when she paints.

I tackled the painting and got to a point where I knew I could finish it back at the hotel. Shen and Lyman returned with the others and we sat in the shade. The woman with Dewey then disclosed she and Dewey were just traveling buddies. Diana and I both noted that she was hanging out with us more than the others, both in the water and out. She seemed in need of separating from the three in the family, or more likely in need of being around others than the family. Dewey is an English teacher in a high school. When I suggested he was a Democrat by his subject of instruction I guessed right. The female friend piped up, "He's for Obama". And you aren't? I wanted to ask but didn't. We exchanged some aspects of our schools and compared the war, gore, and glory of our profession. He was a nice man with nice children, but maybe a tad more conservative than me. The woman's insistence that they were "not together" gave it away. It was a kind of church-language for not having sex.

The boat ride back was a delight because Shen saw dolphins and circled back to encourage then to play with the waves of the boat, which they did, giving me the chance to get some quick video of a fin here and there. The clouds from the morning had moved well over land and were now billowing white peaks, the kind one sees on the ceilings of Rococo churches with small cherubs smiling. I saw a big fish floating in the clouds and was enjoying everything as Diana held my hand and thanked me for being a good husband. It's important to know when to put things right. Her thank you was also her forgiving me.

We beached the boat on shore not far from the hotel, close to Shen's 'Top Notch Diving School'. The others left and didn't say good-bye to us. I find this strange after spending a day with strangers. We were already slipping into there past and their true, impersonal qualities were showing. Dewey seemed surprised when I shook his hand good bye. Shen shook my hand twice so that made up for the lack of manners from the American kids. (Adults can be like kids too.) We took a couple of flyers and told him we'd do what we could about sending business his way. The rest of the evening we packed, showered, ate tortillas with beans and rice, and used up all the remaining fruit in a smoothie. I tried to get on-line. We lay down and began to watch TV when all the electricity went off so we sat there and did something old-fashioned. We conversed about the day, the people we met, the actor who was the artistic director of a community theater/ TV movie star (his wife told how he paid the bills), and Diana's family back in Colombia. The electricity was off so long I got to know whom I had been married to for the past four years. A stupid guest from Europe went up the stairs to tell (complain) Lydia that the lights "weren't working". Duh! I can't imagine that this nitwit looked around the neighborhood, or even at the other rooms in the houses, to see that electricity is a shared commodity that comes though electric wires and does not affect his room exclusively. Lydia was very polite. Diana was dozing fast, and I was counting how many hours would add up to eight hours of sleep. My god, I was so early to bed I could get nine in.

Day five: Leaving At four o'clock I was awake. I know when I've had enough of anything and I wasn't about to miss a chance to get up before the sun and write. I quietly turned on the lights and computer so as to not disturb Diana and went to work. When Diana woke at four forty-five she asked if she could sleep until five. "Why not?" was all I could say. She has this ritual of waking and asking my permission if she can sleep longer, before, during, and after we return from vacations. This always humors me. What if I said, "No, get the hell out of that bed and make me breakfast right now woman". I don't understand her submissiveness. Years of being pistol whipped by feminists had bent me to be the submissive one.

At five the alarm went off and Diana smiled, stretched, and told me she had a wonderful dream. In her dream she had given me a beautiful Arabian horse. Her niece and nephew had come along and were combing the shiny hair. I was in total surprise to a point of near tears with excitement in the dream. Then I said, "Get the hell out of that bed woman, and make me breakfast NOW"! Actually I made her the breakfast shake with half an added banana. I couldn't convince Diana she needn't clean the apartment, but she tidied up things for Lydia out of habit.

We stood out on the single road leading out of Placencia. As the bus pulled up at six-fifteen the jockey opened the rear of the bus and we handed him our bags which he loaded into a space where a seat had been removed. There was already a bicycle in the space, so it was rearranged. The dog that had been lying in the middle of the street had to get up and move, as the bus was the first vehicle to leave town that morning. Some mosquitoes had already bitten Diana. I told her how sweet she was. The bus was a converted school bus from the USA. I have often pondered where old school buses end up. Haven't you? The answer is Central America.

The bus pulled around the corner we had seen the day before on our morning walk and I was reassured we had indeed come to the end of that town and any form of civilization. The road followed a narrow strip of land for miles. We stopped every three or four minutes to pick up passengers because it was the express bus. The local, much slower bus stops every minute to pick up people. (We were actually warned that the seven o'clock bus was much slower because of the number of frequent stops.) A short time into the ride the bus was soon filling up with passengers. A mother with two young children boarded and fumbled her way toward the back of the bus, right behind us. As she took her seat, her six-month-old baby was passed to a man to hold as the mother situated her other, older child. The man was a stranger but was offering a kind, human gesture of compassion for the mother. As soon as the child was taken and the baby saw she was away from her mother, the baby began to cry. In a gush of eloquent parenting the man yelled, "Shut up!" Diana and I couldn't help but be inappropriate as well; we burst out laughing so hard the bus full of people took note. It's not every day such loving-kindness is exhibited toward an innocent baby. These are the kind of parenting skills that are taught in special schools here. Secret agents operate them from the Honduran taxi driver schools. The child was soon breast-feeding and indeed the man's wish came true.

I assume what had inspired the man who verbally whipped the child was the music being played on the bus. At first when we got on pure, good ole American country music was blaring. I thought this somewhat strange, yet we were in an English-speaking nation. It did not matter that we couldn't speak the same English, nor really understand what was being said most of the time by the local people. But Alicia Keys was right there singing her sweet little, high-pitched voice out, right in the middle of Belize. By the time the mother and her two children arrived on the bus the music had evolved into Christian Country music. I mean this was weird. I was the only white guy on the bus; all the music was good ole white, Southern Christian music about praising Jesus and being so grateful he died on the cross for us. I could actually hear a few of the passengers doing some singing along. It was right at the third stanza of "Praise His Holy Name" that the man lashed into the defenseless infant. I have no way of proving this, but I suspect just a tad too much Christian Country Music had been listened to by the passenger who greeted that tiny baby in his loving arms.

The land was so narrow that one could see the inner bay and ocean at once. The bus suddenly took a wild turn straight toward the water, passed a curve, and then suddenly turned in the opposite direction. I looked up just in time to see a gate that could be raised, or lowered, to control the flow of traffic. This was the airport. The runway was so short; traffic had to be stopped by a gate to allow planes to land. The road took a detour along the runway, over the runway, and back around. Then we began to see why the runway had been built. Many developers were building luxury homes with private boat docks. On a piece of land, not more than two city blocks, new gated communities were popping up. Some of the passengers we had picked up began to disembark and walk toward these job sites to begin construction. Female passengers that had boarded would get off at grand houses that had docks and yachts tied to the moorings. They were the cooks and house cleaners for the wealthy homeowners. The bus was nearly empty, as small groups getting off at nondescript dirt roads, while others would board and the bus would almost fill up again. On the way I began to speak to a Hispanic man, a construction worker heading to Dangeria, our first stop. He spoke English and Spanish, had come to Belize from Guatemala, gained his citizenship, and now had a wife and two small children. We asked him the needed information on how to get to and through the border. When we pulled into Dangeria I shook his hand and thanked him. He vanished as we retrieved our bags from the back of the bus.

We entered a bus depot that was all yellow. That's about all I remember except that the bus station employees all wore a yellow shirt that said 'Bus Management' on their backs. We got organized at some seats to wait and I walked to a glass counter that had displays of Haile Selassie and CD's of Reggie Music. A tall handsome Rastafarian was standing in the doorway. His dreads were wrapped up into a white fabric bun on the top of his head. I told him how I had seen Haile Selassie, in person, getting off an airplane in Ireland in 1965. I knew he was a king, or president, at the time from recognizing him in the newspapers and TV, but didn't have a clue what that really was. The man enjoyed me telling him this. He liked me. He told me he wasn't even born in 1965 and we laughed. Before I knew it a crowd of people began to storm toward the door at the back of the bus station. Our bus had arrived and we climbed on board. I found a seat, but a woman came up and told me it was hers already. Diana found a seat and I went to the back of the bus.

This time the music on the bus was all Reggae. The people were much mellower and no Christian Music was causing violent outbursts towards small babies. I stupidly changed seats thinking I'd have more legroom for typing on the computer, so I jumped to the last row, right next to the toilet. A young man in the corner seat motioned his girlfriend to join him, so I was now sandwiched between the latrine and a young girl with my elbow just below her ribs, occasionally rubbing her breasts as I typed away. She would try to move away, I would try to move away, pulling my arm closer to my body, but this would move my arm to touch another part of her body. There was no way of getting around it.

329

I was about to be beaten up for molesting a young woman by her boyfriend. The sweat was beginning to roll down my forehead from embarrassment. The bus's air conditioning kicked in and I could feel a burst of cool air hit my wet brow. God, I was thinking, this could have been a hot trip.

But I was wrong. The bathroom door was locked with a padlock but the wall I was up against was burning hot. Between the young woman, us both feeling like this was way too intimate for total strangers, her boyfriend who was very aware of the older white guy feeling up his girl, and the heat of whatever was about to explode behind that locked door, I was in a very awkward predicament. There was obviously a ton of shit so lethal and dangerous it had to be quarantined behind a secured portal to hell. A hot box of poop was boiling one side of my body while a young man was about to peal the skin off my arm. I stuck to my guns and typed away until they both realized I was an artist dedicated to my craft and nothing could keep me from my self-expression. They knew I was a bit loony for typing on a computer in the back of a bouncing bus anyway.

I had only looked away from my computer a few times to see the landscape. Orange groves and planted pine trees were interspersed with what looked like plantations for small palm trees. These spindly palm trees weren't like those along the beach. The fan-like leaves had died and what looked like black spears shoot up where the green leaves had fallen away. These were dangerous looking trees. I heard from Shen the day before that the British had "developed" Belize for logging (more like raped the natural resources) and made an agreement with the government of Guatemala to build a road from Guatemala City to the coast as a trade route for the timber. This is the source of Guatemalans land claim to Belize still today. The road was never built so when Belize got independence in 1981 the Guatemalan government wanted to take back the land, the entire country in fact. One minor detail is that the road was built, kind of, maybe by Belize and Guatemala on separate sides of the border and at different times, but it is possible to get from Guatemala City to the Belize coast by car. So what's the hubbub all about? I wouldn't give a damn one way or another except that this has personally affected my wife and me on our travels. This so-called "border dispute" since 1981, and before, has forbidden buses to go between the two countries. Trucks and cars are free to come and go as they please, but passenger buses might be smuggling lumber so they are not permitted to cross the borders.

When we got to the capital, Molapan, we went into another yellow waiting room and the men and woman with 'Bus Management' were there to help confuse us. The woman sitting collecting fifty cents to use the restroom was wearing this nifty piece of (Bus Management) identification as well. Back in Daragay the woman who charged me a Belize Dollar wasn't wearing a yellow shirt and I had to pay double to relieve myself. How can one bus station charge a dollar while another in the same country charge half that? It may have been because we were getting closer to the border and the timber industry was so successful that the common people had more money, therefore more economic stability, and greater purchasing power from years of British exporting of the natural resources and giving it right back to the local people. This strong competition in the timber, open-market place drove the price of toilet paper down causing a spike in restrooms being built, thus with less competition. Capitalism took root (no tree puns intended) and Imperialism was defeated as the price for taking a dump was substantially depleted due to the abundance of toilet paper. The history of Belize is very complicated.

The third bus was the last; we had gone from Christian Music in the morning to Reggae in the mid-morning, to nothing by noon. This bus wasn't air conditioned, had no tunes, and was the worst by Belize standards. This was solely due to the fact that we were nearing the border with Guatemala. The people of Belize wanted to keep the Guatemalan's in the dark about their paper wealth. The bus took a million stops, even a ten-minute stop in Cayo. The bus was painfully slow. A young man was lounging on our bags in the back of the bus and I, without trying to be obvious, was turning my head using peripheral vision to see if he was riffling through the top zipper compartments. My paranoia and apprehension were increasing with the border dispute between the two countries fresh on my mind. How the hell would we get through that border without being shot? We didn't want to take sides. We're tourists, that's all!

When the bus pulled into the last town on the border we had to take a taxi to the border. (Remember buses are not allowed near the border.) The taxi was something like six dollars for the short ride. The driver told us he had a friend who specialized in abducting foreigners on the other side who could take us where we wanted to go. We declined. Instead we chose the easy way out. We faced the moneychangers and taxi drivers by ourselves, who told us how dangerous it was and how there were no ATM, and we needed their money and special rates, and who also had a special friend who would take us where we needed to go once we passed through the border. We hadn't even left Belize yet. I love my wife, but she is slightly vulnerable and believes everything she is told by total strangers luring travelers on the border. I did too, or I wouldn't have changed the one hundred dollars at the border by luring moneychangers.

By the time we got to a woman handing us a questionnaire about our stay in Belize our ankles were in bloody shreds where we had kicked off the border dogs. They bite only tourists. The woman was surprisingly friendly and genuine. We did a quick survey about our stay, how long, how much timber was in our bags, and where we entered the country. When I said we entered through Honduras her eyes light up. I have no idea why, assuming the border between these two countries has been well established for hundreds of years, and we used a water taxi, not a bus, to enter the country.

Before we leave the country and I give any misleading explanations about the relations between Honduras and Belize there is one small caveat I need mention - Shoes. The beaches on Belize, that we saw anyway, were strewn with shoes. That is shoes that float, the soles of shoes, not the leather uppers, the rubber bottoms were everywhere on every beach in Belize. This was true and were seen floating in the waters on the way to the snorkeling island of Laughing Bird Caye. This was true even on the island beach we boated to. We saw the bottoms of shoes to a point that I was forced to ask the question of several people. They all gave the same, begrudging answer. "Honduras!" Shen, Lydia, anyone we asked said, "Honduras".   Everyone in Honduras makes sport of throwing their old shoes into the Caribbean Sea, the current and trade winds carry the shoes east to Belize. Barges of trash are dumped in the Caribbean Sea, the waste that floats drifts to Belize. Yet people are barefoot in Belize and buses continue to run between the two countries.

In my panic to not get flustered by the moneychangers at the border I exchanged all my Belize dollars into Quetzals and had to dip into my reserve of United States dollars to get out of Belize. There is a fifteen dollars (US) exit tax. I, in my wisdom of planning had stupidly spent my Belize dollars knowing full well I needed them to get out of the country. We paid the exit tax, took the receipt to a second desk, walked across a dirt road, saw not one bus, and entered into Guatemala. In one last act of love (or defiance) to the continued border dispute, we threw the soles of our shoes behind us, across the border, at the moneychangers. They ducked and we took refuge in the safety of Guatemala and asked for political asylum. All the warnings about a dangerous border were nonsense.

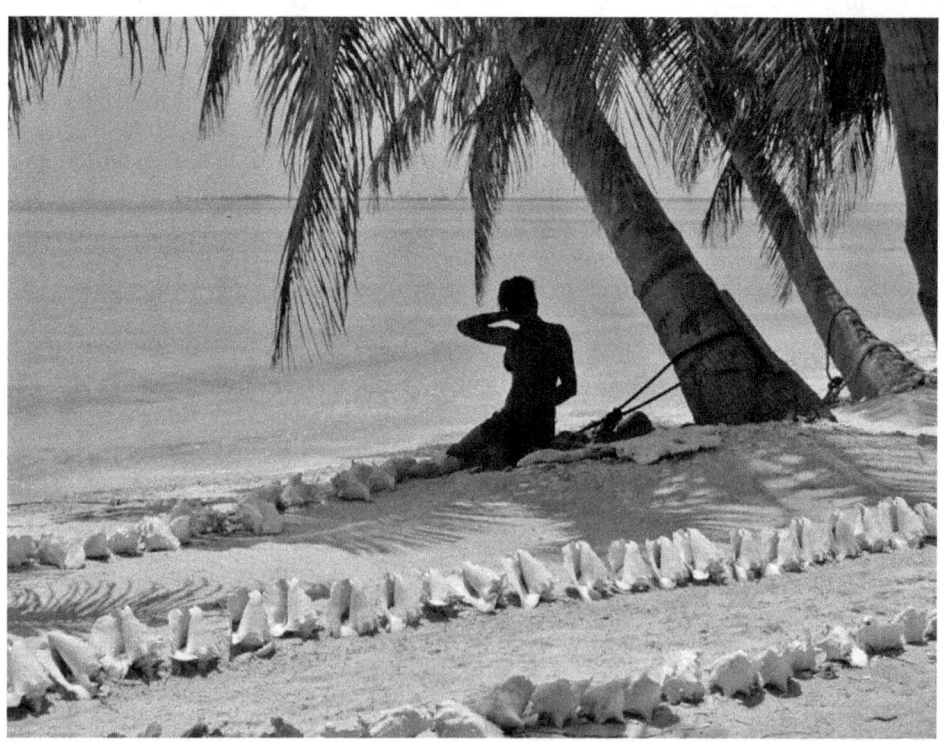

Chapter Nineteen
Guatemala

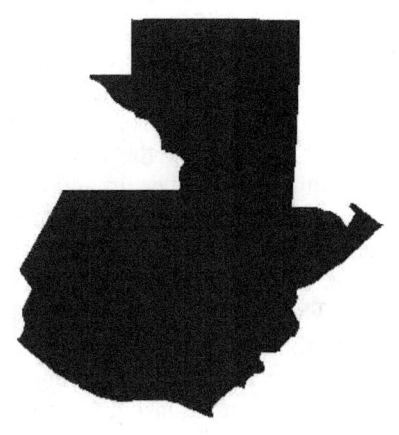

Day One: Three men bite at our heels the very second we left the Belize Immigration office. They didn't even give us a chance to breath for a few minutes until we walked across the border on the dusty gravel to Guatemala. Why the hell weren't there soldiers standing up in towers shooting at these men? Why were they allowed to be between two countries with a border dispute that didn't allow buses to cross? Yet these guys were like the Ice Capades skating wherever they wanted. I wanted them to be in North Korea! Between the two Koreas' they allow buses to cross (with special family visits) but never would you see the kind of chaos that exists on this border. For three minutes big men hounded us until we entered a line for immigration. They magically retreated only to rejoin us when we left the line. I now realize that these were the potential customs agents. They kept asking us if we wanted a taxi, we kept telling them we wanted a van, to be in a group with other travelers, and to not be singled out or victimized by unscrupulous bandits. By the time we got into a four-door truck that we were told was "a van," and were refusing to let our bags be in the back of the truck with one of the very heavy, "big men," I realized that we had not gone through customs and therefore these men were indeed the customs agents. (They may have been double agents.)

I ask you to put me with a group; you put me with a Sumo wrestler sitting in the back of a truck. I ask you for a van, it is a truck. I ask you to be a group; you tell me this is a "group." I ask you for a white flag, you hand me a red flag and tell me it is white. I tell you I want to go to Flores; you tell me I want to go straight to Tikal. I tell you I want a cheap hotel, you tell me there are no cheap hotels in Tikal and you get a commission, so you want to take me to Tikal even though I have said Flores a dozen times. The border agents of Guatemala are bandits but the brain washing of the North Korean gets all the bad press. There is no way this is about timber rights and a road that was never built! This is about tourism and how to bend reality so the experience of the traveler is a luxurious, comfortable one. We never had to open our bags and that was disappointing me more than anything. Who was a border agent or selling rides wasn't really clear.

I had read a few things about this border crossing. I read it's best to stay in Flores, that there were no ATM machines or grocery stores in Tikal, only expensive hotels and restaurants, and the total number of hotels was something like three, minus the hippie campground. Roberto our driver tried his damnedest to change our minds but we pretended to be dumb and stuck to our guns. The big (Sumo) man was dropped off at the gas station where Roberto bought gas and had the big (Sumo) guy buy him a bottle of water. I have no idea who Roberto is and where he came from and how we ended up in his four-door truck, but like a trade wind blowing from Honduras we woke up in his white truck that looked and felt like van by the time the drugs wore off. Diana had a dribble of spittle come out of her lower lip and the drugs were wearing off for her as well. We had been abducted, try as we did to get a van and get through that damn border, we were zooming down the highway in a white four door truck. Roberto was safe, dependable, and passed as many as ("there are none today") six minivans on the road. The minivan service was in full swing; many passengers who paid much less than us were smiling and looking out the windows. They had not been drugged, or lied to. When Roberto waved to the cops parked along the road and no lights began to flash and no one chased us, I calmed down and became human again. "Do you have any children Roberto?" He answered "No."

We were on our way to Flores. We told Roberto the whole story about Diana and the American company that threatened to sue her the summer before. He had lived in the US (Tampa, Florida) for two years in a stained glass factory. His brother is an artist; I showed him my recent paintings. We had a pleasant visit on the drive. The chaos on the border was a faint memory by then. I asked him to take us to a hotel for twenty dollars a day, a fan, no AC, with Wi-Fi. I knew if we stated anything near the truth we wouldn't have found a nice hotel. Along the route, when we came to the split in the road, Roberto said one last time, "This is where we can turn to Tikal or Flores. If we go to Tikal I will charge you an extra ten dollars (US) to go there, because it is a little further than to Flores. The men on the border were all trained to steer tourists toward Tikal so they would get a commission. There are only three hotels there. The hotels in Flores don't give drivers a commission. "Make your decision Flores or Tikal? All those who enter here (Flores) are doomed to an eternity of damnation." We still chose Flores. Suddenly Roberto was beginning to tell us the "truth". He had befriended us, maybe because I showed him my paintings. Somewhere in the mix of lies, fabrications, and a need to make a living, Roberto saw we were people and not just dollar signs. The real Roberto was beginning to offer us small bits of reality.

The drive lasted an hour because Roberto was driving like a crazy man even though the conversation seemed sane. It was further to Flores than Tikal, thus Roberto had to catch up on time. (I am assuming here.) Roberto was, for the first time, attempting to break all speed records and He did. He dropped us at a hotel that was thirty dollars a day. We came to the hotel Roberto told us about; he also showed us a place across the road as a second option. We looked at the room and came back to the front desk. I asked if the owner would lower the price if we stayed three days. The owner, a tall man in his late sixties, seem a bit taken aback by such hard nose bargaining. He lifted the calendar and showed us where he had only one opening and that had been whited-out because of an unusual cancellation. He gave a little chuckle as he showed his discomfort with my selfish attempt and ignorance. We took the room for thirty (US) a night. It has

AC, TV, Wi-Fi, DDT, and a fan at no extra charge. The room resembled a jail cell with windows too high to see out. The young porter carried our heavy bags up the three flights of stairs. We were wise enough to know we need look no further.

After a quick shower, we were out the door to explore and within twenty minutes to re-enter the lobby, where no one was to be seen, I guess because the hotel was entirely full the owner could take the rest of the day off. We had a question for him, but that could wait. We entered an Old Spanish town that is about a square mile large situated on an island. At the end of our street, beyond a row of hotels, there is a lake that surrounds this tiny island of Flores. The shore has a newly built walkway and street with hotels and restaurants on one side. Well-placed stones on the shore make the new construction very attractive. The whole street is new; the stone walk along the shore has low walls and a sloped embankment down to the water. Three water taxis with men sitting under their shaded canopy stood up and offered us a tour around the lake. I motioned no and we walked a few feet when a very old man kindly approached us and in a soft voice (in Spanish) offered us the grand tour for one hundred and fifty Quetzals (Around 20 US dollars). He knew I was asking Diana the price (in English) and continued with a lengthy description of all the features of the tour. At the end of his presentation I offered him one hundred. He came down to one hundred and twenty; I stayed at one hundred and began to walk away. He agreed to one hundred. I had no intentions of a water tour but we had once again, unbeknown to us, been drugged with a potion that made us helplessly weak to the invitations of others seeking money.

Our hour and a half spent floating with Miguel was money well spent. He was a young eighty-seven years old. He told us his wife was still living. She had a stroke and the medication was very costly. Now I was feeling Catholic guilt. Miguel was the most pleasant part of our day. He told us stories, recited poems, and even sang an ancient Mayan song about a man seducing a maiden to go swimming with him. (Miguel was obviously putting the moves on Diana, big time.) We rode in the long, turquoise-green boat, sitting out of the sun in the shade, as the engine was set on the slowest possible speed. We first passed young tourists diving into the lake from wooden platform docks. On the far side of the lake people sat in the shade, men pushed by in wooden dugout boats, and two women sat submerged in the lake up to their waist downing laundry by hand. Miguel showed us the deepest area and told how a professional diver who checked the exact depth of the lake had hired him. A small island of only reeds was where the first hospital of Flores had once stood. The island has a fourteen-year cycle where it rises and then sinks back to its current, submerged, level. We were enthralled. He was a genuine find, friend, and gave me the most soothing vibe I'd felt from anyone in many, many days. If you remember ever having a favorite teacher when you were a child, who exuded patience and love, this was Miguel. He was an angle posing as a water taxi driver.

Miguel had learned the language and ways of the Mayan by spending three days with them when he was a young man. (It must have been a short language and a people with very simple cultural depth for him to learn everything in three days.) He worked for thirty years as a tour guide in Tikal, then as a tour guide on the lake. We didn't want to leave as he pulled the boat up to the island and instructed us on the directions to the large church situated on the crest of a hill. We thanked him and gave a possible commitment to another tour, on another day, to a game preserve with lots of local animals (not taxi drivers).

Passing up a hill through narrow streets we entered a church where a black Christ hung on a cross above the altar. The man working in the church told Diana it was a miracle. The black Christ was a miracle that had miraculously appeared out of an old black log found in the lake. One only needs faith to believe such stories. The church was old but beautiful, in need of a new layer of plaster. I took photographs and we left. We found a food stand and ate two chicken tortillas and a fruit drink. We were happy. The woman at the food stand invited me into the booth to photograph her child sitting in a stroller. The child was chewing on a carrot she kept dropping so I would repeat picking it up and giving it back to her. We sat and ate, watched the men working in the park across from where we sat, and the children running around playing. We walked on the cobble streets, entered a few shops, and soon turned in for an early start tomorrow. We had bought the van ticket to the Mayan ruins of Tikal and had to rise at six o'clock for a seven o'clock pickup. The room was so cold from the air conditioner I wore long pants, a hat, and shocks to bed.

Day Two: Tikal. We sat on the curb in front of the hotel for twenty minutes when a driver approached us. He had been waiting on the other street behind the hotel. The van was full of people. I tried to make a joke, but the blank looks on the faces of the people were a good indication that no one was an English speaker. One man spoke with me. He was from Argentina. The rest of the journey to the ruins was in total silence. I watched as we passed speed bumps in the road and women sat selling food. Each speed bump was an occasion for a small roadside stand. I noticed at one bump a woman was standing shoeing flies away from the food. She did this with such fervor I took note, thinking this must be an exhausting exercise to stand and do all day; waving away flies. I was curious, so in the mirror I kept watching to see what happened once we passed. Sure enough it was all a commercial illusion. She sat down the second we passed. The flies must have been feasting on the food by then. The speed bumps all had signs warning of their approach. Three bumps were on most signs, but my favorite was the two bump signs. They looked too much like breasts for me not to notice and laugh to myself.

The road passed a military base with long walls topped with barbed wire and men stationed in high pillbox lookouts. A shrine to some past conflict was standing on the opposite side from the barracks. What was very cool to me was the shrine wasn't glorifying war, it had the blown up remains of a tank, maybe two tanks, displayed as to show the horror of war; and a sign indicated this message. How different than a tall statue to a dead hero as most commonly seen. The military were very prevalent along that stretch of highway; in addition there were many police trucks. We'd seen this the day before when we passed the same area. Around a curve and along a lengthy stretch of the road a shantytown was lining both sides of the passage. This wasn't a town so much as a long, disconnected patchwork where lots were empty and others would have three of four shakes in close succession. This went on for three or four miles. What distinguished this sector of highway were the people living so close to the road and the amount of dogs lying in the road. These scroungy mutts were all mixed breeds, most seemed to be without owners and living on trash. They were so emaciated that they had no real energy to get up and move for the traffic, so the van would maneuver around them. At some points there were more skinny dogs visible than people.

This all vanished into lush rainforest's as we neared the entrance to the park. At the entrance an orange traffic cone was set in our lane to make us stop. The driver signed a sheet, showed it to a gatekeeper, and returned the sheet to the side of his seat. Then three men standing at the side of the road opened the van door and gave a kind of official speech welcoming us to the park. They didn't wear uniforms; they then began to try and sell us maps and books. (The price was double for the same items for sale inside the park by the rangers.) This irked me as much as the nonsense we had been though the day before on the border. It is like the lawless Wild West, everyone is out to take you. The driver, border agents, military, whoever, just let it all happen. This is free enterprise gone a-muck. No one bought one thing and I was happy. I've been quickly developing an attitude about this kind of free enterprise. A few minutes later the van pulled up to the park real entrance. We walked back from our drop off point, a few hundred yards, to a large building that housed a giant replica of the entire Mayan complex. Diana used the restroom while I looked at the prices in the gift shop. For a five inch wooden carving the price was seventy-five dollars. We entered the park, walked to a booth that asked for our receipts, bought a small map, and were on our way.

I'd like to say that we were spellbound but the distance between all the sites and the deteriorated condition of the temples was enough to convince us that the tickets we had prepaid for the following day, with a guide, wasn't necessary. I had been spoiled the year before when I saw the ruins in Copan, Honduras. If I were writing a guidebook (this is a travel book), I'd tell people to skip Tikal and see the well-preserved site at Copan in Honduras. The hieroglyphics at Copan are definitely better, the mammoth totem-like statues are well preserved/defined, and the area to walk is a fraction of the distance. I feel terrible about this and will lose my sponsorship, and big cash advance from the Guatemalan Government for writing this chapter, but Tikal was a good six hour walk in the jungle and Copan is a four hour walk where all the structures are close, better preserved, and visually much more interesting. Some folks may disagree; Diana never even saw Copan and said it was better. We were exhausted, and saw maybe half the grounds. I did take an hour for a lunch break and a painting of a pyramid called the '*Lost World*'.

As I painted, many people stopped by to look at the work and give positive responses. My favorites are the children who always find art interesting. We could have spent the day showing art. I had my other paintings from the trip with me. A man began to pass them around. He handed them to another man who said "no thank you". He thought I was trying to sell him some art. I found this disturbing; his friend told him I was sharing not selling. Families stopped by, even tour groups, I was feeling a bit overwhelmed because creating art is generally a private act for me. After lunch we once again walked to more temples and archaeological dig sites. The highlight came when we climbed the tallest structure (Temple IV) and could see the tops of four other temples. Unlike Copan the view between sites was obstructed by jungle.

At two o'clock we exited the park, just as the van was leaving, we boarded; handed the driver our voucher and it began to rain. Things happen that way for a reason. I was drenching wet with perspiration; our water was almost gone so we swallowed the last few swigs after sharing a small bags of almonds. Soon I was fast asleep and woke five minutes before we were dropped off at our hotel. Before we came back to the hotel we went straight to the travel agent that sold us the two-day voucher and exchanged it for a trip to the zoo and asked that our water taxi driver (Miguel) be our guide. We also bought two, first class, overnight tickets for a bus to Guatemala City for Monday night. So we all were happy. We didn't ask for any money back, gave the agent more business and more money.

We dropped off our daypacks at the hotel and went walking to a fast food chicken restaurant. It's a chain that we have seen even in New York. I am ashamed to say we bought half a chicken and soft drink. (Sugar drinks) The rest of the day we walked around the outer road of the Island of Flores, got more money at an ATM, went to church, bought a bag of cashews, drifted into a few souvenir shops, and came home to our room. Diana called her mother on the computer-phone. I took a shower and read up on the "Convergence" that is taking place today. Julio, my friend in Antigua, Guatemala has been sending me links and web sites about the alignment of the planets. This is why we are friends, we both love that cosmic, love, new age, spiritual hocus pocus stuff. I have been in touch with him trying to let him know of our where-about and arrival date, still to be determined by the wind and stars.

Day Three: The Zoo. It was a rare treat to sleep in this morning. I woke at seven as we had canceled the plan to get up at four to take a sunrise tour of the ruins. I wonder why? The tour we did schedule was for ten o'clock. This was with a special request for the old man Miguel and his water taxi. We played house when we woke up, I painted, and Diana embroidered. We are on our (all liquid) cleanse fast today. So we are weak and taking it slow and easy. Food is such an emotional part of one's day. It's not just that we wake up and want the nutrients of mommy's milk. We enjoy that milk. We are conditioned from infancy to get into the whole ambiance, preparing the food, sitting with others, etc. But on these "cleanse/fast" days we get up and drink a liquid. We are not full, the stomach is empty, but we do get lots of nutrients as we drink a highly potent mineral liquid. I like to chew food and miss that emotional boost. I have done juice fasting in years past and did some reading up on the subject before I ever tried it. This is the kind of thing a doctor who practices alternative medicine, will totally approve of, while a regular doctor might frown upon it.

We left the hotel at nine fifteen, walked to the corner to take a little stroll when we saw Miguel and the travel agent standing on the sidewalk. We joined them and Miguel asked if we wanted to leave right then. "Yes, why not?" We walked the few blocks to the water and boarded his rickety old boat. The tour began right away. He gave us more information than it's possible to recall. The boat headed in the general direction we had taken two days before. The island of Flores grew smaller as we reached a distance of three or four miles down the lake. Miguel asked us if we'd allow him to join us on land. We agreed to pay his entrance fee. We docked on an island that had a long bridge to the mainland, visible from where we docked. This first area was a small park before the main zoo across the bridge. We disembarked and walked up a small hill to a booth where a man as old as Miguel took the entrance fee. He handed me five slips of paper. There were three of us; I think we were paying for the zoo and the small island. Miguel took us up to the Chicklet tree and squeezed the sap from the end of the leaf. We tasted it; yes this was the same flavor as the chewing gum. As we entered the yard of the park there were wild bores feeding on vegetables inside a shelter. A huge round table stood in the room we entered after passing the animals. Miguel showed us the wood (of the Cedro tree) that was so strong the other old man from the front entrance gate sat on it. The table was nine feet in diameter. We exited the room and passed along a trail where Miguel told us about the medicinal qualities of barks and leaves of the Cedro tree.

A variety of animals in low, fenced-in cages were on exhibit. We saw turtles, alligators, birds in tall cages, and many of the local creatures of the rain forests. I took pictures and followed Miguel's lead through the park. The most interesting animals were in big cages where their escape was impossible. We saw a puma, some small leopard-like cats, and monkeys. I got some good close-ups of the puma, but the big leopard was too lazy to get up and pose for my camera. The tour in the zoo took an hour. There was one other family that we ran into. We felt like we were on an exclusive tour so we were glad to pay for the experience. This zoo is part of a University. Some water slides had been built, they were perched, and an idol on the top of the hill. Miguel told us how the water slides were no longer operational because the lake had gone so low. The end of the slide was three feet this side of the water's edge. Miguel also told us how many people had broken legs, backs, and even died using this water slide. And I was hoping to break a leg! Miguel was asked if he ever used the water slide. He hadn't, that is why he has lived so long.

Diana and I took a break sitting on some benches as we saw the last of the other family and eventually heard their boat leave from down on the dock. We sat and drank our liquid diet supplement as Miguel told us stories. The entire time we only saw the man at the gate, the family of five, and two workers as we re-boarded the boat for the slow ride home. Birds perched along the water's edge and we pulled close to the shore for some close-ups of water lilies. It was a very pleasant three hours. We took a slow boat ride back to the dock where Miguel's son greeted us. He was in his late sixties and looked just like his father. I told the son his father was special, thanked the son for helping us off the boat and waved good-bye to Miguel. We wander into a few shops and ended up back at the hotel just as a few raindrops began to turn the sky darker. We are both so hungry we decided not to watch any TV because the commercials are deadly to one's appetite. I called several people on the phone and have been writing on the computer. I enjoy writing so much I could do this for a living, if there were money involved.

We spent a few hours while I painted and Diana did her embroidery. We were feeling so weak from no solid foods that it was ridiculous. We were getting cabin fever. We left the hotel and boarded a "toot, toot" to the Maxi Bodega, a super market that was situated in a new mall. We wandered the mall just killing time, and then went into the grocery store for food for tomorrow. We smelled food, looked at food, thought about food, but held the line. I hate when I have self-control. The food was enough for three days; we were planning to eat at some point, say tomorrow at brunch. We drink the cleansing shake for breakfast, so the fasting ends more like mid-morning tomorrow. We bought the food pretending we would eat it when we got back to the hotel.

A magnanimous storm rolled in as we were in Maxi Bodega. This forced us to walk the mall one more time until the rain let up and we boarded another "took, took". Again, back to the room, TV, more hunger, until we were forced out to look at restaurants and people eating. I suggested to Diana that the smells were important to enjoy and the heightened, acute awareness of smells was normal. This is our fifth cleansing fast together. We started, primed ourselves a few weeks before we left for Central America. We entered more shops, looking at prices and not buying anything until we get to the open market in Chichicastenango. We sauntered the outer perimeter of the island and ran into a couple we had briefly spoken to the day before in Tikal. This time we visited for about ten minutes. She is from Michigan, he from Mexico. They live in Mexico City where she is a yoga teacher, and he a computer programmer. We bid them a safe journey because they were leaving for Antigua on an overnight bus. They were both small and very timid, but we had a nice visit. Diana and I walked hand in hand along the sidewalk with the water on the outer side. We sat and listened to some marimba players who were set up outside an expensive restaurant. Diana has been very lovey-dovey and wants a lot of kisses. This is the woman I feel in love with. She is free and safe to not worry these last few days. We are in very good harmony the last several days. Our shadows are merging and our footsteps are falling into a uniform dance.

One of the silliest things about this island is the way the church bells are rung. They aren't, or when they are they are barely audible. What are used instead are explosive rockets. When we were waiting for the van to Tikal I made a joke that the exploding rockets were to announce Mass in the church. I thought I was being cute and sarcastic, but Diana asked a woman sweeping her stoop what all the repeated rockets we had been hearing were about. Sure enough, Mass is about to begin. When we finally did go to Saturday Mass we heard the rockets, and saw the big metal tube that shoots the rockets. I am not an explosives buff (only when smuggling them into Belize), but I enjoyed watching an elderly man loading what looked like paper bags the size of a child's lunch, light a long fuse, and step back. Three teenage boys sat and watched the spiritual spectacle.

When we entered the church for mass we saw a young girl who sat in the front in a Quinceanera dress. This was her fifteenth year celebration. We sat in the back of the church where I had a nice view of the rockets being shot off. The first burst was to send the package up into the air; the second was far up in the sky where the rocket actually exploded. What a nice touch for a church to use explosives. The more I thought about this I was sure the church was doing a logic exercise in announcing the beginning of Mass to the outlaying parishioners. The island of Flores is a circle of land in the middle of the lake. A bridge connects the island to the mainland, but it is a short bridge. The majority of people around the island don't live on the island, so the sound carries well over the flat lake to the outreaching community. The bell itself tolls so low someone came up with this plot to sell explosives to the church. It works. When we were on the tour in the morning, far away at the zoo, we could hear the bombs of Christianity. What one would assume is one single explosion is not, several are used. The time we stayed in Mass had a series of explosions numbering perhaps, ten. Why more than a few at the beginning to announce church I can't answer. The smell of gunpowder is fresh; the round plume of smoke up in the air is fascinating. It's just one of those things that make traveling so unreal, but real. I expected the priest to be carrying a sidearm but he wasn't.

Day Four: Food. We both had terrible sleep; it was cold from the air conditioning, and thin sheets that the hotel provides is no different than sleeping naked. I was up at five o'clock trying not to disturb the sleeping princess in the bed next to me. I finished a painting of a Tikal pyramid. At six Diana was awake. I made our breakfast shakes and felt pretty weak from the fast the day before. The sun was strong and I wanted to get in some photographs so we went out into the morning. Five minutes into the walk the sun vanished behind clouds. We circled the island once again, and came back home. I napped and asked Diana if she wanted to see the fruit market in the town across the bridge. The town is called Santa Ana. We rode a "took, took" (taxi) straight up to the market a few blocks away from where we had used an ATM two days before. We had no idea we were so close to such a huge market. See what happens when you venture beyond fear?

This was the real market with no tourists, real working people, and alive with excitement. The descriptive jungle of paths, dark alleys, dirty, clean, bad odors, and good odors, was a true environment of life. In the market nothing goes to waste if it is functional. I saw a vegetable stand where the knife being used was at least ten years old. The blade near the handle was two and a half inches think. The blade at the tip and middle was worn down to a half-inch. We walked past several restaurants, some full of flies, some cleaner than others. One restaurant full of people sitting in the dark had a display of whole cooked chickens for sale. We both stood there and drooled on the glass. That was it. We'd had enough cleansing and wanted to eat, period. We bought a plate of rice, chicken, and cabbage salad. It was ten-thirty in the morning. We sat across from two young workers. Diana spun off into a long conversation as we ate. The young men were all ears. I was too engrossed in the meal to think of what was transpiring. They worked at Tikal was about all I took in. The restaurant wasn't that clean, the walls had what looked like dirty, rubbed hand marks. We were not given napkins so we used the condensation on our glasses of fruit drink to wash up. There was not one fly in the full house. The food was good. It was a delicious experience just to be in the middle of this market and see so much life in a macrocosm.

The market went on at least a half-mile and we walked through in no particular direction, wandering down any isle that looked safe and fun. Every so often we would come to a street, but the sprawling market had no grid, no pattern, was wide and cool in some places with sun coining through, or dark with no lights in other sections. We felt completely safe, people smiled and said hello. Some asked to have their pictures taken. No one was nasty but some people had that worn look from life beating them down. We pranced through as vacationers, pass a place for a second, but people spend entire lives sitting in these booths, never seeing the world, never knowing what is beyond the border of their town. There isn't resentment towards us; there is a bashful resistance to strangers. One fruit stand had a young man who asked me to take his photograph. His mother who was sitting next to him began to duck behind some stacked boxes. She began to giggle as if this was the funniest invasion of privacy in her life. The son was trying to encourage her to look at the camera, but she just laughed and looked for a better place to hide.

We both felt energized from this hour walk. We were in agreement that the tourist things are a bit boring and over-blown, but the real markets and the thousands of interesting faces to see gives one the true life experience that only comes with leaving what is familiar. It was fun, hot, and we were full from food and beginning to feel human again after our fast. We walked all the way home and took a long shower. Eating food and seeing people is a healthy way to spend our last day engaging here. We paid an extra twelve dollars to stay in our room until eight-thirty tonight. We are happy and all set. Now we are going out to paint some of the boats docked along the shore.

Day Four: Antigua. The day we left Flores was spent in and out of the hotel, beginning a new painting of the local boats, and watching TV until our bus' arrival at 9 P.M.. The bus was a trip into hell and back. We saw nothing, it was dark, and the curtains were all drawn the entire time. As I expected, the air conditioning was on and the layers of clothes we brought were put on right away. The driver's assistant told us we could pee, but no one was allowed to poo. The "first class" seats we were told we were paying for did not exist. All the seats were the same and all the seats were uncomfortable. We conferred with the other travels.

As we sat on the curb, waiting for the bus across the street from the best hotel in Flores, we began a conversation with a couple from Poland. We were exchanging travel stories when another couple came up and we all four began to exchange stories. A troupe of four females from Holland came in a taxi, so there was a good sized crowd waiting for the bus. The bus pulled up and we all boarded, the next stop, close by, was when the majority of the passengers loaded in. Every seat was sold. The driver gave the same speech as before to this group of travelers. The first time Diana got up and spoke in English, helping the man get the 'piss, but no poop' message out. These new passengers were locals going to Guatemala City. As the driver told the friendly guidelines, we were all instructed that the bus would only stop in an emergency. It was preferred we all hold that poop until we arrived in the morning to Guatemala City. There were two drivers; we knew one or both of them were heavily armed because of the "dangerous" nature of having to stop could be problematic. I'm thinking we needed an armored car not a public bus. We needed a military escort from the way the journey was being defined. The windows in the bus began to steam up. This wasn't the most reassuring feature, yet I was thinking how this would make the passengers inside much less visible. The curtains were all drawn shut, but condensation was everywhere.

The driver who made all the announcements then told us we would not be able to watch a movie. Why? "It's too dangerous?" You can't poop because that's dangerous, you can't pee because that's dangerous, and you can't eat, drink, or be merry because that's dangerous as well. What isn't dangerous? One of the passengers begged for a movie. The rejecting volley went back and forth until the driver agreed, but only for one hour. One hour with visible lights in the bus was a dangerous time as well. One movie was started and five minutes into it another movie was put on. How that all happened I don't know. Maybe the movie was too dangerous, it was one of those action movies, and the second movie was a love story. At exactly one hour after the movie began the machine was shut off. So I knew we had eight hours of a nine-hour trip remaining.

It was pointless to look inside of the bus at the new passengers since the lights were not allowed to be turned on. I could see no one's face who had boarded because of the "Black out rule", so I wasn't sure if the other passengers on the bus were a paramilitary regiment, or a group of kidnapped tourist with their mouths covered and hands bound. The whole thing began bad and ended the same. As the night progressed I couldn't sleep. I took a sleeping pill only to wake up a few hours later and needing to pee. Thank god no number two was needed. I climbed out of the seat and stumbled over body parts, feet mostly, until I got to the bathroom. There was that same heat coming from the restroom as the bus we rode in Belize. We weren't allowed to use the restroom because it was already full of shit, the radiant heat made that apparent. I was thinking we were not permitted to use the bathroom was because the toilet wouldn't flush. The bus, first came to Flores from Guatemala City, but didn't have a waste station to unload the treasure of the first group of travelers. When I went to relieve myself the toilet was full of pee. It was so full that the pool of liquid was swishing around the bowel and tipping the rim of the bowel. The floor was wet. Now mind you there were no lights allowed so I'm guessing this was a yellow liquid. I may be wrong, but the smell was yellow.

I went back to the seat and was so excited by the prospect of a repeat visit that I couldn't sleep. I took another pill and tried to commit suicide. This was after rolling in my seat for an hour, aware that we did stop a few times to let off passengers, or dead bodies. The air conditioner was so cold I was getting frost bit; yet I was sweating under my clothes. (I sweat when I'm cold. It's true.) I also noticed that it was raining inside the bus. The condensation of the air conditioning had created a tiny microclimate and water had condensed on the vinyl above our seats next to the vent. Drops of water would occasionally splash onto my face. I left my raincoat in the luggage. Now what was I going to do? So I did what any good husband would have done to protect his wife. I asked Diana to change seats with me. Not to worry, the weather was worst in her seat. The rain had an easier drip from the vinyl and was dripping more than my previous seat. I was so glad I had seen this before and selflessly offered myself as a human shield to protect my wife. I propped my head between the window and seat, like I often do in an airplane, stacked the daypacks on the floor so my legs raised my knees above the seat, and took on a fetal position. This actually sounds horrible, but it was the most comfortable I had been all night. I passed into a deep relaxing sleep where drugs had no influence on my behavior. When I woke up Diana said we were in Guatemala City. My neck felt like a frozen, stiff piece of meat, was very sore, and my clothes were wet from rain showers. Was I camping out of doors, or riding a bus?

We left the bus in a hurry because Diana said we had to get right to the bags for their safety. I was so drugged up I could not tell if I was me. Diana took charge and I followed her into the crowded waiting room full of people from a crowded loading dock full of people. We were told a man would be standing and waiting with a sign saying Diana and Dennis. There were a few men, no signs, but a grumpy looking guy took our bags and led us to the van parked outside. Diana found him; but I was too far-gone to know what was going on. I got into the van leaving my bag outside, then Diana suggested a better way to insure the safety of my luggage would be to take it off the busy street and put it in the back of the van, which I did. I have no memory of things after that except my head was rolling around on my shoulders and we were in Guatemala City where thousands of people were walking to their daily jobs.

Now that I'm half awake (Five hours after getting to Antigua) I know the bus driver the night before did the right thing. A bus with lights on inside means that there is breathing bodies inside, there are passengers with valuables, there are potential cash prizes, and moving us with lights is easier to be shot at than a dark bus. I was surprised the driver used the headlights; they can get shot out as well. The number of bus abductions has increased of late. There is a distinct relationship between the use of toilets in buses (but only toilets where people poop) and the hijacking of these buses. Since only peeing has been allowed the number of bus robberies has almost stopped completely. If you noticed any contradictions in the last sentence please ignore them, and the sarcasm.

We were in the van, flying down the side streets of Guatemala City. I was passed out. We got to Antigua and Diana woke me again. I asked the driver if we were near the yellow church. He ignored me. A Dutch passenger asked the driver if he knew where the 'Black Cat' was, he ignored her as well. We both were

344

speaking in Spanish, what was the problem? A yellow church and a black cat are perfectly normal questions to ask any driver. Then Diana got assertive and asked him where he was taking us in Spanish. He broke his purposeful silence and snapped back, "The office". She pressed him, "We need to be dropped at our hotel, and these people want to go to the 'Black Cat Hotel'. In English I began to speak, "He wants to take us to the office so his friends can tell us all that "those other hotels are all full and he knows of a place with a special price". Everyone in the van spoke English but him.

One of the passengers noted we were passing the "Black Cat" at that moment, so we made him stop. The four Dutch women got out, and the remaining four of us convinced the driver to take us to the "Don Quixote Hotel" where I had stayed the year before. He knew right where it was; he spoke to Diana and even helped the four of us unload the luggage. The guy was having a bad day or something. We did note later that he was pretty nasty and had a huge chip on his shoulder from the minute I drooled on him in the bus terminal. The sleeping pills had indeed kicked in by then, and I was not myself. Nor was anyone else in that bus terminal "themselves" as far as I was concerned. The driver realized this lack of awareness in all the people there and became uneasy with so many unaware, and drugged, people. See how well I understand people?

Entering the hotel we negotiated a better price for the room, took our bags up stairs, and were in the room, when there was a knock at the door. My friend Julio was there. We hadn't been there five minutes and he magically appeared. "I just got your email this minute and came right over from the Internet cafe". I had been trying to reach him the day before, and bingo he was there. I introduced him to Diana and we stood talking for a few minutes. I was still drugged from sleeping pills. I had to excuse myself, explaining I needed a shower. We agreed to meet up after I sobered up, later in the day. We went to our room, showered and went straight to bed. I slept fifteen minutes. Diana said it was too noisy to sleep. A couple of hours after our arrival we were out walking the streets. Diana was fully charged by Antigua. She really likes it here. I was just waking up, more like sleepwalking.

One of the aspects where males and females differ is jewelry. One of the aspects that Antigua has is many street peddlers selling jewelry. In our two-hour walk a dozen people selling jewelry approached us. They instantly hand over the jewelry to Diana and she instinctively takes it. They all claim the jade is real. We entered a real jade jewelry shop and asked if the claims on the street were true. "No", was the honest answer. No sooner had we left the jade store than a new man with his arms straddling jade necklaces' began to engage us. He demonstrated with a knife how the jade did not scratch. He even had another piece of jade to show us how "fake jade," scratched. We were being pulled in like a fish eats bait. We refused his offer and walked down the street. I was looking at how much money I really had on me. Eighty Quetzals.

A block later the same man came up again. "I will give you a special offer, how much money you have?" We had already indicated we had no dollars, and very little Guatemala Quetzals. "We don't want anything." It was too late, he handed a new necklace to Diana. He did the same demonstration with this jade necklace. I noticed his knife did scratch the jade this time, and he quickly handed me the glass for me to test the jade myself. I got mad and told Diana, "forget it". I was mad at Diana for spending so much time being stopped by sellers and gave her an angry lecture comparing her to a leaf in the wind. I later explained how I noticed the second piece of jade did scratch and my first reaction of anger was justifiable. But we hit a little bump in the road, my bad, and my fault, excuse me for feeling angry. When a person wants to make a sale and wants to take your last money (we had more in the hotel room), don't do it. It's not even about trust at that point. It's about how stupid one will be to allow the "bargain" to dictate the true rules versus the need to have something.

I am eccentric in my lifestyle. I seldom use restaurants, never buy new clothes in my own country, never need jewelry, but love to buy small remembrances of where I have been. As part of my travel expenses I buy Christmas and birthday gifts for family and friends. This comes into conflict with how Diana was raised, how she spends her money, and what she wants for a home we both share. She has little money this trip, so I am paying and understand this. I've decided to just give her money so she doesn't need to ask me to buy things. Last night we had a fight over her questioning me about my "compensation" to my friend here, Julio. "You didn't take him to a restaurant for driving you around?" This angered me. I have never questioned how Diana operated and balanced her friendships. If anything I have helped her with her gift acquisitions for friends, but I have put my foot down when it comes to buying small gifts every time we go to visit her friends in their homes. Yes, you bring a bottle of vine or cake, but when we were first married she was buying gifts, yet I never saw other people giving her gifts. To buy friendship is distasteful to me. In Colombia Diana claims this is their custom, but I never saw people giving her gifts when we visited. She admits this, expresses some resentment, yet she seems stuck in this evaluation process. When she is evaluating me I get angry. This is ongoing, and it won't change. It may never change. I don't know how to manage my anger other than express it, get it out, like spitting out poison. Diana never expresses anger. She lets it stay inside or drip out as cynicism, or as my private dermatologist.

Our day yesterday was spent mostly recuperating from the bus trip the night before. My system was cleared of sleeping pills by the time I went to bed around eight-thirty. We walked to the grocery store in the rain at night, bought a small container of ice cream, and came home to try and call Diana's family. No one was home. I reached Julio on the computer because he didn't answer his phone. He is a mile away and the best way to reach him is on Facebook, not telephone. In his house he doesn't have electricity and wants to live off the grid. So we communicate by computer when he is in town at the Internet cafe.

Day Five: Antigua. The day was a wandering, unplanned journey from place to place, with only a four o'clock appointment to meet up with Julio. We must have left the hotel close to 9 A.M. because a couple we had been sharing transport and this hotel with had an eight o'clock pick up, but their ride was an hour late. Their names were Alex and Fins (not exactly sure). We met them with the Polish couple as we waited for the bus in Flores, and had a parallel path for two days, even running into them on the street. They were in their early twenties and always kissing each other. Even in the dark bus I saw them kissing. They were in the same van with us to Antigua and came into the hotel on my suggestion. We sat with them and talked for an hour the first day, and then we all sat and went into our own silent worlds, reading, writing, and being together in the sitting room of the hotel.

In the morning we were at the front desk calling my friend's sister in Guatemala City. Alex was waiting to use the phone and called to see why their van was so late. We arranged for a Saturday, ten o'clock pick up with a woman whose name I don't even know. I guess I'll find out. We were told at the front desk our room was booked for next Saturday (one night) but we will get it back on Sunday. The desk clerk, Sandy, helped us call and overheard how long we plan on staying. She also heard our designated pick up in the city and suggested we rendezvous at a better, more convenient place, near our bus drop off. Sergio is the man I know who works here, the same as last year. Sandy is a new employee. (We later found out she is the owner's daughter.) She is a perky, happy person who is always smiling.

We left the hotel and started for the grocery store and entered the vegetable and fruit market where on Wednesday the Indian farmers come to sell their foods. It was so exciting we spent an hour just walking through, talking with people, buying a drink, cashews, and an avocado. I took a photograph of a Brahma cow painted on a wall next to a meat shop. An Indian woman came up to me and asked me to pay fifteen Quetzals for the photograph. She burst out laughing and started to talk to three other woman seated selling vegetables. They were all laughing because when a tourist wants to take their picture they charge them fifteen quetzals. I responded in Spanish that the cow is very beautiful. The woman who asked for the money then asked if I'd take one of the young women sitting nearby to America. I said this wasn't possible because my wife was over there, pointing her out. (Diana was off buying something.) I then said this would cause big problems having two wives. This joking back and forth got a good chuckle from the women sitting there. Diana joined me and I introduced my wife, the Colombian. The woman continued with some joking and Diana joined in. We passed along and as we moved on another woman sat a few feet away from the rest. She sat stone-faced, sad, and in another world just inches from all the merry-making. This kind of detachment is what poverty can do to human beings. As much as I talk about choice to Diana I see at times life beats down the innocent.

The next place we entered was a compound full of tourist shops. This is a big, gated area where there must be over two hundred shops. We walked around like two doctors taking notes as we wrote down all the prices. We know there will be a huge gap between the prices in Chichicastenango but wanted to get a base price. We were making lists of things to buy as well. We didn't buy one thing (yet) and were secretly very joyous from teasing the shopkeepers. (This is due to the aggressive nature of some of the shopkeepers.) I can tell you if you ask a price, and leave, they will suddenly jump and start to cut the prices in half. We had no intentions to buy until Diana came to the jewelry. She bought two sets of earrings, one for herself and one for her mother. I was nearby shooting a photograph for four women. I volunteered to take their picture. They were all related and were happy to have a stranger take the family portrait. I told them I was from the USA. One of the women was a doctor and spoke to me in English. As I was talking with the two older sisters and a cousin, my back was turned for about two minutes when Diana returned having spent some money on jewelry. I promised myself then that when I gave her the money in the morning I wasn't going to judge what she did with it. I hate myself for letting my anger get in the way of my love for my wife as the night before, so I will step back and let go. I thought the money would have lasted three days. It lasted one, but I kept my mouth shut tight.

We spent the entire day looking at prices in shops. I did buy a package of refrigerator magnets from an Indian in the Central Park. At that point in the afternoon, I hadn't spent any money (yet). We came home to the hotel, had lunch, and set out again. When we met with Julio at four-thirty, Diana had spent all the money in the shops and more in the Central Park. I had spent twenty-five Quetzals on gifts all day. I did buy food and soap to wash our clothes, but was feeling on top of my thrift game.

On the street, Julio came up just as I was talking to a Danish architect. We had briefly spoken before as the man sat on the curb doing a watercolor. He was with another man who lived in Sweden. I was joking with the Danish architect about living in a "Socialist" country. He told me about a TV skit he saw on a comedy show, Jon Stewart. We both got a good laugh and then Sara Palin came up. He knew about her and his comment was not flattering. Julio and Diana were talking as I said my good bye to the architect. We all three entered Julio's car and took a back road to his house. It was the same house but it hadn't been cleaned since my last visit. This time he had five dogs living there instead of one. The dogs run the house. I pointed out that he was stepping in dog shit in the living room, but he didn't seem to mind.

We toured the house. My favorite room was the bathroom. The sink had three contraptions of faucets that looked more like ten faucets. These were jimmy-ridged, multi-complicated rubber gaskets, plastic tubes, and a variety of twists and turn that exited into the sink. The bathtub was just as complicated. I have no idea why the water faucets needed so many extra parts added on. It was in that room that Diana gave me a look that only two people who live on the inside of each other's lives can give. Julio continued to tell us how the dog had eaten one of three goats, and one goat had eaten the other goat, and the dogs were still eating the remaining dead goat. If we smelled anything in the yard, it was due to the goat carcass. Not long after that I pointed out the goats head on the floor of his kitchen. Yes, the dogs were still gnawing the head bone indeed.

We entered the garden and Julio showed us the dozen varieties of fruits growing in a lush, thick under growth of flowered plants and weeds. We sampled fruits from the trees and looked into the dark well that had water ten feet deep. I said, "Why don't you pump this water for your tank on the kitchen roof?" to which he replied, "Because I don't have any electricity." I was wondering if there was such a thing as a hand pump and how the water got up there that was already there. He did have water in the bathroom. I used it to wash my hands off after petting the dogs that had been rubbing themselves in the goat carcass. Dogs have a thing about rolling in bad odors like horse manure and goat guts. If you never knew this it is because you haven't been around horse manure or goat guts.

Julio's house isn't a closed environment. Between rooms there are gardens and open areas. Only one room has a real door and that is his bedroom. The so-called kitchen has only two walls and a roof that extends a good distance away from the makeshift stoves. Understand that this is the tropics and there is no need to close off sections of a house, as ventilation is better for keeping the house cool. His unconventional lifestyle is what dictates an unconventional design and lack of general housekeeping. His is the wild, intelligent professor/healer of many stories, cures, potions, and seemingly unrelated topics that merge into his own version of reality.

Mosquitoes were biting Diana so I suggested we all head back to town, ending with an invitation to dinner. We had seen an Indian restaurant while wandering the streets during the day and coincidently Julio knew of a place that wasn't too expensive. He drove up to the same Indian restaurant. We ordered, ate, spoke about life, yoga, spirituality, and Diana got a wealth of 'new age' education. We enjoyed the evening very much. When I went to pay the bill I was stunned. It was eighty dollars. I had seventy-five dollars' worth of Quetzals. I didn't have any more on me and returned to the table to see if Julio or Diana had any cash. They had none. Diana pulled out her credit card and pulled us out of an evening of washing dishes. We put the five dollars balance due on her credit card. We then walked around the block to catch some fresh air after which, Julio drove us back to the hotel. We have a ten o'clock appointment with Julio to go to Guatemala City in the morning. We will be dropping off the car that Julio totaled last December in a car accident and has just repaired enough of the car to drive to a body shop almost an hour away.

Day Six: Julio.   We can't stop talking about Julio. We love him and don't understand how such a wise, spiritual man can live in such chaos. I don't really like to give the descriptions of his house without first explaining his personality. I do not want to give my critical view of his world before first delving into the true essences my friend's nature. Maybe that is just it - nature. Julio is like nature; all beautiful with climate that is a provider and destroyer. His world is far beyond what Diana and I perceive as even livable. He lives within such dynamic contradiction that we go around and around discussing them. He has two cars, three servants, owns his dead mother's home as an income property, lives in a garden of fruits, flowers and vegetables, is very educated, and is extremely spiritual. If I had begun my description of Julio in this way my readers would be very impressed with his credentials. While Julio is all those things, he is also a strange contradiction of madness and genius. He lives by necessity and laziness. He is extremely inventive yet avoids doing things in any traditional way, perhaps to his own detriment.

What I can piece together of his life is not that different than my own. We both once experimented with drugs when younger, studied Eastern Religions, lived off the grid, had many travel experiences, had many relationships, and we are now living a life well earned. I was telling Diana about my life back in Nebraska twenty-five years ago. I lived with a goat, two dogs, and nine cats. I raised chickens, had a vast garden, heated my house with two wood stoves, was very creative, and very, very poor. I was "free" in that I didn't work a regular job. However, I doubt I could ever go back and live that way again. My compromise today is to travel and be frugal, pretend I'm economically poor, but really having all I could ever need. I wanted to make sure I'm never financially desperate ever again. One can't live in my country and live like Julio. Henry David Thoreau didn't stay at Walden Pond his whole life. A friend bailed him out of jail when he got arrested for not paying taxes. So reality is a mixture of romantic myth and cold hard, devilish fact.

Julio lived off his mother's money until she died. His mother funded his education and travels abroad. (I may be wrong, but I think he hasn't "worked" a regular job.) He lived in an ashram in Indian for two years and returned to work in his family's hardware store business. Their No. 1 client was the Guatemalan Calvary. The father sold the business to his brother who was a poor business manager and the two brothers didn't get along. The mother lived in a very exclusive neighborhood of Antioquia, provided a place for her son to live and he in turn took care of her until her death at ninety-two. She was never sick a day of her life, and died from old age. She left Julio the property. He now rents out the house and lives on that small income, which is about to evaporate, as the tenants are about to move out of the house. He lives, rent-free, on land where he has never met the landowner. He ended up on this land because a close American friend, who was embraced by the local Indians, suggested Julio be allowed to take care of this land. The American has since become so old that he lives in a retirement home, has no contact with Julio, and is, shall we say, senile. This leaves Julio in a very vulnerable predicament that Diana and I both find beyond comprehension.

Julio goes to the Internet cafe every night and spends hours online chatting on Facebook, studying astronomy and astrology, and spiritual web sites. How he pays for this we have no idea. I think he has a friend who works, or owns, the Internet cafe. We know that the money he has spent on repairing the car this month is equal to the rent income he gets from his mother's property. As desperate as I make my words sound I know this man will survive and continue to live as he has for decades. He is a saint with personal integrity, and lives in the real garden of paradise. He reminds me of a "homeless" man I knew when I first moved to New York from Nebraska. His name was Jim, who lived in an abandoned factory in one of the most exclusive towns on Long Island. He gathered his own fire wood for heat, grew a few scrawny vegetable and marijuana plants, refused to eat any meat (or meat by-products, or dairy), was living like Saint Francis, and was full of practical wisdom. Jim was a Veteran on a meager income, but he lived within his own integrity. I loved him for this. I admired and respected him ten times more than the rich clients I was driving around while working for a limousine company. The same goes for Julio and most of the people in my professional life. I see it as an honor to know these offbeat characters who don't fit in. If you get to know someone like Julio or Jim you find they live a life of uncompromising integrity. The rest of us live in constant compromise of our values.

Diana and I were talking all morning about agendas and what people use as their priorities. If you know your priorities you've won half the battle. Those who live true to their integrity obtain happiness. We can't judge the vehicle by the external appearances. The car may be polished and brand new, but the mind and soul of the driver is what dictates the way the car is driven. I am attracted to great minds. I believe that we meet people because we need them in our lives. Some might say God does this but I prefer to think God is in everyone to some degree. All the "God stuff" makes me angry. I can relate to religion in some ways because this is a language in and of itself that creates a common bond between people. But when the "God stuff" becomes the "one true way" I know someone is trying to manipulate someone else. The real knowledge of life is pretty simple stuff. The Golden Rule has been, and will be, the best remedy for the journey we all live. I try to compromise and not feel hypocritical. This comes with integrity and knowing one's self. If you know yourself you know God. All the ritualistic hocus pocus, rules, by-laws, and regulations are the tools that religions use to trap victims, thereby creating a system that becomes self-perpetuating. If these tools create self-discipline, that is the essence of God, not the tools. I don't even like to talk about this because it is so personal that no one can truly understand another's agenda - thus Julio and his life. We will see what adventure comes forth today. I am sitting writing about him at the very same table I sat last year, in the same hotel, at the same time of year, and just as intrigued by his story.

The day began with a change. We called Julio and asked if we could just meet him in the afternoon. We knew the drive into Guatemala City would be boring, and to turn around and come back again with all five of us packed into one car seemed a bit too much. Julio understood and at nine-forty Diana and I were off to spend a day in museums. Diana had heard of a convent that had a good collection of art. I'm not sure where she heard this; I only knew we were going there. We found the Convent of Capuchinas. It is now a museum, and no one lives there. Capuchinas is the name given to nuns with white habits that cap the head. These were cloisters that never had contact with the outside world.

The big plaza with a fountain didn't look so bad to spend an entire life in, but the round prison-like sleeping rooms did seem a little confining. The design of their living quarters had a big round central patio with eighteen small rooms that spiraled off the center. Each arched doorway lead to a tiny cell that had an alcove. Below the living quarters was another round room with one central column. This column was ten feet thick, strong enough to support the round patio and building above. The sound in this room was heavenly; it was where the choir sang. We could hear a perfect echo as we did a little singing ourselves. A kitchen was close to the top of the stairs. The kitchen chimney is a typical sight in Antigua. Most of the old houses and structures have a white cylindrical dome with an octagonal set of small openings at the top, like a little house. We can see these from many places in the city, usually behind a tall wall. From inside the kitchen there is a vast dome that stretches up into an apse, something like in a church dome. Looking up from the bottom a round, octagonal had openings like small windows where the smoke exits the building. It appears to be a very functional (rainproof) way to let smoke out of the kitchen. The kitchen itself is a big room. Several fires could be going at once because the kitchen is so large.

On the far side of the courtyard is a church. The church is under renovation and has three big canvas roofs that are located where three domes once filled in the ceiling. On the second floor of the courtyard was an impressive collection of art from the early history of Guatemala, with some of the Rococo Art originating in Spain. There were also sculptures made of wood with painted surfaces. These antiques were from churches that had long vanished. This was world-class exhibition with lights that turned on automatically when one entered a section of the gallery. Low lighting on the floors and soft spot lights gave the small exhibition an intimate feel. The art wasn't overwhelming to look at because it was spaced and situated in a way that leads one to another without crowding. The wooden sculptures were deteriorated with some of the paint worn off, but the original integrity of the art works was still well intact.

In the morning, we had seen a TV show about a mansion here in Antigua called the 'House of a Million Flores' (Flowers). We went off to see if we could get in. We found it but it was a private residence. In a moment of frustration we asked the gatekeeper, or a worker at a gate, if there wasn't a good museum nearby. We saw one on the map, but weren't sure where we even were. The kind man pointed us to a find, a jewel of a museum. He told us about the museum in a hotel and I'm thinking that the hotel has a small museum gallery. It was a vast complex of ruins that had at least seven museums. We paid around six dollars and got lost for three hours wandering this square, quarter of mile series of galleries built within the deteriorated buildings of a convent and church. There were catacombs with real human bones, a silver museum in a long dark hall underground, a museum of modern art, a museum of Pre-Colombian Mayan ceramics displayed with modern glass sculptures, side by side in glass cases that had common themes. An ancient Mayan mask might be in a display with a modern bowl of blown glass where faces were in both objects designs. The art was paired with themes like cougars, birds, women, animals, kings, and other objects. With a few minutes of seeking it was fun to see the common thread that the curators were creating between the ancient and the new. There was music playing in the background and as few as three other people in the gallery. We paid six dollars and really liked this complex of buildings. I had been in Antigua last year, wandered many ruins and never found the qualities of galleries we discovered on this trip. (Diana claims she is the lucky charm. She is, but let's not tell her.) This complex of buildings was the museum ruins of the Hotel Casa Santo Domingo.

If I were writing a tour book I'd say you're a lunatic if you visit Antigua and miss this one. There was a hotel, a theater, and museum, with beautiful banquet rooms where weddings and conferences were held. The hotel itself was hidden within the ruins. This is a five star hotel; so vast we left, and unknowingly reentered three blocks later, only this time from the parking garage. The second time we walked a long underground hallway and came upon the front desk. Again, a world-class joint ya gotta see.

We were given a map for the complex but it was more fun to just discover the different types of exhibitions as we investigated the grounds. Another separate museum feature was handy crafts of the indigenous peoples, their fabrics, foods, customs, and living utensils. This is one of those moments where reading about something in a book isn't as much fun as finding it by mistake. These unplanned pleasures can only happen unexpectedly. Julio had told us about a museum with the largest paintings in Guatemala, and we thought we knew the general direction so we went off. Instead, we found a jade museum inside a jade factory. This wasn't some big sales pitch to force us to look and buy. We had a private tour guide who took us around the three or four galleries patiently showing us interesting aspects of jade, its history, where it can be found, and what the Mayans made with jade. Two Americans, a couple, who were archaeologists, founded the company. They came to Guatemala in the 1970's to start a worldwide jade trade that is now an empire. Nevertheless, what I enjoyed was the educational emphasis versus sales pitches. Yes, there was a sales room at the end of the tour, but I was fine spending forty-five minutes and not wanting anything to buy. There was no pressure at all.

When we left, I was a bit perturbed with Diana's drooling over the jewelry. I don't have a problem telling someone I'm not interested in buying what he or she has to offer. Diana drags this "no" into a lengthy maybe, to an additional fifteen minutes of browsing when I am standing at the door. My body language is definitely saying, "My back is turned away from the sales people, my eyes are looking out the door so let's leave NOW". "If you want to be really honest with yourself you won't be manipulated by others selling something. Don't lead people on. Don't pretend to be interested when you don't even have the money to buy something." (I gave her another lecture.) This is the part of jewelry shopping that kills me. Besides, Diana does not even wear a fraction of what she already owns. Why even spend the time asking one question when pricing is out of your reach? Why go into a store and ask how much something is? Is it me? Am I deficient in the "looking game"? My mother taught me to be quiet when she shopped. She instilled in me the best of patient behaviors. She just didn't prepare me for Diana, the woman I am crazy in love with who drives me crazy with her jewelry addiction. It could be worse and I do get over these silly fits I have.

We returned to the church of San Francisco after deciding that we'd never find the museum Julio had shown us while driving. The day before we saw food stalls so we headed straight to that courtyard. Diana ate a bean tostada and I ate chicken tamale. We then entered the museum of San Francisco on the grounds behind the main church. This was a ruin museum and a museum to Saint Pedro who was canonized in 2002 by Pope Paul the Second. The museum was a dark collection of rooms with a big show room at the end, but very few rooms in all. The halls were lined with testimonials and photographs of people healed by the saint. It was like a children's museum and very poorly kept. I was surprised to see the actual robes of the saint displayed in old badly built, wooden display cases of glass. The paintings were gray and dirty, and the possessions of the saint could have been robbed and no one would have missed them. I wasn't inspired by the exhibition but the man himself inspired me. He worked with the poor and helped many people. I'm like a child about such things; a child who has found out that Santa Clause doesn't exist. I have never seen a miracle. I hope they are true. Because I don't have "faith" I'll never be lucky. I just can't wrap my mind around the "magic." I don't have any millionaire friends and I don't have any miracle friends. I saw all the discarded crutches, canes, and wheel chairs, but I didn't see any cripples walking around. Will someone please slap me? With all the excitement about this new saint it was a real disappointment to see nothing with proper citations or a sense of things preserved.

We walked to a long park called Tanque La Union and bought some more food. This time we ate avocados on tostados, a dry crispy tortilla. We bought natural juices at a grocery store and sat on plastic seats next to the woman selling this food on the street. We had a nice visit with the woman and felt full from the food. This was our dinner at a total cost of about four dollars for both of us. A slow walk put us back through the Central Park, down the shopping streets, to the yellow church (La Merced). This time our four-thirty rendezvous with Julio was within seconds of the designated time. We entered the park and I heard a woman calling my name from a car. It was Julio's cook calling to me from the passenger seat. Julio was in the back seat. His worker was driving and the cook's daughter was with Julio in the back seat. We all joined together squeezing into the car. A drive to the market was where we said good-bye to the three employees of Julio as we dropped them off for their bus.

The events that followed started as one thing and lead in a completely new direction. Julio went to the Internet cafe and caught up on his emails. I sat and read a local English magazine, Diana walked around the shops completely unrestricted by her husband's jewelry phobia. I think Julio would like a female companion, when he showed me some of his contacts while answering a series of woman online.

We got in the car heading for a scenic route around the city Julio had shown me the year before. We came to an elbow in the road and I asked where we were. "This is the Old City. I'll show you." We drove up a hill toward the volcano and a beautiful white church invited us in to take a look. We all went inside and said a greeting. I took photographs. Up the street was a park, and across from there a castle ruin. We approached the guards and asked to see the ruin. But he said, "No, it was closed for the day." As we turned to leave they changed their minds and we were allowed to enter at another gate. The gate was a school and the castle ruin was in the middle of the school. The ruin itself was an apse and supporting structure of a church, more like the piece of a church. It

354

wasn't as big as a two-story garage. The ruin was in the courtyard of a school with classroom surrounding.

Children were everywhere peeking at us from behind doors, waving, passing-by as they curtsied, and asking to have their picture taken. A teacher passed by and we introduced ourselves. I asked him the subjects and level of the school. It was a primary school where the basics were taught. I did a little filming but Diana was reprimanding me for distracting the students inside their classroom. They were waving and smiling for the camera. The teacher had to take care of his students and we left the building.

I asked Julio if the school went in double sessions because it was so late in the day. He said, "No, school begins at five in the evening because these children are working in the fields with their families during the day." In an empty street next to the school there was a lineup of students in a formation. They were practicing marching (in place) with batons. Another group of students were playing an assortment of musical instruments with an inner group of ten to twelve drummers on various sized drums. Four students were playing the glockenspiels. The sound and dancing was pretty disorganized, but the feel of happiness and festivity was in the air. A large group of other students stood watching. I describe this all in a way that tells nothing of the energy and activity at play. The park, the school, and the street, was crawling with students that were like atoms in a random, chaotic dance. Kids were running, punching and running, yelling, laughing, teasing, squeezing, sneezing, and never still. This sounds like a school anywhere. Boys were flirting, girls were blushing, and cliques of girls were discussing who was cute as they were all preparing their bodies and minds for the biological event known as puberty. (Procreation subconsciously of course).

We slipped into the car unnoticed and Julio went up a one-way street. Before the turn I told him it was a one way street, so he turned in the correct direction, only to reverse himself and go the wrong way again, just long enough to turn and go back toward the main intersection. On many occasions Diana and I are saying, "Look out!" But Julio takes it all in stride. Remember we are riding in a foreign country with a man that only has one eye. It can cause a little stress. I asked him how he knew if a street was one way or not. "Oh the cars coming in the opposite directions will blink their lights and let me know." When this has happened he simply pulls to one side, continues to move, and never turns around to get in the legal direction. He continues to drive in the same direction.

It was getting too dark to see any views so we headed back toward the main town. Suddenly, Julio pulled the car into a gated driveway. I thought we would be going inside the gate, but he was parking in one driveway to show us somewhere else. "You've got to see this." It looked like a lumberyard to me. People were filing out a smaller gate and again we warned him of people, the weight of a car on human bones, and bodies in the path of his heavy car. "They have plenty of room," was all he could say to stop our neuroses. Outside the car there wasn't room on the street for a sidewalk and the commuter traffic of the day was squeezing us between a wall and a small wet, rocky path.

Next door to where we parked we entered a small door, bending down to enter a dark room. All I could see were the white teeth of a woman in the dark, she soon turned on a single light bulb and we were hit by the smell of wood and a visual delight of frozen, wooden sculptures; Saints, Christ on the cross, Venus, horses, a zoo of every size and shape of imaginable beings, some being small enough to hold in your hand, some too large to be in the tiny room. All the sculptures were a reddish color due to the unpainted wood. The room was the size of a very small kitchen. Maneuvering was impossible. Four of us were inside. Our bodies couldn't move, but our eyes were spinning from rapid exploration. "Wow," was all we could say. I didn't think about buying anything until Julio asked Diana if she'd like a horse. Diana favored a horse about twelve inches high. It was standing on its hind legs, raising one front leg. You know, that typical famous horse poses.

My first thought was luggage and broken horse legs. It would be impossible to ship or carry without breaking the thin legs. On one lone table, standing like the Trojan horse was a tiny replica of Botero's fat horse sculpture. The solid, fat legs would withstand being run over by Julio's car. That was a find! I loved it. Diana and I had a side conversation on the street after we left the shop. Julio came out and asked if we wanted to buy it. "I don't have enough money," and I didn't. "I'll pay with a check and you pay me back at the hotel," he suggested. We bought a small, copyright-infringement-knock-off of a Botero. Julio paid with a check. I felt like a kid with a new toy.

We had to buy gas for our trip to the ocean the next day so we came back to the hotel for the credit card. I rushed inside, got the cash and credit card, and left the cameras in my bag. Inside the room Sandy had left us a vase full of yellow roses on the bed stand! A small card said, 'Thank you for your nice choice." I was flabbergasted. The management had left us a sign of gratitude. I rushed back to the car, thanking Sandy as I passed the front desk. Julio and Diana were pulled over with the engine running, waiting for me.

Our next stop was to buy food. We stopped at one place, and then realized we had to drive a few blocks around the bus station to enter the market. This took forever and miles of walking in the maze of stalls inside the market. The market was just closing. We half-watched the closing exercise of the daily market game that never stops. The bustle of the market was in full swing. People (all Indians) wrap all their goods under plastic each night to keep away thieves. We noted that the rat population must have had a feast every night. We saw a cat chasing a mouse; the rats must have chased the cats. As unclean as the market was, it was also as clean, only ten inches above the ground. Trash was everywhere. "This could all be recycled and separated", was my suggestion. Julio just laughed at me and said, "That would drive the price of the food up, if food was being saved," to which I replied, "OK, why not feed the poor?" He answered, "By morning, anything eatable will be gone and salvaged by the poor. There is recycling taking place, it's just not obvious". And he was right. There is a system in place. In my western, feed-the-poor-sentiment, I was thinking of improving things, revolutionizing the workers, and putting a socialist state in power. Power to the people! It all fascinates me, but I haven't a clue about the real political solution. What began as a short journey to buy gas, ended as a long journey planning for tomorrow, after filling up the gas tank.

Day Seven: The Beach, Puerto Jan Jose. We woke early by two hours, but we were five minutes late for our nine o'clock appointment with Julio at the front desk. He was here at eight forty-five, and took a short detour to go to the local Internet café while waiting. He has confided in us that he has an Internet girlfriend. She is twenty, or so she says. They live in the same town but he has not physically met her in person. He told us this as we drove to pick up the daughter of his cook, her two daughters, and two more cousins. Three of these girls are close in years, (nine, ten, and eleven), thus a day of giggling and frolicking merriment. The girls were the focus of the day as we were taking them to the beach. This was a first for two of them. The youngest was two and she was kept safe in her mother's arms. She clung to her mother the whole day.

When we were leaving in the morning, like most "planned" excursions this was no different, as we were late, they were slow in getting into the car, and no one was in a hurry. Marta, the cook's daughter, is a widow. Her husband was killed two years ago by a gunshot. "They killed my husband,' was all we were told. This may be why the youngest is so close to the mother. Julio gave me the car keys and I was the designated driver for the day. We opened up the ride with a verse of yellow submarine. Julio and I sang it for the young girls as we set the days tone immediately. The high road around the upper hills of the city is where we exited toward the coast. The road was well built, but in one place a recent mudslide from a volcano eruption had torn out a segment of road. The hills were so lush and green that I see a more verdant country than the rest of Central America.

One of the girls was sitting backwards on the console between Julio and me in the front seat. She got car sick, so we stopped the car. It was a curve, not too dangerous, but enough to cause a police truck to stop and ask if we needed help. The police were very polite and told us we should stop in a better place. Nature called and the stop was too soon to plan. The poor girl spewed her breakfast on the side of the road.

We passed a bicycle race with one hundred bicyclists and their backup vehicles. They had many police escorts on motorcycles. The last one in the race was a young girl who must have been an hour behind the rest, but she had a police motorcycle making sure she was safe. Julio commented that one of the bikes could cost so much that robbery was a motive and protection was well needed. We wound our way down the hills to a long, flat, straight highway that went directly to the port city, Puerto San Jose. The coastal lands were as flat as a tortilla. Expensive, exclusive gated communities would interrupt sugar cane plantation. Some looked not so expensive and the gates were poorly painted and worn. The road was well built and everyone was passing us. I didn't want to get a ticket in a foreign land. There wasn't any police with radar guns, only police trucks with two officers sitting or standing at the side of the road. We could have been in Europe, or the USA, the highway was a highway.

The port city, San Jose, was different. It was congested and full of pedestrians darting across the narrow streets. As soon as we drove into the main business street a man on a bicycle began to chase us, yelling, asking if we wanted a restaurant and beach house. When he caught up to us we told him no, but at the next intersection he was still on our tail. Three times we said no, and he kept up the pursuit. When his lungs gave out he turned away. The next such entrepreneur was on a motorcycle. He chased us; same as the other man, but this time we only had to reject his offer twice. These were desperate people and the poverty was apparent. Many people went without shoes, not just to be fashionable on the beach. It was not anything like Antigua; it was like being back in Honduras, where sidewalks and streets were a war-torn patch of broken and half repaired efforts. It was not a clean place. But I always get amazed at my own false standards. What seemed dangerous and repelling at first was comfortable by the end of the day.

I pictured a beach with shore parking; instead Julio had me pull into a hotel. I was wondering why a hotel? But to park at the beach is too dangerous. The hotel was very old, needed paint and had a few cracked corners; more like every stucco corner was cracked. One central walkway had rooms on both sides, but first we passed through a dark passage where the workers had their rooms, it was two families as far as I could tell. They sat watching TV and eating as we passed with all our food and towels. At the far end of the row of building the young attendant opened a door, handed us a tall fan on a stand, and a pad lock with a key. The room was very, very terrible, moldy smelling, with peeling paint, and two double beds. The toilet was behind a thin transparent curtain. Privacy was out of the question. This was our "safe house". I went along with everything, not asking questions, but letting the day unfold. The dirt courtyard in front of our room had two girls' hand-washing clothes in a sink. They smiled at us and went back to work. Later in the day the same two swept the grounds for small yellow leafs that had fallen. A white, PVC, strand of piping ran from the tops of trees and poles to the wall where three shower heads were hanging with wire supports. It was old and dumpy but a fun place. It's not the place that is important; it's what you make of your situation.

We left our things locked in the room as people took turns changing and going outside. The cameras and food were safe; we went to the beach and saw what we had come to do - play in the surf. I find my first impressions always based on some false assumption where expectations are based on the past, trying to relive what has been. In my mind the beach was compared to Costa Rica, New York, and California, places familiar to me. It was none of those places, but a little bit like everywhere else. Near the city side of the shore there ran a long, two lane concrete path, (sidewalk) with a central divide about five inches high. The sides had a similar barrier. Where the street intersected these divides were not present. The sidewalk was wide, people pushed carts selling drinks as pedestrians shared the same pathway. A kind of bicycle-rickshaw-taxi was peddled up and down the path. The back of the vehicle was a bicycle while a covered, two-passenger seat was built with two large spooked wheels in front. How the thing turned was a mystery to me. Men peddled up and down the beach looking for takers. On the sand four- wheeled sports motorcycles and dune buggies speed up and down the beach. We were immediately spotted and approached by young men asking us if we would buy a ride. We declined, but noticed the young man ran off to bring a newer, better motorcycle, thinking this would change our minds. No, no thank you, not interested, not now, never, get the hell away from us, I'll call the police if you don't leave now, was my mental progression as the pestering continued.

As we neared the water's edge we discovered we were alone. The closer to the water we walked fewer people selling things were around. The four little girls, Diana, Julio and I all entered the water. The shore was steep, so much so it was easy to roll a ball down. The waves would crash a few feet from the shore and swoosh with great force up the incline. Julio and I entered the water to find a deep hole out where the surf was breaking. This was maybe ten feet into the water. I've never been to such a beach. The waves were rough, too rough for the little girls. Marta sat watching with the littlest one plopped on her lap. Soon a giant wave knocked Marta and the baby on their back, then rolling. The baby was crying and we were all laughing at the funny tumble. In one swift moment a wave knocked her away from her mother, rolling her up the sand with the little one swallowing a mouth full of seawater. This caused more leg grabbing by the infant, but eventually she beamed with smiles and laughter like the rest of them.

There were occasions when I wasn't able to keep on my feet because the surf was so strong. There was a strong rip tide. With my feet I could feel just beyond where the shore waves broke, so I stayed pretty close to the shore. A second set of waves broke further out but I wasn't going to visit those waves for the sake of my beloved sport, body surfing. This had to be the result of a storm that was passing. The waves were too strong, too short, too much for Julio, anyone, or even me. But we had fun. Everybody left to return to the hotel while Julio and I lay on the beach talking. It was an intimate moment between us.

He told me more about his youth, his travels, his drug use and when he stopped using, his mother's death, and his current financial predicament. He hasn't ever paid any rent where he is living. We both speculated the property is a in a legal limbo due to a divorce between a husband and wife. The wife owns the land. The husband's relatives came once to ask Julio his name, but that was all they wanted to know. They didn't say move out, stay, pay, how did you get permission to live here - nothing. So we concluded he is safe for the time being and should stay put until the situation changes. A man is building a house on a second half of the property. He has an easement right to use the driveway, but it's not real clear if he has title to the land. Julio is living in a tenuous situation and he is aware of it. I saw his vulnerability and felt like he is well aware of what could or could not be coming. His plan to float is his way of handling this. He doesn't have the money to move, or to pay for a new place, but change will come no matter what.

I am a person who likes to save people. This comes from being the child of an alcoholic. I spent a great deal of time consumed by my mother's spiraling bouts of drinking. Emotionally I wanted to do everything in my power to get her to stop, to a point that I was monitoring her consumption by marking the bottles, by the hour, by the day. Some days she was clean, some days she was a raving maniac, a violent raving maniac. This doesn't leave us when we grow older. We carry the baggage through life and it affects how we relate to others, who we associate with, and what professions we chose in life. The key is to use that energy in positive, healthy ways and learn we have no control over others. Helping others is a healthy thing as long as it is tempered by reason and not losing oneself. With no help from others I would not be where I am today. But there is such a thing as helping others by being there to listen and with Julio, that's all I could do. I was honored to be let inside the otherwise over-confident personality of a man in flux.

The sun was burning my back and I was getting hungry so we went back to find the others. I thought they were getting lunch ready. They were all splashing in a pool. The hotel had a small pool about the size of a large car. All the females were frolicking and laughing. We joined them. The pool had a wall waist high that had a concrete stair leading in and out of it. The edges were good to sit on, while the young girls were small enough to dive into the water. I was getting hungry so I went to start the food. Soon, we were all eating avocado with beans on tostados. We had juice and fruit for dessert. The refried beans are sold in a soft pouch of heavy plastic; spooning out the beans is easy. There is no heat required and we had a feast of food and fun. All the while, Julio was playing with the girls, joking and teasing them. This continued after lunch where they all re-entered the pool. A second larger pool, about the size of a small garage was being filled when we arrived. By the time we finished lunch the second pool had a few feet of water. This is where they all ended up playing. Diana and I sat on the curb outside our room and talked. Marta joined us and told us how Julio had changed after his mother's death. He used to be well kept, well dressed, and much fatter she told us. He was a rich man. This all changed when his mother died. He became eccentric and began to talk about mysticism and astrology. I know this is when he also stopped smoking pot. One would think that egocentric behavior was due to altering his consciousness, yet the opposite was true. It doesn't take a college degree to figure out what happened. It does take a degree to know how to help him. That I can't do, except be a friend.

Diana became much fonder of Julio that day. She saw him playing with the children and softened her view of him. He became more human and less threatening with his wall of Hindu mysticism. He does tend to want to give people direction on health and psychology. But Like all of us, we give advice to others much easier than change our own behavior. As we ate the lunch Julio was telling me he could change my hair color back from being white. "I don't care if my hair is white," I said. "No, you need more Flora in your diet," he said. I told him I have heard one can prevent, or slow the graying process, by eating gelatin every day, so I know of some dietary ways to keep the gray away, other than hair dye, but I really don't care. The same goes for his telling me I can re-grow the hair on my bald head. This is what happens when men get old. I don't like artificial means to make myself look other than what I am. Julio took the avocado shell and the seed and began to rub them in his hair. "This is the best part of the avocado," he kept saying. Sure, if you want to attract fruit flies. Julio can be fun but also overbearing. He often smells like some portion he is wearing. The first day when we got in his car I thought he smelled bad, later to realize that the bad odor was from his dogs. Diana is convinced she got fleabites from sitting in his car and it may well be. I seem to be immune to whatever bites her. I wish I were immune to the emotional duress I get when I feel responsible for her well-being.

At one point I was beginning to want to leave, but Julio and the girls were having too much of a great time. My boredom turned to creative inspiration as I took out the camera and took pictures of the dilapidated hotel. The place was in ruins. I found some rooms on the second floor near the front of the hotel that had old rusted bedsprings, but no mattress. The doors were rusted at the hinges. The bars on the windows were so rusted that time had worn them thin, even to a point where the bars had completely vanished. I was well aware that we had the best room in the hotel, furthest from the entrance, and closest to the beach exit. For its purpose the room was perfect. After a few more hours I returned to the beach where the girls and I buried Julio in sand. I was taking just about as many pictures as I wanted. We all piled into Julio's car and left. The hotel was twelve dollars for the day.

We were in the small beach town of Puerto San Jose. The town gives a feeling that there was once promise and hope, but all has been lost due to depression and lack of new paint. Nowhere were there any signs of economic growth or prosperity. I try to assess what I feel when I come to a new place, and yes, do the usual comparisons as I said, but this was a place unlike anywhere we'd been so far. I'd compare it to Honduras, but that might offend somebody. I am amazed at how someone can own something and never try to keep it up, let alone make it better. But this was the entire town. This was a place that had gone from bad to worse. It was so far removed from Antigua, or Guatemala City, that it could have been Honduras. (There I did it again.) The state of decay was pervasive. The streets were over-crowded with poor, barefoot people. It was intense. We were on a joy ride while starvation was on the other side of the car window. The women running the hotel, and their daughters, were pleasant when we left. The hotel was real bad and dirty, yet they probably thought it was a fine place. Einstein's relativity pops into my mind. How about you?

We passed a military naval base, circled around to the highway, and headed toward Antigua. The erupting volcano that came into view was like a storybook image with one dark plume of smoke rising straight up. I pulled the car over to take a picture. Julio began to raise his voice, telling me the edge of the highway could cut his tires. I wasn't on the edge and knew it. Two days later he inferred I had ruined his tire when I drove off the highway. I questioned his inference and still don't believe I caused him to have a flat tire.

The ride was fun. We passed one rock formation that had a man's profile in it. It reminded me of the great Sphinx of Egypt. High above the highway with a grey sky behind us, the face loomed and looked unattached as we drove past below. The slow incline became steeper as we neared Antigua and the visible face of the volcano. This was the first time Diana saw the entire mountain without clouds. I pulled over again to take a photograph. By now the children were falling asleep in a pile in the back seat, arms, and legs in a tangled web of body parts, all motionless. We took the high road that circled above Antigua, back around to the street that leads into town. I knew right where I was and went straight to Marta's house without any need of direction. I explained to Julio years before that as a limo driver, I was expected to never ask a customer how to return home. I know my way around. The girls were wakened and a drowsy good-bye followed. A cousin who had missed the trip came out to greet us. She gave Julio a big hug. We were back in the hotel and fast asleep within the hour. We lay in bed talking about Julio. Accessing and analyzing until our words were like waves turning in sleep.

That night I woke to the sound of Diana putting on and wearing my raincoat in bed. "What are you doing?" I questioned her. She was jumping and rolling in the bed so much I thought I was inside a tent in the wind. The sound of canvas has a distinct roar when awakened from a good sleep. I was beginning to worry about my wife's sanity until she calmed down and finally fell asleep. I didn't know if I should expect a flood or just believe that it worked for her. She claims it did. She stopped scratching and fidgeting, so it must have worked. Imagine you are wakened by a new noise and in a surreal, dream-like state your wife is in bed with you wearing a raincoat. Wearing a raincoat in bed can have some strong symbolic meanings, none of which I was processing at the time. Somewhere between lunacy and reality lays the truth in life. In this instance, lunacy was winning out, and so did sleep.

Day Seven: Guatemala City.   The alarm was put to use. We had to race for a ride to Guatemala City to meet Loraina, a total stranger. The sun was up sending direct light into the room so I knew it would be good light for taking pictures. We first walked to the central park to get money from an ATM, then on to the street near the bus station. A man was yelling, "Guati, Guati" which I thought was the wrong city. Soon we asked at a corner where the bus came, and three minutes later we entered a bus with a man calling out, "Guati, Guati". (Short for Guatemala City). This is how one learns. The buses leave the terminal about every five minutes and fill up right away. We tucked ourselves into the rear of the bus. At a corner in the middle of town two American females threw their backpacks on the top of the bus and climbed into the rear door. These weren't pushover-gals, but gutsy travelers. I struck up a conversation with the woman closest to me. She was a Californian and working as a Peace Corps volunteer. She worked with education and hygiene in the schools. More people got on board the already cramped bus. A third man sat in a seat and blocked our sight for discussion. The seats were built for two passengers. The Californian and I tried to link up in conversation again, but it wasn't until her stop that she said good-bye and good luck. The road had been rough with curves and lots of other "chicken buses" (A local name given to the buses). The highway came to the crest of a mountain road and flattened into a long, double-width road that runs past several shopping malls. At one of these malls the two Peace Corp volunteers got off the bus. Our shopping mall was two stops later.

This was called the Plaza de Flores. It was an expensive shopping mall that seemed somewhat out of place compared to the rest of the city, but I'd only seen what is called "zone one" the year before, so comparisons were not accurate. We were there a few minutes early so we walked the length of the mall, up to a second level and back. While I was sitting, I saw a young girl nearby with a guitar and asked her if I could play it. I said I was a tiny star in my country. The girl said she was a tiny star in Guatemala as well. We laughed and her mother asked me to play a song. I said no at first then got up some nerve. The girl was dressed in a net cap with low-hung blue jeans, while I looked like a modern hippie. She in turn sang a song. It was in English and she played very well. I was happy to have a brief visit and feel a guitar in my hands. I gave my business (Internet) card to her mother to ease any suspicions of trouble.

As I was talking to the mother and daughter Diana came up to me and introduced me to Loraina. She is the sister of my friend at school. She is a middle-aged, attractive woman who works as an administrator for an office building. She is single and was kind enough to offer us a tour of the city by car. I asked a favor of her, would she drive us to the bus station so we could buy our tickets to Nicaragua. She agreed and said it was on the way anyway. We were going to the museum. She had asked us when we met her in the shopping mall what we liked to do. I suggested a park or museum. Things were looking good. I hadn't really seen this side of life on my last visit to Guatemala. This time I was in a car and able to take more in. The bus station was our first stop. We bought our tickets and set off for the museum arriving forty-five minutes before they closed for lunch. Yes, the museums closed for an hour and a half for a lunch (siesta) break. We went in even though the time was short with a plan to return when they reopened. This was the Museum of Modern Art.

We strolled through the galleries and saw half of the museum. To my delight the entire museum was dedicated to photography. Some of the works were very old, some modern contemporary photographers, all Guatemalan photographers. My favorites were the black and white pictures. At noon the lights were dimmed and we were escorted out of the galleries. The outside of the building was a Spanish design of orange stucco and white lines emphasizing the edges. In the center of the face of the building was an emblem of the country's seal. It was in white against the orange background like the rest of the building. Across a small plaza was another building mirroring the same design as the first building. This was the Museum of Archeology. We had plans to return after our own lunch.

We left the museum and drove a route past the new airport. It seemed strange to have an airport in the middle of the city. The modern buildings were impressive and a lovely sight. Along both sides of the street that followed the airport was a collection of white sculptures. Loraina explained that these were completed in an international competition. The sculptures were built in the gardens behind the Museum of Modern Art and had been very popular. Many people had come to see them as they were being created. We passed a very modern section of the city and Loraina showed us the green-glassed building where she worked. It was twenty-five stories high. This was the business district with modern buildings that fit with the well-cleaned streets. It was all modern. A few blocks later we pulled into a parking lot. Loraina asked us if we wanted typical food. I said yes, but not too expensive. I ate the largest meal I've had in weeks. Diana and Loraina had large plates as well. The credit card was pulled out at the end.

We drove back to the Museum of Modern Art and finished the rest of the photography exhibitions. Our entrance into the Museum of Archeology was stalled because Loraina negotiated a better price. The entrance was a steep twenty-dollar for foreigners. I was a bit surprised at the cost, but even more surprised how well she bargained the price to be lowered. The man at the door welcomed us and we entered an incredible museum. The first exhibition was of small, seven-inch tall, ceramic figures found in the Mayan ruins. These delicate figures were of various people doing simple poses. In all there were some fifty small ceramic pieces. The work was so detailed and exquisite that they looked modern and not at all crude like many of the larger ceramic sculptures. The figures had elegant clothes (like costumes) and portrayed the different profession of ancient Mayan civilization.

The museum had a vast collection of Mayan ceramics, everything from pots to animals and people. In the center of the museum was a fountain with a circular rotunda that opened to the sky. White columns spanned the circle. Around this were huge Mayan sculptures, the same impressive type I'd seen in Copan the year before and missed in Tikal. The museum was one of the best we've seen. It wasn't so much the older building but the collection of works. The last part of the museum walk was dedicated to the clothes of the Indians and their districts within Guatemala. Large glass displays held the wardrobes of the different tribes.

We left the museum at four o'clock. Two and a half hours went by quickly. Outside we walked around to the back of the other building. This was a new treat. Here a collection of white sculptures stood well distanced apart. These were also part of the collection that stood on the street surrounding the airport. The only uniform element was the white marble and overall sizes. The modern designs presented a visual extravaganza. I asked a young teenager to take our picture of us with my camera. He was too far away and I teased him that the picture was terrible. He took several pictures. On our way to the car I asked the boy's father for a family portrait. The parents and children posed for me in front of a sign for the museum. We were all in good spirits.

We drove through the city up to a neighborhood I recognized from the year before when entering the city. We climbed the hills and entered a gated community. The guard was in a small post that was for an entire neighborhood. It wasn't for a single set of houses, but for varied houses of all sizes, each enclave having its own style. Loraina lives with her mother in a small condominium complex. We parked the car in an open garage port and went into their lovely home. The living room was full of antiques. Loraina's mother collects these favored objects. The house had old irons, typing machines, dolls (a variety of unnamed objects) in glass cabinets or stationed in interesting places around the house. On the stairwell landing a tricycle without handlebars functioned as a plant stand. The house was a composite of modern furniture and old antiques. It was somewhat like Diana's mother's homes as far as the conservative furniture, only with lots of nick-knacks. (My favorite kind of visual excitement that my wife doesn't enjoy as much as I do.) We sat and had a piece of cake and some fruit juice. I couldn't keep up with the fast Spanish so I looked at a book about the National Bird of Guatemala, the Quetzal.

Upstairs in the house I thought I heard a person coughing. On a tour of the house we were introduced to a sister who was nine months pregnant and ready to give birth. So ready, she is staying in the upstairs, with instructions from the doctor to stay put, until the precious moment. I took some pictures of the family to give to my friend back in New York. It was getting late so we asked to be driven home. Originally we planned to take the chicken bus back to Antigua but Loraina offered to give us a ride to our hotel. She has a friend who owns a restaurant in Antigua. We were hoping she found her way to his place and safe home after leaving us off.

On the drive back to the hotel Loraina told us of a political controversy the Mayor of Antigua was in. The mayor was trying to limit the use of alcohol by young people in the city. The city is kept pretty sterile for the tourists so the police have a big part in keeping the Guatemalans away. The Mayor is unpopular with the youth faction because he has put laws in place that restrict the sale of alcohol. The open hours of sales of liquor and established distance for liquor stores to churches have been some of the new laws enacted. I know of nothing worse than a drunken teenager, so I must be getting older to agree with restricting a substance.

We thanked Loraina and said our good-byes at the hotel to soon discover we had no toothpaste. A short walk three doors down to a tiny store was the solution. The night was soon upon us. We had an early seven o'clock pick up for our next adventure. Diana wore a raincoat to bed. I never said a word about it. I was glad she didn't smell like vinegar.

Day Eight: Chichicastenango. Julio arrived a few minutes before seven and went down the street to an Internet cafe. A few minutes past seven o'clock the van pulled up to the hotel. We were the second to last pickup. I was sandwiched between a Korean woman and the door in the front seat. Sitting in tight quarters for nearly three hours wasn't fun. I did get to know the Korean enough to learn she was a schoolteacher who left her job to travel Central and South America for five months. We had spoken to her briefly back in Flores some four days before. At that time she was waiting for a ride and standing on the sidewalk back in Flores. I noticed that she spoke weak English on the street, but in the van I was having a pretty good conversation with her. I admire her for traveling alone. Diana commented when we first met her that a woman in Colombia would never travel alone. Here we were four days later sitting cheek to cheek not knowing a new encounter would have taken place. I noted to her we had spoken in Flores on the sidewalk. She then recognized us. Julio and Diana sat in the back and spoke in Spanish most of the way.

Rocks in the road were my favorite part of the ride. The year before I was in the back of a chicken bus, this time I was in full view of everything from the front seat of the van. The bus driver the year before navigated through the switchbacks (lane changes) like a football player. But I could see this year that an additional feature to the road was apparent. Instead of orange cones to designate dangerous areas, rocks had been placed in the road. Where an avalanche was ahead on the road, rocks were placed to veer cars into a new lane. In many places landslides had completely covered the two-lane highway. At those points the traffic was forced over to the opposite side of the highway. I recall the chicken bus driver switching lanes like a hopscotch player. There were other sections where the road had caved in and gapping, open spaces lay below the highway. A cave-like crevice could be seen below the soon-to-cave-in highway. I could see some repair work was in motion, but how would they refill the caved-in, empty space the size of a large garage, was a mystery only a structural engineer could solve. I was just happy the rocks were correctly in place to make us switch lanes. These rocks were large boulders, nothing the size of an orange traffic cone.

A few miles before we got to Chichicastenango we came upon a real snag. A major traffic jam was stopping all traffic. A tractor-trailer truck was jack-knifed in the middle of the road. We were just small enough to squeeze by on the soft dirt that lay between the road and a steep cliff. I could see us falling to our death and me being mistaken as the Korean woman's husband when the bodies were retrieved. The sad thing was three large buses of tourists parked on the side of the steep hill were stopped. They were unable to pass the truck and were parked with all the tourists standing outside. Some of the tourists had taken the situation in hand and began the walk to the town. It was a couple of miles up and down some pretty steep hills. This was not going to be easy for them.

Our van arrived pulling up to the corner in town I knew from the year before. This was the Hotel Saint Thomas, just across from the gas station. We entered the hotel to use the restrooms, which cost five Quetzals. When we were waiting for Diana I saw a couple we had briefly met in Tikal. They were a brother and sister traveling team. I met another photography teacher from the Bronx in the restroom and gave him my card. This kind of cross-pollination is always happening with strangers while traveling.

The Hotel Saint Thomas is a jewel and cost about one hundred dollars a night. The safety in the hotel can be instantly felt compared to the bustling street. To get off the van and retreat to the quiet of the hotel was a way to regroup. This old white hotel has a fountain and a second floor with rooms circling the first of two plazas. It is small and intimate with a band standing on the second floor playing the familiar xylophone music of Guatemala. In the small plaza are Macaws sitting on perches with water and food. Their wings have been clipped so they don't fly away. To the left of the entrance is an expensive looking restaurant where the tables are set amongst the white arches and dining rooms. A young man at the door, that won't let you in unless you buy a ticket, attends to the rest rooms. It costs about one dollar to use. I joked with the attendant that it was cheaper than the rooms for sleeping, but way too small. He thought I was serious. The front door of the hotel is up very steep steps that are right on the crowded street. Hoards of woman and children selling goods stand at the door and rush (more like taunt) the tourists as they walk in and out.

Further down the street the market was more packed with people. We went straight into the heart of it all, near the church. As we were funneled into a pedestrian traffic jam I noticed the problem was a group of women sitting on the sides of the narrow path. They had dominated the walkway with their baskets of food, fruit mostly. I felt some jumbling and pushing in the crowd and thought nothing of it. Later I discovered I had been pick-pocketed. Not to worry, my cash was in my money belt around my waist. I knew there could be problems and prepared myself in advance. The thieves got away with what may have felt like a wad of money. It was my folded shopping list. Diana and I had been walking the shops and markets to compile a list of items and prices. I discovered this after our first shopping volley/battle while sitting on the church steps. Not to worry even more, Diana had been keeping a separate list and she pulled it out.

When we first entered the market I ran into Oscar my guide of the year before. I was all excited to see him again. He was leading a tour of an American family. I asked for his picture and could hear a woman in the back of the line saying, "Let's get moving". Good old American politeness. Oscar didn't recognize me, and it was an awkward moment emphasized by the bitchy woman at the back of the tour. There were six or seven people in a family tour. The nasty woman was insisting that she get her monies worth from Oscar. Julio was talking to a little girl who was trying to sell him a tiny doll. In the mix of comings and goings I bought a tiny doll from the little girl. Her name was Rose. The doll was really a refrigerator magnet. For some reason Diana decided to hold onto the fact that I didn't bargain with the little girl against me, and almost all day she kept referring to me as being too soft, and that she, Diana, would do the negotiating from then on. Now I was thinking how I bought one item, we were buying multiple items in bulk, but that shows how weak I am? The big picture seems to evade Diana at times. The one valuable bit of information we got from Rose was to go to the back of the market because the prices were better where less tourists went. Diana gave me no credit for my fact-finding!

We did go to the back of the market, near the second church, and began our first negotiation. We went to the same stall where I had bought many blankets the year before. The woman was Oscar's family, a distant relative. I don't remember the exact connection. She didn't remember me from Jack. I knew it was she from a photograph I had taken of her holding a blanket. She didn't seem as easy to negotiate with this time so we only bought one item, a blanket with yarned designs of children and houses. As we stood in the stall women came to the edge with blankets in their arms calling us over to their place of business. We tried to negotiate but they kept refusing to go lower, so we walked away. Maybe it was too early in the day.

Around a corner near the side of the church we had better success. Diana did her thing, she got the best sale of the day, and got the price we had studied and written down as our aim. Diana bought ten tablecloths. She took on a stern demeanor and was tough with the woman. This was a side of my wife I seldom see, but she held her ground, so much so that the woman secretly asked Diana not to tell her neighbors the price. We knew we had a good price when fear of the neighbors' sets in. As much bargaining that goes back and forth and the seemingly loose structure of prices that move in vast degrees from high to low, there is really an agreement in the market just what any given item should be sold for. The policing of prices comes in the form of the woman watching whatever is sold and by whom. They know what is going on. They know how low a price can be tolerated by the norms of the community. The tourists are really fooled about the "bargains" (myself included) but the prices overall are better in Chichi compared to Antigua.

After buying the ten tablecloths we took a little retreat on the steps of the church. "Retreat" is used symbolically. Little girls, and old women, selling ceramics that are whistles, or jewelry, hounded us. Julio always started up conversations with the little girls. Oscar passed us again, taking his tour into the church. He told me he did indeed remember me. Oscar told me his wife had opened a small stall and asked us to visit it, giving us the directions. A Mayan shaman stood outside the church waving an incense burner (an old can) and saying his prayers. Indians would come up to the fire burning on the churches terrace and place flowers or make offerings. Sometimes they would talk to the old shaman and make request for a specific needs. These Mayan rituals were an interesting mix of the ancient with the modern. The church was Catholic and the Mayans had embraced both rites.

As we sat on the church steps the Indians at the other white church (on the far side of the market) began to shoot off rockets and firecrackers. The smoke and noise were so loud it was as if we were in the middle of it. Both of the churches are on raised, high platforms that stand above the market. From one doorstep the other church across the market is visible. A procession carrying a saint under a canopy marched out of the church, down the steps, and into the street, as the procession passed through the city we could see the smoke and hear the fireworks that were set off. Maybe ten minutes later, at the far edge of the town, we saw another display of rockets and fireworks. I took inventory of my money and noted we had already spent half of our money for the day (two hundred dollars was our full day's allotment) and we needed to be more selective. We sat eating some nuts Julio offered us, and soon re-entered the battlefield preparing to make a killing.

We decided to head for Oscar's wife's stall located in the entrance of an appliance store called (something like) the Big Rooster. I never got the name right, but when we asked three times in the streets everyone seemed to know what Diana was asking for, even the police.

As we walked, a small boy I had bought a stuffed animal from the year before began to follow us. I didn't think he recognized me, but he tailed us for hours, never making a sale. I didn't want, or need, a stuffed animal. As we sought the small stall we asked about buying a box to ship things home. By asking further we heard that the shipping company wasn't open on Sunday, so we didn't need a box. The Indians were more than willing to sell us the box; it was one of those thick cardboard boxes made in China. It was a pre-used box.

I found the stall by asking who Oscar's wife was. I joked with the woman by drilling her with questions about Oscar. When she confirmed she had two children I shook her hand and said she passed the test. She was indeed Oscar's wife. The only problem was her selection of offerings. She had maybe fifteen items, none that really were what we wanted. I negotiated one items with her, another blanket with a design of small children holding hands. She had t-shirts, baseball hats, and some faded blankets. Who would buy a t-shirt in this exotic market? Some of the items we have bought often smell like smoke, so I suspect that this is either the smoke of a cook fire, or that the items have been used by the Indians before they are sold. Things we buy will need to be washed to get rid of the odor.

We passed the Hotel Saint Thomas, walked a few extra blocks, and found a quiet little store to buy some juice drinks. We had left the market and were in a part of town where no shops for tourists existed. It was a relief to feel left alone. The small store had a table behind the front door with three chairs and we asked permission to use the table and ate our lunch. The husband sat on the other side of the store at another table and the child of the owners was in a walker, rolling himself back and forth across the floor. I took pictures of the child but every time I pointed the camera the man covered his face with his hands. He had given permission to photograph the child but he insisted on covering his face. Julio noted that this was so I didn't steal his soul with my camera. Our lunch was a combination of refried beans with avocado in tortillas, nuts, fruit, and juice drinks. We ate fine and were full.

After lunch we bought a few more items in the market and returned to a long bench in the Hotel Saint Thomas. The music was playing as the water from the fountain reverberated a soothing splashing sound and the birds perched on wire rings chirped, or rather squawked like macaw do.

Diana and Julio sat on the bench and I went out for one last photographic walk-about after paying to use the restroom again. I was looking to buy a pretty blouse we had seen. Diana started the bargaining but the man didn't lower his price. I thought I could do better than Diana (God forgive me), so went looking for the same shop. I never found the shop and bought something we would never need in a million years, a long streamer of fabric with embroidering. I have no idea why, except that my niece might like it. Diana hated it. (God forgive her!)

We stood at our designated pick up location on the street corner and our driver fetched us, walking us a block back to the van. It was two o'clock and we had two huge bags of goods. I had brought along my Chinese plastic bags from the dollar store back in New York. We had bought more than anyone else in the van and packed the things away in the back of the van. I asked an American family if they would let their little girl sit in the front seat so it was more comfortable. "We don't want to be separated", was all I got. The French family understood my reasoning and agreed to take the front seat so I could sit in the back. The mother and daughter sat in the front while the father and son sat behind us. The Americans were safe in the rear of the van. They had exposed guns in their belts and eyed me with suspicion. I had challenged their family values! They were Republicans. I knew it!

The Korean woman was in the back with the French father and child. This time the ride went much smoother. I was still trying to get the kink out of my back from sitting sideways, cheek to cheek, with the Korean. As we passed the truck remaining jack-knifed in the middle of the road I noticed three other buses had parked in the middle of the road, and some of the passengers were dismounting out of a pickup truck. They had hired a truck to take them to the market and back. There were ten to fifteen people standing in the rear of the truck. I thought this was a creative solution and much better than walking, as some passengers had opted to do.

The ride home was still uncomfortable. My body is too long to fit anywhere. (I am six feet tall.) My neck can never lean on a headrest because I am five inches above the stupid things. Even on an airplane you can find me in a second. I am the guy whose head is almost touching the low ceiling. The views were better than my state of being. I would fall asleep only to have my neck spasm and jerk me awake. The countryside is spectacular. The beautiful patchwork of farms and careful rows of crops are a wonderful thing to see.

In one small town the traffic became unbearable so our driver took a side street, up a one-way street, wrong way. He was racing along at a pretty good clip. Other cars kept flashing their lights or waving, pointing, "wrong way," but he kept right along with the direction. He saved us at least twenty minutes. We passed the town square and saw there was festival. The church and plaza were all decked-out with colorful flags. People were crowding the entire area, so the driver kept a skillful eye on pedestrians as he wove a victimless path through them. I was impressed.

On one stretch of highway after the small town I saw an interesting phenomenon. From a long ways off I could see women with fans standing on the edge of the street, one foot out, waving with fans. Imagine a single, long view where many red lights can be seen in one picture frame. (Park Avenue if you know Park Avenue.) What caught my eye were all these moving fans, fans turned downward, and the woman waving traffic to stop and buy food from them. There must have been twenty-five women selling along this stretch of highway. Their food stalls were set up along the road, inches from the edge. These were temporary, moved every day at closing. Cars would pull up and be serviced like a fast food restaurant. A woman waving a brown fan in the shape of a large heart would be standing, one behind the other, in a long line of moving fans. It was a visual delight that I found fun and unusual to see. The consistency of the colors, sizes, and motion of the fans was an activity that one couldn't help but ponder as we neared all this activity along the roadside.

We dropped off Julio at our hotel. We went to our room, and soon found ourselves back on the street. Diana needed something from the pharmacy and we were hungry. In the market we found a last restaurant that was still open. A fat woman sat at the open entrance and greeted us. She was very large, no other way to put it. On a dirty, far wall I could see a black and white portrait of the same woman. I pointed to the picture, then her, and then back at the photograph, then back to her until she laughed. Indeed it was she, only in the picture she was twenty-three, much thinner, and in one of those sidelight, Hollywood poses. The restaurant was still open because they were preparing for a birthday party. The entire extended family was working in the restaurant. They all looked like Rose's sisters or nieces, which I confirmed by asking. Rose introduced her sister and family. We ate a diner of chicken and rice for about a dollar each. I was feeling vindication for spending so much money at the Indian restaurant days before. Now mind you, this was in the market and not up to any kind of standard but that of the local population. Nonetheless, it was very delicious by any standard.

Rose was absolutely delightful. She had put on some music and began to dance alone, waving her gigantic hips in time with the music. We had finished the meal and I got up to join Rose. She danced like me! It was a rock n roll, free-form-style, from the sixties. I knew we were the same age by our dance. Diana often makes fun of my dancing because it is not structured, not a salsa, not anything but moving with the music and mostly bobbing my head and arms. This is one of those areas of cultural difference where I suffer the criticism and mockery. Not only am I humiliated by the smooth style my wife's dances, I suffer deeply from the laughing and pointing out that I look "old". Yes, I am comparatively stiff. My hips are not Latin. My wife knows nothing of my fame as a dancer when I was young and agile. After a few beers I was better than she could have ever been, in MY time, in my generation, with my music, in my country. See how I suffer? It is as if I were one hundred years old telling my wife, "I AM FINE WITH WHO I AM!" Rose and I had a wonderful time as the others prepared for the birthday party, setting up, and stacking gifts on one table. Diana stood clapping her hands in time with the music. The rest of the onlookers were laughing and clapping.

We entered the market to buy some tape, but had to exit and find it on the street. The market was going through the shutting down exercises. The city was having a festival and thousands of people were in the usually quiet street. A carnival had set up behind the market with screaming children riding the fast moving amusement rides. A giant Ferris wheel with glowing lights spun as the night sky darkened. We found an ATM, got cash to pay for the hotel, paid Sandy (the receptionist), and went back out on the streets to see all the people and enjoy the festival.

In the central park people filled the far side and street where a xylophone (marimba) band played on a stage. It was the birthday of the city. The band was playing music as a man ran in a middle row of the crowd. He had a contraption mounted on his head and shoulders as he ducked, carrying the metal object. The metal object, or rack on his back, was lined with fireworks shooting off. He was really dancing in time with the music, but his body was wobbling from all the fireworks. As the music stopped, paused, and restarted, fireworks were shooting off. They were timed to go off when the music paused. The crowd widened the half circle around the stage as the fireworks got dangerously close to the people. The man with the apparatus was wearing a white, protective cloth over his head, which blocked his visibility, making the whole event even more comical. People dashed out of his way as he'd plunge toward the crowd, wait for the music, and begin to dance again. All the while firecrackers were shooting off from his shoulder on this contraption. (I'm sure it had a name in Spanish.) Diana recognized the event and gave it a name, "juoegos pyro-spectacular". She said the custom of dancing with the fireworks on one's back wasn't a Colombian custom, it was exclusive to Guatemala.

People were filing past the crowd, which had spilled onto the church steps. The people were trying to enter the church through the gathering. A crowd of spectators stood on the high, concrete platform just outside the church. Just as in Chichicastenango, and all over Guatemala, the churches are built high above street level. It began to rain and we entered the church. A Mass was about to begin so we found a seat. Some young girls were practicing for the singing with a few older singers and a keyboard player. The girls irritated me because they acted like it was a Broadway show, maybe their world debut. They cooed with the microphone and stood singing like they were on MTV. Another man stood singing like he was on a giant stage with thousands of admirers looking on. He was even more irritating. He spun his arms, opened them, bent backwards and gave his entire emotional repertoire to the uninterested churchgoers. It was a show, not a spiritual exercise. I was very put off. This is what the music industry has done to the young people. They base their posture on what music videos promote. I fully expected the man to garb his crouch, and rub his pants as the girls swung their asses and arched their breasts. It didn't happen. It was church in Guatemala.

All this time, and as the mass began, the fireworks and music outside the church were blasting loud. As the mass began the rockets were going off much louder than before. My favorite part was during the priest's sermon. Increasing loud booms from the rockets seemed to punctuate whatever the priest was saying. As each of his words was spoken a boom was resounding outside, above the church. He was timing his words with the loud booms of the rockets. Adding to the comic element was the large screen in front of us where the church's video system was broadcasting live images of the mass with close-ups of the priest. We were sitting on a side of the church were the altar was obstructed by the inner arches, so the church fathers had installed a large projector screen where all could see the mass. The sounds of the fireworks were so loud not a single word could be heard of the priest's sermon. I found the whole event to be surrealistic. I was making a movie in my head where each word was punctuated with a violent, loud burst. There was war going on outside, as we all sat inside pretending to reverently listen to the inspiring sermon. Funny stuff!

At the end of the mass we left the church and walked the central park. We passed the Americans with whom we shared our van earlier in the day and acknowledged each other. They still had their guns exposed at their sides, except their shirts were tucked behind their holsters this time. They walked like cowboys Republicans. We didn't say anything to each other, just a kind of silent acknowledgment that I was a threat to their family values. I was about to ask them for their NRA registration cards when I was distracted by Diana asking me to buy some ice cream, which I did. We sat in an ice cream store that had a filthy floor because the foot traffic from the rain had brought in all kinds of mud.

We walked home, hand in hand, past a Spanish institution we had been looking for, and heard a free art exhibitions was showing (Loraina told us). The slow walk took us past expensive restaurants with candles burning in the windows. The candles were set inside black cast-iron holders, and very Spanish. One hotel had a winding staircase running from the front entrance to the second floor. We were in an expensive part of town, but one block away it was typical Antigua. Back in our hotel we opened some of the pirated loot we had bought that day. I began to organize our departure in two days, making a new bag and cushioning ceramics with Diana's life jacket. We washed our clothes in the small bathroom sink, hanging them around the room and anything that would hold the clothes. They had to be dry in two days. We plan ahead! Sleep is something we plan for too. My wife wears a raincoat to bed. Pass it on.

Day Nine: Last Day Guatemala. This was a day we could sleep in but this won't be the case tomorrow when we rise at 3:30 AM. We had two things on our agenda today; rope and water. We started out toward the market but took a detour to a museum dedicated to the clothes of the indigenous people here - not a planned event, but the signage gave us the idea. The entrance fee was well within the last days five hundred Quetzal limit. The only problem was the attendant didn't have change for the money I had and allowed us in for less than required. I was trying not to make another ATM withdrawal.

Each Guatemalan city has its own design for the clothes the people wear. A guide approached us as part of the entrance fee. He explained that colors had different symbolic meanings, yellow, for instance was for corn. A particular star pattern on a shirt would represent crops of those areas. There were some twenty-three different Indian dialects but our guide confessed to knowing only English and Spanish. Before the Spanish arrived in the 1500's the looms used by the Indians were narrow, about twenty-four inches, and after the Spaniards introduced a weaving machine men took up the creation of the wide fabrics. Before, men mostly worked the fields, and why this change came about I didn't quite understand. Could it be the size of the looms alone? The guide went on to explain the belts the woman use to hold up the long skirts is twice the size for a married female, the unmarried women have a smaller width.

In the museum our guide greeted us right away. A woman came into a separate stall and sat down beginning to weave for exhibition purposes. As she did this, the male guide spoke and explained the lengthy weaving process. The fabrics can take up to a month or longer to make. From a high pole the weaving apparatus is suspended, swinging down to a strap around the woman buttocks. The weavers usually kneel, but our demonstrator was sitting. The thread is passed back and forth. Two sticks stretch above the fabric and direct the patterns and overall design. Other sticks are used to pat the fabric tighter. It's pure magic to watch this. To remember what and where the different colored threads weave is a mental exercise that astounds me. Some of these people can't read or write but they have a mental capacity of memory that would put a college graduate to shame.

Many of the fabrics have a fuzzy, soft pattern that is within narrow patterns. It gives a kind of crude impression of these particular cloths, but the fuzziness is created by going into the isles of design and "tie dying" the fabric. The weave has open, "unfinished" areas that are tied off so the dye doesn't seep into all the cloth. Yet there is an overall consistent design developed by tying knots of string into sectioned-off strands. The tying of these tiny knots is also a memorized procedure. Our guide went on to tell how some dyes were from plants while others were from insects. The hats of the women are like strands of rope; this represents the serpent god sitting on top of the goddess that is creating weaving. Another type of hat is a multi-purpose fabric that the women wear to keep the sun off their heads or as a shoulder-shawl when it is cold. The Mayans worshiped the sun and moon; these two symbols are in much of the cloth as well. The saw-toothed, zigzag pattern on the shirts of the women is to represent the rays of the sun.

The guide led us from diorama to diorama where dummies with clay pots (instead of heads) stood wearing the cloths. The daily objects of the Indians were also on display. A second section of the museum was individual rooms with cloths, yards of fabrics, and tourists' goodies. The original guide thanked us and introduced us to a woman selling chocolates. We bought one small weaving, almost getting a second, but I told Diana we would go back to the market and find better prices. (Whispering, so the sales clerks wouldn't hear, of course.)

The fabric museum was a few blocks from the local market so we went to find some rope. It took us maybe one minute to find the rope; I bought a second rope a few minutes later, in case I needed more. The rope was going to be used to tie our bags. At a store, set up with counters like a pharmacy, we bought a gallon of water for the bus tomorrow. The store had a long glass counter where people stood behind computers and buyers would read off their lists of needed items. The clerk would then disappear behind a wall of shelves and bring out the goods. We were the only ones buying a solo item while most people were buying in bulk. This store was where I had photographed the cow painted on the wall the day we arrived here in Antigua. None of the same Indian women was there selling. A new set of women sat selling their goods so I am assuming that those who come early get the best spots to sell and to find a repeat vendor would be difficult because the market is always changing. The areas these women sellers take up depend on how many baskets of fruit, beans, or vegetables they have. There seems to be no order to where woman set up, except the isles are more or less established because of the permanent structures of wooden stalls that make a kind of street. The wooden stalls are the only thing permanent about this market.

As we were about to leave the market, heading toward the (tourist) craft market a man came stumbling up to me and put his hand out to shake my hand. In the other hand he had what looked like a few brochures, but he was no salesman representing anything but over-consumption of alcoholic. I declined his handshake and kept walking. As he approached me he was loud and saying 'hi". I sized him up in a millisecond. My rejection caused some protests and without my knowing he bumped up against Diana and elbowed her in the ribs. We just kept walking and entered the gated-off crafts market. All the while he was yelling obscenities at us. "This is my place you f**king Americans, go home." Two big men stood at the entrance to the craft market and made an embarrassed frown-face. They were sellers from the stalls. The drunken man stopped as the men, without even saying a word, moved into the gate, blocking the drunk from following us. It was a slight block, but just enough body language to stop the man who was still yelling at us. We passed one isle into the shops when Diana told me the man had elbowed her in the ribs. "Why didn't you tell me?" She said, "I didn't want to cause any trouble." I said, "We should have called the police, let's go find one." Diana declined any help and went on shopping. She told the man at the handbag stall about the drunk and he gave her a good price. We bought another tapestry, exactly like the one in the museum, for half the price. The people there gave us two small gifts for our troubles with the drunk. The drunken loud ruckus was heard by anyone within earshot. The people were genuinely embarrassed.

We left the market from a different passage, far away from any possible reintroduction to the angry drunk. I didn't know how bad the elbow jab was. It wasn't until she said it was hurting that I was perturbed at her for not making more of this event. Diana became grumpy. I was grumpy and we were keeping a verbal distance from each other. We returned to the hotel to drop off the water and walk with a packed box I wanted to ship home. The box was full of Indian fabrics from Chichicastenango. It was not that large, maybe medium sized, but they wanted two hundred and fifty dollars to send it home. I laughed. That was my only comment. I thanked the woman and chuckled to Diana that we would be carrying this package on the rest of the way to Costa Rica. The value of what we bought was less than the shipping costs. We hailed a 'took, took" back to the hotel, had a snack of cashews, and headed to a museum Loraina had told us about two days before.

To our surprise it was a free exhibition sponsored by the Government of Spain. The only thing we had to do was leave our backpacks in a locked box and sign a guest book. After going through a metal detector we entered a large courtyard with a fountain in the middle. The building was two-storied with arches on the bottom floor and polished, wood columns flowing around the entire second floor. To our right the exhibition began. It was photographs of homes built by money sent from the United States to relatives back here in Guatemala. The homes in the photographs were garish, and ostentatious. The people who built and designed them were attempting to exhibit status and wealth. The odd designs looked even more out of place when situated next to shacks or "normal" dwellings. American flags or eagles would be painted on the walls; even sculptures of the Statue of Liberty were built. A wave of these architectural anomalies has hit the countryside of Guatemala where a son or parent will send money back home to build their dream house.

Diana was reading the captions explaining the theme of the exhibit. Her cynical tone was confusing me. Was the cynicism hers about my country or for the people's houses shown in the exhibition? We were not on the same wavelength to say the least. Maybe I was still angry at her for not telling me about the assault. We quietly walked the entire building, both floors, looking into a library, computer labs, a play room for children, and a conference room where people sat around a large square table. This was a complex, which was built by the Government of Spain for promoting education and cultural exchange. We walked up to the second floor where a beautiful, polished wooden floor was accented by the wooden columns we had seen from the courtyard. This was a fine building where the renovation took on big expense.

We walked to the town's Central Park where we passed an Indian woman from whom Diana had promised to buy ten tablecloths. The woman recognized Diana as she walked by, and politely said, "Later?" I was angry with Diana for not acknowledging the woman and for not at least explaining she did not want to buy the ten tablecloths. I began to lecture Diana as the rains came and we sat in a second floor balcony next to the mayor's chambers. I thought she had been way too impersonal with the Indian woman. I saw the woman's face full of disappointment. This was a rare moment where we both had enough of each other. Diana stormed off, as the rain raged on, and I was left there to chat with the policeman stationed outside the mayor's office on the same level. I told him about the drunken man, leaving out any detail about my being upset with Diana for not reporting this to the police or me. I needed a little time away from my wife and fell asleep on a long bench outside the mayor's office. The policeman didn't wake me and Diana didn't return. I wandered home with the umbrella after stopping at a large cooperative store selling Indians goods. Considering we have not been apart for more than a minute for the last month, I think we are in good shape. A few cross words happens to the best of us. It rains, it rains, it rains and couples have spats. And then the sun comes shining through again.

We waited in the hotel for Julio who didn't show at four-thirty, so we hit the streets for one last walk-about. An Indian woman wanted to sell us a scarf, but the last forty quetzals in my pocket wasn't enough for her. A few blocks away I could see the cooperative store I had visited before, so we entered the store to see what we could find to spend our last money on. We wanted to unload before leaving the country in the morning. (It was maybe seven dollars.)

The cooperative is a huge warehouse that has good prices. The layout of the shop is much disorganized, some tall shelves stand in the rear with clothes, or clothes hang on the walls. The back wall is full of masks, to the right is what I guessed are antique tools. I recognized the antique marimbas with coconuts to amplify the sound. Things were in bad shape. In the middle of the shop was an old boat filled with clothes for sale. These were the used clothes of the Indian women. The prices of these were a fraction of the newer cloths on the racks for sale. Some looked worn; they were displayed with as much glamour as the new clothes. These are clothes tourists hang on their walls for decorations.

It had rained all afternoon and the store had leaks in the roof and walls, so black plastic and water buckets were placed at special location to trap the water. One entire section of wall had all the clothes being displayed removed so water didn't ruin them. The store was a mix of everything Guatemalan. The prices were right for who ever wanted to spend a little or a lot. If there is anything to see this large display of goods can be considered equivalent to a museum visit. We had nothing to do so we browsed and browsed.

As we exited the store we still hadn't spent our money. At the door there were always Indian women trying to sell fabrics, so this was our chance to spend the money. Diana bought two scarves for maybe four dollars. We didn't haggle with the price that much. The women looked at each other like they had made a steal, we were happy to be rid of the last money. The sky was overcast and we felt the usual magnetic pull to the Central Park. Two empty seats on a dry bench were our welcoming sign. The peace and quiet lasted a few minutes until five Indian women came up trying to hock their wares. I began to scream, "This is my place, you mother ***king Indians! Can't you leave us alone for once?" (In my mind only.) Instead I began to point the camera right at eye level and pretend to take their picture. This was the most obnoxious thing I'd done in all the time we'd been in their country. It was my last night and they had to pay for the drunk in the morning. Oddly enough, the women didn't pay any attention to me. Maybe they knew the camera wasn't clicking. They are so aggressive they seem to notice little. In Chichicastenango if you point a camera anywhere the instant response is for the Indians to turn their heads away. If you are pointing the camera at them they flinch. They believe it is a spiritual infringement, and I agree, but money can change that in some cases. I just ask permission, unless I'm in a place where there are too many people for it to matter. Diana had enough of being taunted by the Indians sales women; she felt the same way after shopping at Chichi. It is an exhausting exercise in patience, and guilt, to shop on the streets in Guatemala.

We paid one last visit to the cathedral, where I took a few last photographs. By then it was getting late and the overcast sky was looking like rain again. We walked arm in arm to our hotel. At the desk we found the potion of Rosewater that Julio had promised us. He had come and gone, saying he would return later. I knew he went to the Internet cafe for his online date. We explained to Sandy that we had to go to bed and that if he returned to apologize and tell him we were sleeping. An hour later there was a tap at the door. The other hotel attendant had come to tell us that Julio was there to see us. When we entered the lobby Sandy was telling Julio our message. He apologized for missing the four-thirty appointment, but he had problems with the check he had written so we could buy the wooden horse. The check had bounced. He had to get cash and make sure the woodworker (sculptor) was paid. How this all came about I have no idea. It may have just been an excuse for him being so late, but I was happy to see him.

Diana and I had been discussing some slight issues about Julio and whether he was being honest with us about all the cost of a promised herbal potion. Diana felt he was trying to take advantage of her by trading the potion for her raincoat. (This was after I had talked to him, in secret, about buying the potion for Diana from him the day we were in Chichi.) So there was some stress about Julio, aside from his not showing up on time. We explained to him we needed to be in bed for the 3:30 wake-up. I told him I needed the raincoat I promised him for the bus and would give it to him next time. Diana said, point blank, "I know Dennis paid you for the Rosewater". He looked a little sheepish and I gave him a hug, hoping to let him know everything was still good between us. But we both were wondering if he had tried to take us for a small ride. All the way on our walk back to the hotel Diana was saying he was trying to take advantage of us and he wouldn't bring the purchased Rosewater. I was less skeptical, trying to smooth things over. But missing him because of his lateness was a disappointment. The departure was a kind of silent, anticlimax to our visit together. He turned and walked into the night where the rain had brought a big chill and a less than perfect good-bye. I said we'd see him in a year or so. He was gone. I hope to see him again.

If it's not clear, Julio had asked Diana to trade the Rosewater for her raincoat after I had told him I wanted to buy the Rosewater. I don't keep secrets from Diana so I had already told her I bought her the Rosewater from Julio. Diana concluded that Julio was trying to get paid, in secret by me, and trade the raincoat with her. I had already offered my raincoat to Julio as a gift. Why did he ask Diana to trade her raincoat baffled both of us? I am certain of one thing. There was some strange miscommunication or Julio was really trying to get something from both of us, thinking we would not talk to each other about the "secret" purchase. It was supposed to be a surprise purchase for Diana. I don't know what Julio's intentions were: the flat tire, the bounced check, the late arrival all seemed like ways to get money from us. I hope I am wrong and that our friendship isn't wasted on such silly worries. Our suspicions were too awkward to mention, but too obvious to ignore.

We returned to stuff the bags and get ready for the early awakening. I was fast asleep when the tap at the door came for the van to the bus station in Guatemala City. It was three-thirty in the morning, dark and rainy.

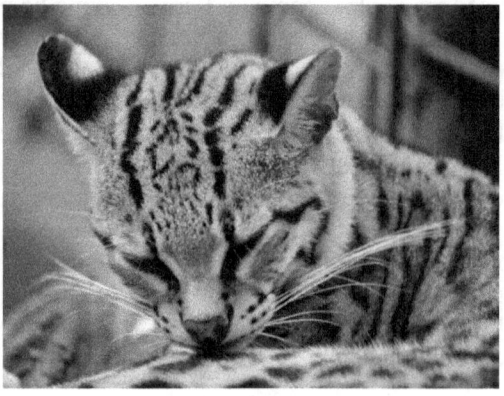

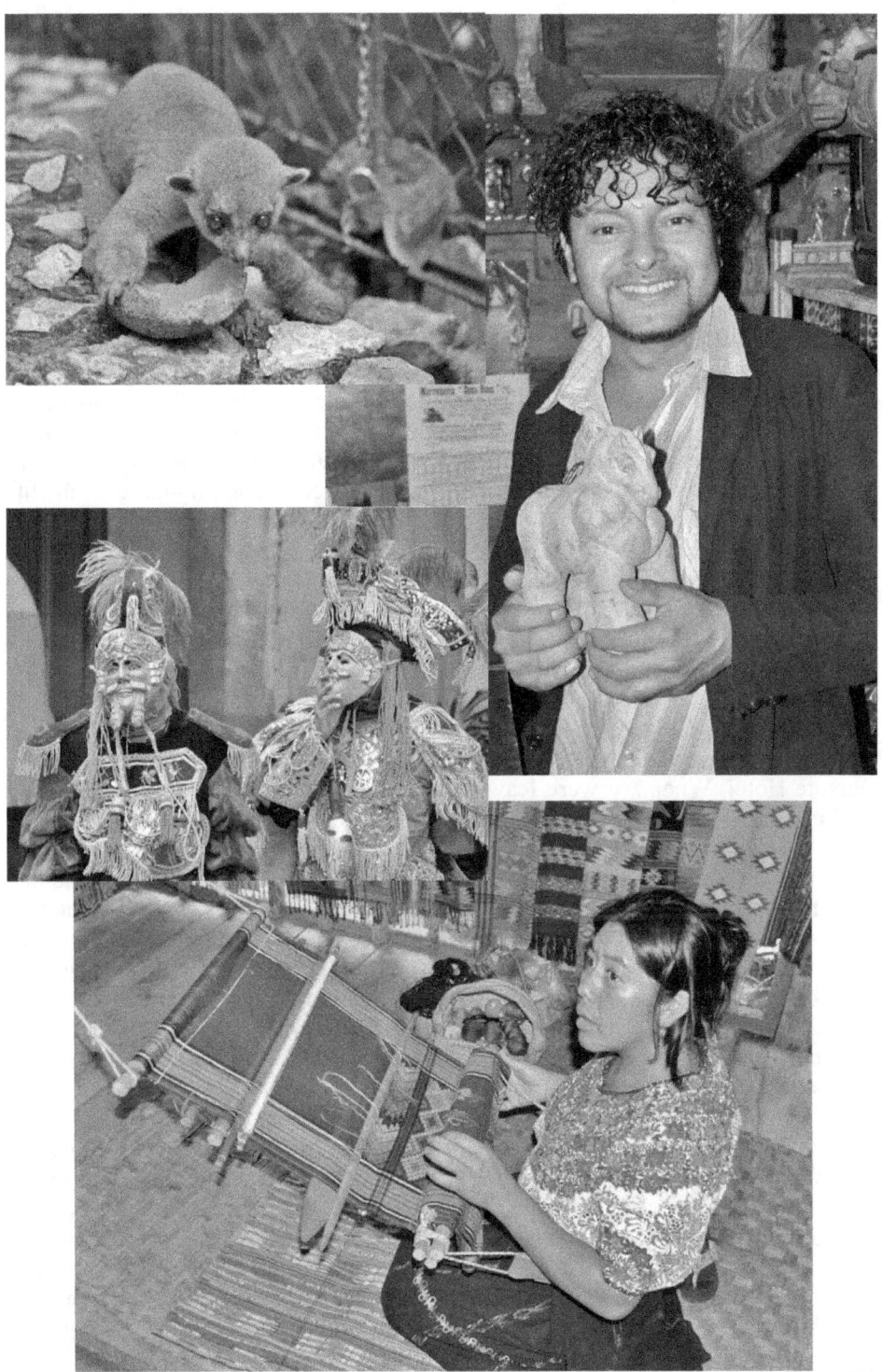

Chapter Twenty
Busland

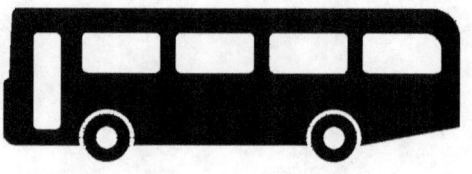

Where is Busland? It is between four countries, Guatemala, El Salvador, Honduras, and Nicaragua. It is a strange land where everything outside the window looks the same, the people, the volcanoes, the lakes, the highway, the trash, and the border crossings. No one speaks and the DVD player runs all day and all night. No one laughs at the funny movies because they are bored beyond comprehension. All the movies blur and morph into one long boring romantic comedy about a young girl and how stupid she really is. There is always a boy and always a surprise ending that was no surprise at all because the people who wrote the scripts never travel in Busland. Only in Busland can you find who you truly are. You are either a content, sentient being or anchored to the TV. Only the Buddha understands Busland. He knows Busland is full of suffering, boredom, and un-enlightenment. He would understand how to tune out a throbbing din like modern movies.

Besides preparing for the trip the night before, we decided it would be a great day to do our cleansing fast. We had access to a toilet all day because the buses are fully equipped. If we were lucky this toilet would work. The van picked us up at 4:00 AM. Who can sleep under such conditions? I wake or toss all night in anticipation of being bored to death on a long journey. Diana didn't sleep either. By the time the man working in the hotel came to awaken us we had already been up and heard his alarm clock upstairs from our room. The shrill, piercing beep-beep-beep is just loud enough to reach every corner of Don Quixote Hotel. When we were leaving, I told the man thank you, and to please send my thanks to Sergio for all his help.

Once in the van we were driven to the west side of Antigua and picked up a woman who said she had been standing and waiting since 3:30AM. She and her husband are Guatemalan. In the dark all I could see were two small silhouettes. He kissed his wife good-bye leaving her to load her luggage into the van alone. She asked the van driver to stop at a restroom. After hours of waiting that was understandable, it was impossible because he was already running late. We curved up, down, around corners at unfathomably break-neck speed and descended the long sloping highway into Guatemala City. The lights of the city were still on and daybreak was creating a haze.

Our first stop was the airport where everyone but another couple, Diana, I, got off. I jumped out to help the driver hand down luggage from the roof of the van. When we got to our stop at the bus station he handed me my bag and I dropped it. *There go the ceramics*, I was thinking. Thankfully nothing broke, I later discovered. We were standing outside the locked bus station door exactly five minutes when the guard opened the door from the inside. They said they would open promptly at 5:30. At 6:00 the agents came in and people formed a line. At 6:30 we boarded, or tried to, but we were sent to the line. We had not checked in. Our bags were searched and our passports scrutinized. A smiling stewardess greeted us and we sat in the lower level of the bus; we were in first class. This bus was up to any US standards and the design with first class below was like a sleek modern European bus. The reclining seats were huge, wide, and stuffed for comfort and sleeping. Every half hour we were offered a drink of juice, so we took the juice and food. We drank the juice; however we stuffed the food into our bags for later on, since we were fasting. Drinking liquids was okay.

This leg of the journey took us five hours as we passed through the border to El Salvador from Guatemala. We only had to sit in the bus. A border agent came in and looked at our passports, which were taken and stamped. I knew this and kept exactly three dollars in Quetzals. The crossing was very pleasant and civilized. As we passed into El Salvador the entire courtesy thing went out the window. We had to file out of the bus form a line on the tile floor, which was so cramped that people were elbowing each other. As we stood there, beggars came up to us and no one tried to stop them from entering the government building. A woman entered the room. She had food for sale that was balanced on her head. Money changers came in and waved hands full of bills in our face. We felt like open targets.

Diana handed her passport to the woman behind the glass and it was stamped immediately. For some reason my passport was held back and I was told to stand aside. I could see the woman had the book open to the page that was stamped the year before, and not this year's entry.

At those moments I just think to myself this is stupidity and bureaucracy at work, be patient and see what kind of trouble this half-brain will try to create for me. And she did. She took the passport to a man sitting at a desk. A Chinese man was sitting at another desk, as if he were being questioned. Another Chinese man, I had struck up a conversation while in line, was also told to step aside. I told the man how I liked China. His English was very weak but we smiled and exchanged pleasantries. This continued as we both stood there waiting for our passports. Diana had her ear next to the window and was listening as the "boss" reprimanded the woman for wasting his time. He handed the agent back my passport. She was indeed looking at last year's expired stamp and had failed to turn to the last page to see *THIS YEAR'S* entry stamp. She thought she caught some guy who had been in the country, illegally, for a year. Too bad. Diana gave the woman a hard time before and after this ordeal. Diana had explained that the stamp was from last year, but I guess the woman needed some drama in her day. As time passed, the two Chinese men became friends, and talked loudly, as if they were yelling from only a few inches apart. Eventually they yelled good-bye to each other and we boarded our bus. The other Chinese man went to a different bus.

The entire time we rode in first class I was typing feverishly on the keyboard. A movie was on but I only remember that a movie was on. As we re-boarded the bus we continued a conversation we had begun with an elderly architect from El Salvador. He told how he had driven through the same border the year before and been robbed at gunpoint not far from there. They took everything in his car and from his person. For this reason he would never drive through the border again. He didn't like to fly, but had been all over the world doing architecture. I showed him the paintings I did during our travels. We exchanged business cards. He made our ride more pleasant as we switched between English and Spanish and conversed.

In San Salvador we exited the bus in the station and stood waiting to be called from a passenger list. We weren't on the list. I got a little worried and insisted we had bought the tickets three days before, which were the first two front seats. There was no first class bus to Nicaragua, but I made sure to get the front seats where I could stretch my legs. This turned out to be a silly, insistent request on my part. As we looked at each other in anger over such poor service, and the fact that they had not announced the king and queen of America would be on their bus, the agent excused herself. The two Chinese men found each other again because a second bus was behind ours and arriving within a few minutes. They talked so loudly they could be heard over the buses that came and went. The stewardess returned twenty minutes later and called out bus routes and city names. I knew the Chinese men didn't have a clue they were being called to board their bus, so I called out to the man I'd been speaking with before and pointed to his bus. He gratefully bowed, many times, and then he left for his bus. My kingly status had been lowered to diplomat at that point.

I encouraged Diana to find out why we were not on the list. "Lean on them," I instructed her. Of course there is another side to all this. We were in the computer, on the list, but the agent didn't want to tell us just simply to make us nervous. This all came crashing down when we entered the bus to find the bus was virtually empty and our insistence on the two front seats was ridiculous. We had the first ten seats to ourselves. I did eventually sit in several seats in hopes of finding greater comfort. It didn't happen. Our first class affair on the morning bus was replaced by uncomfortable seats where no matter how I bent, stretched, or curled into a fetal position, was terrible. The two front seats were just far away enough to not allow my knees to reach and the other seats were too small for me to do anything but get a stiff back. I felt a little stupid about all the hubbub we had made, but I also felt like they were just jerking us around by not telling us the bus was not full. I passed the time and dispersed my anger by typing.

The tax to leave El Salvador was thirteen dollars. We had been in the country maybe four hours but had to pay an exit tax. To enter Honduras, which we were only passing through, we simply handed in the passports, and the same was true for Nicaragua. Honduras didn't ask for any blood money. At the border of Nicaragua we stood outside the bus and a nice man came and looked at our passports. I asked about the stamp and he said, "How long will you be here?" I said, "at most, five days". He said we didn't need anything. I liked him so I trusted him. The rest of my bus travel was a blur. The movies were sickening and I was ashamed my country made such trash. I think the bus attendant, a young woman in her early twenties, had chosen all the movies. They all seemed ridiculously lame. I met a couple from New Zealand while waiting at the border to Nicaragua and the first thing we did was talk about the terrible movies. Then we talked about the Maori in New Zealand. That was a much better topic we all seemed to enjoy. The woman was a lawyer, and one sixteenth Maori. How she came up with that statistic I'll never know. It was equivalent to having a big toe part Maori. We talked about health care, politics, and had a few quick laughs about it all. We soon re-boarded the bus. I have no idea what time it was by then, and only know it was dark and we stood in a strange other-land where one street lamp light our faces.

The bus ride was supposed to take ten hours, but it took almost thirteen. Why? I was hoping you'd ask. Late in the night the driver would pull over for long stretches of time, an hour here, a half hour there, and forty minutes here or there. This wasn't because he needed a nap. Diana was in the front seat and could hear the entire goings on through the glass partition to the driver's compartment. Three buses in front of us on the highway had been held up at gunpoint. The driver wisely waited for other trucks and vehicles to form a caravan for protection. The bus drivers all had some kind of phone network where they would call each other and tell one another where the trouble was. I was too busy changing seats and trying to sleep to know much more. I would sleep long enough to put an extra kink in my neck, wake up, change position, fall asleep, watch three seconds of a movie, close my eyes and dream of riding first class back in Guatemala to El Salvador. It was pretty bad, but not as bad as the eight hours in the shit-bus from Flores to Guatemala City. By the time nightfall had put a black blanket over the land I couldn't see the keyboard of my computer. This bus company had a blackout rule as well, so no one could see inside the bus. No lights were allowed to burn. I practically ruined my eyesight, as it was straining all day as I worked at the computer making a million errors as I typed, and feeling like a drunken man writing spiritual scriptures.

We were keeping to our fast and the attendant kept handing out food and drinks to make everyone feel pampered. All the food we received lasted us the next three days. There were sandwiches, nuts, cakes, cookies, dog biscuits and cat treats. No one barked at the attendant, we just couldn't believe why the ride was taking forever. And of course, in the tradition of sharing information the bus company kept us in the dark, both figuratively and literally.

I aged a few years on that bus ride. I listened to my iPod and dreamed more about first class. We pulled into the bus station some three hours late. I immediately recognized the taxi driver standing outside the bus. He was the same taxi driver I had turned down the year before. I didn't trust him then, only to later find out that he was a partner to the taxi driver I did use, they both ended up at my hotel. This time I knew he had the inside connection to get us out into the night safely. He was parked inside the bus depot. He was the only taxi allowed inside the bus station's heavily guarded gate. I wasn't too crazy about the young man I had hired the year before. By now this man, because he was recognizable, looked like the second coming of Christ. Other than not wearing a beard or long white robe, he looked pretty good. The driver and I loaded the bags in to his trunk. His car didn't start so we helped him jump start his dead battery with a little push, and he drove us across the street to a mini mart where I used the ATM to get Nicaraguan Cordovas. At the mini mart I was swarmed by beggars pointing to their bellies asking for "dollars". I was so tired I wanted to assault one of them, but I used wisdom to think about my future as well as Diana's. I said nothing and went to the car. They came to the car, but my silence got through to them as they stopped tapping on the window while we drove away.

The taxi driver offered me the same hotel as the year before. He promoted the hotel as being owned by Daniel Ortega, the current president of Nicaragua. It was forty-five for two people. Because I was with my wife and wanted to impress her, I asked him to take us to a twenty-five dollar-a-night place. It had no Wi-Fi, two beds, a shower, and a door that locked. That was all we needed. We pulled up to a large gate and the driver tapped on the metal. A few minutes, later a groggy woman dragged her feet to an inner gate ten feet inside the compound, and then to our gate on the street, unlocking them both. It was only 3:00 AM, so why on earth would she be so sleepy? I enjoyed the double security, but not as much as the room. It was nicer than the room back in Antigua, spacious, with a fan and a television. It was clean and comfortable, decorated with small paintings of Nicaragua on the wall. We actually liked this unpretentious room very much. I paid the sleepy innkeeper on the spot.

As we lay there falling asleep we watched some 'Loony Tune' cartoons from about 1930. It was great. I began to wonder if we were really safe. We could have been locked away from the world and never heard from again. We were behind three locked barriers, far enough from the street where our screams could never be heard. I moved our bags in front of the door in a last paranoid attempt to save our lives from a sure kidnapping. I remember seeing a cockroach on the wall behind the bedside table and keeping it to myself. Diana was falling fast asleep, faster than I, and it seemed pointless to mention a silly cockroach in light of a possible kidnapping. Diana had put the TV on a timer. I was so exhausted I couldn't come up with any more terrible plots to keep myself awake. While I was asleep, I heard some kind of falling fruit hit the roof of our room, but dozed off faster than the first time a few minutes before. I dreamed I was on a bus, of all things, traveling through a strange land called Busland. Robberies, falling fruit, teenage romance movies, and cockroaches were running through my head. I think the cockroach literally was running around my head.

A word of advice: The international buses in Central America are the safest way to travel. Bandits target the local "chicken buses" in the middle of the night, not the day; therefore a day trip is always the wisest way to go. A shorter, day trip would have been better for us, but we wanted to do one marathon ride to get to that point where any future bus ride would be thoroughly enjoyed. It is not necessary to travel for thirteen hours on a bus anywhere in the world unless you seek the Buddha's path.

Chapter Twenty One
Nicaragua

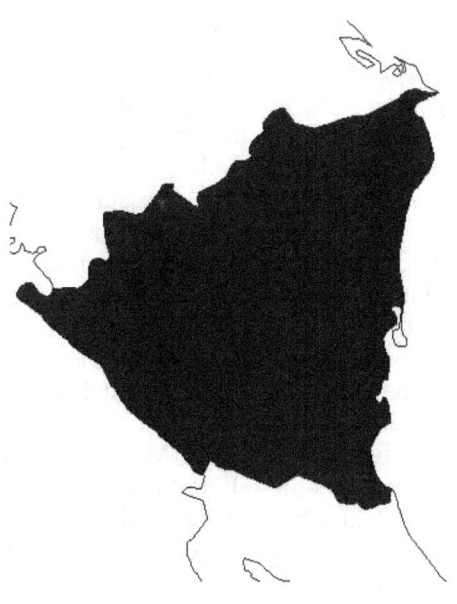

Day One: To describe our room in Managua is easy. Think of a pretty, nicely kept, big, room with a steel roof and tile floors. It was like being in someone's (a female's) house. And we were. The decorations were very homey, quaint, and cute. In the morning I was glad to see we were still alive and looked out the curtains to a beautiful blue sky. The sun was coming in a corner of the room and no one seemed to be awake but us. I opened the door and peeked into a courtyard that was covered with corrugated steel, the same as our roof. Half a dozen motorcycles were parked and in pieces at the back of the courtyard. We showered, made our breakfast shakes, and I went out to see the place. The back of the hotel was a shared motorcycle repair shop. Posters of motorcycle races were all over the walls. Bike parts were piled everywhere. Three rocking chairs were sitting outside our door so I made like Goldilocks and sat in all three deciding which was best.

The woman emerged from her house, another hotel room across the courtyard. In all there were five hotel rooms. We had the best. I am positive from what I saw of the kitchen in her room. A man with a huge potbelly started to sweep the floor like he must have every morning and paid no attention to me. I said good morning to both he and his wife and rocked in the chair enjoying the sun. The woman was wearing a smile and seemed human compared to the zombie skin she wore the night before. The double gates were opened and the man moved his parked truck, outside our door, to the street. He had his grandchild with him, which caused Diana to coo with the baby. She has a way with people that I really love. Babies are a universal talking point. You can even break the ice with a Republican simply by talking baby talk. (Reread what I just wrote, it may have more than one meaning.)

The woman offered to have her husband drive us to the microbus station. We accepted if she would call the taxi driver from the night before and let him know. He didn't answer his phone so we let the appointment stand. Diana made points again with these people by insisting we had to let the other man know. This is what I like about her too. Outside the second gate on the street two young men sat talking to the heavy grandfather. The baby had been passed to grandmother. I went out and sat with the three men and started by asking whom the motorcycle mechanic was. It belonged to the son. I told them about my

Honda back in New York and we passed the time with small talk about motorcycles. The son had once been into racing, but he didn't much care about it anymore. The fact that I was speaking Spanish seemed to make us all feel equalized. I felt at first these people weren't shy so much as respecting that we might want to be left alone. Diana made it clear we were interested in who they were, even if we were just passing through.

The taxi driver, whose name was Oscar, arrived exactly at nine o'clock. I had been telling Diana about the microbus station and she asked Oscar to help us get into the bus. When we arrived he went to one bus for help and two men came over to help us with our bags. They loaded the duffel bags onto the top of the microbus and the other two bags were put on the console between the driver and the front seat. I had paid Oscar before we left the car. In less than a minute a smooth transition took place, we were in the safety of the small bus. The year before it was total chaos. My bags went two separate directions! We waited ten minutes as people selling food came up and asked us if we wanted to buy.

I had a better view of the city of Managua this time, both in the van and my impression. Big pink signs of Daniel Ortega were at the traffic circles saying the future was promising or something like that. The international corporations seem to be taking hold and money is coming into the country through investments. It's like San Salvador in the sense that there was an obvious safe zone where big money has police protection. A modern city with shopping malls is beginning to emerge. What a shame Ronald Reagan couldn't see the way things are going in a Socialist nation he fought against. Sorry Ronnie, the Sandinistas won. I felt even back then that the people would always rise above tyranny. The people of this country are its best asset. There is a spirit alive in Nicaragua.

We passed through the market town of Masaya, or at least on the highway outside the city, and within an hour pulled into Granada. We passed the restaurant where I met a woman named Ruth, who lived in the Bronx, and I waved at her. She waved back. I knew where to exit and asked the driver to let us off when we entered the center of town. He pulled around a corner, stopped, the jockey handed me the bags from the roof, and we were at our hotel in two minutes. This was done with a minimum of stress. The desk clerk was new at Amigos, but no matter, we had the same room I'd been in the year before, upstairs where the breeze is better at night. I said hello to the owner, who recognized me. She wears a brown wig with lots of gray hair showing underneath. She also wears dark, thick glasses. I can never remember her name. In our room we ate a quick lunch and went straight to the central park. We sat and drank tamarindo juice with lots of ice. I recall being astonished at how a simple drink can cool the body so well. I was totally refreshed.

It wasn't long before we walk toward where my artist friend lives; I had painted his portrait the year before. The tourists' zone with restaurants and shops ran for a few blocks along our stroll. The remainder of buildings down to the water is residences. We walked through the tourists' zone, went into an art gallery, and looked at etchings and paintings.

Our next stop was to see the artist Pedro Vargas Mena. A dog barked at us as we stood near a barred window. Inside I could see Pedro walking toward the door, he smiled and waved hello. He and Diana did most of the conversing. He explained to Diana how Granada had been a major transit city in Central America until three tragic events practically demolished it. The Spaniards came first, then pirates, and then the American William Walker. This was a man who wanted to start a new country in the 1800's, that is start a country by force with the gun. He was a self-appointed President for a period of time in 1856, until Honduras and other Central American countries ousted him. He did his devastation in Northern Costa Rica as well. Unlike Antigua being destroyed by natural causes, Granada has suffered due to human ambition.

The history of William Walker is something I'd never heard in my history classes in school. I began to hear about this lunatic American from Jose years before on my first visits to Costa Rica. At first I rejected this as some convoluted folk tale passed down; not believing such a tyrant was so vacant from my history lesson. This is a strange sad, chapter of the history here that makes me wonder why, after so much devastation, these people still admire the United States. I have heard how William Walker plundered these two countries and burned them to the ground. I've always heard about pirates like John Morgan, but this was in the late 1800's, much later.

I didn't know if we were interrupting Pedro by coming unannounced so I suggested we come back tomorrow in the afternoon. He told us he had a good year, had been very busy, and was working at restorations and new projects for wealthy homeowners. Some of the art he had shown me the years before was on display in the major hotel. He invited us to go see the show, explaining further that his home was being renovated and the hotel owner had offered to display his personal works during the renovation for safe storage. We walked a distance of two buildings toward the center of town and entered a very nice hotel, the Grande Plaza Hotel. I asked the price of a room out of curiosity, sixty a night for a back room.

A slow walk to the shore of Lake Nicaragua followed. A group of people was taking a family portrait so I volunteered to take their picture with their camera. We met a firefighter from Florida who was visiting his relatives in Nicaragua. The man seemed unfriendly at first but lightened up as we all began to speak in Spanish. He has been tainted by living in the USA and had a sight defensive posture that soon came down as we proved to be aimless and just making small talk. He was telling us he planned to retire in his home country after twenty years of service with the fire department. We asked the firefighter about a boat ride and he pointed us to two men who had asked him if he wanted to hire a boat.

I had less than twenty dollars, maybe seventeen, and showed the boatman I didn't have the full twenty as we inquired. He took all our money except some small change. Four of us got into a white car and the driver took us to a huge tree where several men lay in hammocks under the shade. This was a couple of miles into the park that runs along the lakes' edge, much further than I had walked the year before. The biggest man introduced us to his father who came up to greet us.

All this time I'm assuming one of the three men would be our boat captain. I asked for a picture of the father and son, the taxi driver disappeared, and a new man came up and took us to his boat.

It was a long thin boat with a row of seats on both sides of the boat. The dock was nothing more than two planks of wood, but surprisingly strong. I tested my footing to make sure. The captain helped us board by leaning one foot on the dock, giving us his hand, and another foot on the boat. We were set. I took off my shirt and sat in the shade of a canvas that covered the sky; Diana sat behind me and began to speak with the friendly man. We were the only passengers. I saw no one pay anyone; this was a community of men who all worked together, and everyone got a cut. They must have been Socialists. I think the big guy got the largest cut for finding the customers, so maybe they were Capitalists.

The captain begins by explaining we were about to enter an archipelago that was formed five hundred years earlier when the volcano outside of Granada erupted, spewing rock and lava all the way to the lake some five miles away. What I thought would be a nature tour by boat soon became quite the opposite. Past the first small island we were shown a mansion owned by the local beer company's founder. He had his own island. This was followed by at least thirty small islands with rich people's mansions. "This guy is an American, this guy is a rich German architect, and another guy owns this company and bought his island for thirty thousand dollars back in the 1960." It went on and on.

We did get some natural flavor when the captain pulled up to a small island where five or six monkeys were hanging by their tails or running to greet the boat. This "monkey island" was a favorite of the tourists who kept the monkeys well fed. The island was too small for them to build their mansion so they were stuck in the trees. Besides, the tourist only gave them food, but no money for building an exclusive mansion. We saw some Ibis birds and Storks. I thought I saw an alligator but was corrected, as there were none in these waters. My imagination was starved for nature, not rich folk's toys.

The boatman was a delight and Diana and he spoke the entire time. I got a few questions in here and there. He then asked our permission to pick up two other passengers, which I thought was so polite. We pulled up to one of the few, abandoned islands and I jumped onto the dock to help with the mooring. A young couple had been standing and kissing on the shore. This continued all the way back to the main dock. They were oblivious to our presence and would have gone much further with their passion had we not come to a point where they had to disembark. I didn't ask what else happened on that empty island. In nine months there may be an answer.

We said thank you to the elderly captain and walked back to the road. The boatman had pointed to the sky and said it was going to rain. We could see the darkening sky and began to walk quickly. I knew we would be drenched in a few minutes so I stopped a taxi driver who was passing. I asked him if he would consider taking us as far as my loose change. He looked at the money; it was a fraction of his usual fare. He paused and said get in. He could see that it was starting to sprinkle on his cab window. Diana told me this would never happen had I suggested my plan to her. Human kindness proved me correct. He drove us as the rain increased, to the corner near Pedro's house. I knew we could take shelter in the hotel, but we pushed on toward the middle of the tourists' street. Then the sky broke and in a burst of lightning a real downpour began. We ducked into a shop where a man sat at a desk selling rare stones; the rest of the shop had tourists' trinkets.

The shop proved to be an interesting stopping point. We had no money but we found some natural wooden bowels that had knots and exposed grain. We liked these assortments of sizes and shapes. It was a find. We needed money, but would come back another day. Our return to the hotel for the bankcards was inevitable. Cash is our lifeblood. A quick visit to the room, a quick visit to the bank machine, and a long rest at the park for a second drink of tamarindo was well deserved. The same woman as in the morning with her daughter moved away from their seats at a table and offered us a place to sit. I seldom take out large amounts of cash in foreign countries. It is wiser to run out of money than to be a target for a thief. There are always plenty of ATM's.

In the central park one side is for tourists sales where stuffed turtles and frogs stand in stiff, awkward positions. This is something unique to the tourist trade of Nicaragua. I have seen this once in Costa Rica and find it very strange. Who would want a stiff turtle standing at a little bar, posed to take a drink? Some are wrestling, dancing, or driving cars. It's pretty strange. I remember the frogs from last year, but this year they must have legalized the turtles and lizards to be stuffed. This is a project for PETA.

We had no food so we began to walk towards the market. Like a Nicaraguan we bought an entire dinner by drifting and looking at what seemed interesting. Eggs were first, then cheese, bread, and avocado. We satisfied our hunger and ended the day with a cold shower in the hotel. I was dreading unheated water, but it was lovely and refreshing. So too, was the breeze on the balcony. We had the place to ourselves. The next room was empty and the key was in the door. I helped myself to the electric outlets and extra fan for the night. No one cared. I sat on a low seat and typed, falling asleep to join Diana who had already dozed off.

Day Two: Masaya.

> The rooster stands on the crest of a roof;
> he calls all to join the day
> The sleeping eye is resting no more;
> for the cock has something to say.

And thus we began this day. On a roof a few yards away from our room a rooster was crowing well before dawn. We had a hot restless night of waking and turning, until we both gave up when the rooster began his calls. The smell of onions and beans was cooking in the hotel's kitchen. I went down stairs to get some ice for our special drink and said good morning to the cook and owner. It was something like six in the morning. The cook didn't recognize me at first, but when I asked, she did. They see a stream of travelers, faces blur into faces, then memory kicks in if you stop and show them they are important to you. It has nothing to do with me.

I asked Diana what she thought of Nicaragua; she said the people were nice. It was the same thing I felt about being here when I arrived. I feel safe in Granada. Not so much so in the capitol, Managua. We have met other travelers who say the people here are much nicer than those in Honduras. Yeah, yeah, it's not wise to generalize but we noticed many times the attitudes in Honduras were cloaked with a grudge. I think this is due to the political oppression of a government and people who have not been liberated yet. Nicaragua and El Salvador both had their revolutions. Honduras has remained in the grip of a military that runs the show. Here in Nicaragua it is refreshing to see Daniel Ortega's smiling face on the political poster that are a kind of warm-pink, a softer, kinder version of the red and black symbol of the Sandinistas. Many businesses along the highway have the red and black flag proudly waving above their entrance. Homes do as well. The pink political signs show the words "Solidarity, and Socialism". The election is next year. Ortega is more open to corporate investment. He ain't no Castro! The country is, oddly, more corporate friendly (from what I saw) than Honduras appears to be. There's a kind of mixed blessing that comes with the 'Americanization" of these countries in Central America. In the USA we export economic stability through corporate growth, but with it we also kill traditional culture, or the way of life lived by peoples for many years. Big money has always greased the wheels. The church and military was the power in the past, but now replaced by corporations that peddle influence, some good, and some bad.

Our first objective in the morning was to find the watch repairman. I had passed him the first night and promised to return for Diana's watch to be fixed. It was too early for the watchman and we decided to not wait but head straight to Masaya to do our tourist shopping. The street leading to the bus terminal is what I refer to as 'desolation row'. It is the filthiest, smelliest, filled-with-derelicts that sit in open doors, place in Granada. In the mornings it is safe for a kitten, at night a rat would eat the kitten. We entered our bus and watched the people coming and going. Outside a woman made food at a stand, and a young girl sold nuts as daily life was in motion.

The ride to Masaya was very mellow; in fact everything seemed mellow in Nicaragua this time. The microbus driver, the big bus driver, and the traffic all seemed to be assigned to 'low'. The bus jockey was a very mellow guy as well, only he had the booming voice of an opera singer. I asked him if he likes to sing, and he said "no". When we arrived at the bus terminal, which was really a dirt field, Diana stated how smelly and dirty it seemed. Yes, but we had to get through the terminal (field) to get to the market. I knew exactly where to go and followed a side street to the backside of the market and passed the row of shoe repairmen I had talked to the year before. I went up to them and reintroduced myself. They remembered me. I asked for another photo and joked how one guy was ugly. They got a good laugh. I sat down as Diana chatted with a second fellow. The first man asked me why I remembered them. "Because I like people. I am a teacher and I like people". He asked me if I return again to please give him a copy of the pictures. I agreed. I've been thinking this would be a nice art project. To travel and return to places and present portraits as gifts. I thought about this the week we left New York, but was too busy to get the pictures made on time. I think about how people work day in and day out, their lives pass and no one notices them.

We began to shop and found a store where the woman wouldn't move her price lower, so we walked down the aisle and found a woman who lowered her price right away. We bought a few ceramic pieces. Around a corner we found another shop where we were also in sight of the first shop, we made another purchase. All this time the first shopkeeper was watching us. We walked by her and she seemed to be emotionless. I kept going, not wanting to rub her nose in anything. I wonder about personalities and what makes people more, or less, compromising. I think success in life has to do with being flexible. At one shop we bought two wooden bowls like the rustic bowels we had seen the day before in the tourist shop. We walked many rows seeking and asking for a particular name of wooden bowls. (I don't recall now.) We found a few shops with these pieces of wood; one woman told us we needed to go to the craftsmen market. We were in a cab within minutes. Before we left her stall we asked how much the taxi would cost. She said, "Twenty Cordova". The taxi driver said fifteen, but went down when we said ten. When we arrived the driver asked for twenty. I protested but his original price quote was for "each" passenger. This is something a traveler needs to be clear about. I had to compromise because I had misunderstood him in error.

The craftsmen market was the best tourist market. It was in what looked like a castle with tall walls and square turrets topping the medieval design. It was a landmark that had been converted into a market just for tourism. The size was a square city block. The prices weren't that much better, but the selection was. The first shop wouldn't bargain, so we moved on. Eventually I bought three more wooden bowls. My favorite is a small, round table piece that opens like a flower. It is about the size of a large glass. The irregular curves and reddish color of the wood make it unusual. The other bowls were more common in shape, but the exposed wood-grain and dark color adds to their character.

Inside the market was a large painted mural. I asked one of the shop keepers where the church and lake were depicted in the painting. These were all a part of the city of Masaya, in different locations around the city. I began to speculate about a taxi tour of these sights, but we asked where the central plaza was instead. We were told it was six blocks away, so off we went walking. We got lost, overshot the plaza, by a few blocks, but in the process found a bus stop that went right back to the first market where we would catch our bus home. I verified this information by asking a friendly beautician in her store. The bus ride would cost us three Cordova, not twenty like the taxi. The central plaza was nearby so onward we continued knowing how to return to the first market. I always like to be able to retrace my route, and know where to find a place.

The central plaza was unlike most where the park is surrounded by a street with stores. In this plaza the church was the dominant structure with a bandstand off to one side. Just before the plaza was a woman on the street selling cheese papusas. We bought two, and then went to sit and eat them on a park bench. I got up to take some pictures and asked a couple sitting on a bench if I could take their picture. They were selling cold drinks in plastic bags. We bought two; delicious, natural fruit drinks and sat down on the same park bench. The woman and man who sold us the drinks passed by and I asked if they were boyfriend and girlfriend. "No, we are married". I pointed to Diana and said so are we.

Inside the large church it was dark. People sat with their heads bowed in depression. The ceiling was made of a dark wood, which added to the heavy feeling. As we walked in, Diana heard some men yelling to each other about the "guy with the camera". So I took some pictures and made sure to keep the camera in the bag as we left the park. I found the church to be stark but the statues were very nice. One was of Saint Margaret. She was beautiful. Usually statues in Catholic Churches have Mary as pretty and simple, but this was a statue that showed a beautiful woman. On the altar, as in every church we saw in Nicaragua, the Virgin was front and center. Christ wasn't hanging on the cross in the middle of the altar. There were smaller crucifixions on the sides, but Mary was the focus of adoration. I liked this touch.

We found the bus stop and returned to the market to buy Diana two sleeveless blouses. The shopping didn't last much longer as we were tired and exhausted by the drain of heat and bargaining. The bus ride home recharged our energy and we were ready to find the bus station to buy our tickets for Costa Rica when we returned to Granada. The bus dropped us off a few blocks from the station, but we had been directed to the wrong bus company. Down the street we found two other bus companies. We passed Ruth's restaurant on the way and said we'd return for a lunch. She remembered me right away and let out a loud hello.

The bus company was the same one I'd used the year before, called Tica Bus. The man selling the tickets was the same man, and he remembered me as well. I noted to him that he was much thinner. He and Diana began a conversation about diet, and how the man had lost weight by cutting out starch and fats, eating fruits and vegetables, and no sugar. He was fifteen pound thinner in one year. We mixed business with the discussion to conclude they did not accept credit cards so we had to go back to the center of town to get the cash.

Ruth was serving other people so we sat down and were attended to by another woman who worked in the restaurant. After the meal, I went and sat with Ruth. She looked glum. "What's wrong?" I said. "Oh, you know, life", wasn't a real answer. "You seem down", I said in English. "Yeah, I guess". "How is your daughter back in New York?" "I spoke with her yesterday." We began small talk and eventually Diana joined us. What was troubling Ruth was the vandalism she had received toward her business. She didn't come out and tell me, she and Diana got into a conversation as I was looking at the traffic. She confided in Diana. People had vandalized her business at night. She stated they were jealous of her success, that she had worked hard to build up a clientele, and that someone had it in for her, maybe a neighboring restaurant. She didn't know whom. She went on to tell Diana that she had built up word-of-mouth advertising with the drivers of the city. She gave them good, lower, prices and her business had flourished. The number of cars and vans that came and went was a testament to her efforts, but she was in an emotional slump. I told her it was me who waved at her the day before from the microbus. "Oh that was you?" she returned. She was beginning to lighten up and smile more. We thanked her and left for the hotel, ATM, and walked back to the bus company to buy our tickets. This took forty minutes with one stop at a new church we had not seen before, along the way. The bus was sold out, so we had to stay an extra day. I wasn't upset at all. The other bus companies left at hours that were too early or too late to attract our business. I wanted to use the Tica Bus anyway.

After we set our date and time we walked toward the center of town to explore another church we'd not seen. The churches in Granada have one common similarity. They look like ruins on the outside, with no paint, but inside they are beautiful. (Only the grand, yellow Cathedral has paint on it.) The church had a faded orange exterior. This church again had the Virgin as the central figure, and to one side was a reproduction of the grotto at Lourdes, France. A woman came up to me and begged for money. This was the only time all summer someone had approached me inside a church. Diana liked the diorama of Lourdes, and I took pictures.

We were looking forward to a return visit with my artist friend and this time I brought all my current watercolor paintings to show Pedro. The five-minute walk to his house proved fruitless because he wasn't home. I asked the woman who answered the door if she was his wife. "No, she worked for him". He had been called out to do an art lesson with some school children and wouldn't be home until late. If we wanted we could return to see him before he left at eight the next morning. At least he had left word, but at eight we were sleeping in. We asked the woman to extend our regards and said another visit, another year perhaps.

The church across the street from Pedro's house became a shelter as the rain began to pour. There was a ceremony where the Eucharist was in a procession around the church under a canopy. We stayed and watched, and then a mass began. I am always interested to see the way different countries express spiritual rituals and how they differ in separate countries. After the mass we entered the street and it began to rain again. Under an awning we shared with an old man he struck up a conversation about his work, a massage professional. He was in his eighties and still working with his hands. He didn't solicit any business, he was just proud of what he did at his age. We all stood in a narrow dry patch as the rain splashed our feet. Fifteen minutes passed and so did the shower.

We slowly made our return to the central park, looking for another drink of tamarindo. It was too late. Our street side food vendors had closed for the day. The hotel kitchen was soon put to use where I shared the kitchen with a woman from France, a woman from Germany, and a woman from Slovakia. We all walked in and around each other trying to negotiate the sink and stove without infringing on anyone's space. I spoke with them on and off as Diana was on the computer/phone with her mother back in Colombia. We had called her from an international phone booth a few minutes before, asking her to turn on her computer so we could make the computer-to-computer call. I made spaghetti. The dining room was too full of hotel guests so I carried our dinner to the lobby where Diana was speaking to her mom.

Later I spoke at length with the woman from Slovakia. I had seen her from our first day there, but now had a chance to speak with her one-on-one as we cooked. Her boyfriend and she were riding bicycles from Mexico to Colombia (there is no direct road). They were writing a blog and gave me their web site; I gave them mine as well. Her English was perfect and she didn't sound European. This was one of their longest stay-over; usually they were on the road cycling a day after a stop. The project at hand was their travel blog and web site. Many times I would pass their room and the man would be typing at his computer. He is a techie and always engrossed in his computer. I know what that can be like. Whenever I walked by the room his head was bowing to the computer. He was like a monk! His name is Kybi.

The balcony was all ours for a second night so I left the door open and sat outside typing. We had switched to the room next door because it had a second bed and better, more electric outlets to charge my cameras. A cold shower was the remedy for such a long day. We slept in comfort and bliss, in separate beds because the heat was too much. The second fan was an extra luxury. I still needed an additional electric outlet so I went back to our first room and plugged the cameras in for charging. I need all my toys fully charged and ready for action. This is one of my nightly rituals.

Day Three: Market in Granada. The hostel (hotel) has a young boy that is the owner's grandson, or some kind of relative. He is a smiling, dark boy whose eyes and teeth beam from his face. He is eight or nine years old with the enthusiasm of a thirty year old. He is cleaning, sweeping, running towels, taking out the trash, and now when we returned from the morning market, he was shining boots out on the sidewalk. These are his father's shoes. The woman that owns "Amigo's" is in her late seventies and doesn't do anything but over-see the operations. This was her private house and now she runs an international guesthouse. We are staying on the second floor of a building in the back that was added on to the original house. We have been lucky in that no one has rented the room next to us for two days so far. It's like having a hotel suite. No one has checked our room; we asked to not clean the sheets every day. The added privacy allows us to leave our door open at night (Regardless of Diana swearing she saw someone walking by, but no way, the sound of anyone coming up the metal stairs is very obvious.) We can be nude in our room and no one can see us because the trees downstairs block any view. From our balcony we can see the far side of the house and lobby, except for the dining room. Most of the view is obstructed by palm leaves. No one has come up here to see the room except a couple that rejected staying in the room. I asked the desk clerk if the larger room up here was the same price. "Yes," she said. "Can we move?" I asked and she said, "Sure". Now we have separate beds and the body heat of my lovely wife is someone I'm suffering without for two nights.

This morning we woke at six, and my lovely wife, who was in a chipper mood, decided to share her rooster call with me while still asleep. We made our shakes and turned on the TV. Daniel Ortega was giving an address to the fire fighters, ambulance drivers, and police. He is much mellower than Chavez. The premise of the speech was 'Preparedness.' The last great earthquake to hit Nicaragua was when Samosa was the dictator. Ortega was saying he was moved to eradicate the dictatorship when he saw how poorly Samosa helped the victims of that earthquake. There were a few jabs at Colombia and the USA, but I do the same. I find him wiser and older, yet not arrogant. This country has improved due to his socialist's policies. If I encountered people being negative towards me because I am an American I might feel the revolution was a bad thing, but really the people have done nothing but show hospitality to us. The people of Nicaragua are special. They fought for their freedom against a tyrant and won. That victory has made them a better country all around.

On our walk to the market we passed the watch-repair man, he was on the opposite side of the street this time. He moves his tiny wooden shop (a box with table) into the shade, and when the sun changes, he switches sides in the afternoon. (He must be a socialist, playing both sides of the street like that.) We gave each other a greeting and asked him where to buy some large plastic bags. He directed us around the corner into the market. I love this dark market. It is mysterious and a little scary, but it is a fun place. Inside the woman selling bags didn't have the size we needed. In hand motions we gestured "bigger". She directed us back to the street and we found just what was needed. The two bags were fifty cents each. I can buy the same bag in the USA for one dollar. They are made in China. They have nice pictures of cities around the world, New York, Paris, etc. They are perfect for moving large amounts of cloths or ceramics wrapped in cloths. The weights of these bags are a fraction of any luggage.

We hadn't finished our appetite for the market yet, so we began to wander, all the while I was shooting photographs. Diana walked up to a woman making tortillas; she bought an arepa with cheese. They had a different name, "chechulilly", or something like that. They were with cheese and corn. The entire production was taking place before our eyes. One woman was husking the corn, another woman mashing and adding water, one shaping them, and a man cooking them in the back of the stall. Because we bought one I was allowed to photograph the entire process. They think I am a little stupid for taking pictures of something they take as so common and boring. As I'm scurrying around, looking for the best light and angle in low light, I was trying to avoid camera motion or blur. The workers were very open and tolerant with me. We continued on and I would ask various people for pictures, some accepted, some declined.

One man yelled for money because I was taking pictures. I said the vegetables were important; I wasn't shooting him in pictures. He began to laugh. He knew I wasn't threatening him in any way. His "fake attitude" melted away into a friendly encounter without any hassle. The streets were fun to walk around. As we walked we bought an avocado. The woman said 20 Cordova; I said ten and stuck to my price. She gave it to me for ten. The people here are like transparent beings. When the real price is doubled, they know I know. It's all done in a free exchange of business where part of the transaction needs that back and forth bargaining. If I buy something I always ask for a picture, rarely am I declined by anyone.

Inside the dark market we ran into the bus jockey from the bus to Masaya we had taken. (I had asked him if he liked to sing.) He was the heavy, shaved-head, jockey yelling, "Masaya, Masaya, Masaya". When I saw him I began to say, "Masaya, Masaya, Masaya". He laughed and shook my hand. Diana told him I was driving her crazy saying this all day. The day before when we entered the bus for our return to Granada, I did the same joke to the bus jockey. He got a good chuckle from my joke. Diana was saying I was being disrespectful, but he knew I was only joking. We get into these little tussles about how I get silly and interact with people. Humor is universal. It works better than money, or politeness, although both work, but humor is what people enjoy the most in life. I know I make my students and wife laugh all the time, or try to. The bus jockey had a freshly shaved face and head, and was looking much cleaner than the day before. His shirt was pressed and had a collar, the day before he wore a dirty t-shirt. We said good-bye because he had to go to work on the same bus we had taken the day before.

We needed shampoo and we were directed to a corner store. Who was there working behind the counter? The watch repairman's wife. She greeted us and we had a family reunion, all smiles, no fighting. She helped us get a cheaper shampoo, because our funds were almost used up. I want to keep a few Cordovas to buy a juice in the park later. I have set aside the exit tax, the taxi money in the morning, and spent money on buying lunch from a vendor on the street. I explained to the woman from whom we bought the cheaper product that I could get to the border without using the ATM. She allowed me to take her photograph. On the way back to the hotel I passed the watchman and showed him the photographs of his wife. We said perhaps our last good bye and now I am sitting on the balcony trying to catch up with the writing. For me the interaction with people is what makes the journey so special.

In Antigua, Guatemala, I gave up on writing every night. There was too much to do and see and I was beginning to feel like I was at work instead of enjoying every second of our travels. I was beginning to dread the evenings because of the two or three hour writing sessions. Last year I didn't have Diana with me and spent a lot of time alone. That was used to fill the time with writing.

Yesterday, we went into a church Diana had not yet seen. I had seen it many times last year, and it dawned on me she is experiencing this place for the first time and I know it already (or just a little bit). What came to my mind was how much fuller my days are, and fun, when I am with Diana. I like being with my wife. I enjoy her company. It sounds a little selfish, but I needed the companionship and made sure she was with me this year, employment, or no employment. I feel like I experience life deeper when I share it. Meanings and mentally stored events that come up in conversations take in a whole, deeper dimension. It is a subtle aspect of love that seems to be missed because so much emphasis is put on romantic love.

The age differences between us often come up. Many times this trip people have referred to me as Diana's father. She politely corrects them, they get embarrassed, and we become an anomaly. We don't fit into the typical framework of couples. In some ways this is strange. She could be young enough to be my child, yes, but she is also willing to live outside the usual framework and embrace our relationship. It puts us on display, but it also gives us a chance to make a statement about LOVE! Diana often refers to romantic love, wanting more romantic love, wanting to feel romantic. I lived through that when I was younger, and I think from my present vantage point (age), much of this is a mental state based on fantasy. I will ask Diana, what do you mean? What exactly do you want? Much of the time I get a "Well you know" answer when I don't know. I want specifics and get this "answer" that I should know the answer. This is the dance of love. The "romantic stuff" is illusion. I'm not trying to be cynical. I try to please her and think most of the time she isn't aware of how much I'm trying. I think I'm working the magic in a more real way that will cause her to appreciate me in a deeper way as she reflects on her time traveling. If all I did was bring her flowers she would be romantically bored, yet she asks, or dreams of receiving flowers every day.

As I sit on the balcony writing, the young boy that works here has been sweeping all the debris off the roof. He is ten or maybe eight years old, but works unlike anyone I've seen. I love this kid! I called him over during a short break and gave him a glass of cold water. He is all smiles. What a gem. He is the cousin of the cook's daughter, or something like that. He may be the owner's grandchild. I just know he works more than the adults here. He is a dynamo.

Diana is suffering from acid reflux. We went out to do some exploring and sat in the park, then moved a block away in a direction we had not been before. In a small plot of earth Diana vomited. She let the banana she had eaten go. "I can't walk, I'm sick." We agreed to meet up later and she went back to the hotel. I was alone with no plan and no one to be with, so I slipped into the past and retraced a small path I had walked the year before.

I first walked in a new neighborhood across a river by a bridge, then back to a street that went to the Museum Of Archeology. I paid and re-entered my solo life. The stone figures I had seen the year before seemed much easier to understand and interpret. My tour guide in Copan had shown me what to look for. I photographed the statues as a black bird sat high on a ledge with his mouth open. It was so hot he didn't want to fly and allowed me to walk within a few feet, still panting and cooling in the shade. I passed a couple that seemed to be at odds with each other. I could sense the woman was tired of being with the same guy. I said hello, he replied. The air was thick between them. It was a strange observation. Maybe if I were with Diana I might not have noticed this.

The traditional hut I had sat in the year before was gone. I sat in a cool place the year before listening to some ceramic chimes. This time I sat inside the courtyard on a rocking chair munching on some peanuts I found in my backpack.

The couple passed me again, still silent. I sat and pondered reincarnation, wondering if a person who retraced his or her own steps invented reincarnation. The tall palms and soft, hot breeze was making me sleepy. I enjoyed this place. I began to imagine what the courtyard would be like, to be imprisoned in such a lovely setting. If I were held captive in such a place I would make dirt sculptures. To keep the rain from destroying the sculptures I would build them under the awnings of the courtyard. I envisioned moving the earth to the tile floors while thinking if I wanted, I could dig a hole and tunnel under the roots of the palms and escape the courtyard. But this would be a prison I did not want to leave. The palm trees held me like a magnet. I would stay there and learn Spanish from the guards. I would not leave but become a monk and dedicate myself to keeping the trees alive. I was in a kind of half sleep enjoying my own thoughts.

Maybe all this daydreaming came from a conversation I had with Art, a Polish man staying in the hotel. He wants to open a language school and teach English based on bible stories. He is a Christian, but he doesn't like the label. He quoted the bible and said that no one can find God, but only through Jesus Christ. I told him I didn't need the bible, that I had God within me. I could tell this was a big challenge for him. He struck me as a man who thought he knew all the answers because he had read them in the bible. He was quoting scriptures and missing the point behind the scriptures. He just rattled off passages from rote memory. It was like talking to a wall. I believe God wants us to be free, not imprison ourselves with words. I think God even wants us to lose the bible stuff. I noted three times in our conversation Art stopped me with a "No, that's not so, because in the bible it says....etc." I called him on that. I told him I don't think Jesus wants us to be proselytized by others, or corrected into submission. The minute someone tries to put a head-trip on me I am sure he or she knows nothing about God. My gut tells me someone wants to control someone else when that kind of narrow interpretation of God's love is at hand.

I don't even care if a person is an atheist. It shows me that person has at least pondered this question better than those who just accept what they are told to believe. It is a very subtle nuance to know if a person is open to others or just trying to fit them into a category for judgment. When Art told me Christ didn't say anything about not being a soldier, and not killing others in war, he really lost me. I told him I was a pacifist and changed the subject to legal issues about Costa Rica. That went much better. I gave him the name of my lawyer in Costa Rica. If he opens his school, and I wish him the best, he will need a good lawyer.

I walked through the museum some more and passed the couple again. "Where are you from?" I asked. "Italy," the male responded. "I know Italy. I've been there five times." We suddenly switched from Spanish to English when I said I was American. "My wife is from Colombia, but she is in the hotel, sick." "My wife is sick too," was his response. I had a good laugh and confirmed that they were indeed having a domestic scrap. "My wife and I have many things that are different about each other." I said, and continued, "That is the dance of love that brings us together and apart." They knew I knew and I took whatever it was with me when I left the room, saying, "chow".

I took photographs of a modern art exhibit in the first courtyard. The paintings were of monk-like figures floating in a golden space. It reminded me of the Buddha because the figures were in long saffron robes and had shaved heads. They also had child-like features, some the size of small children or teenagers. It was very dreamy. I walked home to see my wife after stopping to buy a drink of tamarindo from the lady in the park. At home I ate lunch but Diana was too sick to eat. She sat before the fan watching TV.

The afternoon tedium gave way to a need to explore. I made a phone call to Diana's uncle and my sister on the computer. I received an email from Julio in Guatemala and sent back a thank you for everything. Diana and I set out to make art and paint the big yellow church across from the central plaza. We walked past the woman that sold us the drinks before, where I had my drink of juice without Diana earlier, and promised her we'd return. We went to the far side of the park, crossed the street, and sat on the bottom step of a corner building. I pulled out the paints. The yellow Cathedral was calling me, asking for a portrait.

A corner on the far side of the park served as the perfect vantage point. I sat on the step of a long row of buildings, bending down, with the paper and paints on the ground. Diana sat next to me embroidering her Nativity scene. A tour bus drove by and suddenly my private moment of creativity was a spectacle. I was being photographed. People walked by and were curious, then a few children came up and Diana began to speak with them. They asked me how to paint, then if they could also paint. They were a boy and girl, around seven and ten. I gave them two sheets of paper and we all painted on the ground. The girl painted her house and the boy painted a volcano. We all worked on art for a good hour until it was getting late and time to return to the hotel. I would periodically take breaks and walk around the central park looking for the two men I'd spent time visiting with last year. The children playfully painted their dreams.

Art is such a universal language even a child can speak it. When people see an artist at work they have an instant bond towards him or her. We define ourselves through our cultures where art is the ultimate expression. It is a natural curiosity and almost everyone is attracted to it. Yet, how much art education has been cut from school budgets? The most primitive, basic form of self-expression is being left out of children's development. I believe even the briefest encounter with these willing children on the street will have a lasting, life long, impression. It's like planting little creative seeds that all children desire. It is so healthy that our world would be much better served if art were allowed to flourish in the young. This is not just magical, it is spiritual.

It was when we were making our last pass through the park and leaving that I found my elderly friend from the year before, whose ear was bandaged up. He was sitting between two men I did not know. He knew me right away. I sat with my old friend and Diana took our picture. Another man I met before, who was a schoolteacher, hadn't come to the park that day. We all looked for him. Diana asked my elderly friend how he had lost a large part of his ear. It was from a bee sting. Almost a third of his ear had to be removed from the infection. We sat and told him about our travels and the other two men joined in the conversation. The old man joked with me that I should have a baby with Diana. This happens to us all the time. Someone wants to know how many children, or why none, all a part of brief conversations. By this hour it was getting dark so we said our salutations and walked past the woman who sold us the tamarindo drinks, also saying good-bye. She was closing up for the day.

The street that leads to our hotel has a papusa stand. The woman recognized me from the year before, and she and Diana had a long conversation about making food as I went in the store and paid the husband. There were no lights. I asked why, and he explained that he had problems with the circuits. I explained that I had eaten at his wife's stand the year before and knew he was from El Salvador, where they make papusas. His face lights up because I had remembered such details. The shop was completely different. This time he was the owner and the tables had all been rearranged to fit in more people. They were doing a thriving business based on the papusas sales. The husband joined Diana and I on the sidewalk where the man's wife was feverishly cooking her orders and talking with us. Just as the year before, a line was beginning to form as people stood and waited, as others sat inside the dark shop and ate. The novelty of a food from El Salvador had spread, and business was very good. She had a monopoly on this popular food.

It was our last night in Granada. We walked back to the hotel and sat on the balcony and ate at the small table. No one had rented the room next to ours for three days. We used the extra room at will. Diana would go in and use the TV, I would charge my camera batteries, and use the fan in our room. The laundry we had left out had been rained on but someone was kind enough to take it down for us. In the process my favorite cargo, travel paints disappeared. I think it was a mistake. The lines were all full with other people cloths as well, so to grab something by mistake would be easy. In my comings and goings I met the male partner of the Slovakian woman who was bicycling through Central America. He started talking about Europe; he lives in Prague. We ended up talking computers and web building, a passion we both share. He gave me some ideas about using Java script on my own web site. This is how I learn. He works as a web builder in Prague because the pay is so much better than his home country. Kybi is a longhaired bearded, hippie-like traveler with a warm smile and open personality. I have his web address but haven't looked it up yet.

It was late by the time we lay down to sleep. The electricity had gone out twice, but only for five minutes at a time. The entire city went into a blackout. We had everything packed for Costa Rica and the bus in the morning. I put a bag outside the door, but Diana protested and brought it back in. It was just as well because a huge thunderstorm passed in the middle of the night. I loved it, woke to smile, listen for a while, and drift back to sleep. Diana said she didn't sleep well at all. The storm kept her awake far after it had already passed. Thus is one of the ways I differ from my Colombian wife.

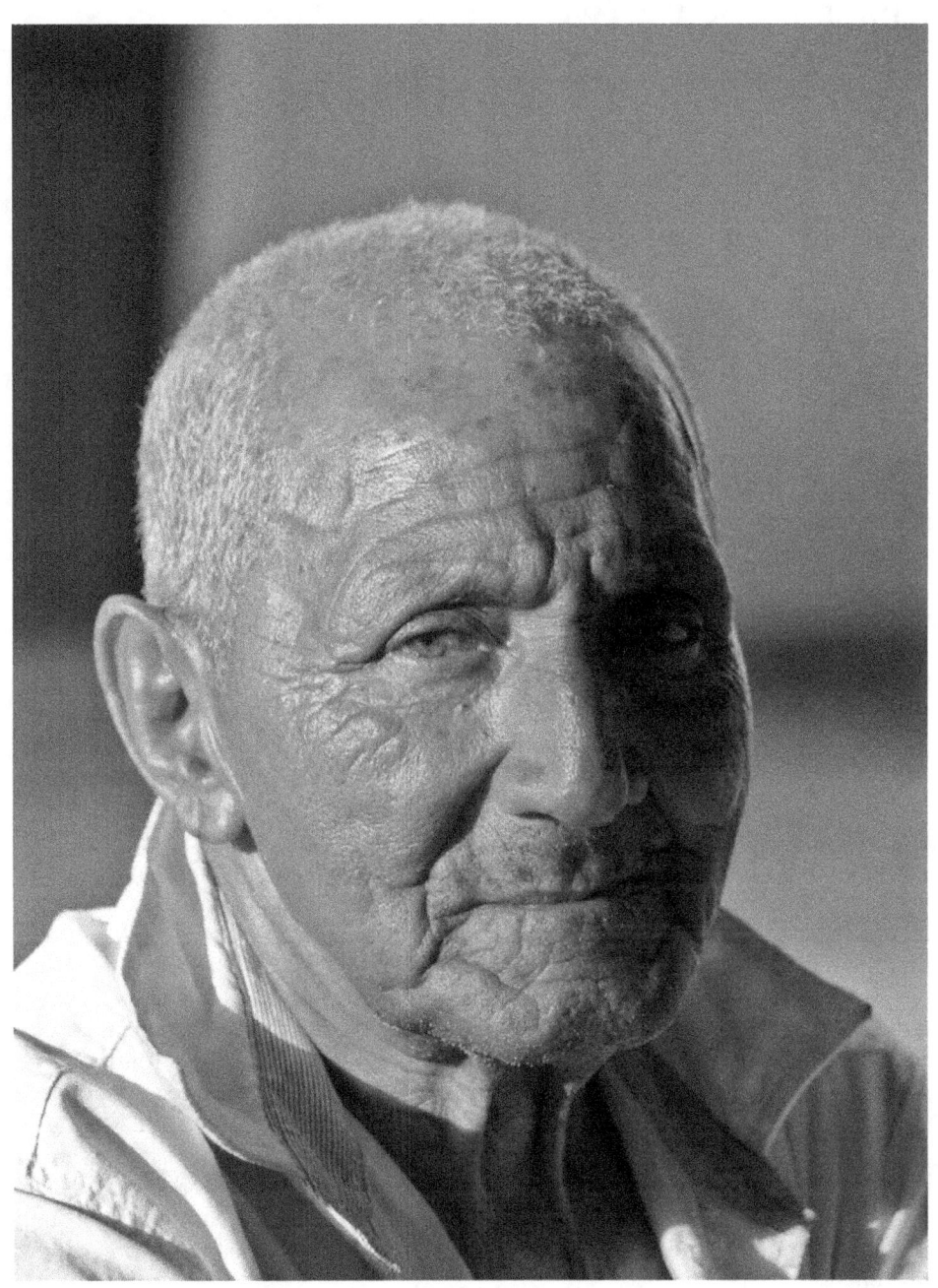

Chapter Twenty Two
Costa Rica

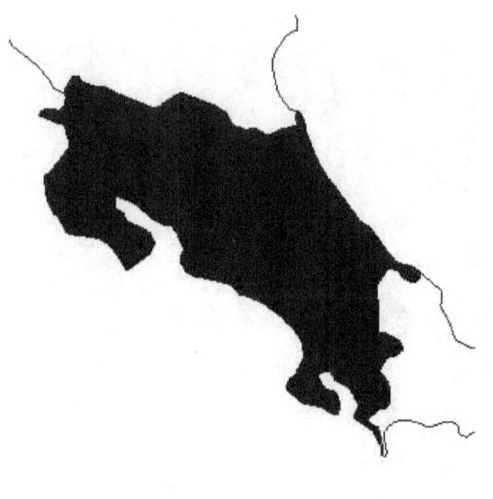

Day One: As much as I love to sleep I too often have trouble sleeping, but it comes in the mornings when I wake up early and can't go back to sleep. So was the case the day we left Granada, Nicaragua. I was up before the rooster, putting a few things into our luggage when I heard his call. Diana looked out the window and saw the rooster standing at crest of the house next door. He was closer than the mornings before. It was a perfect picture. I switched the lens and got out my telephoto lens and shot off a few pictures, making sure the low light would capture the image without camera motion. I leaned the camera on a pole to make the camera stationary.

We had reserved a taxi to the bus station, but the driver never showed up. I thought it was silly to do this anyway. If the man slept in for my small fare I wouldn't hold it against him. I walked to the corner and found a taxi instantly pointing him to the hotel where Diana stood at the door with our bags. The bus station was quiet, many people stood waiting, but no one was conversing. I walked around, looked at the horse drawn carts and the morning's activities. As I crossed the street and began a conversation with a woman sitting in her doorway the bus pulled up. Diana called me back across the street. It was much cooler than the year before, even cooler than the last few mornings. The bus driver handed us four stubs with numbers as we loaded the luggage under the bus. I told him the big plastic bag was ceramics so he placed it on top of all the others.

The ride to the border was an hour plus. It was a bumpy, smelly event. I didn't type because the last two seats were the ones that took motion the most. We had no other options but to sit next to the toilet across the aisle from me. The second I sat down I knew that smell. But I was not sure where I recognized that smell from. It was the toilet smell, yes, then, it hit me. Porta Potty! It was Porta Potty smell - the putrid blue stuff that tries to mask shit smell less than what is really is. My only consolation was that the air conditioner was working well. The bouncing and smell was the difficult part, but hey, we had already been through this ordeal and it was our last stretch of journey. We had the last two seats sold on that bus!

As we boarded the bus I passed a longhaired, bearded, wild-eyed man who was wearing a Jimi Hendrix t-shirt. I noted that I saw the same t-shirt on a man in Honduras. "That's where I got it. In La Ceiba," the young man returned in conversation and I'm thinking to myself, wouldn't it be strange if he robbed the man I saw wearing the t-shirt? This is my mind unrestricted. The man struck me as a bit wild but I like unconventional people. He treated me to conversation even though we were two isles apart. He would crank his neck around and tell me where he had visited. He had been to the same countries as us. He said he was glad to speak English, knew very little Spanish and was from southern Italy. I would have never guessed by the way he was loud and seemingly unashamed of his poor personal hygiene. (Just jokes, Italians please get over it.)

About the time I was winding down conversation with the Italian lad, the bus attendant came up and asked Diana and I if we were getting off at Liberia. "Yes, we are." He goes into a long conversation with Diana that I was getting bits and pieces of. A storm, a bridge, traffic, I could fit together, but the rest of the conversation went too fast. I stopped Diana and asked. "The major bridge to San Jose is out, and traffic must be stopped", she reported. But what does that have to do with us; we are getting off in Liberia (northern Costa Rica)"? "He says we have to leave the bus at the border and get a local bus to Liberia". "But there is only one road to Liberia, local and international buses have to use the same road," I insisted. The attendant was leaving and I asked him to repeat this to Diana. Yes, we would have to get off at the border. I took out my Lonely Planet and showed Diana the highway maps of Costa Rica. "I don't know", was all she could say, but there was clearly only one highway. I got miffed and said we paid for a ticket to Liberia, and would stay on this bus until Liberia. Any change was the bus company's responsibility. (However, this is a very American point of view and total nonsense when it comes to being in a foreign country.)

We were approaching the border and the same attendant came up with another second attendant passing out customs forms. He told us we needed an airline ticket to enter Costa Rica. "What? We don't use airline tickets anymore". All I had was an email, but it was way under the bus somewhere in our bags. I had been through the border the year before and no such request was stated. This guy was double bad news. I had enough exit stamps from Costa Rica in my passport to put up a good argument, so I wasn't about to go rummaging through my bags to locate an email. We had to go through the Nicaraguan border control side first anyway. I tried to be cool-headed, but this was all getting very weird.

On the Nicaraguan side of the border the bus passengers filed out of the bus. I knew the place so I took Diana straight to the restrooms. She needed money for the restroom and I forked over a few extra Cordova I had left. The female restroom attendant looked at me after I left the restroom. I had already used the restroom and wasn't about to pay her again. She knew it. I think when someone needs toilet paper they make him or her pay, or you can bring your own. As Diana went inside I walked over to a moneychanger sitting on a low wall and got twenty dollars' worth of Costa Rican money (Colons). I also got rid of all my Cordova. We sat on the edge of a high sidewalk. The man was not the least bit pushy or yelling in my face. Why did they have to be that way in Guatemala?

I met a couple from Minnesota and told them I was a big Garrison Keller fan (He is a radio host of a show called a Prairie Home Companion.). I made a joke about Republicans and they laughed. "I know you are Democrats because you laughed!" They were. Obama, health care, socialism, and all that stuff came up. I was in blessed company. In the midst of all the conversation a man selling belts had approached Diana and she asked a price for a black belt. The man said six dollars, I said four. This went back and forth. He knew I would not budge, but he didn't acknowledge this, or the sale. Instead he takes out his tools and cuts the belt, shortening it for Diana. I am sitting watching this, wondering if he was about to try and make a scene for cutting off the belt and then selling it to me. He handed me the belt. I said four, and he shook his head yes. It was strange. There was no real agreement made; he just went ahead, cut the belt and handed it over. I knew I was getting punchy; it is stressful to travel through borders. We still had the Costa Rican side to deal with.

Soon an agent came over with a long group of passports tucked from his elbow to his wrist. He called out the names and everyone entered the bus. Diana was third or fourth to be called. I was second to last. The Italian man spoke to us again and he said he had no airline ticket to leave Costa Rica because he was going to Panama. The same was true for a group of three women from Uruguay. It dawned on me that many people pass through Costa Rica and never have plane tickets. They don't even use plane tickets that much. Five minutes later we drove through the border and exited the bus. We stood in a long line that circle around the building. There were three times as many people as the year before and that crossing was insane. The same-armed guard at the door was letting small groups enter another line inside the air-conditioned room.

Inside I stood in one line and Diana in another until we decided which line was moving faster. I handed in both passports together anticipating an argument about an airline ticket. In two seconds our passports were stamped and handed back to us. Thank you was all the woman said. We shrugged our shoulder and smiled at each other, not saying a word. We felt as if we had just slipped into the border to Red China posing as a Taiwan citizens.

As we waited outside a young woman next to us began to go into a panic. I don't know why I was looking at her, but that she was beautiful as she began to make contortions with her face. "What's wrong?" I asked in English. Diana turned and the woman responded in Spanish. She had lost her passport. I felt for our passports, and they were there, but this poor woman was grief stricken. She was going through everything in her hands. She began to cry. A friend with her suggested she look in her bags that were set on the customs inspection bench. A minute later she returned with a big smile. It was indeed in her other bag. There was a ripple of joy that went through all of us waiting and looking on. She turned to me, and as quick as the panic had come she began to speak calmly. "Where are you from?" she said in English. We had a short conversation in Spanish, until we were told to open our bags.

We were outside the same insane line now waiting at a long, low row of benches as our suitcases were taken out, (by ourselves from the bus) and placed for inspection. Three young aggressive looking customs agents looked through everyone's bags. We were on the second cycle of passengers and had to wait in a line while the first set of inspections took place. When the female agent came to my bag she looked through it. When she got to the big plastic bag of wood and ceramics she only lifted the top cloths and moved on to my box. She did the same, only doing a slight inspection. All I said was, "They are fabrics from Guatemala". I looked her in the eyes and told the truth. This was a brief, sweet glance where nothing spectacular was happening. We reloaded the bags and I went up to the bus driver. "What about the bus not going to Liberia?" Diana chimed in. The bus driver ultimately came down to give a funny answer. He responded the attendant was "from Colombia and was crazy". (He knew Diana was Colombian and they had a brief conversation while we were waiting.) We all began to laugh. The attendant over heard this and shook his head, walking away in disgust. He didn't know what he was talking about. I don't think this was some kind of intentional plot to subvert information; he just didn't have real information. He may have never worked on that route before. I was right about the only road into Costa Rica. That was the end of our conflict that never happened. The second inspection stop, where I had been questioned and brought out of the bus the year before, never happened either.

At the border the Italian man did have some trouble getting through. He was in the immigration office a long, long time. It was just before the customs inspection, which we waited forty-five minutes to get. The Italian left the office shaking his head. "Everything ok?" I asked. He made a hand gesture to the effect that it was so-so. He had permission to enter Costa Rica but he had to do some heavy talking and show an email with an airline confirmation. As we stood in the first line he was behind us. We were exchanging stories about crossing borders. We both agreed that Guatemala was the worst, maybe Costa Rica, but we hadn't finished yet. We compared Belize, Honduras, and Guatemala when he explained that he had been detained in Guatemala. "Why?' I asked. "They took my gun away", he said. I asked, "your what?" and he said, "My gun. I bought a gun in Honduras because I felt so unsafe in San Pedro Sula. They wouldn't let me keep it in Guatemala." The nerve, I'm thinking, those silly border agents wouldn't let him keep his firearm. I'm also thinking that meant he was able to smuggle it into Belize, or it would have been taken away. I remarked, "did you show them, did they ask?'" "No, they found it when they searched my bag," He replied. I felt a cold chill despite the hundred-degree heat we were standing in. The conversation ended and I instinctively put some distance between us. He seemed to attract trouble and I wasn't into bonding any more. Oddly enough I was in the bus long before him, pretending I never knew the guy.

After what seemed like more than an hour, we exited the bus onto a highway in Liberia where two taxi drivers asked me if I needed a cab. I was trying to decide which of the two I trusted, but one seemed to magically whisk us away to the local bus station without stress. Before I could say good-bye to the crazy Italian or couple from Minnesota we were gone as the bus pulled away. The border crossing had taken almost three hours; the taxi ride took five minutes. Things were certainly looking up.

I bought the tickets while Diana stood by the curb to watch the bags, all six of them by now. (We started with four, including the backpacks.) We then moved to a line and stood waiting for the bus. It was due in half an hour. A man in front of me looked like someone I could get some information from so I asked him if he knew the hotels in Tamarindo, our next stay-over. He didn't, but his wife would be joining him in a few minutes and she would know. Diana was off buying us something to eat and returned to hand me a greasy chicken empanada. I was starved, so I ate it but was still hungry. Diana was too, so she went off to buy something else. "Get something healthy, like fruit," I said. She came back with a buttery chicken croissant. It had more calories than the empanada. The man in the line asked me what I did as a profession. "A teacher," I said, and he replied, "I am too", he said, as he vigorously shook my hand.

We started to talk shop. He was working in a local school, was Costa Rican, spoke no English, but was totally delightful to be waiting with us. His wife came and he introduced me. Diana had to find a bathroom so I had the five bags with me when the line suddenly moved. The bus had arrived and I was trying to wheel everything to keep up with the line. A woman helped me for a moment, and then Diana arrived. By now we were at the back of the line and I was feeling that there was some injustice at play as all the people rushed past me in the line to the bus. I walked to the front of the line like I owned it and no one said anything.

At the door of the bus another couple was stalled. They had bags and were traveling with luggage as well. All four of us were ordered to the outside and back off the bus with our large bags. The stranger with luggage helped me and I helped him. The luggage was put between the two back seats and our box and bags were placed under the seat. The driver took my tickets and walked to the front of the bus to attend to the other passengers boarding. He came back a minute later and ordered the other travelers who had luggage to sit with their bags. They had moved a few seats forward. The man with the luggage seemed to indicate it was all right, but the attendant made them move a few seats back to be with their bags. The attendant then charged us all an extra thousand Colons for the excess bags. The couple with bags sat across from us, up one row of seats. They were speaking French.

I noticed an instant change when we entered Costa Rica this time, the year before it wasn't as evident that the standard of living, size and conditions of the houses, and new cars on the road were signs of a better economy. I was on a major highway last year, but this year I was on a small road going to Tamarindo, an unknown beach to us. There were fewer people than Nicaragua, no apparent poverty, and everything had a recent coat of paint. I remember the first time I came to Costa Rica. I was thinking how poor it was, how dangerous it was, how I was on a real adventure, and wondered if I was going to get back to the States alive. It's funny what has happened to me since then. It feels safe, rich, industrious, and like home now. Yes the sidewalks are cracked and the roads don't have a curb, but I have seen this country rapidly move into change since my first visit some twelve years ago. After our travels to the other countries we feel very fortunate to be a part of this country and its people. It is the jewel of Central

America. I was "robbed" once in a bus station, because I let a man distract me as my backpack was lifted by a second man. Petty crime is the real offender in this country.

The bus was slow and tedious. The schoolteacher's wife sat with us for a while and Diana got the names of three hotels in Tamarindo. Somewhere along the ride the teacher and his wife left the bus unnoticed. More people left and the seat behind us were vacated, and then refilled by the other two travelers from France. "Where are you from?" I asked. "We are from France," the female answered. "Oh, we loved Paris, it was our favorite city," Diana answered. We started a casual conversation but it was all in Spanish. They were heading to Tamarindo as well, and asked if we knew of a hotel. At some point someone asked if they spoke English because their Spanish was weak. "Oh, we can speak English," they replied and introduced themselves as Tarek and Marie. The ice had been broken and we ventured into a lengthy conversation to pass the time. Twice Tarek asked me, "Do you eat ship?" "Do I what?" I asked, because I thought he was saying "shit." So I said, "No I don't eat shit and I don't eat red meat either" to which he said, 'NO, NO, not shit, ship" and began to make the sound of a lamb. I nodded and said, "Oh, sheep, we call it lamb." We got a good laugh and kept the momentum going with stories and funny tales about border crossings.

Somewhere in all the confusion of the bags, talking to Marie and Tarek, a new bus attendant entered the bus and asked us for our tickets. I didn't have them! I gave them to the first attendant. The young man believed me, but went to the bus driver to verify. I waved at him as if saying, yes, we have been here and we are not lying. That all passed, then we made a stop forty minutes later and a third attendant came on board. (I guess they switch between buses.) I went through the same thing all over again. This time the female wasn't so trusting. Marie showed her torn and wrinkled ticket and verified that we were all together from Liberia; we had given our ticket to the first attendant, but he never returned them. This was all true of course. I usually keep track of papers and tickets, unless I'm going to be asked three times on the same bus ride. The female attendant went back to the driver and once again, I gave the wave. Had I not been with the French travelers, the most cultured people on the planet, I would have thought it was only me who was wondering why three attendants, at three different times, wanted to see our bus tickets. The French proved to be sound-minded people and thought it was crazy as well. I have to admit I love to travel because things like this baffle all logic.

A young man had boarded the bus and kept looking at me. I was about to get defensive, I couldn't tell what the hell he wanted as he kept staring. He broke the stare and asked in Spanish "Do you need a hotel?" I work at a good hotel that is cheap." Suddenly the five of us were out the bus together, in Tamarindo, and being lead up the stairs of a hotel by this young man. He even helped us carry the bags up the two flights of stairs. The bus ticket accusations must have made me edgy because the sudden hospitality was unexpected.

The desk clerk was named Brian. He was extremely accommodating as well as the young man that brought us there. The only problem for us, as announced by Brian, was that the hotel was full. "What about Tsunami (hotel), did you check there?" "No, this is the first place we have been." Brian began to make phone calls for us. In the meantime, I asked him where he was from and he replied, "Chicago." "Oh, I used to live in Omaha," I said. We were practically neighbors, in fact almost relatives by then. He was a very nice, helpful man that we saw for ten minutes as we tried to get our bearings in this new town. The French couple with us sat and smoked cigarettes, as the French are known to do. Brian had arranged for two rooms at the Tsunami Hotel. He called a cab and the four of us lugged all our bags down the steps to the street. Brian again helped us with the suitcases, as did the young man from the bus.

One taxi wasn't big enough so we split up and all went to the first hotel we had already passed on the road into town. The driver said his price and I protested. It was twice what I'd pay in Jaco. We paid anyway later to find out it was a fair price. No one was sticking it to us. By the time we arrived we were speaking to the French couple on a first name basis. "Tarek, what did the taxi driver charge you?" I asked. It was the same. Nothing can bond strangers better than traveling and the uncertainty that comes with a new place.

A scruffy looking man came out and introduced himself. He was Estaban, the hotel manager. He wore shorts, bare feet, and a faded wife-beater t-shirt. He was Costa Rican and just as accommodating as Brian. He showed us the rooms that were thirty-five dollars a night. Marie and Tarek wanted a less expensive room so they returned to the hall where both sides of the corridor had rooms without air conditioning. By that time we lugged the bags up a long incline to the top room, which would be ours, and looked inside. We decided the price and room was fine. It smelled funky, moldy precisely, but it was a step up from the room in Nicaragua with one exception, there was no hot water here, as well.

Exhaustion, mental fatigue, stress, and malaria are all a part of traveling in Central America. We had everything but malaria. The solution? A visit to the beach before we did anything. Diana and I walked to the beach over a wooden bridge, through a mangrove estuary, and to a flat sandy stretch that ran next to the mouth of a river. The tide was thin but rough. This wasn't like Jaco where the waves came and went. There was a strong current mixing with the rivers current. A sudden drop-off a few feet from the shore caused me to wade in waist deep and go no further. Diana stepped into the deep water and panicked. I took her, put her on my lap, and walked back into the shallow water, as she was shaking with fear. The panic on her face was troubling. Without her knowing I had carried her to where it was so shallow (I was on my knees by then) she thought it was deep water. When I put her on the sandy bottom she began to laugh hysterically. The sudden truth was hilarious because a child could have stood up in the shallow waters. Diana realized the folly of her fears and we began to have fun and play together. We had arrived in Tamarindo, Costa Rica.

Our first encounter was with a man on the beach with his two blonde children. They were collecting shells. The beach was full of people and the water was full of surfers. This is a beach one-third the size of Jaco, so things seemed more compact. We picked up a few shells and walked along the shore until we spotted a parking lot. The attendants told us there were ATM's in both directions; one of them being at a super market in the direction of the Tsunami Hotel. We stopped at the hotel to inquire about buses, renting a scooter, tours, and what to do in the area. Estaban was more than willing to help us; most importantly, we found a direct shuttle to Jaco. I was dreading changing local buses three or four times with all our acquired luggage.

A mile or more down the road we found the market. There were no sidewalks and in places the weeds became quite over grown as the trail vanished. Nothing was to be seen but nature - no buildings. The market was a place more spectacular than any in New York. It was a shopping mall with waterfalls, fountains, turtles, fish (giant carp), and a bank. We went to the ATM, got cash to pay for the hotel, and then did our shopping. I made the mistake of taking out fifteen dollars' worth of Colons; kicking myself for the extra bank fees it would cost me when I did a second withdrawal for the correct amount. The currencies in Central America number in the thousands. If we pay ten dollars for an item, in Costa Rica it is five thousand Colons. This never fits into my scheme of money logic and I am constantly making tiny withdrawals from ATM's, thinking I have taken out thousands of dollars.

They say never go to the grocery store on an empty stomach, which is quite true because we bought sixty-five dollars' worth of food. This was the most we had spent in a grocery store since the beginning of our journey. Costa Rica is as expensive as the USA in many ways. Some foods, like chicken, are more expensive while fish is cheaper. The nice thing about this super market was the free samples of food. We walked in and there was cheese on toothpicks, back in the deli section there was more cheese with turkey slices. We hadn't eaten all day and made sure we sampled all the treats, three times when making the rounds. At the checkout the cashier asked me for ID. I had two credit cards, but no passport. Diana said we'd have to use the cash I had just withdrawn. The thought of paying another withdrawal fee motivated me to ask for the manager. The cashier said no, and I pulled out the second credit card and offered to give a signature as proof. The cashier asked the girl in the next register and she verified my signature. Everything was fine. They even called a taxi to take us home.

The taxi driver said it was too dangerous to rent a scooter when I asked how far it would be to some local beaches. I was thinking maybe there were steep hills. "The traffic was way too fast and many accidents," he tried to convince me, but I know a lie when I hear one and this was an attempt for his services, so we ended the topic. We paid the fee, more than it had been the first time we rode a cab in Tamarindo, and went into the hotel. I started to cook in the communal kitchen and Diana went to the room. As we got the shopping bags organized a woman came up and spoke with Diana. She introduced herself as Joanna from Bogota, Colombia. We had seen her before in the hotel and her room was not far from ours. She was with two men. Diana and Joanna hit it off right away. As we ate our dinner the two other men joined us at the table and talked. One was from Colombia, the other from Costa Rica, Jessie and Manfred. Soon Marie, the French woman, was sitting with us. We all visited as Diana and I ate our meal.

Tarek had been on an errand and joined us when he returned. Before we knew it Estaban brought out a ukulele and Tarek and he were singing Bob Marley songs. It was a small party. Tarek had bought some beer and shared it with the Costa Rican, Manfred. I went to my room and brought my paintings down to show everyone.

We talked about politics, the war in Afghanistan, Osama Bin Laden, and religion. Tarek told me he was originally from Morocco and he is a Muslim. This prompted Estaban to go get his Moroccan head dress and put it on. They played with various ways to wrap the turban (if that is what it is called.) As the evening progressed we were all getting to know each other. The Costa Rican man, Manfred, began to speak in Italian with Diana and Marie. Marie and Tarek were speaking French. The two Colombian didn't speak English so we would pass translations back and forth between Spanish and English. It was a real potpourri of languages and fun. We were making jokes and laughing about what makes us all so different. I felt my writing was calling me, so I excused myself and left Diana to visit with the people. An hour, or more, later Diana came up to the room. All the people, but Estaban had gone out to eat dinner together. Diana said the Colombians wanted to visit us in Jaco. "Fine, but never unless we are in the house with them," was my comment. As much as I liked everyone I knew we really didn't know them. The Costa Rican who spoke Italian struck me as being the least grounded, but he was only twenty-six years old.

The majority of that day I felt strange and ungrounded myself. It wasn't until the long walk to the supermarket that I began to feel like myself again. The traveling was getting to me. The disrupted sleep and change of time zones was all adding up. It is a struggle to do so much traveling, change so often, and keep moving from hotel to hotel. I was glad we were about to go back home in Jaco where we could just stay put in our house. As I lay in bed that night I remember thinking how grateful I was to be able to travel, see the world, make new friends, and be myself, at home in my own skin. I remembered times when I was young and totally stressed while traveling, almost traumatized. We had spent almost a month traveling and these people made us feel the most at home. Was it because we were home, or because we had really connected well with so many people all at once?

Day Two: Tamarindo. We both woke at the unlikely hour of four-thirty. I wanted to sleep more so I took a sleeping pill, silly me! I couldn't get back to sleep; and besides, Diana was talking like the rooster back in Nicaragua. I can't sleep when a TV is on, when a rooster crows, or when Diana is talking to me. She often falls asleep faster than me. I used the headphone to drift off with music, but only long enough to feel my mind dip into slumber and pop back awake. I took off the headphones and was trying to sleep again when I heard the flapping of a huge butterfly in the room. I had seen him the night before lying on Diana's bedpost. I warned her she might feel or hear a butterfly in the night. I heard the butterfly and it triggered more alertness. This became a new topic of discussion and I realized I wasn't going back to sleep at all. We got up and began to make the room homey, organized our bags, take the plastic rope off one of the boxes and made a clothes line on the front porch for drying. The wet clothes Diana had washed were hung. I put on some soft music on the portable speakers and we just played house. This has to happen to make a place feel good. It's no different than any animal staking out territory. The animal instinct kicks in and we dig holes. I even took my paintings and taped them to the empty white wall above our beds. Now the room was feeling really domestic. Our breakfast shakes were consumed and a walk to the beach was in order.

I brought the camera and we crossed the wooden bridge over the estuary to the shore. A man asked us to rent his boat for a tour, but Diana politely declined in Spanish. The beach had the morning surfers filing across the waves. I feel envious of the learners who are getting their first long waves. They stand as still as statues with their arms extended. I have had several chances to try; but my longest time to stand was only a few seconds. Nevertheless, I still get this excited rush when I witness this in others. All my life I have wanted to surf, and this started when I was twelve living in Southern California. My parents repeatedly told me it was too dangerous.

We came into the street, walked along the main thoroughfare, and did window-shopping many hours before anyone was open. An occasional security guard would say hello but no one was up yet. A white SUV pulled up and all our friends from the night before asked us to join them for breakfast. We had eaten, and suggested that we were on our way back to the hotel to make tuna sandwiches for our day together at the other beaches. The night before they had offered to give us a ride to some nearby beaches so seven of us will be off to the beach together. Diana and I had some provisions, but we made a quick stop at a market and bought two long, long rolls of French bread. We came back to the hotel and made sandwiches for everybody. They are going to bring the fruit and drinks.

Inside the hotel room the same big brown butterfly scared me to death. I thought it was a bat or something. The room was dark and the butterfly flew out of a pair of pants I picked up. I screamed and Diana turned to see what it was, and then laughed at me for jumping from a butterfly. I was getting some clothes ready for us to leave for the beach.

I had heard of Playa Conch for years. My friend José described it as a white sand beach with all shells. The seven of us drove there. Well, almost there, as a very small river crosses the first beach where we parked. We had to walk a half-mile. An attendant came up and offered to watch the rented SUV that Jessie was driving. All over Central and South America there are men (and woman) who are self-appointed car attendants. I wonder how they stake out their territory on beaches and streets, but there is this unspoken organization of people who will watch your vehicle. They are self-employed and self-appointed. They politely impose their services, which are so cheap that no one seems to mind. You pay them whatever you want. They come up and tell you they are watching the cars. Car thefts and break-ins are so common that Jessie gladly paid.

The beaches were very nice, but nothing like a picture of a long sandy, white, isolated, stretch of beach. It was a small beach with SUV's parked on the hill and people with large coolers drinking beer and eating. There were few tourists. A car path had been bulldozed through a small hill to make the beach accessible. Only four-wheel drive vehicles were high enough to scale the river and steep incline of the dirt path. The sand was made up of shells worn down to tiny bits. I went straight into the water after we found a shady tree to lay our bags and blanket. There were no whole white shells to be seen. Even in the water while snorkeling, I saw no shells. The current of the waves was so strong that I stayed far away from the rocks, but found myself coming too close, as the tide would drag me in large sweeping motions. I did see big fish, small fish, schools of fish, and a murky white sand bottom, but not much else. When I returned from snorkeling I offered them to everyone, but no one else wanted to snorkel. We sat under the tree and began to eat lunch after a length of time sitting and visiting. The merriment from the night before continued.

Diana came up to us under the tree with an elderly woman locked at her side, arm in arm. She was trying to pick up a shell when she asked Diana to help her. They hit it off instantly and Diana brought her to the group to share that it was her birthday. Anglia was eight-two years old this day. Her son had brought her to her favorite beach. Manfred pulled up a tree trunk and Anglia sat and joined us eating. We passed her sandwiches and cookies. We all sang her happy birthday. Eventually, she needed to find her son. He was not far from behind us, and around another tree. We all bid her another happy birthday as she returned to her son.

Jessie proposed we see another beach that Manfred suggested. We drove through a couple small towns of very small beach-villages, and came to a big cove where many yachts were anchored. Manfred pointed out that we should drive to the far, opposite side of the cove, around a bend in the harbor. Through a hill and a forested area we came to a grand hotel across from a long beach. We parked the car and unloaded the gear. This time the beach was a few yards from the car. A street with considerable traffic ran the length of the beach. We found another shade tree and everyone went swimming. Because we were so close to the road we made sure that at least one person was with the blanket at all times.

This was Playa Flamingo. (There are no flamingos in Costa Rica if you were wondering.) Manfred, Tarek, and I all went body surfing. The waves were simple and perfect for an easy catch. There was no rough surf at all. It was very tame. Eventually we ended up back at the blanket, eating, and all of us talking. A bag of cookies was left on the blanket that had a swarm of tiny black ants. This had been found in a matter of minutes and a thin trail of ants lead to a nearby hole. Manfred disappeared and Tarek and Marie went down the beach hand in hand. I sat with Joanna and Diana talking and just enjoying life. Diana and I went hand in hand down the beach next. On our walk we met a teacher from South Dakota. She was on a last vacation before her two sons left for college. She was proud to have taught at all age levels, saying middle school was her favorite. I asked if she liked Obama and health care. "My husband is afraid of it," was all she said. "Republican" was all I said to Diana as we said our good- byes. She didn't like that I bluntly responded, "Well, I'm for it. We need it". We re-entered the surf and played together wondering what had happened to Jessie and Manfred. Tarek and Marie had come back to the blanket and were smoking cigarettes.

I was getting tired of so much company and began to pick up and organize our things. Jessie said he was going to buy gas and he and Joanna left four of us waiting. I picked up everything but the blanket and went to sit on the side of the road waiting for Jessie to return. They returned and Joanna went off to find Manfred. I was confused as to who was a couple. Tarek told me that Joanna and Manfred was a couple and Jessie was there because he worked with Joanna (she was his supervisor). When I first met all three I thought that Jessie and Joanna were the obvious couple because Manfred was so young, and he never seemed to be around Joanna. Then when I saw Manfred kissing Joanna I figured he was her man. There wasn't any love triangle, I was just guessing wrong. But Manfred seemed to be constantly walking up to women and striking up conversations. He would disappear all day long, only to be seen down the beach talking with some young woman. Manfred is twenty-six years old and Joanna is thirty-one. Tarek and I had a private talk in the water about what was going on, or not going on. He divulged that Manfred had been up to the same thing the night before when they all went out to dinner. He said it was disrespectful to Joanna, and I agreed.

I sat at the side of the road creating a paranoid myth that these people were all a team of thieves and they would eventually rob us of all our possessions. Manfred was someone I was questioning from the beginning. Eventually Manfred came back to the shade tree about the same time as Jessie returned with a full tank of gas. Manfred had been at a high-end resort for a few hours swimming in the pool, using the Jacuzzi, and hob-knobbing (with females no doubt). The return of the car seemed to be no incentive to get going as everyone was still standing around. I actually went up and said, "Let's go". I was tired, still tired from all the travel and lack of sleep. I also have a limit as to how long I am comfortably around new people.

The return to the hotel wasn't direct. Tarek had offered to make a Moroccan dinner for all of us and we stopped at the same shopping Mall as the night before. Diana and I said we would make lunch for everyone the next day, so we went around buying the ingredients for chicken spaghetti. We had twenty minutes to wait so Diana and I explored the fountains of the shopping mall. The fish had to be imported from Japan; they were giant, colorful carp. The turtles were local. A protective screen above a waterfall kept the two types of creatures separated. Maybe the turtles like to eat fish, except the fish were twice the size of the turtles. There was an elaborate walkway over the water where the view of the animals below was very pleasant. By the time Tarek and Marie were finished shopping we were all sitting next to the fountain waiting for Manfred and Joanna. They came out with ice cream. Diana privately noted how Manfred was telling Joanna he wanted ice cream and had no money. He got what he wanted. The sun had set by the time we pulled into the hotel Tsunami, while some last wispy red clouds were high above us on the horizon. It must have been a great sunset.

We went to our room to shower and watch TV. Some down time was well deserved by then. Dinner was in preparation when I went up to the hotel desk and got the code for the Wi-Fi. Estaban gave it to me and I got onto the Internet. I made three calls to friends back in the States. I was talking when Diana came up and told me dinner was ready. It had been almost two hours; but the delay was due to running out of propane gas for the stove. Estaban had to run out and buy more. At the dinner table two new co-workers of Joanna and Jessie had joined us. They sat quietly at the far end, feeling a bit left out because we had all been together so much. We had formed a tribe. The couple politely rejected eating, but ate some bread.

The food was a banquet, a Moroccan feast of chicken and potatoes. The spices of Cumin, Cayenne Pepper, and Coriander gave it a special Middle Eastern taste. The smells made us feel like we are from Arabia. Tarek served up all the dishes and most people had two servings, I included. I was full of bread, wine, and Moroccan chicken and rice. He made excuses that it wasn't true to the recipe; he had to improvise with the spices. We thought he was way off because it was delicious. We all ate everything and drank more wine, talking away.

I sat next to Manfred and got to know him better. He said he lived at home with his mother, was looking for a girlfriend, and had just quit his job at HP. I had heard from Diana via Joanna, that they were living together in her apartment, and that they were a couple. They seemed to be a couple when Manfred needed something, but his strange comings and goings had us all wondering. No one said anything. It wasn't really our business. Observation leads to judgment no matter how we try to avoid it. Manfred went on to say he wanted to own a business or be a boss. He was tired to being ordered around by supervisors. The more we talked, he would say, "I don't know.... I'd like to...". The "I don't know" is what stood out, he didn't. Three times he said, "You don't know what the future will bring you." I was thinking, well you do if you make a plan. He said he was enrolled in school and had enough money to float for a while (at his mother's house). His English and Italian were very good, he was a smooth talker, came across as confident and self-assured. I was seeing something a bit different. He seemed a little too self-assured.

The conversation drifted and I began to talk with Marie. Both her parents had been teachers and her father inherited a wine farm, quit his job, and went to live in the south of France. Tarek joined in and told me how Marie wanted him to move there and learn the trade from her father. "What about marriage?" I asked. "Oh that's a problem. My family would never accept me marrying a French woman. We only marry our own." They had been together seven years, met all the families, but there was a cultural barrier. He said they had some problems because of this. I said Diana and I had some of the same conflicts, but not due to family. I enjoyed his open honesty. I was feeling that fate had brought us together on the bus the day before. I invited them to our house in Jaco. They invited us to their house in Paris. It was surely a new friendship.

Six of us sat around talking. The other couple had left, and Manfred disappeared again. I had brought my iPod and speakers down from the room to have dinner music. After dinner we all sat talking and drinking more wine. Tarek is a natural musician, he is always singing bits of songs and his character has a good spirit. He began to sing the Italian song 'Volarie'. I had the Gypsy Kings version, a very bravado, and bold rendition. I put it on; Tarek did a dance and clapped his hands like a Spaniard. We were getting louder and enjoying the music. A Tico staying in the hotel came out of his room and said we were keeping him and his family awake. We apologized and the man went back into the front room. This was our cue to leave and move further back in the hotel, up to Jessie and Joanna's patio, where we wouldn't bother anyone. Yes, I agree we were a bit too loud, but it was only nine thirty. Tarek went and got his computer, we hooked up my speakers, and he played DJ from the Internet. He was playing many new musicians I'd never heard of, and some others we all knew and sang along with. Tarek began to dance, Diana danced with him, Joanna danced, I tried briefly, but I was very tired. Marie joked that this was how Tarek let his feminine side go. He was a good dancer. I excused myself again with my nightly assignment of writing to be taken care of. I could still hear them two doors away as I wrote this book. The drinking and smoking was not my cup of tea. Diana came home much later. I was already fast asleep. Somewhere in the middle of the night I heard the butterfly dancing around the ceiling, turned on the flashlight to see if Diana was in the other bed. She was snoring.

Day Three: Tamarindo.

    In Tamarindo the cock does not crow
    The sound of waves drifts through the air,
    The way of life here is very slow.
    The mix of people, cook and share.
    The sun and sand cannot be compared.

We wake early every day, with today being no exception. Seeing the beach was our first project and collecting shells became our second. We didn't plan this but since there were a few interesting shells, it seemed a fun thing to do. The first shells to catch our eyes were long, thin, pointy shells that were three to four inches in length. Another was a round, modular-like shell that is very common on necklaces. I began to store them in my pockets as Diana handed them to me. My pockets were bulging so much I searched for a trash bin and came up with a plastic bag. We have a big jar in our home and these shells would find a home there with a variety of others we have collected. The beach was bare but the water was full of surfers out catching their first wave of the day. We walked the length of the beach and then turned inland. Unplanned, we had found the "traffic circle," the end of the beach road in Tamarindo. We'd heard of it, seen it on maps, and there it was. Restaurants and gift shops surrounded it; on the beachside it was open to the ocean. We entered a shop with Bob Marley's Reggie songs playing and a dread-locked storekeeper. We walked the isles and noticed all the prices were three times higher than Nicaragua. Wood items are what interested us, but we didn't buy. In another shop we found the only Costa Rican craft that had not been imported. These were masks made by an indigenous tribe. They were excellent and very creative. They immediately caught my eye because of the color and authentic designs. Some were of jaguars and toucans, or devils with long fangs. Most of the wooden souvenirs here are imported from Bali. Even if it says Costa Rica it is the typical carvings sold in Bali. They are long thin faces with drooping eyes. I didn't like them in Bali because they look too touristy. There are other masks and items imported from Bali that try to duplicate the Australian Aboriginal look, but almost nothing is really made in this country other than hammocks. The indigenous masks I liked, are made here, and were two hundred dollars. Ouch!

We returned to the hotel as the shop in front was opening. This shop sells tours, bus rides, shuttles, and rents scooters and surfboards. The first day we were quoted a price of ninety dollars to Jaco. But we only paid eighty, maybe due to using cash. I didn't ask why. We entered the hotel. No one else was up yet so I began to cook the lunch. I started with the filleted chicken. A young Canadian surfer girl, who had been talking to Manfred the night before, passed by and gave me some matches to get the propane-stove lighted. She has long blonde hair and tattoos on her back. Tarek and Marie came out of their nearby room and I offered to make them eggs. We had extra and it was wise to use up the food before we left the next day. I must say I made them a good, wet omelet they enjoyed. Diana did the dishes and cleaned up. The others began to come out of their rooms, but Manfred was still sleeping. He had gone out the night before, without Joanna of course. He got back around three in the morning.

We were sitting and waiting for him to come alive. I went back to the room to just relax. It dawned to me that other than Diana; I haven't been around this many people in a month. Not since leaving my job. I am a person who needs time alone, without that I become cranky. I felt cranky so I went to the room and put on my headphone and drifted away. My second personal peeve is that I hate waiting on others. It is one of my low-tolerance level quirks. We had been with strangers for two days and about to spend a third day together. It was time to feel my own energy and enjoy some solitude. It was an hour well spent. It was a good diversion for Diana because the Colombians are fun for her. She is very open and everybody loves her. The only problem is she begins to talk to me in Spanish and it's too fast for me. Then I realize how much work it has been for Diana to learn English. On our honeymoon I was talking and had to explain my words all the time. There has been a progressive change in the relationship from the constant struggle to understand to a more sympathetic communication. Love is magic; language is what gets in the way.

Tarek and Marie, and the others, all had packed and moved their bags to our room. This took more time. We were the only ones staying that night in the hotel. The checkout hour would be passed when we returned from the day's adventure. Seven bags filled what free space there was in our room. We all loaded into the rented Mercedes SUV and left for a beach while driving past routes we'd seen yesterday. A thin rain began to fall and the sky was getting very dark. The first beach we visited was El Potero. It was raining and the water was brown from a rushing stream that empties onto the beach. The waves were brown and it felt like a dirty place. Out in a bay yachts were moored. The rain increased. There was one restaurant with a bar and tables so we sat under the awning and kept dry. They ordered some beers; Diana and I had brought our own sugar-free drinks. Jessie and Manfred ordered Cheviche as we sat around talking.

I was getting bored, mostly because the Spanish was too fast for me to comprehend, so I went off to take some photographs. Some chickens and a rooster served to be my first subjects. I noticed a large community center with chained link fence as walls. Inside I could see two American women seated and a man standing next to them. The man invited me inside. "We are about to give an art class", one of the woman said. "I'm an art teacher," I returned. There were two children at a nearby table. "Are you in the Peace Corps?" "No." "A church group?" "No." "We are a nonprofit that my husband and I started back in the States to give these children some art lessons." The woman continued that there was no formal art or music in the schools of Costa Rica. Another woman sat nearest to me and said she was a visiting artist from Minnesota. In a disarming moment she asked me how I had lived as an artist. I said, "I was a starving artist until I became a teacher at age forty-five." Usually people aren't interested in such things, but a fellow artist was. I have thought about opening an art school in Jaco after retirement, but said none of this to the people. It seemed self-serving. I asked if they had a business card, they didn't but the artist gave me her card. I was encouraged to stay and help out but I said it was completely out of my hands. "We are on a small tour today. I'm with three Colombians, one Costa Rican, and two French people, but thank you." By the time we finished at the restaurant and passed the community center there were two-dozen children sitting at tables. The woman said it was a concern that no one would show up. They had a good turnout.

We drove what was actually around a small mountain to a small beach. Just around an outcrop of land I found my dream beach. This was a perfect, isolated beach called Playa Pinca. The beach was no more than a mile long with a steep mountain and thick forest at the far end. Modern, luxury homes, mixed amongst small villas lined the beach. There was a river and swamp behind the row of houses that added to the security and isolation. A dirt road ran between the homes and beach, yet there were vast empty lots, so there was no feeling of over-development. We laid our blankets out. Tarek and I went straight into the water. He and I caught several good waves and I gave him some extra hints on how to body surf. The only other people on the beach were an American family who arrived the same time as us. They were walking. The woman was shooting photographs and I said, "It looks like rain." From her English I could tell she was an American, and also by the way she treated her children. Americans are always ordering their children around, being overly involved. They were far enough away on the beach that we could hear them.

Manfred and Jessie walked to the far end of the beach while the ladies sat on the blankets and talked. Tarek and I were out in the water talking about Joanna and Manfred. I explained that I was still confused as to who were a couple or not. Tarek told me he saw Manfred flirting with a lot of women the night they went out to dinner. "This is disrespectful to the women," he said, with me agreeing. He also said that Joanna was spending her money on him, buying food, etc. It wasn't that difficult to tell there was something amuck with how this guy was behaving. Diana and I had already been observing the strange interactions. She thought less of him than I. Tarek said it's not good to judge others.

He and I sat on the blanket with the women. Jessie and Manfred came back and invited us all to get our things together, to walk to the end of the beach. We did so and took a short hike to the cliffs and an estuary that sat a few feet above sea level. During a heavy rain the estuary emptied out to the sea, for now it was ended on a level higher than the beach. A pool formed at the end of the estuary where birds sang and interesting plants grew on the edge. The estuary ran behind one lone house that sat at the end of the beach. The land formed a thin peninsula just wide enough for a strip of land. On the land was the house. Behind the thick mangrove in the estuary was jungle, how far into the land I can only guess, but a cliff with luxury homes stood high up about a quarter of a mile beyond.

The house was a brick structure with round openings; windows were behind the round concrete openings. In essence the entire building was made of bricks for security reasons. The door was barred. The roof was made of industrial, prefabricated concrete panels. This was a fortress where no one could break in. It had to be because it was so isolated from the common occurrence of home burglaries in Costa Rica. On the edge of the estuary Tarek asked Manfred if there were crocodiles. "Of course," he said. We threw branches in the water to see if we could spot any motion. Manfred made jokes and said we should swim in to see if we could find one. The joking volleyed back and forth and we were like a bunch of kids on a school outing. On the opposite side of the pool we thought we spotted what looked like two eyes popping out of the water. After a closer look it was nothing but a floating leaf. Birds gave strange calls and the air was thick with mystery. A light sprinkle of rain began to dust us and we moved onto the property of the brick house. Two shelters stood on the property that had palm roofs, one was round, and the other one at the far end of the property was square and in better condition.

The rain began to turn from sprinkles, to a strong soaking drench. It was time to take shelter. As if everything was meant to be there for us, the high square shelter kept us dry from the storm. No people (the owner) were in the brick house, there was no one to disturb, and so we enjoyed the time and talked for over a half hour waiting for the rain to stop. We had nowhere else to be and we all felt happy to be together. Manfred and I had a lengthy conversation starting with our parents. His father had died a few years back leaving him with his mother. His other two siblings were grown and lived with their spouses. I told him how I had left home at age seventeen because of problems with my parents. We compared life stories. I grew closer to him and felt he was just a young guy trying to make sense of it all. I saw a more vulnerable side to him than the crafty side I'd been seeing. The rain slowed. Tarek and Manfred went to climb on the rocks of the cliff where the beach ended. Marie and I both use Olympus cameras. In the process of asking me how to use her new camera we discovered that our lenses were interchangeable. She was tickled to take my telephoto lens and go out in the lessening rain to use it. She was like a child with a new toy. She was constantly shooting photographs with her new camera.

The group picked up some momentum and started the slow walk back to the car. Marie, Manfred, and Tarek delayed behind and took photos along the beach. I was somewhere in the middle of the tribe taking pictures of the string of houses with cactus and interesting arrangements of color and light. When we all finally loaded into the car the jokes and fun making continued on the drive home. The casual day and slow pace suddenly turned into a frantic drive. Jessie went into a rare driving mode where the beast inside of him came out. I was in the front seat next to him. He became the hulk, not an angry hulk, but a crazed Colombian driver that darts past slow traffic. A semi-truck and trailer full of new cars was practically taking up both sides of the street. The top of the truck was hitting the low branches of all the trees along the route. I began to wonder what type of sudden death a pile of cars would cause for us all. In a strange twist of thought I began to wonder about codes and who set the standards for truck heights. How is it that a truck could drive all the way, hundreds of miles, and be just low enough to pass under low hanging electric wires and trees? A stream of broken leaves was following the path of the truck. Each low branch was nipped by the truck, and broke a ribbon of green leaves flowing along the road. This tiny distraction kept me unaware of the lightning speed as Jessie passed the truck. There were six brand new cars in various colors that passed my peripheral view just enough to catch the glint of sunlight on the chrome. As soon as danger was upon us, it was gone, but Jessie's speed-drive continued. By the time my food was ready to be rapidly erupted, we were pulling into the hotel parking lot.

Our room became the communal dressing quarters. The others had all checked out before we left in the morning and their luggage was still safely in our room. I began to cook our final meal while the others sat around on our porch and ate a plate of nachos' and cheese I readied in the microwave oven. The party continued. Tarek had the music on his laptop and people shifted in and out of the small bathroom shower. Manfred disappeared, as usual, and I focused on the cooking down in the hotel kitchen. I would drift back and forth to grab some nachos, waiting to see when I could jump in the shower. The water for the noodles was boiling and the sauce was on the hot propane stove.

In the morning I had seen a woman sitting on the hotel sofa that is situated in the lobby (more like a covered porch) of the hotel. She wore a red shirt and started to tell me about taking a bus from a nearby town to get medical treatment for an ear infection here in Tamarindo. I asked her where she was from in the States and she told me Santa Cruz, California. This was a brief, passing encounter. But at the time I privately told Diana the woman looked like she suffered from a mental disorder. It is those awkward glimpses between sentences and eye contact that led me to believe she was suffering from more than an ear infection. The woman passed through the kitchen and we began to speak again. Nothing really memorable took place. While I was cooking I asked her about her bus back to where she had come from. I assumed she was going back during the day and she hadn't. She said something about missing the bus and I didn't pay much attention. I kept focused on the cooking. She disappeared into the front of the hotel and I went back to the room to take a quick shower while the stove heated up the food.

The tribe eventually came down to the kitchen table and we sat waiting for the food to cook. Manfred reappeared to take a shower. He had been flirting with a Canadian surfer who was staying the hotel. They had been in the front parking lot. In an either paranoid, or precautions, moment I had moved Manfred's bags onto the front porch of the room, leaving the door locked. I didn't want him in my room unsupervised. He didn't insist on a shower and I welcomed him to join us at the table, which he did. The Canadian female sat at a counter and mixed with us for a while but no one officially invited her to sit with us. We all sat at the table and my dinner of chicken spaghetti was served.

Think of one of those TV commercials where everyone is sitting around a table laughing. The camera stops on a frame where a smile is frozen, teeth are showing from laughter. No one is frowning. The voices rise and fall in bursts of jokes and conversation. Some people are dressed-up; others are in their most casual clothes. The language is mixed and tossed like a salad. The drinks are passed, glasses are filled and refilled. Stories about our youth and families are shared, and no one cares about judgments because we are amongst friends, nothing is serious but the moment and how special it is. We were a family that came together through happenstance. Gravity and coincidence pulled us all into fate and we made the best of the time, knowing how good life could be. Tarek jumped up and made a toast to Diana and me. The other said, "Salude" in a chorus of unity. Four nationalities shared time and food the way life was meant to be shared. In one moment it dawned on me that I was the sole North American. Labels meant nothing. We were citizens of earth, and nationalities weren't what separated us. We shared what we all had in common.

The compliments about the spaghetti came my way. I thought I had put in too much cumin, but apparently not. They all liked the spicy mix of chicken and red tomato sauce. A female who had been in the hotel came out of her room and chose that moment to do her yoga stretches in the middle of the wide corridor. She was on a blanket two rooms away, in full view of all of us. She was facing the opposite direction, which only encouraged more of us to watch. She had a fine body and was showing it off. We tried not to take notice but the poses and contortions while she shifted her thighs into the air caught everyone's eye. This started a series of whispers where the men's eyes were following her thighs, and mouths were drooling. The woman was far enough away to not hear us, but the giggles and exaggerated body gestures caused a few gleeful bursts of laughter. It got to that embarrassing point where laughs were being so suppressed that the situation only got more uncontrollable. I took pictures of Tarek and Jessie straining their necks to see the arched beauty. The woman paid no attention to us. I don't think she even knew we were so enraptured by her sexual twists and turns. The whole group at the table was soon trying not to be so obvious. It was a hilarious juxtaposition of serious yoga and a party of howling wolves miming in silence. Eventually the female went to another room where her friend was staying.

As we sat there a young, nervous male approached the door of the room where the woman had retreated. He tapped on the door, but no one answered. He knocked a little louder looking over his shoulder to see if anyone was watching him. I pretended to not be watching and turned away. No one else was watching this little sideshow. Soon the door opened and the young man looked in both directions while pulling out a tiny plastic bag from his pocket. There was a brief transaction where money was put in one hand and an exchange took place. In a sleight of hand the tiny quantity of green marijuana was passed to the man inside the doorway. This all took less than one minute in total. As quick as the delivery was made it became a shadow in a dark night. I am positive I was the only witness.

The hotel manager, Estaban, passed by and we insisted he get a plate and join us for some spaghetti. He obliged and joined in with the fun. Joanna and Manfred had bought ice cream and what was remaining from their breakfast was shared with all of us for dessert. The female Canadian surfer was still with us and was sitting at the counter talking to the rest of us at the table. We sat eating ice cream as the woman downed three straight shots of rum. She explained that she had no Tylenol and had been hit in the head by a surfboard. She was in a great deal of pain. She showed us a big lump on the back of her skull. We sat and visited with one last gust of energy before they all loaded into Jessie's rented SUV. We hugged our new friend' good-bye and assured each other another time; another place would bring us back together in the circle of life.

As we were saying our good-byes a man walked up and spoke to Diana. He thought she worked for the hotel. He needed to speak with the manager, Estaban. Diana led the man to Estaban and overheard what he had to say. He was from another local hotel and wanted to warn Estaban that the woman in the red shirt had stayed in his hotel for two days and skipped out without paying the bill. He was warning Estaban that she was a drifter and not to be trusted. Diana and I retreated to the room to organize ourselves for the next morning's departure. Back in the room Diana explained all this to me. We knew this woman was harmless and needed some help. I walked to the front of the hotel to give the lone woman some of our extra food. Just at that moment Estaban was speaking to the woman, whose eyes were full of tears. He turned and walked away, not making any eye contact with me. I went up to the woman and handed her some food. "Are you OK?" I asked. This caused a flood of more tears and she said she had nowhere to go. All I could say was, "Maybe this will help." Estaban was returning when I told him, "I gave her something to eat." He had an embarrassed look on his face. I knew he had to evict the woman. She had been camping-out on the sofa in the lobby most of the day. It wasn't clear to me why she hadn't left until the news of her predicament came through the other hotel manager.

Back in the room we lay in bed and wondered what her whole story was. How could a middle-aged woman end up in Costa Rica, be homeless, have no passport or papers, and no food? We never found out the rest of the story. In the morning I looked to see if the sofa had been slept in and it wasn't. Estaban wasn't there when the van pulled up. The other hotel employee who sold us the van ride helped us put our bags into the microbus. I told him to thank Estaban.

The microbus took the four and a half hour ride to our home in Jaco. The driver explained that we would switch to a different van, transfer the luggage, and have a twenty-minute break at a restaurant rest-stop. At that stop we saw many Macaws and local animals. The grounds were a mini-zoo. It was the end of our travels and I was well aware of the amount of energy we had spent. Traveling is work. It may be fun and exciting, but it is work to maneuver through so many new cities, keep safe, and continue to be interested. We would soon be home where life is more familiar. Our second home in Costa Rica has become as comfortable to us as New York. We stepped off the van into our guarded compound with a swimming pool and palm trees.

Day One: Arenal Volcano. After three days, we decided to leave Jaco and do a small tour. Diana had cleaned the house so much the paint was worn off. On a Sunday night we decided to leave first thing Monday morning at seven o'clock. We packed within an hour, just taking the basics, some food and clothes. The cameras are a must as well. I had cabin fever and the restless highway was something I needed again. Diana was happy to go see a new place as well. We had a bag of food and our two backpacks. We didn't forget the toothpaste or deodorant. It was a kind of minimalist venture where the accessories of travel were cut to a bare minimal. All the "extra stuff" we'd been carrying for a month was left behind. We had one change of clothing - just one fresh shirt, our swimsuits, and food.

The bus from Jaco was the same, a two-hour, ride we have known for years. I wrote on the computer or listened to my mp3 player. In San José the bus arrived at Coca Cola and we headed for separate restrooms. We didn't know when the bus for La Fortuna was leaving and we had to walk four or five blocks to another bus terminal. We got directions from a taxi driver on how to get to Arenal. He offered to drive us for thirty-five dollars. The bus was three dollars. While walking to the other bus terminal we stopped to buy Diana some new pajamas. The prices in San José, the capitol, are cheap compared to Jaco.

The walk to the bus terminal was like a short walk through hell. Not for us, but for the unfortunate people whose lives are ruined from drug and alcohol addiction. We passed men laying in groups on the sidewalk, in a kind of "sleep-over" circle of conversation. This is the worst part of San Jose. We stopped at a pharmacy but they were out of what we wanted. The neighborhood was desolate and not a place to linger. When a drunken stranger calls to you, you just keep walking. Men would look up at us, but we passed too fast to let them engage us. This way we became invisible. They would fall back into their drunken stupors, too stoned to know what they needed from a passerby. This sad drama plays out in every city across the earth. It is a sickness that owns no nationality. So many broken hearts live inside themselves unable to share love, so many broken people who have no self-love; they only know how to abuse themselves.

The bus terminal was full of police. We have never seen such good police protection for a bus station. There must have been a good reason for this. The station had an attached restaurant so we went inside to eat and use the restroom.

They are free in restaurants, about fifty cents otherwise. We ordered a chicken and rice dish. At a table nearby two British women came in and we tried to listen in to see what language they spoke. They were definitely Brits. We could hear them reading out loud from the Lonely Planet book.

We sat on a bench and waited, sharing some sugar bread Diana bought in a moment of weakness. Of course I told her all the dangers of sugar as I ate it with her. I felt less guilty by giving half of the bread away to a woman and man sitting at the bench with us.

The line for the bus was already standing when the driver's assistant opened the lower compartment for the luggage. The line emptied and we were left at the bus door, being the first to enter and finding two front seats, as the remaining passengers were loading their luggage. There were few people for such a large bus. Most of the passengers were tourists. The two British women were among them. It wasn't that a number of new people didn't arrive on the bus, the majority of them boarded at bus stops along the way after we left the terminal.

We left San José passing along the familiar highway towards Jaco, them further and further into newer, higher elevations. The houses became large and cleaner; the people seemed to be from another country, and not the beach crowd we are used to in Jaco. We stopped in San Ramon for a fifteen-minute break, but other than the constant stopping and exiting of passengers the ride was eventless. The scenery was what made the trip worthwhile. The higher towns and sweeping hills with farm crops and cattle were breath taking. The clouds opened giving the land that extra burst of sunshine where green pastures are accented and make life feel like a painting by John Constable. As soon as the sun was out it was gone again. The rain clouds burst and a heavy rain was pounding the bus windows by the time we reached the flat lands past San Ramon. Steams were filling as men leaving their daily labors took shelter under the tree branches along the rivers. The rain didn't let up. The bus windows were closed to keep the rain out and steam coated the glass. I was happy to be on the move, happy to find the unexpected landscape around the curves of the thin two-lane road.

By the time we arrived in La Fortuna (In the Arenal vicinity) we had been traveling nine and a half hours from Jaco. The alternative shuttle bus was seventy dollars; we spent ten dollars to get there and paid with time. This is the typical mode that challenges the tourists. It is always cheaper to travel on the local buses, but it is a long, long day of sitting. The front seat has lots of legroom so we had it pretty nice. We stepped out of the bus into a downpour; it was impossible to keep dry. Men wearing white and red shirts immediately invaded the tourists selling them something. I didn't notice what. I was looking for a taxi driver to get us to a cheap hotel. We saw one hotel we'd read about in the Lonely Planet and headed toward the main street. Along the ride we'd seen a sign for a place called Lugi's. As we passed a shop a man politely asked us if we had a hotel. "No, we need one." "I can offer you a special price for a hotel called Lugi's, it is two blocks away and thirty five dollars a night." We felt safe, the man was very professional and there wasn't any high-pressure sale being pushed down our throats. The man continued and we bought an afternoon tour to the volcano for the following day at two o'clock. Things went very smooth. Our salesman was from Holland and had married a Costa Rican woman. He wanted to return to Costa Rica to raise his child. His wife hated her life in Holland and we began to talk about Diana and her life in New York. She isn't that crazy about her life there I told him. The man's name was too Dutch to remember, he worked for the same outfit as the men in the red and white shirts, the Red Lava Tours.

Our Dutch acquaintance even gave us a ride to Lugi's Hotel. What could have been an hour of walking, looking, in the rain were a brief ride and a comfortable beginning to our little vacation. The Red Lava Tours had a nice package. Usually we make our own tours, this was an exception, and the price was forty dollars each. The hotel was a restaurant on the ground floor. The reception desk was at the back of the restaurant with a long hallway leading along a bank of rooms. The rooms faced the volcano. We asked to be moved to the last room on the hall so we could see the volcano from our window. Each room had two rocking chairs perfectly situated to watch the volcano. The erupting red lava was on the opposite side of the sloop, but great puffs of smoke will plume at varied times of the day. It was a wonderful view.

In the room we made our dinner of refried beans, burritos with avocado. It wasn't long before we walked the small town, up the main drag to see the tourists' shops and compare prices. The Baruka masks (Indigenous Costa Rican peoples) were more expensive than in Jaco, but other items were less costly. We saw maybe ten shops in an hour before the sunset. The town of La Fortuna is very small. In my twelve-year-old Lonely Planet book it said there were ten hotels. That number is up to nearly forty now. We saw so many tourists, and tour providers; we can see that the town had gone through a great change. The volcano even looked bigger than my first (and only) visit to Arenal six or seven years before with José and my cousin. As we walked the town we would see some of the same people who had arrived on the bus. I would stop them and ask if they found a hotel and how. Our price seemed to be the most reasonable. We felt lucky.

The night was not long. The room had a giant double sized bathtub that had a broken stopper. So a plastic bag served as a way to keep the water in. The sixties design was dated and the water was slow to fill the tub, but who cares when the TV is on and time is a luxury to be savored. We must have been asleep by ten. The long bus ride had taken its toll.

Day Two: Arenal Volcano. In the morning it was five thirty when I stepped outside the room to begin photographing the volcano in varied phases of light. The higher the light, the more clear the green, but as soon as the volcano looks like it will be clear a cloud will pop up and begin a quick cloaking of its face. If one looks at the volcano every fifteen minutes it will change. Why a constant weather shift plays out so often I don't know. The size of volcanic plume isn't related to the weather that comes and goes. Sometimes a cloud bank will cover the entire mountain and a sudden mushroom cloud will shoot above the weather. The Dutch fellow told me the best time to see the volcano this time of year was in the mornings and I wasn't disappointed.

We made our breakfast shakes and went out to photograph in the morning light. Across a river with a deep gorge we passed over a bridge to a park. The park had a running track and people circling. I was taking pictures of the volcano from many vantage points as we walked. People were on their way to their jobs, smiling and greeting us as we did them. This is a place where a stranger stands out but is welcome and not viewed with suspicion. We passed the tour shop at the bus station and spoke to the Dutch man. We said we might go to the hot springs, but he suggested the waterfalls, saying we'd get better use of our day doing something different than what we paid for coming on our two o'clock tour.

We went back to the hotel, changed into our swimsuits, packed a lunch after a visit to the super market and hired a car to take us to the waterfalls. We heard they were half the price of a local taxi from a man we met in a bakery. We were eating a roll and struck up a conversation with a man sitting next to us. We ran into him again in the central park, and he pointed out where to hire a car on a far corner. At nine o'clock we were in a car and heading for the waterfalls. The fifteen-minute ride coast three dollars, the same price the friendly man in the park had advised us to pay. It is a real joy to feel like the price we pay is the same as the local people. One a long upward climb to the summit of the road we passed luxury hotels, ceramic shops, souvenir shops, horseback riding stables, and a few energetic hikers making their way toward the waterfalls on foot.

At the top there were dozens of four-wheel drive rental vehicles, and giant tour buses in a large parking lot. The entrance building was a beautiful brown, stained wood structure with modern windows where the person behind the glass speaks through a hole in the middle. Across a small bridge the path began. The walk down the cliff was a bit scary in some places. The path was wet and steep but there were chains along the way. The footing was made of bricks that were square with open-earth surfaces. This gave good traction to the wet, muddy path. It had been raining the night before. Additionally, the rain forest had a mist rising from the unseen, but loud, waterfall below. Thousands of plants and vines grew along the path and some giant ferns reminded me of the rain forest in New Zealand. These towering ferns were up to twenty feet tall, looking like we were in an imaginary landscape. Houseplants in the USA were three times their captive cousins' size, growing wild and free. It was green and green and green, in every possible shade.

One small view of the falls gave us a glimpse to what would come. Halfway there an opening in the trees gave us a view of a long, thin, white ribbon of water falling. It was the appetizer. The entire downward trek was twenty minutes. We were told fifteen, but Diana needed to be slow and sure-footed. I was soaked from perspiration by the time we walked up a lookout platform at the breathtaking cascading waters. In the water people swam in the strong current unable to fight the rushing flow of water. It was dangerous and only five or six people entered the water here. Down the platform to another lookout a uniformed man stood holding a rope. He was there to throw the lifeline if someone needed help. He politely stepped aside as I took pictures of the waterfall.

Down a steep embankment with steps, around a bend in the rocks, the majority of the people were swimming in the narrow river. The thin, sandy bank where we stood was almost packed with people. In contrast, a rocky wall jutted up the opposite side of the river. People stood in the water feeding fish that gathered around them. These fishes were fifteen to twenty inches long, fat from the tourists' feedings. The water was crystal clear and freezing cold. I was in the water amazed at how fast my body adapted to the chilly river. I swam to the rock wall and crossed the current to a place where the racing water was calmer. Rocks the sizes of washing machines were scattered up-river, creating a dam where the pool of the main waterfall cascaded into the lower river. The river was ten feet across at its narrowest point. There must have been a hundred tourists, their voices echoing and blending with the roar of the giant waterfall.

We noticed a group of special teenagers who looked like they had mental disabilities and I stopped to speak with one of the councilors. She was from Nova Scotia. I said I knew of Ann Murray, the singer. "Yes, she is the pride of our country". The group was of twenty students, all from Pennsylvania. How a twenty-something teacher from Nova Scotia ended up with this group was a guess. The water was full of people screaming and having a great time. The heat was intolerable and the cold water was blissful.

The hour stay was well worth the effort, which really happened on the climb back. We planned on a forty-five minute climb but it took only thirty. The steps were for people taller than me, and I am tall. Diana had to struggle with each step. On one of our many stops we met a couple from Spain and visited with them for five minutes. They let us take their picture and took one of us with my camera as well. We had brief encounters with many people, all pleasant and spirited. No one was having a bad time. The children seemed most easy to just jump in the frigid water and last to want to leave. They were bouncing up the steep steps like monkeys.

At the top of the stairs we found a lookout platform that provided another view of the falls. A family was singing the Wizard of Oz song, not realizing we were looking down on them from above. When I joined in the singing with, *"Because of the wonderful things he does"*, we all laughed together. More gift shops and showers were stationed at the exit. We waited for our driver, who didn't show on time so I asked the man behind the glass (not curtain) to make a free call for us. We started down the dirt road just to kill time. Remember I hate to wait! The car showed a few minutes later. The driver explained that the waterfalls (Called the Cascades in Spanish) were privately owned by the town of La Fortuna. The profits wisely went into the municipality. The road we were riding on was in the process of being paved with new bricks. A wiser decision yet, since the road had huge, worn erosive groves. The driver dropped us off where we had found him. We crossed the street and entered the central park.

Again we found the same man we had spoken to at the bakery in the morning. We asked deeper, personal questions. He was from Chile and had a small artisans shop on the other side of the park. I was impressed that we asked him what he did, and not him selling his shop to us, despite having three brief conversations. He was a painter, his daughter and son-in-law made stained glass and ceramics. This was cause for us to go and see his art and shop. The man introduced us to his son-in-law and told him to give us fifteen percent off any item. Diana had been tempted to buy some jade pieces way back in Flores, Guatemala. The jade was better in this shop with a polished quality. So I bought a gift for my wife. Aren't I a great guy? I was attracted to the brightly colored ceramics, wood bowls, and paintings. I settled on an unfulfilled want Diana had that had begun way back in another country.

We had an hour before our two o'clock tour so we went home to the hotel to prepare and eat lunch. At two forty-five the van pulled up. We were the second couple to be picked up. The same two women from England we'd seen the day before were on the same tour with us. "Do you know we saw you in the restaurant back in San José?" was my opening question. She asked, "What restaurant?" to which I replied, "The one in the bus station. We were sitting across the way from you." They didn't remember us, but they did know the bus station and restaurant. Our next stop was to pick up two guys from Spain. They seemed completely serious and tight-lipped. That was a first impression. The next stop was three couples. They entered and began to speak in a foreign tongue. "Are you speaking Polish, or Hungarian?" I asked. This got a good laugh. Then one guy started to speak in German with a thick accent. "German," I said. "Yes, but we speak Swiss German. We are from a part of Switzerland that speaks German," he replied. "Oh, I would have never guessed German," I said, getting another group laugh. Our last stop was to pick up our guide. He got in, said very little, and then without any announcement began to give guide information to the two Spaniards. This is how I figured out who he was. He was a quiet fellow; his brother was our driver and another guide. We found this by inference more than any "take-charge" announcements.

A long bumpy road lay between our pickup and destination. Forty-five minutes of driving took us to the far side of the Volcano Arenal within the National Park to a red-earth path. We were dropped off at the end of the paved road and followed the driver who led us ten minutes down to a waterfall. This was not the same size or as easy to get to as the one earlier in the day. It was steep and dangerous from mud and rain. There were no prefabricated bricks to hold our footing. Diana kept up with the group. I was amazed. How can she walk so slow on a city sidewalk and keep pace with all these back-packers? I often tell her attitude is the key to a vigorous stride. She was great.

The waterfall was too delicious to pass up, so I stripped down, changed into my swimsuit and plunged into the water, a second swim in the same day. Diana stayed on the shore. This was a small pool where swimming toward the falls proved impossible because of the current. The leader climbed up the falls and made a jump. He encouraged us all to do so. His name was Luis. I don't jump from waterfalls. I was soon dressing back into warn, dry clothes.

His quiet brother met Diana and I at the top of the steep climb just before the drop to the waterfall. We left before the others knowing that it would be a greater effort for us to scale the steep rocks and path. The waterfall visit lasted an hour or less. There was a pace being set, a rigorous tone set by these athletic brothers. It was something new to contend with, not our usual casual and cautious stroll.

When the others joined us at the top of the ridge Luis showed everyone how to swing on a vine. He called out like Tarzan. Almost everyone tried the vine, but Diana and I passed. We soon were walking along the river that feed the falls, high above, and looking at animals in the brush. A family of small black creatures was scurrying in the brush, but all I saw was a shadow. I was too busy getting the video camera out to really see what I wanted to shoot. They were gone by the time I was ready. Oh well. From then on I was prepared and not disappointed when we came upon some Howler monkeys. High above in the trees a group of black monkeys swung from tree to tree. We followed them for a few minutes until they went away, too far toward the rivers deep ravine. As we walked a light rain began then stopped when we crossed a steel suspension bridge. At the far side of the bridge Luis took out a book and began to make a mound of dirt. This was his demonstration volcano. He told us all he wanted to speak in Spanish and his brother would translate if anyone could not understand. Everyone there spoke enough Spanish to not need the brother. The older, quiet brother stood off to the side under a shelter smoking a cigarette.

Luis gave a lecture that lasted a good half hour. He explained that the volcano had grown substantially in the last five years (I knew I remembered a smaller volcano) and that the newer cone had begun to swallow the older cone. He went on to show photographs of the past twenty years and told how three Americans had been killed in the nineteen nineties by a sudden eruption. Although this is a popular tourist attraction it is a very dangerous place. I asked if there were safety issues for that day. Luis reported the seismographic equipment was quiet, so we were safe. As Luis explained the story he moved more dirt onto his little volcano and showed how the different dates had changed the shape of the Arenal Volcano. It was a very educational lecture and we all stood spell bound. After a closing question and answer period we re-crossed the suspension bridge and headed up a long incline. Diana and I were last by the time all had reached the top. It occurred to me that I was the oldest member of the entire party. Funny but I seldom feel old. My slower accent was a self-signal of aging. Diana was just as slow for other reasons. We make a good team.

Suddenly we passed a luxury home. The path went next to a home that was out of a design magazine. Someone wanted to put their home in the middle of the National Park and did. I think it was part of the scientific research that takes place; it just seemed out of place and way too modern for the jungle. The house offered a long paved drive way back to our road and a walk to an observatory museum. The museum was too small to hold the fourteen of us, so I quickly took a look at the displays of newspapers and geological charts and went outside. As life is full of coincidences so was the fact that the minute we went into the museum it began to pour buckets of rain. Then magically, it slowed as we made a short walk to a hotel observation deck. The rain came stronger as we stood looking at what was supposed to be a spectacular lava flow. The Red Lava Tours was based on this very moment and all we saw was clouds. In fact, only for one minute did we see the faint outline of the volcano, only to be swallowed up by more clouds and rain. Then the lightning began and the rain increased. There were no lights on and the dark only got darker as night fell. We paid for a sunset over the lake and red lava views, but we had a good time anyway. We sat and talked to the two women from England. One was a medical student, and the other a student of something I forgot. Sorry!

Diana and I were starved so I went to the van, got the keys from Luis, and brought back our dinner of refried beans and burritos. We had a banana and some avocado. You are more tired of hearing about our diet than we were of the food. Yes, it was often the same practicality of simple nourishment. This was food for on-the-the go, heating not required. We ate as two other tour groups came up onto the observation deck. Our group stayed the longest. The only part I didn't like was the cigarette smoke. Several people light up and the air were too thick with tobacco smoke. I was offered a chair by the Spaniards but declined. I was flattered because they were being polite, but horrified that this was done because of my age. Besides, my body aches and the slower pace, these are the tiny signs of aging. We continued sitting in the dark in a circle and talked travel stories. We found our way back to the van and headed out of the park. Luis made one more stop at a tree where he turned a flashlight onto a green, red-eyed frog. He said the frogs' eyes were red from eating the marijuana plant, but I never saw any marijuana plants the entire time in Costa Rica. It was offered to me to buy by some street people, but the myth of the red-eyed frog was just that. I don't think frogs eat plants, do they? I am sure they don't smoke plants.

The best part of the tour was to come. Yet, at the time it seemed like the craziest thing to begin to do. We pulled up to a commercial spa, parked the van, and were instructed to take all our shoes off, leave all our clothes behind, and walk down a dark, wet path in our bare feet and bathing suits. This was the most exploratory, sensual, frightening, sensational thing I've done in years. I consider myself a pretty open-minded adventurer but this experience opened me up much more. At the bottom of the path was a hot springs. We stepped into some frigid water to suddenly be washed with hot rushing water of a river. The only light was coming from Luis' tiny headlamp. It was like a star in the night sky and gave off about that much illumination. We were instructed to then sit down on a concrete ledge and fall into the blackness below. This was all a test of true trust toward other human beings. I wouldn't have tried this in daylight! Yet here I was, and amazingly Diana as well, plunging over a five foot drop-off into a pool of unseen hot water. It was an experience that made me feel like I had not been living dangerously enough. I don't like heights so I crossed a suspension bridge in fear. I jumped into a freezing, blind waterfall, and now I was skidding into a hot springs in total darkness. It was terrific but went along with the ride. I was beginning to feel like I was on a real adventure vacation. Writing about it seems silly in comparison to living it. We had a blast.

Two or three other groups of people showed up. There were already people in the dark water when we slid into the water. The two English women were getting more and more nervous about the dark water and the number of wild men in the water with them. The two guides seemed a bit too friendly with their invitation to have the girls spend the night, but first come over for some drinks. I didn't pay as much attention to this as Diana. But I could tell the tour guide of a second group that came to the water was even asking Diana about who she was. She later told me he was asking her who I was, and why we were together. The older guy with gray hair is often seen as a strange partner for a young woman. When she said she was married to me he backed off. All this doesn't anger me, but I did paste the guy right in the nose, making the water so bloody that red was our favorite color that night. The medical student came over and sat with Diana and me saying she wasn't feeling safe and wanted to be near us. We obliged and made it clear she was with us. There were many more men in that water than women. The couples that were with us all seemed to be off to the edge of darken kissing and making whoopee. We pretended not to notice besides it was too dark to see anything. Their silence gave them away.

Part of our group went up over the ledge and did a slippery slide into the deep water. They ran and slipped where the shallow water rushed its strongest. I didn't go that far. I could just see my split skull being rushed to the hospital. There was already one black and blue body floating down stream with the imprint of my wedding ring on his face. What else was about to happen? Nothing actually, it all ended in harmony and no one was taken advantage of. The two women were dropped off last. (We saw them the next day and all had ended fine.) As we boarded the van one of the woman from Switzerland cut her foot, so Luis got out a bandage. It was pretty chaotic in the dark, finding clothes, finding shoes, finding who was with whom, but it was all fun. I saw maybe thirty people in the dark back at the hot springs. The other tour groups brought tiny lights as well, but it was really a blind, sensory experience. No one pressed charges, and no lawsuits. We got home around ten o'clock, rolled into bed and called it an adventurous day.

Day Three: Baldi Hot Springs, Arenal. At dawn the volcano was there just like the day before. This time it was not clear, or rather the sky behind the volcano was gray, yet the volcano was not cloudy. That lasted an hour or so. We got breakfast and took a short walk toward the central park. It started to rain; the hotel was the best option at that point. It was a morning to catch up on emails, wash some clothes, hang them to dry, and do nothing until we headed to the Baldi Hot Springs at eleven. On our brief morning walk we went looking for the driver we'd hired the day before. He wasn't there but we set up an eleven o'clock pick up time with a new driver. This young man was on time and made a better impression on me. At five to eleven we were stepping into his car at the front of our hotel. He told Diana most Costa Rican were lazy, late, and never get ahead in life. This guy was none of that.

The drive was seven minutes and it cost us two dollars each way. We booked a return pickup for six o'clock. I suppose you are wondering why on earth we wanted to stay seven hours at a hot springs. Easy, it was vastly relaxing. Walking into the Baldi Hot Springs was like entering a luxury hotel. Two receptionists stand at a vast wooden counter, smile, and greet you. We had a discount from a tour operator we met on our morning walk and saved seven dollars each on the usual twenty-five dollar entrance fee. If we wanted lunch we could have bought the ticket for thirty dollars each. We brought our own food, fruit, tuna, crackers, and drinks, so we saved a total of twenty-four dollars; a small dining issue that came up later in the day while we were eating. A security guard, very nice guy, politely told us we were not permitted to eat in the park. He may have timed this to when we had already finished, as they seemed too low key about this rule. We didn't know it wasn't permitted. We had seen other people eating while walking around. There were no picnic tables, only fancy restaurants. Farther back on the grounds there were dozens of hidden park benches where a picnic would be hard to spot by a security guard. At any rate we nicely apologized for breaking the rules, let the guard leave, and finished the fruit juice I put away as he spoke.

The grounds have two hotels that are nestled to one side of the park, which makes the pools even more isolated. Upon entering the grounds behind the receptionist, there are two submerged bars where men stand in a "dug out" circle surrounded by water. People sit at submerged bar stools, and order drinks from the bartender. A bridge spans across the water between the two bars and a restaurant is situated to the left. After a small paved driveway stands a restroom and facilities with lockers. We bought a locker, but the towels were received by leaving a twenty-dollar deposit. The deposit was returned at the end of the day, so the towels were free. The dressing room, restrooms, and lockers were in numbers that could accommodate many people. The locker numbers went up into the five hundreds. Ours was five hundred and thirteen.

We stuffed our bag into the locker, cameras, food, clothes and all. We were left with only our bathing suits and bare feet. It started to drizzle and the chill in the air sent us straight to a sauna. The smell of eucalyptus was fresh in the air and the room was over one hundred degrees. We sat sweating in the heat when two men came in. A long conversation about America began. The men were Dutch, one young, one around my age. I started by saying how I agreed with the Dutch Government and how progressive it was, no death penalty, lenient drug laws, and a prison system that really wanted to rehabilitate people. They agreed but said the drug laws were too soft and many problems came from such policies. The fact that Amsterdam attracts so many druggies from the rest of Europe is a problem to them. I countered with the fact that we have prison systems that are made for profit, and few people are rehabilitated, but recycled through again and again. The older man was shocked when I explained that the prison system in the USA had more black inmates than colleges with enrolled young black students. "But Obama will help your country", the younger man said. "Yes" I said, "but some of these problems will take many years to change". This spun off into a Bush versus Obama comparison that is easy to do. Diana got very animated when the conversation went into the lifestyle of most Americans. She vents her frustrations at the language prejudices she has encountered. They left the sauna and we waved hello to them in a larger pool an hour later.

The day passed by visiting almost all the pools. The grounds have twenty-five pools, two restaurants, three wet bars, three waterfalls of thermal waters, four cold pools, a giant Jacuzzi, and wonderful tropical garden with paths through lush, verdant plants with tropical flowers that look unreal. My camera was working overtime in the tropical gardens. (This is where a picnic meal could have been easily eaten and no one would ever know.) There are even three water slides that twist and turn into a giant pool. They ask people not to swim in the thermal pools because the hot water could potentially be dangerous. It was one of the few really luxurious choices on the entire trip that we enjoyed every penny spent.

Baldi is a fine example of a Costa Rican owned business that has international standards. The paved walkways, the inlay stone paths, the sculpted fountains are a beautiful place to visit. At one of the farthest pools we entered the water as a tremendous downpour came. Why run from the rain? We just submerged ourselves in the warm waters and let the rain soak our faces. In this pool a passion fruit tree hung fruits over the water. I was fortunate enough to be under the tree when a ripe yellow fruit dropped into the water. It was soon consumed and thoroughly enjoyed. The smell of passion fruit filled the air at the edge of this pool. So in the rain I ate, kept very warm and allowed the rain to splash my half submerged body. I lay flat on some steps. A few other people came and went; but for the most part we were secluded and happy to be soaking until our skin wrinkled at the toes. Towards five o'clock we found two lounge chairs and sat watching a grand view of the volcano. Baldi Hot Springs is at the base of the Arenal Volcano. Huge plums of gray smoke would shoot above the peak of the volcano; sometimes the top of the volcano would have clouds mixing with volcanic plums. It was great to watch. By five thirty we were unpacking the locker and changing in the dressing room. The last half hour we looked in the gift shop and sat watching people come and go at the front entrance. Our driver was five minutes early. I liked him for this.

The visit to Baldi was totally unplanned. We had originally booked two nights in the hotel. On the third morning we walked around to see if we could find a cheaper hotel and stay an extra day. We had told Tarek and Marie we would be waiting for them on Wednesday in Jaco, but no emails and an instinct to know people tend to be later than sooner opened a new day for us to explore. The hotels were not any cheaper, more expensive, and we decided to stay put at Luigi's. There is a lot of pleasure in walking around and finding that you acquire the best deal for prices. The large double sized bathtub, the view from the balcony, and the location on the main street was enough to keep us satisfied after asking at three other hotels. I was checking for emails from Tarek. On Wednesday morning we got one saying they would be at our house that night. I panicked, but knew we had left word with the security guard to let them in. A second email came saying they would arrive Thursday; they had been having a wonderful time on the Caribbean Coast of Costa Rica.

We got back with enough sunlight to walk around town for a half hour. Then it was back to the room to prepare for the shuttle home at seven in the morning. A small finch had come into the room before we left and I opened the window to let the little guy out. The windows being open all day allowed many mosquitoes to come in so the night was a punctuated by slaps and moans. By morning I was taking my last pictures of the volcano from the balcony. The van was full of people when it arrived so Diana and I were sent to the last seats in the back. I passed the first hour speaking to a man from Berkley, California named Luis. He works as a college recruiter and was on his first visit to Costa Rica. We started by talking about the War On Drugs, the War on Terrorism, and the war on the people who want to let change happen in the USA. He comes from Mexican parents who immigrated to the USA thirty years ago. We had a great talk and he later sent me a link to a website that has some political viewpoints. We had a nice visit as the van rolled up and down mountains and hills. We opted for a seventy dollar four hour ride versus a ten-hour, ten-dollar trip. We are spoiled.

On a half hour stopover for a restroom break the world got very small. As soon as we pulled up I saw the bicyclist couple we had met in Granada, Nicaragua. I had emailed Kybi and visited his web site. When I walked up to him I began by teasing him, saying he never answered my email. He apologized and said he was very busy and seldom staying where there was Internet. They had been camping in the rain and told me how this particular day was clearer, with fewer showers than most. Dasa come out of the gift shop and asked Kybi about buying a decal for his bicycle. She recognized me and smiled hello. I asked Kybi for a photograph, he obliged and admitted that they had NO pictures of the two of them together. I promised to send the photograph to them.

Just as I was talking to Kybi, a recognizable young woman from the waterfalls walked by our group. I said, "Hi Nova Scotia, how are you?" She turned and looked surprised to see me two days after we had met at the waterfalls. "One of us is being followed," I joked. She said she was getting jaded from being around the teenagers. I said I admired her stamina. So in the span of two minutes I reconnected with two separate groups from two separate places. How cosmic! Traveling can be very strange. In New York I go months and never see the same people.

On the ride home we stopped at the bridge where the crocodiles eat food the tourists throw down to them. I priced some masks in a shop and we got our drop off organized with the driver. Door to door is what I like. So we returned home for a second time. I was instantly checking the email to see when Tarek and Marie would arrive. They were scheduled for twelve thirty that day, but arrived at three the next afternoon. If they were having a bad time I would have been upset. Diana went into overdrive cleaning. Don't ask me why.

Day One: Tarek and Marie in Jaco. We could see Tarek and Marie exiting a taxi at the front gate of the condo around five o'clock. They had stopped at the grocery store and brought a few bags of food and some wine. The bus from San Jose took them to the middle of Jaco where they saw a grocery store and got off. We had been cleaning and cooking and soon introduced them to Jose and Eligh. A few hours later we all sat down for a meal of beans and rice. Diana had prepared a special dinner. After Jose and Eligh left we sat around talking and ended with a home movie (DVD) I'd made of one of our trips to Arizona. They were fascinated by the Grand Canyon. The long bus ride had taken its toll on Tarek, and he began to snooze while the movie played. We all decided then, it was time for sleep.

Day Two: Playa Bejuco. In the morning, Tarek caught up with his Internet emails using our broadband connection. We all began to make lunch for a beach outing to Bejuco. Jose has a small piece of property about a mile from the beach, on a thin parcel of land near the main highway. We have been there many times and one of my favorite places to visit. It is an isolated four-mile stretch of beach that has two hotels, a few luxury homes, but mostly open fields and beautiful empty stretches of sandy beach. This is a place away from everything - a place to feel one's own soul.

On our way we stopped at Playa Hermosa, just south of Jaco. Tarek had read that the beach was one of the most surfed locations in all of Costa Rica. This beach is famous for surfing competitions that take place a few times a year. Today, the surf was too rough for anyone to be out in the water. We stood and watched a strong rip tide making swimming a challenge for anyone. Soon we headed south again along the coastal road that follows the shore. It is not a coastal highway, most of the journey one cannot see the shore, but the ocean lay a mile or less to the west. This is the famous Pan-American Highway that runs from Mexico to Panama. In Panama the highway ends in marshy swamp and the road does not continue to Colombia. It seems ridiculous that this last stretch of highway is blank. This could connect the continent of South America to North America but the marshy land is impassable. Another highway through nature may be a knife through her heart.

I was saying that we needed a new beach blanket so Jose suggested taking a few extra minutes and driving to the town of Parita. This extra jaunt would show our guests a real Tico town - some place tourists never go. Fifteen minutes later we pulled into the small village that has typical shops on its main street, but not much more. We found a store that sold old Goodwill clothes and I went rummaging through a pile of sheets and curtains to find a tablecloth. Also, we purchased a big, yellow, square curtain that would serve as an ideal beach blanket. To buy a "real" beach blanket would be absurd. The prices for anything tourists buy are triple. My previous beach blanket was a tablecloth from the local super market. We paid five dollars for the two fabrics and we all got into the car after Jose backed down a slight driveway. Our total weight was too much for the car's load.

The road that runs along the coast at Playa Bejuco is a dirt and sand road. Before we left we filled up the gas tank, so the weight of all the gas and the three adults in the back seat gave Jose's car good sag, so much so, that we were scraping bottom with the gravel and dirt on the beach road. The car was inches from the ground. If the tail pipe wasn't dragging the back wheels were rubbing the wheel wells. I thought we wouldn't make it at many points. Bob Marley was playing on the car's CD and we were singing along, as the car seemed to scrape bottom in time with the music. Tarek is always singing Bob Marley so we put on the music to make him feel at home.

We drove to the farthest point south where the river makes any further progress impossible. We all jumped out of the car, unloaded the gear and began to walk toward a shelter covered with palm leaves. There we set up for the day, putting food in bags, boogie boards, surfboards, and towels under the shade of the hut. I went off by myself as Diana and Marie slowly walked the shore. This beach is where I love to get off by myself and take a good long stroll. I was gathering seashells as I walked. The river that runs to the sea has a long, rushing current that leads a good half-mile to the actual shore. In low tide this is a vast stretch of sand where shells randomly pop their head above the sand. Most of the shells are white with thick edges, but sometimes there are some long thin, pointy shells. It is the place where I most often feel a deep pleasure that comes with solitude. Every time I walk this beach I feel my love for nature and life. I have a good talk with my God. In the distance I could see the spec of two dark bodies on the shore. Diana and Marie were far away. I have a ritual where I stop myself - I stop everything and express gratitude for being alive. This isn't so much directed at God as opening myself up to all that is so beautiful around me. It is a spiritual moment where I absorb the totality of the experience. I am not asking for a blessing, I am accepting the blessing that I often close myself away from by not being aware.

We all had gone in different directions. Tarek was in the water, Jose and Eligh were under the shack, but eventually we all found ourselves wanting food and sitting together again. I pulled out the bread and began to make sandwiches for everyone. The long French bread from the grocery store was cut into sections and we had chicken, cheese, and tomato with mayonnaise. After that we sliced up mangoes and passed them around. It was heavenly.

After lunch we all headed to the water. Jose disappeared into the wild surf with his surfboard, Tarek and I took out the boogie boards, and the women played with Eligh. He was riding his small surfboard in the small waves on shore. Jose leaves Eligh to himself and as a consequence, the child has a great deal of self-confidence. He knows how to handle himself in the surf and has no fear of being left alone in the water. Tarek and I caught some very good waves, yet the surf was tumbling us on occasion. A strong tide was pulling us far from where we had entered the shore. We were like two school kids bouncing and laughing, shouting to each other, "Take this one!" "Here comes a good one!" We went back to the hut with the women and sat waiting for Jose to return as Eligh continued to play by himself in the surf.

Eligh came out of the water and asked me to take him looking for shells so we walked as far as the river, then into the marsh that runs along the river. Diana and Marie caught up with us as we stood at the edge of the river. Diana took a tumble into the river as the soft, sandy ledge gave way. She dropped three feet and we all panicked, wondering about her safety. Her head popped up over the sandy bank and she was laughing. She was not hurt. It is nothing but fun to take an unexpected plunge. Eligh and I found more shells and the woman found their way back to the hut, as Eligh and I soon found our way back as well. Eligh lost his older brother the year before and I asked him if he missed him. He spoke as if he were still alive, but just not with us. In a matter of fact way he explained his death as being a temporary departure. As brief as life is he may have been very correct.

The tide had risen so high that the road we originally unloaded the car at was now covered in water. In a stroke of genius Jose decided to move the car away from the river as a precaution to what had just happened. The tide was the highest I have ever seen it at Bejuco. The strong surf and wind was pushing the waves closer to the line of vegetation near the hut. We gathered all our belongings and loaded the car. We had bits of driftwood, bags of shells, and great memories to take home. I told Tarek this was the real Costa Rica and not where the tourists go. He and Marie had seen a special place.

Just before the highway we stopped and exited the car. Eligh, Jose and I walked through a wet, murky, patch of water to get to his land. The other three passengers walked to the highway to wait for us. It seemed the car wasn't going to make it up the embankment to the highway without scrapping the bottom. Tarek lead the call to abandon ship and walk the short distance. The rain had been falling for many days and the property closest to the road was flooded. Jose wanted to see if his land was flooded as well. He plans on building a home someday and wanted to see if the drainage ditch he had put in was sufficient. It was. His land was dry.

He cut some sugarcane for us to chew on for the drive home. We walked in the ankle-deep waters back to the car. I assessed the reason that the floodwaters had nowhere to exit. The neighbors behind Jose's land had pilled dirt with a bulldozer so there was no place for the water to run. We discussed that perhaps the solution would be an extension of Jose's ditch to the end of the road where all the rainwater would run to the small creek nearby. As we got in the car Tarek was waving to us from the highway and asking, "Was everything OK?" They thought we had some car problems because of the delay. Jose and I stood assessing the water-flooded terrain. All was re-assured everything was all right as we crossed the road and picked them up.

We returned to Jaco and I suggested we take Tarek and Marie to see the sunset on the beach. We saw nothing because it was too cloudy and rain began to fall shortly thereafter. We all went into the swimming pool at the condo to wash off the sand. An hour later we reconvened in the house to enjoy a dinner of pesto and spaghetti. Jose made the fresh pesto sauce in his home and brought it over. It was another feast. We were all hungry beyond imagination. I had so much food my belly was round. We sipped wine and told stories about what we had seen and lived thus far in our lives. I love my family of friends.

Day Two: Tarek and Marie at Manuel Antonio National Park. At six o'clock Diana and I were up and packing for a two-day venture to Manuel Antonio National Park. At six-thirty I tapped on the door to wake Tarek and Marie. We had to catch the nine o'clock bus and had to get enough food and clothes together. I went off to the bank to get some cash, only to make the usual mistake I always do. I took out a tiny amount to discover it was something like thirty dollars. The money in Costa Rica is far beyond my ability because it is always in the thousand and tens of thousands. It's crazy. By eight forty, the four of us, were all walking down the street to the bus stop at the corner of our boulevard.

A taxi driver stopped and asked us if we wanted to ride to the park in his car for thirty dollars. The taxi drivers always lie and say it is longer and more dangerous than humanly possible. This guy even got out of his cab and came up to us sitting on the bus stop bench. He couldn't take no for an answer. Let's see, three dollars or thirty dollars. We would have to be stupid. The bus came and we put a few bags below in the storage compartment. The attendant told me to watch my backpack, emphasizing danger. Tarek and Marie sat in the last seats. I walked back to tell them what the bus attendant had said. Diana and I sat in the middle of the bus. The bumpy ride in the back is what upsets Diana's stomach. She was fast asleep from the Dramamine; and I listened to my mp3 player. We passed all the places we had been the day before. I pointed to Bejuco and Tarek gave a thumb up, recognizing where we were again.

Quapos is the small town before Manuel Antonio. The local bus goes there four times a day from Jaco, but the bus to the National Park runs every half hour. I wanted to buy some more food and watercolor paper so we crossed the street from the bus station and went into a store that sold everything. Marie wanted paper too. The store didn't have what I wanted. I misunderstood the woman's direction to the next store that might have paper. I went off by myself and got lost but finally finding the store I wanted. They didn't have watercolor paper either. I rejoined the group at the bus station. Tarek and Diana went off to find a bank machine and Marie sat on a bench as I went to a fruit stand and bought bananas and mangoes. By the time the next bus arrived we were first to board and headed over the hilly ride to the white sand beach of Manuel Antonio.

This stretch of road over the hills has never appealed to me. Dozens, if not hundreds, of hotels spot the ride. It is where development and nature have their worst clash in Costa Rica. It feels more like California, traffic included. There is one restaurant that is made out of an old train car, another restaurant that is made out of a crashed US Army cargo plane; there are ugly hotels; fancy hotels, and a few places for local people to afford. The drive to the park is an eye sore. The only good thing about these hotels is that they lay on the bus line and it is a US quarter (In Costa Rican Colons) to get to the park and beach that is before the park. Someone wisely thought a bus line would be a lucrative service for all the tourists here.

We arrived at the beach and Tarek and I went off to find a hotel. A guy who works on the beach asked us if we wanted some beach chairs; and next thing we knew he was taking us to hotels. Tarek stopped him and said we didn't need him, but the shirtless fellow assured us it was a free service to us. (The hotel would give him the commission.) We checked five hotels; three were full, one had a cockroach tenant and the last one had only one room and an additional, separate suite. We wanted separate rooms so we negotiated for the two rooms. Diana and I would take the suite; our French companions the smaller room. The first price for the suite was sixty dollars, we got it for forty-five because we wanted the two rooms. We had two double beds, air conditioning, a kitchen and refrigerator. Outside there was a table and we were all set.

Our shirtless buddy left us at the beach. He got no commission. The first thing we did was eating in the room. We had packed avocados, tuna, crackers, fruit and bread. We ate to fill the hunger and stress from looking for a hotel. The best price was the hotel we found. It was lucky all the places were full. Tarek had his Lonely Planet book with him so he was looking at the low-end places. Yet, the hotel we found was less than those listed in the book.

Within the hour we had made our way down a dirt path to the white sand beach that lay outside of Manuel Antonio National Park. This is a very small area with waiters and chair-jockey's selling their wares. We had promised the shirtless hawker we'd use his beach chairs. A muscular well-spoken Tico took us to some chairs and began to dig a hole for an umbrella. "How much is it?" I asked twice as he ignored me. "Twenty dollars." Diana negotiated sixteen. When I joined Tarek in the water he wanted to cancel because of the high cost. I'd already paid.

There are six or seven gift shops, a grocery store, four restaurants, all within a few feet, but there is only one street corner. On that end of the beach there is not much, except beautiful nature, of course. Walking up a slight hill were hotels grouped in a tiny area. These all stand near the entrance to the National Park. The road leading to our hotel was up the slight hill, the road was deteriorated, difficult to walk on, and a car had just as much fun. After this small cluster of commercial buildings on the corner across from the beach, the road continues about a sixteenth of a mile and comes to a roundabout. There is parking for the National Park there, and also in another parking lot next to our hotel back near the park entrance.

We went back and forth to the water and lounge chairs. Waiters from the few restaurants would come up and offer to bring us drinks. At happy hour, Tarek treated Diana and me to a Pina Colada. After many hours, Diana and I walked down the beach to a street lined with souvenir stalls. I found an indigenous, Baruka mask, but told the seller I would return the next day if he could show me a better selection. He assured me that he was getting more in the next day. We returned to the chairs and all decided to go to a restaurant overlooking the bay, high in the mountain. Tarek had read about "The Airplane" and we had passed it on the way on the bus. An hour later we were in a taxi, after showering in our rooms. The driver was guarded and not as friendly as most Tico's.

We walked into "La Avion" (Spanish for airplane), up a flight of stairs to a group of people looking at something in the tree. It was a sloth slowly climbing up the tree. It was going to be a fun evening and this was our opening moment. We joined the crowd and pulled out all the cameras. Marie is a born photographer and is shooting pictures constantly. We had a good view of the bay, so that served as a topic for photography as well. That deck had all the tables filled by customers, so we made our way downstairs to a corner table with a perfect view of the same scenery. The next hour we sipped on Pina Coladas and took pictures of the progressing red sunset over the ocean. Next to our table four French people sat talking, soon to be cross talking with our two French friends. The conversation would drift from English to French to include Diana and myself. It was a fun time. Marie got a little loose from the drinks but we made sure she was safe in the taxi. We headed back to the village of Manuel Antonio where we found a single grocery store, bought lunch for our venture into the park the next day, and began to look for a place to eat.

On one of the corners we entered a restaurant and spent the next few hours enjoying each other's company. Marie sprained her ankle on the sidewalk as we neared the restaurant, so she was feeling slight pain. In the taxi from the "La Avion" she became very animated from the alcohol and sang French songs to the taxi driver. She kept telling the driver how she loved Costa Rica and the people. This driver was friendly and open, joking with us. Throughout the meal Marie would change ice in plastic bags that the bar tender brought over. More wine and good food filled our stomachs and time lessened Marie's ankle pain.

As we sat there a woman at the nearby bar kept looking at us. She was listening in to our conversations and eventually approached the table and began to speak in French. She and Marie immediately went into a deep conversation. The woman was talking very fast with a great deal of emotion. I asked what all the talk was about. It seems the woman had come with a man from France and they had split up a few days before. The man had been acting rude, using her money and rental car, to a point of separation. The man then went to Facebook and began a slanderous attack campaign with her friends. The woman needed to vent and found Marie and Tarek to be good listeners. I was thinking the guy's name was Manfred, and asked, but it wasn't he. Eventually, we found where the woman was staying. It was a hotel where we had tried to find a room. We invited her to join us for breakfast the next morning. We were fast asleep within a half hour of leaving the restaurant. Tarek wanted to be awaked at six-thirty.

Day Three: Tarek and Marie at Manuel Antonio National Park. The next morning at six Diana and I were awake, getting things ready for breakfast and lunch. Tarek went to get Sandrina, the French woman, and we all sat down to scrambled eggs and bread. The hotel rooms' kitchenette had just enough silverware and pans to get by. This had absolutely no effect on the delicious food. We sat and visited while Marie made sandwiches. Sandrina was much calmer and explained she had been going to the restaurant where we met, and she became friends with the waiters and bartender. They warned her against strangers putting drugs in her drinks and told her where to buy the best clothes in Quapos. She didn't seem as vulnerable and had been making friends, us included.

The park has a limit of eight hundred people on weekends, and five hundred during the week. The entrance is not so obvious because it is off the main street, away from the beach. The exit to the park is on the beach with the entrance far from the beach. Inside the park a dirt road leads to the shore, but first goes into the heart of the park. We had to walk up few hills, then down to the water. When I first went to the park, maybe twelve years before, you could enter and exit the park on the shore side. Now, foot traffic was directed to see more of the park than just the ocean. The white sandy beach is where most people spend the day. The entrance fee is ten dollars each. A sign said we must show our passports but no one asked to see them when I bought the tickets. A short fifteen to twenty minute walk puts you at one of the most beautiful white sandy beaches in Costa Rica.

At the park entrance there are men selling guided tours. Some of them come across as if the guide is required. We knew better, paid our entrance fee, and soon left the crowd of park goers. It is a bit confusing at the entrance. Large groups are assembling, monkeys are running around stealing food, and guides are trying to sell a tour. There is always a line to buy the tickets, especially in the mornings.

Marie's sprained ankle was still hurting so she was slower than the rest of us. I walked ahead and struck up a conversation with an American couple from Seattle, Washington. The man's fascination was with bamboo. I asked if he was a biologist. "No, but I do creative landscaping and am on the Board of Directors for the American Bamboo Association." I was impressed and told the man he would see a huge grove of bamboo ahead. The couple had a son who I sat and briefly spoke with as his parents slowed their walk up the slight hill. I sat talking so long that Marie and the crew caught up with me. The crest of the hill is where I sat talking with the young high school student. He didn't like black and white photography because of all the chemicals. I could tell he would be an excellent student to convert to the "old fashioned" art form. Students are often put off by the lack of color and too many chemicals. They think photography should be pushing a button and getting instant results, thus digital photography and its convenience. In black and white photography there are many challenges that involve manual dexterity, something education in general seems to lack. We sit children at desks and wonder why they get bored.

We all made our way down to the beach and situated all our things in the shade of a large tree. It wasn't long before a crowd was standing, looking, and pointing at a group of monkeys. Before anyone could do anything one of the monkeys was in a bag rummaging through, grabbing some food, and up a tree. We ran over to keep more monkeys away, but the terrorist activities had begun. It was already up to level orange, when a stealth group of monkeys were slipping through the underbrush for goodies in bags. As the monkeys made their way down the beach you could see people suddenly standing, walking toward their bags, and making clapping noises. None of this did anything but amuse the monkeys. The only thing that worked was a stick. The raccoons understood sand in the eyes. (This wasn't my idea. The ranger came by and told us that one.) The monkeys were the real threat; they would even jump up on people and take their food. This was fun at first but enjoying a quiet moment on the beach was out of the question. The monkeys went far enough down the beach that I feel asleep for a few minutes, until they retraced the shore path and caused havoc again. They don't even look cute. They have the faces of bandits and little angry people. Some of them are wounded and have limps, or scars, from being attacked by tourists. They reminded me of convicts and so the tourists treated them as such.

Tarek and I went snorkeling. I had made a special effort to bring the heavy load all the way from Jaco, up the hill inside the park; I was going to make sure I used them. We did once. Tarek and I swam to a series of rocks on the edge of the small bay. There was nothing to be seen under the water. I couldn't even see my hand in front of my face. I did see Tarek's foot miss my nose by inches, so I grabbed it and he jumped, thinking a fish had bitten him. I got a good laugh. He wasn't as thrilled. We stood on the rocks and had a long talk, telling each other about our lives, and getting to know each other. We stood talking so long that the tide had receded and more of the rocks were being exposed. We talked about our relationships past and present with woman. A slow swim back to the beach and we were eating the sandwiches. We kept guard watching out for the monkeys. I pulled out a banana and an iguana came running out of the underbrush. He stopped a few feet away and sniffed the air. I threw a piece to the lizard and he ate the banana, sand and all. Another type of lizard saw this and came over to look for a handout as well. This lizard looked like a tiny dragon. Soon a raccoon came walking by and we all jumped to our feet, but it only sniffed the air and kept going.

As we lay on the beach blanket we could hear loud claps of thunder in the direction of our hotel, over the hill. The clouds grew very dark and I made a precipitous prediction for rain. It did indeed, but it was a very light rain. Tarek and Marie went off to look for the waterfall he had read about, despite the condition of Marie's ankle. Sandrina went back to her hotel while Diana and I took a slow walk along a second beach inside the park. This beach is separated by a hilly outcrop and serves as the boundary for the park entrance along the shore. As we walked we saw an increasingly cloudy sky and decided to just go back to the restaurants along the public beach. It was a wise choice because it soon was raining. The path between the park exit and the public beach has a small (very small) river. Here is one of the most ridiculous tourist attractions of all Costa Rica. A man stands at a boat that covers the length of the narrow river; this is a six-foot wide point where the water passes. The man tries to lure tourists into the boat. The boat acts as a bridge really. A drunken man stands there and tries to attract tourists with his charm and wit. The fool can hardly stand up straight but is trying to conduct business. Sadly, or maybe not, all the people walk pass him into the two inch deep stream and get their feet wet rather than encounter the drunk. Never have I seen any one use this service, even when the river was seven inches deep. Of course, the man says there is no charge, but the minute someone walks onto the boat a bear trap springs shut and thus a tourist's trap and an extra expense!

Diana and I found the cheapest, fast food place in the beach zone and sat drinking tamarindo. This fruit drink is out of this world, it is so delicious. We sat there so long while the rain pounded the sandy beach that we ordered three of these drinks. The man actually shook my hand when we left with Tarek and Marie two hours later. He told Diana as we bought the last drink, "Your husband really likes tamarindo." She agreed. We were trying to kill time by buying drinks instead of being squatters. As we sat there a group of young Americans sat at a table in a bar directly behind us. One of the girls even shared the same bench as ours, leaning over to join the party. It was one of these women's birthday. I saw the whole party when first Diana left to change back at the hotel, then to see them sing happy birthday. They all got progressively drunk. Tico men came around like flies. One man presented a gift from his pocket; he probably stole it from a souvenir shop. He made flirtatious advances toward one, then another woman, until he got the message. There were long periods of silence as the liqueur wore deep trenches into their arteries and numbed their brains. No one was speaking and the full burden of drinking came full circle as the hangover begun. Eventually, only three girls were sitting, not laughing, waiting for an answer from heaven to pull them out of their dull nightmare. I was quietly watching this episode of youth unfold. It reminded me of my own stupidity when I was young. Now, two beers is my max, which happens once every few months. With Tarek and Marie we did drink wine. The most wine I have ever seen my wife drink, which are three small glasses.

We all convened at the corner restaurant where we had met Sandrina the night before. Sandrina sat at the same bar stool when we went up and said our last good-byes. We exchange emails. Diana and Marie went off to buy a handbag; and I found a hand-made, stained glass figure of Kokopelli that found its way into my bag for eighteen dollars. Tarek sat at the bar with Sandrina. At five o'clock we got into the bus and rode back to Quapos to get our connection. We walked from the bus to the ticket office, to the Jaco bus, and pulled out of the terminal five minutes later.

All was going well and we had a very delightful, but rainy, ride back to Jaco. The ride home was fine until the bus overshot our stop by about a mile. We had to walk in the rain, in the dark, along a dangerous highway back to the condominiums. Diana and the driver arranged this by misunderstanding each other; also the fact that the electricity and lights on that side of Jaco were completely out. There was no way to see where the condo was. I just knew we were going way past our stop and I was furious for letting Diana screw up a simple bus stop. I had to apologize that night, the next day, the next week, the next month, and the following year, which is yet to come. The apology goes somewhere into the unseen future. I wasn't nice to my wife and my silence gave way to a flurry of words that cannot nor should not be repeated to minors. My embarrassment follows me to this day because my French companions were learning new English words that they never heard in school.

The next morning we all did our usual chores, Tarek went off to find a rental car, Diana cleaned the house, and I wrote this book, trying to be forgiven by my wife for embarrassing her in front of others by my cursing. Marie kept herself busy packing. Somewhere around noon we said our last good-byes until a planned reunion in the unknown future. Before they left I made a public apology to everyone about my anger the night before. Luckily my wife has forgiven me.

Day One: Jaco, Lina, Kybi, and Dasa. As life turns in wheels things all seem to come together and apart in a natural progression when people come and people go. Diana cleans the house and more dirt arrives. We have the cleanest house in the world. I wish it was not so at times. I wish I could see my wife just being lazy, but let's face it, things could be worst. She won't sit still. The one day we had between guests Diana spent cleaning. I get to a point where I'm telling her to leave some items alone, let the dirt have a chance to settle for a few hours. Ceramics on a shelf don't need that kind of daily attention, weekly not even, monthly maybe. I must secretly admit the house looks terrific. When Diana's cousin, Lina, walked in the door she was impressed. The artist in me likes to decorate; my wife thinks this is the domain of the female. I like to have things set on a shelf for years, my wife thinks that items need to be cycled monthly. To keep an object stored away in a box, to be cycled, is a crazy thing to me. In some ways I still think I'm single. I want life to be MY WAY. How silly of me to think I'm Frank Sinatra.

The entire day was about picking up Diana's cousin, Lina. Lina lives in Florida with her mother. We bought the bus tickets two days before. We know how to get the bus at the airport, although there is only a stop on the highway to return back to Jaco. (No station) At nine o'clock we took the bus to meet her cousin. I had to pull Diana away from cleaning. I wrote on the computer most of the ride, until the winding road was too much. At the airport I continued to work on the tiny laptop and was surprised when Diana and Lina walked up to greet me. She was a half hour early. We caught a cab to Alajuela and went to see our friends who own an electronics store. We also left Lina's bag so we could walk around unencumbered. Our first stop was the central market.

The market is a clean, narrow, old-fashioned market with stalls of individual shops. We know where the food is best, went into the restaurant section and found a seat. The lunch was a typical Coat Rica big meal of rice and chicken. After lunch, we went to the church and made a short visit. I know this is important to both women. Ice cream treats followed. Then we sat in the central park for two hours and watched life going by. We returned to the friend's business and took a taxi to the bus stop. The wait was short because I continued to type this story and pass the time as the two women talked. I planned to write some more once I got on the bus. That was short-lived because a man sat next to me in the front seat. He asked to switch seats with Diana because his leg needed extra space, as he uses a cane and the leg was stiff.

His name was conspiracy-theory-Jim. (Not his real name which for all I know could have been a lie, but we'll call him Jim.) I got a few lines typed on the computer when I knew it was going to be impossible, besides I was getting fresh information for this book. Its valuable stuff I can embellish but never make up. Jim started by explaining the US government was trying to kills us but quickly changed the subject to a terrible motorcycle accident that had nearly killed him a year and a half before. A car had clipped his knee, severed his leg and thrown him against his handlebars taking out an eye. He showed me the missing eye socket. He was in the hospital for months and the first few days it was not believed he would live. He described how many surgeries and screws were put into the titanium rod that replaced his left leg. I lost count; even though each time he described his injury he restated the numbers and lengths of every screw. The eye was re-infected after he left the hospital and he went into the gooey details about the extent of the infection and how the doctors thought he was going to have the entire eye socket surgical removed.

The second accident he described was a broken shoulder blade that some "stupid uninsured kid" on another motorcycle caused. I had to ask if this was after the first accident involving a motorcycle. Yes, he had been on his motorcycle with a titanium leg, and one eye, when a "stupid kid" ran into him. He kept showing me his scarred shoulder blade while lifting his shirt and pointing to it. People would look at his animated gestures and listen even though they didn't speak English. I caught Diana's eyes a few rows back. She seemed to be listening. Half the bus was listening to his loud story. Later she said she couldn't really hear what he was saying, only that it was a long, involved story; and she was right.

I tried to steer the conversation into more quiet waters, asking him about his past. He jumped into telling me that the government was lacing the skies with a chemical that was slowly killing off people. "Some people also believe that the government is creating electronic grids with these chemicals so that the electromagnetic communications are clearer;" he bumped it up to a more logical explanation when I protested this was impossible. "I think that could be a more realistic explanation as to why the Air Force is always criss-crossing the skies in the mid-west," I returned. I'm thinking to myself, the government wants people to pay their taxes; therefore, killing them off isn't a wise choice. Jim then went into the 9/11 theories about the third building and how it's collapse was an explosives detonation. "I've seen a movie that supports that," I said. I think we were at least getting closer to a more grounded communication. "When they control the computers it's all over for all of us," he said. I agreed completely on that point.

The conversation began to calm down when I asked him about his life; how he had come to Costa Rica ten years earlier; and what he was doing when he left the United States. He had lived in Austin, Texas and graduated from a college in Ohio. He had traveled to India seven times and talked about living amongst the poor; walking for months and seeing that beautiful country. He told me the men that built the Taj Mahal all had their hands cut off so they would never build another building as beautiful. This came out of speaking about how strict Islam is in Saudi Arabia. Yes, we were jumping from country to country, and subject to subject, but I was fascinated, mostly because he didn't seem crazy, just very hyper. People fascinate me, how they view reality, and their explanations of events. I should have been a psychologist. Art involves a great deal of psychology, so maybe I am in the right field anyway.

He had wanted to get away from selling electric-light fixtures in Austin so he bought an organic herb farm just outside of Austin. He was growing herbs when he decided to cash it all in and move to Costa Rica. But I came to find out this wasn't the whole reason. He continued by saying, "I hope you don't judge me about this." I was afraid I was sitting with a serial killer. (And just between you and me, yes I was passing judgment.) He continued, "I was in a strip tease bar down in Florida and got pulled over for a DWI. They saw me pull out of the place and followed me. They knew I'd been drinking. Well, when my old man died in New Jersey I tried to get a New Jersey license and they told me there was an outstanding warrant because I skipped my parole in Florida". (Yes, a new State and a new fold in the story. Things were getting very wrinkled by then and we were only half way to Jaco.)

He continued further, "I knew this was a problem and I just got fed up with everything and left the country". "Didn't you think this would all catch up with you someday?" I asked. "Well yeah, it did. That F*** George Bush got a law passed that would cutoff anyone with any warrants from their social security pension. So my five hundred dollar a month pension was cut off. A lawyer friend of mine took photographs of my injuries to a judge in Florida and he dropped the charged to a misdemeanor. I still owe the lawyer four thousand dollars. So my pension is reinstated and I now get five hundred dollars a month from the Social Security Administration".

"What did you do in Costa Rica all these ten years?" I asked. "Well I had a restaurant with my x-wife. She took all my money and threw me out for domestic violence. I had a very successful electric fan business until two of my employees ripped me off. One of them would take fans out at night in black plastic bags. I thought I had a room full of fans, but came to find out that half the boxes were empty. I'd been ripped off. Then when I got Dingy Fever I hired a kid who stole everything else I had."

"The woman with me today has been kind enough to take me in." He pointed to her behind us. "I have been hired by a call center near San Jose and start as soon as I straighten out all my Costa Rican legal papers." He then went into a twenty-minute explanation about the Costa Rican social services system and the red tape that lawyers face between the separate agencies. I was getting some useful information if I ever live in this country.

As I sat with Jim, I saw Kybi and Dasa on their bicycles along the highway. I popped my head out the window of the bus and yelled hello to them. They had been emailing us and asked to visit Jaco. We met them in Granada, Nicaragua at Amigo's Hotel. As I stuck my head out and yelled I clipped my eyeglasses on the bus window. My lens went flying out the window and I had a pair of glasses with one eyepiece. Jim and his one eye were beginning to rub off on me. I think his accident-prone karma was rubbing off on me. I was glad to know that Kybi and Dasa were a few miles away from Jaco and continued talking with Jim. He admitted he was a pretty angry guy. He complimented me and said I was "innocent" meaning not corrupted by life. I don't think of myself as innocent, but compared to Jim maybe I was. I noted his negative references to woman, using the "P" word. I asked if he had any children. "No," he had surgical vasectomy years before.

He went into another description about his cameras and shooting photographs of all the seventies rock and roll stars. His pictures were now all mildewed and sitting in his rented house in boxes. I was wondering how such a well-spoken, educated man could end up penniless and living a broken life in Costa Rica. He wasn't a druggie, he said so. He was just a sad story all around. I was exhausted and pretty much intrigued by his story the entire way home. He got off the bus at the town before Jaco and Diana joined me in the empty seat he had occupied. I couldn't begin to re-tell everything. I haven't even told you the entire story, his life as a photographer, his life in India, and his exploits with Costa Rican hookers. How could I tell it all? I need a new novel to cover everything. Jim - minus one eye, and having lived in India reminded me of my friend, Julio, back in Guatemala. I told Jim about Julio losing one eye also. I waved good-bye to him when he was walking away with his cane on the side of the road. He didn't see me.

We got off the bus in the middle of Jaco and went into the super market to buy eggs. Lina wanted something but I don't know what. We took a cab home and found that Kybi and Dasa had just arrived within minutes. We greeted them and did the introductions. I asked them to come to our home for dinner and set an hour appointment to rejoin us. I went home and made a salad and burritos. Diana and Lina started to visit with each other, talking in rapid-fire Spanish, which only a Colombian could follow. I certainly didn't.

Kybi isn't his real name but Dasa is her real name. Kybi is a nickname. In Slovakian language it is short for cyber because he is a cyber-geek. They are a very interesting couple. They have been on the road bicycling for six months. They started in Mexico City. We took out a Lonely Planet book and opened to a map of Central America. One of the most challenging parts of their journey was trekking through the jungles in Northern Guatemala. They had cycled through jungle paths where only four-wheel drive trucks pass. They said their water supply was critically low and monitoring when to drink was important. There was no replenishing supply of fresh water. In one part of Nicaragua they said they were nearly mauled by people grabbing at them asking for food and money.

In Honduras and Nicaragua they cycled through areas that are political separatist's hot zones. Unbeknown to me these two countries have areas that are involved with an armed separatist movement. There is no real government presence, nor any police or military. People ride around in cars and trucks with firearms. Some of these areas were so remote that they had to first get there by boat. In one town they sat with a man holding a rifle. After a visit and him asking them where they were from the man excused himself, and said he had to go to work. They asked him his occupation. In a nonchalant way he simply answered he was a guerilla going on his patrol. They said people never know where Slovakia is so they routinely told them they were Russians. Their blonde hair and light complexions made them look very Russian, so rather than try to explain where Slovakia was they came up with a more identifiable country. Kybi also said that he thought a Russian is more feared so he played that role. If somebody asked if they were American they instantly say no to avoid being a target for kidnapping. I asked if they were ever robbed and Kybi reluctantly disclosed that in Mexico City, soon after their arrival, children stole his GPS off the front handlebars of his bicycle. The children overtook them, surrounding and mobbing them all at once. "We paid the local police one hundred Pesos and they brought it back to us within the hour. The police bought it back from the children."

We sat mesmerized as Kybi told us about his cycling through Iran, Afghanistan, Pakistan, and up into China. He said in Iran the children and streets were lawless. The people would grab at him and push him around. In Afghanistan he met the most polite, hospitable, and gentle people he had ever known. "I would ride into a village and two hundred people would come out to greet me. They would stand in silence and look at me." He went on to tell how they would invite him into their homes, cook for him, and have him sleep there. In Pakistan he had the same kind of hospitality. I had lived in Pakistan so I was very interested in his view of this country. It was similar to mine. The people are wonderful. The common people have the purest hearts and are very generous. I lived there when I was a teenager and still carry fond memories of an exciting time in my life. To hear Kybi's stories rekindled my own memories.

The summer before Kybi and Dasa went to Africa together. They had met three years before when Kybi put an advertisement online, looking for a female cyclist who wanted to trek. Their first adventure was in Indonesia. They interviewed each other and three months later they were traveling together. Now think about this. I boast of how I met Diana online, but these two met, did an interview process, and three months later went off to a foreign land to bicycle around. Romance wasn't on the agenda. (So they say!) They are both physically fit; they have to be able to ride a bike for months on end. They are both well educated. Dasa is actually a doctor and worked in Switzerland before she gave it up to travel and see the world. Kybi has a computer degree and works as a freelance web designer. He's done some jobs on this latest leg of his travels, building a web site for a tour company. He has his computer with him so he is capable of traveling and working at the same time.

The first time we met I saw him sitting for hours at his computer in Amigos hotel in Granada, Nicaragua. I explained to him at dinner that I was wondering why this guy was stuck at the computer and not out sightseeing. He told me he was updating his blog. At that meeting he gave me his web address and I gave him mine. I didn't get to see his photographs until a week later when we arrived in Jaco. (His address is http://foto.kybi.sk). His photographs impressed me. He said he has so many pictures he hasn't even seen them all. I never had a deep contact with him in Granada because we were always coming and going or he was in his hotel room working on his computer. I talked with Dasa one night while I was making dinner in the communal kitchen. We were dodging each other's cooking routine, while talking travel.

I may have mentioned losing my pants in Amigos. It rained one day and our clothes were hanging on the line to dry. When we came home the clothes were in a pile, dry, and off to the side. I didn't notice that the pants were gone until a few days later when I unpacked in Jaco. I thought they were somewhere stuffed out of place. Dasa mentioned that she had lost some clothes at Amigos as well. I didn't bring it up at first, but I was wondering if Dasa had picked up the clothes and put them out of the rain. I was thinking that she might have my pants by mistake and asked. I was wondering if it were she or Art (the Polish Christian that wanted to start a language school). No, in fact, another woman had come to the hotel to pay for the laundry service they advertised at the front of the hotel. This woman had lost a number of clothing items as well. I was laughing because

I found that not only were my clothes missing, but also several other people were missing their clothes from Amigos. These pants I lost were my favorite, light weight, and thin, perfect for hot weather. I wore them almost every day until I lost them. The suspicion lies with the elderly owner, but we may never know who is stealing clothes at Amigos. I can replace the pants. If you ever visit Amigos watch your clothes!

We sat exchanging stories and drinking wine for hours. The different peoples they encountered fascinated me. They said the Mayans, or Indians in Guatemala were very difficult to communicate with. While in other countries the people were helpful and easy to obtain simple needs like shelter and food, the Mayans of Guatemala had a built in suspicion and mistrust for foreigners.

The second night I was visiting with them in Jose's apartment, Dasa and Kybi showed me the route they had taken from Mexico City. (Jose gave them permission to stay in his house while he took his son back to the USA. I made the request.). They use Google Maps to track their progress through a satellite feed on Kybi's global navigator. A red line follows the route and gives a very accurate reading. It showed where in one part of Guatemala, they had to go backwards and double track where there were no roads. They assumed roads were where there were none. The first night Dasa explained the route but it didn't make sense to me until I saw the map. On the program in Google it shows elevations as well. They described the most difficult and challenging uphill climbs were in Guatemala. Dasa showed me where the highest roads zigzagged, moving the image closer and closer to the path they followed.

They continued with more travel stories. In the most remote areas of Guatemala and Honduras the people live like the old Wild West. There is a cowboy mentality where people survive by the gun; everyone is wearing one for protection. These two areas are disenfranchised from their governments and separated by the populated cities. There are few if any roads that economically link these provinces to their own countries. This is where the new separatist movement is taking hold. If you think about it, the areas have no airports, no highways; they are isolated economically and have no police, or military, protection. They must feel like they live in a foreign land. I am curious what political solutions will be needed to connect these two areas; the alternative is a new country that these people want to create. If the two separatist groups from both countries join this would pose a big political problem for both Honduras and Guatemala. (Someday this may be history or, never happen.)

We spent a lot of time talking technology. I had an idea to video their route and put it in a movie. We looked at their web site, I showed them mine, and they showed me other cyclists that were plotting similar journeys on Google Maps. There is a web site where cyclists write each other and tell their stories. I called Dasa and Kybi "earthtronautics" because they travel the earth and document their journey.

One thing they explained to me was how nice it is to be here in Jaco. Here they have been able to stay put and not forced to be in constant motion out in the elements. The first day they only left the complex to get food. It is a luxury for them to be able to sit in a house, cook a meal, and sleep in a real bed. Kybi said one of the distinctions of Costa Rica was how hospitable all the people have been, to such a degree that they have not paid to stay in one hotel. Even in San Jose, the capitol, they found a man on the Internet that allowed people to "couch surf," as he told me. This is a network of people around the globe that sleep in people's houses and crash on their sofa. This is all done on the Internet. This seems like a wonderful way to both meet people and save money.

We talked about the "Fall of Communism." I was wondering how such a strong-gripped system could just one day fall apart. Kybi and Dasa were around seven years old when this happened. There wasn't one gunshot. The Communist party just faded away but the police and all the social services stayed the same. Before the fall of communism they produced a few items in Slovakia, but after the fall, a flood of Western products came in. Instead of two types of blenders there were now ten. They believe that this "soft revolution" would have never happened had big corporations not wanted to go into those countries and sell product. They believe that the profits that went out of these communist countries made the west much richer and they in turn became poorer, or at least, in the short fall. What is "bad" about Capitalism is the wide gap that now exists between the rich and the poor. "Before all the people were equal. Now the rich live like kings and the poor are suffering." Kybi said. He went on, "Before the people were all helping each other and sharing what they had". It seems the general state of low income was an equalizing factor. "Now people are hoarding what they have and not worried about their neighbors," Dasa added.

All this causes me great wonder at the duality of the world. These countries were not "Christian," yet the people shared. When the wall of communism fell the "Christian West" came in and instilled non-sharing lifestyles. Now, what keeps the unbridled capitalism in check? With this expansion comes greater corporate pollution and poverty. Yes, the people have liberty and incentives to work hard and "get ahead". But I wonder if there isn't a balance to come in the future where "business with pollution" is kept in control and people are put first again.

Kybi said a big part of the soft revolution was due to computers and the openness that they provide between nations. Ideals are free to be exchanged when the government doesn't control personal liberties, but this was happening anyway. Maybe not to the extent we in the West have, but the "intelligentsia" (as Kybi put it) was free to push this new spread of Capitalism through and change the government. I found this all very interesting because, as they explained, Communist bloc countries really were (in some ways) a better way of life for the majority of peoples. I was raised with the black and white issue, Capitalism good, Communism bad. I spoke about a Greek man in the beginning of this book who said we have "Corporate Democracy" in the USA. He was right. The future is ripe for change back to a more responsible, people-first oriented system. In the USA today the drum beat of the two parties is NOT causing any solutions to be possible. Democrats think spending money and regulating corporations is the best way to stimulate the economy, while Republicans think less government, more business, and cutting taxes is the solution. Anyone can see both parties have legitimate positions on individual points, but they both are so entrenched in their political positions that compromise is impossible. This stalemate is dangerous for my country. The constant back and forth of these positions with the changing pendulum-swings of election results has crippled my government. Progress gets voted out and conservatives want bring back the past. The two-party system is strangling itself. So we promote Democracy around the world when we have a dysfunctional system. My view is that Social Democracy (modern socialism) has to balance the corporate greed. The idea of having no, or a smaller government, is nearly impossible. Oddly enough both Bush II and Reagan expanded the government.

Dasa and Kybi are very bright young people. I like listening to them speak in Slovakian and go back and forth, having verbal sparring like all couples. Over the last few days I have been able to get a good idea about who they are as people. They don't have a mean bone in their bodies, but they fire words back and forth like missals. He chews her out when she makes errors on the computer. They spend their entire day on the computer; and that is while not riding bikes through several countries. He is always working on his travel blog. She has been working on full color photograph books they send to their parents back in Europe. Dasa creates the books of their travels online and they send them to their parents from a company inside Europe. The parents are not geared toward blogs, or computers, so they like to send a photograph book to the parents. I think it's a very cool gesture. It is one more reason that I like these people and their creativity.

I asked Kybi a lot of questions about the computer. He knows programming code. He was explaining to me the way a computer functions, how it is put together and operates. Some of this I know, but I always learn when listening to a new cyber-geek. He said he did his first programming at age seven. Dasa is a plastic surgeon and she is so smart it comes out in her use of languages. She has been exposed to Spanish for three months and is speaking as well as me after five years. She claims it is due to learning Latin for her studies to become a doctor. They both remind me of my niece and nephew; I am sure, because of the age proximity. They feel like family and we have been able to share so much with them. They eat here, use the washing machine, and if they need something they walk a few houses away and come here.

There is a dog here in the condo complex. The dog is a Chiwawa called Luna (moon). Luna belongs to a Canadian who lives here and is married to a Tica. The man who owns Luna had just gone to Canada for work because the economy is so slow here in Jaco. My Canadian friend got a job in the sand oils fields, but his wife and son are still living here. The dog is without a master and has been coming over to see me several times a day. Lina (Diana's cousin) and Diana have been calling me to the door to come see the dog when she arrives. The dog stands at the door and waits for me to come out, sit down, and be stroked (petted). She is a lap dog. One day I was napping, fast asleep on the sofa when the dog came and stood at the door. Lina and Diana were sitting inside watching to see what the dog would do. She stood at the door and rose on his two hind legs to peak at me laying in the living room. I never woke up and the dog left as if the other woman didn't matter. "Dennis was sleeping so I'm leaving" is what Diana said the dog was thinking. As I am catching up with the writing on the computer, Luna is on my lap. She just sits and doesn't do anything but look out at the world. It's a great life here in Costa Rica. It's like life is supposed to be. Luna says so.

With only days left here we have rented a car for a few days and took Lina, Dasa and Kybi to the cliffs at Bajamar. We go there every time we can now since my first visit there last summer was with Jose. While swimming in the rough surf Kybi lost the fins as a wave knocked him over; I lost my wedding engagement band for the same reason. Last year I lost my wedding ring. I'll replace this ring just as I did my wedding ring. In Colombia they use different hands for the wedding ring than in the USA. I have been wearing two wedding bands, one for each hand to show Diana we are married in both cultures. A wave knocked me so hard I didn't even notice the rings was gone until we were eating a picnic lunch on a blanket. I looked at my empty finger, couldn't feel any absence, but it was gone. Both Kybi and I were knocked very hard by the surf. I was trying to show Kybi how to use the boogie board but it was a disaster. The surf was pounding, the current pulled us toward the cliffs, and the waves were at least fifteen feet high. We gave up and he sat on the cliff watching the surf with Dasa. Diana and I took a long walk. I've been trying to figure how to get another ring from Colombia since we won't be going there for almost a year; maybe through Diana's uncle. Kybi said it's lucky the loss of the ring is the only bad thing that has happened to us all summer. We all feel pretty lucky. Kybi has good sensibility and healthy attitudes. We spent the day at the cliffs until sunset.

Life here is so slow and calming. The heat slows everything down too. The next day we took the rental car to Bejuco, the same beach we took Tarek and Marie, where Jose has his land. We showed the beach to Lina. In my twelve years of visiting Costa Rica I have found secret places where there are no tourists. This is one of my favorite places. (Note to the reader: After reading about these places I have implanted a hidden code that readers will not be able to ever recall the names of my secret locations, so don't ever try to find these places.) We all collected shells and spent the day walking on the beach. The shore was so peaceful it clears my mind of any debris. (Speaking of debris this is one of the cleanest beaches unlike many others. Some beaches have so much garbage that it is sad. Much of this waste is coming from the industrialized, developed world and dumped into the sea.)

I feel refreshed and ready to teach again when we get back to New York. The payoff to teaching is to travel in the summers. Teaching is so intense that it only can be balanced with some time off. Think about this, I have to be the parent for twenty-five students at a time, five hours a day. It isn't easy and I think about my job even when I'm not at my job. Our time here is rapidly dwindling down. In three days we leave. Jose returns just in time to see us for two days. Dasa and Kybi are leaving tomorrow; and Tarek and Marie are back in Paris at their jobs already. Lina leaves for Florida the same day we do. We bought the bus tickets to the airport already. We have one day left to play. The day before we leave we have to pack and clean the house. In a strange way I'm ready for whatever life gives me. It has been wonderful to make new friends and to just be free enough to make sure we can enjoy life.

So the book is going to just fizzle out. There is no grand finale. No one was hurt, robbed, mugged, nor had a car accident. Not one Hollywood-like thing happened in this whole story. Yet, I think it's better than a Hollywood story. It's real. Other than my exaggerations (I hope those are obvious and comical), there isn't any big drama. Lina's visit ended all my angst at my wife, partly because Diana has someone to be with and isn't driving me crazy with all the cleaning. She hasn't even talked to me from the other room since Lina has been here. (You know speaking while I'm working at the computer.) And just as I'm writing about her, she comes over to see what I'm writing about. Isn't that the way life is? We are all electric beings more plugged into each other than we know. We all need each other. We all need to be travelers even if we never leave our hometown. Go up and hug a stranger today. Pretend they are a traveler, or about to go on a long journey and you will never see them again. We should all feel that way towards each other and make the world a better place.

Ending Notes: In the short time since writing this book I have kept in contact with most of our friends, new and old. Denis and Carol in Ireland promise to visit us, but I know Denis is deathly afraid of flying. Susser and Keld are waiting for a free copy of this book before they can visit us. The Italian opera singer, Theodora, send us an occasional email. We plan a rendezvous with Tarek and Marie some time in Paris. Marie is pregnant and they expect a child in a few months. Julio in Guatemala was told he had to move and has a small place and new puppy on the other side of town. He asked me to mention his three gurus; Shri Babaji, Sri Auribindo, and the Cosmic Mother. Lina is back with her mother in Florida. Jose is living between Jaco and Alajuela with Laura and Gloria, the daughter. They have worked out their differences and Jose is working on a sports fishing boat. Eligh is living in Utah with his mother. We will see him next year. Khilani is home with the earth and sky. Diana and I plan a two month venture into Colombia, Peru, and Bolivia the coming summer. And on a very positive note, Dasa and Kybi will have their first child in the near future. The child was conceived in Jaco. They have been married in their home country. I had nothing to do with this, unless you believe in the Divine Mother and how she showers love on all who take shelter while traveling.

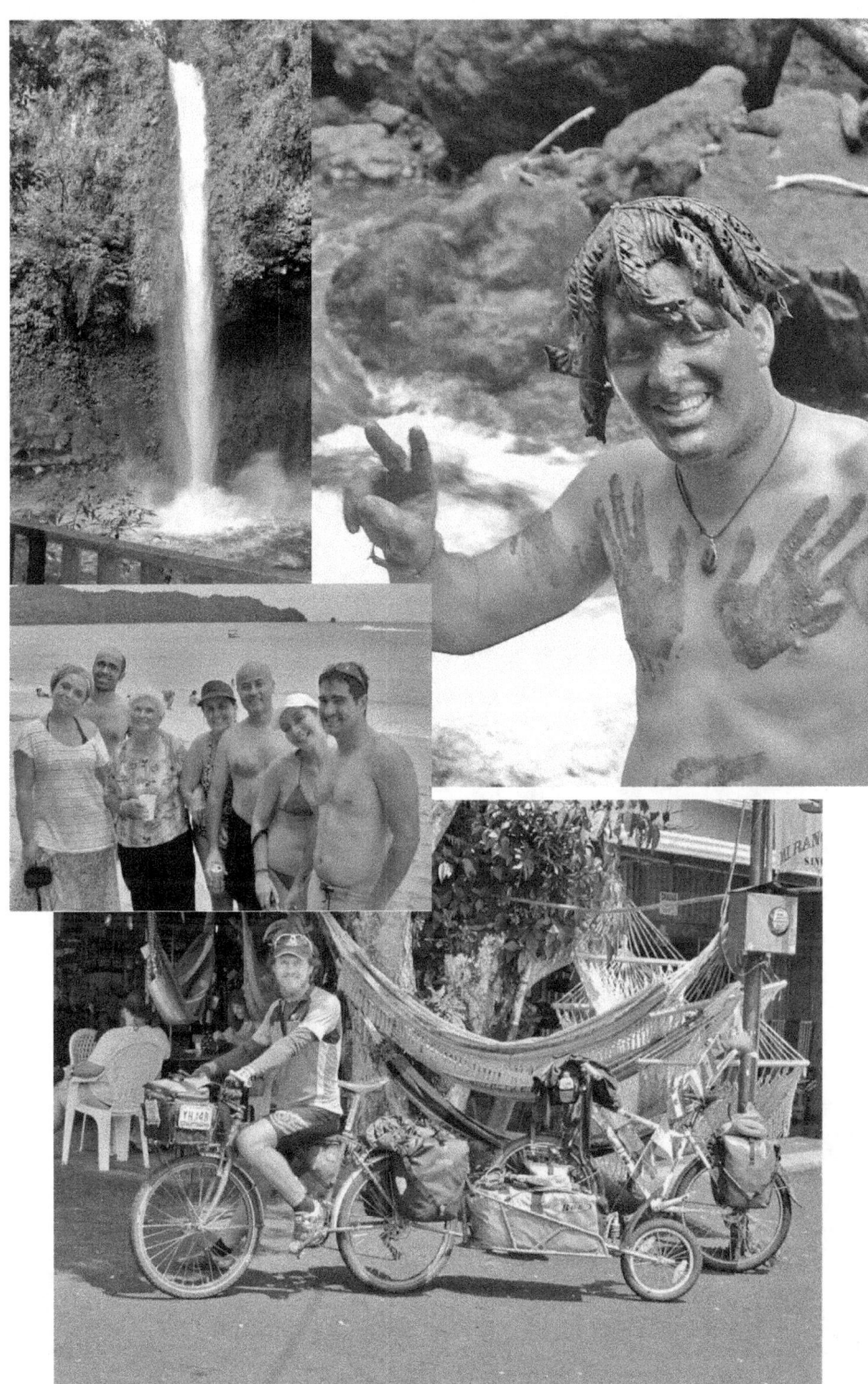

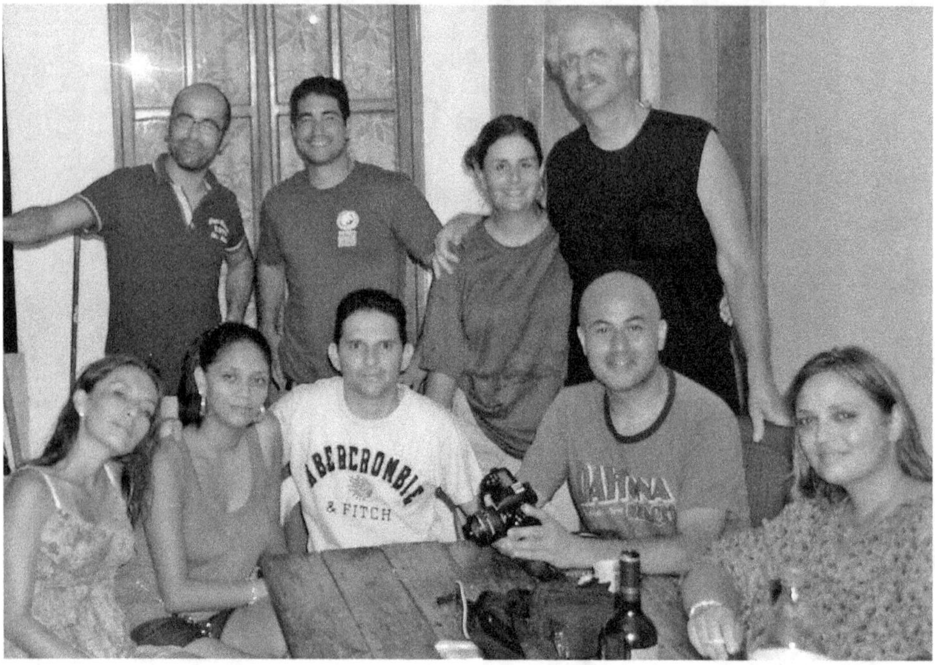
ABERCROMBIE
& FITCH

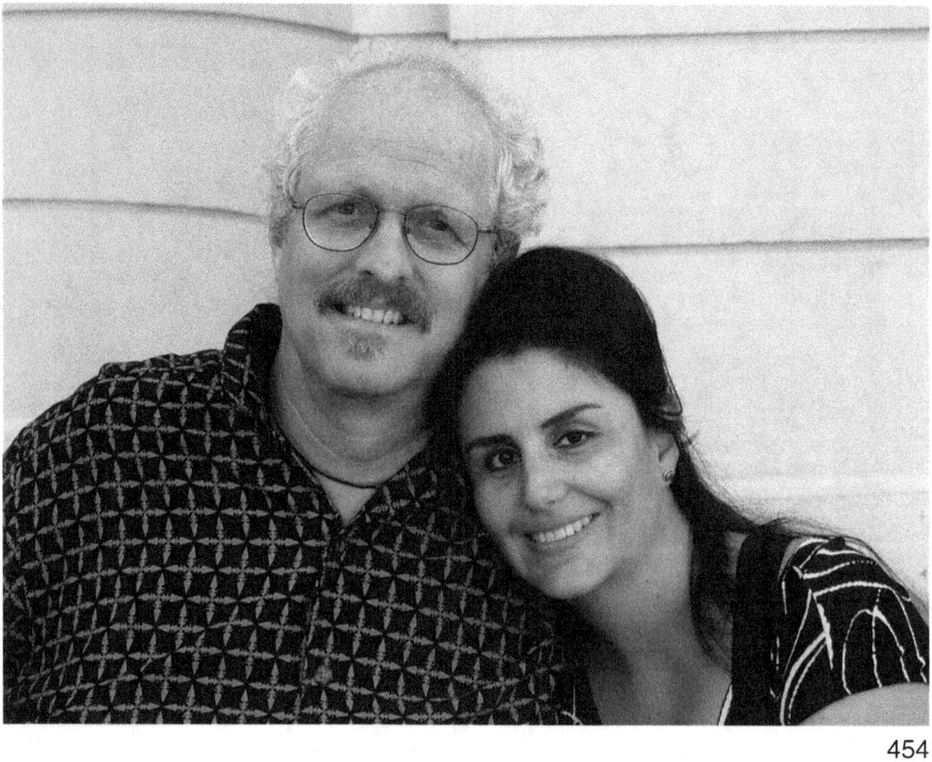

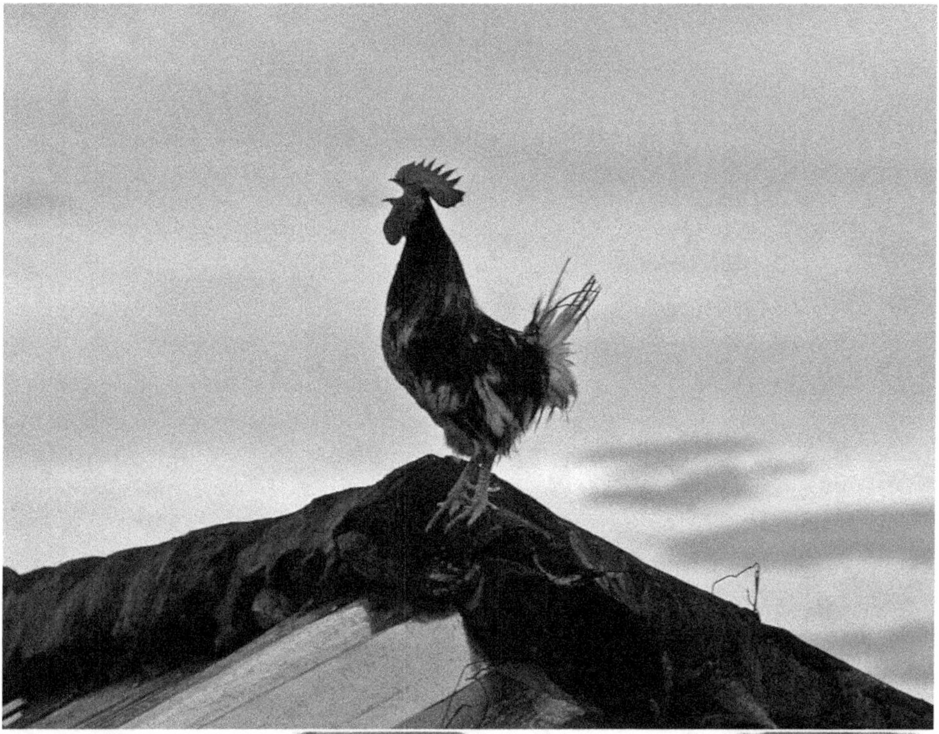

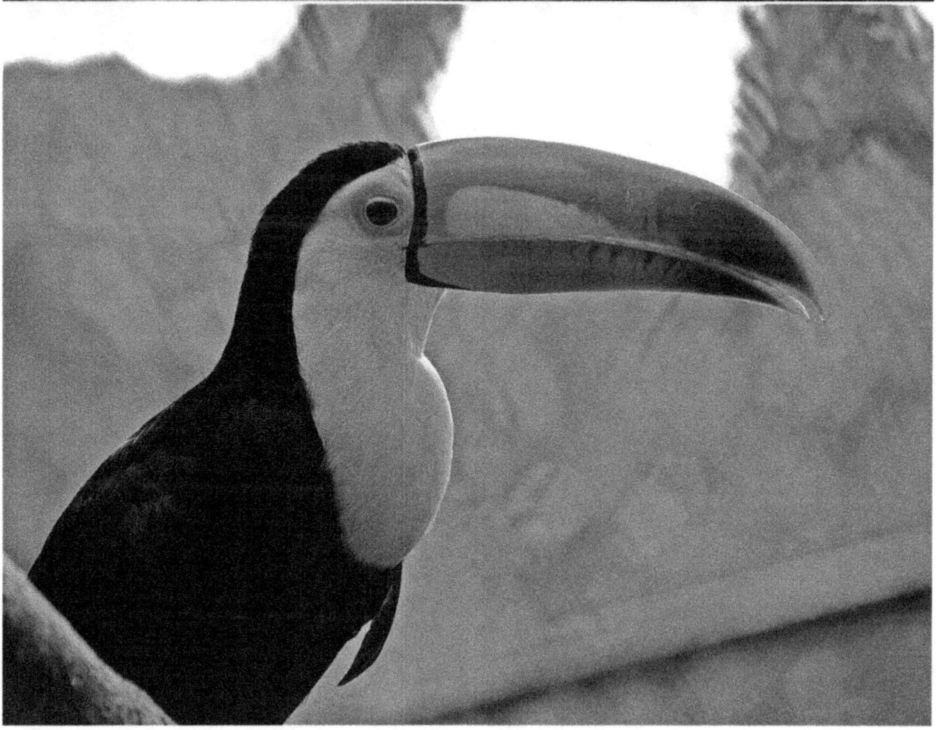

455

www.ingramcontent.com/pod-product-compliance
Lightning Source LLC
Chambersburg PA
CBHW060818170526
45158CB00001B/15